Northwest Vista College
Learning Resource Center
3535 North Ellison Drive
San Antonio, Texas 78251

S0-FKF-397

CAPITAL

IDEAS

150 WRITERS ON THE DEATH PENALTY, FROM THE CODE OF HAMMURABI TO CLARENCE DARROW

SUSAN IVES, EDITOR

WITH A FOREWORD BY JOAN CHEEVER

NORTHWEST VISTA COLLEGE L R C

3 4009 00108218 0

First Gravedigger
**What is he that builds stronger than either
the mason, the shipwright, or the carpenter?**

Second Gravedigger
**The gallows-maker;
for that frame outlives
a thousand tenants.**

Hamlet (c. 1599-1601)
Act 5, Scene 1

peaceCENTER books
1443 S. St. Mary's
San Antonio, TX 78210
210.224.HOPE
www.salsa.net/peace/ebooks

©Copyright 2009, peaceCENTER. All Rights Reserved.

ISBN: 1449511767 EAN-13 9781449511760.

Introduction

capital: c.1225, from L. *capitalis* "of the head," from *caput* (gen. *capitis*) "head." A capital crime (1526) is one that affects the life, or the "head."

idea: 1430, "figure, image, symbol," from L. *idea* "idea," and in Platonic philosophy "*archetype*," from Gk. *idea* "ideal prototype," lit. "look, form," from *idein* "to see," from Proto-Indo-European **wid-es-ya-*, suffixed form of base **weid-* "to see." Sense of "result of thinking" first recorded 1645.

❖

At the peaceCENTER we lament that we live in the belly of the beast, ground zero for executions (as of this writing, 440 in Texas since 1976.) And yet, we are not precisely advocates or activists for the abolition of the death penalty. Instead, we encourage and facilitate community conversations about difficult topics, the death penalty being one we have wrestled with for more than a decade.

conversation: 1340, from O.Fr. *conversation*, from L. *conversationem* (nom. *conversatio*) "act of living with," prp. of *conversari* "to live with, keep company with," lit. "turn about with," from L. *com-* intens. prefix + *vertare*, freq. of *vertere*.

We are not the first one to have this conversation. Indeed, people have been thinking, writing, speaking, preaching, arguing and legislating about the death penalty since humans first recorded their ideas with chisel and stone. Just as we can converse with our friends, colleagues and neighbors, we can "turn about with" these people and ideas from the past.

anthology: 1640, from L. *anthologia*, from Gk. *anthologia* "flower-gathering," from *anthos* "a flower" + *logia* "collection, collecting," from *legein* "gather." Modern sense (which emerged in Late Gk.) is metaphoric, "flowers" of verse, small poems by various writers gathered together.

This anthology gathers 151 writings about the death penalty, covering a span of almost 4,000 years. The entries were selected to illustrate the diversity of thought about capital punishment, to provide a resource for tracing its intellectual history and to provide surprisingly fresh ideas that can inform our contemporary conversations.

The contributors are a varied bunch. In addition to the expected philosophers, scholars, statesmen, clergy, legislators, lawyers, psychiatrists, historians, political scientists and sociologists, there is a goodly number of journalists, playwrights, poets, novelists, soldiers, adventurers, an anarchist or three and even an actress. Two of the writers — the Marquis de Sade and Frank Harris — are best known as pornographers; the connection between the capital punishment and pornography is a conversation all its own.

The entries are arranged in roughly chronological order, although a few exceptions were made to group like entries together, such as the three items about the Spanish Inquisition and the two about lynching. This is not to imply that there is a smooth, unbroken progression of ideas from, say, savagery to enlightenment. The *lex talonis*, eye-for-an-eye law of reciprocity mandated by the Code of Hammurabi still makes sense to many people today, while the solution to crime described by Sir Thomas More in 1516 —eliminate its causes — did not gain popular currency until the rise of the social sciences almost 400 years later. The chapter divisions are in place mainly to make the table of contents less intimidating. Everything in this anthology is in the public domain, which is why it stops where it does.

The entries were selected and edited without considering whether they are for, against, neutral or ambivalent towards capital punishment. They are deliberately presented without commentary, interpretation or context. The challenge implicit in this anthology is that, ultimately, you must struggle to find meaning for yourself.

Within the bounds of clarity, the pieces have only been lightly edited. Basil Montagu, for example, was allowed to keep his archaic spellings —publick, journie, traytor — but his equally old-fashioned Practice of Capitalizing every Noun and Adjective was too Distracting, so was Changed. Likewise, several essays that used the letter f in place of an s were amended, as it *if almoft impoffible to underftand.*

Some of the language is shocking and at times offensive to our 21st Century eyes and ears. However, there is a link between words and deeds. When Bristlecomb wrote about "niggers," McKim about "imbeciles" and even Bellarmine about "heretics," this name-calling served to distance them from the humanity of their victims. Likewise, the nightmarish witness descriptions of executions remind us that there is the suffering of real people behind the often abstract philosophizing. Some of the "flowers" gathered for this anthology have thorns.

This is a work of exploration rather than one of expertise. My only credential is the need to know more, still more and even more. I don't harbor expectations that this anthology will change anyone's mind — after all, it didn't change mine — but I do hope that it will provide the conscientious reader with material to explore the philosophical, societal and emotional origins of his or her deeply held beliefs about capital punishment so that the community conversation can be deep, broad and civil.

Susan Ives
San Antonio, Texas
9-9-09

Foreword
by Joan M. Cheever

It started in 399 BC, with a cup of poison; now in 2009 it's a plastic tube filled with poison, inserted by needle. The irony was not lost on me as I read the fascinating accounts of executions in *Capital Sentences* – a remarkable collection of essays, reports, poems about the history of capital punishment, from the execution of Socrates in 339 B.C. to the 1927 execution of Sacco and Vanzetti.

Not counting the crucifixion of Jesus, witnessed by thousands, the first eyewitness account of an execution was of Socrates – death by drinking a cup of poison in 339 BCE. It is now the method we in America, have decided is "more humane," the method we have carried out in the 1,003 of 1,174 executions in the U.S. since 1982.

Through the years, "we" (society) have experimented with all sorts of ways to kill people – an account of almost every method, by the government and/or those in authority, is described in the pages of *Capital Sentences*.

I was both horrified and mesmerized in reading the eyewitness accounts; inspired by the courage of Archbishop Thomas Cranmer who died, first by placing his hand, responsible for recanting the truth, in the fire that quickly consumed his body and I was disgusted by the tale of Mithridates (1st Century) who was tied in a boat for 17 days, smeared with milk and honey, devoured by flies and maggots.

In 303 A.D., the three failed attempts by Maximus to execute some Christians is described: first, to pack of wild, hungry beasts; secondly, to a previously murderous bear; finally to a fierce lioness. But no animal would touch them.

There are accounts of execution during a Mass in Madrid in 1682; and the dignity displayed by Mary, Queen of Scots who, when told by The Earl of Shrewsbury, at her execution in 1587 that he was praying for her, she abruptly told him to save it. He was the one who would need it after taking part in her murder.

I was astonished, but quickly understood, the brief participation of family members in executions. In "A London Hanging, by a Visiting Frenchman" in 1726, family members tugged "on the feet of their loved ones, so that death will come quicker and they will not suffer."

There are descriptions of execution by guillotine and the execution of Tupac Amaru II in 1781: his tongue was cut out first, the four limbs of his body then tied to four horses pulling in opposite directions, and finally his head was sent to the town of Tinta in Peru, to be placed on a stake for public display.

Included also is a detailed description of a 1922 lynching by fire in an by Juliette V. Harring. "Fuel was brought from everywhere…his eyes bulging from their sockets, rolled from side to side, appealing in vain for help. Some of the crowd yelled and cheered and cried, 'You are burning him too fast!' "

Some of the eyewitness accounts, like these, were so horrible, so incredibly descriptive, that I felt sick. At times I felt as though I was reading porn. Death penalty pornography, sanctioned by those in power.

Thankfully, *Capital Sentences* won't be coming to readers in a brown-paper wrapper, and its publisher, the peaceCENTER of San Antonio, won't be arrested for distributing pornography. It's the truth and is available at all who want to read the true, and often shocking and grisly accounts, of how we, as human beings, from the days of Socrates to present day, kill other people in the name of government. There are descriptions of the crowds climbing into the tens of thousands of Londoners gathered around the hanging tree at Tyburn; across the Atlantic, in America's Midwest, there's a report of 5,000 in attendance in 1842 to watch a hanging in Mineral Point, Wisconsin. And a detailed account of the botched execution by electrocution in 1890 in Buffalo, N.Y. of William Kemmler.

These accounts, written in a compelling and brutally honest manner, are for the most part, an unemotional factual account of that day's free entertainment. It puts the spotlight not just on the condemned, but also on the cheering crowds of thousands, the guards and the executioner himself, who earns his living by chopping off heads. While reading *Capital Sentences*, I wondered if they, too, were deserving of my pity. I am also left wondering, after reading these gruesome accounts of the various ways and methods of execution, who exactly are the people with the truly evil hearts? The condemned or those men who take sick pleasure in inflicting so much pain on so many people through state-sanctioned executions?

I expect some people are so numbed by watching and participating in countless executions, that they don't realize until months or years later, what they have been witnessing. For these people, I now have special empathy, especially in the case of Rev. Carroll Pickett, former chaplain on Texas' Death Row, who witnessed 95 executions before retiring in 1995. In the last hours of an inmates' life, Pickett says his job wasn't to save a man's soul, but, he admits in a 2008 documentary, he was following the orders of the warden who told him his job was to "seduce their (inmates) emotions during the day, so they won't try to fight at midnight." (*At The Death House Door*)

Capital Sentences is a trip through a long, sordid, interesting and painful journey into the history of the death penalty – not just in the U.S. but around the world, from the beginning of time.

My journey began on a hot, October morning in 1994 when I got the "chance" to witness an execution. The following is an excerpt from my eyewitness account of the execution of Walter Key Williams.

❖

I stood there watching him strapped to the gurney five feet away, moments before his execution. Our lives, which had been so intertwined for the past nine years and which had inadvertently overlapped countless times before, were now diverging.

Through an intravenous tube in his right arm, Texas prison officials administered the lethal dose at 12:15 a.m. He closed his eyes, and a tear rolled down his right cheek. He took one last gasp of air, and then his eyes opened. At 12:21 a.m., Walter Key Williams, my client of nine years on Texas' death row, was dead.

The endless motions, legal briefs and evidentiary hearings had done no more than postpone his date with death. Nine minutes after I walked out of the Death House on that hot, still night in Huntsville, the belongings Walter had accumulated during his 11 years on death row were out on the sidewalk in front of the prison unit known as The Walls. Prison officials who had only minutes earlier had stood behind me to witness the execution politely helped lift the six heavy sacks containing Walter's things and put them in the trunk of my rental car. His body was sent to a funeral home in nearby Brenham for burial in a family plot.

I took his case in the fall of 1985 after a frantic telephone call from Robert B. Hirshhorn, a law school classmate. That's how I met Walter, a black 23-year old. I read the transcript and saw his picture. He didn't look like a killer and didn't sound like one either.

Walter killed Danny Liepold, a white convenience store clerk, in a botched robbery attempt. He confessed. His entire trial lasted less than a day and a half. Walter's trial attorneys didn't offer any evidence, either at the guilt-innocence phase or the crucial punishment phase. They testified at one of the evidentiary hearings that it was their trial strategy not to put on any witnesses or offer any mitigating evidence.

One fatal decision was Walter's rejection of a plea bargain: life, which would have translated (after good time) into roughly seven years. Walter said he received conflicting advice. One lawyer urged him to take it; the other said confidently that he could get the case reversed on appeal.

Walter didn't have the personality of a killer. The State of Texas didn't think so either, or they wouldn't have offered him such a sweetheart deal. Nevertheless, the jury returned the verdict in less than an hour and a half.

Walter's faith in the judicial process was misplaced. After an almost decade-long journey through the legal system the case of State v. Williams was over.

Walter asked me to file an application for clemency with Gov. Ann Richards. I knew the odds were against us.

The papers had to be on the governor's desk Monday morning. On Friday night I pounded out a rough draft and went to bed. Awakened at 6 a.m. by the cries of a hungry 9-month-old, I waited for a crucial FedEx delivery. By the time it arrived I had cooked 12 quarts of different kinds of soup. Some people exercise to alleviate stress — I cook.

The nearest FedEx Office, a good 25-minute drive away, closed at 5 p.m. We arrived at 4:57 p.m. — at the wrong store. Racing through red lights, we arrived at 5:04 p.m. The clerk shook his head when I showed him my 11 packets. "Lady, you're too late," he said.

"Please, this is a matter of life and death," I pleaded. When he saw the address he knew I was telling the truth. He assured me the package would arrive on the governor's desk on Monday morning.

Now it was time to get down to Texas to talk about life and prepare for death. I felt unprepared to take it on.

Walter seemed surprised when I met him less than 10 hours before his execution.

In the visiting room at Ellis I, I looked right at him through the screen mesh that separated us and asked what family members would be there with him tonight as he faced the executioner. He was an only child and both his parents were dead. His aunt had died; his uncle was too ill to travel.

"No one," he trembled, his eyes darting around the small cubicle.

"Do you want me to be there?" I asked, not really sure that I wanted to hear the answer.

"Would you? Could you? I didn't want to ask you," he said, his eyes fixed on mine.

I was supposed to have had my name put on a witness list two weeks before the execution. I had tried, but Walter didn't receive my letters and phone calls until the day before his scheduled execution.

Although neither the governor's office nor the Office of the Texas Attorney General objected, the warden's office was not no accommodating. He turned down my request. My personal appeal to the director of the entire prison system, Texas Department of Corrections director Wayne Scott, fell on deaf ears.

He responded to my pleas with a barrage of questions: "Where do you live? How do I know you are even a real lawyer" His purpose was clear – to get me to surrender.

I called Mr. Scott and informed him I was prepared to delay his "perfectly scheduled execution" by getting a federal judge to sign a temporary retraining order. His anger was predictable. "Miss Cheever, are you threatening to *sue* me? Are you *threatening* me?"

"Oh no sir. I am *informing* you that I will sue you at 10 p.m. So that my client doesn't have to die alone."

"Well, I've decided to give you 90 minutes with your client tonight. I never do that for anyone. I suggest you get over to the prison right now. Your time is running."

To the guards I was apparently the enemy. They decided they would require me to remain standing for the entire 90 minutes. It was only after I appealed to the prison chaplain that a chair appeared.

Walter whispered, "Look, party food. Isn't that sick? Sure enough, the guard's table was laden with homemade cookies, brownies, cakes and pies.

Glancing at his Koran and prayer rug nearby, I asked him if he wanted to pray.

"No," he said. "I just want to talk. Have you heard from the governor's office yet?"

I hadn't. He laughed and told me not to apologize. But I did, saying I was sorry I wasn't a better lawyer. And I apologized for prolonging the inevitable. He told me to stop. "Look, I think you and Robert are the best lawyers anyone could ask for. I'm very lucky. I needed that time to get ready for tonight. And you gave me that time. Thank you."

The 90 minutes turned into 2 ½ hours – I don't know how. No one tapped me on the shoulder and asked me to leave. We laughed, we cried and at times we just fell silent.

We talked about gangs, growing up in San Antonio's East Side and the seduction of the street. We talked about the Federal crime bill and the lack of funding for after school basketball programs. We talked about my children and his regret at not having any. We talked about his mother, his father, his aunt and uncle. We talked about his addiction to drugs and alcohol. We talked about Danny Liepold, the convenience store clerk, and Walter talked about how sorry he was for ending the clerk's short life. We talked about forgiveness.

And then we talked about a subject that was never taught in law school.

Tonight I was prepared to talk to Walter about death and the afterlife.

"Why did this happen to me? Why did my life go so wrong? Why tonight?" Walter asked.

My only answer: "You know, Walter, God wanted another angel tonight, and he picked you."

"Do you think so? Do you think that's where I'm going?" he asked, with tears running down his cheeks.

Tearfully I answered, "You've asked for forgiveness and you're truly sorry. There's no doubt in my mind."

My time was up. As I left the Death House, the warden stopped me to say that Mr. Scott had reconsidered. I would be allowed in. "Be outside the administration building at 11:30 p.m. Bring I.D. And nothing else."

When I returned to the Death House I saw Walter, clothed in store-bought blue pants, a prison shirt, wearing his prayer cap and high-tops, lying on the table. Five white leather straps kept his body motionless. Separating us was a glass partition. One microphone dangled over my head and one above Walter's.

"Godspeed and goodbye, Walter, remember, you're almost home," I said, choking back the tears. He turned and thanked me. He asked for forgiveness from "any and everybody I've ever hurt."

With a nod from a prison official, the poison flowed. His eyes closed and then opened, and I knew he was gone. Life had been suspended in that small, cramped chamber, and now it resumed. The room suddenly seemed brighter.

Officially, death occurred six minutes later, when a short man with a stethoscope around his neck, identified as a medical examiner, entered. He opened Walter's shirt and listened vainly for a heartbeat.

I felt a hand on my shoulder. It was a prison official's. He said it was time to leave.

As I left the House of Death, I noticed a clump of white flowers next to the sidewalk. They seem to have been planted just for the occasion.

When I worked as a briefing attorney in the Texas Court of Criminal Appeals I never winced when I saw my research turned into affirmations in death penalty cases. At first, I thought that Walter's case was different than the dozens that had crossed my desk. Now I suspect that most are the same.

The difference is that I got to know Walter, to hear his story about his drunken father who beat his mother; about how he started using drugs and hanging out with gangs when a distant family member told him that he was the product of an affair between his father and a girlfriend; how ten days before his crime spree his wife was gang raped, then left him. How he had never been violent before. How he was transformed, redeemed and forgiven. I did not know that before. I cannot forget it now.

I have read many books about the death penalty. I've written one myself. I always wondered what would have happened had Walter's death sentence been reversed and he had been released from prison. Would he have killed again? Two years after Walter's execution I began researching my book *Back From The Dead*, the story of 589 former death row inmates who, through the lottery of fate, were given a second chance at life in 1972 when the death penalty was abolished; it returned to the United States four years later. I probably know as much about the death penalty as anyone in Texas.

Yet, this anthology continually surprised me with things I did not know. There is a long tradition of thinking, writing and speaking about capital punishment that has been buried in dusty archives on library shelves.

This writing and witnessing has the power to inform us today. I am proud to have been a part of it.

Joan Cheever is an award-winning legal affairs journalist and a former managing editor of The National Law Journal. She received her Bachelor's degree from Southern Methodist University; a Master's in journalism from Columbia University and her law degree from St. Mary's University. She is a member of the bar in the states of Texas, New York and Connecticut. "Back From The Dead: One woman's search for the men who walked off America's death row" was published by John Wiley & Sons in 2006. For more information, visit Cheever's website: www.backfromthedeadusa.com

TABLE OF CONTENTS

Witnesses to executions are rendered in Italics

PART II: The Best of Times, the Worst of Times

PART III: After the Enlightenment

PART IV: Modern Times

IN THE BEGINNING

Code of Hammurabi (1790 BCE)

When Anu the Sublime, King of the Anunaki, and Bel, the lord of Heaven and earth, who decreed the fate of the land, assigned to Marduk, the over-ruling son of Ea, God of righteousness, dominion over earthly man, and made him great among the Igigi, they called Babylon by his illustrious name, made it great on earth, and founded an everlasting kingdom in it, whose foundations are laid so solidly as those of heaven and earth; then Anu and Bel called by name me, Hammurabi, the exalted prince, who feared God, to bring about the rule of righteousness in the land, to destroy the wicked and the evil-doers; so that the strong should not harm the weak; so that I should rule over the black-headed people like Shamash, and enlighten the land, to further the well-being of mankind.

The Code of Laws (excerpts)

1. If anyone ensnare another, putting a ban upon him, but he cannot prove it, then he that ensnared him shall be put to death.

2. If anyone bring an accusation against a man, and the accused go to the river and leap into the river, if he sink in the river his accuser shall take possession of his house. But if the river prove that the accused is not guilty, and he escape unhurt, then he who had brought the accusation shall be put to death, while he who leaped into the river shall take possession of the house that had belonged to his accuser.

3. If anyone bring an accusation of any crime before the elders, and does not prove what he has charged, he shall, if it be a capital offense charged, be put to death.

5. If a judge try a case, reach a decision, and present his judgment in writing; if later error shall appear in his decision, and it be through his own fault, then he shall pay twelve times the fine set by him in the case, and he shall be publicly removed from the judge's bench, and never again shall he sit there to render judgment.

6. If anyone steal the property of a temple or of the court, he shall be put to death, and also the one who receives the stolen thing from him shall be put to death.

7. If anyone buy from the son or the slave of another man, without witnesses or a contract, silver or gold, a male or female slave, an ox or a sheep, an ass or anything, or if he take it in charge, he is considered a thief and shall be put to death.

8. If anyone steal cattle or sheep, or an ass, or a pig or a goat, if it belong to a god or to the court, the thief shall pay thirtyfold therefore; if they belonged to a freed man of the king he shall pay tenfold; if the thief has nothing with which to pay he shall be put to death.

9. If anyone lose an article, and find it in the possession of another: if the person in whose possession the thing is found say, "A merchant sold it to me, I paid for it before witnesses," and if the owner of the thing say, "I will bring witnesses

who know my property," then shall the purchaser bring the merchant who sold it to him, and the witnesses before whom he bought it, and the owner shall bring witnesses who can identify his property. The judge shall examine their testimony — both of the witnesses before whom the price was paid, and of the witnesses who identify the lost article on oath. The merchant is then proved to be a thief and shall be put to death. The owner of the lost article receives his property, and he who bought it receives the money he paid from the estate of the merchant.

16. If anyone receive into his house a runaway male or female slave of the court, or of a freedman, and does not bring it out at the public proclamation of the major domus, the master of the house shall be put to death.

21. If anyone break a hole into a house he shall be put to death before that hole and be buried.

22. If anyone is committing a robbery and is caught, then he shall be put to death.

25. If fire break out in a house, and someone who comes to put it out cast his eye upon the property of the owner of the house, and take the property of the master of the house, he shall be thrown into that self-same fire.

129. If a man's wife be surprised with another man, both shall be tied and thrown into the water, but the husband may pardon his wife and the king his slaves.

130. If a man violate the wife (betrothed or child-wife) of another man, who has never known a man, and still lives in her father's house, and sleep with her and be surprised, this man shall be put to death, but the wife is blameless.

153. If the wife of one man on account of another man has their mates murdered, both of them shall be impaled.

154. If a man be guilty of incest with his daughter, he shall be driven from the place.

155. If a man betroth a girl to his son, and his son have intercourse with her, but he (the father) afterward defile her, and be surprised, then he shall be bound and cast into the water.

157. If anyone be guilty of incest with his mother after his father, both shall be burned.

194. If a man give his child to a nurse and the child die in her hands, but the nurse unbeknown to the father and mother nurse another child, then they shall convict her of having nursed another child without the knowledge of the father and mother and her breasts shall be cut off.

195. If a son strike his father, his hands shall be hewn off.

196. If a man put out the eye of another man, his eye shall be put out.

197. If he break another man's bone, his bone shall be broken.

200. If a man knock out the teeth of his equal, his teeth shall be knocked out.

206. If during a quarrel one man strike another and wound him, then he shall swear, "I did not injure him wittingly," and pay the physicians.

209. If a man strike a free-born woman so that she lose her unborn child, he shall pay ten shekels for her loss.

210. If the woman die, his daughter shall be put to death.

227. If anyone deceive a barber, and have him mark a slave not for sale with the sign of a slave, he shall be put to death, and buried in his house. The barber shall

swear, "I did not mark him wittingly," and shall be guiltless.

229 If a builder build a house for someone, and does not construct it properly, and the house which he built fall in and kill its owner, then that builder shall be put to death.

230. If it kill the son of the owner, the son of that builder shall be put to death.

231. If it kill a slave of the owner, then he shall pay slave for slave to the owner of the house.

244. If anyone hire an ox or an ass, and a lion kill it in the field, the loss is upon its owner.

245. If anyone hire oxen, and kill them by bad treatment or blows, he shall compensate the owner, oxen for oxen.

246. If a man hire an ox, and he break its leg or cut the ligament of its neck, he shall compensate the owner with ox for ox.

282. If a slave say to his master: "You are not my master," if they convict him, his master shall cut off his ear.

The Law of Moses (C. 1600 BCE)

Exodus 21

[12] Anyone who strikes a man and kills him shall surely be put to death. [13] However, if he does not do it intentionally, but God lets it happen, he is to flee to a place I will designate. [14] But if a man schemes and kills another man deliberately, take him away from my altar and put him to death.

[15] Anyone who attacks his father or his mother must be put to death.

[16] Anyone who kidnaps another and either sells him or still has him when he is caught must be put to death.

[17] Anyone who curses his father or mother must be put to death.

[18] If men quarrel and one hits the other with a stone or with his fist and he does not die but is confined to bed, [19] the one who struck the blow will not be held responsible if the other gets up and walks around outside with his staff; however, he must pay the injured man for the loss of his time and see that he is completely healed.

[20] If a man beats his male or female slave with a rod and the slave dies as a direct result, he must be punished, [21] but he is not to be punished if the slave gets up after a day or two, since the slave is his property.

[22] If men who are fighting hit a pregnant woman and she gives birth prematurely but there is no serious injury, the offender must be fined whatever the woman's husband demands and the court allows. [23] But if there is serious injury, you are to take life for life, [24] eye for eye, tooth for tooth, hand for hand, foot for foot, [25] burn for burn, wound for wound, bruise for bruise.

[26] If a man hits a manservant or maidservant in the eye and destroys it, he must let the servant go free to compensate for the eye. [27] And if he knocks out the tooth

of a manservant or maidservant, he must let the servant go free to compensate for the tooth.

[28] If a bull gores a man or a woman to death, the bull must be stoned to death, and its meat must not be eaten. But the owner of the bull will not be held responsible. [29] If, however, the bull has had the habit of goring and the owner has been warned but has not kept it penned up and it kills a man or woman, the bull must be stoned and the owner also must be put to death. [30] However, if payment is demanded of him, he may redeem his life by paying whatever is demanded. [31] This law also applies if the bull gores a son or daughter. [32] If the bull gores a male or female slave, the owner must pay thirty shekels of silver to the master of the slave, and the bull must be stoned.

Deuteronomy 19

[1] When the LORD your God has destroyed the nations whose land he is giving you, and when you have driven them out and settled in their towns and houses, [2] then set aside for yourselves three cities centrally located in the land the LORD your God is giving you to possess. [3] Build roads to them and divide into three parts the land the LORD your God is giving you as an inheritance, so that anyone who kills a man may flee there.

[4] This is the rule concerning the man who kills another and flees there to save his life—one who kills his neighbor unintentionally, without malice aforethought. [5] For instance, a man may go into the forest with his neighbor to cut wood, and as he swings his ax to fell a tree, the head may fly off and hit his neighbor and kill him. That man may flee to one of these cities and save his life. [6] Otherwise, the avenger of blood might pursue him in a rage, overtake him if the distance is too great, and kill him even though he is not deserving of death, since he did it to his neighbor without malice aforethought. [7] This is why I command you to set aside for yourselves three cities.

[8] If the LORD your God enlarges your territory, as he promised on oath to your forefathers, and gives you the whole land he promised them, [9] because you carefully follow all these laws I command you today—to love the LORD your God and to walk always in his ways—then you are to set aside three more cities. [10] Do this so that innocent blood will not be shed in your land, which the LORD your God is giving you as your inheritance, and so that you will not be guilty of bloodshed.

[11] But if a man hates his neighbor and lies in wait for him, assaults and kills him, and then flees to one of these cities, [12] the elders of his town shall send for him, bring him back from the city, and hand him over to the avenger of blood to die. [13] Show him no pity. You must purge from Israel the guilt of shedding innocent blood, so that it may go well with you.

[14] Do not move your neighbor's boundary stone set up by your predecessors in the inheritance you receive in the land the LORD your God is giving you to possess. [15] One witness is not enough to convict a man accused of any crime or offense he may have committed. A matter must be established by the testimony of two or three witnesses.

[16] If a malicious witness takes the stand to accuse a man of a crime, [17] the two men involved in the dispute must stand in the presence of the LORD before the priests and the judges who are in office at the time. [18] The judges must make a thorough investigation, and if the witness proves to be a liar, giving false testimony against his brother, [19] then do to him as he intended to do to his brother. You must purge the evil from among you. [20] The rest of the people will hear of this and be afraid, and never again will such an evil thing be done among you. [21] Show no pity: life for life, eye for eye, tooth for tooth, hand for hand, foot for foot.

Leviticus 24

[13] Then the LORD said to Moses: [14] "Take the blasphemer outside the camp. All those who heard him are to lay their hands on his head, and the entire assembly is to stone him. [15] Say to the Israelites: 'If anyone curses his God, he will be held responsible; [16] anyone who blasphemes the name of the LORD must be put to death. The entire assembly must stone him. Whether an alien or native-born, when he blasphemes the Name, he must be put to death.

[17] "If anyone takes the life of a human being, he must be put to death. [18] Anyone who takes the life of someone's animal must make restitution—life for life. [19] If anyone injures his neighbor, whatever he has done must be done to him: [20] fracture for fracture, eye for eye, tooth for tooth. As he has injured the other, so he is to be injured. [21] Whoever kills an animal must make restitution, but whoever kills a man must be put to death. [22] You are to have the same law for the alien and the native-born. I am the LORD your God.' "

[23] Then Moses spoke to the Israelites, and they took the blasphemer outside the camp and stoned him. The Israelites did as the LORD commanded Moses.

The Ancient Hebrew Law of Homicide
Mayer Sulzburger (1915)

The law of homicide is an index to certain sides of national character. Where there is a small, powerful class able to monopolize rule and government, the rights of the great mass of common people are weak and ill-assured. In such a society there is much violence. Arrogant and turbulent spirits are in perpetual rivalry, and compete for mastery. The stronger steadily eliminate the weaker. Life is held cheap. The chiefs, who are always risking their own lives, compel their underlings, who have no great stake in the contest, to risk theirs. It is a kind of feudal system, in which each chief is the head of a clan or other organization with whose aid he hopes to retain or to achieve pre-eminence.

Out of such a condition the early laws of homicide arise.

Clans in juxtaposition are never quite at peace with each other. There may be a kind of truce, but this is liable to be broken at any moment. The murder of a clansman by a member of another clan is *casus belli,* for the sufficient reason that it weakens the assailed clan. If unpunished, the act tends to be repeated, and this process would, in a relatively short time, bring the weakened clan under subjection to the aggressor clan.

In such a state of society the law of retaliation (the *lex talionis*) becomes inevitable. The assailing clan must be weakened as much as the assailed, if the latter is to retain its relative strength and position. What we call *lex talionis* is therefore, primarily, a means for the defense of the clan, an inter-clan rule. It is one of the early stages of what we now call international law, which even yet knows no final arbitrament but the sword.

The period when this rule began to be applied antedates even primitive history. We know of no stage in which men did not form a kind of society, however small or rude it may have been. And so soon as this point has been reached, individual action ceases to be unrestrained, and must accept limitations useful for society. A member of the blood-covenant may no longer slay his fellow-member. However determined his purpose, the *hatan damim* (member of the blood-covenant guild) must forgo it when he learns that the intended victim is also a member. (Exodus 4:24-6)

From the very beginning of organized society, there must have developed two sets of laws, one for those within and the other for those without the clan. The latter is simple and short. A member of clan A has weakened clan B by killing one of its members. Clan B must retaliate by weakening the aggressor clan at least as much.

This policy, however wise as against another clan, would be ruinous if applied within the clan. One member has killed another, and has thereby reduced the strength of the clan. If the aggressor be killed, its strength is further reduced. The direct clan-interest is that the aggressor be kept alive, unless he is likely to further imperil the community. It is this contingency which creates a necessity for devising a lesser punishment than death for homicide within the clan, and hence is evolved the system of imposing a money penalty on the homicide— *wergild*. It is this contingency, too, which creates a necessity for ascertaining the circumstances of the tragedy and its underlying motive. Hence follows a subdivision of homicide into murder, which even within the clan may continue to be a capital offence, and manslaughter, which may readily be compounded for.

Two systems of homicide law are thus made more or less co-existent: an external homicide law, which is the *lex talionis,* a kind of war, and an internal homicide law, which seeks to ascertain the very right of each case—what we would call justice.

This co-existence of two discordant systems of law in each of the many clans composing a state or kingdom, tends steadily to undermine the *lex talionis.* With the progress of the state, the relations of its several parts become closer and closer, and the comity between them increases. The justice of the internal law becomes more and more apparent, and with the growth of peaceful relations between the several clans, the idea of the unity of the state is strengthened.

The feeling which individuals had for their clan is gradually transferred to the state or kingdom, and it is seen that all the clans together constitute one great clan, which is called the state. When this point is reached the *lex talionis* dies a natural death.

This progress, though curtly described, is very slow, and is reached, not by a leap, but by slow stages. For long ages the *lex talionis* continues to be recited as regulating the relations of men within the clan, and yet it is all the while undergoing decomposition. The Code of Hammurabi, if taken literally, would present a shuddering spectacle. Its notions of retaliation betoken fierce barbarism. It is reasonably certain, however, that in very early times its crude literalness was modified, and that the law as administered in later ages was far different from the bald meaning of its words. The marked intermediate stage, which is most important in the consideration of our subject, may be called the *wergild* stage, or, to use the Hebrew term, the *kofer* stage.

When a kingdom has travelled a certain distance on the road to unity, it perceives that a state of war between its parts, however mild or modified, is injurious to its progress. The same necessity which compelled the clan to work out an internal homicide law milder than the external homicide law, presses upon the state. For its purposes the several clans cannot be hostile to each other, but must constitute one great national family. The distinction between external homicide law and internal homicide law cannot exist for it. Human nature, however, is more powerful than governmental logic; ancient notions and customs are not to be done away with in a day, nor can hereditary feuds be converted into brotherly feeling by mere fiat. Force is necessary, and the growing state exerts it to prevent bloody inter-clan feuds. The first mode of prevention is always the insistence on *wergild* between the two clans, that is, the injured clan, instead of going to war, must accept a money composition for the loss of its member. The central state must, however, have acquired great stability and power before it can effect this end.

When this stage is reached, the kingdom has surmounted a danger leading to disintegration. By way of compensation perhaps, this improvement leads to another danger. Wealth has acquired a new force. It now enables its owner to kill the member of another clan with much less danger to his own life than before. With the growth of a state's wealth this peril grows more and more formidable. Hired assassins will form a class, and individual safety will be greatly impaired. The weakness of the *kofer* system will become more and more apparent, and the moral power of the internal homicide law will make its way.

When the proper point is reached, the state overthrows the *kofer* law and substitutes for it the inquiry into the circumstances and motive of every homicide, which results in the doctrine that homicide is so great an offence against the state that the private wrong is submerged, and that it is incapable of private composition, no matter what the reparation offered. Then only is the state fully organized to carry on a civil government.

We have no adequate means to ascertain when the pre-Hebraic inhabitants of Palestine passed through these stages. The probability is that long before they were conquered by the Hebrews, they had reached the *wergild* stage.

The Code of Hammurabi of Babylonia (circa 2250 B. C.) has as yet no general state-law punishing homicide. This crime must therefore have been under the jurisdiction of recognized constituent elements of the state, such as clans or the like, which severally protected their clansmen's lives against assault from without and within. There are indications that the *kofer* stage had been reached.

A History of Greece from the Earliest Times to the Present, Telemachus Thomas Timayenis (624 BCE / 1883)

But about the beginning of the seventh century B.C. the exclusive political privileges of the nobility began to be curtailed. Hence, in B.C. 624, one Drako was entrusted with the task of revising and reducing to writing the laws of Athens, in order to put a check to the growing insubordination of the inferior classes. Drako did not alter the constitution, but simply codified and published the already existing laws which were falling into disuse, at the same time making some necessary changes. The general belief that he made death the punishment for all misdemeanors is not correct; he decreed the infliction of fines for certain offenses, and under his regulations the death-penalty was of rarer occurrence than it had previously been. To the Greeks of the succeeding centuries, animated by a milder spirit in their criminal legislation, the laws of Drako seemed unnecessarily harsh, and they were popularly said to have been written, not with ink, but with blood. Yet the laws in force before Drako's time made no distinction between the various degrees of murder, whether committed by accident, in anger, in self-defense, or in revenge, but prescribed the penalty of death or banishment for all; whereas Drako first laid down specific and different punishments.

To the Greeks of the succeeding centuries, animated by a milder spirit in their criminal legislation, the laws of Drako seemed unnecessarily harsh, and they were popularly said to have been written, not with ink, but with blood.

His laws did not, however, remove the causes of discontent nor end the danger of revolution. In the year 612 B.C. Kylon, an Athenian patrician, attempted to usurp the supreme power at Athens. The conspiracy failed, Kylon was forced to flee, and many of his adherents were slain. Nevertheless, this occurrence became a source of lasting trouble to the state.

Megakles, a member of the great and powerful family of the Alkmæionidæ, was at that time *archon eponymos*, or chief of the archons then officiating. The friends of Kylon accused him and the rest of the Alkmæionidæ of having violated the sanctuaries of the gods, by putting to death some of Kylon's followers who had taken refuge at the altar in the Acropolis. The Alkmæionidæ refused to undergo a trial for this alleged offense, and the city was in consequence violently disturbed by contending factions of a religious as well as of a political character. Just at this crisis Solon appeared on the scene as the savior of his country.

Tao Te Ching, by Lao-tzu (6th Cen. BCE)

73

He whose boldness appears in his daring (to do wrong, in defiance of the laws) is put to death; he whose boldness appears in his not daring (to do so) lives on. Of these two cases the one appears to be advantageous, and the other to be injurious.

But when Heaven's anger smites a man,
Who the cause shall truly scan?

On this account the sage feels a difficulty (as to what to do in the former case). It is the way of Heaven not to strive, and yet it skillfully overcomes; not to speak, and yet it is skillful in (obtaining a reply; does not call, and yet men come to it of themselves. Its demonstrations are quiet, and yet its plans are skillful and effective. The meshes of the net of Heaven are large; far apart, but letting nothing escape.

74

The people do not fear death; to what purpose is it to (try to) frighten them with death? If the people were always in awe of death, and I could always seize those who do wrong, and put them to death, who would dare to do wrong?

There is always One who presides over the infliction death. He who would inflict death in the room of him who so presides over it may be described as hewing wood instead of a great carpenter. Seldom is it that he who undertakes the hewing, instead of the great carpenter, does not cut his own hands!

The Analects, Confucius (500 BCE)

Chi K'ang asked Confucius about government. Confucius replied, "To govern means to rectify. If you lead on the people with correctness, who will dare not to be correct?"

Chi K'ang, distressed about the number of thieves in the state, inquired of Confucius how to do away with them. Confucius said, "If you, sir, were not covetous, although you should reward them to do it, they would not steal."

Chi K'ang asked Confucius about government, saying, "What do you say to killing the unprincipled for the good of the principled?" Confucius replied, "Sir, in carrying on your government, why should you use killing at all? Let your evinced desires be for what is good, and the people will be good. The relation between superiors and inferiors is like that between the wind and the grass. The grass must bend, when the wind blows across it."

The History of The Peloponnesian War, Thucydides (431 BCE)

However, I have not come forward either to oppose or to accuse in the matter of Mitylene; indeed, the question before us as sensible men is not their guilt, but our interests. Though I prove them ever so guilty, I shall not, therefore, advise their death, unless it be expedient; nor though they should have claims to indulgence, shall I recommend it, unless it be dearly for the good of the country. I consider that we are deliberating for the future more than for the present; and where Cleonis is positive as to the useful deterrent effects that will follow from making rebellion capital, I, who consider the interests of the future quite as much as he, as positively maintain the contrary. And I require you not to reject my useful considerations for his specious ones: his speech may have the attraction of seeming the more just in your present temper against Mitylene; but we are not in a court of justice, but in apolitical assembly; and the question is not justice, but how to make the Mitylenians useful to Athens.

Now of course communities have enacted the penalty of death for many offences far lighter than this: still hope leads men to venture, and no one ever yet put himself in peril without the inward conviction that he would succeed in his design. Again, was there ever city rebelling that did not believe that it possessed either in itself or in its alliances resources adequate to the enterprise? All, states and individuals, are alike prone to err, and there is no law that will prevent them; or why should men have exhausted the list of punishments in search of enactments to protect them from evildoers? It is probable that in early times the penalties for the greatest offences were less severe, and that, as these were disregarded, the penalty of death has been by degrees in most cases arrived at, which is itself disregarded in like manner. Either then some means of terror more terrible than this must be discovered, or it must be owned that this restraint is useless; and that as long as poverty gives men the courage of necessity, or plenty fills them with the ambition which belongs to insolence and pride, and the other conditions of life remain each under the thraldom of some fatal and master passion, so long will the impulse never be wanting to drive men into danger. Hope also and cupidity, the one leading and the other following, the one conceiving the attempt, the other suggesting the facility of succeeding, cause the widest ruin, and, although invisible agents, are far stronger than the dangers that are seen.

> **Either then some means of terror more terrible than this must be discovered, or it must be owned that this restraint is useless**

Fortune, too, powerfully helps the delusion and, by the unexpected aid that she sometimes lends, tempts men to venture with inferior means; and this is especially the case with communities, because the stakes played for are the highest, freedom or empire, and, when all are acting together, each man irrationally magnifies his own capacity. In fine, it is impossible to prevent, and only great simplicity can hope to prevent, human nature doing what it has once set its mind upon, by force of law or by any other deterrent force whatsoever.

We must not, therefore, commit ourselves to a false policy through a belief in the efficacy of the punishment of death, or exclude rebels from the hope of repentance and an early atonement of their error. Consider a moment. At present, if a city that has already revolted perceive that it cannot succeed, it will come to terms while it is still able to refund expenses, and pay tribute afterwards. In the other case, what city, think you, would not prepare better than is now done, and hold out to the last against its besiegers, if it is all one whether it surrender late or soon? And how can it be otherwise than hurtful to us to be put to the expense of a siege, because surrender is out of the question; and if we take the city, to receive a ruined town from which we can no longer draw the revenue which forms our real strength against the enemy?

We must not, therefore, sit as strict judges of the offenders to our own prejudice, but rather see how by moderate chastisements we may be enabled to benefit in future by the revenue-producing powers of our dependencies; and we must make up our minds to look for our protection not to legal terrors but to careful administration. At present we do exactly the opposite. When a free community, held in subjection by force, rises, as is only natural, and asserts its independence, it is no sooner reduced than we fancy ourselves obliged to punish it severely; although the right course with freemen is not to chastise them rigorously when they do rise, but rigorously to watch them before they rise, and to prevent their ever entertaining the idea, and, the insurrection suppressed, to make as few responsible for it as possible."

Only consider what a blunder you would commit in doing as Cleon recommends. As things are at present, in all the cities the people is your friend, and either does not revolt with the oligarchy, or, if forced to do so, becomes at once the enemy of the insurgents; so that in the war with the hostile city you have the masses on your side. But if you butcher the people of Mitylene, who had nothing to do with the revolt, and who, as soon as they got arms, of their own motion surrendered the town, first you will commit the crime of killing your benefactors; and next you will play directly into the hands of the higher classes, who when they induce their cities to rise, will immediately have the people on their side, through your having announced in advance the same punishment for those who are guilty and for those who are not. On the contrary, even if they were guilty, you ought to seem not to notice it, in order to avoid alienating the only class still friendly to us. In short, I consider it far more useful for the preservation of our empire voluntarily to put up with injustice, than to put to death, however justly, those whom it is our interest to keep alive. As for Cleon's idea that in punishment the claims of justice and expediency can both be satisfied, facts do not confirm the possibility of such a combination."

> **I consider it far more useful for the preservation of our empire voluntarily to put up with injustice, than to put to death, however justly, those whom it is our interest to keep alive.**

Confess, therefore, that this is the wisest course, and without conceding too much either to pity or to indulgence, by neither of which motives do I any more than Cleon wish you to be influenced, upon the plain merits of the case before you, be persuaded by me to try calmly those of the Mitylenians whom Paches sent off as guilty, and to leave the rest undisturbed. This is at once best for the future, and most terrible to your enemies at the present moment; inasmuch as good policy against an adversary is superior to the blind attacks of brute force."

The Laws, Plato (360 BCE)

Book V

The shepherd or herdsman, or breeder of horses or the like, when he has received his animals will not begin to train them until he has first purified them in a manner which befits a community of animals; he will divide the healthy and unhealthy, and the good breed and the bad breed, and will send away the unhealthy and badly bred to other herds, and tend the rest, reflecting that his labours will be vain and have no effect, either on the souls or bodies of those whom nature and ill nurture have corrupted, and that they will involve in destruction the pure and healthy nature and being of every other animal, if he should neglect to purify them. Now the case of other animals is not so important- they are only worth introducing for the sake of illustration; but what relates to man is of the highest importance; and the legislator should make enquiries, and indicate what is proper for each one in the way of purification and of any other procedure. Take, for example, the purification of a city—there are many kinds of purification, some easier and others more difficult; and some of them, and the best and most difficult of them, the legislator, if he be also a despot, may be able to effect; but the legislator, who, not being a despot, sets up a new government and laws, even if he attempt the mildest of purgations, may think himself happy if he can complete his work. The best kind of purification is painful, like similar cures in medicine, involving righteous punishment and inflicting death or exile in the last resort. For in this way we commonly dispose of great sinners who are incurable, and are the greatest injury of the whole state. But the milder form of purification is as follows: when men who have nothing, and are in want of food, show a disposition to follow their leaders in an attack on the property of the rich—these, who are the natural plague of the state, are sent away by the legislator in a friendly spirit as far as he is able; and this dismissal of them is euphemistically termed a colony. And every legislator should contrive to do this at once.

Book IX

Such are the preludes which we sing to all who have thoughts of unholy and treasonable actions, and to him who hearkens to them the law has nothing to say. But to him who is disobedient when the prelude is over, cry with a loud voice,—He who is taken in the act of robbing temples, if he be a slave or stranger, shall have his evil deed engraven on his face and hands, and shall be beaten with as many stripes as may seem good to the judges, and be cast naked beyond the borders of the land. And if he suffers this punishment he will probably return to his right mind and be improved; for no penalty which the law inflicts is designed for evil, but always makes him who suffers either better or not so much worse as he would have been. But if any citizen be found guilty of any great or unmentionable wrong, either in relation to the gods, or his parents, or the state, let the judge deem him to be incurable, remembering that after receiving such an excellent education and training from youth upward, he has not abstained from the greatest of crimes. His punishment shall be death, which to him will be the least of evils; and his example will benefit others, if he perish ingloriously, and be cast beyond the borders of the land. But let his children and family, if they avoid the ways of their father, have glory, and let honorable mention be made of them, as having nobly and manfully escaped out of evil into good. None of them should have their goods confiscated to the state, for the lots of the citizens ought always to continue the same and equal.

Touching the exaction of penalties, when a man appears to have done anything which deserves a fine, he shall pay the fine, if he have anything in excess of the lot which is assigned to him; but more than that he shall not pay. And to secure exactness, let the guardians of the law refer to the registers, and inform the judges of the precise truth, in order that none of the lots may go uncultivated for want of money. But if any one seems to deserve a greater penalty, let him undergo a long and public imprisonment and be dishonored, unless some of his friends are willing to be surety for him, and liberate him by assisting him to pay the fine. No criminal shall go unpunished, not even for a single offence, nor if he have fled the country; but let the penalty be according to his deserts—death, or bonds, or blows, or degrading places of sitting or standing, or removal to some temple on the borders of the land; or let him pay fines, as we said before. In cases of death, let the judges be the guardians of the law, and a court selected by merit from the last year's magistrates. But how the causes are to be brought into to court, how the summonses are to be served, the like, these things may be left to the younger generation of legislators to determine; the manner of voting we must determine ourselves.

Crito, Plato (360 BCE)

Socrates. Then will they [the laws] not say: "You, Socrates, are breaking the covenants and agreements which you made with us at your leisure, not in any haste or under any compulsion or deception, but having had seventy years to think of them, during which time you were at liberty to leave the city, if we were not to your mind, or if our covenants appeared to you to be unfair. You had your choice, and might have gone either to Lacedaemon or Crete, which you often praise for their good government, or to some other Hellenic or foreign State. Whereas you, above all other Athenians, seemed to be so fond of the State, or, in other words, of us her laws (for who would like a State that has no laws), that you never stirred out of her: the halt, the blind, the maimed, were not more stationary in her than you were. And now you run away and forsake your agreements. Not so, Socrates, if you will take our advice; do not make yourself ridiculous by escaping out of the city. . . .

"For he who is a corrupter of the laws is more than likely to be corrupter of the young and foolish portion of mankind. Will you then flee from well-ordered cities and virtuous men? And is existence worth having on these terms? Or will you go to them without shame, and talk to them, Socrates? And what will you say to them? What you say here about virtue and justice and institutions and laws being the best things among men? Would that be decent of you? Surely not.

[. . .] "Listen, then, Socrates, to us who have brought you up. Think not of life and children first, and of justice afterwards, but of justice first, that you may be justified before the princes of the world below. For neither will you nor any that belong to you be happier or holier or juster in this life, or happier in another, if you do as Crito bids. Now you depart in innocence, a sufferer and not a doer of evil; a victim, not of the laws, but of men. But if you go forth, returning evil for evil, and injury for injury, breaking the covenants and agreements which you have made with us, and wronging those whom you ought least to wrong, that is to say, yourself, your friends, your country, and us, we shall be angry with you while you live, and our brethren, the laws in the world below, will receive you as an enemy; for they will know that you have done your best to destroy us. Listen, then, to us and not to Crito."

This is the voice which I seem to hear murmuring in my ears, like the sound of the flute in the ears of the mystic; that voice, I say, is humming in my ears, and prevents me from hearing any other. And I know that anything more which you may say will be in vain. Yet speak, if you have anything to say.

WITNESS TO AN EXECUTION
Death of Socrates, Plato (399 BCE)

When Crito heard, he signaled to the slave who was standing by. The boy went out, and returned after a few moments with the man who was to administer the poison which he brought ready mixed in a cup. When Socrates saw him, he said, "Now, good sir, you understand these things. What must I do?"

"Just drink it and walk around until your legs begin to feel heavy, then lie down. It will soon act." With that he offered Socrates the cup.

The latter took it quite cheerfully without a tremor, with no change of color or expression. He just gave the man his stolid look, and asked, "How say

you, is it permissible to pledge this drink to anyone? May I?"

The answer came, "We allow reasonable time in which to drink it."

I understand', he said, "we can and must pray to the gods that our sojourn on earth will continue happy beyond the grave. This is my prayer, and may it come to pass." With these words, he stoically drank the potion, quite readily and cheerfully. Up till this moment most of us were able with some decency to hold back our tears, but when we saw him drinking the poison to the last drop, we could restrain ourselves no longer. In spite of myself, the tears came in floods, so that I covered my face and wept — not for him, but at my own misfortune at losing such a man as my friend. Crito, even before me, rose and went out when he could check his tears no longer.

Apollodorus was already steadily weeping, and by drying his eyes, crying again and sobbing, he affected everyone present except for Socrates himself.

He said, "You are strange fellows; what is wrong with you? I sent the women away for this very purpose, to stop their creating such a scene. I have heard that one should die in silence. So please be quiet and keep control of yourselves." These words made us ashamed, and we stopped crying.

Socrates walked around until he said that his legs were becoming heavy, when he lay on his back, as the attendant instructed. This fellow felt him, and then a moment later examined his feet and legs again. Squeezing a foot hard, he asked him if he felt anything. Socrates said that he did not. He did the same to his calves and, going higher, showed us that he was becoming cold and stiff. Then he felt him a last time and said that when the poison reached the heart he would be gone.

As the chill sensation got to his waist, Socrates uncovered his head (he had put something over it) and said his last words: "Crito, we owe a cock to Asclepius. Do pay it. Don't forget."

"Of course," said Crito. "Do you want to say anything else?"

There was no reply to this question, but after a while he gave a slight stir, and the attendant uncovered him and examined his eyes. Then Crito saw that he was dead, he closed his mouth and eyelids.

This was the end of our friend, the best, wisest and most upright man of any that I have ever known.

Nicomachean Ethics, Aristotle (350 BCE)

Now 'justice' and 'injustice' seem to be ambiguous, but because their different meanings approach near to one another the ambiguity escapes notice and is not obvious as it is, comparatively, when the meanings are far apart, e.g. (for here the difference in outward form is great) as the ambiguity in the use of kleis for the collar-bone of an animal and for that with which we lock a door. Let us take as a starting-point, then, the various meanings of 'an unjust man.' Both the lawless man and the grasping and unfair man are thought to be unjust, so that evidently both the law-abiding and the fair man will be just. The just, then, is the lawful and the fair, the unjust the unlawful and the unfair

Since the unjust man is grasping, he must be concerned with goods—not all goods, but those with which prosperity and adversity have to do, which taken absolutely are always good, but for a particular person are not always good. Now men pray for and pursue these things; but they should not, but should pray that the things that are good absolutely may also be good for them, and should choose the things that are good for them. The unjust man does not always choose the greater, but also the less-in the case of things bad absolutely; but because the lesser evil is itself thought to be in a sense good, and graspingness is directed at the good, therefore he is thought to be grasping. And he is unfair; for this contains and is common to both.

Since the lawless man was seen to be unjust and the law-abiding man just, evidently all lawful acts are in a sense just acts; for the acts laid down by the legislative art are lawful, and each of these, we say, is just. Now the laws in their enactments on all subjects aim at the common advantage either of all or of the best or of those who hold power, or something of the sort; so that in one sense we call those acts just that tend to produce and preserve happiness and its components for the political society. And the law bids us do both the acts of a brave man (e.g. not to desert our post nor take to flight nor throw away our arms), and those of a temperate man (e.g. not to commit adultery nor to gratify one's lust), and those of a good-tempered man (e.g. not to strike another nor to speak evil), and similarly with regard to the other virtues and forms of wickedness, commanding some acts and forbidding others; and the rightly-framed law does this rightly, and the hastily conceived one less well. This form of justice, then, is complete virtue, but not absolutely, but in relation to our neighbor. And therefore justice is often thought to be the greatest of virtues, and 'neither evening nor morning star' is so wonderful; and proverbially 'in justice is every virtue comprehended.' And it is complete virtue in its fullest sense, because it is the actual exercise of complete virtue. It is complete because he who possesses it can exercise his virtue not only in himself but towards his neighbor also; for many men can exercise virtue in their own affairs, but not in their relations to their neighbor. This is why the saying of Bias is thought to be true, that 'rule will show the man,' for a ruler is necessarily in relation to other men and a member of a society. For this same reason justice, alone of the virtues, is thought to be 'another's good,' because it is related to our neighbor; for it does what is advantageous to another, either a ruler or a copartner. Now the worst man is he who exercises his wickedness both towards himself and towards his friends, and the best man is not he who exercises his virtue towards himself but he who exercises it towards another; for this is a difficult task. Justice in this sense, then, is not part of virtue but virtue entire, nor is the contrary injustice a part of vice but vice entire. What the difference is between virtue and justice in this sense is plain from what we have said; they are the same but their essence is not the same; what, as a relation to one's neighbor, is justice is, as a certain kind of state without qualification, virtue.

A History of Continental Criminal Law: Aristotle, Carl Ludwig von Bar (350 BCE / 1883)

Aristotle's theory of criminal law is unique; it stands quite by itself in ancient times. All other ancient philosophy vouchsafed no independent rights to the individual as against the State, and rather, when necessary, allowed the individual to be absolutely sacrificed to the harmony of the whole without further thought or justification. But Aristotle regarded criminal law not only from the viewpoint of the State inflicting the punishment, but also from the viewpoint of the criminal who has to suffer the punishment. He does not arbitrarily adopt the position (of which Plato availed himself in his discussion of ideals) that punishment is a benefit to the criminal.

Aristotle makes a distinction between justification in punishing and obligation to punish. He bases the former upon a contract entered into by the offender. The offender has encroached too far, since justice consists in no one having too much and no one having too little. The offender, by the commission of the crime, makes an involuntary contract whereby his undue proportion shall be reduced by the judge. This undue proportion, however, which he has taken, does not consist in the advantage which he has obtained, but rather in the encroachment which he has made upon justice; and so the punishment must often be greater than the (external) injury caused by the crime. Accordingly, Aristotle derives punishment not from a justice equalizing matters in accordance with a geometric proportion, but rather from a justice equalizing matters in accordance with an arithmetic proportion. In other words, criminal justice is merely a lateral branch of civil justice and has to do with the reparation of injury. But as the example used by Aristotle — an insult to a magistrate — shows, it is an ideal injury which is contemplated. While the question, whence the State receives the right of criminally punishing, is not directly answered by Aristotle, yet from his treatment of suicide, we perceive that he regarded the injury suffered by the individual as also suffered by the State, and from this must have been inclined to derive the right of the State to inflict punishment.

The relation between justification in punishing and obligation to punish is not clearly marked by Aristotle. When he considers punishment from the latter viewpoint, it has for him an entirely different significance. Here in Aristotle, as in Plato, punishment signifies a healing of the offender. So sharply marked is this meaning that, in his opinion, vengeance is

Punishment counteracts the prevalent desire of the masses for profit at the expense of others, and opposes the prospect of pleasure with one of unhappiness and sorrow.

regarded as the best method of punishment, because of the special satisfaction of the party exercising vengeance. However, this idea is later not uniformly adhered to. It becomes associated with the idea of deterrence. Punishment counteracts the prevalent desire of the masses for profit at the expense of others, and opposes the prospect of pleasure with one of unhappiness and sorrow. It is not clear whether the mere deterrence of the party punished is contemplated — a thing reconcilable with the idea of his reformation — or whether the deterrence of others is meant — a thing which, at least in its intended results, is not reconcilable with the idea of the offender's reformation. The banishment of incorrigibles as a last resort is merely advanced as a viewpoint favored by others, and Aristotle himself does not express an opinion.

Conspiracy of Catiline, Gaius Sallustius Crispus (63)

Caesar, when it came to his turn, being asked his opinion by the consul, spoke to the following effect:

Julius Caesar's Speech

"It becomes all men, Conscript Fathers, who deliberate on dubious matters, to be influenced neither by hatred, affection, anger, nor pity. The mind, when such feelings obstruct its view, cannot easily see what is right; nor has any human being consulted, at the same moment, his passions and his interest. When the mind is freely exerted, its reasoning is sound; but passion, if it gain possession of it, becomes its tyrant, and reason is powerless.

"I could easily mention, Conscript Fathers, numerous examples of kings and nations, who, swayed by resentment or compassion, have adopted injudicious courses of conduct; but I had rather speak of those instances in which our ancestors, in opposition to the impulse of passion, acted with wisdom and sound policy.

"In the Macedonian war, which we carried on against King Perses, the great and powerful state of Rhodes, which had risen by the aid of the Roman people, was faithless and hostile to us; yet, when the war was ended, and the conduct of the Rhodians was taken into consideration, our forefathers left them unmolested, lest any should say that war was made upon them for the sake of seizing their wealth, rather than of punishing their faithlessness. Throughout the Punic Wars, too, though the Carthaginians, both during peace, and in suspensions of arms, were guilty of many acts of injustice, yet our ancestors never took occasion to retaliate, but considered rather what was worthy of themselves, than what might justly be inflicted on their enemies.

"Similar caution, Conscript Fathers, is to be observed by yourselves, that the guilt of Lentulus, and the other conspirators, may not have greater weight with you than you own dignity, and that you may not regard your indignation more than your character. If, indeed, a punishment adequate to their crimes be discovered, I consent to extraordinary measures; but if the enormity of their crime exceeds, whatever can be devised, I think that we should inflict only such penalties as the laws have provided.

"Most of those, who have given their opinions before me, have deplored, in studied and impressive language, the sad fate that threatens the republic; they have recounted the barbarities of war, and the afflictions that would fall on the vanquished; they have told us that maidens would be dishonored, and youths abused; that children would be torn from the embraces of their parents; that matrons would be subjected to the pleasure of the conquerors; that temples and dwelling-houses would be plundered; that massacres and fires would follow; and that every place would be filled with arms, corpses, blood, and lamentation. But to what end— in the name of the eternal gods! — was such eloquence directed? Was it intended to render you indignant at the conspiracy? A speech, no doubt, will inflame him whom so frightful and monstrous a reality has not provoked! Far from it: for to no man does evil, directed against himself, appear a light matter; many, on the contrary, have felt it more seriously than was right.

"But to different persons, Conscript Fathers, different degrees of license are allowed. If those who pass a life sunk in obscurity, commit any error, through excessive anger, few become aware of it, for their fame is as limited as their fortune; but of those who live invested with extensive power, and in an exalted station, the whole world knows the proceedings. Thus in the highest position there is the least liberty of action; and it becomes us to indulge neither partiality nor aversion, but least of all animosity; for what in others is called resentment, is in the powerful termed violence and cruelty.

"I am indeed of opinion, Conscript Fathers, that the utmost degree of torture is inadequate to punish their crime; but the generality of mankind dwell on that which happens last, and, in the case of malefactors, forget their guilt, and talk only of their punishment, should that punishment have been inordinately severe. I feel assured, too, that Decimus Silanus, a man of spirit and resolution, made the suggestions which he offered, from zeal for the state, and that he had no view, in so important a matter, to favor or to enmity; such I know to be his character, and such his discretion. Yet his proposal appears to me, I will not say cruel (for what can be cruel that is directed against such characters?), but foreign to our policy. For assuredly, Silanus, either your fears, or their treason, must have induced you, a consul elect, to propose this new kind of punishment. Of fear it is unnecessary to speak, when, by the prompt activity of that distinguished man our consul, such numerous forces are under arms, and as to the punishment, we may say, what is indeed the truth, that in trouble and distress, death is a relief from suffering, and not a torment; that it puts an end to all human woes; and that, beyond it, there is no place either for sorrow or joy.

"But why, in the name of the immortal gods, did you not add to your proposal, Silanus, that, before they were put to death, they should be punished with the scourge? Was it because the Porcian law forbids it? But other laws forbid condemned citizens to be deprived of life, and allow them to go into exile. Or was it because scourging is a severer penalty than death? Yet what can be too severe, or too harsh, towards men convicted of such an offence? But if scourging be a milder punishment than death, how is it consistent to observe the law as to the smaller point, when you disregard it as to the greater?

"But who, it may be asked, will blame any severity that shall be decreed against these parricides of their country? I answer that time, the course of events, and fortune, whose caprice governs nations, may blame it. Whatever shall fall on the traitors, will fall on them justly; but it is for you, Conscript Fathers, to consider well what you resolve to inflict on others. All precedents productive of evil effects, have had their origin from what was good; but when a government passes into the hands of the ignorant or unprincipled, any new example of severity, inflicted on deserving and suitable objects, is extended to those that are improper and undeserving of it. The Lacedaemonians, when they had conquered the Athenians, appointed thirty men to govern their state. These thirty began their administration by putting to death, even without a trial, all who were notoriously wicked, or publicly detestable; acts at

> **All precedents productive of evil effects, have had their origin from what was good; but when a government passes into the hands of the ignorant or unprincipled, any new example of severity, inflicted on deserving and suitable objects, is extended to those that are improper and undeserving of it.**

which the people rejoiced, and extolled their justice. But afterwards, when their lawless power gradually increased, they proceeded, at their pleasure, to kill the good and bad indiscriminately, and to strike terror into all; and thus the state, overpowered and enslaved, paid a heavy penalty for its imprudent exultation.

"Within our own memory, too, when the victorious Sylla ordered Damasippus, and others of similar character, who had risen by distressing their country, to be put to death, who did not commend the proceeding? All exclaimed that wicked and factious men, who had troubled the state with their seditious practices, had justly forfeited their lives. Yet this proceeding was the commencement of great bloodshed. For whenever any one coveted the mansion or villa, or even the plate or apparel of another, he exerted his influence to have him numbered among the proscribed. Thus they, to whom the death of Damasippus had been a subject of joy, were soon after dragged to death themselves; nor was there any cessation of slaughter, until Sylla had glutted all his partisans with riches.

"Such excesses, indeed, I do not fear from Marcus Tullius, or in these times. But in a large state there arise many men of various dispositions. At some other period, and under another consul, who, like the present, may have an army at his command, some false accusation may be credited as true; and when, with our example for a precedent, the consul shall have drawn the sword on the authority of the senate, who shall stay its progress, or moderate its fury?

"Our ancestors, Conscript Fathers, were never deficient in conduct or courage; nor did pride prevent them from imitating the customs of other nations, if they appeared deserving of regard. Their armor, and weapons of war, they borrowed from the Samnites; their ensigns of authority, for the most part, from the Etrurians; and, in short, whatever appeared eligible to them, whether among allies or among enemies, they adopted at home with the greatest readiness, being more inclined to emulate merit than to be jealous of it. But at the same time, adopting a practice from Greece, they punished their citizens with the scourge, and inflicted capital punishment on such as were condemned. When the republic, however, became powerful, and faction grew strong from the vast number of citizens, men began to involve the innocent in condemnation, and other like abuses were practiced; and it was then that the Porcian and other laws were provided, by which condemned citizens were allowed to go into exile. This lenity of our ancestors, Conscript Fathers, I regard as a very strong reason why we should not adopt any new measures of severity. For assuredly there was greater merit and wisdom in those, who raised so mighty an empire from humble means, than in us, who can scarcely preserve what they so honorably acquired. Am I of opinion, then, you will ask, that the conspirators should be set free, and that the army of Catiline should thus be increased? Far from it; my recommendation is, that their property be confiscated, and that they themselves be kept in custody in such of the municipal towns as are best able to bear the expense; that no one hereafter bring their case before the senate, or speak on it to the people; and that the senate now give their opinion, that he who shall act contrary to this, will act against the republic and the general safety."

When Caesar had ended his speech, the rest briefly expressed their assent, some to one speaker, and some to another, in support of their different proposals; but Marcus Porcius Cato, being asked his opinion, made a speech to the following purport:

Marcus Porcius Cato's Speech

"My feelings, Conscript Fathers, are extremely different, when I contemplate our circumstances and dangers, and when I revolve in my mind the sentiments of some who have spoken before me. Those speakers, as it seems to me, have considered only how to punish the traitors who have raised war against their country, their parents, their altars, and their homes; but the state of affairs warns us rather to secure ourselves against them, than to take counsel as to what sentence we should pass upon them. Other crimes you may punish after they have been committed; but as to this, unless you prevent its commission, you will, when it has once taken effect, in vain appeal to justice. When the city is taken, no power is left to the vanquished.

"But, in the name of the immortal gods, I call upon you who have always valued your mansions and villas, your statues and pictures, at a higher price than the welfare of your country; if you wish to preserve those possessions, of whatever kind they are, to which you are attached; if you wish to secure quiet for the enjoyment of your pleasures, arouse yourselves, and act in defense of your country. We are not now debating on the revenues, or on injuries done to our allies, but our liberty and our life is at stake.

"Often, Conscript Fathers, have I spoken at great length in this assembly;

often have I complained of the luxury and avarice of our citizens, and, by that very means, have incurred the displeasure of many. I, who never excused to myself, or to my own conscience, the commission of any fault, could not easily pardon the misconduct, or indulge the licentiousness, of others. But though you little regarded my remonstrances, yet the republic remained secure; its own strength was proof against your remissness. The question, however, at present under discussion, is not whether we live in a good or bad state of morals; nor how great, or how splendid, the empire of the Roman people is; but whether these things around us, of whatever value they are, are to continue our own, or to fall, with ourselves, into the hands of the enemy.

"In such a case, does any one talk to me of gentleness and compassion? For some time past, it is true, we have lost the real names of things; for to lavish the property of others is called generosity, and audacity in wickedness is called heroism; and hence the state is reduced to the brink of ruin. But let those, who thus misname things, be liberal, since such is the practice, out of the property of our allies; let them be merciful to the robbers of the treasury; but let them not lavish our blood, and, while they spare a few criminals, bring destruction on all the guiltless.

"Caius Caesar, a short time ago, spoke in fair and elegant language, before this assembly, on the subject of life and death; considering as false, I suppose, what is told of the dead; that the bad, going a different way from the good, inhabit places gloomy, desolate, dreary, and full of horror. He accordingly proposed that the property of the conspirators should be confiscated, and themselves kept in custody in the municipal towns; fearing, it seems, that, if they remain at Rome, they may be rescued either by their accomplices in the conspiracy, or by a hired mob; as if, forsooth, the mischievous and profligate were to be found only in the city, and not through the whole of Italy, or as if desperate attempts would not be more likely to succeed where there is less power to resist them. His proposal therefore, if he fears any danger from them, is absurd; but if, amidst such universal terror, he alone is free from alarm, it the more concerns me to fear for you and myself.

"Be assured, then, that when you decide on the fate of Lentulus and the other prisoners, you at the same time determine that of the army of Catiline, and of all the conspirators. The more spirit you display in your decision, the more will their confidence be diminished; but if they shall perceive you in the smallest degree irresolute, they will advance upon you with fury. Do not suppose that our ancestors, from so small a commencement, raised the republic to greatness merely by force of arms. If such had been the case, we should enjoy it in a most excellent condition; for of allies and citizens, as well as arms and horses, we have a much greater abundance than they had. But there were other things which made them great, but which among us have no existence; such as industry at home, equitable government abroad, and minds impartial in council, uninfluenced by any immoral or improper feeling. Instead of such virtues, we have luxury and avarice, public distress, and private superfluity; we extol wealth, and yield to indolence; no distinction is made between good men and bad; and ambition usurps the honors due to virtue. Nor is this wonderful; since you study each his individual interest, and since at home you are slaves to pleasure, and here to money or favor; and hence it happens that an attack is made on the defenseless state.

"But on these subjects I shall say no more. Certain citizens, of the highest rank, have conspired to ruin their country; they are engaging the Gauls, the bitterest foes of the Roman name, to join in a war against us; the leader of the enemy is ready to make a descent upon us; and do you hesitate, even in such circumstances how to treat armed incendiaries arrested within your walls? I advise you to have mercy upon them; they are young men who have been led astray by ambition; send them away, even with arms in their hands. But such mercy, and such clemency, if they turn those arms against you, will end in misery to yourselves. The case is, assuredly, dangerous, but you do not fear it; yes, you fear it greatly, but you hesitate how to act, through weakness and want of spirit, waiting one for another, and trusting to the immortal gods, who have so often preserved your country in the greatest dangers. But the protection of the gods is not obtained by vows and effeminate supplications; it is by vigilance, activity, and prudent measures, that general welfare is secured. When you are once resigned to sloth and indolence, it is in vain that you implore the gods; for they are then indignant and threaten vengeance.

Titus Manlius Torquatus, during a war with the Gauls, ordered his own son to be put to death, because he had fought with an enemy contrary to orders. . . do you hesitate what sentence to pass on the most inhuman of traitors?

In the days of our forefathers, Titus Manlius Torquatus, during a war with the Gauls, ordered his own son to be put to death, because he had fought with an enemy contrary to orders. That noble youth suffered for excess of bravery; and do you hesitate what sentence to pass on the most inhuman of traitors? Perhaps their former life is at variance with their present crime. Spare, then, the dignity of Lentulus, if he has ever spared his own honor or character, or had any regard for gods or for men. Pardon the youth of Cethegus, unless this be the second time that he has made war upon his country. As to Gabinius, Statilius, Coeparius, why should I make any remark upon them? Had they ever possessed the smallest share of discretion, they would never have engaged in such a plot against their country.

"In conclusion, Conscript Fathers, if there were time to amend an error, I might easily suffer you, since you disregard words, to be corrected by experience of consequences. But we are beset by dangers on all sides; Catiline, with his army, is ready to devour us; while there are other enemies within the walls, and in the heart of the city; nor can any measures be taken, or any plans arranged, without their knowledge. The more necessary is it, therefore, to act with promptitude. What I advise, then, is this: that since the state, by a treasonable combination of abandoned citizens, has been brought into the greatest peril; and since the conspirators have been convicted on the evidence of Titus Volturcius, and the envoys of the Allobroges, and on their own confession, of having concerted massacres, conflagrations, and other horrible and cruel outrages, against their fellow-citizens and their country, punishment be inflicted, according to the usage of our ancestors, on the prisoners who have confessed their guilt, as on men convicted of capital crimes."

❖ ❖ ❖

When Cato had resumed his seat, all the senators of consular dignity, and a great part of the rest, applauded his opinion, and extolled his firmness of mind to the skies. With mutual reproaches, they accused one another of timidity, while Cato was regarded as the greatest and noblest of men; and a decree of the senate was made as he had advised. [. . .]

When the senate, as I have stated, had gone over to the opinion of Cato, the consul, thinking it best not to wait till night, which was coming on, lest any new attempts should be made during the interval, ordered the triumvirs to make such preparations as the execution of the conspirators required. He himself, having posted the necessary guards conducted Lentulus to the prison; and the same office was performed for the rest by the praetors.

There is a place in the prison, which is called the Tullian dungeon, and which, after a slight ascent to the left, is sunk about twelve feet underground. Walls secure it on every side, and over it is a vaulted roof connected with stone arches; but its appearance is disgusting and horrible, by reason of the filth, darkness, and stench. When Lentulus had been let down into this place, certain men, to whom orders had been given, strangled him with a cord. Thus this patrician, who was of the illustrious family of the Cornelii, and who had filled the office of consul at Rome, met with an end suited to his character and conduct. On Cethegus, Statilius, Gabinius, and Coeparius, punishment was inflicted in a similar manner.

WITNESS TO AN EXECUTION
Execution of Mithridates, Plutarch (1st Century)

Mithridates should be put to death in boats; which execution is after the following manner: Taking two boats framed exactly to fit and answer each other, they lay down in one of them the malefactor that suffers, upon his back; then, covering it with the other, and so setting them together that the head, hands, and feet of him are left outside, and the rest of his body lies shut up within, they offer him food, and if he refuse to eat it, they force him to do it by pricking his eyes; then, after he has eaten, they drench him with a mixture of milk and honey, pouring it not only into his mouth, but all over his face. They then keep his face continually turned towards the sun ; and it becomes completely covered up and hidden by the multitude of flies that settle on it. And as within the boats he does what those that eat and drink must needs do, creeping things and vermin spring out of the corruption and rottenness of the excrement and these entering into the bowels of him, his body is consumed. When the man is manifestly dead, the uppermost boat being taken off, they find his flesh devoured, and swarms of such noisome creatures preying upon and, as it were, growing to his inwards. In this way Mithridates, after suffering for seventeen days, at last expired.

On Mercy, Seneca (1st Century)

Above all, however, alike to the highest and the lowest, extends the same admiration for your quality of mercy; for although of other blessings each one experiences or expects a larger or smaller measure in proportion to his lot, yet from mercy men all hope to have the same; nor is there any man so wholly satisfied with his own innocence as not to rejoice that mercy stands in sight, waiting for human errors.

I know, however, that there are some who think that mercy upholds the worst class of men, since it is superfluous unless there has been some crime, and since it alone of all the virtues finds no exercise among the guiltless. But, first of all, just as medicine is used by the sick, yet is held in honor by the healthy, so with mercy — though it is those who deserve punishment that invoke it, yet even the guiltless cherish it. Again, this virtue has scope even in the person of the guiltless, because at times fortune takes the place of guilt; and not only does mercy come to the rescue of innocence, but often of righteousness also, inasmuch as, from the state of the times, there arise certain acts which, while praised, may yet be punished. Then, too, there are a great many people who might be turned back to the path of virtue if they are released from punishment. Nevertheless, pardoning ought not to be too common; for when the distinction between the bad and the good is removed, the result is confusion and an epidemic of vice. Therefore a wise moderation should be exercised which will be capable of distinguishing between curable and hopeless characters. Neither should we have indiscriminate and general mercy, nor yet preclude it; for it is as much a cruelty to pardon all as to pardon none. We should maintain the mean; but since a perfect balance is difficult, if anything is to disturb the equipoise it should turn the scale toward the kindlier side.

WITNESS TO AN EXECUTION
Execution of Aper (284)

A general assembly of the army was appointed to be held at Chalcedon, whither Aper was transported in chains, as a prisoner and a criminal. A vacant tribunal was erected in the midst of the camp, and the generals and tribunes formed a great military council. They soon announced to the multitude that their choice had fallen on Diocletian, commander of the domestics or body-guards, as the person the most capable of revenging and succeeding their beloved emperor. The future fortunes of the candidate depended on the chance or conduct of the present hour. Conscious that the station which he had filled exposed him to some suspicions, Diocletian ascended the tribunal, and raising his eyes towards the Sun, made a solemn profession of his own innocence, in the presence of that all-seeing Deity. Then, assuming the tone of a sovereign and a judge, he commanded that Aper should be brought in chains to the foot of the tribunal. "This man," said he, "is the murderer of Numerian;" and without giving him time to enter on a dangerous justification, drew his sword, and buried it in the breast of the unfortunate præfect. A charge supported by such decisive proof was admitted without contradiction, and the legions, with repeated acclamations, acknowledged the justice and authority of the Emperor Diocletian.

WITNESS TO AN EXECUTION
The Tenth Persecution under Diocletian, Foxe's Book of Martyrs (303)

Victor was a Christian of a good family at Marseilles, in France; he spent a great part of the night in visiting the afflicted, and confirming the weak; which pious work he could not, consistently with his own safety, perform in the daytime; and his fortune he spent in relieving the distresses of poor Christians.

He was at length, however, seized by the Emperor Maximian's decree, who ordered him to be bound, and dragged through the streets. During the execution of this order, he was treated with all manner of cruelties and indignities by the enraged populace. Remaining still inflexible, his courage was deemed obstinacy.

Being by order stretched upon the rack, he turned his eyes towards heaven, and prayed to God to imbue him with patience, after which he underwent the tortures with most admirable fortitude. After the executioners were tired with inflicting torments on him, he was conveyed to a dungeon. In his confinement,

he converted his jailers, named Alexander, Felician, and Longinus. This affair coming to the ears of the emperor, he ordered them immediately to be put to death, and the jailers were accordingly beheaded. Victor was then again put to the rack, unmercifully beaten with batons, and again sent to prison.

Being a third time examined concerning his religion, he persevered in his principles; a small altar was then brought, and he was commanded to offer incense upon it immediately. Fired with indignation at the request, he boldly

stepped forward, and with his foot overthrew both altar and idol. This so enraged the emperor Maximian, who was present, that he ordered the foot with which he had kicked the altar to be immediately cut off; and Victor was thrown into a mill, and crushed to pieces with the stones, A. D. 303.

Maximus, governor of Cilicia, being at Tarsus, three Christians were brought before him; their names were Tarachus, an aged man; Probus, and Andronicus. After repeated tortures and exhortations to recant, they, at length, were ordered for execution.

Being brought to the amphitheatre, several beasts were let loose upon them; but none of the animals, though hungry, would touch them. The keeper then brought out a large bear, that had that very day destroyed three men; but this voracious creature and a fierce lioness both refused to touch the prisoners. Finding the design of destroying them by the means of wild beasts ineffectual, Maximus ordered them to be slain by the sword, on the 11th of October, A. D. 303.

Romanus, a native of Palestine, was deacon of the church of Cæsarea, at the time of the commencement of Diocletian's persecution. Being condemned for his faith at Antioch, he was scourged, put to the rack, his body torn with hooks, his flesh cut with knives, his face scarified, his teeth beaten from their sockets, and his hair plucked up by the roots. Soon after he was ordered to be strangled, Nov. 17, A. D. 303.

Susanna, the niece of Caius, bishop of Rome, was pressed by the Emperor Diocletian to marry a noble pagan, who was nearly related to him. Refusing the honor intended her, she was beheaded by the emperor's order. [. . .]

Peter, a eunuch belonging to the emperor, was a Christian of singular modesty and humility. He was laid on a gridiron, and broiled over a slow fire till he expired. [. . .]

Eulalia, a Spanish lady of a Christian family, was remarkable in her youth for sweetness of temper, and solidity of understanding seldom found in the capriciousness of juvenile years. Being apprehended as a Christian, the magistrate attempted by the mildest means, to bring her over to paganism, but she ridiculed the pagan deities with such asperity, that the judge, incensed at her behavior, ordered her to be tortured. Her sides were accordingly torn by hooks, and her breasts burnt in the most shocking manner, till she expired by the violence of the flames, Dec. A. D. 303.

City of God (*De Civitate Dei*), Augustine of Hippo (5th Century)

However, there are some exceptions made by the divine authority to its own law, that men may not be put to death. These exceptions are of two kinds, being justified either by a general law, or by a special commission granted for a time to some individual. And in this latter case, he to whom authority is delegated, and who is but the sword in the hand of him who uses it, is not himself responsible for the death he deals. And, accordingly, they who have waged war in obedience to the divine command, or in conformity with His laws, have represented in their persons the public justice or the wisdom of government, and in this capacity have put to death wicked men; such persons have by no means violated the commandment, *You shall not kill*. Abraham indeed was not merely deemed guiltless of cruelty, but was even applauded for his piety, because he was ready to slay his son in obedience to God, not to his own passion. And it is reasonably enough made a question, whether we are to esteem it to have been in compliance with a command of God that Jephthah killed his daughter, because she met him when he had vowed that he would sacrifice to God whatever first met him as he returned victorious from battle. Samson, too, who drew down the house on himself and his foes together, is justified only on this ground, that the Spirit who wrought wonders by him had given him secret instructions to do this. With the exception, then, of these two classes of cases, which are justified either by a just law that applies generally or by a special intimation from God Himself, the fountain of all justice, whoever kills a man, either himself or another, is implicated in the guilt of murder.

Summa Theologica, Thomas Aquinas (1264-1275)

Question 64 (Murder), Article 2. Whether it is lawful to kill sinners?

Objection 1. It would seem unlawful to kill men who have sinned. For our Lord in the parable (Matthew 13) forbade the uprooting of the cockle which denotes wicked men according to a gloss. Now whatever is forbidden by God is a sin. Therefore it is a sin to kill a sinner.

Objection 2. Further, human justice is conformed to Divine justice. Now according to Divine justice sinners are kept back for repentance, according to Ezekiel 33:11, "I desire not the death of the wicked, but that the wicked turn from his way and live." Therefore it seems altogether unjust to kill sinners.

Objection 3. Further, it is not lawful, for any good end whatever, to do that which is evil in itself, according to Augustine (*Contra Mendac.* vii) and the Philosopher (*Ethic.* ii, 6). Now to kill a man is evil in itself, since we are bound to have charity towards all men, and "we wish our friends to live and to exist," according to Ethic. ix, 4. Therefore it is nowise lawful to kill a man who has sinned.

On the contrary, It is written (Exodus 22:18): "Wizards thou shalt not suffer to live," and (Psalm 100:8): "In the morning I put to death all the wicked of the land."

I answer that, as stated above (Article 1), it is lawful to kill dumb animals, in so far as they are naturally directed to man's use, as the imperfect is directed to the perfect. Now every part is directed to the whole, as imperfect to perfect, wherefore every part is naturally for the sake of the whole. For this reason we observe that if the health of the whole body demands the excision of a member, through its being decayed or infectious to the other members, it will be both praiseworthy and advantageous to have it cut away. Now every individual person is compared to the whole community, as part to whole. Therefore if a man be dangerous and infectious to the community, on account of some sin, it is praiseworthy and advantageous that he be killed in order to safeguard the common good, since "a little leaven corrupteth the whole lump." (1 Corinthians 5:6).

Reply to Objection 1. Our Lord commanded them to forbear from uprooting the cockle in order to spare the wheat, i.e. the good. This occurs when the wicked cannot be slain without the good being killed with them, either because the wicked lie hidden among the good, or because they have many followers, so that they cannot be killed without danger to the good, as Augustine says (Contra *Parmen.* iii, 2). Wherefore our Lord teaches that we should rather allow the wicked to live, and that vengeance is to be delayed until the last judgment, rather than that the good be put to death together with the wicked. When, however, the good incur no danger, but rather are protected and saved by the slaying of the wicked, then the latter may be lawfully put to death.

Reply to Objection 2. According to the order of His wisdom, God sometimes slays sinners forthwith in order to deliver the good, whereas sometimes He allows them time to repent, according as He knows what is expedient for His elect. This also does human justice imitate according to its powers; for it puts to death those who are dangerous to others, while it allows time for repentance to those who sin without grievously harming others.

Reply to Objection 3. By sinning man departs from the order of reason, and consequently falls away from the dignity of his manhood, insofar as he is naturally free, and exists for himself, and he falls into the slavish state of the beasts, by being disposed of according as he is useful to others. This is expressed in Psalm 48:21: "Man, when he was in honor, did not understand; he hath been compared to senseless beasts, and made like to them," and Proverbs 11:29: "The fool shall serve the wise." Hence, although it be evil in itself to kill a man so long as he preserve his dignity, yet it may be good to kill a man who has sinned, even as it is to kill a beast. For a bad man is worse than a beast, and is more harmful, as the Philosopher states (*Polit.* i, 1 and *Ethic.* vii, 6).

Utopia, Sir Thomas More (1516)

One day, when I was dining with him, there happened to be at table one of the English lawyers, who took occasion to run out in a high commendation of the severe execution of justice upon thieves, "who," as he said, "were then hanged so fast that there were sometimes twenty on one gibbet!" and, upon that, he said, "he could not wonder enough how it came to pass that, since so few escaped, there were yet so many thieves left, who were still robbing in all places." Upon this, I (who took the boldness to speak freely before the Cardinal) said, "There was no reason to wonder at the matter, since this way of punishing thieves was neither just in itself nor good for the public; for, as the severity was too great, so the remedy was not effectual; simple theft not being so great a crime that it ought to cost a man his life; no punishment, how severe soever, being able to restrain those from robbing who can find out no other way of livelihood.

"In this," said I, "not only you in England, but a great part of the world, imitate some ill masters, that are readier to chastise their scholars than to teach them. There are dreadful punishments enacted against thieves, but it were much better to make such good provisions by which every man might be put in a method how to live, and so be preserved from the fatal necessity of stealing and of dying for it."

"There has been care enough taken for that," said he; "there are many handicrafts, and there is husbandry, by which they may make a shift to live, unless they have a greater mind to follow ill courses."

"That will not serve your turn," said I, "for many lose their limbs in civil or foreign wars, as lately in the Cornish rebellion, and some time ago in your wars with France, who, being thus mutilated in the service of their king and country, can no more follow their old trades, and are too old to learn new ones; but since wars are only accidental things, and have intervals, let us consider those things that fall out every day.

There is a great number of noblemen among you that are themselves as idle as drones, that subsist on other men's labor, on the labor of their tenants, whom, to raise their revenues, they pare to the quick. This, indeed, is the only instance of their frugality, for in all other things they are prodigal, even to the beggaring of themselves; but, besides this, they carry about with them a great number of idle fellows, who never learned any art by which they may gain their living; and these, as soon as either their lord dies, or they themselves fall sick, are turned out of doors; for your lords are readier to feed idle people than to take care of the sick; and often the heir is not able to keep together so great a family as his predecessor did. Now, when the stomachs of those that are thus turned out of doors grow keen, they rob no less keenly; and what else can they do? For when, by wandering about, they have worn out both their health and their clothes, and are tattered, and look ghastly, men of quality will not entertain them, and poor men dare not do it, knowing that one who has been bred up in idleness and pleasure, and who was used to walk about with his sword and buckler, despising all the neighborhood with an insolent scorn as far below him, is not fit for the spade and mattock; nor will he serve a poor man for so small a hire and in so low a diet as he can afford to give him."

To this he answered, "This sort of men ought to be particularly cherished, for in them consists the force of the armies for which we have occasion; since their birth inspires them with a nobler sense of honor than is to be found among tradesmen or ploughmen."

"You may as well say," replied I, "that you must cherish thieves on the account of wars, for you will never want the one as long as you have the other; and as robbers prove sometimes gallant soldiers, so soldiers often prove brave robbers, so near an alliance there is between those two sorts of life. But this bad custom, so common among you, of keeping many servants, is not peculiar to this nation. In France there is yet a more pestiferous sort of people, for the whole country is full of soldiers, still kept up in time of peace (if such a state of a nation can be called a peace); and these are kept in pay upon the same account that you plead for those idle retainers about noblemen: this being a maxim of those pretended statesmen, that it is necessary for the public safety to have a good body of veteran soldiers ever in readiness. They think raw men are not to be depended on, and they sometimes seek occasions for making war, that they may train up their soldiers in the art of cutting throats, or, as Sallust observed, "'or keeping their hands in use, that they may not grow dull by too long an intermission."

But France has learned to its cost how dangerous it is to feed such beasts. The fate of the Romans, Carthaginians, and Syrians, and many other nations and cities, which were both overturned and quite ruined by those standing armies, should make others wiser; and the folly of this maxim of the French appears plainly even from this, that their trained soldiers often find your raw men prove too hard for them, of which I will not say much, lest you may think I flatter the English.

Every day's experience shows that the mechanics in the towns or the clowns in the country are not afraid of fighting with those idle gentlemen, if they are not disabled by some misfortune in their body or dispirited by extreme want; so that you need not fear that those well-shaped and strong men (for it is only such that noblemen love to keep about them till they spoil them), who now grow feeble with ease and are softened with their effeminate manner of life, would be less fit for action if they were well bred and well employed. And it seems very unreasonable that, for the prospect of a war, which you need never have but when you please, you should maintain so many idle men, as will always disturb you in time of peace, which is ever to be more considered than war. But I do not think that this necessity of stealing arises only from hence; there is another cause of it, more peculiar to England." [. . .]

If you do not find a remedy to these evils it is a vain thing to boast of your severity in punishing theft, which, though it may have the appearance of justice, yet in itself is neither just nor convenient; for if you suffer your people to be ill-educated, and their manners to be corrupted from their infancy, and then punish them for those crimes to which their first education disposed them, what else is to be concluded from this but that you first make thieves and then punish them?"

While I was talking thus, the Counselor, who was present, had prepared an answer, and had resolved to resume all I had said, according to the formality of a debate, in which things are generally repeated more faithfully than they are answered, as if the chief trial to be made were of men's memories.

"You have talked prettily, for a stranger," said he, "having heard of many things among us which you have not been able to consider well; but I will make the whole matter plain to you, and will first repeat in order all that you have said; then I will show how much your ignorance of our affairs has misled you; and will, in the last place, answer all your arguments. And, that I may begin where I promised, there were four things--"

"Hold your peace!" said the Cardinal; "this will take up too much time; therefore we will, at present, ease you of the trouble of answering, and reserve it to our next meeting, which shall be to-morrow, if Raphael's affairs and yours can admit of it.

"But, Raphael," said he to me, "I would gladly know upon what reason it is that you think theft ought not to be punished by death: would you give way to it? Or do you propose any other punishment that will be more useful to the public? For, since death does not restrain theft, if men thought their lives would be safe, what fear or force could restrain ill men?"

"On the contrary, they would look on the mitigation of the punishment as an invitation to commit more crimes." I answered, "It seems to me a very unjust thing to take away a man's life for a little money, for nothing in the world can be of equal value with a man's life: and if it be said, "that it is not for the money that one suffers, but for his breaking the law," I must say, extreme justice is an extreme injury: for we ought not to approve of those terrible laws that make the smallest offences capital, nor of that opinion of the Stoics that makes all crimes equal; as if there were no difference to be made between the killing a man and the taking his purse, between which, if we examine things impartially, there is no likeness nor proportion. God has commanded us not to kill, and shall we kill so easily for a little money?

> **It seems to me a very unjust thing to take away a man's life for a little money, for nothing in the world can be of equal value with a man's life.**

But if one shall say, that by that law we are only forbid to kill any except when the laws of the land allow of it, upon the same grounds, laws may be made, in some cases, to allow of adultery and perjury: for God having taken from us the right of disposing either of our own or of other people's lives, if it is pretended that the mutual consent of men in making laws can authorize manslaughter in cases in which God has given us no example, that it frees people from the obligation of the divine law, and so makes murder a lawful action, what is this, but to give a preference to human laws before the divine? And, if this is once admitted, by the same rule men may, in all other things, put what restrictions they please upon the laws of God. If, by the Mosaical Law, though it was rough and severe, as being a yoke laid on an obstinate and servile nation, men were only fined, and not put to death for theft, we cannot imagine, that in this new law of mercy, in which God treats us with the tenderness of a father, He has given us a greater license to cruelty than He did to the Jews.

Upon these reasons it is, that I think putting thieves to death is not lawful; and it is plain and obvious that it is absurd and of ill consequence to the commonwealth that a thief and a murderer should be equally punished; for if a robber sees that his danger is the same if he is convicted of theft as if he were guilty of murder, this will naturally incite him to kill the person whom otherwise he would only have robbed; since, if the punishment is the same, there is more security, and less danger of discovery, when he that can best make it is put out of the way; so that terrifying thieves too much provokes them to cruelty."

But as to the question, 'What more convenient way of punishment can be found?' I think it much easier to find out that than to invent anything that is worse; why should we doubt but the way that was so long in use among the old Romans, who understood so well the arts of government, was very proper for their punishment?

They condemned such as they found guilty of great crimes to work their whole lives in quarries, or to dig in mines with chains about them. But the method that I liked best was that which I observed in my travels in Persia, among the Polylerits, who are a considerable and well-governed people: they pay a yearly tribute to the King of Persia, but in all other respects they are a free nation, and governed by their own laws: they lie far from the sea, and are environed with hills; and, being contented with the productions of their own country, which is very fruitful, they have little commerce with any other nation; and as they, according to the genius of their country, have no inclination to enlarge their borders, so their mountains and the pension they pay to the Persian, secure them from all invasions.

Thus they have no wars among them; they live rather conveniently than with splendor, and may be rather called a happy nation than either eminent or famous; for I do not think that they are known, so much as by name, to any but their next neighbors.

Those that are found guilty of theft among the mare-bound to make restitution to the owner, and not, as it is in other places, to the prince, for they reckon that the prince has no more right to the stolen goods than the thief; but if that which was stolen is no more in being, then the goods of the thieves are estimated, and restitution being made out of them, the remainder is given to their wives and children; and they themselves are condemned to serve in the public works, but are neither imprisoned nor chained, unless there happens to be some extraordinary circumstance in their crimes.

They go about loose and free, working for the public: if they are idle or backward to work they are whipped, but if they work hard they are well used and treated without any mark of reproach; only the lists of them are called always at night, and then they are shut up. They suffer no other uneasiness but this of constant labor; for, as they work for the public, so they are well entertained out of the public stock, which is done differently in different places: in some places whatever is bestowed on them is raised by a charitable contribution; and, though this way may seem uncertain, yet so merciful are the inclinations of that people, that they are plentifully supplied by it; but in other places public revenues are set aside for them, or there is a constant tax or poll-money raised for their maintenance.

In some places they are set to no public work, but every private man that has occasion to hire workmen goes to the market-places and hires them of the public, a little lower than he would do a freeman.

If they go lazily about their task he may quicken them with the whip. By this means there is always some piece of work or other to be done by them; and, besides their livelihood, they earn somewhat still to the public.

They all wear a peculiar habit, of one certain color, and their hair is cropped a little above their ears, and a piece of one of their ears is cut off. Their friends are allowed to give them either meat, drink, or clothes, so they are of their proper color; but it is death, both to the giver and taker, if they give them money; nor is it less penal for any freeman to take money from them upon any account whatsoever: and it is also death for any of these slaves (so they are called) to handle arms. Those of every division of the country are distinguished by a peculiar mark, which it is capital for them to lay aside, to go out of their bounds, or to talk with a slave of another jurisdiction, and the very attempt of an escape is no less penal than an escape itself. It is death for any other slave to be accessory to it; and if a freeman engages in it he is condemned to slavery. Those that discover it are rewarded--if freemen, in money; and if slaves, with liberty, together with a pardon for being accessory to it; that so they might find their account rather in repenting of their engaging in such a design than in persisting in it.

These are their laws and rules in relation to robbery, and it is obvious that they are as advantageous as they are mild and gentle; since vice is not only destroyed and men preserved, but they are treated in such a manner as to make them see the necessity of being honest and of employing the rest of their lives in repairing the injuries they had formerly done to society.

Nor is there any hazard of their falling back to their old customs; and so little do travelers apprehend mischief from them that they generally make use of them for guides from one jurisdiction to another; for there is nothing left them by which they can rob or be the better for it, since, as they are disarmed, so the very having of money is a sufficient conviction: and as they are certainly punished if discovered, so they cannot hope to escape; for their habit being in all the parts of it different from what is commonly worn, they cannot flyaway, unless they would go naked, and even then their cropped ear would betray them.

The only danger to be feared from them is their conspiring against the government; but those of one division and neighborhood can do nothing to any purpose unless a general conspiracy were laid amongst all the slaves of the several jurisdictions, which cannot be done, since they cannot meet or talk together; nor will any venture on a design where the concealment would be so dangerous and the discovery so profitable.

None are quite hopeless of recovering their freedom, since by their obedience and patience, and by giving good grounds to believe that they will change their manner of life for the future, they may expect at last to obtain their liberty, and some are every year restored to it upon the good character that is given of them. "

When I had related all this, I added that I did not see why such a method might not be followed with more advantage than could ever be expected from that severe justice which the Counselor magnified so much.

To this he answered, "That it could never take place in England without endangering the whole nation." As he said this he shook his head, made some grimaces, and held his peace, while all the company seemed of his opinion, except the Cardinal, who said, "That it was not easy to form a judgment of its success, since it was a method that never yet had been tried; but if," said he, "when sentence of death were passed upon a thief, the prince would reprieve him for a while, and make the experiment upon him, denying him the privilege of a sanctuary; and then, if it had a good effect upon him, it might take place; and, if it did not succeed, the worst would be to execute the sentence on the condemned persons at last; and I do not see," added he, "why it would be either unjust, inconvenient, or at all dangerous to admit of such a delay; in my opinion the vagabonds ought to be treated in the same manner, against whom, though we have made many laws, yet we have not been able to gain our end."

When the Cardinal had done, they all commended the motion, though they had despised it when it came from me, but more particularly commended what related to the vagabonds, because it was his own observation.

The Prince, Niccolò Machiavelli (1532)

Upon this a question arises: whether it be better to be loved than feared or feared than loved? It may be answered that one should wish to be both, but, because it is difficult to unite them in one person, it is much safer to be feared than loved, when, of the two, either must be dispensed with. Because this is to be asserted in general of men, that they are ungrateful, fickle, false, cowardly, covetous, and as long as you succeed they are yours entirely; they will offer you their blood, property, life, and children, as is said above, when the need is far distant; but when it approaches they turn against you. And that prince who, relying entirely on their promises, has neglected other precautions, is ruined; because friendships that are obtained by payments, and not by greatness or nobility of mind, may indeed be earned, but they are not secured, and in time of need cannot be relied upon; and men have less scruple in offending one who is beloved than one who is feared, for love is preserved by the link of obligation which, owing to the baseness of men, is broken at every opportunity for their advantage; but fear preserves you by a dread of punishment which never fails.

Nevertheless a prince ought to inspire fear in such a way that, if he does not win love, he avoids hatred; because he can endure very well being feared whilst he is not hated, which will always be as long as he abstains from the property of his citizens and subjects and from their women. But when it is necessary for him to proceed against the life of someone, he must do it on proper justification and for manifest cause, but above all things he must keep his hands off the property of others, because men more quickly forget the death of their father than the loss of their patrimony. Besides, pretexts for taking away the property are never wanting; for he who has once begun to live by robbery will always find pretexts for seizing what belongs to others; but reasons for taking life, on the contrary, are more difficult to find and sooner lapse. But when a prince is with his army, and has under control a multitude of soldiers, then it is quite necessary for him to disregard the reputation of cruelty, for without it he would never hold his army united or disposed to its duties. [. . .]

He must keep his hands off the property of others, because men more quickly forget the death of their father than the loss of their patrimony.

Returning to the question of being feared or loved, I come to the conclusion that, men loving according to their own will and fearing according to that of the prince, a wise prince should establish himself on that which is in his own control and not in that of others; he must endeavor only to avoid hatred, as is noted.

[. . .] When the duke occupied the Romagna he found it under the rule of weak masters, who rather plundered their subjects than ruled them, and gave them more cause for disunion than for union, so that the country was full of robbery, quarrels, and every kind of violence; and so, wishing to bring back peace and obedience to authority, he considered it necessary to give it a good governor. Thereupon he promoted Messer Ramiro d'Orco, a swift and cruel man, to whom he gave the fullest power. This man in a short time restored peace and unity with the greatest success. Afterwards the duke considered that it was not advisable to confer such excessive authority, for he had no doubt but that he would become odious, so he set up a court of judgment in the country, under a most excellent president, wherein all cities had their advocates. And because he knew that the past severity had caused some hatred against himself, so, to clear himself in the minds of the people, and gain them entirely to himself, he desired to show that, if any cruelty had been practiced, it had not originated with him, but in the natural sternness of the minister. Under this pretence he took Ramiro, and one morning caused him to be executed and left on the piazza at Cesena with the block and a bloody knife at his side. The barbarity of this spectacle caused the people to be at once satisfied and dismayed.

WITNESS TO AN EXECUTION
The Execution of Archbishop Thomas Cranmer (1556)

But that I know for our great friendships, and long continued love, you look even of duty that I should signify to you of the truth of such things as here chanceth among us; I would not at this time have written to you the unfortunate end, and doubtful tragedy, of Thomas Cranmer late bishop of Canterbury: because I little pleasure take in beholding of such heavy sights. And, when they are once overpassed, I like not to rehearse them again; being but a renewing of my woe, and doubling my grief. For although his former, and wretched end, deserves a greater misery, (if any greater might have chanced than chanced unto him), yet, setting aside his offenses to God and his country, and beholding the man without his faults, I think there was none that pitied not his case, and bewailed not his fortune, and feared not his own chance, to see so noble a prelate, so grave a counsellor, of so long continued honor, after so many dignities, in his old years to be deprived of his estate, adjudged to die, and in so painful a death to end his life. I have no delight to increase it. Alas, it is too much of itself, that ever so heavy a case should betide to man, and man to deserve it.

But to come to the matter: on Saturday last, being 21 of March, was his day appointed to die. And because the morning was much rainy, the sermon appointed by Mr Dr Cole to be made at the stake, was made in St. Mary's church: whither Dr Cranmer was brought by the mayor and aldermen, and my lord Williams: with whom came divers gentlemen of the shire, Sir T. A. Bridges, Sir John Browne, and others. Where was prepared, over against the pulpit, a high place for him, that all the people might see him. And, when he had ascended it, he kneeled him down and prayed, weeping tenderly: which moved a great number to tears, that had conceived an assured hope of his conversion and repentance [. . .]

When praying was done, he stood up, and, having leave to speak, said, 'Good people, I had intended indeed to desire you to pray for me; which because Mr Doctor hath desired, and you have done already, I thank you most heartily for it. And now will I pray for myself, as I could best devise for mine own comfort, and say the prayer, word for word, as I have here written it.' And he read it standing: and after kneeled down, and said the Lord's Prayer; and all the people on their knees devoutly praying with him....

And then rising, he said, 'Every man desireth, good people, at the time of their deaths, to give some good exhortation, that other may remember after their deaths, and be the better thereby. So I beseech God grant me grace, that I may speak something, at this my departing, whereby God may be glorified, and you edified [. . .]

And now I come to the great thing that troubleth my conscience more than nay other thing that ever I said or did in my life: and that is, the setting abroad of writings contrary to the truth. Which here now I renounce and refuse, as things written with my hand, contrary to the truth which I thought in my heart, and written for fear of death, and to save my life, if it might be: and that is, all such bills, which I have written or signed with mine own hand since my degradation: wherein I have written many things untrue. And forasmuch as my hand offended in writing contrary to my heart, therefore my hand shall first be punished: for if I may come to the fire, it shall be first burned. And as for the Pope, I refuse him, as Christ's enemy and antichrist, with all his false doctrine.'

And here, being admonished of his recantation and dissembling, he said, 'Alas, my lord, I have been a man that all my life loved plainness, and never dissembled till now against the truth; which I am most sorry for it.' He added hereunto, that, for the sacrament, he believed as he had taught in his book against the bishop of Winchester. And here he was suffered to speak no more. [. . .]

Then was he carried away; and a great number, that did run to see him go so wickedly to his death, ran after him, exhorting him, while time was, to remember himself. And one Friar John, a godly and well learned man, all the way traveled with him to reduce him. But it would not be. What they said in particular I cannot tell, but the effect appeared in the end: for at the stake he professed, that he died in all such opinions as he had taught, and oft repented him of his recantation.

Coming to the stake with a cheerful countenance and willing mind, he put off his garments with haste, and stood upright in his shirt: and bachelor of divinity, named Elye, of Brazen-nose College, labored to convert him to his former recantation, with the two Spanish friars. And when the friars saw his constancy, they said in Latin to one another 'Let us go from him: we ought not to be nigh him: for the devil is with him.' But the bachelor of divinity was more earnest with him: unto whom he answered, that, as concerning his recantation, he repented it right sore, because he knew it was against the truth; with other words more. Whereby the Lord Williams cried, 'Make short, make short.' Then the bishop took certain of his friends by the hand. But the bachelor of divinity refused to take him by the hand, and blamed all the others that so did, and said, he was sorry that ever he came in his company. And yet again he required him to agree to his former recantation. And the bishop answered, (showing his hand), 'This was the hand that wrote it, and therefore shall it suffer first punishment.'

Fire being now put to him, he stretched out his right hand, and thrust it into the flame, and held it there a good space, before the fire came to any other part of his body; where his hand was seen of every man sensibly burning, crying with a loud voice, 'This hand hath offended.' As soon as the fire got up, he was very soon dead, never stirring or crying all the while.

His patience in the torment, his courage in dying, if it had been taken either for the glory of God, the wealth of his country, or the testimony of truth, as it was for a pernicious error, and subversion of true religion, I could worthily have commended the example, and matched it with the fame of any father of ancient time: but, seeing that not the death, but cause and quarrel thereof, commendeth the sufferer, I cannot but much dispraise his obstinate stubbornness and sturdiness in dying, and specially in so evil a cause. Surely his death much grieved every man; but not after one sort. Some pitied to see his body so tormented with the fire raging upon the silly carcass, that counted not of the folly. Other that passed not much of the body, lamented to see him spill his soul, wretchedly, without redemption, to be plagued forever. His friends sorrowed for love; his enemies for pity; strangers for a common kind of humanity, whereby we are bound one to another. Thus I have enforced myself, for your sake, to discourse this heavy narration, contrary to my mind: and, being more than half weary, I make a short end, wishing you a quieter life, with less honor; and easier death, with more praise.

WITNESS TO AN EXECUTION
Dirk Willems, Martyr's Mirror (1569)

In the year 1569 a pious, faithful brother and follower of Jesus Christ, named Dirk Willems, was apprehended at Asperen, in Holland, and had to endure severe tyranny from the papists. But as he had founded his faith not upon the drifting sand of human commandments, but upon the firm foundation stone, Christ Jesus, he, notwithstanding all evil winds of human doctrine, and heavy showers of tyrannical and severe persecution, remained immovable and steadfast unto the end; wherefore, when the chief Shepherd shall appear in the clouds of heaven and gather together His elect from all the ends of the earth, he shall also through grace hear the words, "Well done, good and faithful servant; thou hast been faithful over a few things, I will make thee ruler over many things; enter thou into the joy of thy Lord."

Concerning his apprehension, it is stated by trustworthy persons, that when he fled he was hotly pursued by a thief-catcher, and as there had been some frost, said Dirk Willems ran before over the ice, getting across with considerable peril. The thief-catcher following him broke through, when Dirk Willems, perceiving that the former was in danger of his life, quickly returned and aided him in getting out, and thus saved his life. The thief-catcher wanted to let him go, but the burgomaster, very sternly called to him to consider his oath, and thus he was again seized by the thief-catcher, and, at said place, after severe imprisonment and great trials proceeding from the deceitful papists, put to death at a lingering fire by these bloodthirsty, ravening wolves, enduring it with great steadfastness, and confirming the genuine faith of the truth with his death and blood, as an instructive example to all pious Christians of this time, and to the everlasting disgrace of the tyrannous papists.

In this connection, it is related as true from the trustworthy memoirs of those who were present at the death of this pious witness of Jesus Christ, that the place where this offering occurred was without Asperen, on the side of Leerdam, and that, a strong east wind blowing that day, the kindled fire was much driven away from the upper part of his body, as he stood at the stake; in consequence of which this good man suffered a lingering death, insomuch that in the town of Leerdam, towards which the wind was blowing, he was heard to exclaim over seventy times, "O my Lord; my God," etc., for which cause the judge or bailiff, who was present on horseback, filled with sorrow and regret at the man's sufferings, wheeled about his horse, turning his back toward the place of execution, and said to the executioner, "Dispatch the man with a quick death." But how or in what manner the executioner then dealt with this pious witness of Jesus, I have not been able to learn, except only, that his life was consumed by the fire, and that he passed through the conflict with great steadfastness, having commended his soul into the hands of God.

WITNESS TO AN EXECUTION
Execution of Mary, Queen of Scots (1587)

First in the hall of the said castle was a stage, raised of seven feet square every way, and about five feet in height. At the two upper corners were two stools set, one for the Earl of Shrewsbury, another for the Earl of Kent; directly between the said stools was placed a block one foot high, covered with black, and before that stood a little cushion stool for the queen to sit on while her apparel was taken off. Round about the stage stood the high sheriff, with others appointed for the purpose.

About nine a.m., came that sweet saint and martyr, led like a lamb to the butchery, attired in a gown of black satin embroidered with a French kind of embroidery of black velvet; her hair seemly trussed up with a veil of white lawn, which covered her head and all her other apparel down to the foot. Being come into the hall, she stayed, and with a smiling countenance asked Shrewsbury why none of her own servants were suffered to be present. He answered that the queen his mistress had so commanded. "Alas," quoth she, "far meaner persons than myself have not been denied so small a favor, and I hope the queen's majesty will not deal so hardly with me."

"Madam," quoth Shrewsbury, "it is so appointed to avoid two inconveniences, the one that it is likely your people will shriek and make some fearful noise in the time of your execution, and so both trouble you and us, or else press with some disorder to get of your blood and keep it for a relic and minister offence that way." "My lord," answered she, "I pray you for my better quietness of mind let me have some of my servants about me, and I will give you my word that they shall not offend in any sort."

Upon which promise two of her women and five of her men were sent for, who coming into the hall, and seeing the place of execution prepared and their sovereign mistress expecting death, they began to cry out in most woeful and pitiful sort; wherewith she held up her hand, willing them for her sake to forbear and be silent, "for," quoth she, "I have passed my word to these lords that you shall be quiet and not offend them:" and presently there appeared in them a wonderful show of subjection, and loyal obedience, as to their natural prince, whom even at the instant of death they honoured with all reverence and duty. For though their breasts were seen to rise and swell as if their wounded hearts would have burst in sunder, yet did they to their double grief forbear their outward plaints to accomplish her pleasure.

As soon as she was upon the stage, there came to her a heretic, called Doctor Fletcher, dean of Peterborough, and told her how the queen his sovereign, moved with an unspeakable care of her soul, had sent him to instruct and comfort her in the true words of God. At which she somewhat turned her face towards him, saying, "Mr. Doctor, I will have nothing to do with you, nor your doctrine;" and forthwith kneeled down before the block, and began her meditation in most godly manner. Then the doctor entered also into a form of new-fashioned prayers; but the better to prevent the hearing of him, she raised her voice, and prayed so loud, as he could not be understood.

The Earl of Shrewsbury then spoke to her, and told her that he would pray with her, and for her. "My lord," quoth she, "if you will pray for me I thank you; but, in so doing, pray secretly by yourself, for we will not pray together." Her mediations ended, she arose up and kissed her two gentlewomen, and bowed her body towards her men, and charged them to remember her to her sweet son, to whom she sent her blessing, with promise to pray for him in heaven; and lastly to salute her friends, and so took her last farewell of her poor servants.

The executioners then began, after their rough and rude manner, to disrobe her, and while they were so doing, she looked upon the noblemen, and smilingly said, "Now truly, my lords, I never had two such grooms waiting on me before!" Then, being ready for the block, one of her women took forth a handkerchief of cambric, all wrought over with gold needlework, and tied it about her face; which done, Fletcher willed her to die in the true faith of Christ. Quoth she, "I believe firmly to be saved by the passion and blood of Jesus Christ, and therein also I believe, according to the faith of the Ancient Catholic Church of Rome, and therefore I shed my blood." She finished her happy and blessed martyrdom to the comfort of all true Catholics, and to the shame and confusion of all heretics.

Of Experience, Michel de Montaigne (1588)

Socrates asked Menon, "What virtue was." "There is," says Menon, "the virtue of a man and of a woman, of a magistrate and of a private person, of an old man and of a child." "Very fine," cried Socrates, "we were in quest of one virtue, and thou hast brought us a whole swarm." We put one question, and they return us a whole hive. As no event, no face, entirely resembles another, so do they not entirely differ: an ingenious mixture of nature. If our faces were not alike, we could not distinguish man from beast; if they were not unlike, we could not distinguish one man from another; all things hold by some similitude; every example halts, and the relation which is drawn from experience is always faulty and imperfect. Comparisons are ever-coupled at one end or other: so do the laws serve, and are fitted to every one of our affairs, by some wrested, biased, and forced interpretation.

Since the ethic laws, that concern the particular duty of every one in himself, are so hard to be framed, as we see they are, 'tis no wonder if those which govern so many particulars are much more so. Do but consider the form of this justice that governs us; 'tis a true testimony of human weakness, so full is it of error and contradiction. What we find to be favor and severity in justice— and we find so much of them both, that I know not whether the medium is as often met with are sickly and unjust members of the very body and essence of justice. Some country people have just brought me news in great haste, that they presently left in a forest of mine a man with a hundred wounds upon him, who was yet breathing, and begged of them water for pity's sake, and help to carry him to some place of relief; they tell me they durst not go near him, but have run away, lest the officers of justice should catch them there; and as happens to those who are found near a murdered person, they should be called in question about this accident, to their utter ruin, having neither money nor friends to defend their innocence. What could I have said to these people? 'Tis certain that this office of humanity would have brought them into trouble.

How many innocent people have we known that have been punished, and this without the judge's fault; and how many that have not arrived at our knowledge? This happened in my time: certain men were condemned to die for a murder committed; their sentence, if not pronounced, at least determined and concluded on. The judges, just in the nick, are informed by the officers of an inferior court hard by, that they have some men in custody, who have directly confessed the murder, and made an indubitable discovery of all the particulars of the fact. Yet it was gravely deliberated whether or not they ought to suspend the execution of the sentence already passed upon the first accused: they considered the novelty of the example judicially, and the consequence of reversing judgments; that the sentence was passed, and the judges deprived of repentance; and in the result, these poor devils were sacrificed by the forms of justice. Philip, or some other, provided against a like inconvenience after this manner. He had condemned a man in a great fine towards another by an absolute judgment. The truth some time after being discovered, he found that he had passed an unjust sentence. On one side was the reason of the cause; on the other side, the reason of the judicial forms: he in some sort satisfied both, leaving the sentence in the state it was, and out of his own purse recompensing the condemned party. But he had to do with a reparable affair; my men were irreparably hanged. How many condemnations have I seen more criminal than the crimes themselves?

How many condemnations have I seen more criminal than the crimes themselves?

All which makes me remember the ancient opinions, "That 'tis of necessity a man must do wrong by retail who will do right in gross; and injustice in little things, who would come to do justice in great: that human justice is formed after the model of physic, according to which, all that is useful is also just and honest: and of what is held by the Stoics, that Nature herself proceeds contrary to justice in most of her works: and of what is received by the Cyrenaics, that there is nothing just of itself, but that customs and laws make justice: and what the Theodorians held that theft, sacrilege, and all sorts of uncleanness, are just in a sage, if he knows them to be profitable to him." There is no remedy: I am in the same case that Alcibiades was, that I will never, if I can help it, put myself into the hands of a man who may determine as to my head, where my life and honor shall more depend upon the skill and diligence of my attorney than on my own innocence. I would venture myself with such justice as would take notice of my good deeds, as well as my ill; where I had as much to hope as to fear: indemnity is not sufficient pay to a man who does better than not to do amiss. Our justice presents to us but one hand, and that the left hand, too; let him be who he may, he shall be sure to come off with loss. In China, of which kingdom the government and arts, without commerce with or knowledge of ours, surpass our examples in several excellent features, and of which the history teaches me how much greater and more various the world is than

I will never, if I can help it, put myself into the hands of a man who may determine as to my head, where my life and honor shall more depend upon the skill and diligence of my attorney than on my own innocence.

either the ancients or we have been able to penetrate, the officers deputed by the prince to visit the state of his provinces, as they punish those who behave themselves ill in their charge, so do they liberally reward those who have conducted themselves better than the common sort, and beyond the necessity of their duty; these there present themselves, not only to be approved but to get; not simply to be paid, but to have a present made to them. No judge, thank God, has ever yet spoken to me in the quality of a judge, upon any account whatever, whether my own or that of a third party, whether criminal or civil; nor no prison has ever received me, not even to walk there. Imagination renders the very outside of a jail displeasing to me; I am so enamored of liberty, that should I be interdicted the access to some corner of the Indies, I should live a little less at my ease; and whilst I can find earth or air open elsewhere, I shall never lurk in any place where I must hide myself. My God! How ill should I endure the condition wherein I see so many people, nailed to a corner of the kingdom, deprived of the right to enter the principal cities and courts, and the liberty of the public roads, for having quarreled with our laws. If those under which I live should shake a finger at me by way of menace, I would immediately go seek out others, let them be where they would. All my little prudence in the civil wars wherein we are now engaged is employed that they may not hinder my liberty of going and coming.

Now, the laws keep up their credit, not for being just, but because they are laws; 'tis the mystic foundation of their authority; they have no other, and it well answers their purpose. They are often made by fools, still oftener by men who, out of hatred to equality, fail in equity, but always by men, vain and irresolute authors. There is nothing so much, nor so grossly, nor so ordinarily faulty, as the laws. Whoever obeys them because they are just, does not justly obey them as he ought. Our French laws, by their irregularity and deformity, lend, in some sort, a helping hand to the disorder and corruption that all manifest in their dispensation and execution: the command is so perplexed and inconstant, that it in some sort excuses alike disobedience and defect in the interpretation, the administration and the observation of it. What fruit then soever we may extract from experience, that will little advantage our institution, which we draw from foreign examples, if we make so little profit of that we have of our own, which is more familiar to us, and, doubtless, sufficient to instruct us in that whereof we have need.

Disputations on Controversial Matters
Saint Robert Bellarmine (1596)

John Huss, in the recorded article 14 of the Council of Constance, session 15, asserted that it is not permitted to hand over an incorrigible heretic to the secular power and to allow the penalty of burning. Luther held the same in article 33 and its assertion. Nor is the error new, for the Donatists also taught the same, like Parmenianus, Petilianus, and Gaudentius (as Augustine testifies, in Book I against the letter of Parmenianus, in Chapter 7, Book II against the Letters of Petilianus, in Chapter 10 of Book II, against the letter of Gaudentius, and in Chapters 17 and 26 of his Letter 50 to Boniface.)

All Catholics teach the contrary, and even some of the heretics. For Calvin, after he had publicly punished as a heretic Michael Servetus with the ultimate penalty, and after it was debated by other sectarians, published a book in which he demonstrates that it is permissible to take notice of heretics with a sword. Also Benedict Aretus, in a history of the punishment of Valentius Gentilis, argues that the same Gentilis was rightly punished by the Magistrate Bernensis. Theodore Beza, indeed, teaches the same, at greater length, in a book on the punishment of heretics by a magistrate.

We, then, will briefly show that incorrigible heretics, and especially recidivists, can and should be expelled by the Church and be punished by the secular powers with temporal punishments and even by death itself.

The first proof is from Scripture: The Scripture of the Old Testament (in Deuteronomy XIII, 12) commands most severely that false prophets who encourage the worship of false gods be put to death, and in Chapter XVII, after saying that in doubtful cases the High Priest should be consulted, soon adds: "If the person is haughty, however, and is unwilling to obey the command of the High Priest, let him die by the sentence of the judge. (Deuteronomy XVII, 12). And, again, in Chapter XVIII, the false prophet is sentenced to be killed.

And, in reality, Elias (or Elijah), Josias (Josiah), Jehu, and others observed this law by killing a great many false prophets, as is clear from III Kings, XVIII, and IV Kings, X and XXIII, there is almost no difference between our heretics and the false prophets of those days. Nor did only the holy Kings and Prophets punish blasphemers with death, but even Nabuchodonosor [now more often spelled Nebuchadnezzar], as is said in Daniel III, promulgated an edict, that whoever should blaspheme the God of Daniel, that is, the true God, should be put to death and his home be destroyed; in the same edict, he performed a most worthy service to the True God, as St. Augustine remarks in his Epistle 50 and elsewhere. In the New Testament, in Matthew XVIII, we find that the Church can excommunicate and treat as aliens and tax-gatherers those who refuse to obey and to allow them to be treated by the secular powers as no longer children of the Church. We have, then, in Romans XIII, 4, that the secular power can punish criminals with sword: "It is not without purpose that the ruler carries a sword; he is God's servant, to inflict His avenging wrath upon the wrongdoer." From these two scriptural passages, it can be clearly inferred that it is permissible that heretics, who by the judgment of all are rebels against the Church and disturbers of public peace, be cut off from the Church and be punished with death by a secular judge.

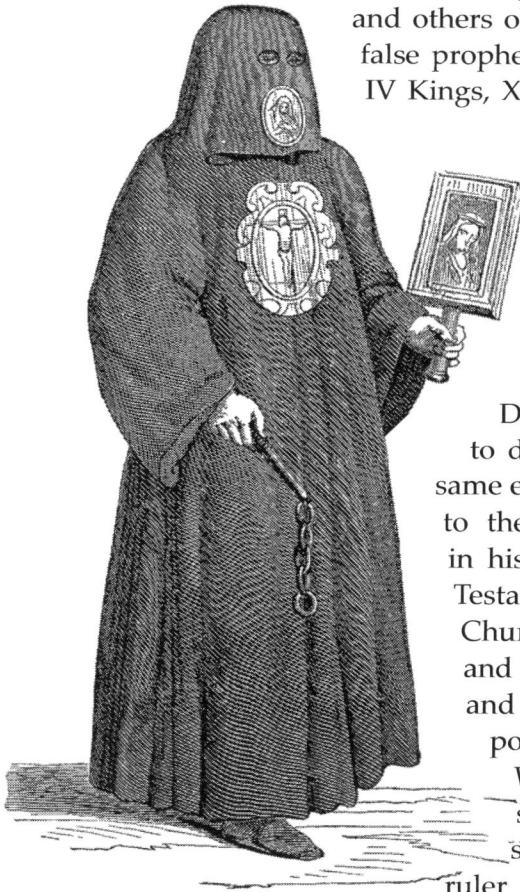

Moreover, Christ and His Apostles have placed heretics in the same category as those matters that can be disposed of, without question, by fire and sword; for in Matthew VII the Lord says: "Be on your guard against false prophets, who come to you in sheep's clothing but underneath are wolves on the prowl." In Acts 20: 29: "I know that when I am gone, savage wolves will come among you who will not spare the flock." It is certain that heretics ought to be known by the title of "wolves," as St. Ambrose explains in his commentary on the beginning of Chapter X of St. Luke. But ravenous wolves are killed for an excellent reason, if they cannot otherwise be driven away; for much more should be made of the lives of the sheep than of the deaths of wolves. Likewise, in John X, 1: "Truly, I assure you: Whoever does not enter the sheepfold through the gate but climbs in some other way is a thief and a marauder." Under the name of thief and marauder heretics are meant, and all subversives and founders of sects, as Chrysostom and Augustine explain; how thieves and marauders should be punished has been explained. Likewise, in II Timothy, II, heresy is compared to a cancer which is not cured by medications but should be excised with a knife, otherwise it will spread progressively and the whole body will be destroyed. Finally, Christ, in John, Chapter II, using a whip forces the merchants to leave the temple. Peter, in Acts V, killed Ananias and Sapphira because they had presumed to lie to the Holy Spirit; and Paul, in Acts XIII, vs. 6-12, struck with blindness the false prophet who was trying to keep Sergius Paulus, the Roman proconsular governor, from the Faith.

The matter is proved, secondly, from the sentences and laws of the Emperors which the Church regularly approved. The Emperor Constantine the First sent into exile Arius and some companions at the request of the Nicene Synod, as the author Sozomenus notes in Book I, Chapter 20 of his History; likewise, he imposed the penalty of death on the Donatists, as Augustine reports in Book I, in a letter opposed to Parmenianus, Chapter 7, and in Epistle 166,

to the Donatists, wherein he enumerates many excellent Emperors who passed many very severe laws against the heretics, and only one, Julian the Apostate, favored heretics.

Then Theodosius, Valentinianus, Martianus, and other very religious Emperors passed laws against heretics by which, on occasion, they sought to punish by fines of pounds of gold, sometimes by confiscation of all their goods, sometimes by exile and scourging, sometimes by imposing the ultimate penalty, as is clear from "C. de hereticis, L. Nanichaeos, L. Ariani, L. Quicumque." by the last of these laws, which is one of Valentinian and Martian, all are to be put to death who attempt to teach perverse doctrine; those, also, who listen to these teachers are punished by fines of some pounds of gold. Justinian, as recorded by Paul the Deacon in Book XVI, by a promulgated law, banished all heretics beyond the boundaries of the entire Empire, while allowing three months for their conversion; later, the Emperor Michael, as is related in Book XXIV of the same Paul the Deacon, established the capital punishment for heretics.

A third proof is had in the laws of the Church: under the headings, "*Ad abolendum*," "*Excommunicamus, extra de hereticis*," and in "*Sexto de hereticis*" in the chapter ahead of it, the Church defines that incorrigible heretics are to be handed over to the secular power, so that they may be punished in a just manner. Likewise, the Council of Constance, in session XV, condemned the opinion of John Huss; and it handed over the same John and Jerome of Prague to the secular power, by whom the two were burned; finally, Leo the Tenth condemned the articles of Luther.

A fourth proof is had in the testimonies of the Fathers. Cyprian, in a book of exhortation on martyrdom, in Chapter 5, after he had recalled from Deuteronomy XIII, that pseudoprophets should be killed, he added, "If this was done under the Old Testament, much more should it be done under the New."

Jerome, in reference to the text in Galatians, Chapter 5, "A little yeast can effect the entire dough," (v. 9) says: "as soon as a spark appears, it should be extinguished, and yeast close to a batch should be removed; spoiled meat should be cut away, and a scabby animal should be driven from a sheepfold, lest the whole house, or mass, or body, or herd burn, be corrupted, spoil, or perish. Arius was one spark, but since he was not immediately extinguished, the whole earth was affected by his flame."

Augustine, in Book II of his Retractions, Chapter 5, and in Epistles 48 and 50, retracts what he had once thought, that heretics should not be forced to believe, and proves at length that it is very useful; he always rules out the punishment of death, not because he thought they did not deserve this, but both because he judged that this was unbecoming the gentleness of the Church and also because no imperial law was in existence, by which heretics were sentenced to death; for the Law, "*Quicumque, C. de hereticis*," was promulgated a little after the death of Augustine.

That, however, Augustine judged it to be just, if heretics were put to death, is beyond question; for, in Book I, in opposition to the letter of Parmenianus, in Chapter 7, he demonstrates that if the Donatists were punished by death, they would be justly so punished. And in Tract 11, on John: "They kill souls, he says, and are afflicted in the body, those who bring about eternal deaths complain that they suffer temporal deaths," by which he says they falsely complain that they are killed by Emperors; nevertheless, even if this were true, they would be complaining unjustly. Finally, in his Letter 50, to Boniface, he writes that the Church does not want any heretic to be put to death: nevertheless, as the House of David could not enjoy peace unless Absalom were done away with and David was consoled by the peace of his realm in his grief over the death of his son: so when, from the laws of Emperors against heretics, the deaths of some follow, the sorrow of the maternal heart of the Church is assuaged by the deliverance of a multitude of people.

St. Leo, in Letter 91, to Turbius, Chapter 1: "Deservedly," he wrote, "our Fathers, in whose time this nefarious heresy broke out throughout the world, acted immediately to drive out the unholy madness from the universal Church; when, also, the Rulers of the world so detested this sacrilegious madness, that they destroyed its author and many of his disciples by the sword of public law; and this interference with Ecclesiastical lenience, which, although content with a judgment that fled from bloody punishments, was nevertheless helped by the severe laws of Christian Rulers, while they who fear corporal punishment sometimes revert to a spiritual remedy." *Optatus Milevitanus*, in Book III, in replying to the calumnies of heretics who were sorrowful over the death of two of theirs killed by the Prefect Macarius: "You see," he wrote, "that similar things were done by Moses, and Phineas, and Elias, and Macharia, because the punishment of the One God emanates from all of them."

St. Gregory, in Book I, Letter 72, to Gennadius, the Exarch of Africa, praises him because he persecuted heretics with weapons, and he urges him to continue.

St. Bernard in Sermon 66, on the Canticle: "They without doubt would be better coerced by the sword of him who, not without cause, carries the sword, than that they be allowed to draw many into their error; for he is a servant of the Lord and vindicator of wrath against him who does evil. Some marvel that they were not only patiently but joyfully led to death, but they scarcely recognize how great is the power of the Devil, not only over the bodies of men but even over their hearts, once he has been allowed to possess them. Is it not better for a man to take himself in hand, than for him willingly to accept force from another."

There is, finally, a proof from reason. First, heretics can be justly excommunicated, as all admit. Therefore, that they [may be] put to death. The consequence is proved from the fact that excommunication is a greater penalty than temporal death. Augustine, in Book I, contra advers. Legis et Prophetarum [against the adversaries of the Law and the Prophets], Chapter 17, says it is more terrible to be given over to Satan through excommunication, than to be struck down by the sword, be consumed by flames, or exposed to being devoured by animals.

Secondly, experience teaches that there is no other remedy; for the Church proceeded gradually, and tried all remedies; first, it fines, then exile, finally, it was driven to the penalty of death; for the heretics show contempt for excommunication and call them "cold thunderbolts;" if you threaten the penalty of fines, they neither fear God nor revere men, since they know that ignorant people will be found who will believe them and feed them. If you confine them to prison or send them into exile, they will corrupt their neighbors with their speech and those who are far away with their books. Therefore, there is only one remedy, send them timely to their place.

Thirdly, forgers, in the judgment of all, deserve death; but heretics are forgers of the Word of God.

Fourthly, by the reasoning of Augustine, in Letter 50, it is more serious for man to fail to keep faith with God, than for a women not to keep faith with a man, but this is punished by death, why not the former?

Fifthly, there are three reasons why, as reason teaches, men are to be put to death, as Galen eloquently teaches in a book whose title is: "That the habits of the soul imitate the temperaments of the body," toward the end of the book.

The first reason is, Lest the evil injure the good, or the innocent be abused by the injurious, in the judgment of all, all are to be executed who are guilty of homicide, adultery, or robbery. The second reason is: That, by the punishment of the few, the many may be corrected: and that those who are unwilling to help society by living may benefit it by dying. And hence, we also see that, in the opinion of all, certain most horrendous crimes are most justly punished by death, even though they do no injury to the neighbor, except by example: crimes like Necromancy, crimes that are abominable and contrary to nature are, therefore, most severely punished, in order that others may know they are monstrous crimes and should not dare to perpetrate the like. Thirdly, because to the very men who are killed it is beneficial to be killed, when, namely, they are becoming ever worse and it is not probable that they will ever revert to sanity of mind.

All these reasons are persuasive that heretics should be put to death; for, in the first place, they injure the neighbor more seriously than any pirate or robber, since they kill souls; even worse, they take away the foundation for all good and fill the state with the upheavals that inevitably result from the diversity of religions.

WITNESS TO AN EXECUTION
Auto da Fe, Madrid (1682)

The officers of the Inquisition, preceded by trumpets, kettledrums, and their banner, marched on the thirtieth of May, in cavalcade, to the palace of the great square, where they declared by proclamation, that, on the thirtieth of June, the sentence of the prisoners would be put in execution.

Of these prisoners, twenty men and women, with one renegade Mahometan, were ordered to be burned; fifty Jews and Jewesses, having never before been imprisoned, and repenting of their crimes, were sentenced to a long confinement, and to wear a yellow cap. The whole court of Spain was present on this occasion. The grand inquisitor's chair was placed in a sort of tribunal far above that of the king.

Among those who were to suffer, was a young Jewess of exquisite beauty, and but seventeen years of age. Being on the same side of the scaffold where the queen was seated, she addressed her, in hopes of obtaining a pardon, in the following pathetic speech: "Great queen, will not your royal presence be of some service to me in my miserable condition? Have regard to my youth; and, oh! consider, that I am about to die for professing a religion imbibed from my earliest infancy!" Her majesty seemed greatly to pity her distress, but turned away her eyes, as she did not dare to speak a word in behalf of a person who had been declared a heretic.

Now Mass began, in the midst of which the priest came from the altar, placed himself near the scaffold, and seated himself in a chair prepared for that purpose.

The chief inquisitor then descended from the amphitheater, dressed in his cope, and having a miter on his head. After having bowed to the altar, he advanced towards the king's balcony, and went up to it, attended by some of his officers, carrying a cross and the Gospels, with a book containing the oath by which the kings of Spain oblige themselves to protect the Catholic faith, to extirpate heretics, and to support with all their power and force the prosecutions and decrees of the Inquisition: a like oath was administered to the counselors and whole assembly. The Mass was begun about twelve at noon, and did not end until nine in the evening, being protracted by a proclamation of the sentence of the several criminals, which were already separately rehearsed aloud one after the other.

After this followed the burnings of the twenty-one men and women, whose intrepidity in suffering that horrid death was truly astonishing. The king's near situation to the criminals rendered their dying groans very audible to him; he could not, however, be absent from this dreadful scene, as it is esteemed a religious one; and his coronation oath obliged him to give a sanction by his presence to all the acts of the tribunal.

The Spanish Inquisition, Count Joseph de Maistre (1822)

Monsieur Le Comte,

IHave had the satisfaction of exciting, both your interest, and your astonishment, in the course of our conversations, on the subject of the Inquisition. You have, therefore, for your own use, and convenience, requested me to commit to writing the different reflections, which I have presented to you, concerning this celebrated institution. [. . .]

The Jews were, at this time, nearly the masters of Spain: and there existed between them, and the Catholic body, a mutual, and mortal, hatred. The Cortes, therefore, now demanded the introduction of severe, and coercive, measures against them. In 1391, they rebelled: and multitudes of them perished. As, however, the danger was, every day, increasing, Ferdinand, surnamed to "the Catholic," conceived, that, in order to save Spain, nothing would contribute more effectually than the Inquisition. To this, Isabella, at first, made strong objection. But, at length, she was induced to consent: and Sixtus IV, in the year 1478, issued out the Bulls of Institution.

Permit me, again, my Lord, before I proceed any farther, to suggest to your consideration another important observation: It is this, that never can any great political disorder, but, above all, any violent attack upon the body of the state, be pre- vented, or repelled, but by the adoption of means, alike violent, and energetic. This is one of the most incontestable axioms in the code of politics. In all real and imminent, dangers, the rule of Roman prudence, "*Videant Consules, ne respublica de trimentum capiat*" {"Let the consuls look to the safety of the state."} is the dictate of enlightened policy. In regard of the methods to be employed, or actually employed, on such occasions, the best are those, I, of course, exclude crime, and injustice, the best are those, which succeed. If you consider only the severities of Torquemada, without calculating the evils, which they prevented, you, in this case, cease to reason.

Wherefore, let us constantly bear in mind this fundamental truth: That the Inquisition, in its origin, was an institution demanded and established by the kings of Spain, under very difficult, and extraordinary, circumstances. This is expressly acknowledged by the Committee of the Cortes. And the reason, which that assembly assigns for its suppression, is simply the consideration, that, as circumstances are now changed, so the Inquisition is now, no longer, necessary.

People have often expressed their surprise at seeing the Inquisitors overload an accused person with a multiplicity of questions, in order to ascertain the fact, whether or not, in his genealogy, he retained any portion, or drop, of Jewish, or Mahometan, blood. "What matters it" they say, "to know, who was the grandfather, or the great-grandfather, of the accused?" What matters it? It, at that time, mattered greatly: because both of the proscribed races, being still intimately connected, and allied, with the great families of the state, must necessarily, either have trembled, or have created terror.

Under these circumstances, it became a concern of prudence to strike, and alarm, the imagination, by constantly holding out the threat of the anathema, attached to the suspicion of Judaism, and Mahomitanism. It is a great mistake to suppose, that, in order to get rid of a powerful enemy, it suffices always merely to arrest him. You must subdue him; or you have done nothing.

With the exception of a small number of enlightened individuals, you hardly ever, in society, meet with a person, who, speaking of the Inquisition, is not impressed with three capital errors; and these so fast riveted to the mind, as not to yield to the very plainest demonstrations. For example, the public, everywhere believe, that the Inquisition is a purely ecclesiastical tribunal, a notion, which, in the first place, is false. Secondly, they believe, that the ecclesiastics, who sit in this tribunal, condemn certain accused criminals to death. This again is false. Thirdly, they believe, that the tribunal condemns men for entertaining mere simple opinions. This, too, is another falsehood.

The tribunal, then, of the Inquisition, is purely, and completely, royal. It is the King alone, who appoints the Inquisitor General. And the Inquisitor General, in his turn, nominates the particular Inquisitors, subject to the approval of the King. The constitutional rules, and order, of the tribunal were drawn up, and published, in the year 1484, by Cardinal Torquemada, "in concert with the King."

The inferior Inquisitors possessed no power to do anything without the approbation of the Grand Inquisitor: neither could the latter do aught without the concurrence, and sanction, of the Supreme Council. This Council was not established by any Bull of the Pope; so that in the case of the General Inquisitor's charge becoming vacant, the members of the tribunal proceeded to act, alone, not as ecclesiastical, but as royal Judges.

The Inquisitor General, in virtue of the Bulls of the Sovereign Pontiff; and the King, in virtue of his royal prerogatives, constitute the authority, which has always regulated the tribunals of the Inquisition. These tribunals are, thus, at once ecclesiastical, and royal; so that, on the supposition of one or other of the two powers receding, the action of these tribunals would, in such case, be necessarily suspended.

The committee of the Cortes, in their Report, have thought proper to represent the two powers, as in a state of equilibrium, in the tribunals of the Inquisition. But, no one, surely, can be the dupe of such misrepresentation, or of the falsehood of this pretended equilibrium. The Inquisition is purely a royal instrument, completely, and exclusively, under the control of the King; and powerless to do evil, save through the fault of his ministers. If the proceedings in any cause are not regular; or the proofs not clear, the King's Councilors can always, where there is question of capital punishments, at once, and by one word, annul the whole process. Neither religion, nor the priesthood, have, in such cases, anything at all to do, in the concern. If unhappily it do so chance, that the accused is punished, without being guilty, the fault, and the injustice, would then be, either in the King, whose laws had unjustly ordained the punishment; or else, in the magistrates, who unjustly inflicted it. But, of this I will cite the proofs, hereafter.

You may remark, my Lord, that, among the numberless declamations, which have been published against the Inquisition, you never trace so much as one word, respecting this distinctive character of the tribunal, a circumstance, however, which, in justice, all writers on the subject ought essentially to have remarked. Thus, Voltaire, for example, in a hundred passages of his works, describes the tribunal, as the instrument exclusively of priestly cruelty, and injustice:

> *Ce sanglant tribunal,*
> *Ce monument affreux du pouvoir monacal,*
> *Que L'Espagne a reçu; mais, qu' elle memc abhorre;*
> *Qui venge les autels, mais qui les déhonore,*
> *Qui, tout couvert de sang, de flammes entoure,*
> *Egorge les mortels avec un fer sacre. ***

Now, this tribunal, although thus frightfully depicted, is, nevertheless, the tribunal of a nation, distinguished for its wisdom, its moderation, and its high sense of honor. It is a tribunal, strictly royal, composed of such members only of the clergy, as are remarkable for their learning, and their abilities; and who, judging of real crimes, in virtue of the public, and pre-existing laws, pronounce their sentence, with a measure of equity, and wisdom, which, perhaps, could nowhere be found in any other Court of Justice. They never condemn any one, however criminal, to death. Hence, then, in what terms, can I express the infamy of the base calumniator, who, in the above verses, thus insolently misrepresents an order of men, who, so far from being cruel, are even remarkable for their clemency, and moderation. But, the truth is, Voltaire had his reasons for hating all authority.

If men were, all of them, wise, and well instructed, the absurdities, and falsehoods, like the foregoing, would excite only their ridicule, and contempt. But, unfortunately, such is not the case. The public, ignorant, and prejudiced, are easily imposed upon, and deceived. And the consequence is, that, cheated by the gross misrepresentations of a host of calumniating writers, they look upon the Inquisition, as a club of stupid and ferocious, monks, who roast men for their own amusement. Nay, it is even true, such is the force of prejudice, and ignorance, that the same erroneous, and unjust, notions, prevail even in the minds of a multitude of individuals, who, in other regards, are distinguished for their good sense. You may find them, moreover, in the works, not unfrequently, of the very defenders of sound, and virtuous, principles.

[. . .] Where, then, in what nation of the globe, does there exist a tribunal, which never condemned any one to death? Or what crime does any civil tribunal commit, which condemns the accused to death, in virtue of a law of the state, ordaining such punishment for the crime, of which he is proved to have been

---

This bloody court,
This frightful monument to monkish power
That Spain has received, but she herself abhors:
Who avenges the altars, but the disgrace;
Who covered with blood, surrounded by flames ,
Slaughtered mortals with a sacred sword.

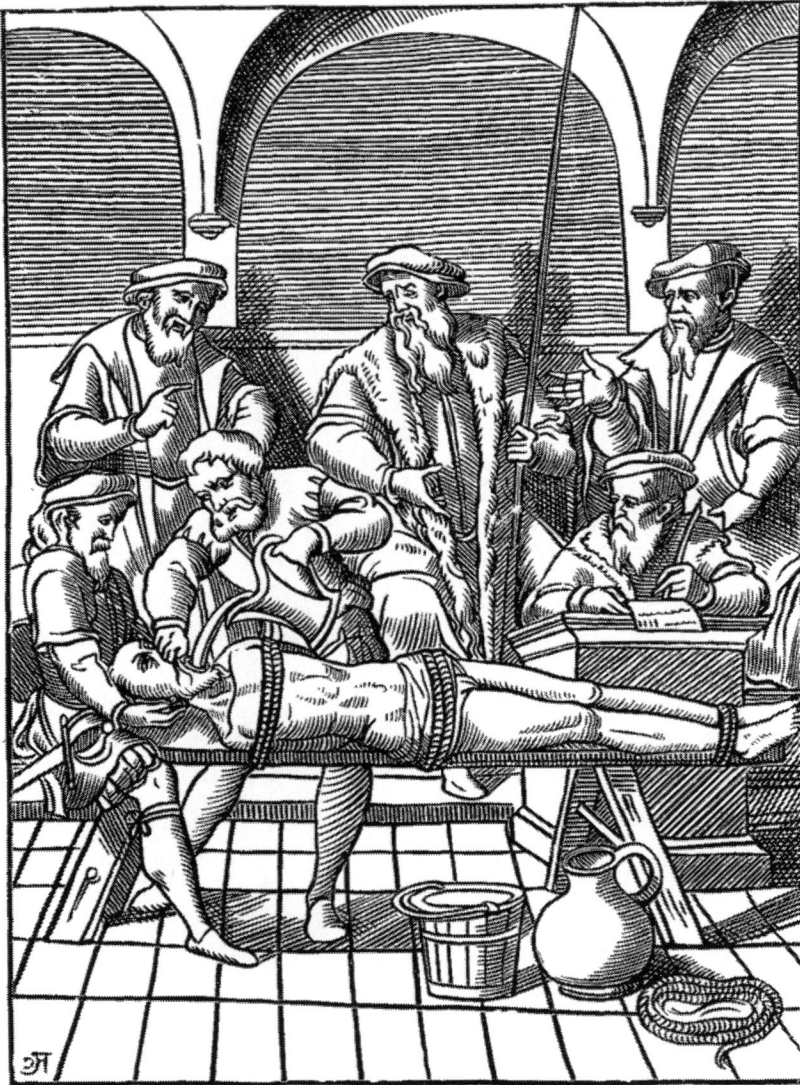

Fig. 341.—The Water Torture.—Fac-simile of a Woodcut in J. Damhoudère's "Praxis Rerum Criminalium;" in 4to, Antwerp, 1556.

guilty? And where, again, is the Spanish law, which ordains, that the Deists shall be put to death? The boldness of such assertion is as impudent an attempt to impose upon the credulity of the public, as injustice, or bigotry, could well have invented.

Amid the numberless errors, which the enemies of our religion have propagated; and with too deplorable success, impressed deeply on the minds of the public, I hardly know any that have surprised me more than the supposition, and belief, that Priests are ever permitted to condemn anyone to death. Men may be excused for not knowing the religions of Fo, of Buddha, or of Somonocondom; although still, whoever undertakes to defame even these preposterous systems, ought, first, in justice, to understand something at least about them. But, for a Christian to be ignorant of the laws of universal Christianity, this, surely, is a

Fig. 345.—The Punishment by Fire.—Fac-simile of a Woodcut of the " Cosmographie Universelle "
of Munster : in folio, Basle, 1552.

disorder, which no apology can justify. For, what eye has not seen that immense, and lucid, Orb, suspended, for eighteen hundred years, between heaven and earth? Or what ear has not heard that eternal axiom of our religion, that *The Church Abhors Blood?* Who does not know, that the Priest is even forbidden to be a surgeon, lest his consecrated hands shed the blood of a man, although it be even for his cure? Who does not know, that, in many Catholic nations, the Priest is dispensed with from appearing as a witness, in the trials of life and death? And that, even in the countries, where such condescendence is not allowed, he is still allowed to enter his protest, that he only appears, as such, in obedience to the laws, and in order to plead for mercy? Never does the Priest erect the scaffold. He ascends it, only as the martyr, or the comforter. He preaches naught but clemency, and pity; and in no corner of the globe, does he shed any other blood, but his own.

"The Church," says Pascal, "the chaste Spouse of the Son of God, is always, in imitation of this merciful Being, prepared, and ready, to shed her blood, for the sake of others; but not to shed that of others, for her own sake. She entertains the most decided horror of bloodshed, proportioned to that particular light, which God has communicated to her. She considers men, not simply as men, but as the images of the God, whom she adores. She cherishes for each, and every, individual, that holy respect, which renders them all, venerable in her sight, as having been purchased, and redeemed, at an infinite price, in order to become, one day, the temples of the Living God. For these reasons it is, that she looks upon the death of an individual, inflicted without an order from God, not only as an act of murder; but as a sacrilege, moreover, depriving her thus of one of her members: because whether the person, thus sacrificed, be one of the faithful or not, she still always considers him, either as being one of her children; or else, capable of becoming such."

It is very well known, that no private individual is permitted to require the death of another. Whence, it became necessary to establish public officers to do this, by the authority of the King, or rather, by that of the Almighty. And hence, again, in order to act as the faithful dispensers of the divine power, in all cases of life, and death, the magistrates have no liberty of judging, and deciding, save by the testimony, and the depositions, of witnesses, in consequence of which, they can neither, in conscience, pass any sentence, but according to the dictate of the law; nor condemn any one to death, but him, whom the law condemns. And then, too, if the order of God obliges them to consign the body of the wretched criminal to punishment, the same order of God obliges them, again, to take care of his guilty soul. In all this, there is nothing but what is right, and completely innocent: and still, so much does the Church abhor the shedding of blood, that she declares all those incapacitated in the service of her altars, who have ever participated in a sentence of death, although this were attended by all the aforesaid religious circumstances.

So much does the Church abhor the shedding of blood, that she declares all those incapacitated in the service of her altars, who have ever participated in a sentence of death.

You cannot, Sir, but admire the beauty, and own the wisdom, of the above theory. Perhaps, however, you may wish, likewise, to know, by experience, the true spirit of the Priesthood, in relation to this interesting object. Well, then, study, and consider, this, in those countries, or places, where the Priesthood once held, or still holds, the sceptre. A series of extraordinary circumstances had formerly established in Germany a multitude of Ecclesiastical Sovereignties. To judge of these, under the heads of clemency, and justice, you need only to call to your recollection the old German proverb; "It is good to live under the Crosier." Proverbs, which are the fruit of public experience, are testimonies, which never deceive us. I, therefore, appeal to this authority, which is still farther confirmed by the sanction of every man, who possesses, either memory, or judgment. Never, under those mild, and pacific, governments was there any question of persecution; nor of any capital sentence against the spiritual enemies of the reigning powers. [. . .]

I must here premise an important observation: It is this, that, in the discussion of all questions, be these what they may, there is nothing so essential as to avoid a confusion of ideas. Wherefore, when we speak, or reason, about the Inquisition, let us always separate, and distinguish, accurately, the conduct of the State from the conduct of the Church. Whatever in this tribunal is rigorous, and frightful, but, above all, the punishment of death, all this is purely the concern of the civil government: it is its affair; and it alone is accountable for it. Whereas, all the clemency, which is so remarkable in this tribunal, is the act and influence, of the Church, which interferes with punishments, only in order, either to suppress, or to mitigate them. Such is its indelible, and never varying, character.

Not only is it an error, it is even a crime, to maintain, or yet to suppose, that the Priesthood can ever pronounce the sentence of death upon any one.

In the history of France, there is a grand event, which is not sufficiently noticed. It is that, which regards the Templars. These unfortunate beings, whether guilty or not, (this is not here the question) petitioned earnestly to be tried by the tribunal of the Inquisition, "knowing well" say their historians, "that, if they could only succeed in obtaining its members for their Judges, they should run no risk of being condemned to death."

The King of France, however, aware of this, and of the inevitable consequences of this appeal of the Templars, formed now his own determination. He shut himself up, alone, with his Council of State; and at once, hastily condemned them to death. This is a fact, which is not, I believe, sufficiently, or generally, known.

At the earlier periods of the Inquisition, and when the greatest severity was chiefly needed, the Inquisitors in Spain used not to inflict any punishment, more rigorous than the confiscation of the criminal's property; and even this was always remitted, whenever he thought proper to abjure his errors, within the term, so called, of Grace." It does not appear quite clear from the instrument, thus referred to, at what exact period, it was, that the tribunal of the Inquisition began to pass the sentence of death. This, however, is not material. It suffices to know, what cannot be called in question, that it could only have acquired this right, by having become a Royal Institution; and that with the sentences of death the Priesthood, from the nature of their character, had not, could not have, anything at all to do.

In our times, the matter is no longer an object of incertitude. It is now well known, that every important sentence, even the sentence of simple arrest, was decided by the advice of the Supreme Council, without whose authority, nothing was, in fact, determined. Now, this is a circumstance, which presupposes, and implies, both the greatest prudence, and the most careful circumspection. But, in short, if it did so happen, that the accused was pronounced a heretic, the tribunal, in this case, after having ordered the confiscation of his property, made him over, for the legal punishment, to the secular arm, that is, to the Council of Castile, a body of men, than whom nothing in any nation, could be more enlightened, more learned, or more impartial. If the proofs, alleged against the accused, did not appear evident; or if even, though guilty, he did not remain obstinate, the only punishment, which then was inflicted on him, was simply an act of abjuration, performed in the church, and attended by certain prescribed ceremonies. It is true, all this implied a certain measure of disgrace to the family of the criminal: and to the criminal himself it involved the incapacity of exercising any public employment. I am, however, perfectly convinced that, in regard of these latter dispositions, they were but the artifices of clemency, invented for the express purpose of sheltering the greatest criminals. Certain facts, which have come to my own knowledge; and above all, the character itself of the tribunal, leave no doubt whatsoever upon my mind in these respects.

The tribunal of the Inquisition is composed of one Supreme head, named the Grand Inquisitor, who is always, either an Archbishop, or a Bishop; of eight Ecclesiastical Councilors, of whom six are always seculars, and two regulars, one of these invariably a Dominican, in virtue of a privilege, granted to the Dominican Order by Philip the Third; the other, a Religious of any other

Order, according to the regulation of Charles the Third. The youngest of the Secular Councilors acts the part of an Attorney- General; and in certain cases, calls in to his assistance two of the Councilors of Castile. I, however, suppose, at the same time, that they are always called together, whenever there is question of any capital punishment. From this plain, and simple, exposition of facts, you cannot but feel, how groundless, and fictitious, are those two phantoms of Voltaire, as well as of thousands of other ignorant, and prejudiced, writers, proclaiming the Inquisition, "a bloody, and frightful, monument of monkish power." There is, surely, nothing very terrific in the circumstance of seeing two humble Religious, united with eleven, or thirteen, Judges: whilst, as for the poor insulted Dominicans, to whom the public prejudice attributes all the odium of the Inquisition, your candor will, I am sure, allow it, these men are wholly undeserving of the unjust imputation, which is thus cast upon them.

It would be difficult to conceive any possible court of justice whose composition is better calculated to prevent, or to efface, even the slenderest suspicion of cruelty.

Whoever considers attentively the whole form, and order, of the tribunal, cannot but be compelled to admit, that it would be difficult to conceive any possible court of justice, whose composition is better calculated to prevent, or to efface, even the slenderest suspicion of cruelty, or rather, I will venture to say it, of simple severity. There is no one, provided he but understands the spirit, and maxims, of the Catholic Priesthood, but must be convinced, that, in its tribunals, mercy will necessarily hold the sceptre.

And let me here suggest to you, in particular, the following observation, that, independently of the favorable presumptions, which arise from the composition alone of the tribunal of the Inquisition, it, moreover, supposes, and presents, an infinite number of particular mitigations, which, all, turn out to the advantage of the accused; and which are known, only by experience. [. . .]

Where the laws of Spain ordain the punishment of death for such or such a crime, the Courts of Justice cannot, of course, oppose them. Thus, if the Inquisition, after the most diligent investigation, and from the clearest evidence, find the accused guilty of the crimes imputed to him, its judgment then, if it be a case of death, regulated by the laws, will, therefore, be followed by death.

But, with this the Tribunal itself has nothing at all to do: and it is, and for ever will be true, that it never condemns any one, however guilty, to death. The civil power acts; and has the authority to act, as it thinks proper. But if, by virtue of the foregoing clause, "dear to the Church" its Judges condemned any innocent man to death, themselves, in such case, would be the great offending criminals. [. . .]

Hence, then, that unceasingly repeated expression, calling the Inquisition "a bloody tribunal" is not merely groundless, but absurd. There does not, there cannot, exist, anywhere, a tribunal, but what, unhappily, is sometimes under the necessity of condemning the criminal to death; and which is irreproachable for doing so, provided it but executes the law upon the most positive, and clearest, evidence, and which even would be justly reproachable, if it did not execute the law, upon such testimony.

It is, moreover, a fact, that the Inquisition does not, itself, condemn any one to the punishment of death, ordained by the dictate of the laws. This is a matter, purely, and essentially, civil, be the appearances ever so much against it. Arid upon this point, the Committee itself of the Cortes agrees with the author of "The Inquisition Unmasked" whom I have cited already. [. . .]

There is not a more common, nor a more favorite, expression among Protestant writers, as well as among the Protestant public, than to call all the criminals, that are condemned by this tribunal, "The Victims of the Inquisition." They are no more "victims," than are all other criminals, who are put to death in virtue of a legal sentence. And it is even true, that the Inquisition never, but at the last extremity, and after every effort to reclaim the accused criminal, makes him over to the civil power. [. . .]

I have thus stated to your Lordship the character of the Inquisition. From it, and from the facts, which I have cited, you will be convinced, how groundless are the notions, which the public, everywhere, entertain of this tribunal; and how unjust, the calumnies, with which the infidel, and the Protestant writers, have so bitterly assailed it.

On Revenge, Sir Francis Bacon (1597)

Revenge is a kind of wild justice; which the more man's nature runs to, the more ought law to weed it out. For as for the first wrong, it doth but offend the law; but the revenge of that wrong, putteth the law out of office. Certainly, in taking revenge, a man is but even with his enemy; but in passing it over, he is superior; for it is a prince's part to pardon. And Solomon, I am sure, saith, it is the glory of a man, to pass by an offence. That which is past is gone, and irrevocable; and wise

men have enough to do, with things present and to come; therefore they do but trifle with themselves, that labor in past matters. There is no man doth a wrong, for the wrong's sake; but thereby to purchase himself profit, or pleasure, or honor, or the like. Therefore why should I be angry with a man, for loving himself better than me? And if any man should do wrong, merely out of ill-nature, why, yet it is but like the thorn or briar, which prick and scratch, because they can do no other. The most tolerable sort of revenge is for those wrongs which there is no law to remedy; but then let a man take heed, the revenge be such as there is no law to punish; else a man's enemy is still before hand, and it is two for one. Some, when they take revenge, are desirous, the party should know, whence it cometh. This is the more generous. For the delight seemeth to be, not so much in doing the hurt, as in making the party repent. But base and crafty cowards, are like the arrow that flieth in the dark.

Cosmus, duke of Florence, had a desperate saying against perfidious or neglecting friends, as if those wrongs were unpardonable; You shall read (saith he) that we are commanded to forgive our enemies; but you never read, that we are commanded to forgive our friends. But yet the spirit of Job was in a better tune: Shall we (saith he) take good at God's hands, and not be content to take evil also? And so of friends in a proportion. This is certain, that a man that studieth revenge, keeps his own wounds green, which otherwise would heal, and do well. Public revenges are for the most part fortunate; as that for the death of Caesar; for the death of Pertinax; for the death of Henry the Third of France; and many more. But in private revenges, it is not so. Nay rather, vindictive persons live the life of witches; who, as they are mischievous, so end they infortunate.

Grotius on the Rights of War and Peace
(*De Jure Belli ac Pacis*) (1625)

XII.

1. Again, others use this argument, that when life is taken, the time for penitence is cut off. But they know that pious magistrates take careful account of this view, and that no one is hurried to capital punishment without giving him time to see and seriously to detest his sins: and that such penitence, although works corresponding do not follow, being intercepted by death, may be accepted by God, the example of the thief crucified with Christ proves. But if it be said that a longer life might have been profitable for a more serious repentance, there may also be found these to whom may deservedly be applied what Seneca says, The only good thing which you can now furnish is the spectacle of your death: and again: Let them cease to be bad men by death, the only way they can. As Eusebius the philosopher also says, Since they can do it no other way, let them at least in this escape the bends of wickedness, and find that refuge.

2. This then, in addition to what we said at the beginning of the work, is our answer to these who held that either all punishment, or at least capital punishments, are without exception forbidden to Christians: which is contrary to what the Apostle teaches us, who includes the use of sword in the royal office, as the exercise of divine vengeance; and who elsewhere bids us to pray that kings may be Christian, and, as kings, be a protection to the innocent. And this, seeing the wickedness of great part of men, even after the propagation of the Gospel, cannot be secured, except, by the death of some, the boldness of others be repressed; since even now, when capital punishments and gibbets are so common, there is scarcely safety for innocence.

> **Even now, when capital punishments and gibbets are so common, there is scarcely safety for innocence.**

3. Still it will not be improper for Christian rulers, at least in some degree, to propose for their imitation the example of Sabaco, king of Egypt, who is reported by Diodorus to have commuted capital punishments for condemnation to the public works, with the happiest success. And Strabe says, that even the peoples about Caucasus punished no crimes with death, not even the greatest. Nor is that of Quintilian to be despised: None will doubt that if guilty men can be brought to a good way of thinking in any way, as it is granted that sometimes they can, it would be better for the State that they should be preserved than capitally punished. Balsamon notes that the Roman laws which enacted the punishment of death, were, by the Christian emperors, changed for the most part into other punishments, that both the condemned might be more thoroughly driven to penitence, and their punishment being prolonged, might be more profitable as example.

XIII

1. But in the enumeration of the ends of punishment by Taurus, it appears that something was overlooked. Gellinis thus quotes him: When therefore there is either great hope that the offender will without punishment correct himself; or, on the other hand, there is no hope that he can be amended and corrected; or, there is no reason to fear that the dignity which is offended will suffer; or, the offense be not such as requires exemplary fear to correct it; then the offense does not seem to be one for which a punishment need be devised. For he speaks as if when one end of punishment is taken away, the punishment should be removed; while on the other hand, all the ends must cease to exist, in order that there may be no ground for punishment. And moreover he omits that end, when a man who is unamendable is removed from life, that he may not commit more or greater crimes: and what he says of loss of dignity, is to be extended to other evils which are to be feared.

2. Seneca spoke better when he said: In punishing wrongs, the law has had these three objects, which the prince also ought to aim at; either to amend him who is punished; or to make others better by the punishment; or to make the rest of mankind more secure by removing the bad. For here, if by the rest, he

Seneca spoke better when he said: In punishing wrongs, the law has had these three objects, which the prince also ought to aim at; either to amend him who is punished; or to make others better by the punishment; or to make the rest of mankind more secure by removing the bad.

means not only these who have been injured, but others who may hereafter be so, you have a complete division of the subject, except that to removing you should add or repressing. For both imprisonment, and any other way of diminishing their power, tends the same way. He has another less perfect partition in another place; as has Quintilian.

XIV

From what has been said, it may be collected, hew unsafe it is for a private Christian man to inflict punishment, and especially capital punishment, either for the sake of his own or of the public good, upon a guilty person; although, as we have said, that is sometimes permitted by the Law of Nations. And hence we must approve of the usage of these peoples by whom navigators are provided with commissions from the public power to suppress pirates, if they find any upon the seas; on which commissions they may act, not as of their own motion, but by public command.

XV

Of much the same kind is the provision which prevails in many places, that not anybody who chooses can take up the accusation of crimes, but only certain persons on whom that office is imposed by the public power; so that no one shall do anything to shed the blood of another, except by the necessity of his office. Accordingly the canon of the Council of Seville provides, that if any one of the faithful shall turn informer, and by his means any one shall be proscribed or put to death, he shall not receive the Communion, even when dying.

XVI

And this too follows from what has been said, that it is not advisable for a truly Christian man, nor is even decent, that he should of his own accord mix himself with public business which involves capital punishment, and seek for a power of life and death, as if he were a sort of God among men. For certainly what Christ says, applies here, that it is dangerous to judge others, since as we judge them, God will judge us.

XVII

1. It is a noted question, whether the human laws, which permit the slaying of certain men, really justify the slayers in the sight of God, or only give them impunity among men. Covarrnvias and Fortunius held the latter, which opinion Vasquius calls shocking. It is not doubtful, as we have said, that, in certain cases the Law can do both the one and the other. But whether the law had

that intention, is to be understood partly from the words of the law, and partly from the matter. For when the law gives indulgence to human feeling, it takes away the punishment of the law, but not the sin, as in the case of a husband who kills the adulterous wife or the adulterer.

2. But if the law look to future danger from the delay of punishment, it is to be conceived to give right and public power to the private person, so that he is no longer a private man.

Of this kind is the law in the Codex under the rubric, When it is lawful for any one without a judge to do justice for himself or for the public service; [Cod. in. 27] where anyone is allowed to suppress by force soldiers who plunder; where too the reason is added, putting such soldiers on the footing of robbers. And a similar law is given respecting deserters. As Tertullian says: Against traitors and public enemies every one is a soldier.

3. There is a difference in the right of killing exiles, outlawed persons: namely, that there, a special opinion has preceded, but in this case, a general edict, which is combined with the evidence of the fact, and has the force of a judicial sentence.

XVIII

Let us now consider whether all vicious acts are such that they may be punished by men. It is certain that they are not all such. For, in the first place, mere internal acts, even if they come to be known, for instance by confession, cannot be punished by men; because, as we have said, it is not congruous to human nature that mere internal acts should give rise to right or obligation. And so the Roman law. But that does not prevent that internal acts, so far as they influence external, may not be taken into account in estimating, not themselves properly, but the external acts which receive from them their character of desert.

XIX

1. In the next place, acts unavoidable to human nature cannot be punished by man. For though nothing is sin which is not done freely, yet to abstain from all sin and always, is above the condition of humanity; and hence sin is said to be natural to man by some of the philosophers, and by many of the Christians. See Seneca, Sopater, Philo, Thucydides, Diodorus.

2. It may even be doubted whether these acts can properly be called sin, which, though they have an appearance of liberty, are not free, when considered in their generality. So Plutarch in Solon. Then again there are other acts which are inevitable, not to human nature properly, but to this particular person at this moment, on account of the constitution of the body affecting the mind, or inveterate habit; which is commonly punished, not in itself, but on account of precedent fault; because either the remedies were neglected, or the diseased thoughts willingly admitted into the mind.

XX

1. Thirdly; these offenses are not to be punished, which neither directly

nor indirectly regard human society or any other man. The reason is, that there is no cause why such sins should not be left to God to punish, who can both know them best, and judge them most justly, and punish them most effectually. Wherefore if such a punishment were instituted, it would be useless, and therefore blamable. From this remark are to be excepted punishments for amendment, which have for their object to make the man better, though the interest of others is not concerned. Also punishments are not to be inflicted on acts opposed to these virtues of which the nature rejects all compulsion, as mercy, liberality, gratitude.

2. Seneca treats this question: Whether ingratitude ought to meet with impunity; and gives many reasons why it ought not [to be punished]; but this as the principal one, which may be extended to other like cases: Since gratitude is a most graceful thing, if it be necessary it ceases to be graceful: that is, it loses its degree of gracefulness, as appears by what follows: We praise a grateful man only as one who returns a deposit or pays a debt without being forced: and again, It could not be a glorious thing to be grateful except it were safe to be ungrateful. As Seneca the father says, I do not want to have [such] a person praised who is accused, but to have him acquitted.

XXI

We must now discuss whether it is ever lawful to excuse or pardon: The Stoics denied it, but with a poor argument: Pardon is the remission of a due penalty, but the wise man does what is due. Here the fallacy is in the word due. For if you understand that he who has transgressed owes the penalty, that is, may be punished without wrong, it will not follow that he who does not punish him, does not do what he ought. But if you say that the punishment is due on the part of the wise man, that is, that he ought by all moans to require it, we deny that that is always the case, and therefore say that the punishment in that sense is not due, but only lawful. And that may be true, both before and after the penal law.

XXII

1. Before the penal law is instituted, it is not doubtful that punishment may have place; because by Natural Law he who has transgressed is in that state in which he may be lawfully punished; but it does not follow that punishment ought to be exacted: because this depends upon the connexion of the ends for which punishment is instituted with punishment itself. Wherefore if these ends are, in moral estimation, not necessary, or if there are, opposed to these, other ends not less useful or necessary, or if the necessary ends of punishment can be obtained in another way, it follows that there is nothing which precisely obliges to exact punishment. We may take an example of the first case in a sin known to few, and of which the public notice is not necessary, or is even hurtful. As Cicero says of a certain Zeuxis, being brought to trial perhaps he ought not to be dismissed, but it was not necessary to bring him to trial. An example of the second case is one who puts forward his own merits or these of his parents, as a

set-off against his fault; so Seneca: an example of the third case, we have in him who is reformed by remonstrance, or who has satisfied the injured person by a verbal acknowledgment, so that punishment is not necessary for these ends.

2. And this is one part of the clemency which liberates the offender from punishment, of which the Hebrew wise man says, Clemency becomes the just man. For since all punishment has in it something opposed not to justice, but to charity, reason easily permits us to abstain from it, except some greater and juster charity oppose insurmountable obstacles. So say Sopater, Cicero, Dio Prusœensis, Favorinus.

XXIII

These cases may occur: that punishment may require absolutely to be exacted, as in crimes of very bad example—or may be fit not to be exacted, as if the public good require it to be omitted—or either course may be allowable: when, as Seneca says, Clemency has free will. Then, say the Stoics, the wise man spares, but does not pardon: as if we might not, with common usage, call that pardon, which they call sparing. In fact, here and elsewhere, as Cicero, Galen and others have noted, a great part of the disputations of the Stoics is about words, which a philosopher ought carefully to avoid. So the writers to Herennius, and Aristotle say.

IT WAS THE BEST OF TIMES
IT WAS THE WORST OF TIMES

Letter XIV To The Jesuits, Blaise Pascal (1656)

What can be a plainer dictate of nature than that "no private individual has a right to take away the life of another?" "So well are we taught this of ourselves," says St. Chrysostom, "that God, in giving the commandment not to kill, did not add as a reason that homicide was an evil; because," says that father, "the law supposes that nature has taught us that truth already." Accordingly, this commandment has been binding on men in all ages.

What can be a plainer dictate of nature than that "no private individual has a right to take away the life of another?"

The Gospel has confirmed the requirement of the law; and the Decalogue only renewed the command which man had received from God before the law, in the person of Noah, from whom all men are descended. On that renovation of the world, God said to the patriarch: "At the hand of man, and at the hand of every man's brother, will I require the life of man. Whoso sheddeth man's blood, by man shall his blood be shed; for man is made in the image of God." (Gen. 9. 5, 6.) This general prohibition deprives man of all power over the life of man. And so exclusively has the Almighty reserved this prerogative in His own hand that, in accordance with Christianity, which is at utter variance with the false maxims of Paganism, man has no power even over his own life. But, as it has seemed good to His providence to take human society under His protection, and to punish the evil-doers that give it disturbance, He has Himself established laws for depriving criminals of life; and thus those executions which, without this sanction, would be punishable outrages, become, by virtue of His authority, which is the rule of justice, praiseworthy penalties.

St. Augustine takes an admirable view of this subject. "God," he says, "has himself qualified this general prohibition against manslaughter, both by the laws which He has instituted for the capital punishment of malefactors, and by the special orders which He has sometimes issued to put to death certain individuals. And when death is inflicted in such cases, it is not man that kills, but God, of whom man may be considered as only the instrument, in the same way as a sword in the hand of him that wields it. But, these instances excepted, whosoever kills incurs the guilt of murder."

It appears, then, fathers, that the right of taking away the life of man is the sole prerogative of God, and that, having ordained laws for executing death on criminals, He has deputed kings or commonwealths as the depositaries of that power — a truth which St. Paul teaches us, when, speaking of the right which sovereigns possess over the lives of their subjects, he deduces it from Heaven in these words: "He beareth not the sword in vain; for he is the minister of God to execute wrath upon him that doeth evil." (Rom. 13. 4.) But as it is God who has put this power into their hands, so He requires

The right of taking away the life of man is the sole prerogative of God.

them to exercise it in the same manner as He does himself; in other words, with perfect justice; according to what St. Paul observes in the same passage: "Rulers are not a terror to good works, but to the evil. Wilt thou, then, not be afraid of the power? Do that which is good: for he is the minister of God to thee for good." And this restriction, so far from lowering their prerogative, exalts it, on the contrary, more than ever; for it is thus assimilated to that of God who has no power to do evil, but is all-powerful to do good; and it is thus distinguished from that of devils, who are impotent in that which is good, and powerful only for evil. There is this difference only to be observed betwixt the King of Heaven and earthly sovereigns, that God, being justice and wisdom itself, may inflict death instantaneously on whomsoever and in whatsoever manner He pleases; for, besides His being the sovereign Lord of human life, it certain that He never takes it away either without cause or without judgment, because He is as incapable of injustice as He is of error. Earthly potentates, however, are not at liberty to act in this manner; for, though the ministers of God, still they are but men, and not gods. They may be misguided by evil counsels, irritated by false suspicions, transported by passion, and hence they find themselves obliged to have recourse, in their turn also, to human agency, and appoint magistrates in their dominions, to whom they delegate their power, that the authority which God has bestowed on them may be employed solely for the purpose for which they received it.

I hope you understand, then, fathers, that, to avoid the crime of murder, we must act at once by the authority of God, and according to the justice of God; and that, when these two conditions are not united, sin is contracted; whether it be by taking away life with his authority, but without his justice; or by taking it away with justice, but without his authority. From this indispensable connection it follows, according to St. Augustine, "that he who, without proper authority, kills a criminal, becomes a criminal himself, chiefly for this reason, that he usurps an authority which God has not given him;" and on the other hand, magistrates, though they possess this authority, are nevertheless chargeable with murder, if, contrary to the laws which they are bound to follow, they inflict death on an innocent man.

Such are the principles of public safety and tranquility which have been admitted at all times and in all places, and on the basis of which all legislators, sacred and profane, from the beginning of the world, have founded their laws. Even Heathens have never ventured to make an exception to this rule, unless in cases where there was no other way of escaping the loss of chastity or life, when they conceived, as Cicero tells us, "that the law itself seemed to put its weapons into the hands of those who were placed in such an emergency."

That such a law was ever enacted, authorizing or tolerating, as you have done, the practice of putting a man to death, to atone for an insult, or to avoid the loss of honor or property, where life is not in danger at the same time – that, fathers, is what I deny was ever done, even by infidels.

But with this single exception, which has nothing to do with my present purpose, that such a law was ever enacted, authorizing or tolerating, as you have done, the practice of putting a man to death, to atone for an insult, or to avoid the loss of honor or property, where life is not in danger at the same time; that, fathers, is what I deny was ever done, even by infidels. They have, on the contrary, most expressly forbidden the practice. The law of the Twelve Tables of Rome bore, "that it is unlawful to kill a robber in the daytime, when he does not defend himself with arms;" which, indeed, had been prohibited long before in the 22d chapter of Exodus. And the law Furem, in the *Lex Cornelia*, which is borrowed from Ulpian, forbids the killing of robbers even by night, if they do not put us in danger of our lives.

Tell us now, fathers, what authority you have to permit what all laws, human as well as divine, have forbidden; and who gave Lessius a right to use the following language? "The book of Exodus forbids the killing of thieves by day, when they do not employ arms in their defense; and in a court of justice, punishment is inflicted on those who kill under these circumstances. In conscience, however, no blame can be attached to this practice, when a person is not sure of being able otherwise to recover his stolen goods, or entertains a doubt on the subject," as Sotus expresses it; "for he is not obliged to run the risk of losing any part of his property merely to save the life of a robber. The same privilege extends even to clergymen." Such extraordinary assurance! The Law of Moses punishes those who kill a thief when he does not threaten our lives, and the law of the Gospel, according to you, will absolve them! What, fathers! Has Jesus Christ come to destroy the law, and not to fulfill it? "The civil judge," says Lessius,"would inflict punishment on those who should kill under such circumstances; but no blame can be attached to the deed in conscience." Must we conclude, then, that the morality of Jesus Christ is more sanguinary, and less the enemy of murder, than that of Pagans, from whom our judges have borrowed their civil laws which condemn that crime? Do Christians make more account of the good things of this earth, and less account of human life, than infidels and idolaters? On what principle do you proceed, fathers? Assuredly not upon any law that ever was enacted either by God or man – on nothing, indeed, but this extraordinary reasoning: "The laws," say you, "permit us to defend ourselves against robbers, and to repel force by force; self-defense, therefore, being permitted, it follows that murder, without which self-defense is often impracticable, may be considered as permitted also."

It is false, fathers, that, because self-defense is allowed, murder may be allowed also. This barbarous method of self-vindication lies at the root of all your errors, and has been justly stigmatized by the Faculty of Louvain, in their censure of the doctrine of your friend Father Lamy, as "a murderous defense— *defensio occisiva*." I maintain that the laws recognize such a wide difference between murder and self-defence that, in those very cases in which the latter is sanctioned, they have made a provision against murder, when the person is in no danger of his life. Read the words, fathers, as they run in the same passage of Cujas: "It is lawful to repulse the person who comes to invade our property; but we are not permitted to kill him." And again: "If any should threaten to strike us, and not to deprive us of life, it is quite allowable to repulse him; but it is against all law to put him to death."

Who, then, has given you a right to say, as Molina, Reginald, Filiutius, Escobar, Lessius, and others among you, have said, "that it is lawful to kill the man who offers to strike us a blow"? Or, "that it is lawful to take the life of one who means to insult us, by the common consent of all the casuists," as Lessius says. By what authority do you, who are mere private individuals, confer upon other private individuals, not excepting clergymen, this right of killing and slaying? And how dare you usurp the power of life and death, which belongs essentially to none but God, and which is the most glorious mark of sovereign authority? These are the points that demand explanation; and yet you conceive that you have furnished a triumphant reply to the whole, by simply remarking, in your thirteenth Imposture, "that the value for which Molina permits us to kill a thief, who flies without having done us any violence, is not so small as I have said, and that it must be a much larger sum than six ducats!" How extremely silly! Pray, fathers, where would you have the price to be fixed? At fifteen or sixteen ducats? Do not suppose that this will produce any abatement in my accusations. At all events, you cannot make it exceed the value of a horse; for Lessius is clearly of opinion, "that we may lawfully kill the thief that runs off with our horse." But I must tell you, moreover, that I was perfectly correct when I said that Molina estimates the value of the thief's life at six ducats; and, if you will not take it upon my word, we shall refer it to an umpire to whom you cannot object. The person whom I fix upon for this office is your own Father Reginald, who, in his explanation of the same passage of Molina (l.28, n. 68), declares that "Molina there determines the sum for which it is not allowable to kill at three, or four, or five ducats." And thus, fathers, I shall have Reginald, in addition to Molina, to bear me out.

It will be equally easy for me to refute your fourteenth Imposture, touching Molina's permission to "kill a thief who offers to rob us of a crown." This palpable fact is attested by Escobar, who tells us "that Molina has regularly determined the sum for which it is lawful to take away life, at one crown." And all you have to lay to my charge in the fourteenth Imposture is, that I have suppressed the last words of this passage, namely, "that in this matter every one ought to study the moderation of a just self-defense." Why do you not complain that Escobar has also omitted to mention these words? But how little tact you have about you! You imagine that nobody understands what you mean by self-defense. Don't we know that it is to employ "a murderous defense"? You would persuade us that Molina meant to say that if a person, in defending his crown, finds himself in danger of his life, he is then at liberty to kill his assailant, in self-preservation. If that were true, fathers, why should Molina say in the same place that "in this matter he was of a contrary judgment from Carrer and Bald," who give permission to kill in self-preservation? I repeat, therefore, that his plain meaning is that, provided the person can save his crown without killing the thief, he ought not to kill him; but that, if he cannot secure his object without shedding blood, even though he should run no risk of his own life, as in the case of the robber being unarmed, he is permitted to take up arms and kill the man, in order to save his crown; and in so doing, according to him, the person does not transgress "the moderation of a just defense." To show you that I am in the right, just allow him to explain himself: "One does not exceed the moderation of a just defense," says he, "when he takes up arms against a thief who has none, or employs weapons which give him the advantage over his assailant. I know there are some who are of a contrary judgment; but I do not approve of their opinion, even in the external tribunal." [. . .]

For a long time the Church refused to be reconciled, till the very hour of death, to those who had been guilty of willful murder, as those are to whom you give your sanction. The celebrated Council of Ancyra adjudged them to penance during their whole lifetime; and, subsequently, the Church deemed it an act of sufficient indulgence to reduce that term to a great many years. But, still more effectually to deter Christians from willful murder, she has visited with most severe punishment even those acts which have been committed through inadvertence, as may be seen in St. Basil, in St. Gregory of Nyssa, and in the decretals of Popes Zachary and Alexander II. The canons quoted by Isaac, Bishop of Langres (tr. 2. 13), "ordain seven years of penance for having killed another in self-defense." And we find St. Hildebert, bishop of Mans, replying to Yves de Chartres, "that he was right in interdicting for life a priest who had, in self-defense, killed a robber with a stone."

After this, you cannot have the assurance to persist in saying that your decisions are agreeable to the spirit or the canons of the Church. I defy you to show one of them that permits us to kill solely in defense of our property (for I speak not of cases in which one may be called upon to defend his life—*se suaquae liberando*); your own authors, and, among the rest, Father Lamy, confess that no such canon can be found. "There is no authority," he says, "human or divine, which gives an express permission to kill a robber who makes no resistance."

And yet this is what you permit most expressly. I defy you to show one of them that permits us to kill in vindication of honor, for a buffet, for an affront, or for a slander. I defy you to show one of them that permits the killing of witnesses, judges, or magistrates, whatever injustice we may apprehend from them. The spirit of the church is diametrically opposite to these seditious maxims, opening the door to insurrections to which the mob is naturally prone enough already. She

[The Church] has invariably taught her children that they ought not to render evil for evil; that they ought to give place unto wrath; to make no resistance to violence; to give unto everyone his due—honor, tribute, submission; to obey magistrates and superiors, even though they should be unjust, because we ought always to respect in them the power of that God who has placed them over us.

has invariably taught her children that they ought not to render evil for evil; that they ought to give place unto wrath; to make no resistance to violence; to give unto everyone his due — honor, tribute, submission; to obey magistrates and superiors, even though they should be unjust, because we ought always to respect in them the power of that God who has placed them over us. She forbids them, still more strongly than is done by the civil law, to take justice into their own hands; and it is in her spirit that Christian kings decline doing so in cases of high treason, and remit the criminals charged with this grave offence into the hands of the judges, that they may be punished according to the laws and the forms of justice, which in this matter exhibit a contrast to your mode of management so striking and complete that it may well make you blush for shame.

As my discourse has taken this turn, I beg you to follow the comparison which I shall now draw between the style in which you would dispose of your enemies, and that in which the judges of the land dispose of criminals. Everybody knows, fathers, that no private individual has a right to demand the death of another individual; and that though a man should have ruined us, maimed our body, burnt our house, murdered our father, and was prepared, moreover, to assassinate ourselves, or ruin our character, our private demand for the death of that person would not be listened to in a court of justice. Public officers have been appointed for that purpose, who make the demand in the name of the king, or rather, I would say, in the name of God. Now, do you conceive, fathers, that Christian legislators have established this regulation out of mere show and grimace? Is it not evident that their object was to harmonize the laws of the state with those of the Church, and thus prevent the external practice of justice from clashing with the sentiments which all Christians are bound to cherish in their hearts? It is easy to see how this, which forms the commencement of a civil process, must stagger you; its subsequent procedure absolutely overwhelms you.

Suppose then, fathers, that these official persons have demanded the death of the man who has committed all the above-mentioned crimes, what is to be done next? Will they instantly plunge a dagger in his breast? No, fathers; the life of man is too important to be thus disposed of; they go to work with more decency; the laws have committed it, not to all sorts of persons, but exclusively to the judges, whose probity and competency have been duly tried. And is one judge sufficient to condemn a man to death? No; it requires seven at the very least; and of these seven there must not be one who has been injured by the criminal, lest his judgment should be warped or corrupted by passion. You are aware also, fathers, that, the more effectually to secure the purity of their minds, they devote the hours of the morning to these functions. Such is the care taken to prepare them for the solemn action of devoting a fellow creature to death; in performing which they occupy the place of God, whose ministers they are, appointed to condemn such only as have incurred his condemnation.

For the same reason, to act as faithful administrators of the divine power of taking away human life, they are bound to form their judgment solely according to the depositions of the witnesses, and according to all the other forms prescribed to them; after which they can pronounce conscientiously only according to law, and can judge worthy of death those only whom the law condemns to that penalty. And then, fathers, if the command of God obliges them to deliver over to punishment the bodies of the unhappy culprits, the same divine statute binds them to look after the interests of their guilty souls, and binds them the more to this just because they are guilty; so that they are not delivered up to execution till after they have been afforded the means of providing for their consciences. All this is quite fair and innocent; and yet, such is the abhorrence of the Church to blood that she judges those to be incapable of ministering at her altars who have borne any share in passing or executing a sentence of death, accompanied though it be with these religious circumstances; from which we may easily conceive what idea the Church entertains of murder. Such, then, being the manner in which human life is disposed of by the legal forms of justice, let us now see how you dispose of it. According to your modern system of legislation, there is but one judge, and that judge is no other than the offended party. He is at once the judge, the party, and the executioner. He himself demands from himself the death of his enemy; he condemns him, he executes him on the spot; and, without the least respect either for the soul or the body of his brother, he murders and damns him for whom Jesus Christ died; and all this for the sake of avoiding a blow on the cheek, or a slander, or an offensive word, or some other offense of a similar nature, for which, if a magistrate, in the exercise of legitimate authority, were condemning any to die, he would himself be impeached; for, in such cases, the laws are very far indeed from condemning any to death. In one word, to crown the whole of this extravagance, the person who kills his neighbor in this style, without authority and in the face of all law, contracts no sin and commits no disorder, though he should be religious and even a priest! Where are we, fathers? Are these really religious, and priests, who talk in this manner? Are they Christians? Are they Turks? Are they men? or are they demons? And are these "the mysteries revealed by the Lamb to his Society?" or are they not rather abominations suggested by the Dragon to those who take part with him?

To come to the point, with you, fathers, whom do you wish to be taken for? — for the children of the Gospel, or for the enemies of the Gospel? You must be ranged either on the one side or on the other; for there is no medium here. "He that is not with Jesus Christ is against him." Into these two classes all mankind are divided. There are, according to St. Augustine, two peoples and two worlds, scattered abroad over the earth. There is the world of the children of God, who form one body, of which Jesus Christ is the king and the head; and there is the world at enmity with God, of which the devil is the king and the head. Hence Jesus Christ is called the King and God of the world, because he has everywhere his subjects and worshippers; and hence the devil is also termed in Scripture the prince of this world, and the god of this world, because he has everywhere his agents and his slaves. Jesus Christ has imposed upon the Church, which is his empire, such laws as he, in his eternal wisdom, was pleased to ordain; and the devil has imposed on the world, which is his kingdom, such laws as he chose to establish. Jesus Christ has associated honor with suffering; the devil with not suffering. Jesus Christ has told those who are smitten on the one cheek to turn the other also; and the devil has told those who are threatened with a buffet to kill the man that would do them such an injury.

Jesus Christ has told those who are smitten on the one cheek to turn the other also; and the devil has told those who are threatened with a buffet to kill the man that would do them such an injury.

Jesus Christ pronounces those happy who share in his reproach; and the devil declares those to be unhappy who lie under ignominy. Jesus Christ says: Woe unto you when men shall speak well of you! And the devil says: Woe unto those of whom the world does not speak with esteem!

Judge, then, fathers, to which of these kingdoms you belong. You have heard the language of the city of peace, the mystical Jerusalem; and you have heard the language of the city of confusion, which Scripture terms "the spiritual Sodom." Which of these two languages do you understand? Which of them do you speak?

Those who are on the side of Jesus Christ have, as St. Paul teaches us, the same mind which was also in him; and those who are the children of the devil— *ex patre diabolo* — who has been a murderer from the beginning, according to the saying of Jesus Christ, follow the maxims of the devil. Let us hear, therefore, the language of your school. I put this question to your doctors: When a person has given me a blow on the cheek, ought I rather to submit to the injury than kill the offender? Or may I not kill the man in order to escape the affront? Kill him by all means- it is quite lawful! Exclaim, in one breath, Lessius, Molina, Escobar, Reginald, Filiutius, Baldelle, and other Jesuits. Is that the language of Jesus Christ? One question more: Would I lose my honor by tolerating a box on the ear, without killing the person that gave it? "Can there be a doubt," cries Escobar, "that so long as a man suffers another to live who has given him a buffet, that man remains without honor?" Yes, fathers, without that honor which the devil transfuses, from his own proud spirit into that of his proud children. This is the honor which has ever been the idol of worldly-minded men.

Leviathan: The Matter, Forme and Power of a Common Wealth Ecclesiasticall and Civil: Chapter XXVIII: Of Punishments and Rewards
Thomas Hobbes (1651)

Apunishment is an evil inflicted by public authority on him that hath done or omitted that which is judged by the same authority to be a transgression of the law, to the end that the will of men may thereby the better be disposed to obedience.

Before I infer anything from this definition, there is a question to be answered of much importance; which is, by what door the right or authority of punishing, in any case, came in. For by that which has been said before, no man is supposed bound by covenant not to resist violence; and consequently it cannot be intended that he gave any right to another to lay violent hands upon his person. In the making of a Commonwealth every man giveth away the right of defending another, but not of defending himself. Also he obligeth himself to assist him that hath the sovereignty in the punishing of another, but of himself not. But to covenant to assist the sovereign in doing hurt to another, unless he that so covenanteth have a right to do it himself, is not to give him a right to punish. It is manifest therefore that the right which the Commonwealth (that is, he or they that represent it) hath to punish is not grounded on any concession or gift of the subjects. But I have also shown formerly that before the institution of Commonwealth, every man had a right to everything, and to do whatsoever he thought necessary to his own preservation; subduing, hurting, or killing any man in order thereunto. And this is the foundation of that right of punishing which is exercised in every Commonwealth. For the subjects did not give the sovereign that right; but only, in laying down theirs, strengthened him to use his own as he should think fit for the preservation of them all: so that it was not given, but left to him, and to him only; and, excepting the limits set him by natural law, as entire as in the condition of mere nature, and of war of every one against his neighbor.

From the definition of punishment, I infer, first, that neither private revenges nor injuries of private men can properly be styled punishment, because they proceed not from public authority.

Secondly, that to be neglected and unpreferred by the public favor is not a punishment, because no new evil is thereby on any man inflicted; he is only left in the estate he was in before.

Thirdly, that the evil inflicted by public authority, without precedent public condemnation, is not to be styled by the name of punishment, but of a hostile act, because the fact for which a man is punished ought first to be judged by public authority to be a transgression of the law.

Fourthly, that the evil inflicted by usurped power, and judges without authority from the sovereign, is not punishment, but an act of hostility, because the acts of power usurped have not for author the person condemned, and therefore are not acts of public authority.

Fifthly, that all evil which is inflicted without intention or possibility of disposing the delinquent or, by his example, other men to obey the laws is not punishment, but an act of hostility, because without such an end no hurt done is contained under that name.

Sixthly, whereas to certain actions there be annexed by nature diverse hurtful consequences; as when a man in assaulting another is himself slain or wounded; or when he falleth into sickness by the doing of some unlawful act; such hurt, though in respect of God, who is the author of nature, it may be said to be inflicted, and therefore a punishment divine; yet it is not contained in the name of punishment in respect of men, because it is not inflicted by the authority of man.

Seventhly, if the harm inflicted be less than the benefit of contentment that naturally followeth the crime committed, that harm is not within the definition and is rather the price or redemption than the punishment of a crime: because it is of the nature of punishment to have for end the disposing of men to obey the law; which end (if it be less than the benefit of the transgression) it attaineth not, but worketh a contrary effect.

Eighthly, if a punishment be determined and prescribed in the law itself, and after the crime committed there be a greater punishment inflicted, the excess is not punishment, but an act of hostility. For seeing the aim of punishment is not a revenge, but terror; and the terror of a great punishment unknown is taken away by the declaration of a less, the unexpected addition is no part of the punishment. But where there is no punishment at all determined by the law, there whatsoever is inflicted hath the nature of punishment. For he that goes about the violation of a law, wherein no penalty is determined, expecteth an indeterminate, that is to say, an arbitrary punishment.

Ninthly, harm inflicted for a fact done before there was a law that forbade it is not punishment, but an act of hostility: for before the law, there is no transgression of the law: but punishment supposeth a fact judged to have been a transgression of the law; therefore harm inflicted before the law made is not punishment, but an act of hostility.

Tenthly, hurt inflicted on the representative of the Commonwealth is not punishment, but an act of hostility: because it is of the nature of punishment to be inflicted by public authority, which is the authority only of the representative itself.

Lastly, harm inflicted upon one that is a declared enemy falls not under the name of punishment: because seeing they were either never subject to the law, and therefore cannot transgress it; or having been subject to it, and professing to be no longer so, by consequence deny they can transgress it, all the harms that can be done them must be taken as acts of hostility. But in declared hostility all infliction of evil is lawful. From whence it followeth that if a subject shall by fact or word wittingly and deliberately deny the authority of the representative of the Commonwealth (whatsoever penalty hath been formerly ordained for treason), he may lawfully be made to suffer whatsoever the representative will: for in denying subjection, he denies such punishment as by the law hath been ordained, and therefore suffers as an enemy of the Commonwealth; that is, according to the will of the representative. For the punishments set down in the law are to subjects, not to enemies; such as are they that, having been by their own act subjects, deliberately revolting, deny the sovereign power.

The first and most general distribution of punishments is into divine and human. Of the former I shall have occasion to speak in a more convenient place hereafter.

Human are those punishments that be inflicted by the commandment of man; and are either corporal, or pecuniary, or ignominy, or imprisonment, or exile, or mixed of these.

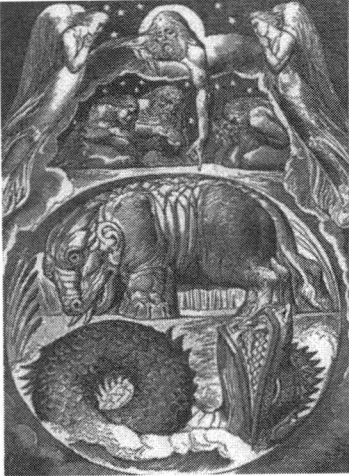

Corporal punishment is that which is inflicted on the body directly, and according to the intention of him that inflicteth it: such as are stripes, or wounds, or deprivation of such pleasures of the body as were before lawfully enjoyed.

And of these, some be capital, some less than capital. Capital is the infliction of death; and that either simply or with torment. Less than capital are stripes, wounds, chains, and any other corporal pain not in its own nature mortal. For if upon the infliction of a punishment death follow, not in the intention of the inflicter, the punishment is not to be esteemed capital, though the harm prove mortal by an accident not to be foreseen; in which case death is not inflicted, but hastened.

Pecuniary punishment is that which consisteth not only in the deprivation of a sum of money, but also of lands, or any other goods which are usually bought and sold for money. And in case the law that ordaineth such a punishment be made with design to gather money from such as shall transgress the same, it is not properly a punishment, but the price of privilege and exemption from the law, which doth not absolutely forbid the fact but only to those that are not able to pay the money: except where the law is natural, or part of religion; for in that case it is not an exemption from the law, but a transgression of it. As where a law exacteth a pecuniary mulct of them that take the name of God in vain, the payment of the mulct is not the price of a dispensation to swear, but the punishment of the transgression of a law indispensable. In like manner if the law impose a sum of money to be paid to him that has been injured, this is but a satisfaction for the hurt done him, and extinguisheth the accusation of the party injured, not the crime of the offender.

Ignominy is the infliction of such evil as is made dishonorable; or the deprivation of such good as is made honorable by the Commonwealth. For there

> **Corporal punishment is that which is inflicted on the body directly, and according to the intention of him that inflicteth it: such as are stripes, or wounds, or deprivation of such pleasures of the body as were before lawfully enjoyed.**
>
> **And of these, some be capital, some less than capital. Capital is the infliction of death; and that either simply or with torment.**

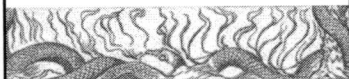

be some things honorable by nature; as the effects of courage, magnanimity, strength, wisdom, and other abilities of body and mind: others made honorable by the Commonwealth; as badges, titles, offices, or any other singular mark of the sovereigns favor. The former, though they may fail by nature or accident, cannot be taken away by a law; and therefore the loss of them is not punishment. But the latter may be taken away by the public authority that made them honorable, and are properly punishments: such are, degrading men condemned, of their badges, titles, and offices; or declaring them incapable of the like in time to come.

Imprisonment is when a man is by public authority deprived of liberty, and may happen from two diverse ends; whereof one is the safe custody of a man accused; the other is the inflicting of pain on a man condemned. The former is not punishment, because no man is supposed to be punished before he be judicially heard and declared guilty. And therefore whatsoever hurt a man is made to suffer by bonds or restraint before his cause be heard, over and above that which is necessary to assure his custody, is against the law of nature. But the latter is punishment because evil, and inflicted by public authority for somewhat that has by the same authority been judged a transgression of the law. Under this word imprisonment, I comprehend all restraint of motion caused by an external obstacle, be it a house, which is called by the general name of a prison; or an island, as when men are said to be confined to it; or a place where men are set to work, as in old time men have been condemned to quarries, and in these times to galleys; or be it a chain or any other such impediment.

Exile (banishment) is when a man is for a crime condemned to depart out of the dominion of the Commonwealth, or out of a certain part thereof, and during a prefixed time, or forever, not to return into it; and seemeth not in its own nature, without other circumstances, to be a punishment, but rather an escape, or a public commandment to avoid punishment by flight. And Cicero says there was never any such punishment ordained in the city of Rome; but calls it a refuge of men in danger. For if a man banished be nevertheless permitted to enjoy his goods, and the revenue of his lands, the mere change of air is no punishment; nor does it tend to that benefit of the Commonwealth for which all punishments are ordained, that is to say, to the forming of men's wills to the observation of the law; but many times to the damage of the Commonwealth. For a banished man is a lawful enemy of the Commonwealth that banished him, as being no more a member of the same. But if he be withal deprived of his lands, or goods, then the punishment lieth not in the exile, but is to be reckoned amongst punishments pecuniary.

> **All punishments of innocent subjects, be they great or little, are against the law of nature: for punishment is only for transgression of the law, and therefore there can be no punishment of the innocent.**

All punishments of innocent subjects, be they great or little, are against the law of nature: for punishment is only for transgression of the law, and therefore there can be no punishment of the innocent. It is therefore a violation, first, of that law of nature which forbiddeth all men, in their revenges, to look at anything but some future good: for there can arrive no good to the Commonwealth by punishing the innocent.

Secondly, of that which forbiddeth ingratitude: for seeing all sovereign power is originally given by the consent of every one of the subjects, to the end they should as long as they are obedient be protected thereby, the punishment of the innocent is a rendering of evil for good. And thirdly, of the law that commandeth equity; that is to say, an equal distribution of justice, which in punishing the innocent is not observed.

But the infliction of what evil soever on an innocent man that is not a subject, if it be for the benefit of the Commonwealth, and without violation of any former covenant, is no breach of the law of nature. For all men that are not subjects are either enemies, or else they have ceased from being so by some precedent covenants. But against enemies, whom the Commonwealth judgeth capable to do them hurt, it is lawful by the original right of nature to make war; wherein the sword judgeth not, nor doth the victor make distinction of nocent and innocent as to the time past, nor has other respect of mercy than as it conduceth to the good of his own people. And upon this ground it is that also in subjects who deliberately deny the authority of the Commonwealth established, the vengeance is lawfully extended, not only to the fathers, but also to the third and fourth generation not yet in being, and consequently innocent of the fact for which they are afflicted: because the nature of this offense consisteth in the renouncing of subjection, which is a relapse into the condition of war commonly called rebellion; and they that so offend, suffer not as subjects, but as enemies. For rebellion is but war renewed. [. . .]

Hitherto I have set forth the nature of man, whose pride and other passions have compelled him to submit himself to government; together with the great power of his governor, whom I compared to LEVIATHAN, taking that comparison out of the two last verses of the one-and-fortieth of Job; where God, having set forth the great power of Leviathan, calleth him king of the proud. "There is nothing," saith he, "on earth to be compared with him. He is made so as not to be afraid. He seeth every high thing below him; and is king of all the children of pride." But because he is mortal, and subject to decay, as all other earthly creatures are; and because there is that in heaven, though not on earth, that he should stand in fear of, and whose laws he ought to obey; I shall in the next following chapters speak of his diseases and the causes of his mortality, and of what laws of nature he is bound to obey.

WITNESS TO AN EXECUTION
Hanging of General Harrison, Samuel Pepys (1660)

To my Lord's in the morning, where I met with Captain Cuttance, but my Lord not being up I went out to Charing Cross, to see Major-General Harrison hanged, drawn; and quartered; which was done there, he looking as cheerful as any man could do in that condition. He was presently cut down, and his head and heart shown to the people, at which there was great shouts of joy. It is said, that he said that he was sure to come shortly at the right hand of Christ to judge them that now had judged him; and that his wife do expect his coming again. Thus it was my chance to see the King beheaded at White Hall, and to see the first blood shed in revenge for the blood of the King at Charing Cross. From thence to my Lord's, and took Captain Cuttance and Mr. Sheply to the Sun Tavern, and did give them some oysters. After that I went by water home, where I was angry with my wife for her things lying about, and in my passion kicked the little fine basket, which I bought her in Holland, and broke it, which troubled me after I had done it. Within all the afternoon setting up shelves in my study. At night to bed.

Hanging Not Punishment Enough, Basil Montagu (1701)

My opinion is, That our present Laws that relate to murtherers, high-way men, and house-breakers, are too favorable, and insufficient for the end they are intended. I fear not to say too favorable, even tho' they extend to death; since that death the law enjoyns, is found unable to deter 'em. Were it not so, our Roads would not be so pester'd with that wicked generation of men, nor our sessions-paper monthly, and the publick news daily full of so many relations of robberies and murthers, and all the pleasure andsatisfaction of travelling destroyed, as it is now, by being so dangerous and unsafe: and (which ought more to be regarded) a frequent interruption given to trade and business, by robbing of packets, and intercepting letters of correspondence and advice to say nothing of the insecurity of sending exchequer and bank- bills by the publick conveyances.

I am sensible,that the English clemency and mildness appear eminently in our laws and constitutions; but since it is found that ill men are grown so much more incorrigible, than in our forefathers days, is it not fit that good men should grow less merciful to them, since gentler methods are ineffectual?

I acknowledge also, that the spirit of Christianity disposes us to patience and forbearance, insomuch that when the roman emperors began to grow Christian, we are informed, that most capital punishments were taken away, and turned into others less sanguinary; either that they might have longer time for repentance, (an indulgence agreeable to the zeal and piety of those good ages) or that the length and continuance of their punishment might be more exemplary. And I acknowledge with the wise Quintilian, that if all men could be made good, as, it must be granted, they sometimes may, it is for the interest of the commonwealth, that they should rather be spared than punished. And I know, that 'tis frequently alledg'd, that you take away a better thing, and that is a man's life, for that which is worse, and that is, your money and goods; but tho' this be speciously enough urged, yet I doubt not, but the publick safety and happiness may lawfully and reasonably be secured by this way, if it can by no other. No doubt, if other methods would do, there had never been recourse to death, since that was questionless reserv'd as the last refuge. But even that now fails, and so fails, that if some remedy be not found to stop this growing evil, we shall shortly not dare to travel in England unless, as in the deserts of Arabia it be in large companies, and arm'd. For to such a height of villany are they arrived, that even some of the nobility themselves have not escaped their hands; and there is no order of men in England but has been sensible of their insolence and rage. And 'tis a very great aggravation of their crime, and a high provocation to those who fall into their power, that they use them in so barbarous and insulting a manner; and so much worse than in former ages, that some men of spirit cannot bear so inhumane treatment, without endangering, and oftentimes losing their lives, as has been too often known, to be prov'd.

So that I must beg leave to say, that they who shew no mercy should find none; and if hanging will not restrain them, hanging them in chains, and starving them, or (if murthers and robbers at the same time, or night incendiaries) breaking them on the wheel, or whipping them to death, a roman punishment should.

I know that torments so unusual and unknown to us may at first surprise us, and appear unreasonable; but I hope easily to get over that difficulty, and make it appear upon examination, that that will be the more probable way to secure us from our fears of them, and the means of preserving great numbers of them, who now yearly by an easie death are taken off at the gallows. For to men so far corrupted in their principles and practices, and that have no expectations beyond the grave (for such, I fear, is the case of most of them) no argument will be so cogent, as pain in an intense degree; and a few such examples made, will be so terrifying, that I persuade myself it would be a law but seldom put in execution.

But then I must add, that I fear it will not have its due effects, if it be too often dispens'd with; since that will be apt to give ground to every offender, to hope he may be of the number of those, who shall escape, and so the good end of the law will be defeated. For if favor or affection, or a man's being of a good family, or money can prevail, and take off the penalty of the statute; if it be not

> **If favor or affection, or a man's being of a good family, or money can prevail, and take off the penalty of the statute; if it be not executed steadily and impartially, with an exact hand . . . it will serve to little purpose.**

executed steadily and impartially, with an exact hand (still giving allowance for extraordinary cases) it will serve to little purpose, since many will be found (as ill men easily flatter themselves) who will not fear a law, that has sharp teeth indeed, but does but sometimes bite. And this, I believe, must be allowed to be the only way to root out our native enemies, as they truly are; as might lately have been seen in a neighboring kingdom, where severity, without the least mixture of mercy, did so sweep high-way men out of the nation, that it has been confidently said, that a man might some time since have openly carried his money without fear of losing it. That he cannot now, is to be charged upon their great numbers of soldiers, without employment and plunder, and in poor pitiful pay; and, it may be, on the very great necessities of the people, and make 'em desperate and careless of their lives.

If death then be due to a man, who surreptitiously steals the value of five shillings (as it is made by a late statute) surely he who puts me in fear of my life, and breaks the King's Peace, and it may be, murthers me at last, and burns my house, deserves another sort of censure; and if the one must die, the other should be made to feel himself die.

Tis a rule in civil law, and reason, that the punishment should not exceed the fault. If death then be due to a man, who surreptitiously steals the value of five shillings (as it is made by a late statute) surely he who puts me in fear of my life, and breaks the King's peace, and it may be, murthers me at last, and burns my house, deserves another sort of censure; and if the one must die, the other should be made to feel himself die.

For as the benefit of the clergy is of late taken from pickpockets, so they are now in the eye of the law upon the same foot with murtherers, highway men, and housebreakers. Their crimes are certainly unequal by the laws of god, and the consent of nations; why then should not their punishment be so too? [. . .]

Besides, the frequent repetitions of the same crimes, even in defiance of the present laws in being, is a just ground of enacting somewhat more terrible; and indeed seems to challenge and require it.

Farther still; at the last great day doubtless there will be degrees of torment, proportionable to men's guilt and sin here; and i can see no reason why we may not imitate the divine justice, and inflict an animadversion suitable to such enormous offenders.

And this, I am persuaded, will best answer the end of sanguinary laws, which are not chiefly intended to punish the present criminal, but to hinder others from being so ; and on that account punishments in the learned languages are called examples, as being design'd to be such to all mankind.

If it be objected, that I propound punishments, that exceed the faults i answer,First, as to high-way men, consider the great terror and fear they put people into; and that contributes largely to their guilt, as appears from that being ever a part of their indictment ; and i apprehend, that the legislative power ought to be highly concern'd, not only for the safety, but for the quiet too of the people.

Besides, those desperate villains hinder trade and commerce, and have made even private visits, and offices of friendship unsafe. They now rob with that impudence, assurance, and leisure, as if they did it legally and with commission ; and as if they came not to steal and rifle, but rather by authority to seize and distrain. They have ruined several, and have brought fear on almost all. They have wounded and maimed divers, have left many bound and naked in cold weather, to the hazard, and often to the loss of their lives.

Then again for housebreakers, the dread of them is greater than can well be express'd, or man the inhabitants of cities and great towns, who are well guarded and secured by their numbers, can imagine. They terrifie innocent people to that high degree, and bring such a consternation on a whole neighborhood, where their haunts are, that they would scarce be more afraid of a foreign invasion. I hope then, we may be allowed to say, it would be a good piece of service to our country, if somewhat more than making a wry mouth, as they ridicule hanging, were appointed for the one and the other.

As for murtherers, as both of them intentionally are, because they are ready armed always for bloody purposes, and have a will not only to rob but to kill too ; as for such, the law of nations is, that like should be returned for like. And since it is an express law of god, that whoso sheds man's blood, by man shall his blood be shed, Gen. 9. 6. A scrupulous man may be tempted to suspect, whether the power that Christian princes generally assume of pardoning wilful murtherers, be not too much, and beyond their commission, since they pardon those whose blood god commands directly and positively to be shed.

I am not ignorant of the common distinction, that the king only remits the loss of his subject ; and among us, that an appeal remains to the party grieved, tho' even that was but lately put in practice. Nevertheless 'tis a known case, that the conditions of appeals are strait and narrow, and clog'd, and that they are constantly discouraged, for a reason easily known, and a flaw in a word or sentence has been commonly found in the appeal, and (it may be) plac'd there on purpose to make it insignificant. I am no enemy to the just prerogative of princes but believe it, when in good hands, to be serviceable and advantageous to the people: but I must say, I am inclined to think, that any usage or custom, memorial or immemorial, that contradicts, or gives leave to dispense with the laws of god is null, and in it self void. I dare not positively say, that this is of that sort, lest I arraign the practice of so many ages, and the best princes; but i think that two eminent civilians declaring, that a murtherer flying to the church, might be drawn from thence, and even by a lay judge, (says one of them) is a very strong argument, that the crime was then look'd upon as exceedingly heinous, since even the exorbitant power of the church, much greater than any secular, was not able to protect those, who were guilty of it.

But still I am sensible, that tho' I argue for severity, in general we ought to be tender of shedding humane blood; for there is such a consanguinity and relation between all mankind, that no one ought to hurt another, unless for some good end to be obtain'd. And bodily punishment, as the civilian welt observes, is greater than any pecuniary mulcts; and every man knows that he who loses his life, is a much greater sufferer than he whose goods are confiscated, or is fined in the most unreasonable manner in the world.

But my design is not, that man's blood should be shed, but that it should not; and I verily believe, that for five men condemned and executed now, you would hardly have one then. For those men out of terror of such a law, would ('tis to be hoped) either apply themselves to honest labor and industry; or else would remove to our plantations, where they are wanted, and so many useful hands would not be yearly lost.

But I must add, that it is not fit, that men in criminal causes, as the civil law well directs, should be condemned, unless the evidence be clearer than the mid-day sun; and no man should expire in such horrid agonies, for whose innocence there is the least pretense.

Now, if with this proviso, executions should happen to be more frequent than i suppose, as nothing is to be wondered at in an age so wicked, let it not be called cruelty, since ill men are to thank themselves for what they knowingly bring on their heads; and 'tis not the law that is to be found fault with, but themselves for coming within the reach of it. For Seneca, as his way is, says very well, that no wise man punishes another so much, because he hath offended, but that others offend not; for (adds he) that which is to come may be hindered, but that which is past cannot. We see then the end of laws, which in scripture language is to be "a terror to the wicked," and every constitution is permitted to secure its own happiness and well-being by the best methods it is able; and the safety and quiet of the people, if it be not the supreme law, is a very considerable one

Isocrates in his *Panathanaic* tells us that his forefathers thought that the war with hurtful beasts is most just and lawful; and the next to that, that with men, like beasts, fierce and hostile by nature, and ever lying in wait for us. And such are these men I am describing; and when a man turns beast, no beast is so cruel as he.

By the imperial constitutions it is declared, that if anyone could apprehend a murtherer, and did not, that he should suffer as a traytor. A very effectual way of bringing malefactors to punishment; and 'twere well, if it were made more penal, for men to harbor and knowingly to receive these transgressors of the laws. And as our proverb says, if there were no receivers, there would be no thieves; so if those men who buy stolen goods at under-rates, and know they are stolen, as in morality and reason they are equally guilty with thieves, if they were to be punished in the same manner they are, this would be to strike at one branch of the root of this wickedness. For doubtless such villainies are carried on by a confederacy, and they are all instruments and subservient one to another, so that if any one part be effectually suppressed, the whole will fall.

And here, to be just, I fear I must say, our English laws do not take sufficient care to make restitution to the injured party, and by that means many prosecutions are hindered, since a man's own goods or money taken from him by violence, are not easily (if at all) to be recovered, even tho' the thief be apprehended and convicted. And this we need not question, occasions many private compositions; and, as most men still have an eye to their own interest, more than to the publick; so they chuse to have their goods restored, rather than to be at the great trouble and charge of prosecution. Nay, which is worse, I am well assured, that some have refused to own their goods (when taken on a thief) before a magistrate, for fear of forfeiting their recognizance, and of long journies, that may sometimes more than double the loss.

Theodicy: Essays on the Goodness of God, the Freedom of Man and the Origin of Evil, Gottfried W. Liebniz (1710)

67. But after all, whatsoever dependence be conceived in voluntary actions, and even though there were an absolute and mathematical necessity (which there is not) it would not follow that there would not be a sufficient degree of freedom to render rewards and punishments just and reasonable. It is true that generally we speak as though the necessity of the action put an end to all merit and all demerit, all justification for praise and blame, for reward and punishment: but it must be admitted that this conclusion is not entirely correct. I am very far from sharing the opinions of Bradwardine, Wyclif, Hobbes and Spinoza, who advocate, so it seems, this entirely mathematical necessity, which I think I have adequately refuted, and perhaps more clearly than is customary. Yet one must always bear testimony to the truth and not impute to a dogma anything that does not result from it. Moreover, these arguments prove too much, since they would prove just as much against hypothetical necessity, and would justify the lazy sophism. For the absolute necessity of the sequence of causes would in this matter add nothing to the infallible certainty of a hypothetical necessity.

68. In the first place, therefore, it must be agreed that it is permitted to kill a madman when one cannot by other means defend oneself. It will be granted also that it is permitted, and often even necessary, to destroy venomous or very noxious animals, although they be not so by their own fault.

69. Secondly, one inflicts punishments upon a beast, despite its lack of reason and freedom, when one deems that this may serve to correct it: thus one punishes dogs and horses, and indeed with much success. Rewards serve us no

less in the managing of animals: when an animal is hungry, the food that is given to him causes him to do what otherwise would never be obtained from him.

In Africa they crucified lions, in order to drive away other lions from the towns and frequented places, and that he had observed in passing through the province of Juelich that they hanged wolves there in order to ensure greater safety for the sheepfolds.

70. Thirdly, one would inflict even on beasts capital punishments (where it is no longer a question of correcting the beast that is punished) if this punishment could serve as an example, or inspire terror in others, to make them cease from evil doing. Rorarius, in his book on reason in beasts, says that in Africa they crucified lions, in order to drive away other lions from the towns and frequented places, and that he had observed in passing through the province of Juelich that they hanged wolves there in order to ensure greater safety for the sheepfolds. There are people in the villages also who nail birds of prey to the doors of houses, with the idea that other birds of the same kind will then not so readily appear. These measures would always be justified if they were of any avail.

71. Then, in the fourth place, since experience proves that the fear of chastisements and the hope of rewards serves to make men abstain from evil and strive to do good, one would have good reason to avail oneself of such, even though men were acting under necessity, whatever the necessity might be. The objection will be raised that if good or evil is necessary, it is useless to avail oneself of means to obtain it or to hinder it: but the answer has already been given above in the passage combating the lazy sophism. If good or evil were a necessity without these means, then such means would be unavailing; but it is not so. These goods and evils come only with the aid of these means, and if these results were necessary the means would be a part of the causes rendering them necessary, since experience teaches us that often fear or hope hinders evil or advances good. This objection, then, differs hardly at all from the lazy sophism, which we raise against the certainty as well as the necessity of future events. Thus one may say that these objections are directed equally against hypothetical necessity and absolute necessity, and that they prove as much against the one as against the other, that is to say, nothing at all.

72. There was a great dispute between Bishop Bramhall and Mr. Hobbes, which began when they were both in Paris, and which was continued after their return to England; all the parts of it are to be found collected in a quarto volume published in London in the year 1656. They are all in English, and have not been translated as far as I know, nor inserted in the *Collection of Works in Latin* by Mr. Hobbes. I had already read these writings, and have obtained them again since. And I had observed at the outset that he had not at all proved the absolute necessity of all things, but had shown sufficiently that necessity would not overthrow all the rules of divine or human justice, and would not prevent

altogether the exercise of this virtue.

73. There is, however, a kind of justice and a certain sort of rewards and of punishments which appear not so applicable to those who should act by an absolute necessity, supposing such necessity existed. It is that kind of justice which has for its goal neither improvement nor example, nor even redress of the evil. This justice has its foundation only in the fitness of things, which demands a certain satisfaction for the expiation of an evil action. The Socinians, Hobbes and some others do not admit this punitive justice, which properly speaking is avenging justice. God reserves it for himself in many cases; but he does not fail to grant it to those who are entitled to govern others, and he exercises it through their agency, provided that they act under the influence of reason and not of passion. The Socinians believe it to be without foundation, but it always has some foundation in that fitness of things which gives satisfaction not only to the injured but also to the wise who see it; even as a beautiful piece of music, or again a good piece of architecture, satisfies cultivated minds. And the wise lawgiver having threatened, and having, so to speak, promised a chastisement, it befits his consistency not to leave the action completely unpunished, even though the punishment would no longer avail to correct anyone. But even though he should have promised nothing, it is enough that there is a fitness of things which could have prompted him to make this promise, since the wise man likewise promises only that which is fitting. And one may even say that there is here a certain compensation of the mind, which would be scandalized by disorder if the chastisement did not contribute towards restoring order. One can also consult what Grotius wrote against the Socinians, of the satisfaction of Jesus Christ, and the answer of Crellius thereto.

74. Thus it is that the pains of the damned continue, even when they no longer serve to turn them away from evil, and that likewise the rewards of the blessed continue, even when they no longer serve for strengthening them in good. One may say nevertheless that the damned ever bring upon themselves new pains through new sins, and that the blessed ever bring upon themselves new joys by new progress in goodness: for both are founded on the principle of the fitness of things, which has seen to it that affairs were so ordered that the evil action must bring upon itself a chastisement. There is good reason to believe, following the parallelism of the two realms, that of final causes and that of efficient causes, that God has established in the universe a connexion between punishment or reward and bad or good action, in accordance wherewith the first should always be attracted by the second, and virtue and vice obtain their reward and their punishment in consequence of the natural sequence of things, which contains still another kind of pre-established harmony than that which appears in the communication between the soul and the body. For, in a word, all that God does, as I have said already, is harmonious to perfection. Perhaps then this principle of the fitness of things would no longer apply to beings acting without true freedom or exemption from absolute necessity; and in that case corrective justice alone would be administered, and not punitive justice. That is the opinion of the famous Conringius, in a dissertation he published on what

is just. And indeed, the reasons Pomponazzi employed in his book on fate, to prove the usefulness of chastisements and rewards, even though all should come about in our actions by a fatal necessity, concern only amendment and not satisfaction, [Greek: *kolasin* or *timorian*.] Moreover, it is only for the sake of outward appearances that one destroys animals accessory to certain crimes, as one razes the houses of rebels, that is, to inspire terror. Thus it is an act of corrective justice, wherein punitive justice has no part at all.

75. But we will not amuse ourselves now by discussing a question more curious than necessary, since we have shown sufficiently that there is no such necessity in voluntary actions. Nevertheless it was well to show that imperfect freedom alone, that is, freedom which is exempt only from constraint, would suffice as foundation for chastisements and rewards of the kind conducive to the avoidance of evil, and to amendment. One sees also from this that some persons of intelligence, who persuade themselves that everything is necessary, are wrong in saying that none must be praised or blamed, rewarded or punished. Apparently they say so only to exercise their wit: the pretext is that all being necessary nothing would be in our power. But this pretext is ill founded: necessary actions would be still in our power, at least in so far as we could perform them or omit them, when the hope or the fear of praise or blame, of pleasure or pain prompted our will thereto, whether they prompted it of necessity, or in prompting it they left spontaneity, contingency and freedom all alike unimpaired. Thus praise and blame, rewards and punishments would preserve always a large part of their use, even though there were a true necessity in our actions. We can praise and blame also natural good and bad qualities, where the will has no part--in a horse, in a diamond, in a man; and he who said of Cato of Utica that he acted virtuously through the goodness of his nature, and that it was impossible for him to behave otherwise, thought to praise him the more.[. . .]

166. [. . .] I confess that one would have some reason to urge that against those who believed that God has no other cause for permitting sin than the design to have something wherewith to exercise punitive justice against the majority of men, and his mercy towards a small number of elect. But it must be considered that God had reasons for his permission of sin, more worthy of him and more profound in relation to us. Someone has dared to compare God's course of action with that of a Caligula, who has his edicts written in so small a hand and has them placarded in so high a place that it is not possible to read them; with that of a mother who neglects her daughter's honor in order to attain her own selfish ends; with that of Queen Catherine de Medicis, who is said to have abetted the love affairs of her ladies in order to learn of the intrigues of the great; and even with that of Tiberius, who arranged, through the extraordinary services of the executioner, that the law forbidding the subjection of a virgin to capital punishment

should no longer apply to the case of Sejanus's daughter. This last comparison was proposed by Peter Bertius, then an Armenian, but finally a member of the Roman communion. And a scandalous comparison has been made between God and Tiberius, which is related at length by Andreas Caroli in his Memorabilia Ecclesiastica of the last century, as M. Bayle observes. Bertius used it against the Gomarists. I think that arguments of this kind are only valid against those who maintain that justice is an arbitrary thing in relation to God; or that he has a despotic power which can go so far as being able to condemn innocents; or, in short, that good is not the motive of his actions.

167. At that same time an ingenious satire was composed against the Gomarists, entitled *Fur praedestinatus, de gepredestineerdedief,* wherein there is introduced a thief condemned to be hanged, who attributes to God all the evil he has done; who believes himself predestined to salvation notwithstanding his wicked actions; who imagines that this belief is sufficient for him, and who defeats by arguments *ad hominem* a Counter-remonstrant minister called to prepare him for death: but this thief is finally converted by an old pastor who had been dismissed for his Arminianism, whom the gaoler, in pity for the criminal and for the weakness of the minister, had brought to him secretly. Replies were made to this lampoon, but replies to satires never please as much as the satires themselves. . . .

WITNESS TO AN EXECUTION
A London Hanging, by a Visiting Frenchman (1726)

Criminals are not executed immediately after their trial, as they are abroad, but are given several days to prepare for death. During that time they may ask for anything that they require either for the soul or for the body. The chaplain of the prison (for there is one) does not leave them, and offers every consolation in his power. The day before the execution those who desire it may receive the sacrament, provided the chaplain thinks that they have sincerely repented and are worthy of it.

On the day of execution the condemned prisoners, wearing a sort of white linen shirt over their clothes and a cap on their heads, are tied two together and placed on carts with their backs to the horses' tails. These carts are guarded and surrounded by constables and other police officers on horseback, each armed with a sort of pike. In this way part of the town is crossed, and Tyburn, which is a good half-mile from the last suburb, is reached, and here stands the gibbet.

One often sees criminals going to their death perfectly unconcerned, others so impenitent that they fill themselves full of liquor and mock at those who are repentant. When all the prisoners arrive at their destination they are to mount on a very wide cart made expressly for the purpose, a cord is passed

The IDLE PRENTICE Executed at Tyburn.

round their necks and the end fastened to the gibbet, which is not very high.

The chaplain who accompanies the condemned men is also on the cart; he makes pray and sings a few verses of the Psalms. Relatives are permitted to mount the cart and take farewell. When the time is up — that is to about a quarter of an hour — the chaplain and relations get off the cart, the executioner covers the eyes and faces of the prisoners with their caps lashes the horses that draw the cart, which slips from under the condemned men's feet, and in this way they remain all hanging together. You often see friends and relations tugging at the hanging men's feet so that they should die quicker and not suffer.

You often see friends and relations tugging at the hanging men's feet so that they should die quicker and not suffer.

The bodies and clothes of the dead belong to the executioner; relatives must, if they wish for them, buy them from him, and unclaimed bodies are sold to surgeons to be dissected. You see most amusing scenes between the people who do not like the bodies to be cut and the messengers the surgeons have sent for bodies; blows are given and returned before they can be got away, and sometimes in the turmoil the bodies are quickly removed and buried.

There is no other form of execution but hanging; it is thought that the taking of life is sufficient punishment for any crime without worse torture. After hanging murderers are, however, punished in a particular fashion. They are first hung on the common gibbet, their bodies are then covered with tallow and fat substances, over this is placed a tarred shirt fastened down with iron bands, and the bodies are hung with chains to the gibbet, which is erected on the spot, or as near as possible to the place, where the crime was committed, and there it hangs till it falls to dust. This is what is called in this country to 'hang in chains.'

Going To Be Hanged, Jonathan Swift (1727)

As clever Tom Clinch, while the rabble was bawling,
Rode stately through Holborn to die in his calling,
He stopt at the George for a bottle of sack,
And promised to pay for it when he came back.
His waistcoat, and stockings, and breeches, were white;
His cap had a new cherry ribbon to tie't.
The maids to the doors and the balconies ran,
And said, "Lack-a-day, he's a proper young man!"
But, as from the windows the ladies he spied,
Like a beau in the box, he bow'd low on each side!
And when his last speech the loud hawkers did cry,
He swore from his cart, "It was all a damn'd lie!"
The hangman for pardon fell down on his knee;
Tom gave him a kick in the guts for his fee:
Then said, I must speak to the people a little;
But I'll see you all damn'd before I will whittle.
My honest friend Wild (may he long hold his place)
He lengthen'd my life with a whole year of grace.
Take courage, dear comrades, and be not afraid,
Nor slip this occasion to follow your trade;
My conscience is clear, and my spirits are calm,
And thus I go off, without prayer-book or psalm;
Then follow the practice of clever Tom Clinch,
Who hung like a hero, and never would flinch.

An Enquiry Concerning Human Understanding
David Hume (1748)

69. Thus it appears, not only that the conjunction between motives and voluntary actions is as regular and uniform as that between the cause and effect in any part of nature; but also that this regular conjunction has been universally acknowledged among mankind, and has never been the subject of dispute, either in philosophy or common life. Now, as it is from past experience that we draw all inferences concerning the future, and as we conclude that objects will always be conjoined together which we find to have always been conjoined; it may

seem superfluous to prove that this experienced uniformity inhuman actions is a source whence we draw inferences concerning them. But in order to throw the argument into a greater variety of lights we shall also insist, though briefly, on this latter topic. The mutual dependence of men is so great in all societies that scarce any human action is entirely complete in itself, or is performed without some reference to the actions of others, which are requisite to make it answer fully the intention of the agent. The poorest artificer, who labors alone, expects at least the protection of the magistrate, to ensure him the enjoyment of the fruits of his labor. He also expects that, when he carries his goods to market, and offers them at a reasonable price, he shall find purchasers, and shall be able, by the money he acquires, to engage others to supply him with those commodities which are requisite for his subsistence. In proportion as men extend their dealings, and render their intercourse with others more complicated, they always comprehend, in their schemes of life, a greater variety of voluntary actions, which they expect, from the proper motives, to cooperate with their own. In all these conclusions they take their measures from past experience, in the same manner as in their reasonings concerning external objects; and firmly believe that men, as well as all the elements, are to continue, in their operations, the same that they have ever found them. A manufacturer reckons upon the labor of his servants for the execution of any work as much as upon the tools which he employs, and would be equally surprised were his expectations disappointed. In short, this experimental inference and reasoning concerning the actions of others enters so much into human life that no man, while awake, is ever a moment without employing it. Have we not reason, therefore, to affirm that all mankind have always agreed in the doctrine of necessity according to foregoing definition and explication of it?

70. Nor have philosophers ever entertained a different opinion from the people in this particular. For, not to mention that almost every action of their life supposes that opinion, there are even few of the speculative parts of learning to which it is not essential. What would become of history, had we not a dependence on the veracity of the historian according to the experience which we have had of mankind? How could politics be a science, if laws and forms of government had not a uniform influence upon society? Where would be the foundation of morals, if particular characters had no certain or determinate power to produce particular sentiments, and if these sentiments had no constant operation on actions? And with what pretense could we employ our criticism upon any poet or polite author, if we could not pronounce the conduct and sentiments of his actors either natural or unnatural to such characters, and in such circumstances? It seems almost impossible, therefore, to engage either in science or action of any kind without acknowledging the doctrine of necessity, and this inference from motive to voluntary actions, from characters to conduct. And indeed, when we consider how aptly natural and moral evidence link together, and form only one chain of argument, we shall make no scruple to allow that they are of the same nature, and derived from the same principles. A prisoner who has neither money nor interest, discovers the impossibility of his escape, as well when he

considers the obstinacy of the gaoler, as the walls and bars with which he is surrounded; and, in all attempts for his freedom, chooses rather to work upon the stone and iron of the one, than upon the inflexible nature of the other. The same prisoner, when conducted to the scaffold, foresees his death as certainly from the constancy and fidelity of his guards, as from the operation of the axe or wheel. His mind runs along a certain train of ideas: The refusal of the soldiers to consent to his escape; the action of the executioner; the separation of the head and body; bleeding, convulsive motions, and death. Here is a connected chain of natural causes and voluntary actions; but the mind feels no difference between them in passing from one link to another: Nor is less certain of the future event than if it were connected with the objects present to the memory or senses, by a train of causes, cemented together by what we are pleased to call a physical necessity. The same experienced union has the same effect on the mind, whether the united objects be motives, volition, and actions; or figure and motion. We may change the name of things; but their nature and their operation on the understanding never change.

Spirit of Laws,
Charles de Secondat, Baron de Montesquieu (1748)

9. Of the Severity of Punishments in different Governments.

The severity of punishments is fitter for despotic governments, whose principle is terror, than for a monarchy or a republic, whose spring is honor and virtue.

In moderate governments, the love of one's country, shame, and the fear of blame are restraining motives, capable of preventing a multitude of crimes. Here the greatest punishment of a bad action is conviction. The civil laws have therefore a softer way of correcting, and do not require so much force and severity.

In those states a good legislator is less bent upon punishing than preventing crimes; he is more attentive to inspire good morals than to inflict penalties.

It is a constant remark of the Chinese authors that the more the penal laws were increased in their empire, the nearer they drew towards a revolution. This is because punishments were augmented in proportion as the public morals were corrupted.

It would be an easy matter to prove that in all, or almost all, the governments of Europe, penalties have increased or diminished in proportion as those governments favored or discouraged liberty.

In despotic governments, people are so unhappy as to have a greater dread of death than regret for the loss of life; consequently their punishments ought to be more severe. In moderate states they are more afraid of losing their lives than apprehensive of the pain of dying; those punishments, therefore, which deprive them simply of life are sufficient.

Men in excess of happiness or misery are equally inclinable to severity; witness conquerors and monks. It is mediocrity alone, and a mixture of prosperous and adverse fortune, that inspires us with lenity and pity.

Men in excess of happiness or misery are equally inclinable to severity; witness conquerors and monks.

What we see practiced by individuals is equally observable in regard to nations. In countries inhabited by savages who lead a very hard life, and in despotic governments, where there is only one person on whom fortune lavishes her favors, while the miserable subjects lie exposed to her insults, people are equally cruel. Lenity reigns in moderate governments.

When in reading history we observe the cruelty of the sultans in administration of justice, we shudder at the very thought of the miseries of human nature.

In moderate governments, a good legislator may make use of everything by way of punishment. Is it not very extraordinary that one of the chief penalties at Sparta was to deprive a person of the power of lending out his wife, or of receiving the wife of another man, and to oblige him to have no company at home but virgins? In short, whatever the law calls a punishment is such effectively.

10. Of the ancient French laws.

In the ancient French laws we find the true spirit of monarchy. In cases relating to pecuniary mulcts, the common people are less severely punished than the nobility. But in criminal cases it is quite the reverse; the nobleman loses his honor and his voice in court, while the peasant, who has no honor to lose, undergoes a corporal punishment.

11. That when people are virtuous few punishments are necessary.

The people of Rome had some share of probity. Such was the force of this probity that the legislator had frequently no further occasion than to point out the right road, and they were sure to follow it; one would imagine that instead of precepts it was sufficient to give them counsels.

The punishments of the regal laws, and those of the Twelve Tables, were almost all abolished in the time of the republic, in consequence either of the Valerian or of the Porcian law. It was never observed that this step did any manner of prejudice to the civil administration.

This Valerian law, which restrained the magistrates from using violent methods against a citizen that had appealed to the people, inflicted no other punishment on the person who infringed it than that of being reputed a dishonest man.

12. Of the power of punishments.

Experience shows that in countries remarkable for the lenity of their laws the spirit of the inhabitants is as much affected by slight penalties as in other countries by severer punishments.

If an inconvenience or abuse arises in the state, a violent government endeavors suddenly to redress it; and instead of putting the old laws in execution, it establishes some cruel punishment, which instantly puts a stop to the evil. But the spring of government hereby loses its elasticity; the imagination grows accustomed to the severe as well as the milder punishment; and as the fear of the latter diminishes, they are soon obliged in every case to have recourse to the former. Robberies on the highway became common in some countries; in order to remedy this evil, they invented the punishment of breaking upon the wheel, the terror of which put a stop for a while to this mischievous practice. But soon after robberies on the highways became as common as ever.

Desertion in our days has grown to a very great height; in consequence of which it was judged proper to punish those delinquents with death; and yet their number did not diminish. The reason is very natural; a soldier, accustomed to venture his life, despises, or affects to despise, the danger of losing it. He is habituated to the fear of shame; it would have been therefore much better to have continued a punishment which branded him with infamy for life; the penalty was pretended to be increased, while it really diminished.

Mankind must not be governed with too much severity; we ought to make a prudent use of the means which nature has given us to conduct them. If we inquire into the cause of all human corruptions, we shall find that they proceed from the impunity of criminals, and not from the moderation of punishments. Let us follow nature, who has given shame to man for his scourge; and let the heaviest part of the punishment be the infamy attending it.

But if there be some countries where shame is not a consequence of punishment, this must be owing to tyranny, which has inflicted the same penalties on villains and honest men.

And if there are others where men are deterred only by cruel punishments, we may be sure that this must, in a great measure, arise from the violence of the government which has used such penalties for slight transgressions.

It often happens that a legislator, desirous of remedying an abuse, thinks of nothing else; his eyes are open only to this object, and shut to its inconveniences. When the abuse is redressed, you see only the severity of the legislator; yet there remains an evil in the state that has sprung from this severity; the minds of the people are corrupted, and become habituated to despotism.

Lysander having obtained a victory over the Athenians, the prisoners were ordered to be tried, in consequence of an accusation brought against that nation of having thrown all the captives of two galleys down a precipice, and of having resolved in full assembly to cut off the hands of those whom they should chance to make prisoners. The Athenians were therefore all massacred, except Adymantes, who had opposed this decree. Lysander reproached Phylocles, before he was put to death, with having depraved the people's minds, and given lessons of cruelty to all Greece.

"The Argives," says Plutarch,"having put fifteen hundred of their citizens to death, the Athenians ordered sacrifices of expiation, that it might please the gods to turn the hearts of the Athenians from so cruel a thought."

There are two sorts of corruptions — one when the people do not observe the laws; the other when they are corrupted by the laws: an incurable evil, because it is in the very remedy itself.

Essays on the Mind (*de l'Espirit*)
Claude Adrien Helvétius (1758)

If pleasure be the only object of man's pursuit, we need only imitate nature, in order to inspire a love of virtue. Pleasure informs us of what she would have done, and pain what she forbids, and man will readily obey her mandates. Why may not the legislature, armed with the same power, produce the same effects? Were men without passions, there would be no means of producing a reformation; but the love of pleasure, against which men, possessed of a probity more venerable than enlightened, have constantly exclaimed, is a bridle by which the passions of the individuals might always be directed to the public good. The hatred most men have for virtue is not then the effect of the corruption of their nature, but of the imperfection of the legislation. It is the legislation, if I may venture to say so, that excites us to vice, by mingling it with pleasure; the great art of the legislator is that of separating them, and making no proportion between the advantage the villain can receive from his crime, and the pain to which he exposes himself. If among the rich men, who are often less virtuous than the indigent, we see few robbers and assassins, it is because the profit obtained by robbery is never to a rich man proportionable to the hazard of a capital punishment: but this is not the case with respect to the indigent; for the disproportion falling infinitely short of being so great, with respect to him, virtue and vice are in a manner placed in an equilibrium.

Not that I would here pretend to insinuate, that men ought to be driven as with a rod of iron. In an excellent legislation, and among a virtuous people, contempt, which deprives man of all consolation, and leaves him desolate in the midst of his native country, is a motive sufficient to form virtuous minds. Every other kind of punishment renders men timid, inactive, and stupid. The kind of virtue produced by the fear of punishment resembles its origin; this virtue is pusillanimous, and without knowledge; or rather fear, which only smothers vice, but produces no virtues. True virtue is founded on the love of esteem and glory, and the fear of contempt, which is more terrible than death itself. I cannot cite here a more apposite example, than the answer which the English Spectator puts into the mouth of a soldier fond of dueling, who thus addresses Pharamond, who reproached him for having disobeyed his orders. "How could I obey such orders?" said the soldier: "Thou punishest indeed with death those who violate them, but with infamy those who obey them! Know, then, that I fear death less than infamy!"

Rambler 114, Samuel Johnson Saturday, 20 April 1750

Audi,
Nulla unquam de morte hominis cunctatio longa est.
Juvenal, VI.220–21.

When man's life is in debate,
The judge can ne'er too long deliberate.
Dryden.

Power and superiority are so flattering and delightful, that, fraught with temptation and exposed to danger as they are, scarcely any virtue is so cautious, or any prudence so timorous, as to decline them. Even those that have most reverence for the laws of right, are pleased with shewing that not fear, but choice, regulates their behavior; and would be thought to comply, rather than obey. We love to overlook the boundaries which we do not wish to pass; and, as the Roman satirist remarks, he that has no design to take the life of another, is yet glad to have it in his hands.

From the same principle, tending yet more to degeneracy and corruption, proceeds the desire of investing lawful authority with terror, and governing by force rather than persuasion. Pride is unwilling to believe the necessity of assigning any other reason than her own will; and would rather maintain the most equitable claims by violence and penalties, than descend from the dignity of command to dispute and expostulation.

It may, I think, be suspected, that this political arrogance has sometimes found its way into legislative assemblies, and mingled with deliberations upon property and life. A slight perusal of the laws by which the measures of vindictive and coercive justice are established, will discover so many disproportions between crimes and punishments, such capricious distinctions of guilt, and such confusion of remissness and severity, as can scarcely be believed to have been produced by publick wisdom, sincerely and calmly studious of publick happiness.

The learned, the judicious, the pious Boerhaave relates, that he never saw a criminal dragged to execution without asking himself, "Who knows whether this man is not less culpable than me?" On the days when the prisons of this city are emptied into the grave, let every spectator of the dreadful procession put the same question to his own heart. Few among those that crowd in thousands to the legal massacre, and look with carelessness, perhaps with triumph, on the utmost exacerbations of human misery, would then be able to return without horror and dejection. For, who can congratulate himself upon a life passed without some act more mischievous to the peace or prosperity of others, than the theft of a piece of money?

It has been always the practice, when any particular species of robbery becomes prevalent and common, to endeavor its suppression by capital denunciations. Thus, one generation of malefactors is commonly cut off, and their successors are frighted into new expedients; the art of thievery is augmented with greater variety of fraud, and subtilized to higher degrees of dexterity, and more occult methods of conveyance. The law then renews the pursuit in the heat of anger, and overtakes the offender again with death. By this practice, capital inflictions are multiplied, and crimes very different in their degrees of enormity are equally subjected to the severest punishment that man has the power of exercising upon man.

The lawgiver is undoubtedly allowed to estimate the malignity of an offense, not merely by the loss or pain which single acts may produce, but by the general alarm and anxiety arising from the fear of mischief, and insecurity of possession: he therefore exercises the right which societies are supposed to have over the lives of those that compose them, not simply to punish a transgression, but to maintain order, and preserve quiet; he enforces those laws with severity that are most in danger of violation, as the commander of a garrison doubles the guard on that side which is threatened by the enemy.

This method has been long tried, but tried with so little success, that rapine and violence are hourly increasing; yet few seem willing to despair of its efficacy, and of those who employ their speculations upon the present corruption of the people, some propose the introduction of more horrid, lingering and terrifick punishments; some are inclined to accelerate the executions; some to discourage pardons; and all seem to think that lenity has given confidence to wickedness, and that we can only be rescued from the talons of robbery by inflexible rigor, and sanguinary justice.

Yet since the right of setting an uncertain and arbitrary value upon life has been disputed, and since experience of past times gives us little reason to hope that any reformation will be effected by a periodical havock of our fellow-beings, perhaps it will not be useless to consider what consequences might arise from relaxations of the law, and a more rational and equitable adaptation of penalties to offenses.

Death is, as one of the ancients observes, to *tôn phoberôn phoberôtaton*, "of dreadful things the most dreadful;" an evil, beyond which nothing can be threatened by sublunary power, or feared from human enmity or vengeance. This terror should, therefore, be reserved as the last resort of authority, as the strongest and most operative of prohibitory sanctions, and placed before the treasure of life, to guard from invasion what cannot be restored. To equal robbery with murder is to reduce murder to robbery, to confound in common minds the gradations of iniquity, and incite the commission of a greater crime to prevent the detection of a less. If only murder were punished with death, very few robbers would stain their hands in blood; but when, by the last act

If only murder were punished with death, very few robbers would stain their hands in blood; but when, by the last act of cruelty no new danger is incurred, and greater security may be obtained, upon what principle shall we bid them forbear?

of cruelty no new danger is incurred, and greater security may be obtained, upon what principle shall we bid them forbear?

It may be urged, that the sentence is often mitigated to simple robbery; but surely this is to confess, that our laws are unreasonable in our own opinion; and, indeed, it may be observed, that all but murderers have, at their last hour, the common sensations of mankind pleading in their favor. From this conviction of the inequality of the punishment to the offense proceeds the frequent solicitation of pardons. They who would rejoice at the correction of a thief, are yet shocked at the thought of destroying him. His crime shrinks to nothing, compared with his misery; and severity defeats itself by exciting pity.

The gibbet, indeed, certainly disables those who die upon it from infesting the community; but their death seems not to contribute more to the reformation of their associates than any other method of separation. A thief seldom passes much of his time in recollection or anticipation, but from robbery hastens to riot, and from riot to robbery; nor, when the grave closes upon his companion, has any other care than to find another.

The frequency of capital punishments therefore rarely hinders the commission of a crime, but naturally and commonly prevents its detection, and is, if we proceed only upon prudential principles, chiefly for that reason to be avoided. Whatever may be urged by casuists or politicians, the greater part of mankind, as they can never think that to pick the pocket and to pierce the heart is equally criminal, will scarcely believe that two malefactors so different in guilt can be justly doomed to the same punishment; nor is the necessity of submitting the conscience to human laws so plainly evinced, so clearly stated, or so generally allowed, but that the pious, the tender, and the just, will always scruple to concur with the community in an act which their private judgment cannot approve.

He who knows not how often rigorous laws produce total impunity, and how many crimes are concealed and forgotten for fear of hurrying the offender to that state in which there is no repentance, has conversed very little with mankind. And whatever epithets of reproach or contempt this compassion may incur from those who confound cruelty with firmness, I know not whether any wise man would wish it less powerful, or less extensive.

If those whom the wisdom of our laws has condemned to die, had been detected in their rudiments of robbery, they might by proper discipline and useful labor, have been disentangled from their habits, they might have escaped all the temptations to subsequent crimes, and passed their days in reparation and penitence; and detected they might all have been, had the prosecutors been certain, that their lives would have been spared. I believe, every thief will confess, that he has been more than once seized and dismissed; and that he has sometimes ventured upon capital crimes, because he knew, that those whom he injured would rather connive at his escape, than cloud their minds with the horrors of his death.

The heart of a good man cannot but recoil at the thought of punishing a slight injury with death.

All laws against wickedness are ineffectual, unless some will inform, and some will prosecute; but till we mitigate the penalties for mere violations of property, information will always be hated, and prosecution dreaded. The heart of a good man cannot but recoil at the thought of punishing a slight injury with death; especially when he remembers, that the thief might have procured safety by another crime, from which he was restrained only by his remaining virtue.

The obligations to assist the exercise of publick justice are indeed strong; but they will certainly be overpowered by tenderness for life. What is punished with severity contrary to our ideas of adequate retribution, will be seldom discovered; and multitudes will be suffered to advance from crime to crime, till they deserve death, because if they had been sooner prosecuted, they would have suffered death before they deserved it. This scheme of invigorating the laws by relaxation, and extirpating wickedness by lenity, is so remote from common practice, that I might reasonably fear to expose it to the publick, could it be supported only by my own observations: I shall, therefore, by ascribing it to its author, Sir Thomas More, endeavor to procure it that attention, which I wish always paid to prudence, to justice, and to mercy.

WITNESS TO AN EXECUTION
An Account of Corsica, James Boswell (1765)

Turin, 22 January, 1765

I set out at eleven. As I went out at one of the ports, I saw a crowd running to the execution of a thief. I jumped out of my chaise and went close to the gallows. The criminal stood on a ladder, and a priest held a crucifix before his face. He was tossed over, and hung with his face uncovered, which was hideous. I stood fixed in attention to this spectacle, thinking that the feelings of horror might destroy those of chagrin. But so thoroughly was my mind possessed by the feverish agitation that I did not feel in the smallest degree from the execution. The hangman put his feet on the criminal's head and neck and had him strangled in a minute. I then went into a church and kneeled with great devotion before an altar splendidly lighted up. Here then I felt three successive scenes: raging love gloomy horror grand devotion. The horror indeed I only should have felt. I jogged on slowly with my *vetturino*, and had a grievous inn at night.

Corte, 18 October 1765

The hangman of Corsica was a great curiosity. Being held in the utmost detestation, he durst not live like another inhabitant of the island. He was obliged to take refuge in the castle, and there he was kept in a little corner turret, where he had just room for a miserable bed and a little bit of fire to dress such victuals for himself as were sufficient to keep him alive; for nobody would have any intercourse with him, but all turned their backs upon him. I went up and looked at him. And a more dirty, rueful spectacle I never beheld. He seemed sensible of his situation and held down his head like an abhorred outcast

It was a long time before they could get a hangman in Corsica, so that the punishment of the gallows was hardly known, all their criminals being shot. At last this creature whom I saw, who is a Sicilian, came with a message to Paoli. The General, who has a wonderful talent for physiognomy, on seeing the man said immediately to some of the people about him, "Behold our hangman." He gave orders to ask the man if he would accept of the office, and his answer was, "My grandfather was a hangman, my father was a hangman. I have been a hangman myself and am willing to continue so." He was therefore immediately put into office, and the ignominious death dispensed by his hands hath had more effect than twenty executions by firearms.

It is remarkable that no Corsican would upon any account consent to be a hangman. Not the greatest criminals, who might have had their lives upon that condition. Even the wretch who for a paltry hire had strangled a woman would rather submit to death than do the same action as the executioner of the law.

Sollacaro, 22-27 October 1765

While I was at Sollacaro, information was received that the poor wretch who strangled the woman at the instigation of his mistress had consented to accept of his life upon condition of becoming hangman. This made a great noise among the Corsicans, who were enraged at the creature and said their nation was now disgraced. Paoli did not think so. He said to me, "I am glad of this. It will be of service. It will contribute to form us to a just subordination. We have as yet too great an equality among us. As we must have Corsican tailors and Corsican shoemakers, we must also have a Corsican hangman."

I could not help being of a different opinion. The occupations of a tailor and a shoemaker, though mean, are not odious. When I afterwards met M. Rousseau in England and made him a report of my Corsican expedition, he agreed with me in thinking that it would be something noble for the brave islanders to be able to say that there was not a Corsican but who would rather suffer death than become a hangman; and he also agreed with me that it might have a good effect to have always a Genoese for the hangman of Corsica.

I must, however, do the Genoese the justice to observe that Paoli told me that even one of them had suffered death in Corsica rather than consent to become hangman.

The Theory of the Moral Sentiments, Adam Smith (1759)

It is thus that man, who can subsist only in society, was fitted by nature to that situation for which he was made. All the members of human society stand in need of each others' assistance, and are likewise exposed to mutual injuries. Where the necessary assistance is reciprocally afforded from love, from gratitude, from friendship, and esteem, the society flourishes and is happy. All the different members of it are bound together by the agreeable bands of love and affection, and are, as it were, drawn to one common center of mutual good offices.

But though the necessary assistance should not be afforded from such generous and disinterested motives, though among the different members of the society there should be no mutual love and affection, the society, though less happy and agreeable, will not necessarily be dissolved. Society may subsist among different men, as among different merchants, from a sense of its utility, without any mutual love or affection; and though no man in it should owe any obligation, or be bound in gratitude to any other, it may still be upheld by a mercenary exchange of good offices according to an agreed valuation.

Society, however, cannot subsist among those who are at all times ready to hurt and injure one another.

Society, however, cannot subsist among those who are at all times ready to hurt and injure one another. The moment that injury begins, the moment that mutual resentment and animosity take place, all the bands of it are broke asunder, and the different members of which it consisted are, as it were, dissipated and scattered abroad by the violence and opposition of their discordant affections. If there is any society among robbers and murderers, they must at least, according to the trite observation, abstain from robbing and murdering one another. Beneficence, therefore, is less essential to the existence of society than justice. Society may subsist, though not in the most comfortable state, without beneficence; hut the prevalence of injustice must utterly destroy it.

Though Nature, therefore, exhorts mankind to acts of beneficence, by the pleasing consciousness of deserved reward, she has not thought it necessary to guard and enforce the practice of it by the terrors of merited punishment in case it should be neglected. It is the ornament which embellishes, not the foundation which supports the building, and which it was, therefore, sufficient to recommend, but by no means necessary to impose. Justice, on the contrary, is the main pillar that upholds the whole edifice. If it is removed, the great, the immense fabric of human society, that fabric which to raise and support seems in this world, if I may say so, to have been the peculiar and darling care of Nature, must in a moment crumble into atoms. In order to enforce the observation of justice, therefore, Nature has implanted in the human breast that consciousness of ill-desert, those terrors of merited punishment which attend upon its violation, as the great safeguards of the association of mankind, to protect the weak, to curb the violent, and to chastise the guilty. Men, though naturally sympathetic, feel so little for another, with whom they have no particular connexion, in comparison of what they feel for themselves; the misery of one, who is merely their fellow creature, is of so little importance to them in comparison even of a small conveniency of their own; they have it so much in their power to hurt him, and may have so many temptations to do so, that if this principle did not stand up within them in his defense, and overawe them into a respect for his innocence, they would, like wild beasts, be at all times ready to fly upon him; and a man would enter an assembly of men as he enters a den of lions.

In every part of the universe we observe means adjusted with the nicest artifice to the ends which they are intended to produce; and in the mechanism of a plant, or animal body, admire how everything is contrived for advancing the two great purposes of nature, the support of the individual, and the propagation of the species. But in these, and in all such objects, we still distinguish the efficient from the final cause of their several motions and organizations. The digestion of the food, the circulation of the blood, and the secretion of the several juices which are drawn from it, are operations all of them necessary for the great purposes of animal life. Yet we never endeavor to account for them from those purposes as from their efficient causes, nor imagine that the blood circulates, or that the food digests of its own accord, and with a view or intention to the purposes of circulation or digestion. The wheels of the watch are all admirably adjusted to the end for which it was made, the pointing of the hour. All their various motions conspire in the nicest manner to produce this effect. If they were endowed with a desire and intention to produce it, they could not do it better. Yet we never ascribe any such desire or intention to them, but to the watchmaker, and we know that they are put into motion by a spring, which intends the effect it produces as little as they do. But though, in accounting for the operations of bodies, we never fail to distinguish in this manner the efficient from the final cause, in accounting for those of the mind we are very apt to confound these two different things with one another. When by natural principles we are led to advance those ends, which a refined and enlightened reason would recommend to us, we are very apt to impute to that reason, as to their efficient cause, the sentiments and actions by which we advance those ends, and to imagine that to be the wisdom of man, which in reality is the wisdom of God. Upon a superficial view, this cause seems sufficient to produce the effects which are ascribed to it; and the system of human nature seems to be more simple and agreeable when all its different operations are in this manner deduced from a single principle.

As society cannot subsist unless the laws of justice are tolerably observed, as no social intercourse can take place among men who do not generally abstain from injuring one another; the consideration of this necessity, it has been thought, was the ground upon which we approved of the enforcement of the laws of justice by the punishment of those who violated them. Man, it has been said, has a natural love for society, and desires that the union of mankind should be preserved for its own sake, and though he himself was to derive no benefit from it. The orderly and flourishing state of society is agreeable to him, and he takes delight in contemplating it. Its disorder and confusion, on the contrary, is the object of his aversion, and he is chagrined at whatever tends to produce it. He is sensible too that his own interest is connected with the prosperity of society, and that the happiness, perhaps the preservation of his existence, depends upon its preservation. Upon every account, therefore, he has an abhorrence at whatever can tend to destroy society, and is willing to make use of every means, which can hinder so hated and so dreadful an event. Injustice necessarily tends to destroy it. Every appearance of injustice, therefore, alarms him, and he runs, if I may say so, to stop the progress of what, if allowed to go on, would quickly put an end to everything that is dear to him. If he cannot restrain it by gentle and fair means, he must beat it down by force and violence, and at any rate must put a stop to its further progress. Hence it is, they say, that he often approves of the enforcement of the laws of justice even by the capital punishment of those who violate them. The disturber of the public peace is hereby removed out of the world, and others are terrified by his fate from imitating his example.

Such is the account commonly given of our approbation of the punishment of injustice. And so far this account is undoubtedly true, that we frequently have occasion to confirm our natural sense of the propriety and fitness of punishment, by reflecting how necessary it is for preserving the order of society. When the guilty is about to suffer that just retaliation, which the natural indignation of mankind tells them is due to his crimes; when the insolence of his injustice is broken and humbled by the terror of his approaching punishment; when he ceases to be an object of fear, with the generous and humane, he begins to be an object of pity. The thought of what he is about to suffer extinguishes their resentment for the sufferings of others to which he has given occasion. They are disposed to pardon and forgive him, and to save him from that punishment, which in all their cool hours they had considered as the retribution due to such crimes. Here, therefore, they have occasion to call to their assistance the consideration of the general interest of society. They counterbalance the impulse of this weak and partial humanity by the dictates of a humanity that is more generous and comprehensive. They reflect that mercy to the guilty is cruelty to the innocent, and oppose to the emotions of compassion which they feel for a particular person, a more enlarged compassion which they feel for mankind.

Sometimes, too, we have occasion to defend the propriety of observing the general rules of justice by the consideration of their necessity to the support of society. We frequently hear the young and the licentious ridiculing the most sacred rules of morality, and professing, sometimes from the corruption, but more frequently from the vanity of their hearts, the most abominable maxims of conduct. Our indignation rouses,

> **We frequently hear the young and the licentious ridiculing the most sacred rules of morality, and professing, sometimes from the corruption, but more frequently from the vanity of their hearts, the most abominable maxims of conduct.**

and we are eager to refute and expose such detestable principles. But though it is their intrinsic hatefulness and detestableness, which originally inflames us against them, we are unwilling to assign this as the sole reason why we condemn them, or to pretend that it is merely because we ourselves hate and detest them. The reason, we think, would not appear to be conclusive. Yet why should it not; if we hate and detest them because they are the natural and proper objects of hatred and detestation? But when we are asked why we should not act in such or such a manner, the very question seems to suppose that, to those who ask it, this manner of acting does not appear to be for its own sake the natural and proper object of those sentiments. We must show them, therefore, that it ought to be so for the sake of something else. Upon this account we generally cast about for other arguments, and the consideration which first occurs to us, is the disorder and confusion of society which would result from the universal prevalence of such practices. We seldom fail, therefore, to insist upon this topic.

All men, even the most stupid and unthinking, abhor fraud, perfidy, and injustice, and delight to see them punished.

But though it commonly requires no great discernment to see the destructive tendency of all licentious practices to the welfare of society, it is seldom this consideration which first animates us against them. All men, even the most stupid and unthinking, abhor fraud, perfidy, and injustice, and delight to see them punished. But few men have reflected upon the necessity of justice to the existence of society, how obvious soever that necessity may appear to be.

That it is not a regard to the preservation of society, which originally interests us in the punishment of crimes committed against individuals, may be demonstrated by many obvious considerations. The concern which we take in the fortune and happiness of individuals does not, in common cases, arise from that which we take in the fortune and happiness of society. We are no more concerned for the destruction or loss of a single man, because this man is a member or part of society, and because we should be concerned for the destruction of society, than we are concerned for the loss of a single guinea, because this guinea is a part of a thousand guineas, and because we should be concerned for the loss of the whole sum. In neither case does our regard for the individuals arise from our regard for the multitude: but in both cases our regard for the multitude is compounded and made up of the particular regards which we feel for the different individuals of which it is composed. As when a small sum is unjustly taken from us, we do not so much prosecute the injury from a regard to the preservation of our whole fortune, as from a regard to that particular sum which we have lost; so when a single man is injured, or destroyed, we demand the punishment of the wrong that has been done to him, not so much from a concern for the general interest of society, as from a concern for that very individual who has been injured. It is to be observed, however, that this concern does not necessarily include in it any degree of those exquisite sentiments which are commonly called love, esteem, and affection, and by which we distinguish our particular friends and acquaintance. The concern which is requisite for this, is no more than the general fellow feeling which we have with every man merely because he is our fellow-creature. We enter into the resentment even of an odious person, when he is injured by those to whom he has given no provocation. Our disapprobation of his ordinary character and conduct does not in this case altogether prevent our fellow-feeling with his natural indignation; though with those who are not either extremely candid, or who have not been accustomed to correct and regulate their natural sentiments by general rules, it is very apt to damp it

Upon some occasions, indeed, we both punish and approve of punishment, merely from a view to the general interest of society, which, we imagine, cannot otherwise be secured. Of this kind are all the punishments inflicted for breaches of what is called either civil police, or military discipline. Such crimes do not immediately or directly hurt any particular person; but their remote consequences, it is supposed, do produce, or might produce, either a considerable inconveniency, or a great disorder in the society. A sentinel, for example, who falls asleep upon his watch, suffers death by the laws of war, because such carelessness might endanger the whole army. This severity may, upon many occasions, appear necessary, and, for that reason, just and proper. When the preservation of an individual is inconsistent with the safety of a multitude, nothing can be more just than that the many should be preferred to the one. Yet this punishment, how necessary soever, always appears to be excessively severe. The natural atrocity of the crime seems to be so little, and the punishment so great, that it is with great difficulty that our heart can reconcile itself to it. Though such carelessness appears very blamable, yet the thought of this crime does not naturally excite any such resentment, as would prompt us to take such dreadful revenge. A man of humanity must recollect himself, must make an effort, and exert his whole firmness and resolution, before he can bring himself either to inflict it, or to go along with it when it is inflicted by others. It is not, however, in this manner, that he looks upon the just punishment of an ungrateful murderer or parricide. His heart, in this case, applauds with ardor, and even with transport, the just retaliation which seems due to such detestable crimes, and which, if, by any accident, they should happen to escape, he would be highly enraged and disappointed. The very different sentiments with which the spectator views those different punishments, is a proof that his approbation of the one is far from being founded upon the same principles with that of the other. He looks upon the sentinel as an unfortunate victim, who, indeed, must, and ought to be, devoted to the safety of numbers, but whom still, in his heart, he would be glad to save; and he is only sorry, that the interest of the many should oppose it. But if the murderer should escape from punishment, it would excite his highest indignation, and he would call upon God to avenge, in another world, that crime which the injustice of mankind had neglected to chastise upon earth.

For it well deserves to be taken notice of, that we are so far from imagining that injustice ought to be punished in this life, merely on account of the order of society, which cannot otherwise be maintained, that Nature teaches us to hope, and religion, we suppose, authorizes us to expect, that it will be punished, even in a life to come. Our sense of its ill desert pursues it, if I may say so, even beyond the grave, though the example of its punishment there cannot serve to deter the rest of mankind, who see it not, who know it not, from being guilty of the like practices here. The justice of God, however, we think, still requires, that he should hereafter avenge the injuries of the widow and the fatherless, who are here so often insulted with impunity. In every religion, and in every superstition that the world has ever beheld, accordingly, there has been a Tartarus as well as an Elysium; a place provided for the punishment of the wicked, as well as one for the reward of the just.

The Social Contract: Or Principles Of Political Right, Jean Jacques Rousseau (1762)

The question is often asked how individuals, having no right to dispose of their own lives, can transfer to the Sovereign a right which they do not possess. The difficulty of answering this question seems to me to lie in its being wrongly stated. Every man has a right to risk his own life in order to preserve it. Has it ever been said that a man who throws himself out of the window to escape from a fire is guilty of suicide? Has such a crime ever been laid to the charge of him who perishes in a storm because, when he went on board, he knew of the danger?

The social treaty has for its end the preservation of the contracting parties. He who wills the end, wills the means also, and the means must involve some risks, and even some losses. He who wishes to preserve his life at others' expense should also, when it is necessary, be ready to give it up for their sake. Furthermore, the citizen is no longer the judge of the dangers to which the law desires him to expose himself; and when the prince says to him: "It is expedient for the State that you should die," he ought to die, because it is only on that condition that he has been living in security up to the present, and because his life is no longer a mere bounty of nature, but a gift made conditionally by the State.

The death penalty inflicted upon criminals may be looked on in much the same light: it is in order that we may not fall victims to an assassin that we consent to die if we ourselves turn assassins. In this treaty, so far from disposing of our own lives, we think only of securing them, and it is not to be assumed that any of the parties then expects to get hanged.

Again, every malefactor, by attacking social rights, becomes on forfeit a rebel and a traitor to his country; by violating its laws be ceases to be a member of it; he even makes war upon it. In such a case the preservation of the State is inconsistent with his own, and one or the other must perish; in putting the guilty to death, we slay not so much the citizen as an enemy. The trial and the judgment are the proofs that he has broken the social treaty, and is in consequence no longer a member of the State. Since, then, he has recognized himself to be such by living there, he must be removed by exile as a violator of the compact, or by death as a public enemy; for such an enemy is not a moral person, but merely a man; and in such a case the right of war is to kill the vanquished.

> **Every malefactor, by attacking social rights, becomes on forfeit a rebel and a traitor to his country.**

But, it will be said, the condemnation of a criminal is a particular act. I admit it: but such condemnation is not a function of the Sovereign; it is a right the Sovereign can confer without being able itself to exert it. All my ideas are consistent, but I cannot expound them all at once.

> **The State has no right to put to death, even for the sake of making an example, any one whom it can leave alive without danger.**

We may add that frequent punishments are always a sign of weakness or remissness on the part of the government. There is not a single ill-doer who could not be turned to some good. The State has no right to put to death, even for the sake of making an example, any one whom it can leave alive without danger.

The right of pardoning or exempting the guilty from a penalty imposed by the law and pronounced by the judge belongs only to the authority which is superior to both judge and law, i.e., the Sovereign; each its right in this matter is far from clear, and the cases for exercising it are extremely rare. In a well-governed State, there are few punishments, not because there are many pardons, but because criminals are rare; it is when a State is in decay that the multitude of crimes is a guarantee of impunity. Under the Roman Republic, neither the Senate nor the Consuls ever attempted to pardon; even the people never did so, though it sometimes revoked its own decision. Frequent pardons mean that crime will soon need them no longer, and no one can help seeing whither that leads. But I feel my heart protesting and restraining my pen; let us leave these questions to the just man who has never offended, and would himself stand in no need of pardon.

Second Treatise of Government, John Locke (1764)

To this purpose, I think it may not be amiss, to set down what I take to be political power; that the power of a MAGISTRATE over a subject may be distinguished from that of a FATHER over his children, a MASTER over his servant, a HUSBAND over his wife, and a LORD over his slave. All which distinct powers happening sometimes together in the same man, if he be considered under these different relations, it may help us to distinguish these powers one from wealth, a father of a family, and a captain of a galley.

POLITICAL POWER, then, I take to be a RIGHT of making laws with penalties of death, and consequently all less penalties, for the regulating and preserving of property, and of employing the force of the community, in the execution of such laws, and in the defense of the common-wealth from foreign injury; and all this only for the public good.

> **POLITICAL POWER, then, I take to be a RIGHT of making laws with penalties of death.**

To understand political power right, and derive it from its original, we must consider, what state all men are naturally in, and that is, a state of perfect freedom to order their actions, and dispose of their possessions and persons, as they think fit, within the bounds of the law of nature, without asking leave, or depending upon the will of any other man.

A state also of equality, wherein all the power and jurisdiction is reciprocal, no one having more than another; there being nothing more evident, than that creatures of the same species and rank, promiscuously born to all the same advantages of nature, and the use of the same faculties, should also be equal one amongst another without subordination or subjection, unless the lord and master of them all should, by any manifest declaration of his will, set one above another, and confer on him, by an evident and clear appointment, an undoubted right to dominion and sovereignty.

[. . .] But though this be a state of liberty, yet it is not a state of license: though man in that state have an uncontrollable liberty to dispose of his person or possessions, yet he has not liberty to destroy himself, or so much as any creature in his possession, but where some nobler use than its bare preservation calls for it. The state of nature has a law of nature to govern it, which obliges every one: and reason, which is that law, teaches all mankind, who will but consult it, that being all equal and independent, no one ought to harm another in his life, health, liberty, or possessions: for men being all the workmanship of one omnipotent, and infinitely wise maker; all the servants of one sovereign master, sent into the world by his order, and about his business; they are his property, whose workmanship they are, made to last during his, not one another's pleasure: and being furnished with like faculties, sharing all in one community of nature, there cannot be supposed any such subordination among us, that may authorize us to destroy one another, as if we were made for one another's uses, as the inferior ranks of creatures are for ours. Every one, as he is bound to preserve himself, and not to quit his station willfully, so by the like reason, when his own preservation comes not in competition, ought he, as much as he can, to preserve the rest of mankind, and may not, unless it be to do justice on an offender, take away, or impair the life, or what tends to the preservation of the life, the liberty, health, limb, or goods of another.

And that all men may be restrained from invading others rights, and

All men may be restrained from invading others rights.

from doing hurt to one another, and the law of nature be observed, which willeth the peace and preservation of all mankind, the execution of the law of nature is, in that state, put into every man's hands, whereby everyone has a right to punish the transgressors of that law to such a degree, as may hinder its violation: for the law of nature would, as all other laws that concern men in this world be in vain, if there were no body that in the state of nature had a power to execute that law, and thereby preserve the innocent and restrain offenders. And if anyone in the state of nature may punish another for any evil he has done, every one may do so: for in that state of perfect equality, where naturally there is no superiority or jurisdiction of one over another, what any may do in prosecution of that law, everyone must needs have a right to do.

And thus, in the state of nature, one man comes by a power over another; but yet no absolute or arbitrary power, to use a criminal, when he has got him in his hands, according to the passionate heats, or boundless extravagancy of his own will; but only to retribute to him, so far as calm reason and conscience dictate, what is proportionate to his transgression, which is so much as may serve for reparation and restraint: for these two are the only reasons, why one man may lawfully do harm to another, which is that we call punishment. In transgressing he law of nature, the offender declares himself to live by another rule than that of reason and common equity, which is that measure God has set to the actions of men, for their mutual security; and so he becomes dangerous to mankind, the tie, which is to secure them from injury and violence, being slighted and broken by him. Which being a trespass against the whole species, and the peace and safety of it, provided for by the law of nature, every man upon this score, by the right he hath to preserve mankind in general, may restrain, or where it is necessary, destroy things noxious to them, and so may bring such evil on any one, who hath transgressed that law, as may make him repent the doing of it, and thereby deter him, and by his

Every man hath a right to punish the offender, and be executioner of the law of nature.

example others, from doing the like mischief.   And in the case, and upon this ground, every man hath a right to punish the offender, and be executioner of the law of nature.

I doubt not but this will seem a very strange doctrine to some men: but before they condemn it, I desire them to resolve me, by what right any prince or state can put to death, or punish an alien, for any crime he commits in their country. It is certain their laws, by virtue of any sanction they receive from the promulgated will of the legislative, reach not a stranger: they speak not to him, nor, if they did, is he bound to hearken to them. The legislative authority, by which they are in force over the subjects of that commonwealth, hath no power over him. Those who have the supreme power of making laws in England, France or Holland, are to an Indian, but like the rest of the world, men without authority: and therefore, if by the law of nature every man hath not a power to punish offenses against it, as he soberly judges the case to require, I see not how the magistrates of any community can punish an alien of another country; since, in reference to him, they can have no more power than what every man naturally may have over another.

Besides the crime which consists in violating the law, and varying from the right rule of reason, whereby a man so far becomes degenerate, and declares himself to quit the principles of human nature, and to be a noxious creature, there is commonly injury done to some person or other, and some other man receives damage by his transgression: in which case he who hath received any damage, has, besides the right of punishment common to him with other men, a particular right to seek reparation from him that has done it: and any other person, who finds it just, may also join with him that is injured, and assist him in recovering from the offender so much as may make satisfaction for the harm he has suffered.

From these two distinct rights, the one of punishing the crime for restraint, and preventing the like offence, which right of punishing is in everybody; the other of taking reparation, which belongs only to the injured party, comes it to pass that the magistrate, who by being magistrate hath the common right of punishing put into his hands, can often, where the public good demands not the execution of the law, remit the punishment of criminal offenses by his own authority, but yet cannot remit the satisfaction due to any private man for the damage he has received. That, he who has suffered the damage has a right to demand in his own name, and he alone can remit: the damnified person has this power of appropriating to himself the goods or service of the offender, by right of self-preservation, as every man has a power to punish the crime, to prevent its being committed again, by the right he has of preserving all mankind, and doing all reasonable things he can in order to that end: and thus it is, that every man, in the state of nature, has a power to kill a murderer, both to deter others from doing the like injury, which no reparation can compensate, by the example of the punishment that attends it from everybody, and also to secure men from the attempts of a criminal, who having renounced reason, the common rule and measure God hath given to mankind, hath, by the unjust violence and slaughter he hath committed upon one, declared war against all mankind, and therefore may be destroyed as a lion or a tyger, one of those wild savage beasts, with whom men can have no society nor security: and upon this is grounded that great law of nature, Whoso sheddeth man's blood, by man shall his blood be shed. And Cain was so fully convinced, that everyone had a right to destroy such a criminal, that after the murder of his brother, he cries out, "Every one that findeth me, shall slay me;" so plain was it writ in the hearts of all mankind.

By the same reason may a man in the state of nature punish the lesser breaches of that law. It will perhaps be demanded, with death? I answer, each transgression may be punished to that degree, and with so much severity, as will suffice to make it an ill bargain to the offender, give him cause to repent, and terrify others from doing the like. Every offense, that can be committed in the state of nature, may in the state of nature be also punished equally, and as far forth as it may, in a commonwealth: for though it would be besides my present purpose, to enter here into the particulars of the law of nature, or its measures of punishment; yet, it is certain there is such a law, and that too, as intelligible and plain to a rational creature, and a studier of that law, as the positive laws of commonwealths; nay, possibly plainer; as much as reason is easier to be understood, than the fancies and intricate contrivances of men, following contrary and hidden interests put into words; for so truly are a great part of the municipal laws of countries, which are only so far right, as they are founded on the law of nature, by which they are to be regulated and interpreted.

> **Each transgression may be punished to that degree, and with so much severity, as will suffice to make it an ill bargain to the offender, give him cause to repent, and terrify others from doing the like.**

To this strange doctrine, viz. that in the state of nature everyone has the executive power of the law of nature, I doubt not but it will be objected, that it is unreasonable for men to be judges in their own cases, that self-love will make men partial to themselves and their friends: and on the other side, that ill nature, passion and revenge will carry them too far in punishing others; and hence nothing but confusion and disorder will follow, and that therefore God hath certainly appointed government to restrain the partiality and violence of men. I easily grant, that civil government is the proper remedy for the inconveniencies of the state of nature, which must certainly be great, where men may be judges in their own case, since it is easy to be imagined, that he who was so unjust as to do his brother an injury, will scarce be so just as to condemn himself for it: but I shall desire those who make this objection, to remember, that absolute monarchs are but men; and if government is to be the remedy of those evils, which necessarily follow from men's being judges in their own cases, and the state of nature is therefore not to how much better it is than the state of nature, where one man, commanding a multitude, has the liberty to be judge in his own case, and may do to all his subjects whatever he pleases, without the least liberty to anyone to question or control those who execute his pleasure and in whatsoever he doeth, whether led by reason, mistake or passion, must be submitted to? Much better it is in the state of nature, wherein men are not bound to submit to the unjust will of another: and if he that judges, judges amiss in his own, or any other case, he is answerable for it to the rest of mankind.

Of Crimes and Punishments, Cesare Beccaria (1764)

The useless profusion of punishments, which has never made men better induces me to inquire, whether the punishment of death be really just or useful in a well governed state? What right, I ask, have men to cut the throats of their fellow creatures? Certainly not that on which the sovereignty and laws are founded. The laws, as I have said before, are only the sum of the smallest portions of the private liberty of each individual, and represent the general will, which is the aggregate of that of each individual. Did anyone ever give to others the right of taking away his life? Is it possible that, in the smallest portions of the liberty of each, sacrificed to the good of the public, can be contained the greatest of all good, life? If it were so, how shall it be reconciled to the maxim which tells us, that a man has no right to kill himself, which he certainly must have, if he could give it away to another?

But the punishment of death is not authorized by any right; for I have demonstrated that no such right exists. It is therefore a war of a whole nation against a citizen whose destruction they consider as necessary or useful to the general good. But if I can further demonstrate that it is neither necessary nor useful, I shall have gained the cause of humanity.

> **The punishment of death is not authorized by any right; for I have demonstrated that no such right exists.**

The death of a citizen cannot be necessary but in one case: when, though deprived of his liberty, he has such power and connections as may endanger the security of the nation; when his existence may produce a dangerous revolution in the established form of government. But, even in this case, it can only be necessary when a nation is on the verge of recovering or losing its liberty, or in times of absolute anarchy, when the disorders themselves hold the place of laws: but in a reign of tranquility, in a form of government approved by the united wishes of the nation, in a state well fortified from enemies without and supported by strength within, and opinion, perhaps more efficacious, where all power is lodged in the hands of a true sovereign, where riches can purchase pleasures and not authority, there can be no necessity for taking away the life of a subject.

If the experience of all ages be not sufficient to prove, that the punishment of death has never prevented determined men from injuring society, if the example of the Romans, if twenty years' reign of Elizabeth, empress of Russia, in which she gave the fathers of their country an example more illustrious than many conquests bought with blood; if, I say, all this be not sufficient to persuade mankind, who always suspect the voice of reason, and who choose rather to be led by authority, let us consult human nature in proof of my assertion.

It is not the intenseness of the pain that has the greatest effect on the mind, but its continuance; for our sensibility is more easily and more powerfully affected by weak but repeated impressions, than by a violent but momentary impulse. The power of habit is universal over every sensible being. As it is by

The death of a criminal is a terrible but momentary spectacle, and therefore a less efficacious method of deterring others than the continued example of a man deprived of his liberty, condemned, as a beast of burden, to repair, by his labor, the injury he has done to society.

that we learn to speak, to walk, and to satisfy our necessities, so the ideas of morality are stamped on our minds by repeated impression. The death of a criminal is a terrible but momentary spectacle, and therefore a less efficacious method of deterring others than the continued example of a man deprived of his liberty, condemned, as a beast of burden, to repair, by his labor, the injury he has done to society. If I commit such a crime, says the spectator to himself, I shall be reduced to that miserable condition for the rest of my life. A much more powerful preventive than the fear of death which men always behold in distant obscurity.

The terrors of death make so slight an impression, that it has not force enough to withstand the forgetfulness natural to mankind, even in the most essential things, especially when assisted by the passions. Violent impressions surprise us, but their effect is momentary; they are fit to produce those revolutions which instantly transform a common man into a Lacedaemonian or a Persian; but in a free and quiet government they ought to be rather frequent than strong. The execution of a criminal is to the multitude a spectacle which in some excites compassion mixed with indignation. These sentiments occupy the mind much more than that salutary terror which the laws endeavor to inspire; but, in the contemplation of continued suffering, terror is the only, or at least predominant sensation. The severity of a punishment should be just sufficient to excite compassion in the spectators, as it is intended more for them than for the criminal.

A punishment, to be just, should have only that degree of severity which is sufficient to deter others. Now there is no man who upon the least reflection, would put in competition the total and perpetual loss of his liberty, with the greatest advantages he could possibly obtain in consequence of a crime. Perpetual slavery, then, has in it all that is necessary to deter the most hardened and determined, as much as the punishment of death. I say it has more. There

A punishment, to be just, should have only that degree of severity which is sufficient to deter others.

are many who can look upon death with intrepidity and firmness, some through fanaticism, and others through vanity, which attends us even to the grave; others from a desperate resolution, either to get rid of their misery, or cease to live: but fanaticism and vanity forsake the criminal in slavery, in chains and fetters, in an iron cage, and despair seems rather the beginning than the end of their misery. The mind, by collecting itself and uniting all its force, can, for a moment, repel assailing grief; but its most vigorous efforts are insufficient to resist perpetual wretchedness.

In all nations, where death is used as a punishment, every example supposes a new crime committed; whereas, in perpetual slavery, every criminal affords a frequent and lasting example; and if it be necessary that men should often be witnesses of the power of the laws, criminals should often be put to death: but this supposes a frequency of crimes; and from hence this punishment will cease to have its effect, so that it must be useful and useless at the same time. I shall be told that perpetual slavery is as painful a punishment as death, and therefore as cruel. I answer, that if all the miserable moments in the life of a slave were collected into one point, it would be a more cruel punishment than any other; but these are scattered through his whole life, whilst the pain of death exerts all its force in a moment. There is also another advantage in the punishment of slavery, which is, that it is more terrible to the spectator than to the sufferer himself; for the spectator considers the sum of all his wretched moments whilst the sufferer, by the misery of the present, is prevented from thinking of the future. All evils are increased by the imagination, and the sufferer finds resources and consolations of which the spectators are ignorant, who judge by their own sensibility of what passes in a mind by habit grown callous to misfortune.

Let us, for a moment, attend to the reasoning of a robber or assassin, who is deterred from violating the laws by the gibbet or the wheel. I am sensible, that to develop the sentiments of one's own heart is an art which education only can teach; but although a villain may not be able to give a clear account of his principles, they nevertheless influence his conduct. He reasons thus: "What are these laws that I am bound to respect, which make so great a difference between me and the rich man? He refuses me the farthing I ask of him, and excuses himself by bidding me have recourse to labor, with which he is unacquainted."

"Who made these laws? The rich and the great, who never deigned to visit the miserable hut of the poor, who have never seen him dividing a piece of moldy bread, amidst the cries of his famished children and the tears of his wife. Let us break those ties, fatal to the greatest part of mankind, and only useful to a few indolent tyrants. Let us attack injustice at its source. I will return to my natural state of independence. I shall live free and happy on the fruits of my courage and industry. A day of pain and repentance may come, but it will be short; and for an hour of grief I shall enjoy years of pleasure and liberty. King of a small number as determined as myself, I will correct the mistakes of fortune, and I shall see those tyrants grow pale and tremble at the sight of him, whom, with insulting pride, they would not suffer to rank with their dogs and horses."

Religion then presents itself to the mind of this lawless villain, and, promising him almost a certainty of eternal happiness upon the easy terms of repentance, contributes much to lessen the horror of the last scene of the tragedy. But he who foresees that he must pass a great number of years, even his whole life, in pain and slavery, a slave to those laws by which he, was protected, in sight of his fellow citizens, with whom he lives in freedom and society, makes an useful comparison between those evils, the uncertainty of his success, and the shortness of the time in which he shall enjoy the fruits of his transgression. The example of those wretches, continually before his eyes, makes a much greater impression on him than a punishment, which instead of correcting, makes him more obdurate.

The punishment of death is pernicious to society, from the example of barbarity it affords.

The punishment of death is pernicious to society, from the example of barbarity it affords. If the passions, or the necessity of war, have taught men to shed the blood of their fellow creatures, the laws, which are intended to moderate the ferocity of mankind, should not increase it by examples of barbarity, the more horrible as this punishment is usually attended with formal pageantry. Is it not absurd, that the laws, which detest and punish homicide, should, in order to prevent murder, publicly commit murder themselves? What are the true and most useful laws? Those compacts and conditions which all would propose and observe in those moments when private interest is silent, or combined with that of the public. What are the natural sentiments of every person concerning the punishment of death? We may read them in the contempt and indignation with which everyone looks on the executioner, who is nevertheless an innocent executor of the public will, a good citizen, who contributes to the advantage of society, the instrument of the general security within, as good soldiers are without. What then is the origin of this contradiction? Why is this sentiment of mankind indelible to the scandal of reason? It is, that, in a secret corner of the mind, in which the original impressions of nature are still preserved, men discover a sentiment which tells them, that their lives are not lawfully in the power of any one, but of that necessity only which with its iron sceptre rules the universe.

What must men think, when they see wise magistrates and grave ministers of justice, with indifference and tranquility, dragging a criminal to death, and whilst a wretch trembles with agony, expecting the fatal stroke, the judge, who has condemned him, with the coldest insensibility, and perhaps with no small gratification from the exertion of his authority, quits his tribunal, to enjoy the comforts and pleasures of life? They will say, "Ah! Those cruel formalities of justice are a cloak to tyranny, they are a secret language, a solemn veil, intended to conceal the sword by which we are sacrificed to the insatiable idol of despotism. Murder, which they would represent to us an horrible crime, we see practiced by them without repugnance or remorse. Let us follow their example. A violent death appeared terrible in their descriptions, but we see that it is the affair of a moment. It will be still less terrible to him who, not expecting it, escapes almost all the pain." Such is the fatal, though absurd reasonings of men who are disposed to commit crimes, on whom the abuse of religion has more influence than religion itself.

If it be objected, that almost all nations in all ages have punished certain crimes with death, I answer, that the force of these examples vanishes when opposed to truth, against which prescription is urged in vain. The history of mankind is an immense sea of errors, in which a few obscure truths may here and there be found.

But human sacrifices have also been common in almost all nations. That some societies only it either few in number, or for a very short time, abstained from the punishment of death, is rather favorable to my argument; for such is the fate of great truths, that their duration is only as a flash of lightning in the long and dark night of error. The happy time is not yet arrived, when truth, as falsehood has been hitherto, shall be the portion of the greatest number.

I am sensible that the voice of one philosopher is too weak to be heard amidst the clamors of a multitude, blindly influenced by custom; but there is a small number of sages scattered on the face of the earth, who will echo to me from the bottom of their hearts; and if these truths should happily force their way to the thrones of princes be it known to them, that they come attended with the secret wishes of all mankind; and tell the sovereign who deigns them a gracious reception, that his fame shall outshine the glory of conquerors, and that equitable posterity will exalt his peaceful trophies above those of a Titus, an Antoninus, or a Trajan.

How happy were mankind if laws were now to be first formed! Now that we see on the thrones of Europe benevolent monarchs, friends to the virtues of peace, to the arts and sciences, fathers of their people, though crowned, yet citizens; the increase of whose authority augments the happiness of their subjects, by destroying that intermediate despotism which intercepts the prayers of the people to the throne. If these humane princes have suffered the old laws to subsist, it is doubtless because they are deterred by the numberless obstacles which oppose the subversion of errors established by the sanction of many ages; and therefore every wise citizen will wish for the increase of their authority.

A Commentary On The Book, *Of Crimes and Punishments*, François-Marie Arouet (Voltaire) (1764)

II. OF PUNISHMENTS

The misfortunes of the wretched in the face of the severity of the law have induced me to look at the criminal code of nations. The humane author of the essay, *Of Crimes and Punishments*, is only too right in complaining that punishment is much too often out of proportion to the crime, and sometimes detrimental to the nation it was intended to serve.

Ingenious punishments, in which the human mind seems to have exhausted itself in order to make death terrible, seem rather the inventions of tyranny than of justice.

The punishment of the wheel was first introduced in Germany in times of anarchy, when those who seized royal power wished to terrify, by the device of an unheard-of torture, whoever would dare to rise up against them. In England they used to rip open the belly of a man convicted of high treason, tear out his heart, slap his cheeks with it, and then throw it into the fire. And what, very frequently, was this crime of high treason? During the civil wars, it was to have been faithful to an unfortunate king, and sometimes had to be explained according to the doubtful rights of a conqueror. In time, manners became milder; it is true that they continue to tear out the heart, but it is always after the death of the criminal. The torture is terrible but the death is easy, if death can ever be easy.

X. OF CAPITAL PUNISHMENT

It is an old saying that a man after he is hanged is good for nothing, and that the punishments invented for the welfare of society should be useful to that society. It is clear that twenty vigorous thieves, condemned to hard labor at public works for the rest of their life, serve the state by their punishment; and their death would serve only the executioner, who is paid for killing men in public. Only rarely are thieves punished by death in England; they are transported overseas to the colonies. The same is true in the vast Russian empire. Not a single criminal was executed during the reign of the autocratic Elizabeth. Catherine II, who succeeded her, endowed with a very superior mind, followed the same policy. Crimes have not increased as a result of this humanity, and almost always, criminals banished to Siberia become good men. The same thing has been noticed in the English colonies. This happy change astonishes us, but nothing is more natural. These condemned men are forced to work constantly in order to live. Opportunities for vice are lacking; they marry and have children. Force men to work and you make them honest. It is well known that great crimes are not committed in the country, except, perhaps, when too many holidays bring on idleness and lead to debauchery.

A Roman citizen was condemned to death only for crimes affecting the welfare of the state. Our teachers, our first legislators, respected the blood of their fellow citizens; we lavish that of ours.

This dark and delicate question has been long discussed: whether judges may punish by death when the law does not expressly require this punishment. This question was solemnly debated before Emperor Henri IV. He judged, and decided that no magistrate could have this power.

There are some criminal cases that are so unusual or so complicated, or are accompanied by such strange circumstances, that the law itself has been forced in more than one country to leave these singular cases to the discretion of the judges. If there really should be one instance in which the law permits a criminal to be put to death who has not committed a capital offense, there will be a thousand instances in which humanity, which is stronger than the law, should spare the life of those whom the law has sentenced to death.

The sword of justice is in our hands; but we ought to blunt it more often than sharpen it. It is carried in its sheath before kings, to warn us that it should be rarely drawn.

There have been judges who loved to make blood flow; such was Jeffreys in England; such in France was a man who was called coupe-tête. Men like these were not born to be judges; nature made them to be executioners.

Principles of Penal Law, William Eden (1771)

I t is impossible to read the histories of executive justice in different governments without shuddering at the very idea of those miseries, which men, with unrelenting ingenuity, have devised for each other. In some countries it hath been usual to sow up criminals in the warm skins of beasts, and in this condition to expose them to wild dogs; in others the limbs are torn asunder by horses; in others recourse is had to crucifixions, burnings, boilings, flayings, famishings, impalements, and other modes of destruction, equally shocking to decency and humanity.

Merciful Heaven,
Thou rather with thy sharp and sulphurous bolt
Split'st the unwedgeable and gnarled oak
Than the soft myrtle: but man, proud man,
Drest in a little brief authority,
Most ignorant of what he's most assured,
His glassy essence, like an angry ape,
Plays such fantastic tricks before high heaven
As make the angels weep [1]

This imputation of tyranny and cruelty hath at different periods been applicable to every government, of which we have any authentic history. Livy, in respect to his Countrymen, hath endeavored to establish a different inference in his account of the punishment of Mettius; "*Exinde duabus admotis quadrigis, in currus earum distentum inligat Mettium; deinde in diuersum iter equi concitati, lacerum in utroque curru corpus, qua inhaeserant uinculis membra, portantes. avertere omnes ab tanta foeditate spectaculi oculos. Primum ultimumque illud supplicium apud Romanos exempli parum memoris legum humanarum fuit: in aliis gloriari licet nulli gentium mitiores placuisse poenas.*"[2]

We know that national benevolence ought to be the concomitant of national liberty, and are therefore inclinable to give credit to this assertion; but it will not be found in any degree reconcilable to the united testimony of many other Historians. The modes of capital punishment, used by the Romans, were at least as numerous, and as exceptionable, as those of other Nations. The head of the malefactor was in some cases fattened within the *furca*, and in this attitude he was whipped to death; and this was distinguished by the name of *supplicium more majorum*. In other cases, as in the execution of Antigonus, the whipping

---

1 Shakespeare, Measure For Measure

2 *Thereupon two four-horse chariots were brought up, and Mettius was bound at full length to each, the horses were driven in opposite directions, carrying off parts of the body in each chariot, where the limbs had been secured by the cords. All present averted their eyes from the horrible spectacle. This is the first and last instance amongst the Romans of a punishment so regardless of humanity. Amongst other things which are the glory of Rome is this, that no nation has ever been contented with milder punishments.*

terminated in beheading. Crucifixion, or the *Servile Supplicium* was in use during many centuries, and first abrogated by Constanstine; the sentence also inflicted whipping, *"verbera intra aut extra pomoerium, arbore infelici suspendito."* The criminal was naked in the execution of these different punishments. Parricides were sewed up in a leather sack with an ape, a cock, a serpent, and a dog, and so cast into the sea. It was also usual to cover some offenders with a mantle dawbed over with pitch, and then to set fire to it: *Cogita, inquit Seneca, illam tunicam alimentis igneis illatam et intextam.* The Emperors introduced a punishment called *"Semi-dissectio." Damnatio in gladium,* or sentence to the public combats, and *damnatio ad bellias,* were also frequent; and the latter appears to have been very fatal; *"præclara ædilitas"* said *Cicero, unus Leo, ducenti Besliarii".*

These cruelties were founded on the twelve tables of the Decemvirs, and were contrary to the republican spirit. Accordingly by the Porcian law, made in the 454th year of Rome, it was ordained, that no Citizen should be put to death. This exemption was in the other extreme, and erroneous in its foundation. Capital executions are in all states necessary.

Nothing, however, but the evident result of absolute necessity, can authorize the destruction of mankind by the hand of man.

The infliction of Death is not therefore to be considered in any instance, as a mode of punishment, but merely as our last melancholy resource in the extermination of those from society, whose continuance among their fellow citizens is become inconsistent with the public safety.

We may pronounce it then contrary both to sentiment and morality, to aggravate capital executions by any circumstances of terror or pain beyond the sufferings inseparable from a violent death.

The punishment of the murderer after trial and conviction was by the Athenians left to the relations of the deceased, who might put him to death if they thought proper; but it was not permitted them to use any degree of torture, or to extort money[3]; Excellent restrictions! which taught the prosecutor to seek justice not revenge; in wrath to remember mercy; and to feel less, what he in his own interests had suffered, than what the Offender was about to suffer.

It was a custom among the Jews to give wine mingled with myrrh to the malefactor at the time of his execution in order, as it is said, to cause a stupor, and deaden the sensibility of the pain.

---

3 Demosthenes hath given a full explanation of this law, which ordered the murderer, if put to death, to be executed in the district, or parish of the deceased

I transcribe the following anecdote from the English State-tryals. "Hugh Peters being carried on a sledge to the scaffold was made to fit therein within the rails, to behold the execution of Mr. Cook. When Mr. Cook was cut down, and brought to be quartered, Col. Turner ordered the Sheriffs men to bring Mr. Peters near, that he might see it; and bye and bye the hangman came to him all besmeared in blood, and, rubbing his bloody hands together, he tauntingly asked, "Come how do you like this work, Mr. Peters, how do you like it". He replied, "Friend you do not well to trample on a dying Man."

Shall we plant thorns in the path of misery? God forbid! Such refinements of inhumanity are admissible only in governments so abominable to their constitution, as to make the mere loss of life desirable.

Solemnity indeed is requisite for the sake of example; but let not death be drawn into "lingering sufferance;" detain not the excruciated soul upon the verge of eternity. A degree of mercy on this point was shewn even by the brutal Caligula, when he laid to an executioner, "*Ita feri, ne mori Se Sentiat.*" [*make him feel that he is dying.*]

Lawgivers should remember that they are, mediately, and in effect, the executioners of every criminal, who suffers death in consequence of any penal statute; and there are certain striking points of view, in which it may be of use to them to consider criminals at the approach of death.

"Master Barnardine, what hoa! Your friend the hangman! You must be so good, Sir, to rise, and be put to death: Pray, Master Barnardine, awake, till you are executed, and sleep afterwards." [4]

The wretch, to whom this last summons is so ludicrously addressed, is represented to us, "as a man, that apprehends death no more dreadfully, but as a drunken dream; careless, reckless, and fearless of what's past, present, or to come."

The crimes of such a man may perhaps have made him unfit to live, but he is certainly unfit to die. The safety of the community, and the preservation of individuals, may call for his execution; but the bosom of humanity will heave in agony at the idea; the eye of religion will turn with horror from the spectacle.

Suppose the sufferer on the contrary to have been a valuable member of society, and to have erred only from some momentary impulse of our imperfect nature; one, who in the recollection of reason hath found repentance; who resigns with cheerfulness that life, which hath become a forfeiture to the law, and looks up in confidence to heaven for that forgiveness, which is not to be found on earth. The last footsteps of such a man, are watered with the tears of his fellow-citizens; and we hear from the mouth of every spectator,

> *"Yes, I do think, that you might pardon him,*
> *And neither heaven, nor man grieve at the mercy."*

---

4 Shakespeare, Measure for Measure, Act 4 ,Scene 3

Memoirs of the Year Two Thousand Five Hundred
Mémoires de l'An 2440
Louis-Sébastien Mercier (1772)

Our form of justice does not command awe, but excites disgust. It is an odious and shocking sight to see a man take off his laced hat, lay down his sword on the scaffold, mount the ladder in a suit of silk or lace, and dance indecently on the body of the wretch that is hanging. Why not give the executioner that formidable aspect he ought to shew? To what purpose is this cold barbarity? The laws thereby lose their dignity, and the punishment its terror. The judge is still more sprucely powdered than the hangman. Shall I here declare the sensations that I have felt? I have trembled, not for the criminal's offense, but for the horrid unconcern of all those that surrounded him. There has been none but that generous man who reconciled the unfortunate sinner to the Supreme Being, who assisted him in drinking the cup of death, that appeared to me to have any remains of humanity. Do we only wish to destroy mankind? **Are we ignorant of the art of terrifying the imagination without violence to humanity?** Learn at length, thoughtless and cruel men, learn to be judges, learn how to prevent crimes; conciliate what is "owing to the law with what is owing to man." I have not the power to speak here of those artful tortures that some criminals have suffered, who seem to have been reserved, so to say, for a privileged punishment. O disgrace to my country! The eyes of that sex which seems made for pity remained the longest fixed on that scene of horrors. Let us draw the curtain. What can I say to those who understand me not?

[. . .] When we examine the validity of that right which human societies have assumed of punishing with death, we are terrified at the imperceptible point which separates equity from injustice. It is to little purpose here that we accumulate arguments; all our lights serve but to lead us astray; we must return to the law of nature only, which has far more regard than our institutions, for the life of a man ; that teaches us, that the law of retaliation is, of all others, the most conformable to right reason. Among rising governments, which have yet the signature of nature, there is scarce any crime punished with death. In the case of murder there is no doubt; for nature tells us, that we should arm ourselves against assassins.

WITNESS TO AN EXECUTION
A Hanging at Tyburn (1777)

The doctor, to all appearance, was rendered perfectly stupid from despair. His hat was flapped all round, and pulled over his eyes, which were never directed to any object around, nor even raised, except now and then lifted up in the course of his prayers. He came in a coach, and a very heavy shower of rain fell just upon his entering the cart, and another just at his putting on his night-cap.

He was a considerable time in praying, which some people standing about seemed rather tired with; they rather wished for some more interesting part of the tragedy. The wind, which was high, blew off his hat, which rather embarrassed him, and discovered to us his countenance, which we could scarcely see before. His hat, however, was soon restored to him, and he went on with his prayers. There were two clergymen attending him, one of whom seemed very much affected; the other, I suppose, was the ordinary of Newgate, as he was perfectly indifferent and unfeeling in everything that he said and did.

The executioner took both the hat and wig off at the same time. Why he put on his wig again I do not know, but he did, and the doctor took off his wig a second time, and then tied on a nightcap which did not fit him; but whether he stretched that, or took another, I could not perceive. He then put on his nightcap himself, and upon his taking it, he certainly had a smile on his countenance. Very soon afterwards there was an end of all his hopes and fears on this side the grave. He never moved from the place he first took in the cart; seemed absorbed in despair, and utterly dejected without any other signs of animation but in praying.

WITNESS TO AN EXECUTION
Execution of Tupac Amaru II
José Antonio de Areche (1781)

I must and do condemn José G. Túpac Amaru to be taken out to the main public square of [Cuzco], dragged out to the place of execution, where he shall witness the execution of the sentences imposed on his wife, Michaela Bastida; his two sons, Hipólito and Fernando Túpac Amaru; his uncle, Francisco Túpac Amaru; and his brother-in-law, Antonio Bastidas, as well as some of the principal captains and aides in his iniquitous and perverse intent or project, all of whom must die on the same day.

And once these sentences have been carried out, the executioner will cut out his tongue, and he will then be tied or bound by strong cords on each one of his arms and feet in such a way that each rope can be easily tied or fastened to others hanging from the saddle straps of four horses, so that, in this position, each one of these horses, facing opposite corners of the square, will pull toward his own direction; and let the horses be urged or jolted into motion at the same time so that his body be divided into as many parts and then, once it is done, the parts should be carried to the hill or high ground known as "Picchu," which is where he came to intimidate, lay siege to, and demand the surrender of this city; and let there be lit a fire which shall be prepared

in advance and then let ashes be thrown into the air and a stone tablet placed there detailing his main crimes and manner of his death as the only record and statement of his loathsome action.

His head will be sent to the town of Tinta where, after being three days on the gallows, it shall be placed on a stake at the most public entrance to the town, one of his arms will go to the town of Tungasuca, where he was chief, where it will be treated in like manner, and the other in the capital of the province of Carabaya; one of the legs shall likewise be sent for the same kind of demonstration to the town of Libitaca in the province of Chumbilcas, while the remaining one shall go to Santa Rosa in the province of Lampa along with the affidavit and order to the respective chief magistrates, or territorial judges that this sentence be proclaimed publicly with the greatest solemnity as soon as it arrives in their hands, and on the same day every year thereafter; and they will give notice in writing of this to their superiors in government who are familiar with the said territories.

Since this traitor managed to arm himself and form an army and forces against the royal arms by making use of or seducing and leading with his falsehood the chiefs who are the second in command in the villages, since these villages, being of Indians, are not governed by such chiefs but rather by mayors who are elected annually by the vote or nomination of the chiefs: let these same electoral communities and the chief magistrates that care to give preference to candidates who know Spanish, and who are of the best behavior, reputation, and customs so that they will treat their subjects well and lovingly, honoring only those who have demonstrated honestly their inclination and faithfulness, eagerness, respect, obedience, submission, and gratitude to the greater glory of our great Monarch through the sacrificed of their lives, properties, or ranches in deference of their country or religion, receiving with brave disdain the threats and offers of the aforesaid reel leader and his military chiefs, yet taking care that these elected leaders are the only ones with the right to the title of chief or governor of their *ayllus* [communities] or towns, and that they cannot transmit their position to their children or other family members.

To this same end, it is prohibited that the Indians wear heathen clothes, especially those who belong to the nobility, since it only serves to symbolize those worn by their Inca ancestors, reminding them of memories which serve no other end than to increase their hatred toward the dominant nation; not to mention that their appear is ridiculous and very little in accordance with the purity of our relics, since they place in different parts images of the sun, which was their primary deity; and this prohibition is to be extended to all the provinces of this southern America, in order to completely eliminate such clothing, especially those items which represent the bestialities of their heathen kings through emblems such and the *unco*, which is a kind of vest; *yacollas*, which are very rich blankets or shawls of black velvet or taffeta; the *macapaycha*, which is a circle in the shape of a crown from which they hand a certain emblem of ancient nobility signified by a tuft or tassel of red-colored alpaca wool, as well as many other things of this kind and symbolism. All of this shall be proclaimed in writing in each province, that they dispose of or surrender to the magistrates whatever clothing of this kind exists in the province, as well as all the paintings or likenesses of their Incas which are extremely abundant in the houses of the Indians who consider themselves to be nobles and who use them to prove their claim or boast of their lineage.

These latter shall be erased without fail since they do not merit the dignity of being painted in such places, and with the same end in mind there shall also be erased, so that no sign remains, any portraits that might be found on walls or other solid objects; in churches, monasteries, hospitals, holy places or private homes, such duties fall under the jurisdiction of the reverend archbishops or bishops of both viceroyalties in those areas pertaining to the churches; and in their place it would be best to replace such adornments with images of the King and our other Catholic sovereigns should that be necessary. Also, the ministers and chief magistrates should ensure that in no town of their respective provinces be performed plays or other public functions of the kind that the Indians are accustomed to put on to commemorate their former Incas; and having carried out the order, these ministers shall give a certified account to the secretaries of the respective governments. In like manner shall be prohibited and confiscated the trumpets or bugles that the Indians use for their ceremonies and which they call *pututos*, being seashells with a strange and mournful sound that celebrate the mourning and pitiful memorial they make for their antiquity; and there shall also be prohibited the custom of using or wearing black clothing as a sign of mourning, a custom that drags on in some provinces in memory of their deceased monarchs and also of the day or time of the conquest which they consider disastrous and we consider fortunate since it brought them into the company of the Catholic Church and the very loving and gentle domination of our Kings.

Thoughts on Executive Justice: with Respect to our Criminal Laws By A Sincere Well-wisher to the Public (Martin Mandan) (1785)

Now, if our Judges of assize really execute their commissions as they ought, what meaneth then the numbers of burglaries, highway robberies, these depredations, by day and night, in our roads, streets, houses, fields? How are our newspapers filled with daily accounts of mischiefs done on the persons and properties of his majesty's subjects, by felons of every denomination?

One reason, and only one, can be given for these things. The law is not in fault, it is wisely contrived to prevent them, by holding forth certain punishment; but that punishment has been rendered so uncertain, or rather the suspension of it so certain, as to prevent the operation of the laws.

I remember to have seen a fellow low at Bristol, who was by trade a viper-catcher. He produced, and opened, a large box, with about one hundred vipers in it, into which he put his hand, and took them up, at least, half a dozen in a bunch. I trembled at the fight, expecting, every instant, to see the man bitten: but my fears were soon removed, by being told, that all their fangs were cut out—so that, if I had pleased, I could myself have handled these horrid creatures with all safety.

Methinks, that our criminal laws are reduced to the state of the aforesaid vipers— their sting is gone, their fangs are out, their terror is lost; and our viper-catchers seem to have so contrived the matter, as that the laws will hurt nobody who chuses to sport with them.

Since I began these sheets, I have had some conversation with an eminent barrister, upon these subjects; and he furnished me with an anecdote, which abundantly illustrates what has been said.

Some years ago, when he went the Norfolk circuit, he accidentally had occasion to fee a fellow who had been capitally convicted, and, having received sentence of death, was remanded to prison. It seems he had been an old offender, and before had had some hair-breadth escapes for his life. My friend expostulated with him, and asked him how he could venture again on his old practices, after so many escapes? "Ah, Sir," said the fellow, "that's the very thing — there are so many chances for us, and so few against us, that I never thought of coming to this.—First," said he, "there are many chances against being discovered — so many more that we are not taken—and if taken, not convicted—and if convicted, not hanged—that I thought myself very safe, with at least twenty to one in my favour."

The argument which this villain used, is, no doubt, in the thoughts of all the rogues in the kingdom, who find equal encouragement to persist in their evil courses, with this fellow; for the newspapers assure them, on relating the conviction and condemnation of the criminals at the several assize-towns, that "they were all reprieved before their lordships left the town." I will not say always, but this is most usually the case.

Nay, I once heard a Judge, in his charge to the grand jury, say to this effect:, that, " Where men robbed on the highway, and did not use much violence, or do any mischief to the persons they robbed, he thought them proper to be recommended as objects of mercy." This, was no doubt carried to the gaol, and received with high applause: and at that very assizes, five or fix highwaymen were convicted on the cleared evidence: but they were all reprieved before the Judge left the town. [. . .]

Some have said, that a scruple of conscience in Judges, prevents the execution of the laws against certain offenses—that they think them too severe for the offense, and therefore constantly reprieve those who are convicted. But I do not apprehend that this is at all the province of a Judge—whatever laws the parliament sees necessary to enact, the Judge, agreeably to his oath of office, is bound to declare and pronounce; and his standing between the judgment and execution, is taking upon himself, not only to be wiser than the law, but a power, which, if wantonly and causelessly exerted, must render the most important and salutary laws contemptible and useless. The Judge, in such a case as this, sets himself above the law, and presumes to exercise an authority with which the constitution has not intruded even the crown itself. We all know how a dispensing power over the penal laws was attempted in the days: of kings who aimed at arbitrary power, by setting themselves above the laws, and wanting to govern without them, and we also know what this ended in. But where is the difference, between the arbitrary prevention of trial, and the arbitrary prevention of execution? The former, perhaps, may be more glaringly arbitrary, but the latter will answer the same end.

That the king has an inherent power to pardon all offences against his crown and dignity, is most certain: and very dreadful would it be, if he had not such a power; for otherwise we should, in very many cases, which might be

Whatever laws the parliament sees necessary to enact, the Judge, agreeably to his oath of office, is bound to declare and pronounce.

mentioned, be liable to suffer, however innocent, if once convicted, through the malice or wickedness of our fellow subjects.

But will anybody contend, that the constitution, by intrusting the crown with the power of pardon for the most salutary purposes, could ever mean to set it above the law, so as that the execution of it should wholly depend on a wanton and arbitrary exercise of this prerogative, to the utter suspension and subversion of all law whatsoever?

So the Judges have a power to reprieve: and thankful may we be that it is so; for, by this, they are enabled to save lives which ought not to be taken away. For instance—a Judge perceives prejudice and malice in the jury, a fixed determination, right or wrong, to convict the prisoner; the evidence by no means proves the case; the Judge, accordingly, in his direction to the jury, takes due notice of this, and leaves the matter to the jury in favor of the prisoner; notwithstanding which, they find the prisoner guilty — here it becomes the Judge's duty to reprieve, and recommend the convict, to the royal mercy, of which such a convict is undoubtedly an object. So, where there is a contradiction and contrariety of evidence, and, though the jury convict, the Judge is by no means satisfied in his own mind of the guilt of the prisoner.

Likewise, in cases where there is a doubt of the law—or where life may depend on vague and uncertain words in an act of parliament, of very doubtful construction — or where facts appear after the condemnation, which incontestably prove the innocence of the convict. In these, and in some few other instances which might be named, the Judge is not only justified in reprieving, but would not execute judgment in mercy if he did not.

But to exercise this power of reprieve wantonly, and indiscriminately, so as to save felons only because they are condemned; to defeat the end of the law by a mere arbitrary dispensation of a Judge, who, to gratify his feelings as a man, violates his oath and duty as a magistrate, is to abuse a most salutary power to the most mischievous purposes. It makes void the law — its terror, and therefore its best use, is no more — the innocent public suffers, the guilty invader of its property triumphs. [. . .]

In France, capital offenses seldom, if ever, meet with a relaxation of the laws—robberies and burglaries especially—and therefore they are very seldom heard of. I believe, in no country but this, are felons safe from the law; and therefore there are ten times the number of felons among us, than in any other country. No other reason can be conceived for this, but the total relaxation of discipline, the little consideration that is paid to the peace and quiet of the public, and the almost certainty of escape from death, which the minds of robbers are impressed. Certainty of punishment carries a terror to the heart, which is not easily overcome; but when that certainty decreases, the terror will decrease in the same proportion.

The Right of Punishing, Immanuel Kant (1790)

The right of administering punishment is the right of the sovereign as the supreme power to inflict pain upon a subject on account of a crime committed by him. The head of the state cannot therefore be punished; but his supremacy may be withdrawn from him. Any transgression of the public law which makes him who commits it incapable of being a citizen, constitutes a crime, either simply as a private crime, or also as a public crime. Private crimes are dealt with by a civil court; public crimes by a criminal court. Embezzlement or speculation of money or goods entrusted in trade, fraud in purchase or sale, if done before the eyes of the party who suffers, are private crimes. On the other hand, coining false money or forging bills of exchange, theft, robbery, etc., are public crimes, because the commonwealth, and not merely some particular individual, is endangered thereby. Such crimes may be divided into those of a base character and those of a violent character. Judicial or juridical punishment is to be distinguished from natural punishment, in which crime as vice punishes itself, and does not as such come within the cognizance of the legislator. Juridical punishment can never be administered merely as a means for promoting another good either with regard to the criminal himself or to civil society, but must in all cases be imposed only because the individual on whom it is inflicted has committed a crime.

The penal law is a categorical imperative; and woe to him who creeps through the serpent-windings of utilitarianism to discover some advantage that may discharge him from the justice of punishment.

For one man ought never to be dealt with merely as a means subservient to the purpose of another, nor be mixed up with the subjects of real right. Against such treatment his inborn personality has a right to protect him, even although he may be condemned to lose his civil personality. He must first be found guilty and punishable, before there can be any thought of drawing from his punishment any benefit for himself or his fellow citizens. The penal law is a categorical imperative; and woe to him who creeps through the serpent-windings of utilitarianism to discover some advantage that may discharge him from the justice of punishment, or even from the due measure of it, according to the Pharisaic maxim: "It is better that one man should die than that the whole people should perish." For if justice and righteousness perish, human life would no longer have any value in the world.

What, then, is to be said of such a proposal as to keep a criminal alive who has been condemned to death, on his being given to understand that, if he agreed to certain dangerous experiments being performed upon him, he would be allowed to survive if he came happily through them? It is argued that physicians might thus obtain new information that would be of value to the commonweal. But a court of justice would repudiate with scorn any proposal of this kind if made to it by the medical faculty; for justice would cease to be justice, if it were bartered away for any consideration whatever.

But what is the mode and measure of punishment which public justice takes as its principle and standard? It is just the principle of equality, by which the pointer of the scale of justice is made to incline no more to the one side than the other. It may be rendered by saying that the undeserved evil which any one commits on another is to be regarded as perpetrated on himself. Hence it may be said: "If you slander another, you slander yourself; if you steal from another, you steal from yourself; if you strike another, you strike yourself; if you kill another, you kill yourself." This is the right of retaliation (*jus talionis*); and, properly understood, it is the only principle which in regulating a public court, as distinguished from mere private judgment, can definitely assign both the quality and the quantity of a just penalty. All other standards are wavering and uncertain; and on account of other considerations involved in them, they contain no principle conformable to the sentence of pure and strict justice.

> **This is the right of retaliation (*jus talionis*); and, properly understood, it is the only principle which in regulating a public court. . . can definitely assign both the quality and the quantity of a just penalty.**

It may appear, however, that difference of social status would not admit the application of the principle of retaliation, which is that of "like with like." But although the application may not in all cases be possible according to the letter, yet as regards the effect it may always be attained in practice, by due regard being given to the disposition and sentiment of the parties in the higher social sphere. Thus a pecuniary penalty on account of a verbal injury may have no direct proportion to the injustice of slander; for one who is wealthy may be able to indulge himself in this offense for his own gratification. Yet the attack committed on the honor of the party aggrieved may have its equivalent in the pain inflicted upon the pride of the aggressor, especially if he is condemned by the judgment of the court, not only to retract and apologize, but to submit to some meaner ordeal, as kissing the hand of the injured person. In like manner, if a man of the highest rank has violently assaulted an innocent citizen of the lower orders, he may be condemned not only to apologize but to undergo a solitary and painful imprisonment, whereby, in addition to the discomfort endured, the vanity of the offender would be painfully affected, and the very shame of his position would constitute an adequate retaliation after the principle of "like with like."

But how then would we render the statement: "If you steal from another, you steal from yourself?" In this way, that whoever steals anything makes the property of all insecure; he therefore robs himself of all security in property, according to the right of retaliation. Such a one has nothing, and can acquire nothing, but he has the will to live; and this is only possible by others supporting him. But as the state should not do this gratuitously, he must for this purpose yield his powers to the state to be used in penal labor; and thus he falls for a time, or it may be for life, into a condition of slavery. But whoever has committed murder, must die. There is, in this case, no juridical substitute or surrogate, that can be given or taken for the satisfaction of justice. There is no likeness or proportion between life, however painful, and death; and therefore there is no equality between the crime of murder and the retaliation of it but what is judicially accomplished by the execution of the criminal. His death, however, must be kept free from all maltreatment that would make the humanity suffering in his person loathsome or abominable.

> **There is no likeness or proportion between life, however painful, and death; and therefore there is no equality between the crime of murder and the retaliation of it but what is judicially accomplished by the execution of the criminal.**

Even if a civil society resolved to dissolve itself with the consent of all its members—as might be supposed in the case of a people inhabiting an island resolving to separate and scatter themselves throughout the whole world—the last murderer lying in the prison ought to be executed before the resolution was carried out. This ought to be done in order that every one may realize the desert of his deeds, and that blood-guiltiness may not remain upon the people; for otherwise they might all be regarded as participators in the murder as a public violation of justice.

The equalization of punishment with crime is therefore only possible by the cognition of the judge extending even to the penalty of death, according to the right of retaliation. This is manifest from the fact that it is only thus that a sentence can be pronounced over all criminals proportionate to their internal wickedness; as may be seen by considering the case when the punishment of death has to be inflicted, not on account of a murder, but on account of a political crime that can only be punished capitally.

A hypothetical case, founded on history, will illustrate this. In the last Scottish rebellion there were various participators in it — such as Balmerino and others — who believed that in taking part in the rebellion they were only discharging their duty to the house of Stuart; but there were also others who were animated only by private motives and interests. Now, suppose that the judgment of the supreme court regarding them had been this: that everyone should have liberty to choose between the punishment of death or penal servitude for life. In view of such an alternative, I say that the man of honor would choose death, and the knave would choose servitude. This would be the effect of their human nature as it is; for the honorable man values his honor more highly than even life itself, whereas a knave regards a life, although covered with shame, as better in his eyes than not to be. The former is, without gainsaying, less guilty than the other; and they can only be proportionately punished by death being inflicted equally upon them both; yet to the one it is a mild punishment when his nobler temperament is taken into account, whereas it is a hard punishment to the other in view of his baser temperament. But, on the other hand, were they all equally condemned to penal servitude for life, the honorable man would be too severely punished, while the other, on account of his baseness of nature, would be too mildly punished. In the judgment to be pronounced over a number of criminals united in such a conspiracy, the best equalizer of punishment and crime in the form of public justice is death. And besides all this, it has never been heard of that a criminal condemned to death on account of a murder has complained that the sentence inflicted on him more than was right and just; and any one would treat him with scorn if he expressed himself to this effect against it. Otherwise it would be necessary to admit that, although wrong and injustice are not done to the criminal by the law, yet the legislative power is not entitled to administer this mode of punishment; and if it did so, it would be in contradiction with itself.

However many they may be who have committed a murder, or have even commanded it, or acted as art and part in it, they ought all to suffer death; for so justice wills it, in accordance with the idea of the juridical power, as founded on the universal laws of reason. But the number of the accomplices in such a deed might happen to be so great that the state, in resolving to be without such criminals, would be in danger of soon also being deprived of subjects. But it will not thus dissolve itself, neither must it return to the much worse condition of nature, in which there would be no external justice. Nor, above all, should it deaden the sensibilities of the people by the spectacle of justice being exhibited in the mere carnage of a slaughtering bench. In such circumstances the sovereign must always be allowed to have it in his power to take the part of the judge upon himself as a case of necessity- and to deliver a judgment which, instead of the penalty of death, shall assign some other punishment to the criminals and thereby preserve a multitude of the people.

The penalty of deportation is relevant in this connection. Such a form of judgment cannot be carried out according to a public law, but only by an authoritative act of the royal prerogative, and it may only be applied as an act of grace in individual cases. Against these doctrines, the Marquis Beccaria has given forth a different view. Moved by the compassionate sentimentality of a humane feeling, he has asserted that all capital punishment is wrong in itself and unjust. He has put forward this view on the ground that the penalty of death could not be contained in the original civil contract; for, in that case, every one of the people would have had to consent to lose his life if be murdered any of his fellow citizens. But, it is argued, such a consent is impossible, because no one can thus dispose of his own life.

All this is mere sophistry and perversion of right. No one undergoes punishment because he has willed to be punished, but because he has willed a punishable action; for it is in fact no punishment when any one experiences what he wills, and it is impossible for anyone to will to be punished. To say, "I will to be punished, if I murder any one," can mean nothing more than, "I submit myself along with all the other citizens to the laws;" and if there are any criminals among the people, these laws will include penal laws. The individual who, as a co-legislator, enacts penal law cannot possibly be the same person who, as a subject, is punished according to the law; for, *qua criminal*, he cannot possibly be regarded as having a voice in the legislation, the legislator being rationally viewed as just and holy. If anyone, then, enact a penal law against himself as a criminal, it must be the pure juridically law-giving reason, which subjects him as one capable of crime, and consequently as another person, along with all the others in the civil union, to this penal law.

The individual who, as a co-legislator, enacts penal law cannot possibly be the same person who, as a subject, is punished according to the law; for, *qua criminal*, he cannot possibly be regarded as having a voice in the legislation, the legislator being rationally viewed as just and holy.

In other words, it is not the people taken distributively, but the tribunal of public justice, as distinct from the criminal, that prescribes capital punishment; and it is not to be viewed as if the social contract contained the promise of all the individuals to allow themselves to be punished, thus disposing of themselves and their lives. For if the right to punish must be grounded upon a promise of the wrongdoer, whereby he is to be regarded as being willing to be punished, it ought also to be left to him to find himself deserving of the punishment; and the criminal would thus be his own judge. The chief error of this sophistry consists in regarding the judgment of the criminal himself, necessarily determined by his reason, that he is under obligation to undergo the loss of his life, as a judgment that must be grounded on a resolution of his will to take it away himself; and thus the execution of the right in question is represented as united in one and the same person with the adjudication of the right.

There are, however, two crimes worthy of death, in respect of which it still remains doubtful whether the legislature have the right to deal with them capitally. It is the sentiment of honor that induces their perpetration. The one originates in a regard for womanly honor, the other in a regard for military honor; and in both cases there is a genuine feeling of honor incumbent on the individuals as a duty. The former is the crime of maternal infanticide; the latter is the crime of killing a fellow-soldier in a duel. Now legislation cannot take away the shame of an illegitimate birth, nor wipe off the stain attaching from a suspicion of cowardice, to an officer who does not resist an act that would bring him into contempt, by an effort of his own that is superior to the fear of death. Hence it appears that, in such circumstances, the individuals concerned are remitted to the state of nature; and their acts in both cases must be called homicide, and not murder, which involves evil intent. In all instances the acts are undoubtedly punishable; but they cannot be punished by the supreme power with death.

An illegitimate child comes into the world outside of the law which properly regulates marriage, and it is thus born beyond the pale or constitutional protection of the law. Such a child is introduced, as it were, like prohibited goods, into the commonwealth, and as it has no legal right to existence in this way, its destruction might also be ignored; nor can the shame of the mother, when her unmarried confinement is known, be removed by any legal ordinance. A subordinate officer, again, on whom an insult is inflicted, sees himself compelled by the public opinion of his associates to obtain satisfaction; and, as in the state of nature, the punishment of the offender can only be effected by a duel, in which his own life is exposed to danger, and not by means of the law in a court of justice. The duel is therefore adopted as the means of demonstrating his courage as that characteristic upon which the honor of his profession essentially rests; and this is done even if it should issue in the killing of his adversary. But as such a result takes place publicly and under the consent of both parties, although it may be done unwillingly, it cannot properly be called murder.

What then is the right in both cases as relating to criminal justice? Penal justice is here in fact brought into great straits, having apparently either to declare the notion of honor, which is certainly no mere fancy here, to be nothing in the eye of the law, or to exempt the crime from its due punishment; and thus it would become either remiss or cruel. The knot thus tied is to be resolved in the following way. The categorical imperative of penal justice, that the killing of any person contrary to the law must be punished with death, remains in force; but the legislation itself and the civil constitution generally, so long as they are still barbarous and incomplete, are at fault. And this is the reason why the subjective motive-principles of honor among the people do not coincide with the standards which are objectively conformable to another purpose; so that the public justice issuing from the state becomes injustice relatively to that which is upheld among the people themselves.

Against Granting the King a Trial, Robespierre (1792)

A new difficulty! To what punishment shall we condemn Louis? The punishment of death is too cruel. No, says another, life is more cruel still. I ask that he may live. Advocates of the king, is it through pity or cruelty that you wish to save him from the penalty of his crimes? As for me, I abhor the penalty of death so lavish in your laws, and I have neither love nor hatred for Louis. Crimes only I hate. I have asked the Assembly, which you still call Constituent, for the abolition of the death penalty, and it is not my fault if the first principles of reason seem to it moral and political heresies. But if you never bethought yourselves to invoke them in favor of so many unfortunates whose offenses are less their own than those of the government, by

what fatality do you remember them only to plead the cause of the greatest of all criminals? You ask an exception to the death penalty for him alone against whom it can be legitimate! Yes, the penalty of death generally is a crime, and for that reason alone, according to the indestructible principles of nature, it can be justified only in cases when it is necessary for the safety of individuals or the social body. Public safety never demands it against ordinary offenses, because society can always guard against them by other means and make the offender powerless to harm it. But a dethroned king in the bosom of a revolution which is anything but cemented by laws, a king whose name suffices to draw the scourge of war on the agitated nation, neither prison nor exile can render his existence immaterial to the public welfare; and this cruel exception to ordinary laws which justice approves can be imputed only to the nature of his crimes.

It is with regret that I utter this fatal truth. But Louis must die, because the country must live. Among a people at peace, free and respected at home and abroad, the counsels to generosity given you might be entertained. But a people whose liberty is still contested after so many sacrifices and combats; a people among whom the laws are still inexorable only toward the unfortunate; a people among whom, the crimes of tyranny are still the subjects of debate, must long for vengeance; and the generosity with which we are flattered would seem too much like that of a band of brigands dividing the spoils.

Journée du 21 Janvier 1793

WITNESS TO AN EXECUTION
The Execution of Louis XVI
Henry Essex Edgeworth (1792)

The King, finding himself seated in the carriage, where he could neither speak to me nor be spoken to without witness, kept a profound silence. I presented him with my breviary, the only book I had with me, and he seemed to accept it with pleasure: he appeared anxious that I should point out to him the psalms that were most suited to his situation, and he recited them attentively with me. The gendarmes, without speaking, seemed astonished and confounded at the tranquil piety of their monarch, to whom they doubtless never had before approached so near.

The procession lasted almost two hours; the streets were lined with citizens, all armed, some with pikes and some with guns, and the carriage was surrounded by a body of troops, formed of the most desperate people of Paris. As another precaution, they had placed before the horses a number of drums, intended to drown any noise or murmur in favour of the King; but how could they be heard? Nobody appeared either at the doors or windows, and in the street nothing was to be seen, but armed citizens — citizens, all rushing towards the commission of a crime, which perhaps they detested in their hearts.

The carriage proceeded thus in silence to the *Place de Louis XV*, and stopped in the middle of a large space that had been left round the scaffold: this space was surrounded with cannon, and beyond, an armed multitude extended as far as the eye could reach. As soon as the King perceived that the carriage stopped, he turned and whispered to me, "We are arrived, if I mistake not." My silence answered that we were. One of the guards came to open the carriage door, and the gendarmes would have jumped out, but the King stopped them, and leaning his arm on my knee, "Gentlemen," said he, with the tone of majesty, "I recommend to you this good man; take care that after my death no insult be offered to him – I charge you to prevent it." [. . .] As soon as the King had left the carriage, three guards surrounded him, and would have taken off his clothes, but he repulsed them with haughtiness – he undressed himself, untied his neckcloth, opened his shirt, and arranged it himself. The guards, whom the determined countenance of the King had for a moment disconcerted, seemed to recover their audacity. They surrounded him again, and would have seized his hands. "What are you attempting?" said the King, drawing back his hands. "To bind you," answered the wretches. "To bind me," said the King, with an indignant air. "No! I shall never consent to that: do what you have been ordered, but you shall never bind me."

The path leading to the scaffold was extremely rough and difficult to pass; the King was obliged to lean on my arm, and from the slowness with which he proceeded, I feared for a moment that his courage might fail; but what was my astonishment, when arrived at the last step, I felt that he suddenly let go my arm, and I saw him cross with a firm foot the breadth of the whole scaffold; silence, by his look alone, fifteen or twenty drums that were placed opposite to me; and in a voice so loud, that it must have been heard it the *Pont Tournant*, I heard him pronounce distinctly these memorable words: "I die innocent of all the crimes laid to my charge; I Pardon those who have occasioned my death; and I pray to God that the blood you are going to shed may never be visited on France."

He was proceeding, when a man on horseback, in the national uniform, and with a ferocious cry, ordered the drums to beat. Many voices were at the same time heard encouraging the executioners. They seemed reanimated themselves, in seizing with violence the most virtuous of Kings, they dragged him under the axe of the guillotine, which with one stroke severed his head from his body. All this passed in a moment. The youngest of the guards, who seemed about eighteen, immediately seized the head, and showed it to the people as he walked round the scaffold; he accompanied this monstrous ceremony with the most atrocious and indecent gestures.

The youngest of the guards, who seemed about eighteen, immediately seized the head, and showed it to the people as he walked round the scaffold; he accompanied this monstrous ceremony with the most atrocious and indecent gestures.

At first an awful silence prevailed; at length some cries of *"Vive la Republique!"* were heard. By degrees the voices multiplied and in less than ten minutes this cry, a thousand times repeated became the universal shout of the multitude, and every hat was in the air.

The Life of Thomas Paine, Moncure Daniel Conway (1793)

[Tom] Paine was in consultation with him on his plan of sending [King] Louis [XVI] to America. Indeed, it is probable that popular suffrage would have ratified the decree. Nevertheless, it was a fair "appeal to the people" which Paine made, after the fatal verdict, in expressing to the Convention his belief that the people would not have done so. For after the decree the helplessness of the prisoner appealed to popular compassion, and on the fatal day the tide had turned.

Four days after the execution the American Minister writes to Jefferson: "The greatest care was taken to prevent a concourse of people. This proves a conviction that the majority was not favorable to that severe measure. In fact the great mass of the people mourned the fate of their unhappy prince." To Paine the death of an "unhappy prince " was no more a subject for mourning than that of the humblest criminal—for, with whatever extenuating circumstances, a criminal he was to the republic he had sworn to administer. But the impolicy of the execution, the resentment uselessly incurred, the loss of prestige in America, were felt by Paine as a heavy blow to his cause—always the international republic. He was, however, behind the scenes enough to know that the blame rested mainly on America's old enemy and his league of foreign courts against liberated France.

The man who, when Franklin said "Where liberty is, there is my country," answered "Where liberty is not, there is mine," would not despair of the infant republic because of its blunders. Attributing these outbursts to maddening conspiracies around and within the new-born nation, he did not believe there could be peace in Europe so long as it was ruled by George III. He therefore set himself to the struggle, as he had done in 1776. Moreover, Paine has faith in Providence.

At this time, it should be remembered, opposition to capital punishment was confined to very few outside of the despised sect of Quakers. In the debate three, besides Paine, gave emphatic expression to that sentiment, Manuel, Condorcet —Robespierre! The former, in giving his vote against death, said: "To Nature belongs the right of death. Despotism has taken it from her; Liberty will return it." As for Robespierre, his argument was a very powerful reply to Paine, who had reminded him of the bill he had introduced into the old National Assembly for the abolition of capital punishment. He did, indeed, abhor it, he said; it was not his fault if his views had been disregarded. But why should men who then opposed him suddenly revive the claims of humanity when the penalty happened to fall upon a King? Was the penalty good enough for the people, but not for a King? If there were any exception in favor of such a punishment, it should be for a royal criminal.

This opinion of Robespierre is held by some humane men. The present writer heard from Professor Francis W. Newman—second to none in philanthropy and compassionateness—a suggestion that the death penalty should be reserved for those placed at the head of affairs who betray their trust, or set their own above the public interests to the injury of a Commonwealth. The real reasons for the execution of the King closely resemble those of Washington for the execution of Major Andre, notwithstanding the sorrow of the country, with which the Commander sympathized. The equal nationality of the United States, repudiated by Great Britain, was in question. To hang spies was, however illogically, a conventional usage among nations. Major Andre must die, therefore, and must be refused the soldier's death for which he petitioned.

For a like reason Europe must be shown that the French Convention is peer of their scornful Parliaments; and its fundamental principle, the equality of men, could not admit a King's escape from the penalty which would be unhesitatingly inflicted on a "Citizen." The King had assumed the title of Citizen, had worn the republican cockade; the apparent concession of royal inviolability, in the moment of his betrayal of the compromise made with him, could be justified only on the grounds stated by Paine—impolicy of slaying their hostage, creating pretenders, alienating America; and the honor of exhibiting to the world, by a salient example, the Republic's magnanimity in contrast with the cruelty of Kings.

On Punishing Murder by Death, Benjamin Rush (1792)

In an essay upon the effects of public punishments upon criminals and upon society, published in the second volume of the American Museum, I hinted, in a short paragraph, at the injustice of punishing murder by death. I shall attempt in the following essay, to support that opinion, and to answer all the objections that have been urged against it.

I. Every man possesses an absolute power over his own liberty and property, but not over his own life. When he becomes a member of political society, he commits the disposal of his liberty and property to his fellow citizens; but as he has no right to dispose of his life, he cannot commit the power over it to any body of men. To take away life, therefore, for any crime, is a violation of the first political compact.

II. The punishment of murder by death is contrary to reason, and to the order and happiness of society.

The punishment of murder by death multiplies murders.

1. It lessens the horror of taking away human life, and thereby tends to multiply murders.

2. It produces murder, by its influence upon people who are tired of life, and who, from a supposition, that murder is a less crime than suicide, destroy a life (and often that of a near connexion) and afterwards deliver themselves up to justice, that they may escape from their misery by means of a halter.

3. The punishment of murder by death multiplies murders, from the difficulty it creates of convicting persons who are guilty of it. Humanity, revolting at the idea of the severity and certainty of a capital punishment, often steps in, and collects such evidence in favor of a murderer, as screens him from justice altogether, or palliates his crime into manslaughter. If the punishment of murder consisted in long confinement, and hard labor, it would be proportioned by the measure of our feelings of justice, and every member of society would be a watchman or a magistrate, to apprehend a destroyer of human life, and to bring him to punishment.

4. The punishment of murder by death, checks the operations of universal justice, by preventing the punishment of every species of murder. Quack doctors--frauds of various kinds--and a licentious press, often destroy life, and sometimes with malice of the most propense nature. If murder were punished by confinement and hard labor, the authors of the numerous murders that have been mentioned, would be dragged forth, and punished according to their deserts. How much order and happiness would arise to society from

such a change in human affairs! But who will attempt to define these species of murder, or to prosecute offenders of this stamp, if death is to be the punishment of the crime after it is admitted, and proved to be willful murder? Only alter the punishment of murder, and these crimes will soon assume their proper names, and probably soon become as rare as murder from common acts of violence.

5. The punishment of murder by death, has been proved to be contrary to the order and happiness of society by the experiments of some of the wisest legislators in Europe. The Empress of Russia, the King of Sweden, and the Duke of Tuscany, have nearly extirpated murder from their dominions, by converting its punishment into the means of benefiting society, and reforming the criminals who perpetrate it.

III. The punishment of murder by death, is contrary to divine revelation. A religion which commands us to forgive and even to do good to our enemies, can never authorize the punishment of murder by death. "Vengeance is mine," said the Lord; "I will repay." It is to no purpose to say here, that this vengeance is taken out of the hands of an individual, and directed against the criminal by the hand of government. It is equally an usurpation of the prerogative of heaven, whether it be inflicted by a single person, or by a whole community. [. . .]

I cannot take leave of this subject without remarking that capital punishments are the natural offspring of monarchical governments. Kings believe that they possess their crowns by a divine right: no wonder, therefore, they assume the divine power of taking away human life. Kings consider their subjects as their property: no wonder, therefore, they shed their blood with as little emotion as men shed the blood of their sheep or cattle. But the principles of republican governments speak a very different language. They teach us the absurdity of the divine origin of kingly power. They approximate the extreme ranks of men to each other. They restore man to his God—to society—and to himself. They revive and establish the relations of fellow-citizen, friend, and brother. They appreciate human life, and increase public and private obligations to preserve it. They consider human sacrifices as no less offensive to the sovereignty of the people, than they are to the majesty of heaven. They view the attributes of government, like the attributes of the Deity, as infinitely more honored by destroying evil by means of merciful than by exterminating punishments. The United States have adopted these peaceful and benevolent forms of government. It becomes them therefore to adopt their mild and benevolent principles. An execution in a republic is like a human sacrifice in religion. It is an offering to monarchy, and to that malignant being, who has been styled a murderer from the beginning, and who delights equally in murder, whether it be perpetrated by the cold, but vindictive arm of the law, or by the angry hand of private revenge.

Philosophy in the Bedroom, Marquis de Sade (1795)

That we cannot devise as many laws as there are men must be admitted; but the laws can be lenient, and so few in number, that all men, of whatever character, can easily observe them. Furthermore, I would demand that this small number of laws be of such a sort as to be adaptable to all the various characters; they who formulate the code should follow the principle of applying more or less, according to the person in question. It has been pointed out that there are certain virtues whose practice is impossible for certain men, just as there are certain remedies which do not agree with certain constitutions. Now, would it not be to carry your injustice beyond all limits were you to send the law to strike the man incapable of bowing to the law? Would your iniquity be any less here than in a case where you sought to force the blind to distinguish amongst colors?

From these first principles there follows, one feels, the necessity to make flexible, mild laws and especially to get rid forever of the atrocity of capital punishment, because the law which attempts a man's life is impractical, unjust, inadmissible.

From these first principles there follows, one feels, the necessity to make flexible, mild laws and especially to get rid forever of the atrocity of capital punishment, because the law which attempts a man's life is impractical, unjust, inadmissible. Not, and it will be clarified in the sequel, that we lack an infinite number of cases where, without offense to Nature (and this I shall demonstrate), men have freely taken one another's lives, simply exercising a prerogative received from their common mother; but it is impossible for the law to obtain the same privileges, since the law, cold and impersonal, is a total stranger to the passions which are able to justify in man the cruel act of murder. Man receives his impressions from Nature, who is able to forgive him this act; the law, on the contrary, always opposed as it is to Nature and receiving nothing from her, cannot be authorized to permit itself the same extravagances: not having the same motives, the law cannot have the same rights. Those are wise and delicate distinctions which escape many people, because very few of them reflect; but they will be grasped and retained by the instructed to whom I recommend them, and will, I hope, exert some influence upon the new code being readied for us.

The second reason why the death penalty must be done away with is that it has never repressed crime; for crime is every day committed at the foot of the scaffold.

The second reason why the death penalty must be done away with is that it has never repressed crime; for crime is every day committed at the foot of the scaffold. This punishment is to be got rid of, in a word, because it would be difficult to conceive of a poorer calculation than this, by which a man is put to death for having killed another: under the present arrangement the obvious result is not one man the less but, of a sudden, two; such arithmetic is in use only amongst headsmen and fools. However all that may be, the injuries we can work against our brothers may be reduced to four types: calumny; theft; the crimes which, caused by impurity, may in a disagreeable sense affect others; and murder.

All these were acts considered of the highest importance under the monarchy; but are they quite so serious in a republican State? That is what we are going to analyze with the aid of philosophy's torch, for by its light alone may such an inquiry be undertaken. Let no one tax me with being a dangerous innovator; let no one say that by my writings I seek to blunt the remorse in evildoers' hearts, that my humane ethics are wicked because they augment those same evildoers' penchant for crime. I wish formally to certify here and now, that I have none of these perverse intentions; I set forth the ideas which, since the age when I first began to reason, have identified themselves in me, and to whose expression and realization the infamous despotism of tyrants has been opposed for uncounted centuries. So much the worse for those susceptible to corruption by any idea; so much the worse for them who fasten upon naught but the harmful in philosophic opinions, who are likely to be corrupted by everything. Who knows? They may have been poisoned by reading Seneca and Charron. It is not to them I speak; I address myself only to people capable of hearing me out, and they will read me without any danger.

WITNESS TO AN EXECUTION
Execution of Governor Wall,
don Manual Alvarez Espriella (1802)

Nothing is now talked of in London but the fate of Governor Wall, who has just been executed for a crime committed twenty years ago. He commanded at that time the English settlement at Goree, an inactive and unwholesome station, little reputable for the officers, and considered as a place of degradation for the men. The garrison became discontented at some real or supposed malpractices in the distribution of stores; and Wall seizing those whom he conceived to be the ringleaders of the disaffected, ordered them, by his own authority, to be so dreadfully flogged, that three of them died in consequence and he himself standing by during the execution, and urging the executioner not to spare, in terms of the most brutal cruelty. An indictment for murder was preferred against him on his return to England; he was apprehended, but made his escape from the officers of justice, and got over to the Continent, where he remained many years. Naples was at one time the place of his residence, and the countenance which he received there from some of his countrymen of high rank perhaps induced him to believe that the public indignation against him had subsided. Partly, perhaps, induced by this confidence, by the supposition that the few witnesses who could have testified against him were dead, or so scattered about the world as to be out of reach, and still more compelled by the pressure of his circumstances, he at length resolved to venture back.

It is said, that some years before his surrender he came to Calais with this intent, and desired one of the king of England's messengers to take him into custody, as he wished to return and stand his trial. The messenger replied that he could not possibly take charge of him, but advised him to signify his intention to the Secretary of State, and offered to carry his letter to the office. Wall was still very solicitous to go, though the sea was at that time so tempestuous that the ordinary packets did not venture out; and the messenger, whose dispatches would not admit of delay, had hired a vessel for himself: finding, however, that this could not be, he wrote as had been suggested ; but when he came to subscribe his name, his heart failed him, his countenance became pale and livid, and in an agony of fear or of conscience he threw down the pen and rushed out of the room. The messenger put to sea; the vessel was wrecked in clearing out of the harbor, and not a soul on board escaped.

This extraordinary story has been confidently related with every circumstantial evidence; yet it seems to imply a consciousness of guilt, and a feeling of remorse, noways according with his after conduct. He came over to England about twelve months ago, and lived in London under a fictitious name: here also a circumstance took place which touched him to the heart. Some masons were employed about his house, and he took notice to one of them that the lad who worked with him appeared very sickly and delicate, and unfit for so laborious an employment. The man confessed that it was true, but said that he had no other means of supporting him, and that the poor lad had no other friend in the world, "For his father and mother," said he, are dead, and his only brother was flogged to death at Goree, by that barbarous villain Governor Wall."

It has never been ascertained what were his motives for surrendering himself: the most probable cause which can be assigned is, that some property had devolved to him, of which he stood greatly in need but which he could not claim till his outlawry had been reversed. He therefore voluntarily gave himself up, and was brought to trial. One of the persons whom he had summoned to give evidence in his favor dropped down dead on the way to the court; it was, however, known that his testimony would have borne against him. Witnesses appeared from the remotest parts of the island whom he had supposed dead. One man who had suffered under his barbarity and recovered, had been hanged for robbery but six months before, and expressed his regret at going to the gallows before Governor Wall, as the thing which most grieved him, "For," said he, "I know he will come to the gallows at last."

The question turned upon the point of law, whether the fact, for that was admitted, was to be considered as an execution — or as a murder. The evidence of a woman who appeared in his behalf, was that which weighed most heavily against him: his attempt to prove that a mutiny actually existed failed; and the jury pronounced him guilty. For this he was utterly unprepared; and, when he heard the verdict, clasped his hands in astonishment and agony, The Bench, as it is called, had no doubt whatever of his guilt, but they certainly thought it doubtful how the jury might decide; and as the case was singular, after passing sentence in the customary form, they respited him, that the circumstances might be more fully considered.

The Governor was well connected, and had powerful friends; it is said also, that as the case turned upon a question of discipline, some persons high in the military department exerted themselves warmly in his favor. The length of time which had elapsed was no palliation, and it was of consequence that it should not be considered as such; but his self-surrender, it was urged, evidently implied that he believed himself justifiable in what he had done. On the other hand, the circumstances which had appeared on the trial were of the most aggravating nature; they had been detailed in all the newspapers, and women were selling the account about the streets at a half-penny each, vociferating aloud the most shocking parts, the better to attract notice. Various editions of the trial at length were published; and the publishers, most unpardonably, while the question of his life or death was still under the consideration of the privy council, stuck up their large notices all over the walls of London, with prints of the transaction, and "Cut his liver out," the expression which he had used to the executioner, written in large letters above. The popular indignation had never before been so excited. On the days appointed for his execution (for he was repeatedly respited) all the streets leading to the prison were crowded by soldiers and sailors chiefly, every one of whom felt it as his own personal cause: and as the execution of the mutineers in the fleet was so recent, in which so little mercy had been shown, a feeling very generally prevailed among the lower classes, that this case was to decide whether or not there was law for the rich as well as for the poor. The deliberations of the privy council continued for so many days that it was evident great efforts were made to save his life; but there can be little doubt, that had these efforts succeeded, either a riot would have ensued, or a more dangerous and deeply founded spirit of disaffection would have gone through the people. Wall, meantime, was lying in the dungeon appointed for persons condemned to death, where, in strict observance of the letter of the law, he was allowed no other food than bread and water. Whether he felt compunction may be doubted—we easily deceive ourselves—form only was wanting to have rendered that a legal punishment which was now called murder, and he may have regarded himself as a disciplinarian, not a criminal; but as his hopes of pardon failed him, he was known to sit up in his bed during the greater part of the night, singing psalms. His offence was indeed heavy, but never did human being suffer more heavily! The dread of death, the sense of the popular hatred, for it was feared that the mob might prevent his execution and pull him in pieces; and the tormenting reflection that his own vain confidence had been the cause—that he had voluntarily placed himself in this dreadful situation—these formed a punishment sufficient, even if remorse were not superadded.

On the morning of his execution, the mob, as usual, assembled in prodigious numbers, filling the whole space before the prison, and all the wide avenues from whence the spot could be seen. Having repeatedly been disappointed of their revenge, they were still apprehensive - of another respite, and their joy at seeing him appear upon the scaffold was so great that they set up three huzzas—an instance of ferocity which had never occurred before. The miserable man, quite overcome by this, begged the hangman to hasten his work. When he was turned off they began their huzzas again; but instead of proceeding to three distinct shouts, as usual, they stopped at the first. This conduct of the mob has been called inhuman and disgraceful; for my own part, I cannot but agree with those who regard it in a very different light. The revengeful joy which animated them, unchristian as that passion certainly is, and whatever may have been its excess, was surely founded upon humanity; and the sudden extinction of that joy, the feeling which at one moment struck so many thousands, stopped their acclamations at once, and awed them into a dead silence when they saw the object of their hatred in the act and agony of death, is surely as honorable to the popular character; as any trait which I have seen recorded of any people in any age or country.

The body, according to custom, was suspended an hour: during this time the Irish basket-women who sold fruit under the gallows were drinking his damnation in a mixture of gin and brimstone! The halter in which he suffered was cut into the smallest pieces possible, which were sold to the mob at a shilling each. According to the sentence, the body should have been dissected; it was just opened as a matter of form, and then given to his relations; for which indulgence they gave 100% to one of the public hospitals. One of the printed trials contains his portrait as taken in the dungeon of the condemned; if it be true that an artist was actually sent to take his likeness under such dreadful circumstances, for the purpose of gain, this is the most disgraceful fact which has taken place during the whole transaction.

A print has since been published called *The Balance of Justice*. It represents the mutineers hanging on one arm of a gallows, and Governor Wall on the other.

WITNESS TO AN EXECUTION
Execution of Governor Wall, J.T. Smith (1802)

As we crossed the press-yard a cock crew, and the solitary clanking of a restless chain was dreadfully horrible. The prisoners had not risen. Upon our entering a cold stone room, a most sickly stench of green twigs, with which an old round-shouldered, goggle-eyed man was endeavouring to kindle a fire, annoyed me almost as much as the canister fumigation of the doctor's Hatton Garden friends.

The prisoner entered. He was death's counterfeit, tall, shrivelled, and pale; and his soul shot so piercingly through the port-holes of his head, that the first glance of him nearly terrified me. I said in my heart, putting my pencil in my pocket, 'God forbid that I should disturb thy last moments!' His hands were clasped, and he was truly penitent. After the yeoman had requested him to stand up, he 'pinioned him,' as the Newgate phrase is, and tied the cord with so little feeling, that the governor, who had not given the wretch the accustomed fee, observed, 'You have tied me very tight,' upon which Dr. Ford ordered him to slacken the cord, which he did, but not without muttering. 'Thank you, sir,' said the governor to the doctor, 'it is of little moment.' He then observed to the attendant, who had brought in an immense iron shovelful of coals to throw on the fire, 'Ay, in one hour that will be a blazing fire;' then, turning to the doctor, questioned him, 'Do tell me, sir: I am informed I shall go down with great force; is that so?' After the construction and action of the machine had been explained, the doctor questioned the governor as to what kind of men he had at Goree. 'Sir,' he answered, 'they sent me the very riff-raff.' The poor soul then joined the doctor in prayer; and never did I witness more contrition at any condemned sermon than he then evinced.

The Nottingham Frame-Breaking Bill
George Gordon, Lord Byron (1808)

A bill intended for the suppression of the riotous proceedings of the Nottingham stocking-weavers, during a season of peculiar distress.

In what state of apathy have we been plunged so long, that now, for the first time, the house has been officially apprised of these disturbances? All this has been transacting within one hundred and thirty miles of London; and yet we — "good easy men! Have deemed full surely our greatness was a ripening" — and have sat down to enjoy our foreign triumphs, in the midst of domestic calamity. But all the cities you have taken, all the armies which have retreated before your leaders, are but paltry subjects of self-congratulation, if your land divides against itself, and your dragoons and executioners must be let loose against your fellow-citizens.

You call these men a mob, desperate, dangerous, and ignorant; and seem to think that the only way to quiet the *"belltat multorum capitum"* [monster of many heads] is to lop off a few of its superfluous heads. But even a mob may be better reduced to reason by a mixture of conciliation and firmness, than by additional irritation and redoubled penalties.

Are we aware of our obligations to a mob? It is "the mob" that labor in your fields, and serve in your houses — that man your navy, and recruit your army — that have enabled you to defy all the world — and can also defy you, when neglect and calumny have driven them to despair. You may call the people a mob, but do not forget that a mob too often speak the sentiments of the people. And here I must remark with what alacrity you are accustomed to fly to the succor of your distressed allies, leaving the distressed of your own country to the care of Providence, or — the parish.

When the Portuguese suffered under the retreat of the French, every arm was stretched out, every hand was opened — from the rich man's largess to the widow's mite, all was bestowed to enable them to rebuild their villages and replenish their granaries. And, at this moment, when thousands of misguided, but most unfortunate fellow-countrymen, are struggling with the extremes of hardship and hunger, as your charity began abroad, it should end at home. A much less sum — a tithe of the bounty bestowed on Portugal, even if these men, (which I cannot admit without inquiry,) could not have been restored to their employments — would have rendered unnecessary the tender mercies of the bayonet and the gibbet. But doubtless our funds have too many foreign claims to admit a prospect of domestic relief — though never did such objects demand it.

I have traversed the seat of war in the Peninsula; I have been in some of the most oppressed provinces of Turkey; but never, under the most despotic of infidel governments, did I behold such squalid wretchedness as I have seen, since my return, in the very heart of a Christian country. And what are your remedies? After months of inaction, and months of action worse than inactivity, at length comes forth the grand specific and never-failing nostrum of all state physicians, from the days of Draco to the present time. After feeling the pulse, and shaking the head over the patient, prescribing the usual course of warm water and bleeding—the warm water of your mawkish policy, and the lancets of your military — these convulsions must terminate in death — the sure consummation of the prescriptions of all political Sangrados.

Setting aside the palpable injustice and the certain inefficiency of the bill,

Will you erect a gibbet in every field, and hang up men like scarecrows?

are there not capital punishments sufficient on your statutes? Is there not blood enough upon your penal code, that more must be poured forth to ascend to heaven, and testify against you? How will you carry this bill into effect? Can you commit a whole country to their own prisons? Will you erect a gibbet in every field, and hang up men like scarecrows? Or will you proceed, (as you must, to bring this measure into effect,) by decimation; place the country under martial law; depopulate and lay waste all around you; and restore Sherwood Forest, as an acceptable gift to the crown, in its former condition of a royal chase, and an asylum for outlaws? Are these the remedies for a starving and desperate populace? Will the famished wretch who has braved your bayonets, be appalled by your gibbets? When death is a relief, and the only relief it appears that you will afford him, will he be dragooned into tranquility? Will that which could not be effected by your grenadiers be accomplished by your executioners?

If you proceed by the forms of law, where is your evidence? Those who have refused to impeach their accomplices, when transportation only was the punishment, will hardly be tempted to witness against them, when death is the penalty. With all deference to the noble lords opposite, I think a little investigation, some previous inquiry, would induce even them to change their purpose. That most favorite state measure, so marvelously efficacious in many and recent instances — temporizing — would not be without its advantage in this. When a proposal is made to emancipate or relieve, you hesitate, you deliberate for years, you temporize, and tamper with the minds of men; but a death-bill must be passed off-hand, without a thought of the consequences.

Sure I am, from what I have heard, and from what I have seen, that to pass the bill, under all the existing circumstances, without inquiry, without deliberation, would only be to add injustice to irritation, and barbarity to neglect The framers of such a bill must be content to inherit the honors of that Athenian lawgiver, whose edicts were said to be written not in ink, but in blood. But suppose it passed; suppose one of these men, as I have seen them, meagre with famine, sullen with despair, careless of a life which your lordships are, perhaps, about to value at something less than the price of a stocking-frame; suppose this man surrounded by those children for whom he is unable to procure bread, at the hazard of his existence, about to be torn forever from a family which he lately supported in peaceful industry, and which it is not his fault that he can no longer so support; suppose this man — and there are ten thousand such, from whom you may select your victims — dragged into court to be tried for this new offence, by this new law; still there are two things wanting to convict and condemn him; and these are, in my opinion, twelve butchers for a jury, and a Jeffereys for a judge!

WITNESS TO AN EXECUTION
An Execution in Rome, Lord Byron (1817)

The day before I left Rome I saw three robbers guillotined. The ceremony—including the masqued priests; the half-naked executioners; the bandaged criminals; the black Christ and his banner; the scaffold; the soldiery; the slow procession, and the quick rattle and heavy fall of the axe; the splash of the blood, and the ghastliness of the exposed heads — is altogether more impressive than the vulgar and ungentlemanly dirty 'new drop,' and dog-like agony of infliction upon the sufferers of the English sentence. Two of these men behaved calmly enough, but the first of the three died with great terror and reluctance, which was very horrible. He would not lie down; then his neck was too large for the aperture, and the priest was obliged to drown his exclamations by still louder exhortations. The head was off before the eye could trace the blow; but from an attempt to draw back the head, notwithstanding it was held forward by the hair, the first head was cut off close to the ears: the other two were taken off more cleanly. It is better than the oriental way, and (I should think) than the axe of our ancestors. The pain seems little; and yet the effect to the spectator, and the preparation to the criminal, are very striking and chilling. The first turned me quite hot and thirsty, and made me shake so that I could hardly hold the opera-glass (I was close, but determined to see, as one should, see everything, once, with attention); the second and third (which shows how dreadfully soon things grow indifferent), I am ashamed to say, had no effect on me as a horror, though I would have saved them if I could.

Capital Punishment And The Ordeal,
Frederick von Schlegel (1810)

Of the Supreme Being, of a righteous and merciful God ruling over all destinies and the powers of nature, the heathen nations of antiquity had indeed some conception, for the government of the world and the conscience of man bear witness of him aloud. But this was but an isolated vestige of the truth, lost in a tissue of errors and fables. It may be maintained that in this respect the Germans were superior to other nations, who, instead of the worship of God and a religion, had but a worship of nature and a mythology. This appears deducible from the following circumstances in particular. By the Germanic law, capital punishment was awarded in but one case; in that of treachery to people and state—to the commonwealth. But it was not the duke or the prince, it was not the assembly of nobles and people who fixed and proclaimed the punishment. They deliberated, perhaps, and decided on the guilt of the party, but the judgment itself was pronounced and awarded in the name of the divinity by a priest of the nation, elected by the assembled nobles and people. Not prince or king, but Woden himself, the father of all, had, so to say, exclusive capital jurisdiction —the power of life and death. Thus they conceived this, their supreme national god, as the avenger of disloyalty and perjury. An idea certainly worthier, and more moral than the best that can be deduced from the popular belief of the Greeks and Romans as to their Jupiter, even when they are not speaking of him in mere fables, but with an approximation to the higher notion of a father of all things. This old Germanic conception of a father of all, as the highest supreme judge and avenger of wrong, had great influence upon the so-called ordeals or judgments of God. In cases which baffled human sagacity, the matter was referred to single combat, or to the trial by fire and water, in the fixed idea and belief that God himself would decide on the result for right and truth. This was an error and custom, that despite the opposition of Christianity, was maintained for many centuries, and of which, at least upon the stage, we are even at the present day sometimes reminded, although not always very happily.

Elements Of The Philosophy of Right,
Georg Wilhelm Friedrich Hegel (1820)

§ 100

The injury [the penalty] which falls on the criminal is not merely implicitly just — as just, it is *eo ipso* [*by the very fact*] his implicit will, an embodiment of his freedom, his right; on the contrary, it is also a right established within the criminal himself, i.e. in his objectively embodied will, in his action. The reason for this is that his action is the action of a rational being and this implies that it is something universal and that by doing it the criminal has laid down a law which he has explicitly recognized in his action and under which in consequence he should be brought as under his right.

§ 101

The annulment of the crime is retribution in so far as (a) retribution in conception is an 'injury of the injury,' and (b) since as existent a crime is something determinate in its scope both qualitatively and quantitatively, its negation as existent is similarly determinate. This identity rests on the concept, but it is not an equality the specific character of the crime and that of its negation; on the contrary, the two injuries are equal only in respect of their implicit character, i.e. in respect of their 'value.'

§ 102

The annulling of crime in this sphere where right is immediate is principally revenge, which is just in its content in so far as it is retributive. But in its form it is an act of a subjective will which can place its infinity in every act of transgression and whose justification, therefore, is in all cases contingent, while to the other party, too, it appears as only particular. Hence revenge, because it is a positive action of a particular will, becomes a new transgression; as thus contradictory in character, it falls into an infinite progression and descends from one generation to another ad infinitum.

§ 103

The demand that this contradiction, which is present here in the manner in which wrong is annulled, be resolved like contradictions in the case of other types of wrong is the demand for a justice freed from subjective interest and a subjective form and no longer contingent on might, i.e. it is the demand for justice not as revenge but as punishment. Fundamentally, this implies the demand for a will which, though particular and subjective, yet wills the universal as such. But this concept of Morality is not simply something demanded; it has emerged in the course of this movement itself.

§ 104

That is to say, crime, and justice in the form of revenge, display (i) the shape which the will's development takes when it has passed over into the distinction between the universal implicit will and the single will explicitly in opposition to the universal; and (ii) the fact that the universal will, returning into itself through superseding this opposition, has now itself become actual and explicit. In this way, the right, upheld in face of the explicitly independent single will, is and is recognized as actual on the score of *its necessity*. At the same time, however, this external formation which the will has here is *eo ipso* a step forward in the inner determination of the will by the concept. The will's immanent actualization in accordance with its concept is the process whereby it supersedes its implicit state and the form of immediacy in which it begins and which is the shape it assumes in abstract right; this means that it first puts itself in the opposition between the implicit universal will and the single explicitly independent will; and then, through the supersession of this opposition (through the negation of the negation), it determines itself in its existence as a will, so that it is a free will not only in itself but for itself also, i.e. it determines itself as self-related negativity. Its personality — and in abstract right the will is personality and no more — it now has for its object; the infinite subjectivity of freedom, a subjectivity become explicit in this way, is the principle of the moral standpoint.

The Saint Petersburg Dialogues, Joseph de Maistre (1821)

To come now to detail, let us start with human justice. Wishing men to be governed by men at least in their external actions, God has given sovereigns the supreme prerogative of punishing crimes, in which above all they are his representatives. [. . .]

This formidable prerogative of which I have just spoken results in the necessary existence of a man destined to inflict on criminals the punishments awarded by human justice; and this man is in fact found everywhere, without there being any means of explaining how; for reason cannot discern in human nature any motive which could lead men to this calling. I am sure, gentlemen, that you are too accustomed to reflection not to have pondered often on the executioner. Who is then this inexplicable being who has preferred to all the pleasant, lucrative, honest, and even honorable jobs that present themselves in hundreds to human power and dexterity that of torturing and putting to death his fellow creatures? Are this head and this heart made like ours? Do they not hold something peculiar and foreign to our nature? For my own part, I do not doubt this. He is made like us externally; he is born like us but he is an extraordinary being, and for him to exist in the human family a particular decree, a FIAT of the creative power is necessary. He is a species to himself. Look at the place he holds in public opinion and see if you can understand how he can ignore or affront this opinion! Scarcely have the authorities fixed his dwelling-place, scarcely has he taken possession of it, than the other houses seem to shrink back until they no longer overlook his. In the midst of this solitude and this kind of vacuum that forms around him, he lives alone with his woman and his offspring who make the human voice known to him, for without them he would know only groans. A dismal signal is given; a minor judicial official comes to his house to warn him that he is needed; he leaves; he arrives at some public place packed with a dense and throbbing crowd. A poisoner, a parricide, or a blasphemer is thrown to him; he seizes him, he stretches him on the ground, he ties him to a horizontal cross, he raises it up: then a dreadful silence falls, and nothing can be heard except the crack of bones breaking under the crossbar and the howls of the victim. He unfastens him; he carries him to a wheel: the shattered limbs interweave with the spokes; the head falls; the hair stands on end, and the mouth, open like a furnace, gives out spasmodically only a few blood-spattered words calling for death to come. He is finished: his heart flutters, but it is with joy; he congratulates himself, he says sincerely, No one can break men on the wheel better than I. He steps down; he stretches out his blood-stained hand, and justice throws into it from a distance a few pieces of gold which he carries through a double row of men drawing back with horror. He sits down to a meal and eats; then to bed, where he sleeps. And next day, on waking, he thinks of anything other than what he did the day before. Is this a man? Yes: God receives him in his temples and permits him to pray. He is not a criminal, yet it is impossible to say, for example, that he is virtuous, that he is an honest man, that he is estimable, and so on. No moral praise can be appropriate for him, since this assumes relationships with men, and he has none.

And yet all grandeur, all power, all subordination rests on the executioner: he is the horror and the bond of human association. Remove this incomprehensible agent from the world, and at that very moment order gives way to chaos, thrones topple, and society disappears. God, who is the author of sovereignty, is the author also of chastisement: he has built our world on these two poles; for Jehovah is the master of the two poles, and on these he makes the world turn. [1 Samuel 2:8]

Thus there is in the temporal sphere a visible and divine law for the punishment of crime, and this law, as stable as the society it upholds, has been carried out invariably from the beginning of time. Evil exists on the earth and acts constantly, and by a necessary consequence it must be continually repressed by punishment; indeed, we see over the whole globe constant action by every government to prevent or punish criminal outrages. The sword of justice has no scabbard; it must always threaten or strike. What then do these complaints about the impunity of crime mean? For whom are the knout, the gallows, the wheels, and the stakes? Obviously for the criminal. The mistakes of courts are exceptions that do not shake the rule: I have, besides, several reflections to offer to you on this point. In the first place, these fatal errors are much less frequent than is imagined. If it is allowed to doubt, opinion is always contrary to authority, and the public ear listens avidly to the slightest suggestions of a judicial murder; a thousand individual passions can fortify this general inclination [. . .]

That an innocent dies is a misfortune like any other; that is to say, it is common to all mankind. That a guilty man escapes is another exception of the same kind. But it always remains true, generally speaking, that there is on the earth a universal and visible order for the temporal punishment of crimes; and I must again draw your attention to the fact that criminals do not by any means cheat justice so often as might be ingenuously supposed in view of the infinite precautions they take to avoid it. There is often in the circumstances that betray the most cunning scoundrels something so unexpected, so surprising, so unforeseeable, that men who are called by their position or reflections to follow this kind of affair tend to believe that human justice is not entirely without a certain supernatural assistance in seeking out the guilty.

Allow me to add one more consideration to bring to an end this chronicle of punishments. Just as it is very possible for us to be wrong when we accuse human justice of sparing the guilty, since those we regard as being such are not really guilty, so it is equally possible on the other side that a man punished for a crime he has not committed has actually merited it by another completely unknown crime. Fortunately and unfortunately, there are several examples of this kind of thing shown by the confessions of criminals, and there are many more, I believe, of which we are ignorant. This last supposition deserves especially close attention, for, although in such a case the judges are extremely blameworthy or unfortunate, Providence, for whom everything, even an obstacle, is a means, makes full use of dishonesty or mistakes to execute the temporal justice we demand; and it is certain that these two suppositions restrict considerably the number of exceptions. You can see, then, how far this assumed equality that I supposed at the beginning is already disrupted by the consideration of human justice alone.

The Rationale of Punishment, Jeremy Bentham (1830)

Analogy Between Crimes And Punishments

Analogy is that relation, connexion, or tie, between two objects, whereby the one being present to the mind, the idea of the other is naturally excited. Likeness is one source of analogy, contrast another. That a punishment may be analogous to an offence, it is necessary that the crime should be attended with some striking characteristic circumstances, capable of being transferred upon the punishment. These characteristic circumstances will be different in different crimes. In some cases they may arise from the instrument whereby the mischief has been done; in others, from the object to which the mischief is done; in others, from the means employed to prevent detection. The examples which follow arc only intended clearly to explain this idea of analogy. I shall point out the analogy between certain crimes and certain punishments, without absolutely recommending the employment of those punishments in all cases. It is not a sufficient reason for the adoption of a punishment, that it is analogous: other considerations ought to be always regarded.

§ 1. First Source of Analogy: The same Instrument used in the Crime as in the Punishment

Incendiarism, inundation, poisoning: in these crimes, the instrument employed is the first circumstance which strikes the mind. In their punishment, the same instrument may be employed. With respect to incendiarism, we may observe, that this crime should be considered as limited to those cases in which some individual has perished by fire: if no life has been lost, nor any personal injury been suffered, the offense ought to be treated as an ordinary waste; whether an article of property has been destroyed by fire, or any other agent, does not make any difference. The amount of the damage ought to be the measure of the crime. Does a man set fire to a solitary and uninhabited house? This would be an act of destruction, and ought not to be ranked under the definition of incendiarism, If the punishment of fire had been reserved for incendiaries, the law would have had in its favor both reason and analogy; but in the legislation of barbarous times, it has been generally employed throughout Europe, for the crimes of magic and heresy: the first, an offense purely imaginary; the second, a simple difference of religious opinion, perfectly innocent, often useful, and with respect to which, the only effect of punishment is to produce insincerity. Fire may be employed as an instrument of punishment, without occasioning death. This punishment is variable in its nature through all the degrees of severity of which there can be any need. It would be necessary carefully to determine in the text of the law, the part of the body which ought to be exposed to the action of the fire; the intensity of the fire; the time during which it is to be applied, and the paraphernalia to be employed to increase the terror of the punishment. In order to render the description more striking, a print might be annexed, in which the operation should be represented. Inundation is an offense less common than incendiarism: in some countries it is altogether unexampled; it can only be perpetrated in countries that are intersected by water confined by artificial banks. It is susceptible of every degree of aggravation, from the highest to the lowest.

If the offense consist merely in inundation, in effect it amounts only to a simple destruction of property. It is by the destruction of life that this crime is raised to that degree of atrocity which requires severe punishment. A most evident analogy points out the means of punishment; that is, the drowning of the criminal, with such accompanying circumstances as will add to the terror of the punishment. In a penal code which should not admit the punishment of death, the offender might he drowned and then restored to life. This might be made a part of the punishment.

It may be asked, ought poison to be employed as a means of punishment for a poisoner? In some respects there is no punishment more suitable. Poisoning is distinguished from other murders, by the secrecy with which it may be perpetrated, and the cool determination which it supposes.

Of these two circumstances, the first increases the force of temptation and the evil of the crime; the second proves that the criminal, attentive to his own interest, is capable of serious reflection upon the nature of the punishment.

The idea of perishing by the same kind of death which he prepares, is the more frightful for him: in every step of his preparations, his imagination will represent to him his own lot. In this point of view, the analogy would produce its full effect. There are, however, many difficulties. Poisons are uncertain in their operation: it would be necessary, therefore, to fix a time after which the punishment should be abridged by strangulation. If the effect of the poison should be to produce sleep, the punishment may not be sufficiently exemplary: if it produce convulsions and distortions, it may prove hateful. If the poison administered by the criminal has not proved fatal, he may be made to take an antidote before the penal poison has produced death. The dose and the time may be fixed by the Judges, according to the report of skilful physicians. The horror attached to this crime would most probably render this punishment popular. And if there is one country in which this crime is more common than others, it is there that this punishment, which possesses so striking an analogy with the crime, would be most suitable.

§2. Second Source of Analogy: For a Corporal Injury, a similar Corporal Injury. — "An eye for an eye, a tooth for a tooth."

In crimes producing irreparable bodily injuries, the part of the body injured will afford the characteristic circumstance. The analogy will consist in making the offender suffer an evil similar to that which he has maliciously and willfully inflicted. It will, however, be necessary to provide for two cases: that in which the offender does not possess the member of which he has deprived the party he has attacked, and that in which the loss of the member would be more or less prejudicial to him than to the party injured. If the injury has been of an ignominious nature, without permanent mischief, similar ignominy may be employed in the punishment, when the rank of the party and other circumstances permit.

§ 3. Third Source of Analogy: Punishment of the Offending Member.

In crimes of deceit, the tongue and the hand are the usual instruments. An exact analogy in the punishment may be drawn from this circumstance. In punishing the crime of forgery, the hand of the offender may be transfixed by an iron instrument fashioned like a pen; and in this condition he may be exhibited to the public, previously to undergoing the punishment of imprisonment. In the utterance of calumny, and the dissemination of false reports, the tongue is the instrument employed. The offender might in the same manner be publicly exposed with his tongue pierced. These punishments may be made more formidable in appearance than in reality, by dividing the instruments in two parts, so that the part which should pierce the offending member need not be thicker than a pin. whilst the other part of the instrument may be much thicker, and appear to penetrate with all its thickness. Punishments of this kind may appear ridiculous; but the ridicule which attaches to them enhances their merit. This ridicule will be directed against the cheat, whom it will render more despicable, whilst it will increase the respect due to upright dealing.

§ 4. Fourth Source of Analogy: Imposition of Disguise Assumed.

Some offences are characterized by the assumption of a disguise to facilitate their commission: a mask, or crape over the face, has commonly been used. This circumstance constitutes an aggravation of the offense: it increases the alarm produced, and diminishes the probability of detection; and hence arises the propriety of additional punishment. Analogy would recommend the imprinting on the offender a representation of the disguise assumed. This impression might be made either evanescent or indelible, according as the imprisonment by which it may be accompanied, is to be either temporary or otherwise. If evanescent, it might be produced by the use of a black wash: if indelible, by tatooing. The utility of this punishment would be most particularly felt in cases of premeditated murder, rape, irreparable personal injury, and theft, when accompanied with violence and alarm.

§5. Other Sources of Analogy.

There are other characteristic circumstances, which do not, like the foregoing, fit into classes; which may, however, according to the nature of the different offenses, be employed as a foundation for analogy. In the fabrication of base coin, the art of the delinquent may furnish an analogous source of punishment. He has made an impression upon the metal he has employed; — a like impression may be made on some conspicuous part of his face. This mark may be either evanescent or indelible, according as the imprisonment by which it is to be accompanied is either temporary or perpetual. At Amsterdam, vagabonds and idle persons are committed to the House of Correction, called the Rasp House. It is said, that among other species of forced labor in which such characters are employed, there is one reserved for those who are incorrigible by other means: which consists in keeping a leaky vessel, in which the idle prisoner is placed, dry, by means of a pump at which he must work, if he would keep himself from being drowned. Whether this punishment is in use or not, it is an example of an analogous punishment carried to the highest degree of rigor. If such a method of punishment is adopted, it ought to be accompanied with precise regulations for adjusting the punishment to the strength of the individual undergoing it. The place in which a crime has been committed may furnish a species of analogy. Catherine II condemned a man who had committed some knavish trick at the Exchange, to sweep it out every day that it was used, during six months.

Capital Punishment

Capital punishment may be distinguished into — 1st, simple; 2nd afflictive.

I call it simple when, if any bodily pain be produced, no greater degree of it is produced than what is necessary to produce death.

I call it afflictive when any degree of pain is produced more than what is necessary for that purpose.

It will not be necessary, upon the present occasion, to attempt to give an exhaustive view of all the possible modes by which death might be produced without occasioning any, or the least possible quantity of collateral suffering. The task would be almost an endless one: and when accomplished, the only use to which it could be applied would be that of affording an opportunity of selecting out of the catalogue the mode that seemed to possess the desired property in the greatest perfection, which may readily be done without any such process.

The mode in use in England is far from being the best that could be devised. In strangulation by suspension, the weight of the body alone is seldom sufficient to produce an immediate and entire obstruction of respiration. The patient, when left to himself, struggles for some time: hence it is not uncommon for the executioner, in order to shorten his sufferings, to add his own weight to that of the criminal. Strangling by the bowstring may to some, perhaps, appear a severer mode of execution; partly from the prejudice against every usage of despotic governments, partly by the greater activity exerted by executioners in this case than in the other. The fact however is that it is much less painful than the other, for it is certainly much more expeditious. By this means the force is applied directly in the direction which it must take to effect the obstruction required: in the other case, the force is applied only obliquely; because the force of two men pulling in that manner is greater than the weight of one man.

It is not long, however, even in hanging, before a stop is put to sense; as is well enough known from the accounts of many persons who have survived the operation. This probably is the case a good while before the convulsive strugglings are at an end; so that in appearance the patient suffers more than he does in reality.

With respect to beheading, there are reasons for supposing that the stop put to sensation is not immediate: a portion of sensibility may still be kept up in the spinal marrow a considerable time after it is separated from the brain. It is so, at least, according to all appearance, for different lengths of time in different animals and insects, which continue to move after their heads are separated from their bodies. [. . .]

If the particular nature of the several species of punishments of this description be examined, as well those that have for a long time past been abolished, such as crucifixion and exposure to wild beasts, as those that have been in use in various parts of modern Europe, such as burning, empaling, tearing to pieces, and breaking on the wheel, it will be found in all of them that the most afflictive part consists in their duration: but this circumstance is not of a nature to produce the beneficial effect that may have been expected from it.

When any particular species of punishment is denounced, that part of it which takes the strongest hold of the imagination is its intensity: its duration makes a much more feeble impression. A slight apparent addition of organical suffering made to the ordinary, mode of inflicting the punishment of death, produces a strong effect upon the mind: the idea of the duration of its pain is almost wholly absorbed by the terrors of the principal part of the punishment.

In the legal description of a punishment its duration is seldom (distinctly) brought to view; it is not mentioned, because in itself it is naturally uncertain: it depends partly upon the physical strength of the patient, and partly upon various other accidental circumstances. To this remarkable and important feature of this species of punishment there is no means by which the attention can be drawn and fixed upon it: upon those who reflect, it produces no impression; upon those who do not reflect, it is altogether lost.

It is true that the duration of any particular punishment might be fixed by law: the number of hours or minutes might be determined, which should be employed in performing the several prescribed manipulations. This obviously would be a mode of fixing the attention upon this particular feature of the punishment: but even this mode, perfect as it may appear to be, would be found very inadequate to produce the desired effect. By the help of pictures, the intensity of any particular species of punishment may be more or less faithfully represented; but to represent its duration is impossible. The flames, the rack and all the engines of torture, together with the convulsive throes of the half-expiring and wretched sufferer, may be depicted, but time cannot. A punishment that is to be made to last for two hours will not appear different from a punishment that is to last only a quarter of an hour. The deficiencies of art may, to a certain degree, be compensated for by the imagination: but even then the reality will be left far behind.

It is true that upon bystanders the duration of the punishment is calculated to make a strong impression: but even upon them, after a certain time, the prolongation loses its effect, and gives place to a feeling directly opposite to that which it is desirable to produce — sentiments of pity and sympathy for the sufferer will succeed, the heart of the spectator will revolt at the scene he witnesses, and the cry of suffering humanity will be heard. The physical suffering will not be confined to the offender: the spectators will partake of it: the most melancholy accidents, swoonings, and dangerous convulsions will be the accompaniments of these tragic exhibitions. These sanguinary executions, and the terrific accounts that are spread concerning them, are the real causes of that deep-rooted antipathy that is felt against the laws and those by whom they are administered; an antipathy which tends to multiply offences by favoring the impunity of the guilty.

The only reason that can be given by any government, that persists in continuing to employ a mode of punishing so highly penal, is that the habitual condition of the people is so wretched that they are incapable of being restrained by a more lenient kind of punishment.

Will it be said that crimes are more frequent in countries in which punishments such as those in question are unknown. The contrary is the fact. It is under such laws that the most ferocious robbers are found: and this is readily accounted for. The fate with which they are threatened hardens them to the feelings of others as well as their own. They are converted into the most bitter enemies, and every barbarity they inflict is considered as a sort of reprisal.

Upon this subject; as upon so many others, Montaigne was far beyond the age in which he lived. All beyond simple death (he says) appears to me to be cruelty. The legislator ought not to expect that the offender that is not to be deterred by the apprehension of death, and by being beheaded and hanged, will be more effectually deterred by the dread of being exposed to a slow fire, or the rack. And I do not know indeed but that he may be rendered desperate.

By the French Constituent Assembly afflictive punishments were abolished. In the Code Napoleon, beheading is the mode prescribed for inflicting the punishment of death. And it is only in the case of parricide, and of attempts made upon the life of the sovereign, that to the simple punishment of death the characteristic afflictive punishment of cutting off the hand of the offender is added.

In this country, the only crime for which afflictive punishment is in use, is that of high treason. The judgment in high treason consists of seven different operations of the afflictive kind. 1. Dragging at a horse's tail along the streets from the prison to the place of execution. 2. Hanging by the neck, yet not so as entirely to destroy life. 3. Plucking out and burning of the entrails while the patient is yet alive. 4. Beheading. 5. Quartering. 6. Exposure of the head and quarters in such places as the King directs. This mode of punishment is not now in use. In favor of nobility; the judgment has been usually changed into beheading: in favor of the lower classes, into hanging.

I wish that upon this part of our subject we could end here; but unfortunately there remains to be mentioned an afflictive mode of punishment most excruciating, and more hideous than any of which we have hitherto spoken, and which is still in use. It is not in Europe that it is employed, but in European colonies — in our own West India Islands.

The delinquent is suspended from a post by means of a hook inserted under his shoulder, or under his breast bone. In this manner the sufferer is prevented from doing anything to assist himself, and all persons are prohibited, under severe penalties, from relieving him. He remains in this situation, exposed to the scorching heat of the day, where the sun is almost vertical, and the atmosphere almost without a cloud, and to the chilling dews of the night; his lacerated flesh attracts a multitude of insects, which increase his torments, and under the fever produced by these complicated sufferings, joined to hunger and thirst, all raging in the most intense degree, till he gradually expires.

When we reflect on this complication of sufferings, their intensity surpasses everything that the imagination can figure to itself and consider that their duration continues not merely for many hours, but for many days it will be found to be by far the most severe punishment ever yet devised by the ingenuity of man.

The persons to whom this punishment has been hitherto appropriated, are Negro slaves, and their crime, what is termed rebellion, because they are the weakest, but which, if they were the strongest, would be called an act of self-defense. The constitutions of these people are, to their misfortune, in certain respects so much harder than ours, that many of them are said to have lingered ten or twelve days under these frightful torment.

It is said that this punishment is nothing more than is necessary for restraining that people, and keeping them in their servile state; for that the general tenor of their lives is such a scene of misery, that simple death would be generally a relief, and a death less excruciating would scarce operate as a restraint.

This may perhaps be true. It is certain that a punishment to have any effect upon man must bear a certain ratio to the mean state of his way of living, in respect of sufferings and enjoyments. But one cannot well help observing where this leads. The number of slaves in these colonies is to that of freemen as about six to one; them may be about three hundred thousand blacks and fifty thousand whites; here there are three hundred thousand persons kept in a way of life that upon the whole appears to them worse than death, and this for the 'sake of keeping fifty thousand persons in a way of life not remarkably more nappy than that which, upon an average, the same number of persons would be in where there was no slavery;

When we reflect on this complication of sufferings, their intensity surpasses everything that the imagination can figure to itself and consider that their duration continues not merely for many hours, but for many days it will be found to be by far the most severe punishment ever yet devised by the ingenuity of man.

on the contrary, it is found that men in general are fond, when they have the opportunity, of changing that scene for this. On the other hand, it is not to be disputed that sugar and coffee, and other delicacies, which are the growth of those islands, add considerably to the enjoyments of the people here in Europe; but taking all these circumstances into consideration, if they are only to be obtained by keeping three hundred thousand men in a state in which they cannot be kept but by the terror of such executions: are there any considerations of luxury or enjoyment that can counterbalance such evils.

At the same time, what admits of very little doubt is that the defenders of these punishments, in order to justify them, exaggerate the miseries of slavery, and the little value set by the slaves upon life. If they were really reduced to such a state of misery as to render necessary laws so atrocious, even such laws would be insufficient for their restraint; having nothing to lose, they would be regardless of all consequences; they would be engaged in perpetual insurrections and massacres. The state of desperation to which they would be reduced would daily produce the most frightful disorders. But if existence is not to them a matter of indifference, the only pretence that there is in favor of these laws falls to the ground. Let the colonists reflect upon this; if such a code be necessary, the colonies are a disgrace and an outrage on humanity: if not necessary, these laws are a disgrace to the colonists themselves.

Capital Punishment Examined

In making this examination, the following plan will be pursued. The advantageous properties of capital punishment will in the first place be considered: we shall afterwards proceed to examine its disadvantageous properties.

We shall, in the last place, consider the collateral ill effects resulting from this mode of punishment: effects more remote and less obvious, but sometimes more important, than those which are more immediate and striking.

The task thus undertaken would be an extremely ungrateful and barren one, were it not that the course of the examination will lead us to make a comparison between this and other modes of punishment, and thus to ascertain which is entitled to the preference. On the subject of punishment, the same rule ought in this respect to be observed as on the subject of taxes. To complain of any particular tax as being an injudicious one, is to sow the seeds of discontent, and nothing more: to be really useful, this in itself mischievous discovery, should be accompanied by the indication of another tax which will prove equally productive, with less inconvenience.

Advantageous Properties of the Punishment of Death

1 . The most remarkable feature in the punishment of death, and that which it possesses in the greatest perfection, is the taking from the offender the power of doing further injury. Whatever is apprehended, either from the force or cunning of the criminal, at once vanishes away. Society is in a prompt and complete manner delivered from all alarm.

2. It is analogous to the offense in the case of murder; but there its analogy terminates.

3. It is popular in respect of that same crime, and in that alone.

4. It is exemplary in a higher degree perhaps than any other species of punishment, and in countries in which it is sparingly employed, an execution makes a deep and lasting impression.

It was the opinion of Beccaria that the impression made by any particular punishment was in proportion to its duration, and not to its intensity. "Our sensibility" (he observes) "is more readily and permanently affected by slight but reiterated attacks than by a violent but transient affection. For this reason the putting an offender to death forms a less effectual check to the commission of crimes than the spectacle of a man kept in a state of confinement, and employed in hard labor, to make some reparation by his exertions for the injury he has inflicted on society."

Notwithstanding such respectable authority, I am apt to think the contrary is the case. This opinion is founded principally on two observations. 1. Death in general is regarded by most men as the greatest of all evils, and they are willing to submit to any other suffering whatever in order to avoid it. 2. Death, considered as a punishment, is almost universally reckon too severe, and men plead, as a measure of mercy, for the substitution of any other punishment in lieu of it. In respect to duration, the suffering is next to nothing. It must, therefore, I think, be some confused and exaggerated notion of the intensity of the pain of death, especially of a violent death, that renders the idea of it so formidable. It is not without reason, however, that with respect to the higher class of offenders, M. Beccaria considers a punishment of the laborious kind, moderate we must suppose in its degree, will make a stronger impression than the most excruciating kind of death that can be devised. But for the generality of men, among those who are attached to life by the ties of reputation, affection, enjoyment, hope, capital punishment appears to be more exemplary than any other.

5. Though the apparent suffering in the punishment of death is at the highest pitch, the real suffering is perhaps less than in the larger portion of afflictive punishment. In addition to their duration, they leave after them a train of evils which injure the constitution of the patient, and render the remainder of his life a complication of sufferings. In the punishment of death the suffering is momentary: it is a negation of all sensation.

When the last moment only is considered, penal death is often more gentle than natural death, and, so far from being an evil, presents a balance of good. The suffering endured must be sought for in some anterior period. The suffering consists in apprehension. This apprehension commences from the moment the delinquent has committed the crime; it is redoubled when he is apprehended. It increases at every stage of the process which renders his condemnation more certain, and is at its height in the interval between sentence and execution.

The more solid argument in favor of the punishment of death, results from the combined force of the above considerations. On the one hand, it is to men in general of all punishment of the greatest apparent magnitude, the most impressive and the most exemplary; and on the other hand, to the wretched class of beings that furnish the most atrocious criminals, it is less rigorous than it appears to be. It puts a speedy termination to an uneasy, unhappy, dishonored existence, stript of all true worth: — *Heu! Heu! quam male est extra legem viventibus.* [*Alas! Alas! The outlaw has a hard life.*(Petronius)]

Desirable Penal Qualities Which Are Wanting In Capital Punishment

1. The punishment of death is not convertible to profit: it cannot be applied to the purpose of compensation. In so far as compensation might be derived from the labor of the delinquent, the very source of the compensation is destroyed.

2. In point of frugality it is pre-eminently defective. So far from being convertible to profit, to the community it produces a certain loss, both in point of wealth and strength. In point of wealth, a man chosen at random is worth to the public that portion of the whole annual income of the state which results from its division by the number of persons of which it consists. The same mode of calculation will determine the loss in respect of strength. But the value of a man who has been proved guilty of someone or other of those crimes for which capital punishment is denounced, is not equal to that of a man taken at random. Of those by whom a punishment of this sort is incurred, nine out of ten have divested themselves of all habits of regular industry; they are the drones of the hive: and with respect to them, death is therefore not an ineligible mode of punishment, except in comparison with confinement and hard labor, by which there is a chance of their being reformed and rendered of some use to society.

3. Equability is another point, and that a most important one, in which this punishment is eminently deficient. To a person taken at random, it is upon an average a very heavy punishment, though still subject to considerable variation. But to a person taken out of the class of first-rate delinquents, it is liable to still greater variation. To some it is as great as to a person taken at random; but to many it is next to nothing.

Death is the absence of all pleasures indeed, but at the same time of all pains. When a person feels under temptation to commit a crime punishable with death, his determination to commit it or not to commit it is the result of the following calculation. He ranges on one side the clear portion of happiness he thinks himself likely to enjoy in case of his abstaining: on the other — he places the clear happiness he thinks himself likely to enjoy in case of his committing the crime, taking into the account the chance there appears to him to be, that the punishment threatened will abridge the duration of that happiness.

Now then, if in the former case there appears to be no clear happiness likely to accrue to him, much more if there appears to be a clear portion of unhappiness; in other words, if the clear portion of happiness likely to befall him appears to be equal to zero, or much more if it appears to be negative, the pleasure that constitutes the profit of the crime will act upon him with a force that has nothing to oppose it. The probability of seeing it brought to an abrupt period by death will subtract more or less from the balance; but at any rate there will be a balance.

Now this is always the case with a multitude of malefactors. Rendered averse to labor by natural indolence or disuse, or hurried away by the tide of some impetuous passion, they do look upon the pleasures to be obtained by honest industry as not worth living for, when put in competition with the pains: or they look upon life as not worth keeping, without some pleasure or pleasures which, to persons in their situation, are not attainable but by a crime.

I do not say that this calculation is made with all the formality with which I have represented it. I do not say that in casting up the sum of pains on the one side and pleasures on the other, exact care is always used to take every item into the account. But however, well or ill, the calculation is made: else a man could not act as he is supposed to do.

Now then, in all these cases, which unhappily are but too frequent, it is plain the punishment of death can be of no use.

It may be said, no more would any other punishment. For any other punishment, to answer its purpose, must have the effect of deterring or otherwise disabling the person in question from committing the like crimes in future. If then he is thus deterred or disabled, he is reduced to a situation in which, by the supposition, death was to him an event desirable upon the whole. Being then in his power, he will produce it.

The conclusion, however, is not necessary. There are several reasons why the same impulse which is strong enough to dispose a man to meet death at the bands of justice should not be strong enough to dispose him to bring on himself that event with his own hand.

In the first place, the infliction of it as a punishment is an event by no means certain. It is in itself uncertain; the passion he is supposed to be influenced by, withdrawing his attention from the chances that are in favor of its happening, makes it look still more uncertain.

In the next place, although it were certain, it is at any rate distant: and the mortification he undergoes, from the not possessing the object of his passion, is present.

Thirdly, death is attended with much more pain when a man has to inflict it on himself with his own hand, than when all he does is simply to put himself in a situation in which it will be inflicted on him by the hands of another, or by the operation of some physical cause. To put himself in such a situation, requires but a single and sudden volition, and perhaps but a single act in consequence, during the performance of which he may keep his eyes shut, as it were, against the prospect of the pain to which he is about to subject himself. The moment of its arrival is at an uncertain distance. The reverse is the case where a man is to die by his own hand. His resolution must be supported during the whole period of time that is necessary to bring about the event. The manner is foreseen and the time immediate. It may be necessary that even after a part of the pain has been incurred, the resolution should go on and support itself, while it prompts him to add further pain before the purpose is accomplished.

Accordingly, when people are resolved upon death, it is common for them, when they have an opportunity, to choose to die rather by the hand of another than by their own. Thus Saul chose to die by the hand of his armor-bearer; Tiberius Gracchus by that of his freeman. So again the emperor Nero by one of his minions.

Fourthly, when a man is prompted to seek relief in death, it is not so much by the sudden vehemence of some tempestuous passion, as by a close persuasion that the miseries of his life are likely to be greater than the enjoyments; and, in consequence, when the resolution is once taken, to rest satisfied without carrying it immediately into effect; for there is not a more universal principle of human conduct, than that which leads a man to satisfy himself for awhile with the power, without proceeding immediately, perhaps without proceeding ever, to the act. It is the same feeling which so often turns the voluptuous man to a miser.

Now this is likely enough to be the condition of those who, instead of death, may have been sentenced to another punishment. They defer the execution of their design from hour to hour: sometimes for want of means, sometimes for want of inclination, till at last some incident happens that puts in their heads a train of thought which in the end diverts them from their resolution. In the mental as well as in the material part of the human frame, there is happily a strong disposition to accommodate itself by degrees to the pressure of forced and calamitous situations. When a great artery is cut or otherwise disabled, the circumjacent smaller ones will stretch and take upon themselves the whole duty of conveying to the part affected the necessary supplies. Loss of sight improves the faculty of feeling. A left hand learns to perform the offices of the right, or even the feet, of both. An inferior part of the alimentary canal has learned to perform the office, and even to assume the texture of the stomach.

The mind is endowed with no less elasticity and docility, in accommodating itself to situations which at first sight appeared intolerable. In all sufferings there are occasional remissions, which in virtue of the contrast are converted into pleasure. How many instances are there of men who, having suddenly fallen from the very pinnacle of grandeur into the gulphs of misery, have, when the old sources of enjoyment were irrecoverably dry, gradually detached their minds from all recollections of their customary enjoyments, and created for themselves fresh sources of happiness. The Comte de Lauzun's Spider, the straw-works of the Bicêtre, the skillfully wrought pieces of carved work made by the French prisoners, not to mention others, are sufficient illustrations of this remark.

Variability is a point of excellence in which the punishment of death is more deficient than in any other. It subsists only in one degree; the quantity of evil can neither be increased or lessened. It is peculiarly defective in the case of

the greater part of the most malignant and formidable species of malefactors —
that of professed robbers and highwaymen.[5]

4. The punishment of death is not remissable[6] Other species of afflictive
punishments it is true are exposed to the same objection, but though irremissible
they are not irreparable. For death there is no remedy.

No man, how little soever he may have attended to criminal procedure,
but must have been struck at the very slight circumstances upon which the life
of a man may depend; and who does not recollect instances in which a man has
been indebted for his safety to the occurrence of some unlooked-for accident
which has brought his innocence to light. The risk incurred is doubtless greater
under some systems of jurisprudence than under others. Those which allow
the torture to supply the insufficiency of evidence derived from other sources:
those in which the proceedings are not public, are, if the expression may be used,
surrounded with precipices. But it may be said, is there or could there be devised
any system of penal procedure which could insure the Judge from being misled
by false evidence or the fallibility of his own judgment? No; absolute security in
this branch of science is a point which, though it can never be attained may be
much more nearly approached than it has hitherto been. Judges will continue

---

5 "Are you not aware that we are subject to one disease more than other men ?" said
a malefactor upon the rack to his companion, who shrieked- from pain. When one
observes the courage or brutal insensibility, when in the very act of being turned off, of
the greater part of the malefactors that are executed at Newgate, it is impossible not to
feel persuaded that they have been accustomed to consider this mode of ending their
days as being to them a natural death — as an accident or misfortune, by which they
ought no more to be deterred from their profession than soldiers or sailors are from
theirs, by the apprehension of bullets or of shipwreck.

6 There is an evil resulting from the employment of death as a punishment which may be
properly noticed here. It destroys one source of testimonial proof. The archives of crime
are in a measure lodged in the bosoms of criminals. At their death, all the recollections
which they possess relative to their own crimes and those of others perish. Their death is
an act of impunity for all those who might have been detected by their testimony, whilst
innocence must continue oppressed, and the right can never be established because a
necessary witness is subtracted.

Whilst a criminal process is going forward the accomplices of the accused flee
and hide themselves. It is an interval of anxiety and tribulation. The sword of justice
appears suspended over their heads. When his career is terminated, it is for them an
act of jubilee and pardon. They have a new bond of security, and they can walk erect.
The fidelity of the deceased is exalted among his companions as a virtue, and received
among them for the instruction of their young disciples, with praises for his heroism.

In the confines of a prison, this heroism would be submitted to a more
dangerous proof than the interrogatories of the tribunals. Left to himself, separated from
his companions, a criminal ceases to possess this feeling of honor which unites him to
them. It needs only a moment of repentance to snatch from him those discoveries which
he only can make; and without his repentance, what is more natural than a feeling of
vengeance against those who caused him to lose his liberty, and who, though equally
culpable with himself, yet continue in the enjoyment of liberty! He need only listen to
his interest, and purchase by some useful information some relaxation of the rigor of his
punishment.

fallible, witnesses to depose falsehood or to be deceived; whatever number may depose to the same fact, the existence of that fact is not rendered certain; as to circumstantial evidence, that which is deemed incapable of explanation, but by supposing the existence of the crime, may be the effect of chance or of arrangements made with the view of producing deception. The only sort of evidence that appears entitled to perfect conviction, is the voluntary confession of the crime by the party accused, but this is not frequently made, and does not produce absolute certainty, since instances have not been wanting, as in the case of witchcraft, in which individuals have acknowledged themselves guilty, when the pretended crime was impossible. [. . .]

Judges will continue fallible, witnesses to depose falsehood or to be deceived; whatever number may depose to the same fact, the existence of that fact is not rendered certain.

The danger attending the use of capital punishment appears in a more striking point of view when we reflect on the use that may be made of it by men in power, to gratify their passions, by means of a judge easily intimidated or corrupted. In such cases, the iniquity covered with the robe of justice may escape, if not all suspicion, at least the possibility of proof. Capital punishment, too, affords to the prosecutor as well as to the Judge, an advantage that in all other modes is wanting: I mean, greater security against detection, by stifling by death all danger of discovery arising from the delinquent, at least: while he lives, to whatever state of misery he may be reduced, the oppressed may meet with some fortunate event by which his innocence may be proved, and he may become his own avenger. A judicial assassination, justified in the eyes of the public by a false accusation, with almost complete certainty assures the triumph of those who have been guilty of it. In a crime of an inferior degree, they would have had everything to fear; but the death of the victim seals their security.

The danger attending the use of capital punishment appears in a more striking point of view when we reflect on the use that may be made of it by men in power, to gratify their passions, by means of a Judge easily intimidated or corrupted.

If we reflect on those very unfrequent occurrences, but which may at any time recur, those periods at which the Government degenerates into anarchy and tyranny, we shall find that the punishment of death, established by law, is a weapon ready prepared, which is more susceptible of abuse than any other mode of punishment. A tyrannical government, it is true, may always reestablish this mode of punishment after it has been abolished by the Legislature. But the introducing what would then become an innovation, would not be unattended with difficulty: the violence of which it was to be the precursor, would be too much exposed, the tocsin would be sounded. Tyranny is much more at its ease when exercised under the sanction of law, when there is no appearance of any departure from the ordinary course of justice, and when it finds the minds of people already reconciled and accustomed to this mode of punishment. The Duke of Alba, ferocious as he was, would not have dared to sacrifice so many thousand victims in the Low Countries, if it had not been a commonly received opinion that heresy was a crime which merited the punishment of death. Biren, not less cruel than the Duke of Alba, Biren, who peopled the deserts of Siberia with exiles, caused them previously to be mutilated, that being the most severe punishment that was in use in that country; he very rarely ventured to punish them capitally, because capital punishment was not in use. So little do even the most arbitrary despots dare to violate established customs. Hence we may draw a strong reason for seizing upon periods of tranquility for destroying these dangerous instruments, which, though no longer dreaded when covered with rust, are with such facility brought into use again, when passion invites their employment.

The objection arising from the irremissibility of the punishment of death, applies to all cases, and can be removed only by its complete abolition. Upon this occasion it is necessary to bear in mind that there are two branches of security, for each of which it is necessary to make provision. Security against the errors and corruptions in judicial procedure, and security against crimes. If the latter were not to be attained but at the expense of the former, there would be no room for hesitation. With respect to crimes, from whom is it that the terror is felt? From every person that is capable of committing a crime, that is to say, from all men, and at all times. With respect to the errors and corruptions of justice, these are the exceptions, the accidental and rare occurrences.

This punishment is far from being popular: and it becomes less and less so every day in proportion as mankind become more enlightened, and their manners more softened. The people flock in crowds to an execution; but this eagerness, which at first might appear so disgraceful to humanity, does not proceed from the pleasure expected from the sight of men in the agonies of death, it arises from the pleasure of having the passions strongly excited by a tragic scene. There is, however, one case in which it does seem to be popular, and that in a very high degree; I mean the case of murder. The attachment seems to be grounded partly on the fondness for analogy, partly on the principle of vengeance, and partly perhaps by the fear which the character of the criminal is apt to inspire. Blood it is said will have blood, and the imagination is flattered with the notion of the similarity of the suffering, produced by the punishment,

The people flock in crowds to an execution; but this eagerness, which at first might appear so disgraceful to humanity, does not proceed from the pleasure expected from the sight of men in the agonies of death, it arises from the pleasure of having the passions strongly excited by a tragic scene.

with that inflicted by the criminal.

In other cases, the punishment of death is unpopular, and this unpopularity produces different dispositions, all equally contrary to the ends of justice ; a disposition on the part of the individuals injured not to prosecute the offenders, for fear of bringing them to the scaffold; a disposition on the part of the public to favor their escape; a disposition on the part of the witnesses to withhold their testimony, or to weaken its effect; a disposition on the part of the Judges to allow of a merciful prevarication in favor of the accused; and all these anti-legal dispositions render the execution of the laws uncertain, without referring to that loss of respect which follows upon its being considered meritorious to prevent their execution.

Recapitulation And Comparison Of The Punishment Of Death, With Those Punishments Which May Be Substituted For It.

The punishment of death, it has been observed, possesses four desirable properties.

1. It is in one case analogous to the offense.

2. In that same case it is popular.

3. It is in the highest degree efficacious in preventing further mischief from the same source.

4. It is exemplary, producing a more lively impression than any other mode of punishment.

The two first of these properties exist in the case of capital punishment when applied to murder; and with reference to that species of offense alone are they sufficient reasons for persevering in its use; certainly not: each of them, separately considered, is of very little importance. Analogy is a very good recommendation, but not a good justification. If in other respects any particular mode of punishment be eligible, analogy is an additional advantage: if in other respects it be ineligible, analogy alone is not a sufficient recommendation: the value of this property amounts to very little, because, even in the case of murder, other punishments may be devised, the analogy of which will be sufficiently striking.

In respect also of popularity, the same observations apply to this mode of punishment. Every other mode of punishment that is seen to be equally or more efficacious will become equally or more popular. The approbation of the multitude will naturally be in proportion to the efficacy of the punishment.

The third reason, that it is efficacious in preventing further mischief from the same source, is somewhat more specious, but not better founded. It has been asserted, that in the crime of murder it is absolutely necessary; that there is no other means of averting the danger threatened from that class of malefactors. This assertion is, however, extremely exaggerated: its groundlessness may be seen in the case of the most dangerous species of homicide. Assassination for lucre, a crime proceeding from a disposition which puts indiscriminately the life of every man into immediate jeopardy. Even these malefactors are not so dangerous nor so difficult to manage as madmen; because the former will commit homicide only at the time that there is something to be gained by it, and that it can be perpetrated with a probability of safety. The mischief to be apprehended from madmen is not narrowed by either of these circumstances. Yet it is never thought necessary that madmen should be put to death. They are not put to death: they are only kept in confinement; and that confinement is found effectually to answer the purpose.

In *fine*, I can see but one case in which it can be necessary, and that only occasionally: in the case alleged for this purpose by M. Beccaria; the case of rebellion or other offence against government of a rebellious tendency, when, by destroying the chief you may destroy the faction, where discontent has spread itself widely through a community, it may happen that imprisonment will not answer the purpose of safe custody. The keepers may be won over to the insurgent party, or if not won over, they may be overpowered. They may be won over by considerations of a conscientious nature, which is a danger almost peculiar to this case; or they may be won over by considerations of a lucrative nature, which danger is greater in this case than in any other, since party projects may be carried on by a common purse.

What, however, ought not to be lost sight of in the case of offences of a political nature is, that if by the punishment of death one dangerous enemy is exterminated, the consequence of it may be the making an opening for a more formidable successor. Look, said the executioner to an aged Irish man, shewing him the bleeding head of a man just executed for rebellion: "Look at the head of your son."

"My son (replied he) has more than one head." It would be well for the legislator before he appoints capital punishment, even in this case, to reflect on this instructive lesson.

The fourth reason is the strongest. The punishment of death is exemplary, preeminently exemplary: no other punishment makes so strong an impression. This assertion, as has been already noticed, is true with respect to the majority of mankind, it is not true with respect to the greatest criminals.

It appears however to me that the contemplation of perpetual imprisonment, accompanied with hard labor and occasional solitary confinement, would produce a deeper impression the minds of persons in whom it is more eminently desirable that that impression should be produced, than, even death itself. We have already observed that to them life does not offer the same attractions as it does to persons of innocent and industrious habits. Their very profession leads them continually to put their existence in jeopardy; and intemperance, which is almost natural to them inflames their brutal and uncalculating courage. All the circumstances that render death less formidable to them, render, laborious restraint proportionably more irksome. The more their habitual state of existence is independent, wandering, and hostile to steady and laborious industry, the more they will be terrified by a state of passive submission and of laborious confinement, a mode of life, in the highest degree repugnant to their natural inclinations.

Giving to each of these circumstances their due weight, the result appears to be that the prodigal use made by legislators of the punishment of death has been occasioned more by erroneous judgments [arising from the situation in which they are placed with respect to the other classes of the community] than from any blameable cause. Those who make laws belong to the highest classes of the community, among whom death is considered as a great evil, and an ignominious death as the greatest of evils. Let it be confined to that class, if it were practicable the effect aimed at might be produced; but it shews a total want of judgment and reflection to apply it to a degraded and wretched class of men, who do not set the same value upon life, to whom indigence and hard labor is more formidable than death, and the habitual infamy of whose lives renders them insensible to the infamy of the punishment.

If, in spite of these reasons, which appear to be conclusive, it be determined to preserve the punishment of death, in consideration of the effects it produces *in terrorum*, it ought to be confined to offenses which, in the highest degree, shock the public feeling — for murders, accompanied with circumstances of aggravation, and particularly when their effect may be the destruction of numbers ; and in these cases expedients by which it may be made to assume the most tragic appearance may be safely resorted to, in the greatest extent possible, without having recourse to complicated torments.

Collateral Evil Effects Of The Frequent Use Of The Punishment Of Death

The punishment of death, when applied to the punishment of offences in opposition to public opinion, far from preventing offenses tends to increase them by the hope of impunity. This proposition may appear paradoxical; but the paradox vanishes when we consider the different effects produced by the unpopularity of the punishment of death. In the first place it relaxes prosecution in criminal matters, and in the next place foments three vicious principles.

1. It makes perjury appear meritorious, by founding it on humanity;

2. It produces contempt for the laws, by rendering it notorious that they are not executed;

3. It renders convictions arbitrary and pardons necessary.

The relaxation of criminal procedure results from a series of transgressions on the part of the different public functionaries, whose concurrence is necessary to the execution of the laws: each one alters the part allotted to him, that he may weaken or break the legal chain by which he is bound, and substitute his own will for that of the legislator; but all these causes of uncertainty in criminal procedure are so many encouragements to malefactors.

Lectures on Witchcraft, Comprising A History of the Delusion In Salem in 1692, Charles W. Upham (1831)

D r. Turner, in his history of the Anglo Saxons says that they had laws against sorcerers and witches, but that they did not punish them with death. There was an English statute against witchcraft, in the reign of Henry VIII and another in that of Elizabeth. Up to this time, however, the legislation of parliament on the subject, was merciful and judicious — for it did not attach to the guilt of witchcraft the punishment of death, unless it had been used to destroy life ; that is, unless it had become murder.

On the demise of Elizabeth, James of Scotland ascended the throne. His pedantic and eccentric character is well known. He had an early and decided inclination towards abstruse and mysterious speculations. Before he had reached his twentieth year, he undertook to accomplish what only the most sanguine and profound theologians have ever dared to attempt. He expounded the *Book of Revelation*. When he was about twenty-five years of age, he published a work on *The Doctrine of Devils and Witchcraft*. Not long after he succeeded to the British crown. It may easily be imagined that the subject of demonology, soon became a fashionable and prevailing topic of conversation in the royal saloons and throughout the nation. It served as a medium through which obsequious courtiers could convey their flattery to the ears of their accomplished and learned sovereign.

His majesty's book was reprinted and extensively circulated. It was of course praised and recommended in all quarters. The parliament, actuated by a base desire to compliment the vain and superstitious king, enacted a new and much more severe statute against witchcraft, in the very first year of his reign. It was under this law that so many persons here and in England, were deprived of their lives. The blood of hundreds of their innocent fellow creatures was thus unrighteously shed! It was a fearful price which these servile lawgivers paid for the favor of their prince.

But this was not the only evil that was brought about by courtly deference to the prejudices of King James. It was under his direction that our present translation of the scriptures was made. To please his royal majesty, and to strengthen the arguments in his work on demonology, the word 'witch' was used to represent expressions in the original Hebrew, that conveyed an entirely different idea, and it was freely inserted in the headings of the chapters. A person having a 'familiar spirit,' was a favorite description of a witch in the king's book. The translators, forgetful of their high and solemn unction, endeavored to establish this definition by inserting it into their version. Accordingly, they introduced it in several places; in the eleventh verse of the eighteenth chapter of Deuteronomy, for instance: 'a consuiter with familiar spirits.' There is no word in the Hebrew which corresponds with 'familiar.' And this is the important, the essential word in the definition. It conveys the idea of alliance, stated connexion, confederacy, or compact, which is characteristic and distinctive of a witch. The expression in the original signifies 'a consulter with spirits' — especially as was the case with the ' Witch of Endor,' a consulter with departed spirits.

It was a shocking perversion of the word of God, for the purpose of flattering a frail and mortal sovereign! King James lived to see and acknowledge the error of his early opinions, and he would gladly have counteracted their bad effects; but it is easier to make laws and translations than it is to alter and amend them.

While the law of the land required the capital punishment of witches, no blame ought to be attached to judges and jurors for discharging their respective duties in carrying it into execution. It will not do for us to assert that they ought to have refused, let the consequences to themselves have been what they would, to sanction and give effect to such inhuman and unreasonable enactments. We cannot consistently take this ground, for there is nothing more certain than, that with their notions, our ancestors had at least as good reasons to advance in favor of punishing witchcraft with death, as we have for punishing any crime whatsoever in the same awful and summary manner.

We appeal, in defense of our capital punishments, to the text of Moses, 'Whoso sheddeth man's blood, by man shall his blood be shed.' The apologist of our fathers, for carrying into effect the law making witchcraft a capital offense, tells us in reply, in the first place, that this passage is not of the nature of a precept, but merely of an admonition; that it does not enjoin any particular method of proceeding, but simply describes the natural consequences of cruel and contentious conduct; and that it amounts only to this; that quarrelsome, violent and bloodthirsty persons will be apt to meet the same fate they bring upon others; that the duelist will be likely to fall in private combat; the ambitious conqueror to perish, and the warlike nation to be destroyed, on the field of battle. If this is not considered by us a sufficient and satisfactory answer, he advances to our own ground, points to the same text where we place our defense, and puts his finger on the following plain and authoritative precept: 'Thou shall not suffer a witch to live.' Indeed we must acknowledge that the capital punishment of witches is as strongly supported and fortified by the Scriptures of the Old

Testament, at least as they appear in our present version, as the capital punishment of any crime whatever.

If we adopt another line of argument, and say that it is necessary to punish some particular crimes with death, in order to maintain the security of society, or hold up an impressive warning to others, here also we find that our opponent has full as much to offer in defense of our fathers, as can be offered in our own defense. He describes, to us the tremendous and infernal power, which was universally believed by them to be possessed by a witch, a power which, as it was not derived from a natural source, could not easily be held in check by natural restraints; neither chains nor dungeons could bind it down, or confine it. You might load the witch with irons, you might bury her in the lowest cell of a feudal prison, and still it was believed that she could send forth her imps, or her spectre, to ravage the fields, and blight the meadows, and throw the elements into confusion, and torture the bodies, and craze the minds of any who might be the objects of her malice. [. . .] Can it be wondered at, that under such circumstances, the law, connecting capital punishment with the guilt of witchcraft, was resorted to, as the only means to protect society and warn others from entering into the dark, wicked and malignant compact?[7]

On Witchcraft, Harriet Martineau (1836)

This poor creature was wrought upon by threats, delusions, and (as she long afterwards protested) by the scourge, applied by Mr. Parris's own dignified hands, to confess she was in league with the devil. A confession — indisputable evidence as it appeared — was all that was wanted to decide the success of the experiment. Few doubted against such proof; and of those few, some concealed their skepticism, and kept as quiet as possible, and others, probably, secured their own safety by pretending to be bewitched, and thus aided the delusion. This sort of evidence abounded in proportion to the spread of the mischief; for the lives of those who confessed were spared. Fifty-five persons thus escaped death. In their case the motive to confession is clear; but it was long a mystery to us in instances where confession was the highway

---

7   It is not probable that even King James' Parliament would have been willing to go to the length of Selden in his *Table Talk,* who takes this ground in defense of the capital punishment of witches. "The law against witches does not prove there be any, but it punishes the malice of those people that use such means to take away men's lives. If one should profess that by turning his hat thrice and crying buz, he could take away a man's life, (though in truth he could do no such thing,) yet this were a just law made by the state, that whoever should turn his hat thrice, and cry buz, with an intention to take away a man's life, shall be put to death."

to the stake or the gibbet, as in England and Scotland. The effecting: anecdote told by Sir George Mackenzie, however, makes all plain. One of these confessors told him, "under secresie," that she had not confessed because she was guilty, but, being a poor creature who wrought for her meat, and being defamed for a witch, she knew she would starve; for no person thereafter would either give her meat or lodging, and that all men would beat her and hound dogs at her, and that therefore she desired to be out of the world. She had heard of a place where the wicked cease from troubling.

WITNESS TO AN EXECUTION
The Execution of Davy Crockett,
Lt. Col. José Enrique de la Peña (1836)

DAVID CROCKETT

Some seven men survived the general carnage and, under the protection of General Castrillón, they were brought before Santa Anna. Among them was one of great stature, well proportioned, with regular features, in whose face there was the imprint of adversity, but in whom one also noticed a degree of resignation and nobility that did him honor. He was the naturalist David Crockett, well known in North America for his unusual adventures, who had undertaken to explore the country and who, finding himself in Béjar at the very moment of surprise, had taken refuge in the Alamo, fearing that his status as a foreigner might not be respected. Santa Anna answered Castrillón's intervention in Crockett's behalf with a gesture of indignation and, addressing himself to the sappers, the troops closest to him, ordered his execution. The commanders and officers were outraged at this action and did not support the order, hoping that once the fury of the moment had blown over these men would be spared; but several officers who were around the president and who, perhaps, had not been present during the danger, became noteworthy by an infamous deed, surpassing the soldiers in cruelty. They thrust themselves forward, in order to flatter their commander, and with swords in hand, fell upon these unfortunate, defenseless men just as a tiger leaps upon his prey. Though tortured before they were killed, these unfortunates died without complaining and without humiliating themselves before their torturers.

On The Punishment Of Death: A Fragment, Percy Bysshe Shelley (1839)

The first law which it becomes a Reformer to propose and support, at the approach of a period of great political change, is the abolition of the punishment of death. It is sufficiently clear that revenge, retaliation, atonement, expiation, are rules and motives, so far from deserving a place in any enlightened system of political life, that they are the chief sources of a prodigious class of miseries in the domestic circles of society. It is clear that however the spirit of legislation may appear to frame institutions upon more philosophical maxims, it has hitherto, in those cases which are termed criminal, done little more than palliate the spirit, by gratifying a portion of it; and afforded a compromise between that which is bests--the inflicting of no evil upon a sensitive being, without a decisively beneficial result in which he should at least participates--and that which is worst; that he should be put to torture for the amusement of those whom he may have injured, or may seem to have injured. Omitting these remoter considerations, let us inquire what, DEATH is; that punishment which is applied as a measure of transgressions of indefinite shades of distinction, so soon as they shall have passed that degree and color of enormity, with which it is supposed no, inferior infliction is commensurate.

And first, whether death is good or evil, a punishment or a reward, or whether it be wholly indifferent, no man can take upon himself to assert. That that within us which thinks and feels, continues to think and feel after the dissolution of the body, has been the almost universal opinion of mankind, and the accurate philosophy of what I may be permitted to term the modern Academy, by showing the prodigious depth and extent of our ignorance respecting the causes and nature of sensation, renders probable the affirmative of a proposition, the negative of which it is so difficult to conceive, and the popular arguments against which, derived from what is called the atomic system, are proved to be applicable only to the relation which one object bears to another, as apprehended by the mind, and not to existence itself, or the nature of that essence which is the medium and receptacle of objects.

The popular system of religion suggests the idea that the mind, after death, will be painfully or pleasurably affected according to its determinations during life. However ridiculous and pernicious we must admit the vulgar accessories of this creed to be, there is a certain analogy, not wholly absurd, between the consequences resulting to an individual during life from the virtuous or vicious, prudent or imprudent, conduct of his external actions, to those consequences which are conjectured to ensue from the discipline and order of his internal thoughts, as affecting his condition in a future state. They omit, indeed, to calculate upon the accidents of disease, and temperament, and organization, and circumstance, together with the multitude of independent agencies which affect the opinions, the conduct, and the happiness of individuals, and produce determinations of the will, and modify the judgment, so as to produce effects the most opposite in natures considerably similar. These are those operations in the order of the whole of nature, tending, we are prone to believe, to some definite mighty end, to which the agencies of our peculiar nature are subordinate; nor is there any reason to suppose, that in a future state they should become suddenly exempt from that subordination. The philosopher is unable to determine whether our existence in a previous state has affected our present condition, and abstains from deciding whether our present condition will affect us in that which may be future. That, if we continue to exist, the manner of our existence will be such as no inferences nor conjectures, afforded by a consideration of our earthly experience, can elucidate, is sufficiently obvious. The opinion that the vital principle within us, in whatever mode it may continue to exist, must lose that consciousness of definite and individual being which now characterizes it, and become a unit in the vast sum of action and of thought which disposes and animates the universe, and is called God, seems to belong to that class of opinion which has been designated as indifferent.

To compel a person to know all that can be known by the dead concerning that which the living fear, hope, or forget; to plunge him into the pleasure or pain which there awaits him; to punish or reward him in a manner and in a degree incalculable and incomprehensible by us; to disrobe him at once from all that intertexture of good and evil with which Nature seems to have clothed every form of individual existence, is to inflict on him the doom of death.

A certain degree of pain and terror usually accompany the infliction of death.
A certain degree of pain and terror usually accompany the infliction of death. This degree is infinitely varied by the infinite variety in the temperament and opinions of the sufferers. As a measure of punishment, strictly so considered, and as an exhibition, which, by its known effects on the sensibility of the sufferer, is intended to intimidate the spectators from incurring a similar liability, it is singularly inadequate.

Firstly, persons of energetic character, in whom, as in men who suffer for political crimes, there is a large mixture of enterprise, and fortitude, and disinterestedness, and the elements, though misguided and disarranged, by which the strength and happiness of a nation might have been cemented, die in such a manner, as to make death appear not evil, but good. The death of what is called a traitor, that is, a person who, from whatever motive, would abolish the government of the day, is as often a triumphant exhibition of suffering virtue, as the warning of a culprit. The multitude, instead of departing with a panic-stricken approbation of the laws which exhibited such a spectacle, are inspired with pity, admiration and sympathy; and the most generous among them feel an emulation to be the authors of such flattering emotions, as they experience stirring in their bosoms. Impressed by what they see and feel, they make no distinctive between the motives which incited the criminals to the action for which they suffer, or the heroic courage with which they turned into good that which their judges awarded to them as evil or the purpose itself of those actions, though that purpose may happen to be eminently pernicious. The laws in this case lose their sympathy, which it ought to be their chief object to secure, and in a participation of which consists their chief strength in maintaining those sanctions by which the parts of the social union are bound together, so as to produce, as nearly as possible, the ends for which it is instituted.

Secondly—persons of energetic character, in communities not modeled with philosophical skill to turn all the energies which they contain to the purposes of common good, are prone also to fall into the temptation of undertaking, and are peculiarly fitted for despising the perils attendant upon consummating, the most enormous crimes. Murder, rapes, extensive schemes of plunder are the actions of persons belonging to this class; and death is the penalty of conviction. But the coarseness of organization, peculiar to men capable of committing acts wholly selfish, is usually found to be associated with a proportionate insensibility to fear or pain. Their sufferings communicate to those of the spectators, who may be liable to the commission of similar crimes a sense of the lightness of that event, when closely examined which, at a distance, as uneducated persons are accustomed to do, probably they regarded with horror. But a great majority of the spectators are so bound up in the interests and the habits of social union that no temptation would be sufficiently strong to induce them to a commission of the enormities to which this penalty is assigned.

The more powerful, and the richer among them,— and a numerous class of little tradesmen are richer and more powerful than those who are employed by them, and the employer, in general, bears this relation to the employed— regard their own wrongs as, in some degree, avenged, and their own rights secured by this punishment, inflicted as the penalty of whatever crime. In cases of murder or mutilation, this feeling is almost universal. In those, therefore, whom this exhibition does not awaken to the sympathy which extenuates crime and discredits the law which restrains it, it produces feelings more directly at war with the genuine purposes of political society. It excites those emotions which it is the chief object of civilization to extinguish forever, and in the extinction of which alone there can be any hope of better institutions than those under which men now misgovern one another. Men feel that their revenge is gratified, and that their security

> **It excites those emotions which it is the chief object of civilization to extinguish forever, and in the extinction of which alone there can be any hope of better institutions than those under which men now misgovern one another.**

is established by the extinction and the sufferings of beings, in most respects resembling themselves; and their daily occupations constraining them to a precise form in all their thoughts, they come to connect inseparably the idea of their own advantage with that of the death and torture of others. It is manifest that the object of sane polity is directly the reverse; and that laws founded upon reason, should accustom the gross vulgar to associate their ideas of security and of interest with the reformation, and the strict restraint, for that purpose alone, of those who might invade it.

The passion of revenge is originally nothing more than an habitual perception of the ideas of the sufferings of the person who inflicts an injury, as connected, as they are in a savage state, or in such portions of society as are yet undisciplined to civilization, with security that that injury will not be repeated in future. This feeling, engrafted upon superstition and confirmed by habit, at last loses sight of the only object for which it may be supposed to have been implanted, and becomes a passion and a duty to be pursued and fulfilled, even to the destruction of those ends to which it originally tended. The other passions, both good and evil. Avarice, Remorse, Love, Patriotism, present a similar appearance; and to this principle of the mind over-shooting the mark at which it aims, we owe all that is eminently base or excellent in human nature; in providing for the nutriment or the extinction of which, consists the true art of the legislator.

Nothing is more clear than that the infliction of punishment in general, in a degree which the reformation and the restraint of those who transgress the laws does not render indispensable, and none more than death, confirms all the inhuman and unsocial impulses of men. It is almost a proverbial remark, that those nations in which the penal code has been particularly mild, have been distinguished from all others by the rarity of crime. But the example is to be admitted to be equivocal. A more decisive argument is afforded by a consideration of the universal connexion of ferocity of manners, and a contempt of social ties, with the contempt of human life. Governments which derive their institutions from the existence of circumstances of barbarism and violence, with some rare exceptions perhaps, are bloody in proportion as they are despotic, and form the manners of their subjects to a sympathy with their own spirit.

The spectators who feel no abhorrence at a public execution, but rather a self-applauding superiority, and a sense of gratified indignation, are surely excited to the most inauspicious emotions. The first reflection of such a one is the sense of his own internal and actual worth, as preferable to that of the victim, whom circumstances have led to destruction. The meanest wretch is impressed with a sense of his own comparative merit. He is one of those on whom the tower of Siloam fell not—he is such a one as Jesus Christ found not in all Samaria, who, in his own soul, throws the first stone at the woman taken in adultery. The popular religion of the country takes its designation from that illustrious person whose beautiful sentiment I have quoted. Anyone who has stript from the doctrines of this person the veil of familiarity, will perceive how adverse their spirit is to feelings of this nature.

[Note: The savage and the illiterate are but faintly aware of the distinction between the future and the past; they make actions belonging to periods so distinct, the subjects of similar feelings; they live only in the present, or in the past, as it is present. It is in this that the philosopher excels one of the many; it is this which distinguishes the doctrine of philosophic necessity from fatalism; and that determination of the will, by which it is the active source of future events, from that liberty or indifference, to which the abstract liability of irremediable actions is attached, according to the notions of the vulgar.

This is the source of the erroneous excesses of Remorse and Revenge; the one extending itself over the future, and the other over the past; provinces in which their suggestions can only be the sources of evil. The purpose of a resolution to act more wisely and virtuously in future, and the sense of a necessity of caution in repressing an enemy, are the sources from which the enormous superstitions implied in the words cited have arisen. P.B.S.]

Sonnets Upon The Punishment Of Death, William Wordsworth (1839)

I. THIS Spot--at once unfolding sight so fair
    Of sea and land, with yon grey towers that still
    Rise up as if to lord it over air--
    Might soothe in human breasts the sense of ill,
    Or charm it out of memory; yea, might fill
    The heart with joy and gratitude to God
    For all his bounties upon man bestowed:
    Why bears it then the name of "Weeping Hill?"
    Thousands, as toward yon old Lancastrian Towers,
    A prison's crown, along this way they past
    For lingering durance or quick death with shame,
    From this bare eminence thereon have cast
    Their first look--blinded as tears fell in showers
    Shed on their chains; and hence that doleful name.

II TENDERLY do we feel by Nature's law
    For worst offenders: though the heart will heave
    With indignation, deeply moved we grieve,
    In after thought, for Him who stood in awe
    Neither of God nor man, and only saw,
    Lost wretch, a horrible device enthroned
    On proud temptations, till the victim groaned
    Under the steel his hand had dared to draw.
    But oh, restrain compassion, if its course,
    As oft befalls, prevent or turn aside
    Judgments and aims and acts whose higher source
    Is sympathy with the unforewarned, who died
    Blameless—with them that shuddered o'er his grave,
    And all who from the law firm safety crave.

III   THE Roman Consul doomed his sons to die
Who had betrayed their country. The stern word
Afforded (may it through all time afford)
A theme for praise and admiration high.
Upon the surface of humanity
He rested not; its depths his mind explored;
He felt; but his parental bosom's lord
Was Duty,—Duty calmed his agony.
And some, we know, when they by wilful act
A single human life have wrongly taken,
Pass sentence on themselves, confess the fact,
And, to atone for it, with soul unshaken
Kneel at the feet of Justice, and, for faith
Broken with all mankind, solicit death.

IV   IS 'Death,' when evil against good has fought
With such fell mastery that a man may dare
By deeds the blackest purpose to lay bare?
Is Death, for one to that condition brought,
For him, or any one, the thing that ought
To be 'most' dreaded? Lawgivers, beware,
Lest, capital pains remitting till ye spare
The murderer, ye, by sanction to that thought
Seemingly given, debase the general mind;
Tempt the vague will tried standards to disown,
Nor only palpable restraints unbind,
But upon Honour's head disturb the crown,
Whose absolute rule permits not to withstand
In the weak love of life his least command.

V   NOT to the object specially designed,
Howe'er momentous in itself it be,
Good to promote or curb depravity,
Is the wise Legislator's view confined.
His Spirit, when most severe, is oft most kind;
As all Authority in earth depends
On Love and Fear, their several powers he blends,
Copying with awe the one Paternal mind.
Uncaught by processes in show humane,
He feels how far the act would derogate
From even the humblest functions of the State;
If she, self-shorn of Majesty, ordain
That never more shall hang upon her breath
The last alternative of Life or Death.

VI   YE brood of conscience—Spectres! that frequent
         The bad Man's restless walk, and haunt his bed--
         Fiends in your aspect, yet beneficent
         In act, as hovering Angels when they spread
         Their wings to guard the unconscious Innocent--
         Slow be the Statutes of the land to share
         A laxity that could not but impair
         'Your' power to punish crime, and so prevent.
         And ye, Beliefs! coiled serpent-like about
         The adage on all tongues, "Murder will out,"
         How shall your ancient warnings work for good
         In the full might they hitherto have shown,
         If for deliberate shedder of man's blood
         Survive not Judgment that requires his own?

VII   BEFORE the world had past her time of youth
         While polity and discipline were weak,
         The precept eye for eye, and tooth for tooth,
         Came forth—a light, though but as of daybreak,
         Strong as could then be borne. A Master meek
         Proscribed the spirit fostered by that rule,
         Patience 'his' law, long-suffering 'his' school,
         And love the end, which all through peace must seek.
         But lamentably do they err who strain
         His mandates, given rash impulse to control
         And keep vindictive thirstings from the soul,
         So far that, if consistent in their scheme,
         They must forbid the State to inflict a pain,
         Making of social order a mere dream.

VIII   FIT retribution, by the moral code
         Determined, lies beyond the State's embrace,
         Yet, as she may, for each peculiar case
         She plants well-measured terrors in the road
         Of wrongful acts. Downward it is and broad,
         And, the main fear once doomed to banishment,
         Far oftener then, bad ushering worse event,
         Blood would be spilt that in his dark abode
         Crime might lie better hid. And, should the change
         Take from the horror due to a foul deed,
         Pursuit and evidence so far must fail,
         And, guilt escaping, passion then might plead
         In angry spirits for her old free range,
         And the "wild justice of revenge" prevail.

IX   THOUGH to give timely warning and deter
       Is one great aim of penalty, extend
       Thy mental vision further and ascend
       Far higher, else full surely shalt thou err.
       What is a State? The wise behold in her
       A creature born of time, that keeps one eye
       Fixed on the statutes of Eternity,
       To which her judgments reverently defer.
       Speaking through Law's dispassionate voice the State
       Endues her conscience with external life
       And being, to preclude or quell the strife
       Of individual will, to elevate
       The grovelling mind, the erring to recall,
       And fortify the moral sense of all.

X   OUR bodily life, some plead, that life the shrine
       Of an immortal spirit, is a gift
       So sacred, so informed with light divine,
       That no tribunal, though most wise to sift
       Deed and intent, should turn the Being adrift
       Into that world where penitential tear
       May not avail, nor prayer have for God's ear
       A voice--that world whose veil no hand can lift
       For earthly sight. "Eternity and Time,"
       'They' urge, "have interwoven claims and rights
       Not to be jeopardised through foulest crime:
       The sentence rule by mercy's heaven-born lights."
       Even so; but measuring not by finite sense
       Infinite Power, perfect Intelligence.

XI   AH, think how one compelled for life to abide
       Locked in a dungeon needs must eat the heart
       Out of his own humanity, and part
       With every hope that mutual cares provide;
       And, should a less unnatural doom confide
       In life-long exile on a savage coast,
       Soon the relapsing penitent may boast
       Of yet more heinous guilt, with fiercer pride.
       Hence thoughtful Mercy, Mercy sage and pure,
       Sanctions the forfeiture that Law demands,
       Leaving the final issue in 'His' hands
       Whose goodness knows no change, whose love is sure,
       Who sees, foresees; who cannot judge amiss,
       And wafts at will the contrite soul to bliss.

XII   SEE the Condemned alone within his cell
        And prostrate at some moment when remorse
        Stings to the quick, and, with resistless force,
        Assaults the pride she strove in vain to quell.
        Then mark him, him who could so long rebel,
        The crime confessed, a kneeling Penitent
        Before the Altar, where the Sacrament
        Softens his heart, till from his eyes outwell
        Tears of salvation. Welcome death! while Heaven
        Does in this change exceedingly rejoice;
        While yet the solemn heed the State hath given
        Helps him to meet the last Tribunal's voice
        In faith, which fresh offences, were he cast
        On old temptations, might for ever blast.

XIII   CONCLUSION
        YES, though He well may tremble at the sound
        Of his own voice, who from the judgment-seat
        Sends the pale Convict to his last retreat
        In death; though Listeners shudder all around,
        They know the dread requital's source profound;
        Nor is, they feel, its wisdom obsolete--
        (Would that it were!) the sacrifice unmeet
        For Christian Faith. But hopeful signs abound;
        The social rights of man breathe purer air,
        Religion deepens her preventive care;
        Then, moved by needless fear of past abuse,
        Strike not from Law's firm hand that awful rod,
        But leave it thence to drop for lack of use:
        Oh, speed the blessed hour, Almighty God!

XIV   APOLOGY
        THE formal World relaxes her cold chain
        For One who speaks in numbers; ampler scope
        His utterance finds; and, conscious of the gain,
        Imagination works with bolder hope
        The cause of grateful reason to sustain;
        And, serving Truth, the heart more strongly beats
        Against all barriers which his labour meets
        In lofty place, or humble Life's domain.
        Enough;--before us lay a painful road,
        And guidance have I sought in duteous love
        From Wisdom's heavenly Father. Hence hath flowed
        Patience, with trust that, whatsoe'er the way
        Each takes in this high matter, all may move
        Cheered with the prospect of a brighter day.

William Wordsworth, His Life, Works, And Influence
George McLean Harper (1916)

In 1839 and 1840 [Wordsworth] composed a series of fourteen sonnets (fifteen if we include the one addressed to Americans) on the singular subject of capital punishment. Parliament had recently reduced the list of offences punishable with death, which had formerly included a large number of crimes for which a few weeks' imprisonment is now the utmost penalty. Some members of the House of Commons favored a further reduction, so that murder and treason should be the only capital offenses. Wordsworth, as is usual with persons of a theoretical and highly dogmatic character, was accustomed to judge all proposed changes by what he thought would happen in consequence of the same tendency being carried to its logical extreme.

He was utterly un-English in his inability to allow for the modifications which compromise and vicissitude cause in human affairs. His sonnets against the abolition of capital punishment were a clog upon a course of sound and greatly needed legislation. They operated, if they had any practical result, against specific reforms which he himself probably would have approved, had not his vision of ultimate consequences excited his fears. What he dreaded was that before long the death penalty for murder might be changed to imprisonment, and at length all the terrors of the law mitigated until the distinction between right and wrong became obscured. His old friend Basil Montagu was one of the most persevering advocates of the reform, which was in part effected. The sonnets do more honor to Wordsworth's courage than to his political sense. His argumentation is of a very high order, and it would be unjust to charge him with inhumanity.

The sonnets do more honor to Wordsworth's courage than to his political sense

As to the poetical quality of the work, I think it may be said truly that more of it has never been displayed on a subject so incapable of rewarding its exercise. The sonnets serve, moreover, to show us more startlingly than any other of his writings, what a large place in Wordsworth's outlook was now held by belief in the immortality of the soul. What does it matter, he seems to say, whether life be long or short, happily or painfully ended, if the soul is fit for eternity? To minds like his, reform, when insisted upon with much eagerness, appears a dangerous concession to materialism. Why seek happiness and equal justice in this world, when the only important life is yet to come ?

The fourteen sonnets were originally printed in the December number of *The Quarterly Review*, 1841, in an essay on "The Sonnets of William Wordsworth," by Sir Henry Taylor. The remaining one, " Men of the Western World," was occasioned by reports of lynching in America, which seemed to confirm Wordsworth's view that relaxation of the law, through the working of sentimentality or of democratic ideas, tended to bring about a terrible anarchic reaction.

WITNESS TO AN EXECUTION
Going To See A Man Hanged,
William Makepeace Thackeray (1840)

X-- , who had voted with Mr. Ewart for the abolition of the punishment of death, was anxious to see the effect on the public mind of an execution, and asked me to accompany him to see Courvoisier killed. We had not the advantage of a sheriffs order, like the "six hundred noblemen and gentlemen" who were admitted within the walls of the prison; but determined to mingle with the crowd at the foot of the scaffold, and take up our positions at a very early hour.

As I was to rise at three in the morning, I went to bed at ten, thinking that five hours' sleep would be amply sufficient to brace me against the fatigues of the coming day. But, as might have been expected, the event of the morrow was perpetually before my eyes through the night, and kept them wide open. I heard all the clocks in the neighborhood chime the hours in succession; a dog from some court hard by kept up a pitiful howling; at one o'clock, a cock set up a feeble melancholy crowing; shortly after two the daylight came peeping grey through the window-shutters; and by the time that X– arrived, in fulfilment of his promise, I had been asleep about half-an-hour. He, more wise, had not gone to rest at all, but had remained up all night at the Club along with Dash and two or three more. Dash is one of the most eminent wits in London, and had kept the company merry all night with appropriate jokes about the coming event. It is curious that a murder is a great inspirer of jokes. We all like to laugh and have our fling about it; there is a certain grim pleasure in the circumstance — a perpetual jingling antithesis between life and death, that is sure of its effect.

In mansion or garret, on down or straw, surrounded by weeping friends and solemn oily doctors, or tossing unheeded upon scanty hospital beds, there were many people in this great city to whom that Sunday night was to be the last of any that they should pass on earth here. In the course of half-a-dozen dark wakeful hours, one had leisure to think of these (and a little, too, of that certain supreme night, that shall come at one time or other, when he who writes shall be stretched upon the last bed, prostrate in the last struggle, taking the last look of dear faces that have cheered us here, and lingering – one moment more – ere we part for the tremendous journey); but, chiefly, I could not help thinking, as each clock sounded, what is he doing now— has he heard it in his little room in Newgate yonder – Eleven o'clock. He has been writing until now, can hold out no longer, and is very weary. "Wake me at four," says he, "for I have still much to put down." From eleven to twelve the gaoler hears how he is grinding his teeth in his sleep. At twelve he is up in his bed and asks, "Is it the time?" He has plenty more time yet for sleep; and he sleeps, and the bell goes on tolling. Seven hours more – five hours more. Many a carriage is clattering through the streets, bringing ladies away from evening parties; many bachelors are reeling home after a jolly night; Covent Garden is alive; and the light coming through the cell-window turns the gaoler's candle pale. Four hours more! "Courvoisier," says the gaoler, shaking him, "it's four o'clock now, and I've woke you as you told me; but there's no call for you to get up yet." The poor wretch leaves his bed, however, and makes his last toilet; and then falls to writing, to tell the world how he did the crime for which he has suffered. This time he will tell the truth and the whole truth.

They bring him his breakfast "from the coffee-shop opposite -- tea, coffee, and thin bread and butter." He will take nothing, however, but goes on writing. He has to write to his mother — the pious mother far away in his own country — who reared him and loved him; and even now has sent him her forgiveness and her blessing. He finishes his memorials and letters, and makes his will, disposing of his little miserable property of books and tracts that pious people have furnished him with. "*Ce 6 Juillet, 1840. Francois Benjamin Courvoisier vous donne ceci, mon ami, pour souvenir.*" He has a token for his dear friend the gaoler; another for his dear friend the under-sheriff. As the day of the convict's death draws nigh, it is painful to see how he fastens upon everybody who approaches him, how pitifully he clings to them and loves them.

While these things are going on within the prison (with which we are made accurately acquainted by the copious chronicles of such events which are published subsequently), X—'s carriage has driven up to the door of my lodgings, and we have partaken of an elegant *dejeuner* that has been prepared for the occasion. A cup of coffee at half-past three in the morning is uncommonly pleasant; and X— enlivens us with the repetition of the jokes that Dash has just been making. Admirable, certainly — they must have had a merry night of it, that's clear; and we stoutly debate whether, when one has to get up so early in the morning, it is best to have an hour or two of sleep, or wait and go to bed afterwards at the end of the day's work. That fowl is extraordinarily tough -- the wing, even, is as hard as a board; a slight disappointment, for there is nothing else for breakfast. "Will any gentleman have some sherry and soda-water before he sets out? It clears the brains famously." Thus primed, the party sets out. The coachman has dropped asleep on the box, and wakes up wildly as the hall-door opens. It is just four o'clock. About this very time they are waking up poor — pshaw! Who is for a cigar? X— does not smoke himself; but vows and protests, in the kindest way in the world, that he does not care in the least for the new drab-silk linings in his carriage. Z— , who smokes, mounts, however, the box.

"Drive to Snow Hill." says the owner of the chariot. The policemen, who are the only people in the street, and are standing by, look knowing — they know what it means well enough.

How cool and clean the streets look, as the carriage startles the echoes that have been asleep in the corners all night. Somebody has been sweeping the pavements clean in the night-time surely; they would not soil a lady's white satin shoes, they are so dry and neat. There is not a cloud or a breath in the air, except Z—'s cigar, which whiffs off, and soars straight upwards in volumes of white pure smoke. The trees in the squares look bright and green – as bright as leaves in the country in June. We who keep late hours don't know the beauty of London air and verdure; in the early morning they are delightful — the most fresh and lively companions possible. But they cannot bear the crowd and the bustle of mid-day. You don't know them then — they are no longer the same things. We have come to Gray's Inn; there is actually dew upon the grass in the gardens; and the windows of the stout old red houses are all in a flame.

As we enter Holborn the town grows more animated; and there are already twice as many people in the streets as you see at mid-day in a German *Residenz* or an English provincial town. The gin shop keepers have many of them taken their shutters down, and many persons are issuing from them pipe in hand. Down they go along the broad bright street, their blue shadows marching after them; for they are all bound the same way, and are bent like us upon seeing the hanging.

It is twenty minutes past four as we pass St. Sepulchre's: by this time many hundred people are in the street, and many more are coming up Snow Hill. Before us lies Newgate Prison; but something a great deal more awful to look at, which seizes the eye at once, and makes the heart beat, is — —

There it stands black and ready, jutting out from a little door in the prison. As you see it, you feel a kind of dumb electric shock, which causes one to start a little, and give a sort of gasp for breath. The shock is over in a second; and presently you examine the object before you with a certain feeling of complacent curiosity. At least, such was the effect that the gallows produced upon the writer, who is trying to set down all his feelings as they occurred, and not to exaggerate them at all.

After the gallows-shock had subsided, we went down into the crowd, which was very numerous, but not dense as yet. It was evident that the day's business had not begun. People sauntered up, and formed groups, and talked; the newcomers asking those who seemed habitués of the place about former executions; and did the victim hang with his face towards the clock or towards Ludgate Hill? And had he the rope round his neck when he came on the scaffold, or was it put on by Jack Ketch afterwards — and had Lord W— taken a window, and which was he -- I may mention the noble Marquis's name, as he was not at the exhibition. A pseudo W— was pointed out in an opposite window, towards whom all the people in our neighborhood looked eagerly, and with great respect too.

The mob seemed to have no sort of ill-will against him, but sympathy and admiration. This noble lord's personal courage and strength have won the plebs over to him. Perhaps his exploits against policemen have occasioned some of this popularity; for the mob hate them, as children the schoolmaster.

Throughout the whole four hours, however, the mob was extraordinarily gentle and good-humored. At first we had leisure to talk to the people about us; and I recommend X—'s brother senators of both sides of the House to see more of this same people and to appreciate them better. Honourable Members are battling and struggling in the House; shouting, yelling, crowing, hear-hearing, pooh-poohing, making speeches of three columns, and gaining "great Conservative triumphs," or "signal successes of the Reform cause," as the case may be. Three hundred and ten gentlemen of good fortune, and able for the most part to quote Horace, declare solemnly that unless Sir Robert comes in, the nation is ruined. Three hundred and fifteen on the other side swear by their great gods that the safety of the empire depends upon Lord John; and to this end they quote Horace too. I declare that I have never been in a great London crowd without thinking of what they call the two "great" parties in England with wonder. For which of the two great leaders do these people care, I pray you? When Lord Stanley withdrew his Irish Bill the other night, were they in transports of joy, like worthy persons who read the *Globe* and the *Chronicle*? Or when he beat the Ministers, were they wild with delight, like honest gentlemen who read the *Post* and the *Times*? Ask yonder ragged fellow, who has evidently frequented debating-clubs, and speaks with good sense and shrewd good-nature. He cares no more for Lord John than he does for Sir Robert; and, with due respect be it said, would mind very little if both of them were ushered out by Mr. Ketch, and took their places under yonder black beam. What are the two great parties to him, and those like him? Sheer wind, hollow humbug, absurd clap-traps; a silly mummery of dividing and debating, which does not in the least, however it may turn, affect his condition. It has been so ever since the happy days when Whigs and Tories began; and a pretty pastime no doubt it is for both. August parties, great balances of British freedom: are not the two sides quite as active, and eager, and loud, as at their very birth, and ready to fight for place as stoutly as ever they fought before – But lo! In the meantime, whilst you are jangling and brawling over the accounts, *Populus*, whose estate you have administered while he was an infant, and could not take care of himself – *Populus*, has been growing and growing, till he is every bit as wise as his guardians.

Talk to our ragged friend. He is not so polished, perhaps, as a member of the "Oxford and Cambridge Club;" he has not been to Eton; and never read Horace in his life; but he can think just as soundly as the, best of you; he can speak quite as strongly in his own rough way; he has been reading all sorts of books of late years, and gathered together no little information. He is as good a man as the common run of us; and there are ten million more men in the country, as good as he – ten million, for whom we, in our infinite superiority, are acting as guardians, and to whom, in our bounty, we give – exactly nothing. Put yourself in their position, worthy sir. You and a hundred others find yourselves in some lone place, where you set up a government. You take a chief, as is natural; he is the cheapest order-keeper in the world. You establish half-a-dozen worthies, whose families you say shall have the privilege to legislate for you for ever; half-a-dozen more, who shall be appointed by a choice of thirty of the rest: and the other sixty, who shall have no choice, vote, place, or privilege at all. Honorable sir, suppose that you are one of the last sixty: how will you feel, you who have intelligence, passions, honest pride, as well as your neighbor; how will you feel towards your equals, in whose hands lie all the power and all the property of the community – Would you love and honor them, tamely acquiesce in their superiority, see their privileges, and go yourself disregarded without a pang? You are not a man if you would. I am not talking of right or wrong, or debating questions of government. But ask my friend there, with the ragged elbows and no shirt, what he thinks – You have your party, Conservative or Whig, as it may be. You believe that an aristocracy is an institution necessary, beautiful, and virtuous. You are a gentleman, in other words, and stick by your party.

And our friend with the elbows (the crowd is thickening hugely all this time) sticks by his. Talk to him of Whig or Tory, he grins at them: of virtual representation, pish! He is a democrat, and will stand by his friends, as you by yours; and they are twenty millions, his friends, of whom a vast minority now, a majority a few years hence, will be as good as you. In the meantime we shall continue electing, and debating, and dividing, and having every day new triumphs for the glorious cause of Conservatism, or the glorious cause of Reform, until --

❖ ❖ ❖

What is the meaning of this unconscionable republican tirade -- *apropos* of a hanging -- Such feelings, I think, must come across any man in a vast multitude like this. What good sense and intelligence have most of the people by whom you are surrounded; how much sound humor does one hear bandied about from one to another! A great number of coarse phrases are used, that would make ladies in drawing-rooms blush; but the morals of the men are good and hearty. A ragamuffin in the crowd (a powdery baker in a white sheep's-wool cap) uses some indecent expression to a woman near: there is an instant cry of shame, which silences the man, and a dozen people are ready to give the woman protection.

The crowd has grown very dense by this time, it is about six o'clock, and there is great heaving, and pushing, and swaying to and fro; but round the women the men have formed a circle, and keep them as much as possible out of the rush and trample. In one of the houses, near us, a gallery has been formed on the roof. Seats were here let, and a number of persons of various degrees were occupying them. Several tipsy dissolute-looking young men, of the Dick Swiveller cast, were in this gallery. One was lolling over the sunshiny tiles, with a fierce sodden face, out of which came a pipe, and which was shaded by long matted hair, and a hat cocked very much on one side. This gentleman was one of a party which had evidently not been to bed on Sunday night, but had passed it in some of those delectable night-houses in the neighborhood of Covent Garden.

The debauch was not over yet, and the women of the party were giggling, drinking, and romping, as is the wont of these delicate creatures; sprawling here and there, and falling upon the knees of one or other of the males. Their scarves were off their shoulders, and you saw the sun shining down upon the bare white flesh, and the shoulder-points glittering like burning-glasses. The people about us were very indignant at some of the proceedings of this debauched crew, and at last raised up such a yell as frightened them into shame, and they were more orderly for the remainder of the day. The windows of the shops opposite began to fill apace, and our before-mentioned friend with ragged elbows pointed out a celebrated fashionable character who occupied one of them; and, to our surprise, knew as much about him as the Court Journal or the Morning Post. Presently he entertained us with a long and pretty accurate account of the history of Lady – , and indulged in a judicious criticism upon her last work. I have met with many a country gentleman who had not read half as many books as this honest fellow, this shrewd *proletaire* in a black shirt. The people about him took up and carried on the conversation very knowingly, and were very little behind him in point of information. It was just as good a company as one meets on common occasions. I was in a genteel crowd in one of the galleries at the Queen's coronation; indeed, in point of intelligence, the democrats were quite equal to the aristocrats. How many more such groups were there in this immense multitude of nearly forty thousand, as some say – How many more such throughout the country? I never yet, as I said before, have been in an English mob without the same feeling for the persons who composed it, and without wonder at the vigorous orderly good sense and intelligence of the people.

The character of the crowd was as yet, however, quite festive. Jokes bandying about here and there, and jolly laughs breaking out. Some men were endeavouring to climb up a leaden pipe on one of the houses. The landlord came out, and endeavoured with might and main to pull them down. Many thousand eyes turned upon this contest immediately. All sorts of voices issued from the crowd, and uttered choice expressions of slang. When one of the men was pulled down by the leg, the waves of this black mob-ocean laughed innumerably; when one fellow slipped away, scrambled up the pipe, and made good his lodgment on the shelf, we were all made happy, and encouraged him by loud shouts of admiration. What is there so particularly delightful in the spectacle of a man clambering up a gas pipe? Why were we kept for a quarter of an hour in deep interest gazing upon this remarkable scene -- Indeed it is hard to say: a man does not know what a fool he is until he tries; or, at least, what mean follies will amuse him. The other day I went to Astley's and saw a clown come in with a fool's-cap and pinafore, and six small boys who represented his schoolfellows. To them enters schoolmaster; horses clown, and flogs him hugely on the back part of his pinafore. I never read anything in Swift, Boz, Rabelais, Fielding, Paul de Kock, which delighted me so much as this sight, and caused me to laugh so profoundly. And why? What is there so ridiculous in the sight of one miserably rouged man beating another on the breech? Tell us where the fun lies in this and the before-mentioned episode of the gas pipe? Vast, indeed, are the capacities and ingenuities of the human soul that can find, in incidents so wonderfully small, means of contemplation and amusement. [. . .]

But yonder, glittering through the crowd in Newgate Streets—the Sheriff's carriages are slowly making their way. We have been here three hours! Is it possible that they can have passed so soon? Close to the barriers where we are, the mob has become so dense that it is with difficulty a man can keep his feet. Each man, however, is very careful in protecting the women, and all are full of jokes and good-humor. The windows of the shops opposite are now pretty nearly filled by the persons who hired them. Many young dandies are there with moustaches and cigars; some quiet fat family parties, of simple honest tradesmen and their wives, as we fancy, who are looking on with the greatest imaginable calmness, and sipping their tea. Yonder is the sham Lord W − , who is flinging various articles among the crowd; one of his companions, a tall, burly man, with large moustaches, has provided himself with a squirt, and is aspersing the mob with brandy-and-water. Honest gentleman! High-bred aristocrat! Genuine lover of humor and wit! I would walk some miles to see thee on the treadmill, thee and thy Mohawk crew!

We tried to get up a hiss against these ruffians, but only had a trifling success; the crowd did not seem to think their offense very heinous; and our friend, the philosopher in the ragged elbows, who had remained near us all the time, was not inspired with any such savage disgust at the proceedings of certain notorious young gentlemen, as I must confess fills my own particular bosom. He only said, "So-and-so is a lord, and they'll let him off," and then discoursed about Lord Ferrers being hanged. The philosopher knew the history pretty well, and so did most of the little knot of persons about him, and it must be a gratifying thing for young gentlemen to find that their actions are made the subject of this kind of conversation.

Scarcely a word had been said about Courvoisier all this time. We were all, as far as I could judge, in just such a frame of mind as men are in when they are squeezing at the pit-door of a play, or pushing for a review or a Lord Mayor's show. We asked most of the men who were near us, whether they had seen many executions -- most of them had, the philosopher especially; whether the sight of them did any good -- "For the matter of that, no; people did not care about them at all; nobody ever thought of it after a bit." A countryman, who had left his drove in Smithfield, said the same thing; he had seen a man hanged at York, and spoke of the ceremony with perfect good sense, and in a quiet sagacious way.

J. S −, the famous wit, now dead, had, I recollect, a good story upon the subject of executing, and of the terror which the punishment inspires. After Thistlewood and his companions were hanged, their heads were taken off, according to the sentence, and the executioner, as he severed each, held it up to the crowd, in the proper orthodox way, saying, "Here is the head of a traitor!" At the sight of the first ghastly head the people were struck with terror, and a general expression of disgust and fear broke from them. The second head was looked at also with much interest, but the excitement regarding the third head diminished. When the executioner had come to the last of the heads, he lifted it up, but, by some clumsiness, allowed it to drop. At this the crowd yelled out, "Ah, Butter-fingers!" The excitement had passed entirely away. The punishment had grown to be a joke − butter-fingers was the word — a pretty commentary, indeed, upon the august nature of public executions, and the awful majesty of the law.

It was past seven now; the quarters rang and passed away; the crowd began to grow very eager and more quiet, and we turned back every now and then and looked at St. Sepulchre's clock. Half-an-hour, twenty-five minutes. What is he doing now? He has his irons off by this time. A quarter: he's in the press-room now, no doubt. Now at last we had come to think about the man we were going to see hanged. How slowly the clock crept over the last quarter! Those who were able to turn round and see (for the crowd was now extraordinarily dense) chronicled the time, eight minutes, five minutes; at last -- ding, dong, dong, dong! -- the bell is tolling the chimes of eight.

❖ ❖ ❖

Between the writing of this line and the last, the pen has been put down, as the reader may suppose, and the person who is addressing him has gone through a pause of no very pleasant thoughts and recollections. The whole of the sickening, ghastly, wicked scene passes before the eyes again; and, indeed, it is an awful one to see, and very hard and painful to describe.

As the clock began to strike, an immense sway and movement swept over the whole of that vast dense crowd. They were all uncovered directly, and a great murmur arose, more awful, bizarre, and indescribable than any sound I had ever before heard. Women and children began to shriek horribly.

I don't know whether it was the bell I heard; but a dreadful quick feverish kind of jangling noise mingled with the noise of the people, and lasted for about two minutes. The scaffold stood before us, tenantless and black; the black chain was hanging down ready from the beam. Nobody came. "He has been respited," some one said; another said, "He has killed himself in prison."

Just then, from under the black prison-door, a pale quiet head peered out. It was shockingly bright and distinct; it rose up directly, and a man in black appeared on the scaffold, and was silently followed by about four more dark figures. The first was a tall grave man: we all knew who the second man was. "That's he— that's he!" you heard the people say, as the devoted man came up.

I have seen a cast of the head since, but, indeed, should never have known it. Courvoisier bore his punishment like a man, and walked very firmly. He was dressed in a new black suit, as it seemed: his shirt was open. His arms were tied in front of him. He opened his hands in a helpless kind of way, and clasped them once or twice together. He turned his head here and there, and looked about him for an instant with a wild imploring look. His mouth was contracted into a sort of pitiful smile. He went and placed himself at once under the beam, with his face towards St. Sepulchre's. The tall grave man in black twisted him round swiftly in the other direction, and, drawing from his pocket a night-cap, pulled it tight over the patient's head and face. I am not ashamed to say that I could look no more, but shut my eyes as the last dreadful act was going on which sent this wretched guilty soul into the presence of God.

If a public execution is beneficial—and beneficial it is, no doubt, or else the wise laws would not encourage forty thousand people to witness it—the next useful thing must be a full description of such a ceremony, and all its entourages, and to this end the above pages are offered to the reader. How does an individual man feel under it—In what way does he observe it—how does he view all the phenomena connected with it—What induces him, in the first instance, to go and see it—and how is he moved by it afterwards? The writer has discarded the magazine "we" altogether, and spoken face to face with the reader, recording every one of the impressions felt by him as honestly as he could.

I must confess, then (for "I" is the shortest word, and the best in this case), that the sight has left on my mind an extraordinary feeling of terror and shame. It seems to me that I have been abetting an act of frightful wickedness and violence, performed by a set of men against one of their fellows; and I pray God that it may soon be out of the power of any man in England to witness such a hideous and degrading sight. Forty thousand persons (say the Sheriffs), of all ranks and degrees—mechanics, gentlemen, pickpockets, members of both Houses of Parliament, street-walkers, newspaper-writers, gather together before Newgate at a very early hour; the most part of them give up their natural quiet night's rest, in order to partake of this hideous debauchery, which is more exciting than sleep, or than wine, or the last new ballet, or any other amusement they can have. Pickpocket and Peer each is tickled by the sight alike, and has that hidden lust after blood which influences our race.

Government, a Christian government, gives us a feast every now and then: it agrees—that is to say, a majority in the two Houses agrees—that for certain crimes it is necessary that a man should be hanged by the neck. Government commits the criminal's soul to the mercy of God, stating that here on earth he is to look for no mercy; keeps him for a fortnight to prepare, provides him with a clergymen to settle his religious matters (if there be time enough, but government can't wait); and on a Monday morning, the bell tolling, the clergyman reading out the word of God, "I am the resurrection and the life," "The Lord giveth and the Lord taketh away"— on a Monday morning, at eight o'clock, this man is placed under a beam, with a rope connecting it and him; a plank disappears from under him, and those who have paid for good places may see the hands of the government agent, Jack Ketch, coming up from his black hole, and seizing the prisoner's legs, and pulling them, until he is quite dead—strangled.

Many persons, and well-informed newspapers, say that it is mawkish sentiment to talk in this way, morbid humanity, cheap philanthropy, that any man can get up and preach about. There is *The Observer*, for instance, a paper conspicuous for the tremendous sarcasm which distinguishes its articles, and which falls cruelly foul of the *Morning Herald*. "Courvoisier is dead, "says the *Observer*: "he died as he had lived — a villain; a lie was in his mouth. Peace be to his ashes. We war not with the dead." What a magnanimous *Observer*! From this, *Observer* turns to the *Herald*, and says, "Fiat *justitia, ruat cælum*. So much for the *Herald*.

We quote from memory, and the quotation from the Observer possibly is, -- "*De mortuis nil nisi bonum;* " or, "*Onme ignotum pro magnifico;* " or, "*Sero nunquam est ad bonos mores via;*" or, "*Ingenuas didicisse fideliter artes emollit mores nec sinit esse feros:*" all of which pithy Roman apophthegms would apply just as well.

"Peace be to his ashes. He died, a villain." This is both benevolence and reason. Did he die a villain? — *The Observer* does not want to destroy him body and soul, evidently, from that pious wish that his ashes should be at peace. Is the next Monday but one after the sentence the time necessary for a villain to repent in—May a man not require more leisure – a week more – six months more—before he has been able to make his repentance sure before Him who died for us all – – for all, be it remembered—not alone for the judge and jury, or for the sheriffs, or for the executioner who is pulling down the legs of the prisoner — but for him too, murderer and criminal as he is, whom we are killing for his crime. Do we want to kill him body and soul? Heaven forbid! My Lord in the black cap specially prays that Heaven may have mercy on him; but he must be ready by Monday morning.

Look at the documents which came from the prison of this unhappy Courvoisier during the few days which passed between his trial and execution. Were ever letters more painful to read—At first, his statements are false, contradictory, lying. He has not repented then. His last declaration seems to be honest, as far as the relation of the crime goes. But read the rest of his statement, the account of his personal history, and the crimes which he committed in his young days, — then "how the evil thought came to him to put his hand to the work" — it is evidently the writing of a mad, distracted man. The horrid gallows is perpetually before him; he is wild with dread and remorse. Clergymen are with him ceaselessly; religious tracts are forced into his hands; night and day they ply him with the heinousness of his crime, and exhortations to repentance. Read through that last paper of his; by Heaven, it is pitiful to read it.

See the Scripture phrases brought in now and anon; the peculiar terms of tract-phraseology (I do not wish to speak of these often meritorious publications with disrespect); one knows too well how such language is learned – imitated from the priest at the bedside, eagerly seized and appropriated, and confounded by the poor prisoner.

But murder is such a monstrous crime (this is the great argument) — when a man has killed another it is natural that he should be killed. Away with your foolish sentimentalists who say no — it is natural. That is the word, and a fine philosophical opinion it is — philosophical and Christian. Kill a man and you must be killed in turn: that is the unavoidable sequitur. You may talk to a man for a year upon the subject, and he will always reply to you, "It is natural, and therefore it must be done. Blood demands blood."

Does it? — The system of compensations might be carried on ad infinitum — an eye for an eye, a tooth for a tooth, as by the old Mosaic law. But (putting the fact out of the question, that we have had this statute repealed by the Highest Authority), why, because you lose your eye, is that of your opponent to be extracted likewise? Where is the reason for the practice? And yet it is just as natural as the death dictum, founded precisely upon the same show of sense. Knowing, however, that revenge is not only evil, but useless, we have given it up on all minor points. Only to the last we stick firm, contrary though it be to reason and to Christian law.

There is some talk, too, of the terror which the sight of this spectacle inspires, and of this we have endeavoured to give as good a notion as we can in the above pages. I fully confess that I came away down Snow Hill that morning with a disgust for murder, but it was for the murder I saw done. As we made our way through the immense crowd, we came upon two little girls of eleven and twelve years: one of them was crying bitterly, and begged, for Heaven's sake, that some one would lead her from that horrid place. This was done, and the children were carried into a place of safety. We asked the elder girl — and a very pretty one – what brought her into such a neighborhood? The child grinned knowingly, and said, "We've koom to see the mon hanged!" Tender law, that brings out babes upon such errands, and provides them with such gratifying moral spectacles!

This is the 20th of July, and I may be permitted for my part to declare that, for the last fourteen days, so salutary has the impression of the butchery been upon me, I have had the man's face continually before my eyes; that I can see Mr. Ketch at this moment, with an easy air, taking the rope from his pocket; that I feel myself ashamed and degraded at the brutal curiosity which took me to that brutal sight; and that I pray to Almighty God to cause this disgraceful sin to pass from among us, and to cleanse our land of blood.

Concerning Political Justice and Its Influence On Morals And Happiness, William Godwin (1842)

Of The Future History Of Political Societies

Government can have no more than two legitimate purposes, the suppression of injustice against individuals within the community, and the common defense against external invasion. The first of these purposes, which alone can have an uninterrupted claim upon us, is sufficiently answered, by an association, of such an extent, as to afford room for the institution of a jury, to decide upon the offenses of individuals within the community, and upon the questions and controversies, respecting property, which may chance to arise. It might be easy indeed for an offender, to escape from the limits of so petty a jurisdiction; and it might seem necessary, at first, that the neighboring parishes,or jurisdictions, should be governed in a similar manner, or at least should be willing, whatever was their form of government, to cooperate with us, in the removal or reformation of an offender, whose present habits were alike injurious to us and to them. But there will be no need of any express compact, and still less of any common centre of authority, for this purpose.

General justice, and mutual interest, are found more capable of binding men, than signatures and seals. In the mean time, all necessity for causing the punishment of the crime to pursue the criminal, would soon, at least, cease, if it ever existed. The motives to offense would become rare: its aggravations few: and rigor superfluous. The principal object of punishment, is restraint upon a dangerous member of the community; and the end of this restraint would be answered, by the general inspection, that is exercised by the members of a limited circle, over the conduct of each other, and by the gravity and good sense that would characterize the censures of men, from whom all mystery and empiricism were banished. No individual would be hardy enough in the cause of vice, to defy the general consent of sober judgment that would surround him. It would carry despair to his mind, or, which is better, it would carry conviction. He would be obliged, by a force not less irresistible than whips and chains, to reform, his conduct.

Political Superintendence Of Opinion

A principle, which has entered deeply into the systems of the writers on political law, is that of the duty of governments to watch over the manners of the people. "Government," say they, "plays the part of an unnatural stepmother, not of an affectionate parent, when she is contented by rigorous punishments to avenge the commission of a crime, while she is wholly inattentive beforehand, to imbue the mind with those virtuous principles, which might have rendered punishment unnecessary. It is the business of a sage and patriotic magistracy, to have its attention ever alive to the sentiments of the people, to encourage such as are favorable to virtue, and to check in the bud, such as may lead to disorder and corruption.

How long shall government be employed to display its terrors, without ever having recourse to the gentleness of invitation? How long shall she deal in retrospect and censure, to the utter neglect of prevention and remedy? These reasonings have, in some respects, gained additional strength, by means of the latest improvements, and clearest views, upon the subject of political truth. It is now more evident, than it was in any former period, that government, instead of being an

> **How long shall [government] deal in retrospect and censure, to the utter neglect of prevention and remedy?**

object of secondary consideration, has been the principal vehicle of extensive and permanent evil to mankind. It was unavoidable therefore to say, "since government can produce so much positive mischief, surely it can do some positive good." But these views, however specious and agreeable they may in the first instance appear, are liable to very serious question. If we would not be seduced by visionary good, we ought here, more than ever, to recollect the fundamental principles laid down and illustrated in this work, "that government is, in all cases, an evil," and "that it ought to be introduced as sparingly as possible." Man is a species of being, whose excellence depends upon his individuality; and who can be neither great nor wise, but in proportion as he is independent.

Limitations Of The Doctrine Of Punishment Which Result From The Principles Of Morality

It cannot be reformation. Reformation is improvement and nothing can take place in a man worthy the name of improvement, otherwise than by an appeal to the unbiased judgment of his mind, and the essential feelings of his nature. If I would improve a man's character, who is there that knows not, that the only effectual mode is, by removing all extrinsic influences and incitements, by inducing him to observe, to reason and enquire, by leading him to the forming a series of sentiments that are truly his own, and not slavishly modeled upon the sentiments of another?

To conceive that compulsion and punishment are the proper means of reformation, is the sentiment of a barbarian; civilization and science are calculated to explode so ferocious an idea. It was once universally admitted and approved; it is now necessarily upon the decline.

Punishment must either ultimately succeed in imposing the sentiments it is employed to inculcate upon the mind of the sufferer; or it must forcibly alienate him against them.

The last of these can never be the intention of its employer, or have a tendency to justify its application. If it were so, punishment ought to follow upon deviations from vice, not deviations from virtue. Yet to alienate the mind of the sufferer from the individual that punishes, and from the sentiments he entertains, is perhaps the most common effect of punishment.

Let us suppose, however, that its effect is of an opposite nature; that it produces obedience, and even a change of opinion. What sort of a being does it leave the man thus reformed? His opinions are not changed upon evidence. His conversion is the result of fear. Servility has operated that within him, which liberal enquiry and instruction were not able to do. Punishment undoubtedly may change a man's behavior. It may render his external conduct beneficial from injurious, though it is no very promising expedient for that purpose. But it cannot improve his sentiments, or lead him to the form of right proceeding but by the basest and most despicable motives. It leaves him a slave, devoted to an exclusive self-interest, and actuated by fear, the meanest of the selfish passions. But it may be said, "however strong may be the reasons I am able to communicate to a man in order to his reformation, he may be restless and impatient of expostulation, and of consequence render it necessary that I should retain him by force, till I can properly instill these reasons into his mind." It must be remembered that the idea here is not that of precaution, to prevent the mischiefs he might perpetrate, for that belongs to another of the three ends of punishment, that of restraint. But, separately from this idea, the argument is peculiarly weak. If the reasons I have to communicate be of an energetic and impressive nature, if they stand forward perspicuous and distinct in my own mind, it will be strange if they do not, at the outset, excite curiosity and attention in him to whom they are addressed. It is my duty to choose a proper season to communicate them, and not to betray the cause of justice by an ill-timed impatience. This prudence I should infallibly exercise, if my object were to obtain something interesting to myself; why should I be less quick-sighted when I purpose the benefit of another? It is a miserable way of preparing a man for conviction, to compel him by violence to hear an expostulation which he is eager to avoid. These arguments prove, not that we should lose sight of reformation, if punishment for any other reason appear to be necessary; but that reformation cannot reasonably be made the object of punishment.

Punishment for the sake of example is a theory that can never be justly maintained. The suffering proposed to be inflicted, considered absolutely, is either right or wrong. If it be right, it should be inflicted for its intrinsic recommendations. If it be wrong, what sort of example does it display? To do a thing for the sake of example is, in other words, to do a thing today, in order to prove that I will do a similar thing tomorrow. This must always be a subordinate consideration. No argument has been so grossly abused as this of example. We found it, under the subject of war, employed to prove the propriety of my doing a thing otherwise wrong, in order to convince the opposite party that I should, when occasion offered, do something else that was right. He will display the best example, who carefully studies the principles of justice, and assiduously practices them. A better effect will be produced in human society by my conscientious adherence to them, than by my anxiety to create a specific expectation respecting my future conduct. This argument will be still further enforced, if we recollect what has already been said, respecting the inexhaustible differences of different cases, and the impossibility of reducing them to general rules.

The third object of punishment according to the enumeration already made, is restraint. If punishment be, in any case, to be admitted, this is the only object it can reasonably propose to itself. The serious objections to which, even in this point of view, it is liable, have been stated in another stage of the enquiry: the amount of the necessity tending to supersede these objections, has also been considered. The subject of this chapter is of great importance, in proportion to the length of time that may possibly elapse, before any considerable part of mankind shall be persuaded, to exchange the present complexity of political institution, for a mode which promises to supersede the necessity of punishment. It is highly unworthy of the cause of truth, to suppose that, during this interval, I have no active duties to perform, that I am not obliged to cooperate for the present welfare of the community, as well as for its future regeneration. The temporary obligation that arises out of this circumstance exactly corresponds with what was formerly delivered on the subject of duty. Duty is the best possible application of a given power to the promotion of the general good. But my power depends upon the disposition of the men by whom I am surrounded. If I were enlisted in an army of cowards, it might be my duty to retreat, though, absolutely considered, it should have been the duty of the army to come to blows. Under every possible circumstance, it is my duty to advance the general good, by the best means which the circumstances under which I am placed will admit.

[. . .] the consideration of restraint, as the only justifiable ground of punishment, will furnish us with a simple and satisfactory criterion by which to measure the justice of the suffering inflicted. The infliction of a lingering and tormenting death cannot be vindicated upon this hypothesis; for such infliction can only be dictated by sentiments of resentment on the one hand, or by the desire to exhibit a terrible example on the other.

To deprive an offender of his life in any manner, will appear to be unjust, as it seems always sufficiently practicable, without this, to prevent him from further offense. Privation of life, though by no means the greatest injury that can be inflicted, must always be considered as a very serious injury; since it puts a perpetual close upon the prospects of the sufferer, as to all the enjoyments, the virtues, and the excellence of a human being. In the story of those whom the merciless laws of Europe doom to destruction, we sometimes meet with persons who, subsequently to their offense, have succeeded to a plentiful inheritance, or who, for some other reason, appear to have had the fairest prospects of tranquility and happiness opened upon them. Their story, with a little accommodation, may be considered as the story of every offender.

If there be any man whom it may be necessary, for the safety of the whole, to put under restraint, this circumstance is a powerful plea to the humanity and justice of those who conduct the affairs of the community, in his behalf. This is the man who most stands in need of their assistance. If they treated him with kindness, instead of supercilious and unfeeling neglect, if they made him understand with how much reluctance they had been induced to employ the force of the society against him, if they represented the true state of the case with calmness, perspicuity, and benevolence, to his mind, if they employed those precautions, which an humane disposition would not fail to suggest, to keep from him the motives of corruption and obstinacy, his reformation would be almost infallible. These are the prospects to which his wants and his misfortunes powerfully entitle him; and it is from these prospects that the hand of the executioner cuts him off forever. It is a mistake to suppose, that this treatment of criminals, tends to multiply crimes. On the contrary, few men would enter upon a course of violence, with the certainty of being obliged, by a slow and patient process, to amputate their errors. It is the uncertainty of punishment under the existing forms that multiplies crimes. Remove this uncertainty, and it would be as reasonable to expect that a man would willfully break his leg, for the sake of being cured by a skilful surgeon. Whatever gentleness the intellectual physician may display, it is not to be believed that men can part with rooted habits of injustice and vice, without considerable pain.

The true reasons, in consequence of which these forlorn and deserted members of the community are brought to an ignominious death, are, first, the peculiar iniquity of the civil institutions of that community, and, secondly, the supineness and apathy of their superiors. In republican and simple forms of government, punishments are rare, and the punishment of death almost unknown. On the other hand, the more there is in any country of inequality and oppression, the more punishments are multiplied. The more the institutions of society contradict the genuine sentiments of the human mind, the more severely is it necessary to avenge their violation. At the same time the rich and titled members of the community, proud of their fancied eminence, behold, with total unconcern, the destruction of the destitute and the wretched, disdaining to recollect that, if there be any intrinsic difference between them, it is the offspring of their different circumstances, and that the man whom they now so much despise, might have been found as accomplished and susceptible as they, if he had only changed situations. When we behold a company of poor wretches brought out for execution, reflection will present to our affrighted fancy all the hopes and possibilities which are thus brutally extinguished; the genius, the daring invention, the unshrinking firmness, the tender charities and ardent benevolence, which have occasionally, under this system, been sacrificed, at the shrine of torpid luxury and unrelenting avarice.

WITNESS TO AN EXECUTION
A Hanging in Wisconsin (1842)

William Caffee -- Newspaper account of his hanging for the murder of Samuel Southwick -- North Western Gazette & Galena Advertiser, Galena, Illinois, Friday, November 4, 1842.

Execution Of Caffee, Mineral Point, W.I.

The execution of Caffee, for the murder of Southwick, took place today, in the presence of an immense throng of spectators. The crowd commenced gathering yesterday, and continued to pour in from all directions in solid phalanx until the fatal hour. It would be difficult to estimate the number of spectators present; it could not be much less than four or five thousand. It was painful to contemplate such a crowd, assembled for such a purpose. Five thousand people assembled in the peaceful and quiet village of Mineral Point to witness what! The agony and dying throes of a fellow man. Good God! What a curiosity.

The crowd was not made up of any particular class, but was composed indiscriminately of both high and low, rich and poor, men white with the frosts of age, and tottering upon the verge of eternity were here, and young men in throngs were here. The pious and the good were here. The aged and discreet matron was here. The virgin, "chaste as the icicle that hangs on Dian's temple," were here. Infants, muling and puking in their nurse's arms, were here by the acre. In a word, every age, sex, color and condition was fully represented here today.

The execution took place upon the low ground below the town, surrounded by an amphitheatre of hills, which were literally covered by the eager multitude. The scaffold was constructed upon the old plan, and consisted of a square frame work, placed upon the ground, into which was inserted two upright posts about twelve feet high and four feet apart; across the top of these posts went a beam, with a large iron hook inserted, to which was attached the rope. Between the upright posts, and about six feet from the ground was fixed a platform or trap door, about four feet square, hung with hinges upon one side and kept in a horizontal position by a pin passing through one of the upright posts and under the edge of the platform. To this pin was attached a lever for the purpose of drawing it out and letting fall the trap. The ascent to the scaffold was by means of a flight of stairs.

Agreeable to the requisition of George Messersmith, Esq. Sheriff, Capt. Shaw attended from the South part of the county, with a company of thirty men, in uniform, armed with muskets, a company of Dragoons armed with pistols and sabres, was organized at Mineral Point, under Major Gray, a strong guard of citizens was also organized and stationed round the jail during the fore part of the day, and were afterwards incorporated into Capt. Shaw's company.

At 2 o'clock, p.m. the procession formed in front of the jail in the following order:

Dragoons under Maj. Gray; Infantry; Waggon containing coffin; Infantry; Dragoons under Col. Sublett.

Prisoner was then led forth from the jail in a long white robe, with a white cap upon his head, and a rope round his neck, leaning upon the arm of the Sheriff; he walked to the wagon and stepped into it with little or no assistance, and seated himself upon the coffin; the Sheriff and his deputies took seats in the wagon; a dead march was struck up, and the procession moved forward to the place of execution. Here the military were stationed round the gallows at the distance of some thirty feet, to keep off the crowd. Prisoner was then assisted from the wagon, and with a firm step ascended with the Sheriff to the scaffold. The Rev. Mr. Wilcox, who was in frequent attendance upon the prisoner during his last hours, now ascended the scaffold and prayed with him for the last time; the Prisoner, in the meantime, leaning upon one of the posts of the gallows, and manifesting no emotion. Upon being asked by the Sheriff if he had any thing to say, he answered no, and requested that the rope might be adjusted "with a good long slack," and his doom forthwith sealed. The Sheriff then adjusted the rope, drew the cap down over the prisoner's face, and descended from the scaffold, putting his hand to lever, the fatal pin was drawn out, and prisoner launched into eternity.

From the time of prisoner's arrest, down to the last moment of his existence, he maintained the utmost coolness; and manifested such a contempt of death, as to invest him with a sort of terrible grandeur; making good upon the scaffold his previous boast, that he could stare the grim messenger out of countenance.

Saturday last he was visited by his brothers and some other of his relatives, who were much afflicted at the meeting; he alone remaining unmoved, and conversing in the most trivial manner. Today his brothers visited him for the last time; prisoner asked forgiveness for his levity when they last saw him; said he was now disposed to forgive and ask forgiveness of all mankind, and was not without hope of happiness hereafter.

Much credit is due the Sheriff for the manner in which he performed his duty to day, as well as for his untiring vigilance since the prisoner was first placed in his custody.

WITNESS TO AN EXECUTION
The Execution of the Mexican Assassins of the New Mexico Governor, Lewis H. Garrard (1847)

On Friday, the ninth, the sky was unspotted, save by hastily-fleeting clouds; and, as the rising sun loomed over the Taos Mountain, the bright rays, shining on the yellow and white mud houses, reflected cheerful hues while the shades of the toppling peaks receding .from the plain beneath drew within themselves. The humble valley wore an air of calm repose, The plaza was deserted; woe-begone donkeys drawled forth sacrilegious brays as the warm sunbeams roused them from hard, grassless ground to scent among straw or bones their breakfast: a señora in her nightdress and disheveled hair—which, at the fandango, was the admiration of the moustached *señors* and half-wild *voluntarios*—could here and there be seen at this early hour, opening her house, previous to the preparation of the fiery chile colorado.

As onward sped the day, so did the crowd of morning drinkers at Estis's Tavern to renew their libations to Bacchus. Poor Mexicans hurried to and fro, casting suspicious glances around; *los Yankees* at *El Casa Americano* drank their juleps and puffed their cigarillos in silence.

The sheriff (Metcalfe, formerly a mountaineer, son-in-law to Estis) was in want of the wherewith to hang the criminals, so he borrowed our rawhide lariats and two or three hempen picket cords of a teamster. In a room adjoining the bar, we put the hangman's noose on one end, tugging away quite heartily.. . .

The prison was at the edge of town; no houses intervened between it and the fields to the north. One hundred and fifty yards distant a scaffold of two upright posts and a crossbeam was erected.

At the portal were several *compañeros*, discussing, in a very light way, the "fun," as they termed it, on hand—they almost wishing a rescue would be attempted so as to gratify their propensity for excitement,

The word was passed, at last, that the criminals were coming. Eighteen soldiers received them at the gate, with their muskets at port arms—the six abreast, with the sheriff on the right—nine soldiers on each side—Hatcher, Loyu Simonds, Chadwick, myself, and others, eight in all, formed in line a pace behind, as the rear guard, with our trusty mountain rifles at rest in the bended elbow of the left arm, the right hand resting on the stock, to be drawn up to the face, and all ready to fight on our own responsibility at the least intimation of danger.

The poor *pelados* marched slowly, with down-cast eyes, arms tied behind, and bare heads, with the exception of white cotton caps stuck on the back part, to be pulled over the face as the last ceremony.

The *azoteas* —roofs—in our vicinity, were covered with women and children, to witness the first execution by hanging in the valley of Taos, save that of Montojo, the insurgent leader. No men were near; a few, afar off, stood moodily looking on.

On the flat jail roof was placed a mountain howitzer, loaded and ranging the gallows. Near was the complement of men to serve it, one holding in his hand a lighted match.

The two hundred and thirty soldiers (deducting the eighteen forming the guard) were paraded in front of the jail and in sight of the gibbet, so as to secure the prisoners awaiting trial, Lieutenant Colonel Willock, on a handsome charger, from his position commanded a view of the whole.

When within fifteen paces of the gallows, the side guard, filing off to the right and left, formed, at regular distances from each other, three sides of a hollow square; the mountaineers and myself composed the fourth and front side, in full view of the trembling prisoners, who marched up to the tree, under which was a government wagon with two mules attached. The driver and sheriff assisted them in, ranging them on a board, placed cross the hinder end, which maintained its balance, as they were six-and even number—two on each extremity and two in the middle. The gallows was so narrow they touched. The ropes, by reason of size and stiffness despite the soaping given them, were adjusted with difficulty; but, though the indefatigable efforts of the sheriff and a lieutenant, all preliminaries were arranged. The former, officiating as deputy sheriff for the occasion, seemed to enjoy the position—but the blue uniform looked sadly out of place on a hangman.

With rifles grounded, we awaited the consummation of the fearful tragedy. No crowd was around to disturb; a death-like stillness reigned. The spectators on the *azoteas* seemed scarcely to move—their eyes directed to the painful sight of the doomed wretches, with harsh halters now circling their necks.

The sheriff and assistant sat down; and, succeeding a few moments of intense expectation, the heart-wrung victims said a few words to their people. But one said that they had committed murder and deserved death. In their brief, but earnest appeals, which I could but imperfectly comprehend, the words, *"mi padre, mi madre"* could be distinguished. The one sentenced for treason showed a spirit of martyrdom worthy of the cause for which he died — the liberty of his country; and, instead of the cringing, contemptible recantation of the others, his speech was firm asserations of his own innocence, the unjustness of his trial, and the arbitrary conduct of his murderers. With a scowl, as the cap was pulled over his face, the last words he uttered between his gritting teeth were, *"Caraho, los Americanos!"*

Bidding each other *"adios,"* with a hope of meeting in Heaven, at word from the sheriff the mules were started, and the wagon drawn from under the tree. No fall was given, and their feet remained on the board till the ropes drew taut. The bodies swayed back and forth, and, coming in contact with each other, convulsive shudders shook their frames; the muscles, contracting, would relax, and again contract, and the bodies writhed most horribly.

While thus swinging, the hands of two came together, which they held with a firm grasp till the muscles loosened in death.

Speech before the National Assembly
Victor Hugo (1848)

IRegret, gentlemen, that this question of the abolition of capital punishment—the most important question, perhaps, of all before this body,—comes up at a time when we are little prepared for its discussion. For myself, I have but few words to say on the subject, but they will proceed from convictions profound and long entertained. You have established the inviolability of the domicile: we ask you to establish inviolability higher and more sacred—the inviolability of human life! Gentlemen, a constitution, and above all, a constitution made by France and for France, is necessarily an important step in civilization. If it is not that, it is nothing. Consider, then, this penalty of death. What is it but the special and eternal type of barbarism? Wherever the penalty of death is most in vogue, barbarism prevails. Wherever it is rare, civilization reigns. Gentlemen, these are in disputable facts. The modification of the penalty was a great forward step.

The eighteenth century, to its honor, abolished the torture. The nineteenth century will abolish the death penalty! You may not abolish it today. But, doubt not, you will abolish it tomorrow; or else your successors will abolish it. You have inscribed at the head of the preamble of your constitution the words, "IN PRESENCE OF GOD;" and would you begin by depriving that God of the right which to Him only belongs—the right of life and death? Gentlemen, there are three things which are God's, not man's: the irrevocable, the irreparable, the indissoluble. Woe to man if he introduces them into his laws! Sooner or later they will force society to give way under their weight; they derange the equilibrium essential to the security of laws and of morals; they take from human justice its proportions; and then it happens,—think of it, gentlemen!—it happens that the law revolts the conscience.

I have ascended this tribune to say but a word, a decisive word, and it is this: After the Revolution of February came a great thought to the French people! The day after they had burned the Throne, they sought to burn the Scaffold! But this sublime idea they were prevented from carrying into execution. In the first article of this constitution you have consecrated the people's first thought; you have cast down the Throne! Now consecrate its second thought, and cast down the Scaffold! Vote for the entire abolition of the penalty of death.

WITNESS TO AN EXECUTION
The Execution of Tapner, Victor Hugo (1856)

Tapner, an assassin, an incendiary, and a robber, is condemned to death. At the present day, my lord and the facts I have just mentioned would suffice to prove what I say in every upright and healthy conscience the penalty of death is abolished. Tapner being condemned, a general outcry is heard, petitions multiply, and one, energetically asserting the inviolability of human life, is signed by 600 of the most enlightened inhabitants of the island. It is worthy of notice that not a single minister of any form of Christian worship has added his signature to these petitions. These men are probably ignorant that the cross was a gibbet. The people cry 'Pardon!' but the priest cries 'Death! Let us pity the priests, and pass on. The petitions were duly forwarded to you, my lord, and you granted a respite. In such cases a respite signifies a commutation of the punishment. The island breathes: the gibbet will not be erected. Not so: the gibbet is erected. Tapner is hanged.

After reflection.

Why?

Why is that refused to Guernsey which has been so frequently granted to Jersey? Why the concession to one island and the refusal to the other? Why is mercy to be granted here and the executioner sent there? Why this difference where the cases were parallel? What was the meaning of this respite, which is now only an aggravation? Is there any mystery connected with it? Of what use is reflection?

Things have been said, my lord, before which I turn away my head. No, what has been said cannot be.

Whatever may be the state of the case, you have commanded, these are the words of the despatch, that justice should take its course. Whatever it may be, all is now at an end. Whatever may happen, Tapner, after three respites and three reflections, was yesterday, on the 10th February, hanged; and the following, my lord, is an account of the day's proceedings :

There was a garden attached to the prison, and there the scaffold was erected. A breach was made in the wall in order to enable the crowd to pass. At eight o'clock in the morning, the crowd invaded the neighboring streets, two hundred spectators, privileged ones being stationed in the garden. The man appeared in the breach. He looked bravely around, and walked with a firm step; he was pale, and a red rim encircled his eyes. The month that had just passed away had added twenty years to his age. This man of thirty years looked at least fifty. A white cotton nightcap was pulled over his head, but was raised up so as to show his forehead.

These are the words of an eyewitness: he was dressed in the brown great-coat which he generally wore on his trial, and on his feet he had a pair of old slippers; he walked all round the garden on a walk ready gravelled for the occasion. The constables, the sheriff, the deputy sheriff, and the Queen's

Procureur, surrounded him. His hands were tied, but not securely, as you will see. Nevertheless, according to the English custom, whilst his hands were crossed over his breast by these cords, another cord tied his elbows together behind his back. Beside him the chaplains, who had refused to sign the petition for pardon, were weeping. The gravelled walk led to the ladder. The noose was ready, suspended. Tapner ascended the steps: the executioner was trembling. Tapner placed himself under the running noose, and put his neck through it, and his hands being insecurely tied, as he saw the executioner was unequal to the occasion and went clumsily to work, he himself assisted him. Then, as if he foresaw what was about to happen, adds the same witness, he said, "Do tie my hands tighter."

"It is of no use!" said the executioner. Tapner, standing thus in the running noose, with his feet over the bolt, the executioner pulled down the cap over his eyes, and nothing more was seen of his countenance than his mouth, in the act of praying. After a few seconds, just about the time it would take to turn round, the man of great actions pressed the spring of the trap. A vacant space was then left under the convict's feet, and he fell suddenly into it; the cord stretched, the body turned, and the man was thought to be dead. "It was supposed," said the eyewitness, "that Tapner had been killed outright by breaking his neck. He fell from a height of four feet, and with his full weight, he being a tall man." My informant adds, "This notion, which was a great relief to all present, was hardly felt for as much as two minutes." On a sudden, this man, who was not yet a corpse, but was already a spectre, was seen to move; his legs were raised and lowered, one after the other, as if they were feeling for a footing in the empty space beneath him. What was now seen was becoming truly horrible. The man's hands, which had nearly become untied, spread apart and joined themselves together again, as if to ask for assistance. The cord which tied the elbows together had been broken in the shock of the fall. During the convulsions that took place, the cord by which he was suspended began to oscillate. The elbows of the wretched man presently grazed against the edge of the trap, and his hands clung to it; his right knee then leant against it; his body half raised itself; and the hanged man leant over the crowd. He fell back again, and this scene was twice repeated. He then raised his cap, and the crowd could see his face. This had now lasted too long, and it became necessary to put a stop to it. The executioner, who had descended, mounted the platform again, and I still quote the words of the eyewitness, made the dying man quit his hold. The executioner and the spectre struggled for a moment, and the executioner gained the mastery. Then this man, a convict himself, precipitated himself into the hole where Tapner was hanging, clasped his two knees, and hung from his feet. The cord still swung for a moment, carrying the dying man and the executioner the crime and the law backwards and forwards. At length, the executioner let go his hold, and all was over. The man was dead.

You see, my lord, things went off very well. It was a very complete affair. If they wished for a shriek of horror, they certainly had it.

The town being built like an amphitheater, the people could witness the scene from their houses. Everybody was anxiously looking into the garden.

The crowd were exclaiming, "Shame! Shame!" Some women fainted.

Whilst all this was going on, Fouquet, who had been respited in 1851, has since repented. The executioner turned Tapner into a corpse; mercy has made Fouquet a man once more.

A last detail.

In the interval between Tapner's falling into the hole, occasioned by removing the trap door, and the moment when the executioner, feeling that the last death struggle was over, dropped from the feet of the corpse, twelve minutes intervened. Let it be calculated what this amounts to, if indeed there be any who know by what dial the hours of agony may be reckoned.

It was in this way, my lord, that Tapner died.

The theory of example is satisfied. The philosopher alone is sad, and asks if this is justice, 'taking its course.'

We must assume that philosophy is wrong. The death was frightful, but the crime was a hideous one.

Society is bound to defend itself, is it not true? Where should we be if, &c., &c., &c.? The boldness of malefactors would be unlimited. Nothing but atrocities and crimes of violence would be heard of. It is necessary to repress all this. In fine, it is your opinion, my lord, that the Tapners should be hanged. Let the will of the statesman be done!

Listen, my lord, it is horrible. We inhabit you and I the infinitely small. I am but an exile, and you are only a Minister. I am ashes, and you are dust. Being both atoms, we may speak together. From one nothingness to another, home truths may be told. Well, be it known to you, whatever be the actual splendors of your political position, my lord, this rope tied round a man's throat, that trap door which opens under his feet, that hope one entertains that he will break his neck in falling, that face which turns blue under the lugubrious veil of the gibbet, those bloodshot eyes which start from their sockets, that tongue which is thrust out of his mouth, that groan of anguish which the noose stifles, that distracted soul which struggles in its prison-house, the skull, without being able to escape; those convulsed knees, seeking some place against which they may press; those hands bound, and mutely appealing for help; and that other man, that dark shadow, who throws himself on this shuddering and palpitating mass of humanity, who clings to the wretch's knees, and who hangs himself to the hanging man; all this, my lord, is frightful. You said, let justice take its course. You gave these orders as they are wont to be given, and these repetitions but little affect you. To hang a man is to you very much like drinking a glass of water. You did not recognize the enormity of the act. It is one of the occurrences of daily life to a great statesman; nothing more. My lord, keep your thoughtless acts for the earth; do not offer them to eternity. Believe me, do not trifle with depths like these; do not throw anything of yourself into them. It is an act of imprudence. With regard to these depths, I am nearer them than you are. I see them. Take care, *Exul sicut mortuus*. I speak to you from within the tomb.

Bah! What matters it? A man hanged, and then a rope to be taken away, a scaffold to be unnailed, a corpse to be buried; what does it all amount to? We will fire a gun off; there will be a little smoke in the east, and nothing more will be said about it. Guernsey, Tapner—we must have a microscope to see little things like these. But that rope, that scaffold, that corpse, that wretched gibbet, hardly seen, that misery, these are immensity. It is a social question, much higher than any political question. It is yet more, it is something that no longer exists on earth. What is really of no importance is your firing of guns, your politics, your smoke. The assassin, who, between sunrise and sunset, has been assassinated, this is the frightful thing; a soul which takes its flight, holding a piece of the rope torn from the gibbet, this is really formidable. Statesmen, between the signing of two protocols, between two meals, between two smiles, you carelessly press with your white-gloved thumb the spring of the gallows, and the trap gives way under the feet of the hanging man.

Do you know what that trap is? It is eternity which is dawning, it is the unfathomable and the unknown; it is the great shadow which opens unexpectedly and terribly upon your littleness.

Go on. It is well. Let us see men of the old school at work. As the past will not pass away, let us look back at it. Let us see all its members in succession. At Tunis, we have impaling; under the Czar, the knout; under the Pope, garroting; in France, the guillotine; in England, the gibbet; in Asia and America, the slave market. Ah! All this will fade away. We anarchists, we demagogues, we bloodthirsty men, we declare unto you, unto you, the Conservatives, that human liberty is august, human intelligence is holy, human life is sacred, and the human soul is Divine. After this, will you still hang?

Take care. Futurity draws near. You believe that which is dead to be living, and that which is living you believe to be dead. The old society still holds its position; but I tell you, that is dead. You have deceived yourselves. You have placed your hand on the spectre in the night, and you have made it your bride. You turn your backs on life, and presently it will rise from behind you. When we pronounce those words, Progress, Revolution, Liberty, Humanity, you smile, unhappy men! And you show us the night, in which we are, and in which you are. Truly, do you know what the night means? Learn its meaning, for ere long, ideas will emerge from it, vast and radiating. Yesterday democracy was France, tomorrow it will be Europe. The present eclipse masks the mysterious aggrandizement of the planet.

AFTER THE ENLIGHTENMENT

Essays On The Punishment Of Death
Charles Spear (1844)

"Government has not been slow to punish crime, nor has society suffered for want of dungeons and gibbets. But the prevention of crime and the reformation of the offender, have nowhere taken rank among the first objects of legislation."
[William Ellery] Channing

D r. Franklin relates the story of a horse-stealer, who, on being asked by his judge what he had to say why sentence of death should not be passed, replied, 'that it was hard to hang a man for only stealing a horse.' 'Man,' replied the judge, 'thou art not to be hanged only for stealing a horse, but that horses may not be stolen.' This anecdote shows the true nature of capital punishment. The good of the offender is always unthought of in its infliction. One great object is entirely disregarded.

It may be said of our penal code generally, that it is rather retrospective than prospective. The future good of the criminal is not considered. The idea is well expressed in our motto, by Channing. Our prisons should be places of emendation; not mere gloomy cells, but hospitals to heal the moral disorders of the soul. Until this is done, we cannot expect any beneficial results from the confinement of the culprit. When we hear of the perpetration of a crime, we are too apt to think only of punishment. What suffering can be too great for such a wretch! Is the exclamation which bursts from almost every lip. The sentiment is worthy of the unlovely doctrines which produce and cherish it. A more benevolent system would excite a different feeling. What can be done to reclaim the unhappy offender? What means can be taken to enlighten his mind, and meliorate his heart? What discipline is best adapted to his mental and moral disorder? What will lead him back to virtue and to happiness most speedily, and with the least pain?

Such is the feeling of the mind enlightened by the generous doctrine we have endeavored to establish. Could it but enter the heart of every legislator; did it but guide the hand that constructs the cell of the poor captive; did it apportion his pallet of straw and his scanty meal; did it determine the completeness and the duration of his exclusion from the light of day and the pure breeze of heaven; did it apply his manacles, (if, disdaining to treat a human being with more indignity than is practiced towards the most savage brutes, it did not dash his chains to the earth,) what a different aspect would these miserable mansions soon assume! What different inhabitants would they contain! Prisons would not then be the hot-beds of vice, in which the youthful offender grows into the hardened criminal, and the want of shame succeeds the abolition of principle, but hospitals of the mind, in which its moral disorder is removed by the application of effectual remedies.

That capital punishment has no good moral effect by way of example will be shown in the essay on the *Influence of Public Executions.* A very able writer has given us the following definitions of punishment and revenge. According to his reasoning, both bear the following definition: "The infliction of pain in consequence of the violation or neglect of duty." The question then arises, where is the difference? The real difference consists not in the pain and suffering endured, nor in the person or law that inflicts it, but in the motive with which it is administered. Punishment is prospective, referring to future consequences; but revenge is retrospective, having reference only to a past offence.

Punishment by death originated among savages. Among them, however, it was called by its right name: revenge.

Punishment by death originated among savages. Among them, however, it was called by its right name: revenge. In the savage state, the murderer is considered the lawful prey of any relative or friend of the slain, who may please to take revenge; but the community takes no part in the transaction. Now, society pursues the murderer for the same object. Revenge is still the same, whether inflicted by the hand of the savage, or by the most enlightened government. The great object seems to be to inflict evil merely because an evil has taken place. We do not say that all view the matter in this light, but that the community do generally. For, what are the expressions that we hear when persons are convicted for murder? "Hang them! They deserve it! They did not spare — let them not be spared! Let them die!" "Die and be damned," was the recent answer of one.

To say, as some do, that we have a right to take away the life of a human being, because he or she hath taken away the life of another, is a fallacious mode of reasoning. It appears like justifying one crime by another. It is comparing ourselves with ourselves; not with the law of God, which is the standard of moral rectitude. Let us apply this sophistical mode of reasoning to some of the other commandments, say the eighth, ninth, and tenth.

Have we a right to steal from one who hath been guilty of theft? Have we a right to bear false witness against one who hath been guilty of perjury? Or to covet the goods of one who hath coveted the goods of his neighbor? In this way we might make void, not only the Sixth Commandment, but also all the rest which respect the duty of man to man. By these commandments all theft, all perjury, all covetousness, and all shedding of human blood, are expressly forbidden! If the Sixth Commandment had said, "Thou shalt not kill, except it be one who hath killed another," or words to that effect, it would have given some colorable right to take away the life of the murderer. But as it now stands, and will forever stand, it gives no such right. The badness of the character of the criminal will not justify the violation of the commandment by others. The prohibition is peremptory, decisive, universal, and unconditional. The 'just vengeance of the law' is an expression which shows the real character of capital punishment. When presented, however, in its real import, it is generally disclaimed. Mr. (John Louis) O'Sullivan, speaking on this subject, says, "Evil in its nature, this spirit of revenge which lies at the root of our laws of capital punishment, is, however, the fruitful source of abundant retributive evil, in its eventual consequences, to those themselves who yield to its indulgence. Thus is it ever, by an eternal and universal moral law which has no less certain applicability to societies than to individuals. The suicidal reaction of these laws back on the community which frames and enforces them—by desecrating the idea of the inviolable sanctity of human life—by weakening the force of that instinct against the willful shedding of the blood of our fellow man. which is the strongest safeguard to the personal security of us all—by sanctioning and suggesting the infliction of death as a rightful punishment for human offenses by demoralizing the public heart, and familiarizing it with the idea of these cold, formal, and deliberate judicial murders—by setting such a high social example of the indulgence of revenge in this world, and of comparative indifference to the too probable fate of the human soul in the next—has been, it is believed, sufficiently shown, to claim from all the recognition of the high moral, of which these evil fruits from evil seed afford so signal an illustration."

"It is from an abuse of language," says (William) Eden on the *Principles of Penal Law*, "that we apply the word punishment to human institutions. Vengeance belongeth not to man." But the best proof to show that capital punishment is revengeful is the admission of a magistrate to Mr. (Edward) Livingston. "He acceded to the propriety of the proposed reform, in all cases but murder; which he excepted on the ground of the difficulty of keeping the offender, and the severity of the substitute of solitary confinement. But when these two objections had been satisfactorily answered, he replied by one of the usual exclamations by which some men—with what is far worse than merely a shocking levity, heartlessness, and irreflection—are wont to dismiss the subject, that the murderer deserves death! And blood must be shed for blood!" and added, very frankly, "I must confess that there is some little feeling of revenge at the bottom of my opinion on the subject."

"If all other reasoners," adds Mr. Livingston, "were equally candid, there would be less difficulty in establishing true doctrines. Passion first made revengeful laws, and revenge once incorporated with the system of justice, reproduced its own image, after passion had expired."

More might be added in proof of the revengeful nature of capital punishment, but it would be unnecessary. It must be seen that the reformation of the offender is entirely overlooked. And, in all penal inflictions, this should be a great, a paramount object; and when once the true idea of the inviolability of human life is seen and understood, the life of even the most abandoned will be preserved, and society, instead of cutting off the offender, will endeavor to ameliorate his condition, and restore him to community.

What a noble work! And that it may be accomplished, will be seen by the illustrations of kindness which may be found at the close of the present volume. Mr. (Robert) Rantoul gives an instance of a boy, who was convicted of highway robbery. "He was convicted and sentenced to death, but, in consideration of his age, and other circumstances, his sentence was commuted to imprisonment for life. In the State prison he became a good boy, and was pardoned, and restored to society, to virtue and to usefulness. He acquired a good reputation in the neighborhood where he lived, and died a Christian death among his friends, in

March, 1835."

It has been said, but it is the language of unreflecting levity, that the criminal convicted of a capital offence, under our laws, is generally depraved and worthless, and that, therefore, the sacrifice of a few such lives is of very little consequence to society, and it is not an object fit to engage the attention of the government of a great state, even if these laws might be repealed without injury. It is impossible that any legislator can entertain so inhuman a sentiment. Felons, however fallen, still are men, and have the better title to commiseration the more deeply they are sunk in guilt. If these wretches were princes, says Goldsmith, there would be thousands ready to offer their ministry; but the heart that is buried in a dungeon is as precious as that seated on a throne. Suppose that one only may be caught up from the gulf of vice, misery and perdition, and restored to repentance, virtue and usefulness, this would be gain enough to reward all the exertions that may be made to effect the reform for there is upon earth no gem so precious as the human soul.

Humanitarian Doctrines: Their Bearing on the Theory Of Capital Punishment, based on Professor Karl Josef Anton Mittermaier's "Todstraffe" (1846)

The Reformation undermined faith in authority, and roused the spirit of inquiry. But before this inquisitive spirit was applied to the principles of Legislation in general, and of Penal Legislation in particular, the political structures of ancient empires had to be shaken to their foundations; wars, both foreign and domestic, of the most devastating character, had to be waged, and the views of mankind, on Criminal Law entirely revolutionized.

The first impulse to this movement was given in England. The two tempests of 1649 and 1688 purified the atmosphere. They tore up by the roots and cast aside prejudices of the most inveterate kind. Whilst this was being done in England, we find that in Germany the princes were holding the people with a firmer grasp. The nation was being crushed to atoms, and the power of united action destroyed.

Those who have carefully studied the growth and development of a single legislative principle or idea, from its first germ until it is embodied in a legal enactment, must have been struck with its slow and almost imperceptible progress. This is easily accounted for. The human race, in their collective capacity, are always engaged in working out the practical solution of many problems at the same time. Even the theoretical inquiry into the principles of legislation does not take place until it is called forth by the growth and development of the nation. This accounts for the fact that in Germany even Leibnitz, with his universal and comprehensive genius, never inquired into the history, principle, and object of Penal Legislation. He was by no means an indifferent spectator of historical events or the policy and fate of his own country. In order to divert Louis XIV from his intended encroachments on the liberty and political existence of other nations, he personally suggested to that monarch a plan for the conquest of Egypt — a plan which, after the lapse of a century, Napoleon I attempted to carry out. And besides his manifold scientific inquiries, Leibnitz conducted long and protracted negotiations with Roman Catholic divines, particularly Bossuet, the famous French bishop and councilor of State, for reconciling Roman Catholicism with Protestantism — a project which may be taken up again after the lapse of another century. Besides, he wrote a history of the House of Brunswick, in order to pave the way to this Sovereign, the Elector of Hanover, to the throne of Great Britain. But how far justice was realized, civilization advanced in the history, or the then existing enactments of the Penal Law of Germany or other countries, seems never to have occupied the mind of this great thinker.

England was the country which gave the first impulse to speculations on the principle and object of Penal Legislation; but it was by French, and not by English authors, that the subject was first broached. Those French authors of eminence who came to England in Queen Anne's time, especially Voltaire and Montesquieu, could not but be struck with the working of the Constitution, and that well-preserved inheritance — national self-government — which conquered the Stuarts, survived the tempests of the Commonwealth, the Restoration, and the Revolution of 1688. Voltaire and Montesquieu both lived in this country, both owed much to their personal intercourse with some of the great English statesmen of the time — especially the Earl of Shaftesbury and Lord Bolingbroke, — both exercised a wholesome influence on reforming the Penal Legislation of their country, and enlightening mankind on the principles of Legislation in general.

Voltaire attacked with stern and fearless violence, with bitter satire, whatever he found or thought to be bad in the institutions of France, and stood forth an undaunted defender of those who had been unjustly condemned to death. He demonstrated with irrefutable logic that the prevailing severity of the Penal Law was not required by justice, and was a disgrace to his age.

Montesquieu, taking a higher aim, showed in that section of his justly celebrated work *The Spirit of Law* which treats of Penal Law, and contains both a review of past, and a survey of contemporaneous Legislation, that severity has always missed its ends, and that punishments ought to be graduated in the same proportion as misdemeanors and crimes. It is true that he has not exhausted the subject, nor are his pithy concluding sentences — as, for instance, this one: "*Enfin tout ce que la loi appelle une peine c'est effectivement une peine*" [*Finally, everything that the law calls a sentence is actually a sentence.*]— free from paradoxical exaggeration; but he has, nevertheless, the great merit of having laid down in an impressive manner, that Penal Legislation, in order to attain its ends, must combine leniency in its enactments with certainty in their execution.

Returning to England, we must pay due homage to the practical philanthropy of our countryman, John Howard (born at Enfield, 1726; died in Turkey, 1790), who, with true British singleness of purpose and perseverance, devoted his life to the mitigation of the sufferings of his fellow men. The portions of his philanthropic work in which we are at present most concerned are his endeavors to improve the condition of prisoners. The office of a gaoler had in process of time lost its character as a public service, and degenerated into a lucrative privilege. The gaolers were not paid by the State, and gradually acquired the right of obtaining payment from the prisoners themselves. In fact, the gaolers sold favors at a high price to all who were able to pay, or facilitated their escape from prison; whereas to the poor who had no *solatium* to offer, food of inferior quality — often quite unfit for human sustenance — was given. The prisons themselves, from an accumulation of filth, became hotbeds for fever and pestilence. One of the innumerable abuses was that those prisoners from whom the gaolers thought they might be able to extort money were kept much longer in confinement than the sentence warranted. In fact, the prisoners were entirely in the hands of the gaolers. Parliament in emphatic terms expressed its thanks and those of the country to the great philanthropist; and soon after, the flagrant abuse was abolished by the "Howard-Popham Bill" which was passed June 2, 1774.

The published results of Howard's inquiries in England and other countries show that the abuses in the management of prisons were much more flagrant in England than elsewhere, because here alone the officials had perverted into a vested right and lucrative privilege what in its very nature is a responsible service, and ought to be kept under the severest control. But, on the other hand, Howard's life, and the results of his philanthropic endeavors, confirm the recognized fact, that in England every abuse has at last to yield to the energy of a persevering reformer, and that the inherent vitality of this State is great enough to admit of every reform being carried to its ultimate results, while the Commonwealth itself grows with increased vigor and renewed energy.

Howard's contemporary, Jeremy Bentham, took a higher aim, and tended more directly to the mitigation of penalties, and the abolition of capital punishment.

Most of Bentham's works were first published in French, at the beginning of the present century, by his particular friend M. Dumont; but from the preface of one of these books we learn that the manuscripts from which *La Théorie des Peines* was taken were written as early as the year 1775.

In order to do justice to Bentham's views we have, however, only to refer to those of his works which were published by himself. These are *The Rationale of Punishment*, published in London, 1830, and Jeremy Bentham to his *Fellow-Citizens of France on Death Punishment*, published in London, 1881.

In *The Rationale of Punishment* he endeavors to strike a balance between the good and bad qualities of capital punishment as a penalty, under the following heads :

I. Advantageous Properties of the Punishment of Death.

1. It takes from the offender the power of doing further injury.

2. It is analogous to the offence in the case of murder — but there its analogy terminates.

3. It is popular in respect to that crime, and that alone.

4. It is exemplary in a higher degree, perhaps, than any other species of punishment.

II. Desirable Penal Qualities which are wanting in Capital Punishment.

1. The punishment of death is not convertible to profit; it cannot be applied to the purpose of compensation. Insofar as compensation might be derived from the labor of the delinquent, the very source of the compensation is destroyed.

2. In point of frugality it is preeminently defective. Bentham considers the life of an individual as an element of wealth and strength to the community to which he belongs, and accordingly his death as a loss. This objection to Capital Punishment, however, is greatly weakened by the consideration that the criminal is in this respect of less value to the community than an average man, or of no value at all; in the latter case his death would not be a loss.

3. Equability is another point, and that a most important one, in which the punishment is eminently deficient. To a person taken at random, it is, upon an average, a very heavy punishment, though still subject to considerable variation. But to a person taken out of the class of first-rate delinquents, it is liable to still greater variation. To some it is as great as to a person taken at random; but to many it is next to nothing.

4. Variability is a point of excellence in which the punishment of death is more deficient than in any other. It subsists only in one degree.

5. The Punishment of Death is not remissible. No infallible system of jurisprudence having yet been devised, no test for the evidence of witnesses having yet been laid down to render testimony equally conclusive for proving a fact, an action, or an intention, as a mathematical proof for a given proposition. Error is possible in all judgments. In every other case of judicial error, compensation can be made to the injured person. Death admits of no compensation.

In a footnote to this head, Bentham states another defect of capital punishment, which appears of sufficient importance to form a distinct head by itself. It is, in fact, so momentous an objection, that we think it necessary to transcribe the paragraph *in extenso*:

"There is an evil resulting from the employment of death as a punishment which may be properly noticed here. It destroys one source of testimonial proof. The archives of crime are, in a measure, lodged in the bosoms of criminals. At their death, all the recollections which they possess relative to their own crimes and those of others perish. Their death is an act of impunity for all those who might have been detected by their testimony, whilst innocence must continue oppressed, and the right can never be established, because a necessary witness is subtracted.

"Whilst a criminal process is going forward, the accomplices of the accused flee and hide themselves. It is an interval of anxiety and tribulation. The sword of justice appears suspended over their heads. When his career is terminated, it is for them an act of jubilee and pardon. They have a new bond of security, and they can walk erect. The fidelity of the deceased is exalted among his companions as a virtue, and received among them, for the instruction of their young disciples, with praises for his heroism.

"In the confines of a prison, this heroism would be submitted to a more dangerous proof than the interrogatories of the tribunals. Left to himself, separated from his companions, a criminal ceases to possess this feeling of honor which unites him to them. It .needs only a moment of repentance to snatch from him those discoveries which he only can make; and without his repentance, what is more natural than a feeling of vengeance against those who cause him to lose his liberty, and who, though equally culpable with himself, yet continue in the enjoyment of liberty? He need only listen to his interest, and purchase, by some useful information, some relaxation in the rigor of his punishment."

(Besides, another defect of capital punishment as a penalty, which follows from its not being remissible, is that it may be used by men in power to gratify their passions by means of a corruptible judge.) In such cases, as Bentham says, "the iniquity covered with the robe of justice may escape, if not all suspicion, at least the possibility of proof. Capital punishment, too, affords to the prosecutor as well as to the judge, an advantage that in all other modes is wanting: I mean greater security against detection, by stifling by death all danger of discovery arising from the delinquent, at least; while he lives, to whatever state of misery he may be reduced, the oppressed may meet with some fortunate event by which his innocence maybe proved, and he may become his own avenger.

"A judicial assassination, justified in the eyes of the public by a false accusation, with almost complete certainty assures the triumph of those who have been guilty of it. In a crime of an inferior degree, they would have had everything to fear; but the death of the victim seals their security."

"The objection arising," says our author, "from the irremissibility of the punishment of death applies to all cases, and can be removed only by its complete abolition."

After striking the balance between the good and evil qualities of the penalty, Bentham arrives at no decisive and definite conclusion; or, to speak more exactly, he arrives at various conclusions by no means consistent with each other. He says that there is only one case in which capital punishment is necessary — namely, that of rebellion against government.

But by subsequent consideration, he weakens and almost annihilates his argument again; and to the reasons by which he effects this another could be added:

"In *fine*, I can see but one case in which it can be necessary and that only occasionally: in the case alleged for this purpose by M. Beccaria — the case of rebellion or other offense against government of a rebellious tendency, when, by destroying the chief, yon may destroy the faction. Where discontent has spread itself widely through a community, it may happen that imprisonment will not answer the purpose of safe custody. The keepers may be won over to the insurgent party, or, if not won over, they may be overpowered. They may be won over by considerations of a conscientious nature, which is a danger almost peculiar to this case; or they may be won over by considerations of a lucrative nature, which danger is greater in this case than in any other, since party projects may be carried on by a common purse.

"What, however, ought not to be lost sight of in the case of offenses of a political nature is, that if by the punishment of death one dangerous enemy is exterminated, the consequence of it may be the making an open door for a more formidable successor. 'Look,' said the executioner to an aged Irishman, showing him the bleeding head of a man just executed for rebellion: 'Look at the head of your son I ' 'My son,' replied he, 'has more than one head.' It would be well for the legislator before he appoints capital punishment, even in this case, to reflect on this instructive lesson." (Bentham, *The Rationale of Punishment*)

Bentham proposes that capital punishment should be confined to that class of the community from which the legislators are taken. And on the following page he proposes to confine Capital Punishment to the grayest offences—to murders, accompanied with circumstances of aggravation, and particularly when their effect may be the destruction of numbers; and in these cases, expedients by which it may be made to assume the most tragic appearance may be safely resorted to in the greatest extent possible, without having recourse to complicated torments.

But no wavering, no uncertainty, no want of decision are met with in the second treatise, viz., his address, published under the title: *Jeremy Bentham to his Fellow-Citizens of France on Death Punishment*. In this address in he says: "Now, then, as to this same question. The punishment of death, shall it be abolished? I answer, Yes. Shall there be an exception to this rule? I answer. So far as regards subsequential offenses, No,—meaning by subsequential, an offence committed on any day subsequent to that which stands appointed by the law as that after which no such act of punishment shall be performed."

Justice requires us to say that, whatever may have been the inducement which made Bentham at the date of this address a decided advocate for the abolition of capital punishment, it was certainly not the ambition of the demagogue, who, in order to farther his own selfish designs, flatters the popular passions of the day.

The leaders of the French popular party after the Revolution of 1830, desired that exemplary — that is, capital — punishment should be inflicted upon the advisers of Charles X. The defenders of these Ministers — Villele, Peyronnet, Polignac — in order to ward off the danger, proposed that capital punishment should be abolished. Although legally a new law could avail nothing for men who had committed offenses before it came into operation, still there would have been an important point gained for the ex-Ministers, if the punishment of death had at that time been abolished. Their defenders would in that case have had much greater chance of success. Whosoever, under these circumstances, proposed the abolition of Capital Punishment, as Jeremy Bentham did, exposed himself courageously to the enmity of the popular leaders, and certainly was by no means their vile and selfish flatterer.

Jeremy Bentham died more than thirty years ago, but no impartial judgment has yet been pronounced on the man or his works. The most of those who know anything of him follow either in the wake of his blind admirers, or take the aspersions of his slanderers for granted. Those who follow tradition as their guide, take the term utilitarianism as a true and proper designation for Bentham's philosophical and political system. They have no hesitation in denouncing him as a shrewd and thoroughly selfish fellow. That such men should take the trouble to learn that the term utilitarianism was not invented by Bentham himself, but by his enemies, can hardly be expected. But whether or not the word is appropriate as a general expression of Bentham's system, one thing is certain, that few men have been less guilty of low selfishness than Jeremy Bentham. His very faults show that, on the contrary, he was a man of benevolence and generosity.

In our opinion, at least, the fundamental defect in Bentham's system consists in his regarding the greatest happiness of the greatest number, or, as in other passages he still more pithily expresses it, his "greatest happiness principle," as the ultimate aim and end of all government. But let a State be as democratically constituted as it may, the number of its rulers, the legislative assembly included, is certainly a small minority of the citizens. In order to carry out Bentham's plan, this small minority would have to decide in the name of all what their greatest happiness is, and to regulate all public affairs according to this standard. But the individual's standard of happiness being various and manifold, and the very essence of freedom consisting in the individual right of every one to form a standard of happiness for himself, and to shape his conduct accordingly, provided that no individual is allowed to encroach upon the personal sphere of another, it necessarily follows that Bentham's "greatest happiness principle" would turn out to be the foundation of the most unbearable despotism.

Limiting ourselves to Bentham's works on Penal Legislation, we have a few objections to offer.

1. He is wanting in due respect to man. Our meaning will be best illustrated by the quotation of a single sentence: "Constantine prohibited by law the branding criminals on the face, alleging that it is a violation of the law of nature to disfigure the majesty of the human face—the majesty of the face of a scoundrel! "

The author might have spared himself the trouble of writing many painful chapters of his work if he had admitted that mutilating, disfiguring, defacing the human form, must be excluded from the Penal Code of every civilized nation.

Mr. Grote, in his history of Greece, already referred to, has laid it down as one of the chief characteristics of the Grecian mind that mutilation of the person, both in warfare and as a penalty, was "not only not practiced, but considered unseemly among non-Hellenes." And in our days, public opinion, whose silent growth and wholesome influence is much underrated both by Bentham and some living authors, would stamp that legislator with the indelible stigma of a barbarian who would vote for legalizing the infliction of such penalties.

2. Our second objection to Bentham's proposed Penal Code refers to his

introduction of sham punishments. As an illustration of our meaning, we again quote from *The Rationale of Punishment*. After recommending as penalties for deceit or forgery transfixing the hand or tongue of the culprit, he goes on to say: "These punishments may be made more formidable in appearance than in reality by dividing the instrument into two parts, so that the part which should pierce the offending member need not be thicker than a pin, whilst the other part of the instrument may be much thicker, and appear to penetrate with all its thickness."

Such a ruse would, however, soon prove quite useless, for the true extent of the injury inflicted could not be kept secret; and when the actual amount of the injury became known, greater harm would be done to public morality by this want of truthfulness in a legal act than good could be expected from the magnified appearance of the injury. A lawful penalty must be a reality and not a sham.

But after mentioning these defects, it is only fair to acknowledge that Bentham's works on Penal Legislation afford proofs of great learning and penetration, solidity of judgment, and activity of mind. He has paved the way for reformers by throwing the light of his criticisms on many abuses and prejudices. But of his proposed penal arrangements, nothing has been so generally introduced as solitary prisons, called by Bentham "Panopticons." Observation and experience have already shown that such arrangements are almost indispensable where the reformation of the criminal is an object in the penalty inflicted. But the final verdict on the value of solitary confinement has not yet been pronounced.

No man has devoted himself with greater energy to the mitigation of our Penal Code than Sir Samuel Romilly. The difficulties he had to contend against in order to carry through Parliament the bill for the abolition of capital punishment for picking pockets to the amount of five shillings may be learned by our readers from his memoirs or from the annals of our Penal Legislation. It is, however, a significant fact that the House of Commons, in 1808, forced upon him the omission of the following preamble to that bill: "Whereas the extreme severity of Penal Laws has not been found effectual for the prevention of crimes; but, on the contrary, by increasing the difficulty of convicting offenders, in some cases affords them impunity, and in most cases renders their punishment extremely uncertain" — and that of four successive Bills for the mitigation of punishment, only one passed the House of Lords, in which Lords Eldon, Ellenborough, and Sidmouth, were the jealous Conservative guardians of the Constitution and the sanctity of the criminal code. After Sir Samuel's lamented death, in 1818, Sir James Mackintosh followed in the same path of mitigation, with almost equal devotedness, and had to contend with Herculean labor against opposition and difficulty. Meanwhile, Thomas Fowell Buxton, the brother-in-law of Mrs. Fry (of well-deserved fame for her efforts to mitigate the sufferings of prisoners), assisted her valiantly in her endeavors, and published, in 1818, his enquiry whether crime and misery are produced or prevented by our present system of prison discipline.

It was a hard struggle indeed. The abuses in the administration of our gaols, the Draconian severity of our Penal Legislation, did not yield to the efforts of one, but demanded the perseverance of several generations of reformers. While by the suspension of cash payments the promissory notes of the Bank of England for more than twenty years were forced upon the nation as legal tender, and thereby the price of commodities raised to an unknown height— while the shipping interest was protected by the navigation acts — the landed interest by the corn bills, and almost every manufacturing interest enjoyed its particular protection—a policy which most effectually diminished the foreign demand for English produce, and tended to reduce the workmen to starvation —our Government saw no effective remedy against the daily increasing spirit of discontent save by maintaining the full severity of our Penal Code.

And still more were they hardened in their obstinacy when the discontentment brought about by hunger was increased by the harangues of political agitators, who pointed to reforms in the representation of the people as the only effective panacea for all evils. The great majority in both Houses of Parliament obstinately defended the severe enactments of our Penal Law, although they might have learned at every sitting of the assizes, and almost in every single trial, that this unpopular severity rendered these enactments inoperative and became an insurance of impunity for by far the greater number of culprits. The fact that severity was injurious to the public interest was not allowed, as we have seen in Sir Samuel Romilly's case, to be recorded in our Parliamentary Acts. But the stem reality was not abolished by the affected blindness of our legislators. And so deep-rooted is inveterate prejudice, that even long after the Reform Bill was carried, a Whig Ministry, and a prominent reformer in this Ministry, obstinately resisted the due limitation of death punishment. When Lord John Russell's Bill to reduce the number of capital offences was being considered in committee on May 19, 1837, Mr. William Ewart moved an amendment confining the penalty of death to the single case of deliberate murder. The Ministry resisted and carried the original bill by a majority of one vote. When brought before the House of Lords, Lord Brougham observed that nothing but pressure of time prevented his endeavoring to amend the measure by extending the remission of the Death Penalty to all crimes except that of murder; and his lordship did not know that he should venture to except that — so convinced was he that capital punishment tended to the increase of crime and to the impairing of justice.

No better proof can be given that a legislative measure has fairly taken hold of the public mind—no more effective means can be devised for carrying a lawful purpose into effect—than the formation of a society.

The Society for the Abolition of Capital Punishment was founded in 1828, under the patronage of the Duke of Sussex, by Messrs. J. Sydney Taylor, W. Allen, Peter Bedford, J. Thomas Barry, Sir Fowell Buxton, and the Right Hon. Dr. Lushington. Through their instrumentality petitions have been presented to both Houses of Parliament. On May 24, 1880, a petition, signed by upwards of a thousand bankers of Edinburgh, Dublin, Manchester, Liverpool, &c. &c. [the list comprises 288 towns], was presented to the House of Commons by

Henry Brougham. The petition contained the following remarkable statement: "That your petitioners find by experience that the infliction of death, or even the possibility of the infliction of death, prevents the prosecution, conviction, and punishment of the criminal, and thus endangers the property which it is intended to protect."

In consequence of this and other petitions to Parliament, death punishment for forgery was abolished.

In connection with this part of our subject we must refer our readers to the second report of the Royal Commissioners on Criminal Law, 1886.

Although in reviewing the progress of opinion with regard to Penal Legislation, we here give a prominent place to England, and have brought down our historical survey near to the present time, it must not be implied that other countries have been altogether indifferent to the subject. In fact, it appears from our short account of Bentham's career and writings, how closely English views on this subject were related to those of France, and to what extent the ideas expressed in either country obtained influence in the other. Most of our readers will admit that this steadily increasing mutual influence of European nations upon each other is one of the prominently characteristic features of our age.

The philosophy of Penal Legislation has in no country been more carefully investigated than in Italy. Cesare Bonesano de Beccaria [bom 1738 : died 1794] wrote and published [first edition anonymously, Monaco, 1764,] his celebrated and influential work, *Dei Delitti e delle Pene*. We learn that he was a member of a society of men of letters at Milan, who edited a periodical, *Il Caffé*. The judicial murder of Calas, at Toulouse, caused at that time a European sensation; one of the French authors, who, as editors of the great *Encyclopédie*, were afterwards styled "Encyclopedists," is said to have written to a member of the Milan literary society: "Now is the time to rise against religious intolerance and the exaggerated severity of Penal Legislation."

Most of the members of the literary club were struck with this idea, and, before all others, Beccaria, who, a zealous reader of French authors — especially Condillac, Helvetius, Montesquieu — was induced to write his work *Dei Delitti e delle Pene*, which afterwards made him famous, and up to the present time has been considered one of the most important treatises on Penal Legislation. In a letter written prior to the publication of this book, which Morellet, the French translator of Beccaria, has preserved, this author says of himself that he was mainly actuated by three sentiments — viz., love of literary fame, love of liberty, and compassion for the unhappy condition of mankind, who were enslaved by many errors.

Beccaria's work was not intended to be a complete system of Penal Law, but was mainly directed against the most flagrant errors and abuses of contemporaneous legislation. The author insists particularly on abolition of punishment of death and abolition of torture. The wide circulation which this work obtained, the fame and influence which have attended it, justify us in giving a short analysis of the chapter relating to Capital Punishment: "The right to punish which is vested in the sovereign is founded on the interest that everybody has in the maintenance of justice. Justice is defined to be the bond which unites the interests of individuals for mutual protection—perpetual warfare of everybody against his neighbor being the natural consequence of an isolated state. The power of dispensing justice is vested in the sovereign. In order to constitute this power every man was required to surrender a portion of his liberty—especially a portion of those rights which regard his own person. "The aggregate of these, the smallest portions possible, forms the right of punishing; all that extends beyond this, is abuse, not justice."

The small portion of his liberty which every individual is supposed to have ceded to the sovereign cannot include the right to dispose of the individual's life. Besides, the end professed to be aimed at by capital punishment can be better attained by less violent means.

For the death of a citizen cannot be necessary, save in one case, when, though deprived of his liberty, he is still powerful enough, through his connections, to endanger the security of the nation. But such a state of things supposes complete anarchy, in which the arbitrary will of individuals supplants law. Such an exceptional state of things may require exceptional remedies, may justify extraordinary energy, and even violence exerted by single individuals; but laws are given for a state of tranquility, and in these happier times there can be no necessity for taking away the life of an individual.

The author then asserts that it is not the intensity of a pain which produces the greatest effect on the mind of man, but its continuance, and thereby implies that in his view the main object of punishment is to operate as a deterrent on those who are likely to commit the offense for which the punishment has been inflicted. As a deterring example, the execution of a culprit lasts only a short time; whereas, by perpetual slavery (Beccaria's mode of punishing the greatest crimes), every criminal affords a frequent and lasting example.

He then meets the objection: perpetual slavery is as painful a punishment as death, and the sovereign has accordingly just as little right to inflict the former as the latter punishment. His answer is, that perpetual slavery might be even a greater evil than death, if it were possible to concentrate in one point all the miserable moments in the life of a slave. But these miseries being spread over a long period, while the pain of death is confined to a moment, makes slavery by far the milder of the two modes of suffering. Besides, habit exercises its mitigating influence by rendering the culprits callous, and hope, this cheering companion of mortals, by flattering visions of a brighter future. Accordingly, slavery is in reality a milder punishment than it appears to be to the spectators, who estimate the privations of the slave without taking into account the alleviating influences.

Another objection to capital punishment is the example it affords of barbarity. "If the passions or the necessity of war have taught men to shed the blood of their fellow creatures, the laws which are intended to moderate the ferocity of mankind should not increase it by the examples of barbarity, the more horrible as this punishment is usually attended with formal pageantry." But in enumerating Beccaria's reasons against the infliction of death, without giving an idea of his impressive style and his lively eloquence, we have only done half justice to the anther of this hook, which, in a large measure, owes its success and the diffusion of its principles to the animated style in which it appeals to the feelings of mankind — a success which has been even enhanced by the ingenuity and dexterity with which susceptibilities have been spared, and the existing powers flattered.

The work appeared in about thirty Italian editions, and was translated into most of the European languages. From 1767 to 1778, four editions of the English translation were issued in this country.

The work of another Italian—*La Seienza della Legialaziane, di Gaetano Filangieri*—is remarkable in more than one respect. The author, third son of Caesar, Prince of Arianelli, in the kingdom of Naples, was born in the year 1752. He was educated for the bar, and practiced first as an advocate in the courts at Naples; afterwards, when by his family connections he obtained royal favor, he was appointed gentleman of the Chamber in 1777, and held besides a commission in the Royal Noble Guard.

After writing some essays on law and politics, he published, 1782, the first and second books of the *Seienza della Legislazione*, which were received with a burst of applause and soon reprinted in four subsequent editions. Whilst the author held high offices he was the favorite of his sovereign; whilst he carried into effect his vast plan of a general reform in the legislation of his country, being checked neither by favor nor persecution, he wrote his great theoretical work *On The Science of Legislation*, which, however, in the thirty-sixth year of his age (1788), he was, by death, prevented from completing.

No writer on the history of Frederick I and Maria Theresa, no writer on the history of the French Revolution who desires to make himself acquainted with its causes and the events immediately preceding, can dispense with reading this book. There is one striking passage in the introduction which we think no reader of our day can peruse without being reminded of the gentle breeze which, after long sultry summer days, is the certain precursor of the coming storm; we mean the passage which alludes to the oration delivered by the Bishop of Aix before Louis XVI, on the day of his coronation.

Not only on account of its author, and as an illustration of the history of its time, is the book remarkable, but it was besides "singular in its kind, and equally singular was its fortune. In the bosom of superstition, and in some degree of civil and religious slavery, it has run through no less than seven different editions. It has been twice published in the German language, has appeared in two French versions, has been translated into Spanish, and is at last naturalized in the happiest and freest government in the world." [*from the preface to the 1806 translation by R. Clayton.*]

The third book of the *Seienza della Legislazione* treats Criminal Law, and is divided into two parts, of which the first refers to the procedure, and the second treats of crimes and punishments.

Filangieri differs from Beccaria with regard to the punishment of death, and opposes his reasoning without mentioning his name. Filangieri asserts that the sovereign has the right of inflicting Death Punishment, and attempts to prove his assertions in the following manner: "Man in a state of nature has a right to his life. He cannot resign that right, but he can forfeit it by misdeeds, and he does forfeit it by a murderous assault upon his fellow man.

"In a state of nature no individual is appointed to perform special functions; consequently it is the right and duty of every man to punish the transgressor of natural laws, and everybody is justified in killing that individual who by his misdeeds has forfeited his life.

"This natural right to kill the transgressor is by every individual transferred to the sovereign, and consequently vested in him so soon as the state of nature is transformed into a civil state. The right of the sovereign to inflict the punishment of death arises from this transference of the right of every individual to kill his neighbor—by no means from the cession of the natural right which every man has to his own person."

Those of our readers who are not conversant with the philosophy of Right, will be prone to take this reasoning of Filangieri as idle hair-splitting sophistry; but how can these champions of so-called common sense and sober matter of fact explain that in all civilized states, in respect to one case at least, impunity is granted to the perpetrator of intended homicide? No judge, no legally empaneled jury, will condemn a man for having killed his neighbor who assaulted him with murderous intent, provided that no other mode of saving his own life was possible. Common sense suggests no objection to such an absolving verdict; and Filangieri's theory justifies it by the assumption that man is allowed to return to his natural right whenever he finds it impossible to have recourse to the authority whose competency he recognizes by the very act of his being a member of a community.

Filangieri does not advocate the abolition of capital punishment, but limits the infliction of death to a few crimes, viz., murder with intent after cold-blooded deliberation (*a sangue freddo*), treason, and high treason.

The infliction of this penalty is to be accompanied with melancholy solemnity, but divested of all avoidable cruelty.

Before leaving Filangieri, we will quote one passage of his book, from which it will appear that he derives the right of punishing from, the nature of man. He says (chap xxix. b. 8) : "Those phenomena, which we term moral, those sentiments, those passions which manifest themselves in us unconsciously, are only so many links of the invisible chain which nature has made for great designs. Nature—to use an expression of Aristotle (*Republica, Lib. I.*) — has special means for every special purpose, and we are enabled in some way to trace out one of her purposes by recognizing the corresponding means. What object, I ask, could our hatred have to the perpetrator of a crime which does not concern ourselves, our relatives, or friends? Which of us does not suffer from seeing a crime unpunished? Which of us does not rejoice when justice condemns the perpetrator to his deserved punishment? Which of us, on hearing the narrative of an atrocious crime, would not wish to have in his own grasp the wretch who has committed it, in order to avenge the wrong done to the unfortunate man totally unknown to us? To be sincere, we must confess that at such a time no motive of self-interest actuates us."

Although of these two Italian writers Filangieri had more learning and depth, Beccaria's treatise made a greater impression on his contemporaries, and had more influence on legislation.

Among the governments of Italy, that of Tuscany was most impressed with Beccaria's views. In harmony with the spirit of reform, characteristic of all his predecessors of the dynasty of Lorraine, Leopold, Grand Duke of Tuscany, reformed the legislation of his country. By the Code published 1786, he abolished punishment of death. The preamble of the act by which the Code was introduced asserts that no capital punishment had been inflicted in Tuscany for fourteen years before (1772), that severe punishments are productive of mischief; that the reformation of the criminal ought to be one of the main ends of justice; that the legislator ought never to despair of attaining this end; and that in Tuscany, at least, reformation was more certainly attainable by means of good prisons than by Capital Punishment, which the people of Tuscany detested.

It has been shown that the number of crimes has not increased since the abolition of capital punishment. When, however, Leopold ascended the Imperial Throne of Austria in 1790, riots broke out in some parts of the country, and presented the opportunity which the adversaries of reform had long desired. They succeeded in prevailing upon the Emperor to enact the law of 1790, by which capital punishment was re-introduced for riotous disobedience. The law of August 30, 1796, signed by the Grand Duke Ferdinand, was still more severe, and menaced certain crimes against religion, besides assassination, murder, infanticide, with capital punishment. The real cause of this retrograde legislation must be referred to the timid character of the Grand Duke, and the agitations both of a reactionary and a French revolutionary party. It is a remarkable fact that, according to trustworthy authorities, the number of capital crimes was not increased under the law of 1786; nor were such crimes committed by foreigners; whence it appears how unfounded was the fear that, after the abolition of capital punishment, foreigners would rush into that country where punishment by death was abolished, in order to commit murders. Even after the enactment of capital punishment, no execution took place, because of the indisposition of the courts of law to convict, and on account of the mercy which was granted to condemned criminals. We shall refer in another portion of this work to the subsequent legislation regarding capital punishment in Tuscany.

The publication of Beccaria's work, and the abolition of capital punishment in Tuscany, encouraged, not only in Italy, but throughout the whole of Europe, the advocates of the abolition of death punishment, or, at least, its limitation to the grayest crimes. In Germany, the first example was set by Austria. The benevolent Emperor Joseph II had his misgivings regarding the lawfulness of death penalty, but did not venture on its abrogation. He accordingly, in 1781 and 1788, gave orders in council that passed sentences should not be carried into execution without his special mandate. These orders in council were kept secret, in order not to weaken the deterring influence of the law upon individuals predisposed to crime. Very few executions took place after 1781, but death punishment was not actually abolished before the promulgation of the new Penal Code of April, 1787. The Emperor Francis re-enacted Capital Punishment, at first for high treason only (1796), but afterwards for many crimes, by the Code (*Strafgesetzbuch*) of 1803. The Emperor apologized, after his own fashion, for so doing, by a decree of the Court, October 29, 1803; he could not help, in the same decree, recognizing the fact that the number of crimes committed had not increased since the abolition of Death Punishment; but he considered it, nevertheless, necessary to threaten the penalty again, as a check on those criminals whose hardened disposition was manifested by the atrocity of their offenses.

We reserve for a future portion of this work what we have to say respecting the subsequent fate of death punishment in Austria. The French Revolution, and the events arising from it, filled the rulers and statesmen of the time with fear, and made them think that the menace of the severest penalties, especially death punishment, was- alone sufficient as a deterrent from crime. In the Prussian Code, *Allgemeines Landreckt fur die Konige Preussischen Staaten* published 1788, confirmed 1794, capital punishment is accordingly threatened for many, especially political, misdemeanors and crimes, in such a manner as to show that the legislator had no other object save that of deterring.

The Penal Code of Bavaria also maintained capital punishment. Feuerbach, the author of this code, followed his own penal theory, according to which, in order to render the menace effective, the temptation to the grossest crime ought to be checked by the menace of the greatest evil — death.

In France, Beccaria's ideas were received with applause by the French nation before the Revolution; but after 1790, Le Pelletier Saint-Fargeau, reporter of the Committees for Legislation and Constitution in the National Assembly, moved that punishment of death be abolished, with the solitary exception of those political culprits who had been declared rebels. Robespierre delivered a speech in favor of abolition, but the measure was lost by a majority of votes. After the execution of Louis XVI, which increased the number of those in favor of abolition, Condorcet, in the Convention, moved (1793) that punishment of death for all common crimes should be abolished. The speeches delivered on the occasion show that the disposition of at least a fraction of that assembly was not unfavorable to the motion. But the decree of the Year IV, enacting the abolition of death punishment was rendered meaningless by the addition that the act should not come into operation before the proclamation of general peace. Cruel sentences of transportation were substituted for Death Punishment until, December 29th, 1801, capital punishment was legally re-enacted. The Code Napoleon of 1810 ordains the extreme penalty for thirty-six crimes; the motives assigned for its imposition reveal the heartless cruelty of the Emperor. During the Restoration some good books were published, showing the unlawfulness of death punishment. But a Minister of Charles X was bold enough to declare that the Chamber had no right to discuss the lawfulness of capital punishment. It was not until 1830 that the debates on the subject possessed much general interest. Of those discussions which took place after that date we shall speak in a subsequent chapter.

The development of the views on our subject in the North American States was peculiar. Ever since 1682 the inhabitants of Pennsylvania have repeatedly expressed their desire that capital punishment should be limited to murder. The Quakers especially endeavored to show that the penalty was altogether unlawful, or that it should at least be confined to the gravest crime. A sort of compromise between the legislature of Pennsylvania and the Quakers resulted in the limitation of the penalty to murder. After the lapse of three years, the law was provisionally renewed, and at last, in 1794, definitively enacted. The discussion in the Pennsylvanian legislature had an influence on surrounding states. A translation of Beccaria's work was read with avidity, and his views supplied fresh impulse to the movement in favor of abolition. But violent opponents of the measure were not wanting. The combatants on both sides quoted Scripture in favor of their respective views, but without satisfactory results. Accordingly, as one or the other party prevailed, the abolition of death punishment, or its retention, was constituted the law in the various states. Livingston, by his energetic struggle against death punishment, exercised a very powerful influence in flavor of abolition. We refer specially to his report of 1822, and to that other report which forms the introduction to his Criminal Code. It is true that a great deal may be said against his views on the Philosophy of Right, but his comprehensive genius, the proofs afforded of his learning and practical experience, and the spirited manner in which he demolished the arguments of his antagonists, made a deep impression in America, and even now fully deserve the attention of the legal profession in every country.

In connection with this part of our subject it is worthy of notice that in America, especially in Pennsylvania, the conviction first gained ground that murder, if punished with death, ought to be distinguished as murder of the first and second degree. This view was soon incorporated into the codes of other American states.

Besides, the policy of executing criminals in the presence of a few selected individuals, and not before the public, was first advocated in America. The question is continually kept before the American public by means of petitions, motions in the legislative assemblies, and public meetings. This continual agitation on the subject has naturally produced an immense mass of materials relating to our question.

Capital Punishment, Margaret Fuller (1846)

Review of: A Defence of Capital Punishment, and an Essay on the Ground and Reason of Punishment, with Special Reference to the Penalty of Death, George Barrel Cheever, New York, 1846.

We have had this book before us for several weeks, but the task of reading it has been so repulsive that we have been obliged to get through it by short stages, with long intervals of rest and refreshment between, and have only just reached the end. We believe, however, we are now possessed of its substance, so far as it is possible to admit into any mind matter wholly uncongenial with its structure, its faith, and its hope.

Meanwhile, others have shown themselves more energetic in the task, and notices have appeared that express, in part, our own views. Among others an able critic has thus summed up his impressions: — "Of the whole we will say briefly, that its premises are monstrous, its reasoning sophistical, its conclusions absurd, and its spirit diabolic."

❖ ❖ ❖

These writers profess to occupy the position of defense; surely never was one sustained so in the spirit of offense.

1st. They appeal either to the natural or regenerate man, as suits their purpose. Sometimes all traditions and their literal interpretations are right; sometimes it is impossible to interpret them aright, unless according to some peculiar doctrine, and the natural inference of the common mind would be an error.

2d. They strain, but vainly, to show the New Testament no improvement on the Old, and themselves in harmonious relations to both. On this subject we would confidently leave the arbitration to a mind — could such a one be found — sufficiently disciplined to examine the subject, and new both to the New Testament and this volume, as that of Rammohun Roy might have been, whether its views are not of the same strain that Jesus sought to correct and enlighten among the Jews, and whether the writers do not treat the teachings of the new dispensation most unfairly, in their desire to wrest them into the service of the old.

3d. Wherever there is a weak place in the argument, it is filled up by abuse of the opposite party. The words "absurd," "infidel," "blasphemer. . ." "shallow philosophy," "sickly sentimentalism," and the like, are among the favorite missiles of these defenders of the truth. They are of a sort whose frequent use is generally supposed to argue the want of a shield of reason and a heart of faith.

And this brings us to a more close consideration of the spirit of this book, characterized by our contemporary as "diabolic." And we, also, cannot excuse ourselves from marking it as, in this respect, one of the worst books we have ever seen.

❖ ❖ ❖

We wish most sincerely this book had been a wise and noble one. To ascertain just principles, it is necessary that the discussion should be full and fair, and both sides ably argued. After this has been done, the sense of the world can decide. It would be a happiness for which it might seem that man at this time of day is ripe, that the opposing parties should meet in open lists as brothers, believing each that the other desired only that the truth should triumph, and able to clasp hands as men of different structure and ways of thinking, but fellow-students of the divine will. O, had we but found such an adversary, above the use of artful abuse, or the feints of sophistry, able to believe in the noble intention, of a foe as of a friend, how cheerily would the trumpets ring out while the assembled world echoed the signal words, "God Speed The Right!" The tide of progress rolls onward, dwelling more and more with the lives of those who would fain see all men called to repentance. It must be a strong arm, indeed, that can build a dam to stay it even for a moment. None such do we see yet; but we should rejoice in a noble and strong opponent, putting forth all his power for conscience's sake. God speed the Right!

Hurrah For Hanging!, Walt Whitman (1846)

We are going to say some bold truths! We are going to dash at once into the impassioned errors of probably four out of every five who will read this article!

If ever the present system of criminal law, and the treatment of criminals, offered an instance of one of its fruits, that instance is the precocious monster Freeman, the butcher of five human beings last week in Cayuga County in this state—as we have already published the dark and dreadful narrative. Reader! You may meet such a remark as the foregoing, with a scowl, or an impatient jibe—but if we are not, in our own mind, clear in its truth, may we never get sight of Heaven hereafter.

The present excited state of public feeling will, of course, lead the representatives of society in due time to paddle in his blood, as he in that of his victims. The murder will surely be revenged.

The present excited state of public feeling will, of course, lead the representatives of society in due time to paddle in his blood, as he in that of his victims. The murder will surely be revenged. We can therefore do no harm by seizing the occasion to draw as profitable a lesson as we may from the whole case. It is no inviting task; but few tasks are inviting.

Let us examine somewhat of the murderer's life:

So far as anything can be gathered from the facts brought to light, Freeman seems to be an uneducated, friendless outcast. He has never had the benefit of any kind of teaching or counsel; and never lived within any fixed moral or religious influences. His whole character is of the most blindly brutal cast—a mere human animal. At the early age of nineteen, he is accused of a crime of which he says he is not guilty, and through the influence of Mr. Van Ness, is sent to the State Prison for five years! Now consider how few of better fortune, even of virtuous and religious character, would not deeply feel the wrong and injustice of such proceedings, and be roused to the fiercest hate against those who had been instrumental in bringing them to it. How much more terrible the effect then on this neglected, ignorant and depraved Negro, in whom the brute had been allowed to rule the man.

For five long and weary years he is shut up in prison, and left to brood over his wrongs. He can make no distinction between the inevitable mistakes of the law and human testimony, and what he imagines is a determination to crush him. He thinks only of his laborious imprisonment day after day, month after month, till it has taken possession of all his thoughts; and the purpose of revenge, which to him is justice, has become to him the very breath of life. If society had dealt tenderly with him during this awful period; if some ministering angel had come and heard his sorrowful story, and sought to bring him under kindly influences, and taught him the beautiful Christian law, "Love your enemies; bless those who curse you;" if this had been done, he might have been saved, and his victims been still in the midst of the living.

But this was not done. The neglected wretch was left to his fate, left to be haunted by his foul passions, and at last to be turned out to do their own bidding without a word of warning, or one friend to guide or bless. Is it a matter of wonder then, that the result is what we have seen? Is it strange that the wild beast prevailed?

That the wretch had worked himself into a terribly calm and blind ferocity, appears from the whole account of the murder. The idea of revenge seems to have swallowed up all things else. He seems to have become perfectly bewildered and blinded by his purpose of blood. He not only strikes the object of his spite, the man who did him the supposed wrong, but indiscriminately, as though running the bloody muck. With a frightful coolness, he plunges his knife into all whom he meets, sacrificing guilty and innocent alike. He destroys those who never did him harm, whom he never saw, and against whom he could have had no possible hatred or ill feeling! This very horror of the butchery, shows how thoroughly diseased and confused the whole moral being of the murderer had become.

What remains then? Hang him! In the work of death, let the law keep up with the murderer, and see who will get the victory at last. Homicides are increasing in every part of the land. We are amazed that the gallows don't stop 'em! Let its advocates not be backward, however. Let them stick it out staunchly, and kill and slay the faster—and, even if the more they hang the more they prepare to hang, let them keep it up still—for is not such the command of God?

Letters to the Daily News, Charles Dickens (1846)

23 Feb 1846

GENTLEMEN. I choose this time for addressing to you, the first of two or three letters on the subject of Capital Punishment, because it seems to me that the importance of the question is very strongly presented to the public mind just now, by a recent execution in Ireland: and the recent acquittal, in England, of one of the most cruel murderers of whom we have any record. And although there can be no doubt that such a theme, of all others, should be considered with the calmest reference to its own broad Right and Wrong, and not with a limited appeal to its illustration in this or that instance: still, I apprehend that cases like these resolve themselves so directly into the general question, as to have a legitimate and very powerful bearing on it; and that no better occasion can be seized for reviving its discussion, than when such circumstances are generally remembered.

I wish to be distinctly understood, in the outset, as writing in no spirit of sympathy with the criminal. It will be a part of my purpose to endeavor to show, that the morbid and odious sentimentality which has been exhibited of late years, in favor of ruffians utterly unworthy of it, but drawing nigh to the gallows, is one of the evil concomitants of the Punishment of Death. And I desire to consider it, with a reference to the criminal, only in two points of view. To these, I will confine this introductory letter.

I wish to be distinctly understood, in the outset, as writing in no spirit of sympathy with the criminal.

First. Whether one of the two great objects of all punishment (reserving the second for its proper place) be not to reform the offender. Secondly. Whether an irrevocable doom—which nothing can recall, which no human power can set right if it be wrong, which may be wrongfully inflicted with the most just intention and which has been wrongfully inflicted with the most just intention, as we all know, more than once—should ever be pronounced by men of fallible and erring judgment, on their fellow creatures.

It may be urged that, in the preparation of a criminal for death, and in his devout reception of religious comfort, and in his full confession and late repentance, his reformation is achieved and worked out. Reverend ordinaries, at Newgate and elsewhere, have said so. Hosts of angels have been imagined, in enthusiastic sermons, waiting to conduct the murderer to Heaven; and strange parallels have even been suggested, in such discourses, between the Scaffold and the Cross. GOD forbid that I should presume to measure, or doubt, the mercy in store for the worst criminal ever executed! But I do distinctly challenge and dispute this kind of reformation. Besides that the reformation brought about by legal punishment, should be, to be satisfactory, a living, lasting, growing one: working on, in degradation and humility, from day to day; and striving, in its chains, and labor, and long-distant Hope, to make some atonement always; besides this, I doubt the possibility of a great change being wrought in any man's heart and nature, in the flush and fever of that flying interval between the Warrant and the Noose. I see the dreadful hurry of the time, expressed in every word and action that comes leaking through the prison walls, to be caught up by the thirsty crowd outside. I see Hope living on, and know it must live on, in some faint shape, until the Bell begins to toll. I see the restless mind wandering away, miserably, from the main theme of the repentant letter, written in the cell; and while it tells of trust and steadfastness, having power to settle nowhere. I see the abject clinging on to life, which clutches at the hangman's hand, and blesses him beneath the beam. I see, in everything, the same wild, rapid, incoherent dream: of which I believe the penitence and preparation to be, at least, as unsettled and unsubstantial as any other part. And I believe this, because of the natural constitution of the human mind, and its ordinary workings at such a frightful pass.

"I can give you no hope of life," said a gentlemen to a criminal in Newgate, on the night before the day appointed for his execution. "Unless I had solemnly given the promise elsewhere, that I would tell you so, I should not be here. But, by much entreaty, I have obtained a respite: that there may be time to inquire into what I have represented as a doubtful point. Can you bear the thought of living, only for another week?" "O God, sir!" cried the man, "a week is a long time to live!" And being smitten, as if he were only a week old then, he fell down, senseless, on the ground

Upon the second question, whether an irrevocable punishment be, on principle, justifiable; ordained, as it necessarily is, by men of fallible judgment, whose powers of arriving at the truth are limited, and in whom there is the capacity of mistake and false deduction; upon this question alone, I submit that a firm and efficient stand may be made against the punishment of Death. Better that hundreds of guilty persons should escape scot-free (which, supposing any other punishment to be substituted in its place, they never could or would), than that one innocent person should suffer. Better, I will even say, that hundreds of guilty persons should escape, than that the possibility of any innocent man or woman having been sacrificed, should present itself, with the least appearance of cooler of reason, to the minds of any class of men!

Take the case of SEERY, the man just now executed in Ireland; in that unhappy country, where it is considered most essential to assert the law, and make examples through its means. My impression of the case, so far as I know it from the public reports, is, that the man was guilty; but that is nothing to the purpose. There are these facts in it:

The prosecutor was shot at, by night; and identified the wretched man who has suffered, as the person who fired at him: against whom there was some other evidence, but all of a circumstantial and constructible nature. Before that miserable man went to his death, he set on record, a deliberate and solemn protest against the justice of his sentence, and called upon his Maker before whom he would so soon appear, with all his sins upon his head, to bear witness to his innocence. Since his death, the prosecutor (an honourable and credible witness, no doubt), has repeated his "positive and unalterable conviction," that he was not mistaken in his previous identification, and that SEERY was the man who fired at him.

Will anyone deny that there is, here, the possibility of mistake? I entreat all who may chance to read this letter, to pause for an instant, and ask themselves whether they can remember any occasion, on which they have, in the broad day, and under circumstances the most favorable to recognition, mistaken one person for another: and believed that in a perfect stranger, they have seen, going away from them or coming towards them, a familiar friend. I beg them to consider whether such mistakes be not so common, in all men's experience, as to render it highly probable that every Irish peasant in whose remembrance this dying declaration lives and burns, can easily recall one such for himself. And then I put this question—Is such an execution calculated to assist the law: to diffuse a wholesome respect for it: to repress atrocious crimes against the person: to awaken any new sense of the sacredness of human life?

Contending, at present, against the justifiability of the punishment of death, on this second ground which I have stated: I submit that probability of mistake is not required. The barest possibility of mistake is a sufficient reason against the taking of a life which nothing can restore; whereas, it would weigh but as a shred of gossamer against the infliction of any other punishment, within the power of man to repair.

The barest possibility of mistake is a sufficient reason against the taking of a life which nothing can restore; whereas, it would weigh but as a shred of gossamer against the infliction of any other punishment, within the power of man to repair.

With this, I leave the question of capital punishment in its reference to the convict sentenced, and shall beg leave, in another letter, to consider it in its bearings on society and crime. But, as a part of its effects upon society, I would, in conclusion, entreat your readers to reflect, whether such a declaration as that made by Seery before his execution, would be likely to have awakened a general sympathy among the Irish people, or any strong conviction of his innocence (unless afterward revived and borne out by newly discovered circumstances), but for its being surrounded by the awful dignity of death.

9 March 1846

GENTLEMEN, I will take for the subject of this letter, the effect of Capital Punishment on the commission of crime, or rather of murder; the only crime with one exception (and that a rare one) to which it is now applied. Its effect in preventing crime, I will reserve for another letter: and a few of the more striking illustrations of each aspect of the subject, for a concluding one.

Some murders are committed in hot blood and furious rage; some, in deliberate revenge; some, in terrible despair; some (but not many) for mere gain; some, for the removal of an object dangerous to the murderer's peace or good name; some, to win a monstrous notoriety.

On murders committed in rage, in the despair of strong affection (as when a starving child is murdered by its parent) or for gain, I believe the punishment of death to have no effect in the least. In the two first cases, the impulse is a blind and wild one, infinitely beyond the reach of any reference to the punishment. In the last, there is little calculation beyond the absorbing greed of the money to be got. Courvoisier, for example, might have robbed his master with greater safety and with fewer chances of detection, if he had not murdered him. But, his calculations going to the gain and not to the loss, he had no balance for the consequences of what he did. So, it would have been more safe and prudent in the woman who was hanged a few weeks since, for the murder in Westminster, to have simply robbed her old companion in an unguarded moment, as in her sleep. But, her calculation going to the gain of what she took to be a Bank note; and the poor old woman living between her and the gain; she murdered her.

On murders committed in deliberate revenge, or to remove a stumbling block in the murderer's path, or in an insatiate craving for notoriety, is there reason to suppose that the punishment of death has the direct effect of an incentive and an impulse?

A murder is committed in deliberate revenge. The murderer is at no trouble to prepare his train of circumstances, takes little or no pains to escape, is quite cool and collected, perfectly content to deliver himself up to the Police, makes no secret of his guilt, but boldly says, "I killed him. I'm glad of it. I meant to do it. I am ready to die." There was such a case the other day. There was such another case not long ago. There are such cases frequently. It is the commonest first exclamation on being seized. Now, what is this but a false arguing of the question, announcing a foregone conclusion, expressly leading to the crime, and inseparably arising out of the punishment of death? "I took his life. I give up mine to pay for it. Life for life; blood for blood. I have done the crime. I am ready with the atonement. I know all about it; it's a fair bargain between me and the law. Here am I to execute my part of it; and what more is to be said or done?"

It is the very essence of the maintenance of this punishment for murder, that it does set life against life. It is in the essence of a stupid, weak, or otherwise ill-regulated mind (of such a murderer's mind, in short), to recognize in this set off, a something that diminishes the base and coward character of murder. In a pitched battle, I, a common man, may kill my adversary, but he may kill me. In a duel, a gentleman may shoot his opponent through the head, but the opponent may shoot him too, and this makes it fair. Very well. I take this man's life for a reason I have, or choose to think I have, and the law takes mine. The law says, and the clergyman says, there must be blood for blood and life for life. Here it is. I pay the penalty.

A mind incapable, or confounded in its perceptions—and you must argue with reference to such a mind, or you could not have such a murder—may not only establish on these grounds an idea of strict justice and fair reparation, but a stubborn and dogged fortitude and foresight that satisfy it hugely. Whether the fact be really so, or not, is a question I would be content to rest, alone, on the number of cases of revengeful murder in which this is well known, without dispute, to have been the prevailing demeanor of the criminal: and in which such speeches and such absurd reasoning have been constantly uppermost with him. "Blood for blood," and "life for life," and such like balanced jingles, have passed current in people's mouths, from legislators downwards, until they have been corrupted into "tit for tat," and acted on.

Next, come the murders done to sweep out of the way a dreaded or detested object. At the bottom of this class of crimes, there is a slow, corroding, growing hate. Violent quarrels are commonly found to have taken place between the murdered person and the murderer: usually of opposite sexes. There are witnesses to old scenes of reproach and recrimination, in which they were the actors; and the murderer has been heard to say, in this or that coarse phrase, "that he wouldn't mind killing her, though he should be hanged for it"—in these cases, the commonest avowal.

It seems to me, that in this well-known scrap of evidence, there is a deeper meaning than is usually attached to it. I do not know, but it may be—I have a strong suspicion that it is—a clue to the slow growth of the crime, and its gradual development in the mind. More than this: a clue to the mental connexion of the deed, with the punishment to which the doer of that deed is liable, until the two, conjoined, give birth to monstrous and misshapen Murder.

The idea of murder, in such a case, like that of self-destruction in the great majority of instances, is not a new one. It may have presented itself to the disturbed mind in a dim shape and afar off; but it has been there. After a quarrel, or with some strong sense upon him of irritation or discomfort arising out of the continuance of this life in his path, the man has brooded over the unformed desire to take it. "Though he should be hanged for it." With the entrance of the Punishment into his thoughts, the shadow of the fatal beam begins to attend—not on himself, but on the object of his hate. At every new temptation, it is there, stronger and blacker yet, trying to terrify him. When she defies or threatens him, the scaffold seems to be her strength and "vantage ground." Let her not be too sure of that; "though he should be hanged for it."

Thus, he begins to raise up, in the contemplation of this death by hanging, a new and violent enemy to brave. The prospect of a slow and solitary expiation would have no congeniality with his wicked thoughts, but this throttling and strangling has. There is always before him, an ugly, bloody, scarecrow phantom, that champions her, as it were, and yet shows him, in a ghastly way, the example of murder. Is she very weak, or very trustful in him, or infirm, or old? It gives a hideous courage to what would be mere slaughter otherwise; for there it is, a presence always about her, darkly menacing him with that penalty whose murky secret has a fascination for all secret and unwholesome thoughts. And when he struggles with his victim at the last, "though he should be hanged for it," it is a merciless wrestle, not with one weak life only, but with that ever-haunting, ever-beckoning shadow of the gallows, too; and with a fierce defiance to it, after their long survey of each other, to come on and do its worst.

Present this black idea of violence to a bad mind contemplating violence; hold up before a man remotely compassing the death of another person, the spectacle of his own ghastly and untimely death by man's hands; and out of the depths of his own nature you shall assuredly raise up that which lures and tempts him on. The laws which regulate those mysteries have not been studied or cared for, by the maintainers of this law; but they are paramount and will always assert their power.

Out of one hundred and sixty-seven persons under sentence of death in England, questioned at different times, in the course of years, by an English clergyman in the performance of his duty, there were only three who had not been spectators of executions.

We come, now, to the consideration of those murders which are committed, or attempted, with no other object than the attainment of an infamous notoriety. That this class of crimes has its origin in the punishment of death, we cannot question; because (as we have already seen, and shall presently establish by another proof) great notoriety and interest attach, and are generally understood to attach, only to those criminals who are in danger of being executed.

One of the most remarkable instances of murder originating in mad self-conceit; and of the murderer's part in the repulsive drama, in which the law appears at such great disadvantage to itself and to society, being acted almost to the last with a self-complacency that would be horribly ludicrous if it were not utterly revolting; is presented in the case of Hocker.

Here is an insolent, flippant, dissolute youth: aping the man of intrigue and levity: over-dressed, over-confident, inordinately vain of his personal appearance: distinguished as to his hair, cane, snuff-box, and singing-voice: and unhappily the son of a working shoemaker. Bent on loftier flights than such a poor house-swallow as a teacher in a Sunday school can take; and having no truth, industry, perseverance, or other dull work-a-day quality, to plume his wings withal; he casts about him, in his jaunty way, for some mode of distinguishing himself—some means of getting that head of hair into the print-shops; of having something like justice done to his singing-voice and fine intellect; of making the life and adventures of Thomas Hocker remarkable; and of getting up some excitement in connection with that slighted piece of biography. The Stage? No. Not feasible. There has always been a conspiracy against the Thomas Hockers, in that kind of effort. It has been the same with Authorship in prose and poetry. Is there nothing else? A Murder, now, would make a noise in the papers! There is the gallows to be sure; but without that, it would be nothing. Short of that, it wouldn't be fame. Well! We must all die at one time or other; and to die game, and have it in print, is just the thing for a man of spirit. They always die game at the Minor Theatres and the Saloons, and the people like it very much. Thurtell, too, died very game, and made a capital speech when he was tried. There's all about it in a book at the cigar shop now. Come, Tom, get your name up! Let it be a dashing murder that shall keep the wood-engravers at it for the next two months. You are the boy to go through with it, and interest the town!

The miserable wretch, inflated by this lunatic conceit, arranges his whole plan for publication and effect. It is quite an epitome of his experience of the domestic melodrama or penny novel. There is the Victim Friend; the mysterious letter of the injured Female to the Victim Friend; the romantic spot for the Death-Struggle by night; the unexpected appearance of Thomas Hocker to the Policeman; the parlor of the Public House, with Thomas Hocker reading the paper to a strange gentleman; the Family Apartment, with a song by Thomas Hocker; the Inquest Room, with Thomas Hocker boldly looking on; the interior of the Marylebone Theatre, with Thomas Hocker taken into custody; the Police Office with Thomas Hocker "affable" to the spectators; the interior of Newgate, with Thomas Hocker preparing his defense; the Court, where Thomas Hocker, with his dancing-master airs, is put upon his trial, and complimented by the Judge; the Prosecution, the Defense, the Verdict, the Black Cap, the Sentence— each of them a line in any Playbill, and how bold a line in Thomas Hocker's life!

It is worthy of remark, that the nearer he approaches to the gallows—the great last scene to which the whole of these effects have been working up— the more the overweening conceit of the poor wretch shows itself; the more he feels that he is the hero of the hour; the more audaciously and recklessly he lies, in supporting the character. In public—at the condemned sermon—he deports himself as becomes the man whose autographs are precious, whose portraits are innumerable; in memory of whom, whole fences and gates have been borne away, in splinters, from the scene of murder. He knows that the eyes of Europe are upon him; but he is not proud—only graceful. He bows, like the first gentleman in Europe, to the turnkey who brings him a glass of water; and composes his clothes and hassock, as carefully as good Madame Blaize could do. In private—within the walls of the condemned cell—every word and action of his waning life, is a lie. His whole time is divided between telling lies and writing them. If he ever have another thought, it is for his genteel appearance on the scaffold; as when he begs the barber "not to cut his hair too short, or they won't know him when he comes out." His last proceeding but one is to write two romantic love letters to women who have no existence. His last proceeding of all (but less characteristic, though the only true one) is to swoon away, miserably, in the arms of the attendants, and be hanged up like a craven dog.

Is not such a history, from first to last, a most revolting and disgraceful one; and can the student of it bring himself to believe that it ever could have place in any record of facts, or that the miserable chief-actor in it could have ever had a motive for his arrogant wickedness, but for the comment and the explanation which the Punishment of Death supplies!

It is not a solitary case, nor is it a prodigy, but a mere specimen of a class. The case of Oxford, who fired at Her Majesty in the Park, will be found, on examination, to resemble it very nearly, in the essential feature. There is no proved pretense whatever for regarding him as mad; other than that he was like this malefactor, brimful of conceit, and a desire to become, even at the cost of the gallows (the only cost within his reach) the talk of the town. He had less invention than Hocker, and perhaps was not so deliberately bad; but his attempt was a branch of the same tree, and it has its root in the ground where the scaffold is erected.

Oxford had his imitators. Let it never be forgotten in the consideration of this part of the subject, how they were stopped. So long as attempts invested them with the distinction of being in danger of death at the hangman's hands, so long did they spring up. When the penalty of death was removed, and a mean and humiliating punishment substituted in its place, the race was at an end, and ceased to be.

WITNESS TO AN EXECUTION
Horsemonger Lane Execution, Charles Dickens (1849)

Sir—I was a witness of the execution at Horsemonger-Lane this morning. I went there with the intention of observing the crowd gathered to behold it, and I had excellent opportunities of doing so, at intervals all through the night, and continuously from daybreak until after the spectacle was over.

I do not address you on the subject with any intention of discussing the abstract question of capital punishment, or any of the arguments of its opponents or advocates. I simply wish to turn this dreadful experience to some account for the general good, by taking the readiest and most public means of adverting to an intimation given by Sir G. Grey in the last session of Parliament, that the Government might be induced to give its support to a measure making the infliction of capital punishment a private solemnity within the prison walls (with such guarantees for the last sentence of the law being inexorably and surely administered as should be satisfactory to the public at large), and of most earnestly beseeching Sir G. Grey, as a solemn duty which he owes to society, and a responsibility which he cannot forever put away, to originate such a legislative change himself.

I believe that a sight so inconceivably awful as the wickedness and levity of the immense crowd collected at that execution this morning could be imagined by no man, and could be presented in no heathen land under the sun. The horrors of the gibbet and of the crime which brought the wretched murderers to it, faded in my mind before the atrocious bearing, looks and language, of the assembled spectators. When I came upon the scene at midnight, the shrillness of the cries and howls that were raised from time to time, denoting that they came from a concourse of boys and girls already assembled in the best places, made my blood run cold. As the night went on, screeching, and laughing, and yelling in strong chorus of parodies on Negro melodies, with substitutions of "Mrs. Manning" for "Susannah," and the like,

The horrors of the gibbet and of the crime which brought the wretched murderers to it, faded in my mind before the atrocious bearing, looks and language, of the assembled spectators.

were added to these. When the day dawned, thieves, low prostitutes, ruffians and vagabonds of every kind, flocked on to the ground, with every variety of offensive and foul behavior. Fightings, faintings, whistlings, imitations of Punch, brutal jokes, tumultuous demonstrations of indecent delight when swooning women were dragged out of the crowd by the police with their dresses disordered, gave a new zest to the general entertainment. When the sun rose brightly—as it did— it gilded thousands upon thousands of upturned faces, so inexpressibly odious in their brutal mirth or callousness, that a man had cause to feel ashamed of the shape he wore, and to shrink from himself, as fashioned in the image of the Devil. When the two miserable creatures who attracted all this ghastly sight about them were turned quivering into the air, there was no more emotion, no more pity, no more thought that two immortal souls had gone to judgment, no more restraint in any of the previous obscenities, than if the name of Christ had never been heard in this world, and there were no belief among men but that they perished like the beasts.

I have seen, habitually, some of the worst sources of general contamination and corruption in this country, and I think there are not many phases of London life that could surprise me. I am solemnly convinced that nothing that ingenuity could devise to be done in this city, in the same compass of time, could work such ruin as one public execution, and I stand astounded and appalled by the wickedness it exhibits. I do not believe that any community can prosper where such a scene of horror and demoralization as was enacted this morning outside Horsemonger-Lane Gaol is presented at the very doors of good citizens, and is passed by, unknown or forgotten. And when, in our prayers and thanksgivings for the season, we are humbly expressing before God our desire to remove the moral evils of the land, I would ask your readers to consider whether it is not a time to think of this one, and to root it out.

The Philosophy of Poverty
Pierre-Joseph Proudhon (1847)

The farther we delve into this system of illusory compromises between monopoly and society—that is, as we have explained in 1 of this chapter, between capital and labor, between the patriciate and the proletariat—the more we discover that it is all foreseen, regulated, and executed in accordance with this infernal maxim, with which Hobbes and Machiavel, those theorists of despotism, were unacquainted: EVERYTHING BY THE PEOPLE AND AGAINST THE PEOPLE. While labor produces, capital, under the mask of a false fecundity, enjoys and abuses; the legislator, in offering his mediation, thought to recall the privileged class to fraternal feelings and surround the laborer with guarantees; and now he finds, by the fatal contradiction of interests, that each of these guarantees is an instrument of torture. It would require a hundred volumes, the life of ten men, and a heart of iron, to relate from this standpoint the crimes of the State towards the poor and the infinite variety of its tortures. A summary glance at the principal classes of police will be enough to enable us to estimate its spirit and economy.

After having sown trouble in all minds by a confusion of civil, commercial, and administrative laws, made the idea of justice more obscure by multiplying contradictions, and rendered necessary a whole class of interpreters for the explanation of this system, it has been found necessary also to organize the repression of crimes and provide for their punishment. Criminal justice, that particularly rich order of the great family of non-producers, whose maintenance costs France annually more than six million dollars, has become to society a principle of existence as necessary as bread is to the life of man; but with this difference — that man lives by the product of his hands, while society devours its members and feeds on its own flesh.

It is calculated by some economists that there is:

In London	1 criminal	to every	89 inhabitants.
In Liverpool	1 "	"	45 "
In Newcastle	1 "	"	27 "

But these figures lack accuracy, and, utterly frightful as they seem, do not express the real degree of social perversion due to the police. We have to determine here not only the number of recognized criminals, but the number of offenses. The work of the criminal courts is only a special mechanism which serves to place in relief the moral destruction of humanity under the monopoly system; but this official exhibition is far from including the whole extent of the evil. Here are other figures which will lead us to a more certain approximation.

The police courts of Paris disposed:

In 1835 of	106,467 cases.
In 1836 "	128,489 "
In 1837 "	140,247 "

Supposing this rate of increase to have continued up to 1846, and to this total of misdemeanors adding the cases of the criminal courts, the simple matters that go no further than the police, and all the offences unknown or left unpunished,—offenses far surpassing in number, so the magistrates say, those which justice reaches—we shall arrive at the conclusion that in one year, in the city of Paris, there are more infractions of the law committed than there are inhabitants. And as it is necessary to deduct from the presumable authors of these infractions children of seven years and under, who are outside the limits of guilt, the figures will show that every adult citizen is guilty, three or four times a year, of violating the established order.

Thus the proprietary system is maintained at Paris only by the annual consummation of one or two millions of offenses! Now, though all these offenses should be the work of a single man, the argument would still hold good: this man would be the scapegoat loaded with the sins of Israel: of what consequence is the number of the guilty, provided justice has its contingent?

Violence, perjury, robbery, cheating, contempt of persons and society, are so much a part of the essence of monopoly; they flow from it so naturally, with such perfect regularity, and in accordance with laws so certain, — that it is possible to submit their perpetration to calculation, and, given the number of a population, the condition of its industry, and the stage of its enlightenment, to rigorously deduce therefrom the statistics of its morality. The economists do not know yet what the principle of value is; but they know, within a few decimals, the proportionality of crime. So many thousand souls, so many malefactors, so many condemnations: about that there can be no mistake. It is one of the most beautiful applications of the theory of chances, and the most advanced branch of economic science. If socialism had invented this accusing theory, the whole world would have cried calumny.

> **The economists do not know yet what the principle of value is; but they know, within a few decimals, the proportionality of crime.**

Yet, after all, what is there in it that should surprise us? As misery is a necessary result of the contradictions of society, a result which it is possible to determine mathematically from the rate of interest, the rate of wages, and the prevailing market prices, so crimes and misdemeanors are another effect of this same antagonism, susceptible, like its cause, of estimation by figures. The materialists have drawn the silliest inferences from this subordination of liberty to the laws of numbers: as if man were not under the influence of all that surrounds him, and as if, since all that surrounds him is governed by inexorable laws, he must not experience, in his freest manifestations, the reaction of those laws!

The same character of necessity which we have just pointed out in the establishment and sustenance of criminal justice is found, but under a more metaphysical aspect, in its morality.

In the opinion of all moralists, the penalty should be such as to secure the reformation of the offender, and consequently free from everything that might cause his degradation. Far be it from me to combat this blessed tendency of minds and disparage attempts which would have been the glory of the greatest men of antiquity. Philanthropy, in spite of the ridicule which sometimes attaches to its name, will remain, in the eyes of posterity, the most honorable characteristic of our time: the abolition of the death penalty, which is merely postponed; the abolition of the stigma; the studies regarding the effects of the cellular system; the establishment of workshops in the prisons; and a multitude of other reforms which I cannot even name — give evidence of real progress in our ideas and in our morals. What the author of Christianity, in an impulse of sublime love, related of his mystical kingdom, where the repentant sinner was to be glorified above the just and the innocent man — that utopia of Christian charity has become the aspiration of our skeptical society; and when one thinks of the unanimity of feeling which prevails in respect to it, he asks himself with surprise who then prevents this aspiration from being realized.

Alas! It is because reason is still stronger than love, and logic more tenacious than crime; it is because here as everywhere in our civilization there reigns an insoluble contradiction. Let us not wander into fantastic worlds; let us embrace, in all its frightful nudity, the real one.

Le crime fait la honte, et non pas l'echafaud, [*It is the crime which causes the shame, not the scaffold.*] says the proverb. By the simple fact that man is punished, provided he deserved to be, he is degraded: the penalty renders him infamous, not by virtue of the definition of the code, but by reason of the fault which caused the punishment. Of what importance, then, is the materiality of the punishment? Of what importance all your penitentiary systems? What you do is to satisfy your feelings, but is powerless to rehabilitate the unfortunate whom your justice strikes. The guilty man, once branded by chastisement, is incapable of reconciliation; his stain is indelible, and his damnation eternal. If it were possible for it to be otherwise, the penalty would cease to be proportional to the offence; it would be no more than a fiction, it would be nothing. He whom misery has led to larceny, if he suffers himself to fall into the hands of justice, remains forever the enemy of God and men; better for him that he had never been born; it was Jesus Christ who said it: "*Bonum erat ei, si natus non fuisset homo ille.*" And what Jesus Christ declared, Christians and infidels do not dispute: the irreparability of shame is, of all the revelations of the Gospel, the only one which the proprietary world has understood. Thus, separated from nature by monopoly, cut off from humanity by poverty, the mother of crime and its punishment, what refuge remains for the plebeian whom labor cannot support, and who is not strong enough to take?

To conduct this offensive and defensive war against the proletariat a public force was indispensable: the executive power grew out of the necessities of civil legislation, administration, and justice. And there again the most beautiful hopes have changed into bitter disappointments.

The Death Penalty Is Atheistical In Doctrine, W.Y. Emmet (1849)

For when it is contended, that the citizen "has given up to the government a portion of his own individual rights, for the general good," the doctrine of this argument is, "I have the right to take my own life; I owe no obligation to any one for its existence! I have the perfect right to do what I will with what is mine own."

Is not this sentiment an atheistical one? Surely it is. For if I have this right, I owe God nor anyone else any obligation for its possession. For if I do owe God, or any other being obligation for its possession, then I have not this right to dispose of it without the consent of him to whom I am indebted for its possession.

If this doctrine of right to dispose of my own life be denied, then I answer, the argument that the government has the right, fails forever. For if the individual had not this right himself, he could not dispose of it to the government by contract! And if not thus invested in the government, then its exercise by the government is usurpation and tyranny.

We deny man's right to make such contract. Man is endowed by his Creator with certain inalienable rights. Then he holds these inalienable rights, by a tenure which he cannot alienate, but must hold at the will and pleasure of the donor.

We also deny the existence of any such contract. Our constitutions declare "all rights not specially delegated are reserved." Let the contract be shown to exist, and then we will meet it. We deny that our fathers possessed this right, and therefore if they had made any such contract with the government, it would have been a wrong, a nullity. And therefore they could not have imposed on their posterity any obligation to submit to, or continue that wrong, even if it were found to exist in the constitutions of our country. But we ask, is it possible that American citizens, who declare the "right to life" inalienable, have bartered it away? Where is the traitor? Have we indeed bartered away any of our rights? No! We have only vested government with power to protect, and preserve them inviolate. We have not attempted to surrender or barter away these rights which we have declared inalienable. Have we contracted away that life with which the Creator has invested us, as His gift, which He only may recall, at His pleasure? And that gift too, on which all other gifts, rights, and privileges depend? No! No!! It is preposterous. Then, "we have not 'voluntarily' consented to hold our lives, and the tenure of our earthly existence, at the discretion or caprice of a legislative majority, whose erratic legislation no man can calculate."

The object of establishing legal government is the preservation of all the rights of all over whom it is established, which are embraced in the enjoyment of Life. "Property may be diminished by the operation of government, and restored again. Liberty may be taken away for a time, and restored again. The wound inflicted may be healed, and the wrongs may be redressed, or atoned for! But life once taken by man, cannot be restored by man. And it is atheistical presumption, to interfere with God's prerogative, to give and recall his gift.

We see by the foregoing remarks that the "death penalty" is contrary to the great first principles recognized in the Declaration of Independence, which forms the basis of our Republican Government. For if "men are and of right ought to be (not only alive but) free," then no further interference with even their liberty, ought to be allowed by law, than what is absolutely necessary for the general good. For the only object of penal law is, or should be, to secure the general good; not to gratify the violent passions of men. And in seeking the general good, it must not be overlooked that the criminal himself is an integral part of those whose good is to be sought. He is one of that society whose rights are to be protected inviolate. Criminal law, then, must consult the best good of the criminal himself, the best good of his family, or those with whom he is connected, as well as the other portions of society. Punishment in its very nature implies this. Punishment is not retaliation, nor revenge, nor cruelty; but the "infliction of pain or evil, with a view to the good of the offender."

> **For the only object of penal law is, or should be, to secure the general good; not to gratify the violent passions of men. And in seeking the general good, it must not be overlooked that the criminal himself is an integral part of those whose good is to be sought. He is one of that society whose rights are to be protected inviolate.**

This is a well-established doctrine of political as well as of divine law. Seneca, the great ancient moralist, said "the end of all correction is the amendment of wicked men, or to prevent the influence of evil example." Dyraond quotes this from Seneca with approbation, and asks, "is it for his own advantage, or others, or both, that the offender is punished? Both! Primarily his own! We should feel toward the mentally diseased, as we do toward the physically diseased."

The great question to be settled is, what will best secure these ends of government? In answering this question, we shall first show that the "death penalty" defeats all these objects of penal legislation.

Model Prisons, Thomas Carlyle (1850)

I take the liberty of asserting that there is one valid reason, and only one, for either punishing a man or rewarding him in this world; one reason, which ancient piety could well define: That you may do the will and commandment of God with regard to him; that you may do justice to him. This is your one true aim in respect of him; aim thitherward, with all your heart and all your strength and all your soul, thitherward, and not else whither at all! This aim is true, and will carry you to all earthly heights and benefits, and beyond the stars and Heavens. All other aims are purblind, illegitimate, untrue; and will never carry you beyond the shop counter, nay very soon will prove themselves incapable of maintaining you even there. Find out what the Law of God is with regard to a man; make that your human law, or I say it will be ill with you, and not well! If you love your thief or murderer, if Nature and eternal Fact love him, then do as you are now doing. But if Nature and Fact do not love him? If they have set inexorable penalties upon him, and planted natural wrath against him in every god—created human heart—then I advise you, cease, and change your hand.

Reward and punishment? Alas, alas, I must say you reward and punish pretty much alike! Your dignities, peerages, promotions, your kingships, your brazen statues erected in capital and county towns to our select demigods of your selecting, testify loudly enough what kind of heroes and hero-worshippers you are. Woe to the People that no longer venerates, as the emblem of God himself, the aspect of Human Worth; that no longer knows what human worth and unworth is! Sure as the decrees of the eternal, that people cannot come to good. By a course too clear, by a necessity too evident, that people will come into the hands of the unworthy; and either turn on its bad career, or stagger downwards to ruin and abolition. Does the Hebrew People prophetically sing "*Ou' clo'*!" in all thoroughfares, these eighteen hundred years in vain?

To reward men according to their worth: alas, the perfection of this, we know, amounts to the millennium! Neither is perfect punishment, according to the like rule, to be attained,--nor even, by a legislator of these chaotic days, to be too zealously attempted. But when he does attempt it—yes, when he summons out the Society to sit deliberative on this matter, and consult the oracles upon it, and solemnly settle it in the name of God; then, if never before, he should try to be a little in the right in settling it!—In regard to reward of merit, I do not bethink me of any attempt whatever, worth calling an attempt, on the part of modern Governments; which surely is an immense oversight on their part, and will one day be seen to have been an altogether fatal one. But as to the punishment of crime, happily this cannot be quite neglected. When men have a purse and a skin, they seek salvation at least for these; and the Four Pleas of the Crown are a thing that must and will be attended to. By punishment, capital or other, by treadmilling and blind rigor, or by whitewashing and blind laxity, the extremely disagreeable offences of theft and murder must be kept down within limits.

And so you take criminal caitiffs, murderers, and the like, and hang them on gibbets "for an example to deter others." Whereupon arise friends of humanity, and object. With very great reason, as I consider, if your hypothesis be correct. What right have you to hang any poor creature "for an example"? He can turn round upon you and say, "Why make an 'example' of me, a merely ill-situated, pitiable man? Have you no more respect for misfortune? Misfortune, I have been told, is sacred. And yet you hang me, now I am fallen into your hands; choke the life out of me, for an example! Again I ask, Why make an example of me, for your own convenience alone?" All "revenge" being out of the question, it seems to me the caitiff is unanswerable; and he and the philanthropic platforms have the logic all on their side.

The one answer to him is: "Caitiff, we hate thee; and discern for some six thousand years now, that we are called upon by the whole Universe to do it. Not with a diabolic but with a divine hatred. God himself, we have always understood, 'hates sin,' with a most authentic, celestial, and eternal hatred. A hatred, a hostility inexorable, unappeasable, which blasts the scoundrel, and all scoundrels ultimately, into black annihilation and disappearance from the sum of things. The path of it as the path of a flaming sword: he that has eyes may see it, walking inexorable, divinely beautiful and divinely terrible, through the chaotic gulf of Human History, and everywhere burning, as with unquenchable fire, the false and death-worthy from the true and life-worthy; making all Human History, and the Biography of every man, a God's Cosmos in place of a Devil's Chaos. So is it, in the end; even so, to every man who is a man, and not a mutinous beast, and has eyes to see. To thee, caitiff, these things were and are, quite incredible; to us they are too awfully certain, the Eternal Law of this Universe, whether thou and others will believe it or disbelieve. We, not to be partakers in thy destructive adventure of defying God and all the Universe, dare not allow thee to continue longer among us. As a palpable deserter from the ranks where all men, at their eternal peril, are bound to be: palpable deserter, taken with the red band fighting thus against the whole Universe and its Laws, we—send thee back into the whole universe, solemnly expel thee from our community; and will, in the name of God, not with joy and exultation, but with sorrow stern as thy own, hang thee on Wednesday next, and so end."

Other ground on which to deliberately slay a disarmed fellow-man I can see none. example, effects upon the public mind, effects upon this and upon that: all this is mere appendage and accident; of all this I make no attempt to keep account, sensible that no arithmetic will or can keep account of it; that its "effects," on this hand and on that, transcend all calculation. One thing, if I can calculate it, will include all, and produce beneficial effects beyond calculation, and no ill effect at all, anywhere or at any time: What the Law of the Universe, or Law of God, is with regard to this caitiff? That, by all sacred research and consideration, I will try to find out; to that I will come as near as human means admit; that shall be my exemplar and "example;" all men shall through me see that, and be profited beyond calculation by seeing it.

What this Law of the Universe, or Law made by God, is? Men at one time read it in their Bible. In many Bibles, books, and authentic symbols and monitions of nature and the world (of fact, that is, and of human speech, or wise interpretation of fact), there are still clear indications towards it. Most important it is, for this and for some other reasons, that men do, in some way, get to see it a little! And if no man could now see it by any Bible, there is written in the heart of every man an authentic copy of it direct from Heaven itself: there, if he have learnt to decipher Heaven's writing, and can read the sacred oracles (a sad case for him if he altogether cannot), every born man may still find some copy of it.

"Revenge," my friends! Revenge, and the natural hatred of scoundrels, and the ineradicable tendency to *revancher* oneself upon them, and pay them what they have merited: this is forevermore intrinsically a correct, and even a divine feeling in the mind of every man. Only the excess of it is diabolic; the essence I say is manlike, and even godlike—a monition sent to poor man by the Maker himself. Thou, poor reader, in spite of all this melancholy twaddle, and blotting out of Heaven's sunlight by mountains of horsehair and officiality, hast still a human heart. If, in returning to thy poor peaceable dwelling-place, after an honest hard day's work, thou wert to find, for example, a brutal scoundrel who for lucre or other object of his, had slaughtered the life that was dearest to thee; thy true wife, for example, thy true old mother, swimming in her blood; the human scoundrel, or two-legged wolf, standing over such a tragedy: I hope a man would have so much divine rage in his heart as to snatch the nearest weapon, and put a conclusion upon said human wolf, for one! A palpable messenger of Satan, that one; accredited by all the Devils, to be put an end to by all the children of God. The soul of every god-created man flames wholly into one divine blaze of sacred wrath at sight of such a Devil's messenger; authentic firsthand monition from the Eternal Maker himself as to what is next to be done. Do it, or be thyself an ally of Devil's messengers; a sheep for two-legged human wolves, well deserving to be eaten, as thou soon wilt be!

My humane friends, I perceive this same sacred glow of divine wrath, or authentic monition at first hand from God himself, to be the foundation for all criminal law, and official horsehair-and-bombazine procedure against scoundrels in this world. This first-hand gospel from the Eternities, imparted to every mortal, this is still, and will forever be, your sanction and commission for the punishment of human scoundrels. See well how you will translate this message from Heaven and the Eternities into a form suitable to this world and its times. Let not violence, haste, blind impetuous impulse, preside in executing it; the injured man, invincibly liable to fall into these, shall not himself execute it: the whole world, in person of a minister appointed for that end, and surrounded with the due solemnities and caveats, with bailiffs, apparitors, advocates, and the hushed expectation of all men, shall do it, as under the eye of God who made all men. How it shall be done? This is ever a vast question, involving immense considerations. Thus Edmund Burke saw, in the Two Houses of Parliament, with King, Constitution, and all manner of Civil-Lists, and Chancellors' wigs and Exchequer budgets, only the "method of getting twelve just men put into a jury box:" that, in Burke's view, was the summary of what they were all meant for. How the judge will do it? Yes, indeed: but let him see well that he does do it:

for it is a thing that must by no means be left undone! A sacred gospel from the Highest: not to be smothered under horsehair and bombazine, or drowned in platform froth, or in any wise omitted or neglected, without the most alarming penalties to all concerned!

Neglect to treat the hero as hero, the penalties—which are inevitable too, and terrible to think of, as your Hebrew friends can tell you—may be some time in coming; they will only gradually come. Not all at once will your thirty thousand needlewomen, your three million paupers, your Connaught fallen into potential cannibalism, and other fine consequences of the practice, come to light; though come to light they will; and *"Ou' clo'!"* itself may be in store for you, if you persist steadily enough. But neglect to treat even your declared scoundrel as scoundrel, this is the last consummation of the process, the drop by which the cup runs over; the penalties of this, most alarming, extensive, and such as you little dream of, will straightway very rapidly come. Dim oblivion of Right and Wrong, among the masses of your population, will come; doubts as to Right and Wrong, indistinct notion that Right and Wrong are not eternal, but accidental, and settled by uncertain votings and talkings, will come. Prurient influenza of platform benevolence, and "paradise to all-and-sundry," will come. In the general putrescence of your "religions," as you call them, a strange new religion, named of Universal Love, with Sacraments mainly of—Divorce, with Balzac, Sue and Company for Evangelists, and Madame Sand for Virgin, will come—and results fast following therefrom which will astonish you very much!

"The terrible anarchies of these years," says Crabbe, in his *Radiator*, "are brought upon us by a necessity too visible." By the crime of Kings—alas, yes; but by that of Peoples too. Not by the crime of one class, but by the fatal obscuration, and all but obliteration of the sense of Right and Wrong in the minds and practices of every class. What a scene in the drama of universal history, this of ours! A world-wide loud bellow and bray of universal misery; lowing, with crushed maddened heart, its inarticulate prayer to Heaven: very pardonable to me, and in some of its transcendent developments, as in the grand French Revolution, most respectable and ever-memorable. For injustice reigns everywhere; and this murderous struggle for what they call 'Fraternity,' and so forth has a spice of eternal sense in it, though so terribly disfigured! Amalgam of sense and nonsense; eternal sense by the grain, and temporary nonsense by the square mile: as is the habit with poor sons of men. Which pardonable amalgam, however, if it be taken as the pure final sense, I must warn you and all creatures, is unpardonable, criminal, and fatal nonsense; with which I, for one, will take care not to concern myself!

"Dogs should not be taught to eat leather," says the old adage: no; and where, by general fault and error, and the inevitable nemesis of things, the universal kennel is set to diet upon leather; and from its keepers, its 'Liberal Premiers,' or whatever their title is, will accept or expect nothing else, and calls it by the pleasant name of progress, reform, emancipation, abolition-principles, and the like—I consider the fate of said kennel and of said keepers to be a thing settled. Red republic in Phrygian nightcap, organization of labor a la Louis

Blanc; street-barricades, and then murderous cannon-volleys a la Cavaignac and Windischgratz, follow out of one another, as grapes, must, new wine, and sour all-splitting vinegar do: vinegar is but *vin-aigre*, or the self-same 'wine' grown sharp! If, moreover, I find the Worship of Human Nobleness abolished in any country, and a new astonishing Phallus-Worship, with universal Balzac-Sand melodies and litanies in treble and in bass, established in its stead, what can I compute but that Nature, in horrible throes, will repugn against such substitution—that, in short, the astonishing new Phallus-Worship, with its finer sensibilities of the heart, and 'great satisfying loves,' with its sacred kiss of peace for scoundrel and hero alike, with its all-embracing Brotherhood, and universal Sacrament of Divorce, will have to take itself away again!

The Ancient Germans, it appears, had no scruple about public executions; on the contrary, they thought the just gods themselves might fitly preside over these; that these were a solemn and highest act of worship, if justly done. When a German man had done a crime deserving death, they, in solemn general assembly of the tribe, doomed him, and considered that Fate and all Nature had from the beginning doomed him, to die with ignominy. Certain crimes there were of a supreme nature; him that had perpetrated one of these, they believed to have declared himself a prince of scoundrels. Him once convicted they laid hold of, nothing doubting; bore him, after judgment, to the deepest convenient Peat-bog; plunged him in there, drove an oaken frame down over him, solemnly in the name of gods and men: "There, prince of scoundrels, that is what we have had to think of thee, on clear acquaintance; our grim good-night to thee is that! In the name of all the gods lie there, and be our partnership with thee dissolved henceforth. It will be better for us, we imagine!"

My friends, after all this beautiful whitewash and humanity and prison-discipline; and such blubbering and whimpering, and soft Litany to divine and also to quite other sorts of Pity, as we have had for a century now—give me leave to admonish you that that of the Ancient Germans too was a thing inexpressibly necessary to keep in mind. If that is not kept in mind, the universal Litany to Pity is a mere universal nuisance, and torpid blasphemy against the gods. I do not much respect it, that purblind blubbering and litanying, as it is seen at present; and the litanying over scoundrels I go the length of disrespecting, and in some cases even of detesting. Yes, my friends, scoundrel is scoundrel: that remains forever a fact; and there exists not in the earth whitewash that can make the scoundrel a friend of this Universe; he remains an enemy if you spent your life in whitewashing him. He won't whitewash; this one won't. The one method clearly is, that, after fair trial, you dissolve partnership with him; send him, in the name of Heaven, whither he is striving all this while and have done with him. And, in a time like this, I would advise you, see likewise that you be speedy about it! For there is immense work, and of a far hopefuler sort, to be done elsewhere.

Neapolitan Trials for Political Offenses, William Ewart Gladstone (1851)

There is a general impression that the organization of the governments of Southern Italy is defective — that the administration of justice is tainted with corruption — that instances of abuse or cruelty, among subordinate public functionaries, are not uncommon, and that political offenses are punished with severity, and with no great regard to the forms of justice. I advert to this vague supposition of a given state of things, for the purpose of stating that, had it been accurate, I should have spared myself this labor. The difference between the faintest outline that a moment's handling of the pencil sketches, and the deepest coloring of the most elaborately finished portrait, but feebly illustrates the relation of these vague suppositions to the actual truth of the Neapolitan case.

It is not mere imperfection, not corruption in low quarters, not occasional severity, that I am about to describe: it is incessant, systematic, deliberate, violation of the law by the power appointed to watch over and maintain it. It is such violation of human and written law as this, carried on for the purpose of violating every other law, unwritten and eternal, human and divine; it is the wholesale persecution of virtue, when united with intelligence, operating upon such a scale, that entire classes may, with truth, be said to be its object; so that the government is in bitter and cruel, as well as utterly illegal, hostility to whatever in the nation really lives and moves, and forms the main-spring of practical progress and improvement; it is the awful profanation of public religion, by its notorious alliance, in the governing powers, with the violation of every moral law, under the stimulants of fear and vengeance; it is the perfect prostitution of the judicial office, which has made it, under veils only too threadbare and transparent, the degraded recipient of the vilest and clumsiest forgeries, got up willfully and deliberately, by the immediate advisers of the crown, for the purpose of destroying the peace, the freedom, ay, and even if not, by capital sentences, the life, of men among the most virtuous, upright, intelligent, distinguished, and refined (of the whole community; it is the savage and cowardly system of moral, as well as in a lower degree of physical, torture, through which the sentences extracted from the debased courts of justice, are carried into effect.

The effect of all this is, total inversion of all the moral and social ideas. Law, instead of being respected, is odious. Force, and not affection, is the foundation of government. There is no association, but a violent antagonism, between the idea of freedom and that of order. The governing power, which teaches, of itself, that it is the image of God upon earth, is clothed, in the view of the overwhelming majority of the thinking public, with all the vices, for its attributes.

I have seen and heard the strong and too true expression used: "This is the negation of God, erected into a system of government." I confess my amazement at the gentleness of character, which has been shown by the Neapolitan people, in times of revolution. It really seems as if the hell-born spirit of revenge had no place whatever in their breasts. I know that, at any rate, some illustrious victims are supported by the spirit of Christian resignation, by their cheerful acceptance of the will of God. But the present persecution is awfully aggravated, as compared with former ones ; it differs, too, in this, that it seems to be specially directed against those men of moderate opinions, whom a government well stocked even with worldly prudence, whom Machiavelli, had he been minister, would have made it his study to conciliate and attach. These men, therefore, are being cleared away; and the present efforts to drive poor human nature to extremes, cannot wholly fail in stirring up the ferocious passions, which never, — to my belief — since the times of the heathen tyrants, have had so much to arouse, or so much to palliate, when aroused, their fury.

The law of Naples, as I have been informed, requires that personal liberty shall be inviolable, except under a warrant from a court of justice, authorized for the purpose. I do not mean the constitution, but the law anterior to and independent of the constitution. This warrant, I understand, must proceed upon actual depositions, and must state the nature of the charge; or it must be communicated immediately afterwards — I am not sure which. In utter defiance of this law, the government, of which the prefect of police is an important member, through the agents of that department, watches and dogs the people, pays domiciliary visits, very commonly at night, ransacks houses, seizing papers and effects, and tearing up floors, at pleasure, under pretense of searching for arms, and imprisons men, by the score, by the hundred, by the thousand, without any warrant whatever, sometimes without even any written authority at all, or anything beyond the word of a policeman; constantly without any statement whatever of the nature of the offense.

Nor is this last fact wonderful. Men are arrested, not because they have committed, or are believed to have committed, any offense; but because they are persons whom it is thought convenient to confine, and to get rid of; and against whom, therefore, some charge must be found or fabricated. The first process commonly is to seize them and imprison them; and to seize and carry off books, papers, or whatever else these degraded hirelings may choose. The correspondence of the prisoner is then examined, as soon as may be found convenient; and he is himself examined upon it; in secret, without any intimation of the charges, which as yet in fact do not exist; or of the witnesses, who do not exist, either. In

Men are arrested, not because they have committed, or are believed to have committed, any offense; but because they are persons whom it is thought convenient to confine, and to get rid of; and against whom, therefore, some charge must be found or fabricated.

this examination, he is allowed no assistance whatever; nor has he, at this stage, any power of communication with a legal adviser! He is not examined only, but, as I know, insulted at will, and in the grossest manner, under pretense of examination, by the officers of the police. And do not suppose this is the fault of individuals. It is essential to the system, of which the essential aim is, to create a charge. What more likely than that, smarting under insult, and knowing with what encouragement, and for whose benefit, it is offered, the prisoner should, for a moment, lose his temper, and utter some expression disparaging to the sacred majesty of the government? If he does, it goes down in the minutes against him: if he does not, but keeps his self-command, no harm is done to the great end in view.

His correspondence is examined, as well as himself. Suppose him a man of cultivated intelligence: he has probably watched public affairs, and followed their vicissitudes. His copies of letters, or the letters to him which he may have kept, will contain allusions to them. The value of this evidence, as evidence, would, of course, depend upon giving full effect to all these allusions, taken in connection one with another. But not so: any expression which implies disapproval, (since nothing is easier than to construe disapproval into disaffection — disaffection into an intention of revolution or of regicide) is entered on the minutes. Suppose there happens to be some other, which entirely destroys the force of the former, and demonstrates the loyalty of the victim: it is put by, as of no consequence; and if he remonstrate, it is in vain. In countries where justice is regarded, acts are punished, and it is deemed unjust to punish thoughts; but, in this case, thoughts are forged, in order that they may be punished.

I here speak of what I know to have happened, and have imagined or heightened nothing.

For months, or for a year, or for two years, or three, as the case may be, these prisoners are detained before their trials; but very generally for the longer terms. I do not happen to have heard of any one tried at Naples on a political charge, in these last times, with less than sixteen or eighteen months of previous imprisonment. I have seen men still waiting, who had been confined for six and twenty months; and this confinement, as I have said, began by an act not of law, but of force in defiance of law. There may be cases — doubtless there are — of arrest under warrant, after depositions; but it is needless to enter upon what is, I believe, purely exceptional. I do not scruple to assert, in continuation, that, when every effort has been used to concoct a charge, if possible, out of the perversion and partial production of real evidence, this often fails; and then the resort is to perjury and to forgery.

The miserable creatures to be found in most communities, but especially in these where the government is the great agent of corruption, upon the people, the wretches who are ready to sell the liberty and life of fellow subjects for gold, and to throw their own souls into the bargain, are deliberately employed by the executive power, to depose, according to their inventions, against the man whom it is thought desirable to ruin. Although, however, practice should, by this time, have made perfect, these depositions are generally made in the coarsest and clumsiest manner; and they bear upon them the evidences of falsehood, in absurdities and self-contradictions, accumulated even to nausea. But what then? Mark the calculation. If there is plenty of it, some of it, according to the vulgar phrase, will stick. Do not think I am speaking loosely. I declare my belief that the whole proceeding is linked together, from first to last; a depraved logic runs through it. Inventors must shoot at random, therefore they take many strings to their bow. It would be strange indeed, and contrary to the doctrine of chances, if the whole forged fabric were dissolved and overthrown by self-contradiction.

Now let us consider practically what takes place. Suppose nine tenths too absurd to stand even before the Neapolitan courts; of this portion some is withdrawn by the police, and not carried into the trial, at all, after they have been made aware, through the prisoner's or his counsel's assistance, of its absurdity; the rest is overlooked by the judges. In any other country it would, of course, lead to inquiry, and to a prosecution for perjury. Not so there; it is rather regarded as so much of well-meant and patriotic effort, which, through untoward circumstances, has failed. It is simply neutralized, and stands at zero. But there remains the one tenth not self-contradicted. Well, but surely, you will say, the prisoner will be able to rebut that, if false, by counter evidence. Alas! He may have counter evidence mountains high; but he is not allowed to bring it. I know this is hardly credible; but it is true. The very men tried while I was at Naples, named and appealed to the counter evidence of scores and hundreds of men of all classes and professions— military, clergy, government functionaries, and the rest; but in every instance, with, I believe, one single exception, the court, the grand criminal court of justice, refused to hear it; and, in that one case, the person, when called, fully bore out the statement of the prisoner. Of course, the assertion of the accused, however supported by the evidence of station and character, goes for nothing, against the small remaining fragment, not self-destroyed, of the fictions of the vilest wretch, however such a fragment be buried beneath presumptions of falsehood; and this fragment, being thus secured from confutation, forms the pillow on which the consciences of the judges, after the work of condemnation, calmly and quietly repose.

Defence Of Slavery! A Series Of Letters To Harriet Beecher Stowe, Nicholas Brimblecomb, Esq. (1853)

MADAM: — In my last I alluded to the laws of the Southern States concerning slavery. I shall proceed, in this, to some further references to these laws by way of illustrating the exalted nature and character of the institution. It has already fully appeared that slaves are, by law, things — merchandise, like cattle, tobacco, corn, and the like. It follows, as a matter of course, that they have no civil rights, and cannot be parties to civil suits. "A slave," says a competent authority, "cannot be a party before a judicial tribunal in any species of action against his master; no matter how atrocious may have been the injury which he has received from him."

To this there appears to be only one exception — that is, when a slave claims to be free. The slave possessing nothing and holding nothing, he of course is not, and cannot be, a competent party to a suit at law; and this prevails wherever slavery exists in the country. And all this, madam, is perfectly consistent and proper. When we undertake to make horses parties to a civil suit, then it will be time enough to talk about affording this privilege to slaves, both horses and niggers being alike cattle. Another exceedingly wholesome law in the slave code is, that while niggers may testify for or against other niggers, whether bond or free, yet no nigger, bond or free, can testify for or against a white man; and this law obtains in every slave state in the Union.

Nothing can be wiser than this. It, in fact, gives the owner of slaves absolute power whenever he pleases to exercise it. He can work and punish his slaves to all intents and purposes, and be secure from any harm from law. All the master has to do is, like Mr. Legree, just to exclude all white persons from his plantation or premises, and then he may reign there like a prince of absolute authority. The *grand seignior* himself has not more complete power over his subjects, and over the ladies of his *seraglio*, than has the slaveholder over the men and women of his establishment. The case of Legree is a fine specimen of this elegant state of things. Remote from other plantations, and being surrounded only by his own niggers, he lived a king, with subjects under his absolute power, and over whom he exercised entire control. He could whip at his pleasure, and proceed to the extreme of killing whenever he chose, and by whatever means he chose, while all this excellent liberty he used without let or hindrance. He had his laws, and no one trampled upon them with impunity.

In case of trial for delinquency or shortcoming, he was himself prosecutor, witness, judge, and jury. He had his executioners whenever he thought proper to make use of them. He had his place of execution whenever he wished to inflict capital punishment; and he had his different modes of punishment by death, whether he proposed to kill by hanging, whipping, cutting, bleeding, burning, or otherwise.

The execution of old Tom presents a fine illustration of Mr. Legree's eligible position. He approaches his nigger, and seizing him by the collar, exclaims, "Do you know I have made up my mind to kill you?" Now, this was the language of a man who knew that he had absolute authority, and who

well knew that he was above all law that could reach him. In view of Tom's continued and abominable obstinacy in refusing to inform about the missing slaves, Legree addresses him again, saying, "I have made up my mind! I'll conquer ye, or kill ye! I'll count every drop of blood there is in ye, and take 'em one by one, till ye give up."

It is perfectly obvious that allowing niggers to testify against a white man would effectually destroy this very desirable and necessary prerogative in masters of taking, now and then, the lives of their slaves. It is for this reason, we cannot doubt, that this grand prohibition exists. It becomes necessary, at times, to cull off niggers; while yet, for the sake of appearances, the law must seem to disallow it. Thus the statute of Louisiana asserts that "the slave is entirely subject to the will of his master, who may correct and chastise him, though not with unusual rigor, or so as to maim or mutilate him, or to expose him to danger of loss of life, or to cause his death." This is the law ostensibly; and, as I have just remarked, it is so framed — not that the law designs to punish masters who kill their slaves, but that it may appear to discountenance and punish such treatment of slaves. That noble statute making colored testimony illegal, as brought against a white man, completely nullifies the other; and it virtually whispers to slave owners that they may punish so as to kill, if they will only do it out of sight of white witnesses. Mr. Legree, with many of the rest of us, availed himself of this advantage, and killed his niggers as he would kill other animals; that is, whenever he thought proper.

Why, of course, it must be so; you cannot separate this feature from our sublime system of servitude. It is a strictly logical and irresistible consequence. If you own a man as a piece of property, you may do what you will with him, as with other property. If you may kill your pig, you may kill your nigger; both for the same irresistible reason — they are both alike your own. True, you must be more careful in killing your nigger than in butchering your pig. You must look around before proceeding, and satisfy yourself that your wife, or children, or neighbors, are not looking on. The barn, with the doors closed, is a suitable place; or you may take him into the neighboring thicket; or you may order the nigger up at midnight, and just take him out in one of the outhouses, and stick him. There are a thousand opportunities, as slaveholders well know; and the slave law, while it seems to forbid, grants, however, all desirable indulgence. It virtually suggests that we may kill, under the proper circumstances.

That sapient upstart, young George Shelby, had to be reminded of this when he was about to bury old Tom. Fixing his eyes on Legree, he exclaimed, "Sir, this innocent blood shall have justice. I will proclaim this murder. I will go to the first magistrate and expose you!" A smart boy! — very, very smart boy this! He was determined to bring Mr. Legree to immediate justice.

"Do!" responded Mr. Legree, snapping his fingers scornfully. "I'd like to see ye doing it. Where ye going to get witnesses? How ye going to prove it? Come, now!" Mr. George Shelby thus saw himself headed, and that his officiousness would be of no manner of use. Mr. Legree was safe; there was no law to touch him; and you represent George as feeling that he would have rent the heavens with his heart's indignant cry for justice. Why, madam, he might as well have rent the heavens with his indignant cry against the blessed institution itself.

I hereby advertise you that killing niggers is a feature of this system — it is entirely congenial with it, part and parcel of it, and a logical result of it. Give a man the right of property in a hundred sheep, and he may kill off every one of them. So give a man the right of property in a hundred niggers, and he may just as surely kill off every one of them when he chooses to do so. Our glorious slave laws will bear him out in doing it; only, as I have already shown, those laws must, for the sake of the popular sentiment of mankind, have a show of opposition to such killing, while, by a covert provision, they grant the requisite permit. That covert provision is the dignified statute forbidding colored testimony against white people.

This is exactly the thing — this is all we want. It is a most capital provision. Under it we can do just what we please with our slaves —just what we please, Mrs. Stowe. There is our prerogative. We are kings and queens of absolute power among our niggers, and we greatly rejoice in our elevated estate.

Karl Marx, The New York Tribune (1853)

*T*he *Times* of Jan. 25 contains the following observations under the head of *Amateur Hanging*: "It has often been remarked that in this country a public execution is generally followed closely by instances of death by hanging, either suicidal or accidental, in consequence of the powerful effect which the execution of a noted criminal produces upon a morbid and unmatured mind."

Of the several cases which are alleged by *The Times* in illustration of this remark, one is that of a lunatic at Sheffield, who, after talking with other lunatics respecting the execution of Barbour, put an end to his existence by hanging himself. Another case is that of a boy of 14 years, who also hung himself. The doctrine to which the enumeration of these facts was intended to give its support, is one which no reasonable man would be likely to guess, it being no less than a direct apotheosis of the hangman, while capital punishment is extolled as the *ultima ratio* of society. This is done in a leading article of the "leading journal."

The Morning Advertiser, in some very bitter but just strictures on the hanging predilections and bloody logic of *The Times*, has the following interesting data on 43 days of the year 1849:

This table, as *The Times* concedes, shows not only suicides, but also murders of the most atrocious kind, following closely upon the execution of criminals. It is astonishing that the article in question does not even produce a single argument or pretext for indulging in the savage theory therein propounded; and it would

Executions of:		Murders and Suicides:	
Millan	March 20	Hannah Sandles	March 22
		M. G. Newton	March 22
Pulley	March 26	J. G. Gleeson —	March 27
		4 murders at Liverpool	
Smith	March 27	Murder and suicide	April 2
		at Leicester	
Howe	March 31	Poisoning at Bath	April 7
		W. Bailey	April 8
Landick	April 9	J. Ward murders	April 13
		his mother	
Sarah Thomas	April 13	Yardley	April 14
		Doxey, parricide	April 14
		J. Bailey kills his	April 17
		2 children, himself	
J. Griffiths	April 18	Charles Overton	April 18
J. Rush	April 21	Daniel Holmsden	May 2

be very difficult, if not altogether impossible, to establish any principle upon which the justice or expediency of capital punishment could be founded, in a society glorying in its civilization.

Punishment in general has been defended as a means either of ameliorating or of intimidating. Now what right have you to punish me for the amelioration or intimidation of others? And besides, there is history — there is such a thing as statistics — which prove with the most complete evidence that since Cain the world has neither been intimidated nor ameliorated by punishment. Quite the contrary. From the point of view of abstract right, there is only one theory of punishment which recognizes human dignity in the abstract, and that is the theory of Kant, especially in the more rigid formula given to it by Hegel. Hegel says: "Punishment is the right of the criminal. It is an act of his own will. The violation of right has been proclaimed by the criminal as his own right. His crime is the negation of right. Punishment is the negation of this negation, and consequently an affirmation of right, solicited and forced upon the criminal by himself." [Hegel, *Philosophy of Right*]

There is no doubt something specious in this formula, inasmuch as Hegel, instead of looking upon the criminal as the mere object, the slave of justice, elevates him to the position of a free and self-determined being. Looking, however, more closely into the matter, we discover that German idealism here, as in most other instances, has but given a transcendental sanction to the rules of existing society. Is it not a delusion to substitute for the individual with his real motives, with multifarious social circumstances pressing upon him, the abstraction of "free-will" — one among the many qualities of man for man himself! This theory, considering punishment as the result of the criminal's own will, is only a metaphysical expression for the old *"jus talionis"* [the right of retaliation by inflicting punishment of the same kind] eye against eye, tooth against tooth, blood against blood.

Plainly speaking, and dispensing with all paraphrases, punishment is nothing but a means of society to defend itself against the infraction of its vital conditions, whatever may be their character. Now, what a state of society is that, which knows of no better instrument for its own defense than the hangman, and which proclaims through the "leading journal of the world" its own brutality as eternal law? Mr. A. Quételet, in his excellent and learned work, *l'Homme et ses Facultés*, says: "There is a budget which we pay with frightful regularity — it is that of prisons, dungeons and scaffolds . . . We might even predict how many individuals will stain their hands with the blood of their fellow men, how many will be forgers, how many will deal in poison, pretty nearly the same way as we may foretell the annual births and deaths." And Mr.Quételet, in a calculation of the probabilities of crime published in 1829, actually predicted with astonishing certainty, not only the amount but all the different kinds of crimes committed in France in 1830. That it is not so much the particular political institutions of a country as the fundamental conditions of modern bourgeois society in general, which produce an average amount of crime in a given national fraction of society, may be seen from the following table, communicated by Quételet, for the years 1822-24. We find in a number of one hundred condemned criminals in America and France:

Age	Philadelphia	France
Under twenty-one years	19	19
Twenty-one to thirty	44	35
Thirty to forty	23	23
Above forty	14	23
Total	100	100

Now, if crimes observed on a great scale thus show, in their amount and their classification, the regularity of physical phenomena — if as Mr. Quételet remarks, "it would be difficult to decide in respect to which of the two" (the physical world and the social system) "the acting causes produce their effect with the utmost regularity" — is there not a necessity for deeply reflecting upon an alteration of the system that breeds these crimes, instead of glorifying the hangman who executes a lot of criminals to make room only for the supply of new ones?

A London Fête, Coventry Patmore (1854)

All night fell hammers, shock on shock;
With echoes Newgate's granite clang'd:
The scaffold built, at eight o'clock
They brought the man out to be hang'd.
Then came from all the people there
A single cry, that shook the air;
Mothers held up their babes to see,
Who spread their hands, and crow'd for glee;
Here a girl from her vesture tore
A rag to wave with, and join'd the roar;
There a man, with yelling tired,
Stopp'd, and the culprit's crime inquired;
A sot, below the doom'd man dumb,
Bawl'd his health in the world to come;
These blasphemed and fought for places;
Those, half-crush'd, cast frantic faces,
To windows, where, in freedom sweet,
Others enjoy'd the wicked treat.
At last, the show's black crisis pended;
Struggles for better standings ended;
The rabble's lips no longer curst,
But stood agape with horrid thirst;
Thousands of breasts beat horrid hope;
Thousands of eyeballs, lit with hell,
Burnt one way all, to see the rope
Unslacken as the platform fell.
The rope flew tight; and then the roar
Burst forth afresh; less loud, but more
Confused and affrighting than before.
A few harsh tongues for ever led
The common din, the chaos of noises,
But ear could not catch what they said.
As when the realm of the damn'd rejoices
At winning a soul to its will,
That clatter and clangour of hateful voices
Sicken'd and stunn'd the air, until
The dangling corpse hung straight and still.
The show complete, the pleasure past,
The solid masses loosen'd fast:
A thief slunk off, with ample spoil,
To ply elsewhere his daily toil;
A baby strung its doll to a stick;
A mother praised the pretty trick;
Two children caught and hang'd a cat;
Two friends walk'd on, in lively chat;
And two, who had disputed places,
Went forth to fight, with murderous faces.

Capital Punishment Speech, Wendell Phillips (1859)

Extract from a Speech of Wendell Phillips before a committee of the Legislature of Massachusetts, appointed to consider the propriety of abolishing Capital Punishment. March 16, 1859.

Gentlemen, for one hundred years the progress of all legislation has been to throw away those extreme penalties; and, in proportion as it has done so, crime has diminished. This shows that society does not need the gallows for protection; and, if it does not need it for protection, it has no right to it. These gentlemen will not contend, of course, that society has a right to take life from caprice, from whim, from taste, but only from necessity. If we show you that when it has been withdrawn from a crime that crime has diminished; then, I say, we show you a competent and sufficient argument why it should be abolished.

We have the experience of Russia, of Tuscany, of Belgium, of Sir James Mackintosh in India, where they have given up the death penalty; yet murder did not increase.

We have got outside of the Bible now. We have the experience of two hundred years in England that every crime from which the penalty of the gallows was taken off has diminished. We have the experience of Russia, of Tuscany, of Belgium, of Sir James Mackintosh in India, where they have given up the death penalty; yet murder did not increase. You say, these experiments were local, and for a short time. True, but they were all one way. Society has never tried the gallows, but to fail. Now, all we ask of Massachusetts is, that, as she has tried the one and not succeeded, she shall now try the other.

We used to punish highway robbery with death. Then that crime was frequent; but things got to such a state that a man was more likely to be struck with lightning, sitting in his parlor in any town of the commonwealth, than to be hanged for committing highway robbery. We took off the penalty of death, and then highway robbery diminished; there were more cases before than since. In the states that have abolished the death penalty, the result has been entirely satisfactory — and every humane man must rejoice at it. Take Michigan, and those states that have rescinded the penalty—they are no worse off than Massachusetts. I say that this is a state preeminently fitted to try this experiment.

We are the great Normal School of all civil government—Massachusetts. We have the most moral people on the face of the earth; we have the best circumstances for an experiment in civil government; we have a people with wealth equally divided; we have common schools; we are a people with a high moral tone; we have a homogeneous population; it is easy to get a living here, and poverty, therefore, does not drive to crime, as in some other places; our circumstances are all favorable to morality. We are in a better state to try such an experiment —than Michigan, far better than Belgium, Tuscany, or Russia; yet they tried it, and were successful, and why will not we?

All the great lights of jurisprudence are on our side — Franklin, Livingston, Rush, Lafayette, Beccaria, Grotius — I might mention forty eminent names, all throwing their testimony against the gallows. Lafayette said, "I shall demand the abolition of the penalty of death, until you show me the infallibility of human testimony." He thought it was enough to discredit the gallows that men might be hung by mistake. There have been two or three scores of such cases in the history of jurisprudence.

Now, with all this experience on our side, with the fact that we are the very best government in the world to try the experiment; with the testimony of Lord Brougham — a man not biased by any peculiar circumstances, by any religious fanaticism, by any sentimental enthusiasm — that this idea of deterring from offenses by example is a failure; that education is the only thing; that the prison ought to be a moral hospital; that the man is to be taken possession of, and restrained by moral influences — shall we be behind such a man as Lord Brougham? It seems that we ought not to be.

All experience points one way. The old barbarous practices have gradually given place to others more humane and merciful. Once a prisoner was not allowed to swear his witnesses; then they would not allow him counsel; now he may swear his witnesses, and is entitled to counsel—yet the government is safe. Men used to say, "We cannot get rid of the gallows. Why, murder is so rife in the land that if you don't have the very worst punishment that man can devise, no man's life will be safe." If this was so, why didn't you impale the criminal, as in Algiers, or crucify him, as the Romans did? Why didn't you make the gallows as cruel as possible? If you wanted the terror of example, if you wanted the blood to freeze in the hearts of men, why did you not make the punishment as cruel as you could? That is not the spirit of the age.

The question is not now how we shall most frighten men, but how we shall take life the easiest. It has even been proposed, from motives of humanity, to give chloroform to the man about to be executed. If you want to frighten people, adopt the cruelest punishment you can invent; and yet, if you should do so, if you should take pains to make your punishments as severe and cruel as possible, the humanity of the nineteenth century would rebuke you. If you can come down one step—if you can give up the rack and the wheel, impaling, tearing to death with wild horses, why cannot you come down two, and adopt imprisonment? Why cannot you come down three, and, instead of putting the man in a jail, make your prisons, as Brougham recommends, moral hospitals, and educate him? Why cannot you come down four, and put him under the influence of some community of individuals, who will labor to awaken again the moral feelings and sympathies of his nature?

Who knows how many steps you can come down? We came down one when we gave up burning at the stake; we came down another when we gave up the tearing of the body to pieces with red-hot pincers; we came down another when we gave up the torture of the wheel. You cannot tolerate these things now. Society has been forced, by the instinct of humanity, against its logic, to put away these cruel penalties.

Men have been crying out continually against this instinct of mercy, which sought to make the dungeon less terrible; they feared to remove a cobweb from that dungeon's cruelty, lest the world should go to pieces. Yet the world swept it down, and is safer today than ever before. Now we ask you to abolish the gallows. It is only one step further in the same direction. Massachusetts has got up to the wall. She has thrown it away for almost all offenses— she only retains it for one or two. We ask you to take one more step in the same direction. Take it, because the civilized world is taking it, in many quarters! Take it, because the circumstances of the time prove you may take it safely! Take it, because it is well to try experiments for humanity, and this is a favorable community to try them in!

WITNESS TO AN EXECUTION
The Execution of John Brown
John T. L. Preston letter (1859)

Charles Town, Dec. 2, 1859:
The execution is over; we have just returned from the field and I sit down to give you some account of it. The weather was very favorable: the sky was a little overcast, with a gentle haze in the atmosphere that softened without obscuring the magnificent prospect afforded here

Between eight and nine o'clock, the troops began to put themselves in motion to occupy the positions assigned to them on the field, as designated on the plan I send you. Col. Smith had been assigned the superintendence of the execution, and he and his staff were the only mounted officers on the ground, until the Major General and his staff appeared. By ten o'clock all was arranged. The general effect was most imposing, and, at the same time, picturesque.

The cadets were immediately in rear of the gallows with a howitzer on the right and left, a little behind, so as to sweep the field. They were uniformed in red flannel shirts, which gave them a gay, dashing, Zouave look, and was exceedingly becoming, especially at the battery. They were flanked obliquely

by two corps, the Richmond Grays (Greys) and Company F, which if inferior in appearance to the cadets, were superior to any other company I ever saw outside of the regular army. Other companies were distributed over the field, amounting in all to about 800 men. The military force was about 1,500.

The whole enclosure was lined by cavalry troops posted as sentinels, with their officers--one on a peerless black horse, and another on a remarkable-looking white horse, continually dashing round the enclosure. Outside this enclosure were other companies acting as rangers and scouts. The jail was guarded by several companies of infantry, and pieces of artillery were put in position for its defense.

Shortly before eleven o'clock the prisoner was taken from the jail, and the funeral cortege was put in motion. First came three companies, then the criminal's wagon, drawn by two large white horses. John Brown was seated on his coffin, accompanied by the sheriff and two other persons. The wagon drove to the foot of the gallows, and Brown descended with alacrity and without assistance, and ascended the steep steps to the platform. His demeanor was intrepid, without being braggart. He made no speech; whether he desired to make one or not, I do not know. Had he desired it, it would not have been permitted. Any speech of his must, of necessity, have been unlawful, and as being directed against the peace and dignity of the Commonwealth, and as such could not be allowed by those who were then engaged in the most solemn and extreme vindication of law.

His manner was without trepidation, but his countenance was not free from concern, and it seemed to me to have a little cast of wildness. He stood upon the scaffold but a short time, giving brief adieus to those about him, when he was properly pinioned, the white cap drawn over his face, the noose adjusted and attached to the hook above, and he was moved blindfold a few steps forward. It was curious to note how the instincts of nature operated to make him careful in putting his feet as if afraid he would walk off the scaffold. The man who stood unblanched on the brink of eternity was afraid of falling a few feet to the ground. He was now all ready. The sheriff asked him if he should give him a private signal before the fatal moment. He replied in a voice that seemed to me unnaturally natural, so composed was its tone, and so distinct its articulation, that "it did not matter to him, if only they would not keep him too long waiting." He was kept waiting, however. The troops that had formed his escort had to be put into their position, and while this was going on, he stood for some ten or fifteen minutes blindfold, the rope around his neck, and his feet on the treacherous platform, expecting instantly the fatal act. But he stood for this comparatively long time upright as a soldier in position, and motionless.

I was close to him, and watched him narrowly, to see if I could perceive any signs of shrinking or trembling in his person, but there was none. Once I thought I saw his knees tremble, but it was only the wind blowing his loose trousers. His firmness was subjected to still further trial by hearing Colonel Smith announce to the sheriff, "We are all ready, Mr. Campbell." The sheriff did not hear, or did not comprehend; and in a louder tone the same announcement was made. But the culprit still stood ready until the sheriff, descending the flight of steps, with a well-directed blow of a sharp hatchet, severed the rope that held up the trap door, which instantly sank beneath him, and he fell about three feet; and the man of strong and bloody hand, of fierce passions, of iron will, of wonderful vicissitudes, the terrible partisan of Kansas, the capturer of the United States Arsenal at Harper's Ferry, the would-be Catiline of the South, the demi-god of the abolitionists, the man execrated and lauded, damned and prayed for, the man who in his motives, his means, his plans, and his successes, must ever be a wonder, a puzzle, and a mystery---John Brown---was hanging between heaven and earth.

There was profound stillness during the time his struggles continued, growing feebler and feebler at each abortive attempt to breathe. He knees were scarcely bent, his arms were drawn up to a right angle at the elbow, with the hands clenched; but there was no writhing of the body, no violent heaving of the chest. At each feebler effort at respiration his arms sank lower, and his legs hung more relaxed, until at last, straight and lank he dangled, swayed to and fro by the wind.

It was a moment of deep solemnity, and suggestive of thoughts that make the bosom swell. The field of execution was a rising ground, and commanded the outstretching valley from mountain to mountain, and their still grandeur gave sublimity to the outline, while it so chanced that white clouds resting upon them, gave them the appearance that reminded more than one of us of the snow peaks of the Alps. Before us was the greatest array of disciplined forces ever seen in Virginia; infantry, cavalry and artillery combined, composed of the old Commonwealth's noblest sons, and commanded by her best officers; and the great canopy of the sky overarching all, came to add its sublimity ever present, but only realized when other great things are occurring beneath each.

But the moral of the scene was its grand point. A sovereign state had been assailed, and she had uttered but a hint, and her sons had hastened to show that they were ready to defend her. Law had been violated by actual murder and attempted treason, and that gibbet was erected by law, and to uphold law was this military force assembled. But, greater still---God's Holy Law and righteous Providence was vindicated, "Thou shalt not kill"--- "Whoso sheddeth man's blood, by man shall his blood be shed." And here the gray-haired man of violence meets his fate, after he has seen his two sons cut down before him, in the same career of violence into which he had introduced them. So perish all such enemies of Virginia! All such enemies of the Union! All such foes of the human

Law had been violated by actual murder and attempted treason, and that gibbet was erected by law, and to uphold law was this military force assembled. But, greater still—God's Holy Law and righteous Providence was vindicated, "Thou shalt not kill"— "Whoso sheddeth man's blood, by man shall his blood be shed."

race! So I felt, and so I said, with solemnity and without one shade of animosity, as I turned to break the silence, to those around me. Yet, the mystery was awful, to see the human form thus treated by men, to see life suddenly stopped in its current, and to ask one's self the question without answer--"And what then?"

In all that array there was not, I suppose, one throb of sympathy for the offender. All felt in the depths of their hearts that it was right. On the other hand, there was not one single word or gesture of exultation or of insult. From the beginning to the end, all was marked by the most absolute decorum and solemnity. There was no military music, no saluting by troops as they passed one another, nor anything done for show. The criminal hung upon the gallows for nearly forty minutes, and after being examined by a whole staff of surgeons, was deposited in a neat coffin to be delivered to his friends, and transported to Harper's Ferry, where his wife awaited it. She came in company with two persons to see her husband last night, and returned to Harper's Ferry this morning. She is described by those who saw her as a very large, masculine woman, of absolute composure of manner. The officers who witnessed their meeting in the jail said they met as if nothing unusual had taken place, and had a comfortable supper together.

Brown would not have the assistance of any minister in jail during his last days, nor their presence with him on the scaffold. In going from prison to the place of execution, he said very little, only assuring those who were with him that he had no fear, nor had he at any time in his life, known what fear was. When he entered the gate of the enclosure, he expressed his admiration of the beauty of the surrounding country, and pointing to different residences, asked who were the owners of them.

There was a very small crowd to witness the execution. Governor Wise and General Taliaferro had both issued proclamations exhorting the citizens to remain at home and guard their property, and warned them of possible danger. The train on the Winchester Railroad had been stopped from carrying passengers; and even passengers on the Baltimore Railroad were subjected to examination and detention. An arrangement was made to divide the expected crowed into recognized citizens, and those not recognized; to require the former to go to the right, and the latter to the left. Of the latter there was not a single one. it was told last night there were not in Charles Town ten persons besides citizens and military.

There is but one opinion as to the completeness of the arrangements made on the occasion, and the absolute success with which they were carried out. I have said something about the striking effect of the pageant as a pageant, but the excellence of it was that everything was arranged solely with the view of efficiency, and not for effect upon the eye. Had it been intended as a mere spectacle, it could not have been made more imposing, or had actual need occurred, it was the best possible arrangement.

You may be inclined to ask was all this necessary? I have not time to enter upon the question now. Governor Wise thought it necessary, and he said he had reliable information. The responsibility of calling out the force rests with him. It only remained for those under his orders to dispose the force in the best manner. That this was done is unquestionable, and, whatever credit is due for it, may fairly be claimed by those who accomplished it.

WITNESS TO AN EXECUTION
The Execution of John Brown
Thomas J. "Stonewall" Jackson (1859)

John Brown was hung today at about 11½ a.m. He behaved with unflinching firmness. The arrangements were well made under the direction of Col. Smith. Brown's wife visited him last evening. The body is to be delivered to her. The gibbet was southeast of the town in a large field. Brown rode on the head of his coffin, from his prison to the place of execution. The coffin was of black walnut, enclosed in a poplar box of the same shape as the coffin.

He was dressed in carpet slippers of predominating red, white socks, blacks pants, black frock coat, black vest & black slouch hat. Nothing around his neck beside his shirt collar. The open wagon in which he rode was strongly guarded on all sides. Capt. Williams, formerly one of the assistants of the Institute, marched immediately in front of the wagon. The jailer and high sheriff and several others rode in the wagon with the prisoner.

Brown had his arms tied behind him, & ascended the scaffold with apparent cheerfulness. After reaching the top of the platform, he shook hands with several who were standing around him. The sheriff placed the rope around his neck, then threw a white cap over his head & asked him if he wished a signal when all should be ready—to which he replied that it made no difference, provided he was not kept waiting too long.

In this condition he stood on the trap door, which was supported on one side by hinges, and on the other (south side) by a rope, for about 10 minutes, when Col. S. told the Sheriff "all is ready," which apparently was not comprehended by the Sheriff, and the Col. had to repeat the order, when the rope was cut by a single blow, and Brown fell through about 25 inches, so as to bring his knees on a level with the position occupied by his feet before the rope was cut. With the fall his arms below the elbow flew up, hands clenched, & his arms gradually fell by spasmodic motions—there was very little motion of his person for several minutes, after which the wind blew his lifeless body to & fro.

His face, upon the scaffold, was turned a little east of south, and in front of him were the cadets commanded by Major Gilham. My command was still in front of the cadets, all facing south. One howitzer I assigned to Mr. Truheart on the left of the cadets, and with the other I remained on the right. Other troops occupied different positions around the scaffold, and altogether it was an imposing but very solemn scene.

I was much impressed with the thought that before me stood a man, in the full vigor of health, who must in a few minutes be in eternity. I sent up a petition that he might be saved. Awful was the thought that he might in a few minutes receive the sentence "Depart ye wicked into everlasting fire." I hope that he was prepared to die, but I am very doubtful—he wouldn't have a minister with him.

His body was taken back to the jail, and at 6 p.m. was sent to his wife at Harper's Ferry. When it reached Harper's Ferry the coffin was opened and his wife saw the body—the coffin was again opened at the depot, before leaving for Baltimore, lest there should be an imposition.

Burning Human Beings Alive at the Stake
William Henry Fey (1860)

As the slaves augment, while their chances of escape and incentives to restlessness multiply through steam traveling and the increased intercourse with the Free States, stringent measures for keeping them in subjection, outside even the horrible slave code, become more common. Among these, preeminent for savage cruelty, stands the growing custom of burning men at the stake. The poor wretches, born of forced prostitution, unable to read or write, being kept in dark ignorance, denied the rank of human beings, and pronounced chattels, are logically not amenable to law; but notwithstanding, are subject not only to the demoniac statutes but to lynch law, such as is without parallel in the nineteenth century.

That such burnings are inevitable under the system, is not to be disputed; and so no special indignation should be expressed in regard to them, or any other forms of savage punishment included. It is difficult to reach the facts regarding plantation horrors, the dissemination of intelligence in the South being comparatively so limited. But enough is known to warrant the affirmation, that burning slaves alive for "crimes" is to some extent systematically pursued in the South, although there is no such punishment on the statute book. The journals in the North, have published from time to time, such accounts of these roastings as escaped into the circle of publicity; but yet, notwithstanding, the following debate took place in the House of Representatives, on the 7th March, 1860, as reported in *The Congressional Globe* of the 8th:

"Mr. VAN WYCK—Sir, I will indulge in no unkind remark to wound the feelings of any man, but the charge must be met, and history vindicated, let the consequences fall where and as they may. One other gentleman spoke of Massachusetts burning witches in the ancient times. Does he not know that your own people burn slaves at the stake, and it seems to waken no horror in your minds.

Mr. DAVIS, of Miss. (interrupting)—I pronounce the gentleman a liar and scoundrel. I pronounce the gentleman's assertion false—utterly false.

Mr. VAN WYCK— My time is short, and I hope not to be interrupted.

Mr. DAVIS, of Miss.—You have no right to utter such foul and false slanders.

Mr. GABTBELL—I rise to a point of order. It is that no member upon this floor has a right to libel the people of any section of this country, and then deny to the representatives of that people the right to reply. I pronounce the assertion made by the gentleman false and founded. (Cries of "Order"on the Republican side.)

Mr. VAN WYCK—I have heard such words before, and I am not to be disturbed nor interfered with by any blustering of that sort. I am not here to libel any part of the Union.

Mr. DAVIS—Will you go outside the District of Columbia and test the question of personal courage with any Southern man?

Mr. VAN WYCK—I travel anywhere, and without fear of anyone. For the first eight weeks of this session you stood upon this floor, continually libeling the North, and the people of the Free States, charging them with treason and all manner of crimes; and now you are thrown into a great rage when I tell you a few facts.

The debate on slave-burning had its origin, as may be seen, in the assertion by a member—that Massachusetts burned witches centuries since. But even this off-set to the barbarities of the South in the nineteenth century is wanting, for Massachusetts put witches to death not by burning. But in proof of the accuracy of Mr. Van Wyck's statement, that the South does now burn slaves alive, the following cases are on record. *The Union Springs Gazette* of Alabama, of the 18th January, 1859, gives an account of the burning of a slave for murdering his master, said to be kind and humane:

"The deceased has the reputation of having, even to fault, ever been a kind and humane master. On the day before the murder, Mr. J. had whipped this boy, Milford, or had him whipped, for some misdemeanor, and had him chained or locked till Monday morning, when he went to him, took off his chain, and told him to 'go to the mill and go to work.' The boy made some impudent reply, when Mr. J. told him if he did not stop his insolence he would knock him down with a lock, and turned to walk away. The boy then took an axe that was lying near and struck Mr. J. on the head, and knocked him down, dropped the axe and walked away a few steps, then turned and went back, took the axe and struck him three times more on the head, and retired a short distance and sat down, making no attempt to escape.

"A public meeting of the citizens, indiscriminately, was called on Wednesday, to determine what should be done with the Negro, when the proposition was made to burn him alive, everyone, to the number of 200 or 800, voting for it. That evening, at 8 o'clock, in the presence of 500 persons, he was chained to a tree and burned. Just before the fire was set, he confirmed the above statement in every particular. He stated also, that he had determined to kill his master some time before—that his having him whipped the day before had not instigated him to the brutal deed—that he had his knife open in his pocket to do the deed when his master should come to unfasten him, but his heart failed him; but that when he told him that if he did not stop his insolence he would knock him down, he proceeded to execute his fell purpose. The culprit ceased to show any signs of life two and half minutes from the time the torch was applied."

"The kind and humane master," according to the Southern journal, had the slave whipped and chained—kindness and humanity it would seem in the South, meaning whips and chains. Another instance of slave burning is thus recited, the incentive for the murder committed by the slave, being the same as in the above, that of corporeal punishment; whether the master in this case was a model of kindness, is not related.

On the first day of last year, 1859, at the annual Negro sales at Troy (Ky.), Mr. James Calaway, the brother-in-law of one Simon B. Thornhill, who, it seems, had been murdered by a slave in revenge for some punishment, mounted a box in the street, and exhorted the people to do speedy justice upon the murderer, and closed by saying, "All that feel as I do will follow me." Eight hundred or a thousand followed him. They went to the jail, took out the prisoner, and in the jailyard itself drove down a stake, to which they chained him hand and feet. Fine split wood was piled around him, and he was miserably burned to death. "He gave," says a correspondent of *The Maysville* (Ky.) *Eagle*, "some of the most hideous screams I ever heard come from any human being."

The Philadelphia Bulletin, of April 11, 1860, presents this statement of a case in the present year: "A SLAVE BURNED AT A STAKE. *The Vicksburg Sun* has come in possession of the following facts in relation to the burning of a Negro man at Mr. Woolfolk's plantation on Deer Creek. It seems that the Negro thus summarily dealt with was a vicious, self-willed fellow, and becoming offended at a woman (black) on the same plantation, walked up to her as she was working in the field and deliberately plunged the knife into her breast. Upon perpetrating this bloody deed he fled to the woods, not, however, before giving several other Negroes to understand that their time would come next, and after them two white men living hard by. Dogs were put on his tracks, and after a chase of several hours he was captured, though not without a desperate struggle—the pursuers being put to all they knew to take him alive. The residents of the vicinity decided to burn him at the stake, which was done in the presence of all the Negroes on that and several of the adjoining plantations, all of whom seemed terrified out of their wits on viewing so awful a scene. The spirit of the doomed Negro never was subdued. He died cursing his judges—his last words being that he would "take vengeance on them when they met each other in h-ll"

Mr. C. E. Fuller, of the State of Michigan, obtained from Mr. J. F. Norrell, the account of the burning of two slaves, in the township of Extra, in Ashley County, Arkansas, in September, 1857, one of the slaves having belonged to Mr. Norrell. They were suspected of murder and arson. Mr. Fuller says: "Ike" (one of the suspected) was whipped nearly to death, in order to extort from " him a confession; but he persisted in denying any knowledge of the affair. Mr. N. then poured on his bleeding back spirits of turpentine, and set it on fire. Ike then confessed that he and a Negro, named Jack, were guilty. The slaves were taken by the "regulators," chained to stakes, and burnt to death with fat pine wood. It is worthy of remark, that the considerate regulators took up a subscription, to indemnify the owners for the value of the slaves, so roasted by the supreme lynch law of the South.

The Montgomery Alabama Mail thus speaks of a Negro-burning fete, which was likely to come off on the 16th of March, of the present year, 1860. "We hear that it has now been ascertained who committed the murder of Alfred Jones, on Saturday night, in this county. It seems, that two or three days previous to this murder, he gave one of his Negroes, Adam, a whipping, and that the Negro "then said, it would be the last one he would ever give him, and persuaded another boy to hold his master's horse, while he knocked him on the head with an axe. The two Negroes we understand, will be burned to death on Friday, the 16th instant."

The New York Times quotes the following: BY A SLAVE—*The Atlanta Georgia Intelligencer* gives the substance of a letter from Hon. W. R. Nicholl, of Oglethorpe County, Georgia, detailing a horrible murder perpetrated by a Negro, in the employ of Mr. Wm. P. Smith. Jim, the Negro, was ordered by Mr. Smith to do a piece of work, which he refused to do, peremptorily. An altercation ensued, and Mr. Smith told the Negro, if he wished to quarrel with him, to go to the house. The two started together, Mr. Smith walking in front. Just as he entered the gate, the Negro asked Mr. Smith what he intended to do with him. As he made no reply, the Negro sprang upon him, and stabbed him sixteen times, jumping upon his victim as he fell. Mrs. Smith, with some Negroes who were in the house, witnessed the scene and managed, finally, to drag the murderer away. He fled to a straw-house, where he was captured the next morning. Mr. Smith died soon afterward. The people had determined to burn his murderer alive."

This is the case of which the following telegraphic report appeared in The Philadelphia Bulletin, of June 12, 1860, showing that the design of the lynch-legists had been put in execution.

"ACOCSTA, GA., June 12—MURDER OF A GEORGIA PLANTER BY HIS SLAVE—THE SLAVE BURNT AT A STAKE—A man, named William Smith, a planter in Oglethorpe County, Georgia, was murdered by a slave on Saturday. The slave was captured, and burnt at a stake on Monday." Referring to this case, *The Atlanta Georgia Intelligencer* says: "Mr. Smith had treated this Negro with great kindness—had raised him, and never struck him a lick. He was, doubtless, demented, and instigated by the devil. His fate should be an awful warning to others of his color, who are alike ungrateful." If demented mean insane, this Georgia editor justifies the burning of an insane man.

The St. Louis Evening News, of the 14th of March, 1860, copies from a journal of that city, of the 22d of July, 1859, an account of the burning at the stake, by a mob, at Marshall, Saline County, Missouri, on the 19th of the latter month, of a Negro, who had been condemned to be hung by the legal tribunal for the murder of a gentleman, named Hinton. He was taken by the mob from the sheriff, who was conveying him to prison, chained to a stake, dry wood was piled around, and he was burned to death. As the flames gathered about his limbs and body, he commenced the most frantic shrieks and appeals for mercy— for death; he seized his chains, they were hot, and burned the flesh off his hands; he would drop and catch them again and again. There must have been upward of one thousand people present. The mob, at the same time, hung two other Negroes whom they had taken out of jail.

The statute book of the South, cruel as it is, does not meet the wants of the sovereign people there; so they break open jails, and burn and hang at pleasure.

The New York Tribune, of March 12, 1860, contained an account of a slave burning, in Charleston, S. C., upon the authority of the late John Parish, of Philadelphia, a preacher of the Society of Friends. His statement is, "That a slave was burnt to death, at a stake, in Charleston, surrounded by a multitude of spectators, some of whom were people of the first rank. The poor object was heard to cry, as long as he could breathe, 'Not guilty, not guilty!' "

In reference to this case, a correspondent of another New York paper signing himself J. Jeffreys, states that he was present at the burning, and justifies it, because the crime was the rape of a young lady, entrusted to the slave to take to school, for which he had been tried, and condemned to be hanged; the day, however, came for the execution, but the people, says Mr. Jeffreys, rose en masse, high and low, and determined that "hanging was too good for him;" and gives a description of how the Negro was chained to an iron bar, and roasted to death. "He lived," says Mr. Jeffreys, "about ten or twelve minutes, and caved in: and the cry was, 'Pile on the fagots'; others ought to be served the same way, white or black. I would lend a hand to pile on the fagots for the same crime, in this enlightened day."

The New York Tribune, of April 21, 1860, contains the following:

OHIO, April 18, 1860. To the Editor of *The N. Y. Tribune*: "SIR: On the 18th of August last, I saw a Negro hung by a mob, in Springfield, Mo. The cause of the lynching was an outrage committed upon the person of a lady residing near that city. On the same evening, a member of the Missouri Legislature, residing in Springfield, informed me that five years before he saw two Negroes burned at the stake, in Jasper, one of the western counties in that State. He gave me full details of the affair, asserting that many slaves were brought in from the adjacent country to witness it; that the victims seemed to lose their consciousness immediately after the flame struck their faces, etc. I have every reason to believe that my informant is a reliable gentleman, and will cheerfully furnish his name to any one desiring it."A. D. RICHARDSON.

The Montgomery, Alabama, Herald, of a late date, contained the following: "WE THINK SO TOO. The Editors of *The Hayneville, Alabama, Chronicle*, very justly observes: 'It is questionable ' whether burning Negroes by whites has any better effect than to brutalize the feelings of the community. Several have already been burned in Montgomery County, without, it seems, decreasing crime among them."

Here we have the authority of two Alabama newspapers, that several slaves have been roasted alive in one county. If that be taken as the average of the number of burnings through the South, the cases would number by thousands. Nearly all the instances above cited, are recent. Others of older date could be given, for example:

About twenty years ago, an overseer in Goochland County, Virginia, was tried and imprisoned for having burned a slave to death. In 1836, a freeman of color, named Macintosh, was burned at the stake at St. Louis, Missouri, by a mob who took him from the jail, and burned him alive in the presence of three thousand people. He was twenty minutes dying. He was steward of a steamboat, and his crime was the killing of a man who had arrested him on a charge of rescuing another freeman of color who was under arrest.

A correspondent of The Cincinnati Herald, in July, 1845, wrote to that paper an account of the burning of the house of an overseer, near Oakland Cottage, Mississippi, by slaves who had been emancipated by the will of their master, but were exasperated and desperate at being still held in bondage. A white child was burned to death in the overseer's house. The incendiaries, eight or nine in number, were seized by the neighbors, and two of them immediately hanged. The rest were chained to the floor of a log-house, and therein slowly roasted to death. This statement was extensively published in the papers at the time, and was not denied or refuted.

A correspondent of *The New Orleans Picayune*, writing from Jackson, Mississippi, 20th December, 1855, gave the account of a Negro who was chained to a stake and burned alive for having attempted to commit a rape upon a young lady. The execution was at Lexington.

The Montgomery, Alabama, Mail, of April 8, 1856, says: "We learn, that the Negro who murdered Mr. Capeheart, was burned to death yesterday at Mount Meigs. He acknowledged himself guilty."

In the *Travels in the South* of Dr. Parsons, of Boston, published in 1856, an account is copied by him from *The Sumter, Alabama, Whig*, of a then recent slave-burning in that county. The slave Dave belonged to J. D. Thornton, and was accused of murdering a young lady. Thornton and his friends took the slave, by stratagem, from jail: "they left in high glee," says *The Whig*; "he was tied to a stake, with fat, light wood piled around him, and the torch was applied in the presence of two thousand persons." *The Whig* denied the rumors afloat, that Dave was tortured—burning alive not being considered torture in Alabama.

Dr. Parsons also gives another instance which occurred not long before his visit to Georgia, the details of which he had from eye-witnesses. A slave, who had been cruelly whipped, wounded his mistress with a hatchet: he was given to the mob for punishment; they whipped him for five successive days, fifty lashes a day, and on a Sunday he was taken from the jail, stripped naked, and tied by his hands to the limb of a large oak tree, near the courthouse. A fire of hard pine shavings was then kindled beneath him, and while burning to death, he was stabbed and cut by knives fastened to poles, the executioners shouting that this was the punishment of every slave who would murder his mistress. Ten thousand people were present at this scene, which took place in 1855.

John Kingsley, of Portsmouth, Ohio, published a statement on the 7th of January, 1857, of the burning at the stake of a Negro, which he witnessed the preceding week in Carter County, Kentucky. The victim was the slave of William McMinnis. He was suspected of planning an insurrection, and before being burned received two hundred lashes to extort a confession, which he did not make.

It will thus be seen, that lynch law is universal in the South, and will not wait for the hangman, but executes punishment of a kind utterly unknown to Christendom elsewhere, and supposed to pertain alone to the cruelties of past ages. Such atrocities in the nineteenth century belong exclusively to Slave States, and to the aboriginal savages only. They are a part of the system, and cannot be dissociated therefrom. Are they not reasons for restricting Slavery within its present limits, covering, as it does, nearly two-thirds of the surface of the States, and threatening with blood and fire, to spread itself to the Pacific?

WITNESS TO AN EXECUTION
Execution of 38 Sioux, Isaac Heard (1863)

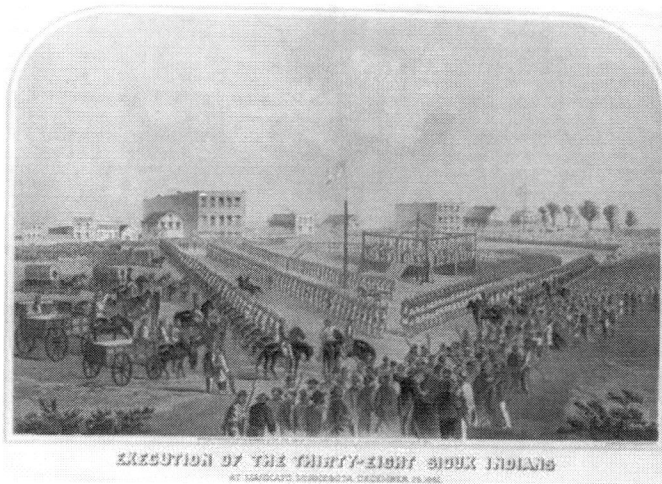

EXECUTION OF THE THIRTY-EIGHT SIOUX INDIANS
AT MANKATO MINNESOTA DECEMBER 26, 1862.

On Wednesday [Dec. 24, 1862] each Indian set apart for execution was permitted to send for two or three of his relatives or friends confined in the same prison for the purpose of bidding them a final adieu, and to carry such messages to absent relatives as each person might be disposed to send. Major Brown was present during the interviews, and describes them as very sad and affecting. Each Indian had some word to send to his parents or family. When speaking of their wives and children, almost every one was affected to tears.

Good counsel was sent to the children. They were in many cases exhorted to an adoption of Christianity and the life of good feeling toward the whites. Most of them spoke confidently of their hopes of salvation. [. . .]

There is a ruling passion with many Indians, and Tazoo could not refrain from its enjoyment even in this sad hour Ta-ti-mi-ma was sending word to his relatives not to mourn for his loss. He said he was old and could not hope to live long under any circumstances, and his execution would not shorten his days a great deal, and dying as he did, innocent of any white man's blood, he hoped would give him a better chance to be saved; therefore he hoped his friends would consider his death but as a removal from this to a better world. "I have every hope," said he, "of going direct to the abode of the Great Spirit, where I shall always be happy."

This last remark reached the ears of Tazoo, who was also speaking to his friends, and he elaborated upon it in this wise: "Yes, tell our friends that we are being removed from this world over the same path they must shortly travel. We go first, but many of our friends may follow us in a very short time. I expect to go direct to the abode of the Great Spirit, and to be happy when I get there; but we are told that the road is long and the distance great; therefore, as I am slow in all my movements, it will probably take a long time to reach the end of the journey, and I should not be surprised if some of the young, active men we will leave behind us will pass me on the road before I reach the place of my destination."

In shaking hands with Red Iron and Akipa, Tazoo said: "Friends, last summer you were opposed to us. You were living in continual apprehension of an attack from those who were determined to exterminate the whites. Yourselves and families were subjected to many taunts, insults, and threats. Still you stood firm in our friendship for the whites and continually counseled the Indians to abandon their raid against the whites. Your course was condemned at the time, but now you see your wisdom. You were right when you said the whites could not be exterminated, and the attempt indicated folly; you and your families were prisoners, and the lives of all in danger. Today you are here at liberty, assisting in feeding and guarding us, and thirty-nine men will die in two days because they did not follow your example and advice."

Several of the prisoners were completely overcome during the leave-taking, and were compelled to abandon conversation. Others again (and Tazoo was one) affected to disregard the dangers of their position, and laughed and joked apparently as unconcerned as if they were sitting around a camp-fire in perfect freedom.

On Thursday, the women who were employed as cooks for the prisoners, all of whom had relations among the condemned, were admitted to the prison. This interview was less sad, but still interesting. Locks of hair, blankets, coats, and almost every other article in possession of the prisoners, were given in trust for some relative or friend who had been forgotten or overlooked during the interview of the previous day. The idea of allowing women to witness their weakness is repugnant to an Indian, and will account for this. The messages were principally advice to their friends to bear themselves with fortitude and refrain from great mourning. The confidence of many in their salvation was again reiterated.

Late on Thursday night, in company with Lieutenant Colonel Marshall, the reporter visited the building occupied by the doomed Indians. They were quartered on the ground floor of the three-story stone building erected by the late General Leech.

They were all fastened to the floor by chains, two by two. Some were sitting up, smoking and conversing, while others were reclining, covered with blankets and apparently asleep. The three half-breeds and one or two others, only, were dressed in citizens' clothes. The rest all wore the breech-clout, leggins, and blankets, and not a few were adorned with paint. The majority of them were young men, though several were quite old and gray-headed, ranging perhaps toward seventy. One was quite a youth, not over sixteen. They all appeared cheerful and contented, and scarcely to reflect on the certain doom which awaited them. To the gazers, the recollection of how short a time since they had been engaged in the diabolical work of murdering indiscriminately both old and young sparing neither sex nor condition, sent a thrill of horror through the veins. Now they were perfectly harmless, and looked as innocent as children. They smiled at your entrance, and held out their hands to be shaken, which yet appeared to be gory with the blood of babes. Oh treachery, thy name is Dakota.

Father Ravoux spent the whole night among the doomed ones, talking with them concerning their fate, and endeavoring to impress upon them a serious view of the subject. He met with some success, and during the night several were baptized, and received the communion of the Church.

At daylight the reporter was there again. That good man, Father Ravoux, was still with them; also Rev. Dr. Williamson; and whenever wither of these worthy men addressed them, they were listened to with marked attention. The doomed ones wished it to be known among their friends, and particularly their wives and children, how cheerful and happy they all had died, exhibiting no fear of this dread event. To the skeptical it appeared not as an evidence of Christian faith, but as a steadfast adherence to their heathen superstitions.

They shook hands with the officers who came in among them, bidding them goodbye as if they were going on a long and pleasant journey. They had added some fresh streaks of vermilion and ultramarine to their countenances, as their fancy suggested, evidently intending to fix themselves off as gay as possible for the coming exhibition. They commenced singing their death-song, Tazoo leading, and nearly all joining. It was wonderfully exciting.

At half past seven all persons were excluded from the room except those necessary to help prepare the prisoners for their doom. Under the superintendence of Major Brown and Captain Redfield, their irons were knocked off, and one by one were tied by cords, their elbows being pinioned behind and the wrists in front, but about six inches apart. This operation occupied till about nine-o'clock. In the mean time the scene was much enlivened by their songs and conversation, keeping up the most cheerful appearance. As they were being pinioned, they went round the room shaking hands with the soldiers and reporters, bidding them goodbye, etc. White Dog requested not to be tied, and said that he could keep his hands down; but of course his request could not be complied with. [. . .]

After all were properly fastened, they stood up in a row around the room, and another exciting death-song was sung. They then sat down very quietly and commenced smoking again. Father Ravoux came in, and after addressing them a few moments, knelt in prayer, reading from a prayer book in the Dakota language, which a portion of the condemned repeated after him. During this ceremony nearly all paid the most strict attention, and several were affected even to tears. [. . .] The caps were then put upon their heads. These were made of white muslin taken from the Indians when their camps were captured, and which had formed part of the spoils they had taken from the murdered traders. They were made long, and looked like a meal sack, but, being rolled up, only came down to the forehead, and allowed their painted faces yet to be seen.

They received these evidences of their near approach to death with evident dislike. When it had been adjusted on one or two, they looked around on the others who had not yet received it with an appearance of shame. Chains and cords had not moved them — their wear was not considered dishonorable —- but this covering of the head with a white cap was humiliating. There was no more singing, and but little conversation and smoking now. All sat around the room, most of them in a crouched position, awaiting their doom in silence, or listening to the remarks of Father Ravoux, who still addressed them. Once in a while they brought their small looking-glasses before their faces to see that their countenances yet preserved the proper modicum of paint. The three half-breeds were the most affected, and their dejection of countenance was truly pitiful to behold.

At precisely ten o'clock, the condemned were marshaled in a procession and, headed by Captain Redfield, marched out into the street, and directly across through files of soldiers to the scaffold, which had been erected in front, and were delivered to the officer of the day, Captain Burt. They went eagerly and cheerfully, even crowding and jostling each other to be ahead, just like a lot of hungry boarders rushing to dinner in a hotel. The soldiers who were on guard in their quarters stacked arms and followed them, and they in turn, were followed by the clergy, reporters, etc.

As they commenced the ascent of the scaffold the death-song was again startled, and when they had all got up, the noise they made was truly hideous. It seemed as if pandemonium had broken loose. It had a wonderful effect in keeping up their courage. One young fellow, who had been given a cigar by one of the reporters just before marching from their quarters, was smoking it on the stand, puffing away very coolly during the intervals of the hideous "Hi-yi-yi, Hi-yi-yi," and even after the cap was drawn over his face he managed to get it up over his mouth and smoke. Another was smoking his pipe. The noose having been promptly adjusted over the necks of each by Captain Libby, all was ready for the fatal signal.

The solemnity of the scene was here disturbed by an incident which, if it were not intensely disgusting, might be cited as a remarkable evidence of the contempt of death which is the traditional characteristic of the Indian. One of the Indians, in the rhapsody of his death-song, conceived an insult to the spectators which it required an Indian to conceive, and a dirty dog of an Indian to execute. The refrain of his song was to the effect that if a body was found near New Ulm with his head cut off, and placed in a certain indelicate part of the body, he did it. "It is I," he sung, "it is I;" and suited the action to the word by an indecent exposure of his person, in hideous mockery of the triumph of that justice whose sword was already falling on his head.

The scene at this juncture was one of awful interest. A painful and breathless suspense held the vast crowd, which had assembled from all quarters to witness the execution.

Three slow, measured, and distinct beats on the drum by Major Brown, who had been announced as signal officer, and the rope was cut by Mr. Duly (the same who killed Lean Bear, and whose family were attacked)—the scaffold fell, and thirty-seven lifeless bodies were left dangling between heaven and earth. One of the ropes was broken, and the body of Rattling Runner fell to the ground. The neck had probably been broken, as but little signs of life were observed; but he was immediately hung up again. While the signal-beat was being given, numbers were seen to clasp the hands of their neighbors, which in several instances continued to be clasped till the bodies were cut down.

As the platform fell, there was one, not loud, but prolonged cheer from the soldiery and citizens who were spectators, and then all were quiet and earnest witnesses of the scene. For so many, there was but little suffering; the necks of all, or nearly all, were evidently dislocated by the fall, and the after struggling was slight. The scaffold fell at a quarter past ten o'clock, and in twenty minutes the bodies had all been examined by Surgeons Le Boutillier, Sheardown, Finch, Clark, and others, and life pronounced extinct.

The bodies were then cut down, placed in four army wagons, and, attended by Company K as a burial party, and under the command of Lieutenant Colonel Marshall, were taken to the grave prepared for them among the willows on the sandbar nearly in front of the town. They were all deposited in one grave, thirty feet in length by twelve in width, and four feet deep, being laid on the bottom in two rows with their feet together, and their heads to the outside. They were simply covered with their blankets, and the earth thrown over them. The other condemned Indians were kept close in the quarters, where they were chained, and not permitted to witness the executions.

WITNESS TO AN EXECUTION
Guillotining in Paris, George Alfred Townsend (1864)

The guillotining which I witnessed in Paris, in the month of June, 1864, may be deemed worthy of an extended description:

The news had gone abroad that la Pommerais would not be pardoned. It was also generally credited that this would be the last execution ever held in Paris, since there is a general desire for the abolition of capital punishment in France, and a conviction that the Legislature, at its next session, will substitute life-imprisonment. This, with the rarity of the event, and that terrible allurement of blood which distinguishes all populaces, brought out all the excitable folk of the town; and at dusk, on the night before the expiation, the whole neighborhood of La Roquette was crowded with men and women. All classes of Parisians were there — the blouses, or workingmen, standing first in number; the students from the *Latin Quartier* being well represented, and idlers, and well-dressed nondescripts without enumeration — distributing themselves among women, dogs, and babies.

Venders of *galeaux*, mussels, and fruit were out in force. The "Savage of Paris," clothed in his war plumes, paint, greaves, armlets, and moccasins, was selling razors by gaslight; here and there ballad-mongers were singing the latest songs, and boys, with chairs to let, elbowed into the intricacies of the crowd, which amused itself all the night long by smoking, drinking, and hallooing. At last, the mass became formidable in numbers, covering every inch of ground within sight of the prison, and many soldiers and sergeants *de ville*, mounted and on foot, pushed through the dense mass to restore order.

At midnight, a body of cavalry forced back the people from the square of *La Roquette*. A number of workmen, issuing from the prison gates, proceeded to set up the instrument of death by the light of blazing torches. The flame lit up the dark jail walls, and shone on the helmets and cuirasses of the sabre-men, and flared upon spots of the upturned faces, now bringing them into strong, ruddy relief, now plunging them into shadow. When the several pieces had been framed together, we had a real guillotine in view — the same spectre at which thousands of good and bad men had shuddered; and the folks around it, peering up so eagerly, were descendants of those who stood on the *Place de la Concorde* to witness the head of a king roll into the common basket. Imagine two tall, straight timbers, a foot apart, rising fifteen feet from the ground. They are grooved, and spring from a wide platform, approached by a flight of steps. At the base, rests a spring-plank or *bascule*, to which leather thongs are attached to buckle down the victim, and a basket or pannier filled with sawdust to receive the severed head. Between these, at their summit, hangs the shining knife in its appointed grooves, and a cord, which may be disconnected by a jerk, holds it to its position. Two men will be required to work the instrument promptly — the one to bind the condemned, the other to drop the axe. The *bascule* is so arranged that the whole weight and length of the trunk will rest upon it, leaving the head and neck free, and when prone it will reach to the grooves, leaving space for the knife to pass below it. The knife itself is short and wide, with a bright concave edge, and a rim of heavy steel ridges it at the top; it moves easily in the greased grooves, and may weigh forty pounds. It has a terrible fascination, hanging so high and so lightly in the blaze of the torches, which play and glitter upon it, and cast stains of red lights along its keen blade, as if by their brilliance all its past blood-marks had become visible again. A child may send it shimmering and crashing to the scaffold, but only God can fasten together the warm and throbbing parts which it shall soon dissever. And now that the terrible creature has been recreated, the workmen slink away, as if afraid of it, and a body of soldiers stand guard upon it, as if they fear that it might grow thirsty and insatiate as in the days of its youth. The multitude press up again, reinforced every hour, and at last the pale day

climbs over the jail walls, and waiting people see each other by its glimmer. The bells of *Notre Dame* peal out; a hundred towers fall into the march of the music; the early journals are shrieked by French newsboys, and folks begin to count the minutes on their watches. There are men on the ground who saw the first guillotine at work. They describe the click of the cleaver, the steady march of victims upon the scaffold-stairs, the rattle of the death-cart turning out of the rue *Saint Honoré*, the painted executioners, with their dripping hands, wiping away the jets of blood from the hard, rough faces; nay! The step of the young queen, white-haired

It has a terrible fascination, hanging so high and so lightly in the blaze of the torches, which play and glitter upon it, and cast stains of red lights along its keen blade, as if by their brilliance all its past blood-marks had become visible again.

with care, but very beautiful, who bent her body as she had never bent her knee and paid the penalty of her pride with the neck which a king had fondled.

At four minutes to six o'clock on Thursday morning, the wicket in the prison gate swung open; the condemned appeared, with his hands tied behind his back, and his knees bound together. He walked with difficulty, so fettered; but other than the artificial restraints, there was no hesitation nor terror in his movements. His hair, which had been long, dark, and wavy, was severed close to his scalp; his beard had likewise been clipped, and the fine moustache and goatee, which had set off his most interesting face, no longer appeared to enhance his romantic, expressive physiognomy. Yet his black eyes and cleanly cut mouth, nostrils, and eyebrows, demonstrated that Couty de la Pommerais was not a beauty dependent upon small accessories. There was a dignity even in his painful gait; the coarse prison shirt, scissored low in the neck, exhibited the straight columnar throat and swelling chest; for the rest, he wore only a pair of black pantaloons and his own shapely boots. As he emerged from the wicket, the chill morning air, laden with the dew of the truck gardens near at hand, blew across the open spaces of the suburbs, and smote him with a cold chill. He was plainly seen to tremble; but in an instant, as if by the mere force of his will, he stood motionless, and cast a first and only glance at the guillotine straight before him. It was the glance of a man who meets an enemy's eye, not shrinkingly, but half-defiant, as if even the bitter retribution could not abash his strong courage — he seemed to feel that forty thousand men and women, and young children were looking upon him to see how he dared to die, and that for a generation his bearing should go into fireside descriptions. Then he moved on between the files of soldiers at his shuffling pace, and before him went the *aumonier* or chaplain, swaying the crucifix, behind him the executioner of Versailles — a rough and bearded man — to assist in the final horror.

It was at this intense moment a most wonderful spectacle. As the prisoner had first appeared, a single great shout had shaken the multitude. It was the French word *"Voila!"* which means "Behold!" "See!" Then every spectator stood on tiptoe; the silence of death succeeded; all the close street was undulant with human emotion; a few house roofs near by were dizzy with folks who gazed down from the tiles; all the way up the heights of *Pere la Chaise*, among the pale chapels and monuments of the dead, the thousands of stirred beings swung and shook like so many drowned corpses floating on the sea. Every eye and mind turned to the little structure raised among the trees, on the space before *La Roquette*, and there they saw a dark, shaven, disrobed young man, going quietly toward his grave.

He mounted the steps deliberately, looking towards his feet; the priest held up the crucifix, and he felt it was there, but did not see it; his lips one moment touched the image of Christ, but he did not look up nor speak; then, as he gained the last step, the *bascule* or swingboard sprang up before him; the executioner gave him a single push, and he fell prone upon the plank, with his face downward; it gave way before him, bearing him into the space between the upright beams, and he lay horizontally beneath the knife, presenting the back of his neck to it. Thus resting, he could look into the

With a quick, keen sound, the steel became detached; it fell hurtling through the grooves; it struck something with a dead, dumb thump; a jet of bright blood spurted into the light, and dyed the face of an attendant horribly red; and Couty de la Pommerais's head lay in the sawdust of the *pannier*, while every vein in the lopped trunk trickled upon the scaffold-floor!

pannier or basket, into whose sawdust lining his head was to drop in a moment. And in that awful space, while all the people gazed with their fingers tingling, the legitimate Parisian executioner gave a jerk at the cord which held the fatal knife. With a quick, keen sound, the steel became detached; it fell hurtling through the grooves; it struck something with a dead, dumb thump; a jet of bright blood spurted into the light, and dyed the face of an attendant horribly red; and Couty de la Pommerais's head lay in the sawdust of the *pannier*, while every vein in the lopped trunk trickled upon the scaffold-floor! They threw a cloth upon the carcass and carried away the pannier; the guillotine disappeared beneath the surrounding heads; loud exclamations and acclaims burst from the multitude; the venders of trash and edibles resumed their cheerful cries, and a hearse dashed through the mass, carrying the warm body of the guillotined to the cemetery of *Mt. Parnasse*. In thirty minutes, newsboys were hawking the scene of the execution upon all the quays and bridges. In every café of Paris some witness was telling the incidents of the show to breathless listeners, and the crowds which stopped to see the funeral procession of the great Marshal Pelissier divided their attention between the warrior and the poisoner — the latter obtaining the preponderance of fame.

WITNESS TO AN EXECUTION
The Execution Of The Lincoln Conspirators
Clara E. Laughlin (1865)

An attempt to stay the execution through a writ of habeas corpus failed through suspension by the President — in whom this power is vested — an order to that effect proceeding from the Executive Office at ten o'clock on Friday morning. It was confidently believed, almost up to the hour of execution, that some influence would avail to save Mrs. Surratt, and the tension at the penitentiary was horrible.

Since a little after eight o'clock soldiers, spectators, newspaper men, clergy, had been assembling at the prison to wait in the blistering heat — and wait — and wait. Soldiers stood, almost shoulder to shoulder, along the high wall surrounding the prison yard. Down below, in the grassy enclosure, were many more soldiers forming three sides of a large square, the fourth side of which was the penitentiary's front. Within the square the gallows stood, its platform, reached by fifteen steps, ten feet above the ground; the beam, from which four nooses dangled, ten feet above that again. Down at the gallows' foot were four new wooden boxes at the edges of four freshly dug graves.

The wait was long, in the brazen sun, and nearly everyone but the soldiers carried an umbrella. At last, when it was not far from two o'clock, the barred door of the penitentiary opened and a woman walked out, a middle-aged woman dressed in black, bonneted and heavily veiled. On either side of

her walked a bare-headed priest, behind her walked four soldiers with muskets. In the strained silence the low tones of the priests muttering the service for the dying were audible to every ear.

Then came a sound of clanking chains; a small, shambling German dragged his fetters toward the gallows. Two officers walked before him, a Lutheran clergyman walked beside him, a squad of armed soldiers brought up the rear. Next came a tottering boy, with an Episcopalian rector accompanying him. And last walked in the wasted shadow of a splendid young giant, with a shock of tawny hair and big blue eyes which made one spectator say he looked "rather the barbarian striding in his conqueror's triumph than the assassin going to the gallows."

The condemned were seated on the gallows while the warrants were read to them by General Hartranft. When he had finished, Dr. Gillette spoke on behalf of Payne, not in pleading nor extenuation, but merely to thank the prison officials for their kind treatment of him — which was not so ironical as it sounds, because the boy seems to have made himself liked, and his attendants, while they were powerless to mitigate the severity of his irons, probably did whatever they could to show him kindness.

During Dr. Gillette's prayer, the boy's big blue eyes filled with tears, and he followed in the closing sentences of it with deep emotion — the first he had shown since his arrest Dr. Olds then said for Davy Herold that he tendered his forgiveness to all who had wronged him, and asked the forgiveness of all whom he had wronged. He also thanked the officers and guards for kindnesses rendered him, and said that he hoped he died in charity with all men and at peace with God. Dr. Butler spoke and prayed for Atzerodt, and there was no more to be said; Mrs. Surratt's confessors, after the custom of their Church, remaining silent.

In a few moments the awful preparations were completed, the signal was given, the two traps fell, and four souls went home to a Tribunal which may safely temper justice with mercy.

Hardly more than an hour after the appearance of the black-robed woman at the prison door, four nameless graves were full and the grassy yard was quiet again under the fiercely beating rays of the summer sun.

Toward the end of that year there was laid beside them the body of Wirz, the keeper of Andersonville, who was hanged for atrocities of which he is now believed innocent. In 1867 the five bodies were taken up and removed to one of the storehouses in the Arsenal grounds. The body of Booth was laid beside them, and the old penitentiary where it had for two years had sepulture was torn down.

Objections To Capital Punishment, Horace Greeley (1867)

My Friends:

My objections to Capital Punishment may be summed up in a few words. They are:

1. I hate vengeance. If I am ever revengeful, I hate myself for being so. Vengeance is a barbarous, cruel, malignant passion, which I would not teach my children, nor any children. The gallows does teach it — always did teach it — always will teach it The boy who runs to see a man hung, will be taught thereby to seek to injure every one he deems his enemy, or who he supposes has injured or wronged him. This is Paganism — possibly Judaism— it is not Christianity, as I have learned that religion. I revere the cross, and detest the gallows.

> **Vengeance is a barbarous, cruel, malignant passion, which I would not teach my children, nor any children. The gallows does teach it — always did teach it — always will teach it.**

2. I dread human fallibility. Men are prejudiced, passionate, and too often irrational. Today they shout "Hosanna" and tomorrow howl "Crucify him!" I would save them from the harsher consequences of their own frenzy. Our Saviour is by no means a solitary example of the unjust execution of the innocent and just. Socrates, Cicero, Sir Walter Raleigh, Algernon Sidney, John Huss, Michael Servetus, Louis XVI, the Duc d'Enghein, Marshal Ney, Riego, Nagy Sandor, Maximilian, are among the conspicuous instances of victims of the

law of blood. We have recorded instances of innocent men convicted of murder on their own confession — of men, convicted, sentenced and hung, for offenses whereof they were nowise guilty.

Men may suffer unjustly, even though death be stricken from the list of our legal penalties; but to be imprisoned and stripped of property, is quite endurable, compared with the infliction of an ignominious death, in the presence and for the delectation of a howling mob of exulting human brutes. So long as man is liable to error, I would have him reserve the possibility of correcting his mistakes, and redressing the wrongs he is misled into perpetrating.

3. I would affirm and inculcate, as widely and impressively as possible, the sanctity of human life. Unlike the French wit, I would have society set its enemies a salutary example. I believe that legal executions incite to, rather than diminish, murders.

In Defense of the Death Penalty, John Stuart Mill (1868)

Speech delivered before the British Parliament on April 21, 1868 in opposition to a bill banning capital punishment.

It would be a great satisfaction to me if I were able to support this Motion. It is always a matter of regret to me to find myself, on a public question, opposed to those who are called—sometimes in the way of honor, and sometimes in what is intended for ridicule—the philanthropists. Of all persons who take part in public affairs, they are those for whom, on the whole, I feel the greatest amount of respect; for their characteristic is, that they devote their time, their labor, and much of their money to objects purely public, with a less admixture of either personal or class selfishness, than any other class of politicians whatever.

On almost all the great questions, scarcely any politicians are so steadily and almost uniformly to be found on the side of right; and they seldom err, but by an exaggerated application of some just and highly important principle. On the very subject that is now occupying us we all know what signal service they have rendered. It is through their efforts that our criminal laws—which within my memory hanged people for stealing in a dwelling house to the value of 40s.- laws by virtue of which rows of human beings might be seen suspended in front of Newgate by those who ascended or descended Ludgate Hill—have so greatly relaxed their most revolting and most impolitic ferocity, that aggravated murder is now practically the only crime which is punished with death by any of our lawful tribunals; and we are even now deliberating whether the extreme penalty should be retained in that solitary case.

This vast gain, not only to humanity, but to the ends of penal justice, we owe to the philanthropists; and if they are mistaken, as I cannot but think they are, in the present instance, it is only in not perceiving the right time and place for stopping in a career hitherto so eminently beneficial. Sir, there is a point at which, I conceive, that career ought to stop. When there has been brought home to any one, by conclusive evidence, the greatest crime known to the law; and when the attendant circumstances suggest no palliation of the guilt, no hope that the culprit may even yet not be unworthy to live among mankind, nothing to make it probable that the crime was an exception to his general character rather than a consequence of it, then I confess it appears to me that to deprive the criminal of the life of which he has proved himself to be unworthy—solemnly to blot him out from the fellowship of mankind and from the catalogue of the living—is the most appropriate, as it is certainly the most impressive, mode in which society can attach to so great a crime the penal consequences which for the security of life it is indispensable to annex to it. I defend this penalty, when confined to atrocious cases, on the very ground on which it is commonly attacked--on that of humanity to the criminal; as beyond comparison the least cruel mode in which it is possible adequately to deter from the crime.

If, in our horror of inflicting death, we endeavor to devise some punishment for the living criminal which shall act on the human mind with a deterrent force at all comparable to that of death, we are driven to inflictions less severe, indeed, in appearance, and therefore less efficacious, but far more cruel in reality. Few, I think, would venture to propose, as a punishment for aggravated murder, less than imprisonment with hard labor for life; that is the fate to which a murderer would be consigned by the mercy which shrinks from putting him to death. But has it been sufficiently considered what sort of a mercy this is, and what kind of life it leaves to him? If, indeed, the punishment is not really inflicted—if it becomes the sham which a few years ago such punishments were rapidly becoming—then, indeed, its adoption would be almost tantamount to giving up the attempt to repress murder altogether.

But if it really is what it professes to be, and if it is realized in all its rigor by the popular imagination, as it very probably would not be, but as it must be if it is to be efficacious, it will be so shocking that when the memory of the crime is no longer fresh, there will be almost insuperable difficulty in executing it. What comparison can there really be, in point of severity, between consigning a man to the short pang of a rapid death, and immuring him in a living tomb, there to linger out what may be a long life in the hardest and most monotonous toil, without any of its alleviations or rewards—debarred from all pleasant sights and sounds, and cut off from all earthly hope, except a slight mitigation of bodily restraint, or a small improvement of diet? Yet even such a lot as this, because there is no one moment at which the suffering is of terrifying intensity, and, above all, because it does not contain the element, so imposing to the imagination, of the unknown, is universally reputed a milder punishment than death--stands in all codes as a mitigation of the capital penalty, and is thankfully accepted as such. For it is characteristic of all punishments which depend on duration for their efficacy—all, therefore, which are not corporal or pecuniary—that they are more rigorous than they seem; while it is, on the contrary, one of the strongest recommendations a punishment can have, that it should seem more rigorous than it is; for its practical power depends far less on what it is than on what it seems.

There is not, I should think, any human infliction which makes an impression on the imagination so entirely out of proportion to its real severity as the punishment of death. The punishment must be mild indeed which does not add more to the sum of human misery than is necessarily or directly added by the execution of a criminal. As my hon. friend the Member for Northampton (Mr.Gilpin) has himself remarked, the most that human laws can do to anyone in the matter of death is to hasten it; the man would have died at any rate; not so very much later, and on the average, I fear, with a considerably greater amount of bodily suffering. Society is asked, then, to denude itself of an instrument of punishment which, in the grave cases to which alone it is suitable, effects its purposes at a less cost of human suffering than any other; which, while it inspires more terror, is less cruel in actual fact than any punishment that we should think of substituting for it.

My hon. friend says that it does not inspire terror, and that experience proves it to be a failure.

But the influence of a punishment is not to be estimated by its effect on hardened criminals. Those whose habitual way of life keeps them, so to speak, at all times within sight of the gallows, do grow to care less about it; as, to compare good things with bad, an old soldier is not much affected by the chance of dying in battle. I can afford to admit all that is often said about the indifference of professional criminals to the gallows. Though of that indifference one-third is probably bravado and another third confidence that they shall have the luck to escape, it is quite probable that the remaining third is real. But the efficacy of a punishment which acts principally through the imagination, is chiefly to be measured by the impression it makes on those who are still innocent; by the horror with which it surrounds the first promptings of guilt; the restraining influence it exercises over the beginning of the thought which, if indulged, would become a temptation; the check which it exerts over the graded declension towards the state—never suddenly attained— in which crime no longer revolts, and punishment no longer terrifies.

As for what is called the failure of death punishment, who is able to judge of that? We partly know who those are whom it has not deterred; but who is there who knows whom it has deterred, or how many human beings it has saved who would have lived to be murderers if that awful association had not been thrown round the idea of murder from their earliest infancy? Let us not forget that the most imposing fact loses its power over the imagination if it is made too cheap. When a punishment fit only for the most atrocious crimes is lavished on small offenses until human feeling recoils from it, then, indeed, it ceases to intimidate, because it ceases to be believed in.

The failure of capital punishment in cases of theft is easily accounted for; the thief did not believe that it would be inflicted. He had learnt by experience that jurors would perjure themselves rather than find him guilty; that judges would seize any excuse for not sentencing him to death, or for recommending him to mercy; and that if neither jurors nor judges were merciful, there were still hopes from an authority above both. When things had come to this pass it was high time to give up the vain attempt. When it is impossible to inflict a punishment, or when its infliction becomes a public scandal, the idle threat cannot too soon disappear from the statute book. And in the case of the host of offenses which were formerly capital, I heartily rejoice that it did become impracticable to execute the law.

If the same state of public feeling comes to exist in the case of murder; if the time comes when jurors refuse to find a murderer guilty; when judges will not sentence him to death, or will recommend him to mercy; or when, if juries and judges do not flinch from their duty, Home Secretaries, under pressure of deputations and memorials, shrink from theirs, and the threat becomes, as it became in the other cases, a mere *brutum fulmen*; then, indeed, it may become necessary to do in this case what has been done in those—to abrogate the penalty. That time may come—my hon. friend thinks that it has nearly come.

I hardly know whether he lamented it or boasted of it; but he and his friends are entitled to the boast; for if it comes it will be their doing, and they will have gained what I cannot but call a fatal victory, for they will have achieved it by bringing about, if they will forgive me for saying so, an enervation, an effeminacy, in the general mind of the country. For what else than effeminacy is it to be so much more shocked by taking a man's life than by depriving him of all that makes life desirable or valuable?

Is death, then, the greatest of all earthly ills? *Usque adeone mori miserum est?* Is it, indeed, so dreadful a thing to die? Has it not been from of old one chief part of a manly education to make us despise death--teaching us to account it, if an evil at all, by no means high in the list of evils; at all events, as an inevitable one, and to hold, as it were, our lives in our hands, ready to be given or risked at any moment, for a sufficiently worthy object? I am sure that my hon. Friends know all this as well, and have as much of all these feelings as any of the rest of us; possibly more. But I cannot think that this is likely to be the effect of their teaching on the general mind. I cannot think that the cultivating of a peculiar sensitiveness of conscience on this one point, over and above what results from the general cultivation of the moral sentiments, is permanently consistent with assigning in our own minds to the fact of death no more than the degree of relative importance which belongs to it among the other incidents of our humanity.

The men of old cared too little about death, and gave their own lives or took those of others with equal recklessness. Our danger is of the opposite kind, lest we should be so much shocked by death, in general and in the abstract, as to care too much about it in individual cases, both those of other people and our own, which call for its being risked. And I am not putting things at the worst, for it is proved by the experience of other countries that horror of the executioner by no means necessarily implies horror of the assassin. The stronghold, as we all know, of hired assassination in the 18th century was Italy; yet it is said that in some of the Italian populations the infliction of death by sentence of law was in the highest degree offensive and revolting to popular feeling.

Much has been said of the sanctity of human life, and the absurdity of supposing that we can teach respect for life by ourselves destroying it. But I am surprised at the employment of this argument, for it is one which might be brought against any punishment whatever. It is not human life only, not human life as such, that ought to be sacred to us, but human feelings. The human capacity of suffering is what we should cause to be respected, not the mere capacity of existing. And we may imagine somebody asking how we can teach people not to inflict suffering by ourselves inflicting it? But to this I should answer—all of us would answer—that to deter by suffering from inflicting suffering is not only possible, but the very purpose of penal justice. Does fining a criminal show want of respect for property, or imprisoning him, for personal freedom? Just as unreasonable is it to think that to take the life of a man who has taken that of another is to show want of regard for human life. We show, on the contrary, most emphatically our regard for it, by the adoption of a rule that he who violates that right in another forfeits it for himself, and that while no other crime that he can commit deprives him of his right to live, this shall.

> **To deter by suffering from inflicting suffering is not only possible, but the very purpose of penal justice.**

There is one argument against capital punishment, even in extreme cases, which I cannot deny to have weight—on which my hon. friend justly laid great stress, and which never can be entirely got rid of. It is this—that if by an error of justice an innocent person is put to death, the mistake can never be corrected; all compensation, all reparation for the wrong is impossible. This would be indeed a serious objection if these miserable mistakes—among the most tragical occurrences in the whole round of human affairs—could not be made extremely rare.

The argument is invincible where the mode of criminal procedure is dangerous to the innocent, or where the Courts of Justice are not trusted. And this probably is the reason why the objection to an irreparable punishment began (as I believe it did) earlier, and is more intense and more widely diffused, in some parts of the Continent of Europe than it is here. There are on the Continent great and enlightened countries, in which the criminal procedure is not so favorable to innocence, does not afford the same security against erroneous conviction, as it does among us; countries where the Courts of Justice seem to think they fail in their duty unless they find somebody guilty; and in their really laudable desire to hunt guilt from its hiding places, expose themselves to a serious danger of condemning the innocent. If our own procedure and Courts of Justice afforded ground for similar apprehension, I should be the first to join in withdrawing the power of inflicting irreparable punishment from such tribunals.

But we all know that the defects of our procedure are the very opposite. Our rules of evidence are even too favorable to the prisoner; and juries and judges carry out the maxim, "It is better that ten guilty should escape than that one innocent person should suffer," not only to the letter, but beyond the letter. Judges are most anxious to point out, and juries to allow for, the barest possibility of the prisoner's innocence. No human judgment is infallible; such sad cases as my hon. friend cited will sometimes occur; but in so grave a case as that of murder, the accused, in our system, has always the benefit of the merest shadow of a doubt.

And this suggests another consideration very germane to the question. The very fact that death punishment is more shocking than any other to the imagination, necessarily renders the Courts of Justice more scrupulous in requiring the fullest evidence of guilt. Even that which is the greatest objection to capital punishment, the impossibility of correcting an error once committed, must make, and does make, juries and Judges more careful in forming their opinion, and more jealous in their scrutiny of the evidence. If the substitution of penal servitude for death in cases of murder should cause any declaration in this conscientious scrupulosity, there would be a great evil to set against the real, but I hope rare, advantage of being able to make reparation to a condemned person who was afterwards discovered to be innocent. In order that the possibility of correction may be kept open wherever the chance of this sad contingency is more than infinitesimal, it is quite right that the Judge should recommend to the Crown a commutation of the sentence, not solely when the proof of guilt is open to the smallest suspicion, but whenever there remains anything unexplained and mysterious in the case, raising a desire for more light, or making it likely that further information may at some future time be obtained.

I would also suggest that whenever the sentence is commuted the grounds of the commutation should, in some authentic form, be made known to the public. Thus much I willingly concede to my hon. friend; but on the question of total abolition I am inclined to hope that the feeling of the country is not with him, and that the limitation of death punishment to the cases referred to in the Bill of last year will be generally considered sufficient. The mania which existed a short time ago for paring down all our punishments seems to have reached its limits, and not before it was time. We were in danger of being left without any effectual punishment, except for small of offenses. What was formerly our chief secondary punishment—transportation—before it was abolished, had become almost a reward. Penal servitude, the substitute for it, was becoming, to the classes who were principally subject to it, almost nominal, so comfortable did we make our prisons, and so easy had it become to get quickly out of them. Flogging—a most objectionable punishment in ordinary cases, but a particularly appropriate one for crimes of brutality, especially crimes against women—we would not hear of, except, to be sure, in the case of garrotters, for whose peculiar benefit we reestablished it in a hurry, immediately after a Member of Parliament had been garroted. With this exception, offenses, even of an atrocious kind, against the person, as my hon. and learned friend the Member for Oxford (Mr.Neate) well remarked, not only were, but still are, visited with penalties so ludicrously inadequate, as to be almost an encouragement to the crime.

I think, Sir, that in the case of most offences, except those against property, there is more need of strengthening our punishments than of weakening them; and that severer sentences, with an apportionment of them to the different kinds of offences which shall approve itself better than at present to the moral sentiments of the community, are the kind of reform of which our penal system now stands in need. I shall therefore vote against the Amendment.

WITNESS TO AN EXECUTION
Mark Twain Witnesses a Hanging (1868)

I find some changes since I was here last. The little wildcat mines are abandoned and forgotten, and the happy millionaires in fancy (I used to be one of them) have wandered penniless to other climes, or have returned to honest labor for degrading wages. But the majority of the great silver mines on the Comstock lode are flourishing—

Novel Entertainment.

But I am tired talking about mines. I saw a man hanged the other day. John Melanie, of France. He was the first man ever hanged in this city (or country either), where the first twenty six graves in the cemetery were those of men who died by shots and stabs.

I never had witnessed an execution before, and did not believe I could be present at this one without turning away my head at the last moment. But I did not know what fascination there was about the thing, then. I only went because

I thought I ought to have a lesson, and because I believed that if ever it would be possible to see a man hanged, and derive satisfaction from the spectacle, this was the time. For John Melanie was no common murderer -- else he would have gone free. He was a heartless assassin. A year ago, he secreted himself under the house of a woman of the town who lived alone, and in the dead watches of the night, he entered her room, knocked her senseless with a billet of wood as she slept, and then strangled her with his fingers. He carried off all her money, her watches, and every article of her wearing apparel, and the next day, with quiet effrontery, put some crepe on his arm and walked in her funeral procession.

Afterward he secreted himself under the bed of another woman of the town, and in the middle of the night was crawling out with a slung-shot in one hand and a butcher knife in the other, when the woman discovered him, alarmed the neighborhood with her screams, and he retreated from the house. Melanie sold dresses and jewelry here and there until some of the articles were identified as belonging to the murdered courtesan. He was arrested and then his later intended victim recognized him.

After he was tried and condemned to death, he used to curse and swear at all who approached him; and he once grossly insulted some young Sisters of Charity who came to minister kindly to his wants. The morning of the execution, he joked with the barber, and told him not to cut his throat — he wanted the distinction of being hanged.

This is the man I wanted to see hung. I joined the appointed physicians, so that I might be admitted within the charmed circle and be close to Melanie. Now I never more shall be surprised at anything. That assassin got out of the closed carriage, and the first thing his eye fell upon was that awful gallows towering above a great sea of human heads, out yonder on the hill side and his cheek never blanched, and never a muscle quivered! He strode firmly away, and skipped gaily up the steps of the gallows like a happy girl. He looked around upon the people, calmly; he examined the gallows with a critical eye, and with the pleased curiosity of a man who sees for the first time a wonder he has often heard of. He swallowed frequently, but there was no evidence of trepidation about him — and not the slightest air of braggadocio whatever. He prayed with the priest, and then drew out an abusive manuscript and read from it in a clear, strong voice, without a quaver in it. It was a broad, thin sheet of paper, and he held it apart in front of him as he stood. If ever his hand trembled in even the slightest degree, it never quivered that paper. I watched him at that sickening moment when the sheriff was fitting the noose about his neck, and pushing the knot this way and that to get it nicely adjusted to the hollow under his ear — and if they had been measuring Melanie for a shirt, he could not have been more perfectly serene. I never saw anything like that before. My own suspense was almost unbearable — my blood was leaping through my veins, and my thoughts were crowding and trampling upon each other. Twenty moments to live — fifteen to live — ten to live — five — three — heaven and earth, how the time galloped! — and yet that man stood there unmoved though he knew that the sheriff was reaching deliberately for the drop while the black cap descended over his quiet face! — then down through the hole in the scaffold the strap-bound figure shot like a dart! — a dreadful shiver started at the shoulders, violently convulsed the whole body all the way down, and died away with a tense drawing of the toes downward, like a doubled fist — and all was over!

I saw it all. I took exact note of every detail, even to Melanie's considerately helping to fix the leather strap that bound his legs together and his quiet removal of his slippers — and I never wish to see it again. I can see that stiff, straight corpse hanging there yet, with its black pillow-cased head turned rigidly to one side, and the purple streaks creeping through the hands and driving the fleshy hue of life before them. Ugh!

Letter to Marvin H. Bovee, Elizabeth Cady Stanton (1868)

You ask me if I believe in capital punishment. Indeed I do not. When men are dangerous to the public, they should be imprisoned; that done, the remaining consideration is the highest good of the prisoner. Crime is a disease; hence our prisons should be moral seminaries, where all that is true and noble in man should be nurtured into life. Our jails, our prisons, our whole idea of punishment is wrong, and will be until the mother soul is represented in our criminal legislation. It makes me shudder to think of the cruelties that are inflicted on criminals in the name of justice, and of the awful waste of life and force — of the crushing out of hundreds and thousands of noble men and promising boys in these abominable Bastilles of the nineteenth century.

As to the gallows, it is the torture of my life. Every sentence and every execution I hear of, is a break in the current of my life and thought for days. I make my son the victim. I am with him in the solitude of that last awful night, broken only by the sound of the hammer and the coarse jeers of men, in preparation for the dismal pageant of the coming day. I see the cold sweat of death upon his brow, and weigh the mountain of sorrow that rests upon his soul, with its sad memories of the past and fearful forbodings of the world to come. I imagine the mortal agony, the death-struggle, and I know ten thousand mothers all over the land weep, and pray, and groan with me over every soul thus lost. Woman knows the cost of life better than man does. **There will be no gallows, no dungeons, nor needless cruelty in solitude, when mothers make the laws.** God bless you in your noble work.

I have felt so much on this subject that I have often said to my husband, if there is such a thing as the transmigration of souls, mine has been in some tortured prisoner, for, ever since I began to think, I have felt the most intense sympathy for the inmates of our jails and prisons. When I was a little girl, twelve years old, there was a public hanging in the town where I lived. From the day the man was placed in our county jail he occupied all my thoughts. I went to see him every day, taking him flowers and fruit, cakes and candy; and knowing the jailor's wife, she would often let me in the cell to talk and read to him. He was as gentle and tractable as a child; and, as the awful day approached, I felt that I could not let him die; and as everybody outside called him a horrible wretch, I saw that he could only be saved by some special interposition, and, fearing he was too wicked for Heaven to make any, I decided to do it myself. I watched the building of the gallows on a distant hill, and decided at the last to cut the rope, so that when he fell it would break. So on the morning of the day I hastened early to the spot. There was no rope there, and nothing that I could do. Oh! how I wept, and prayed, and wondered what I could do on that cold December morning. At length I heard the distant music, saw the military surround the gallows, saw the poor man ascend it, heard the prayer, saw the death-struggle, and in anguish hurried home, and there I lay for many weeks in a terrible fever; and every execution I now read of in our public journals, brings back that terrible memory.

Whenever you visit our legislature, having in view the modification of our penal code, I will gladly do all in my power to help you banish that relic of barbarism from our land.

The Program of the International Brotherhood
Mikhail Bakunin (1869)

Convinced as we are that individual and social evil resides much less in individuals than in the organization of material things and in social conditions, we will be humane in our actions, as much for the sake of justice as for practical considerations, and we will ruthlessly destroy what is in our way without endangering the revolution. We deny society's free will and its alleged right to punish. Justice itself, taken in its widest, most humane sense, is but an idea, so to say, which is not an absolute dogma; it poses the social problem but it does not think it out. It merely indicates the only possible road to human emancipation, that is the humanization of society by liberty in equality. No positive solution can be achieved only by an increasingly rational organization of society. This solution, which is so greatly desired, our ideal for all, is liberty, morality, intelligence, and the welfare of each through the solidarity of all: human fraternity, in short.

Every human individual is the involuntary product of a natural and social environment within which he is born, and to the influence of which he continues to submit as he develops. The three great causes of all human immorality are: political, economic, and social inequality; the ignorance resulting naturally from all this; and the necessary consequence of these, slavery.

Since the social organization is always and everywhere the only cause of

Since the social organization is always and everywhere the only cause of crimes committed by men, the punishing by society of criminals who can never be guilty is an act of hypocrisy or a patent absurdity.

crimes committed by men, the punishing by society of criminals who can never be guilty is an act of hypocrisy or a patent absurdity. The theory of guilt and punishment is the offspring of theology, that is, of the union of absurdity and religious hypocrisy. The only right one can grant to society in its present transitional state is the natural right to kill in self-defense the criminals it has itself produced, but not the right to judge and condemn them. This cannot, strictly speaking, be a right, it can only be a natural, painful, but inevitable act, itself the indication and outcome of the impotence and stupidity of present-day society. The less society makes use of it, the closer it will come to its real emancipation. All the revolutionaries, the oppressed, the sufferers, victims of the existing social organization, whose hearts are naturally filled with hatred and a desire for vengeance, should bear in mind that the kings, the oppressors, exploiters of all kinds, are as guilty as the criminals who have emerged from the masses; like them, they are evildoers who are not guilty, since they, too, are involuntary products of the present social order. It will not be surprising if the rebellious people kill a great many of them at first. This will be a misfortune, as unavoidable as the ravages caused by a sudden tempest, and as quickly over; but this natural act will be neither moral nor even useful.

History has much to teach us on this subject. The dreadful guillotine of 1793, which cannot be reproached with having been idle or slow, nevertheless did not succeed in destroying the French aristocracy. The nobility was indeed shaken to its roots, though not completely destroyed, but this was not the work of the guillotine; it was achieved by the confiscation of its properties. In general, we can say that carnage was never an effective means to exterminate political parties; it was proved particularly ineffective against the privileged classes, since power resides less in men themselves than in the circumstances created for men of privilege by the organization of material goods, that is, the institution of the State and its natural basis, individual property.

Therefore, to make a successful revolution, it is necessary to attack conditions and material goods; to destroy property and the State. It will then become unnecessary to destroy men and be condemned to suffer the sure and inevitable reaction which no massacre has ever failed and ever will fail to produce in every society.

WITNESS TO AN EXECUTION
The Algerian Executioner (1873)

Severe justice is the only condition on which French supremacy can be maintained in the country, and probably for the general Arab populace, the rule of the Gauls is a judicious one. But it is to be questioned whether the rule of *talion* is the right one for the Kabyles. In 1871, at the height of the French troubles with the Commune, formidable revolts were going on among the descendants of those untamable wretches whom Saint Arnaud smoked out in a cave. In July the garrison at Setif heard the plaint of a friendly cadi, named D'joudi, who had been wantonly attacked for his loyalty to the French by some organized mutineers under Mohammed Ben-Hadad. The poor wretch had been obliged to flee, with his women and his flocks, into the protection of his country's oppressors. Since the *chassepot* has succeeded in reducing the Kabyles once more to a superficial obedience, the courts have been busy with the sentences of their insubordinate leaders.

France imitates England's sanguinary policy in her treatment of rebellious and semi-civilized tribes. Eight of the leaders of the Kabyle revolt of 1871 have been condemned to death, and a number of others have been sentenced to various terms of imprisonment. The Kabyles will take their revenge when another European war places the Algiers colonists at their mercy. [. . .]

Yes, the fact must be admitted: these rugged mountaineers, so proud, and, according to their own code, so honorable, never blush to prepare imitations of the circulating medium, which they only know as an appurtenance and invention of their civilized conquerors. In his rude hovel, with all the sublimities of Nature around him, this child of the wilderness looks up to the summits of the

He appeared to modern visitors as a modest coffee-house keeper in the Arab quarters, who would serve you, for two cents, a cup of coffee with the hand that had wielded the *yataghan*.

Atlas, "with peaky tops engrailed," and immediately thereafter looks down again to attend to the engrailing of his neat five-franc pieces, which can hardly be told from the genuine. This multiplication of finance was punished under the beys with death. The Bey of Constantina arrested in one day the men of three tribes notorious for counterfeiting, and decapitated a hundred of them. There was lately to be seen at Constantina the executioner who was charged with this punishment, the very individual who cut off the ingenious heads of all these poor money-makers, and did not "cut them off with a shilling." He appeared to modern visitors as a modest coffee-house keeper in the Arab quarters, who would serve you, for two cents, a cup of coffee with the hand that had wielded the *yataghan*. He was an old Turk, with wide gray moustaches, dressed in a remarkable and theatrical fashion. He wore a yellow turban of colossal size, and an ample orange girdle over a dress of light green. Poor Tobriz—that was his name—was violently opposed to the introduction of the guillotine in Algeria. In the days of his prosperity an enormous sabre was passed through his flaming girdle. In the early years of the French conquest, Tobriz was employed in the decapitations, which were executed with a saw, and must have been a horrible spectacle. He remembered well the execution of the hundred counterfeiters in one night, and their heads exposed in the market.

Judicial And Executive Systems, Herbert Spencer (1874)

§ 522.

That we may be prepared for recognizing the primitive identity of military institutions with institutions for administering justice, let us observe how close is the kinship between the modes of dealing with external aggression and internal aggression, respectively.

We have the facts, already more than once emphasized, that at first the responsibilities of communities to one another are paralleled by the responsibilities to one another of family-groups within each community; and that the kindred claims are enforced in kindred ways. Various savage tribes show us that, originally, external war has to effect an equalization of injuries, either directly in kind or indirectly by compensations. Among the Chinooks, "has the one party a larger number of dead than the other, indemnification must be made by the latter, or the war is continued; " and among the Arabs "when peace is to be made, both parties count up their dead, and the usual blood-money is paid for excess on either side." By which instances we are shown that in the wars between tribes, as in the family-feuds of early time? A death must be balanced by a death, or else must be compounded for; as it once was in Germany and in England, by specified numbers of sheep and cattle, or by money.

Not only are the wars which societies carry on to effect the righting of alleged wrongs, thus paralleled by family feuds in the respect that for retaliation in kind there may be substituted a penalty adjudged by usage or authority; but they are paralleled by feuds between individuals in the like respect. From the first stage in which each man avenges himself by force on a transgressing neighbor, as the whole community does on a transgressing community, the transition is to a stage in which he has the alternative of demanding justice at the hands of the ruler. We see this beginning in such places as the Sandwich Islands, where an injured person who is too weak to retaliate, appeals to the king or principal chief; and in quite advanced stages, option between the two methods of obtaining redress survives. The feeling shown down to the 13th century by Italian nobles, who regarded it as disgraceful to submit to laws rather than do themselves justice by force of arms, is traceable throughout the history of Europe in the slow yielding of private rectification of wrongs to public arbitration.

A capitulary of Charles the Bald bids them [the freemen] go to court armed as for war, for they might have to fight for their jurisdiction; and our own history furnishes an interesting example in the early form of an action for recovering land: the "grand assize " which tried the cause, originally consisted of knights armed with swords. Again we have evidence in such facts as that in the 12th century in France, legal decisions were so little regarded that trials often issued in duels. Further proof is yielded by such facts as that judicial duels (which were the authorized substitutes for private wars between families) continued in France down to the close of the 14th century; that in England, in 1768, a legislative proposal to abolish trial by battle, was so strongly opposed that the measure was dropped; and that the option of such trial was not disallowed till 1819.

We may observe, also, that this self-protection gradually gives place to protection by the State, only under stress of public needs—especially need for military efficiency. Edicts of Charlemagne and of Charles the Bald, seeking to stop the disorders consequent on private wars, by insisting on appeals to the ordained authorities, and threatening punishment of those who disobeyed, sufficiently imply the motive; and this motive was definitely shown in the feudal period in France, by an ordinance of 1296, which "prohibits private wars and judicial duels so long as the king is engaged in war."

Once more the militant nature of legal protection is seen in the fact that, as at first, so now, it is a replacing of individual armed force by the armed force of the State—always in reserve if not exercised. "The sword of justice " is a phrase sufficiently indicating the truth that action against the public enemy and action against the private enemy are in the last resort the same.

Thus recognizing the original identity of the functions, we shall be prepared for recognizing the original identity of the structures by which they are carried on.

§ 527.

[. . .] Originally the ruler, with or without the assent of the assembled people, not only decides: he executes his decisions, or sees them executed. For example, in Dahomey, the king stands by, and if the deputed officer does not please him, takes the sword out of his hand and shows him how to cut off a head. An account of death-punishment among the Bedouins ends with the words—"the executioner being the sheikh himself." Our own early history affords traces of personal executive action by the king; for there came a time when he was interdicted from arresting anyone himself, and had thereafter to do it in all cases by deputy. And this interprets for us the familiar truth that, through his deputies the sheriffs, who are bound to act personally if they cannot themselves find deputies, the monarch continues to be theoretically the agent who carries the law into execution: a truth further implied by the fact that execution in criminal cases, nominally authorized by him though actually by his minister, is arrested if his assent is withheld by his minister. And these facts imply that a final power of judgment remains with the monarch, notwithstanding delegation of his judicial functions. How this happens we shall see on tracing the differentiation.

Naturally, when a ruler employs assistants to hear complaints and redress grievances, he does not give them absolute authority; but reserves the power of revising their decisions. We see this even in such rude societies as that of the Sandwich Islands, where one who is dissatisfied with the decision of his chief may appeal to the governor, and from the governor to the king; or as in ancient Mexico, where "none of the judges were allowed to condemn to death without communicating with the king, who had to pass the sentence."

§ 532.

Such being the origin and nature of laws, it becomes manifest that the cardinal injunction must be obedience. Conformity to each particular direction presupposes allegiance to the authority giving it; and therefore the imperativeness of subordination to this authority is primary.

That direct acts of insubordination, shown in treason and rebellion, stand first in degree of criminality, evidently follows. This truth is seen at the present time in South Africa. According to a horrible law of the Zulu despots, when a chief is put to death they exterminate also his subjects. It was illustrated by the ancient Peruvians, among whom a rebellious city or province was laid waste, and its inhabitants exterminated; and again by the ancient Mexicans, by whom one guilty of treachery to the king was put to death, with all his relations to the fourth degree. A like extension of punishment occurred in past times in Japan, where, when the offense is committed against the state, punishment is inflicted upon the whole race of the offender. Of efforts thus wholly to extinguish families guilty of disloyalty, the Merovingians yielded an instance: King Guntchram swore that the children of a certain rebel should be destroyed up to the ninth generation.

And these examples naturally recall those furnished by Hebrew traditions. When Abraham, treating Jahweh as a terrestrial superior (just as existing Bedouins regard as god the most powerful living ruler known to them), entered into a covenant under which, for territory given, he, Abraham, became a vassal, circumcision was the prescribed badge of subordination; and the sole capital offense named was neglect of circumcision, implying insubordination:

Jahweh elsewhere announcing himself as "a jealous god," and threatening punishment "upon the children unto the third and fourth generation of them that hate me." And the truth thus variously illustrated, that during stages in which maintenance of authority is most imperative, direct disloyalty is considered the blackest of crimes, we trace down through later stages in such facts as that, in feudal days, so long as the fealty of a vassal was duly manifested, crimes, often grave and numerous, were overlooked.

Less extreme in its flagitiousness than the direct disobedience implied by treason and rebellion, is, of course, the indirect disobedience implied by breach of commands. This, however, where strong rule has been established, is regarded as a serious offense, quite apart from, and much exceeding, that which the forbidden act intrinsically involves. Its greater gravity was distinctly enunciated by the Peruvians, among whom, says Garcilasso, "the most common punishment was death, for they said that a culprit was not punished for the delinquencies he had committed, but for having broken the commandment of the Inca, who was respected as God."

The like conception meets us in another country where the absolute ruler is regarded as divine. Sir R. Alcock quotes Thunbers to the effect that in Japan, "most crimes are punished with death, a sentence which is inflicted with less regard to the magnitude of the crime than to the audacity of the attempt to transgress the hallowed laws of the empire." And then, beyond the criminality which disobeying the ruler involves, there is the criminality involved by damaging the ruler's property, where his subjects and their services belong wholly or partly to him. In the same way that maltreating a slave, and thereby making him less valuable, comes to be considered as an aggression on his owner—in the same way that even now among ourselves a father's ground for proceeding against a seducer is loss of his daughter's services; so, where the relation of people to monarch is servile, there arises the view that injury done by one person to another, is injury done to the monarch's property. An extreme form of this view is alleged of Japan, where cutting and maiming of the king's dependents "becomes wounding the king, or regicide." And hence the general principle, traceable in European jurisprudence

The general principle, traceable in European jurisprudence from early days, that a transgression of man against man is punishable mainly, or in large measure, as a transgression against the State.

from early days, that a transgression of man against man is punishable mainly, or in large measure, as a transgression against the State. It was thus in ancient Rome: "Every one convicted of having broken the public peace, expiated his offense with his life." An early embodiment of the principle occurs in the Salic law, under which "to the *wehrgeld* is added, in a great number of cases . . . the *fred*, a sum paid to the king or magistrate, in reparation for the violation of public peace;" and in later days, the fine paid to the State absorbed the *wehrgeld*. Our own history similarly shows us that, as authority extends and strengthens, the guilt of disregarding it takes precedence of intrinsic guilt. "The king's peace" was a privilege which attached to the sovereign's court and castle, but which he could confer on other places and persons, and which at once raised greatly the penalty of misdeeds committed in regard to them. Along with the growing check on the right of private revenge for wrongs—along with the increasing subordination of minor and local jurisdictions—along with that strengthening of a central authority which these changes imply, "offenses against the law become offenses against the king, and the crime of disobedience a crime of contempt to be expiated by a special sort of fine." And we may easily see how, where a ruler gains absolute power, and especially where he has the prestige of divine origin, the guilt of contempt comes to exceed the intrinsic guilt of the forbidden act.

A significant truth may be added. On remembering that Peru, and Japan till lately, above named as countries in which the crime of disobedience to the ruler was considered so great as practically to equalize the flagitiousness of all forbidden acts, had societies in which militant organization, carried to its extreme, assimilated the social government at large to the government of an army; we are reminded that even in societies like our own, there is maintained in the army the doctrine that insubordination is the cardinal offense. Disobedience to orders is penal irrespective of the nature of the orders or the motive for the disobedience; and an act which, considered in itself, is quite innocent, may be visited with death if done in opposition to commands.

Crimes and Punishments, James Anson Farrer (1880)

It is of interest to trace some of the practical results which followed Beccaria's treatise during the thirty years that he lived after its publication; that is, from the year 1764 to 1794.

The country in which the first attempt was made to apply his principles to practice was Russia, where Catharine II was anxious to establish a uniform penal code, based on the liberal ideas of the time, which then found more favor in St. Petersburg than they did at Paris. For this purpose in 1767 she summoned to Moscow from all the provinces of Russia those 652 deputies who formed the nearest approach in the history of that country to a Russian Parliament. In the instructions that were read to this assembly, as the basis for the proposed codification of the laws, the principles propounded were couched not only in the spirit but often in the very words of the author of the ' Crimes and Punishments.' The following are examples:

☐ Laws should only be considered as a means of conducting mankind to the greatest happiness.

☐ It is incomparably better to prevent crimes than to punish them.

☐ The aim of punishment is not to torment sensitive beings.

□ All punishment is unjust that is unnecessary to the maintenance of public safety.

□ In methods of trial the use of torture is contrary to sound reason. Humanity cries out against the practice and insists on its abolition.

□ Judgment must be nothing but the precise text of the law, and the office of the judge is only to pronounce whether the action is contrary or conformable to it.

□ In the ordinary state of society the death of a citizen is neither useful nor necessary.

The following especially is from Beccaria: Would you prevent crimes, contrive that the laws favor less different orders of citizens than each citizen in particular? Let men fear the laws and nothing but the laws. Would you prevent crimes, provide that reason and knowledge be more and more diffused? To conclude: the surest but most difficult method of making men better is by perfecting education.

Although these instructions were not so much laws as suggestions of laws, it is obvious what their effect must have been when published and diffused throughout Russia. That they were translated into Latin, German, French, and Italian proves the interest that was taken in Europe by this first attempt to apply the maxims of philosophy to practical government.

In France, Beccaria's book became widely popular, and many writers helped to propagate his ideas, such as Servan, Brissot, Lacretelle, and Pastoret. Lacretelle attributes the whole impulse of criminal law reform to Beccaria, while regretting that Montesquieu had not said enough to attract general attention to the subject. His book is said to have so changed the spirit of the old French criminal tribunals, that, ten years before the Revolution, they bore no resemblance to their former selves. All the younger magistrates gave their judgments more according to the principles of Beccaria than according to the text of the law. The result of the agitation appeared in the Royal Ordinances of 1780 and 1788, directed to the diminution of torture, the only reforms which preceded the Revolution. It is said that the last time anyone was tortured in France was in the year 1788, the last year of the *ancien regime*. At the very beginning of the Revolution, more than a hundred different offences ceased to incur the penalty of death.

The most successful adoption of Beccaria's principles of punishment occurred in Tuscany, under the Grand Duke Leopold. When he ascended the ducal throne, the Tuscans were the most abandoned people of all Italy. Robberies and murders were none the less frequent for all the gallows, wheels, and tortures which were employed to repress them. But Leopold, in 1786, resolved to try Beccaria's plan, for which purpose he published a code, proportioning punishments to crimes, abolishing mutilation and torture, reducing the number of acts of treason, lessening confiscations, destroying the right of asylum, and above all abolishing capital punishment even for murder. The result was, says a contemporary, that Tuscany, from having been the land of the greatest crimes and villainies, became '"the best ordered State of Europe." During twenty years only five murders were committed in Tuscany, whilst at Rome, where death continued to be inflicted with great pomp, as many as sixty were committed within the space of three months.

Torture was definitely and totally abolished in Portugal in 1776, in Sweden in 1786, and in Austria in 1789. In the latter country, indeed, it had been abolished by Maria Theresa sixteen years before in her German and Polish provinces; and the Penal Code of Joseph II, published in 1785, was an additional tribute to the cause of reform. Secret orders were even given to the tribunals to substitute other punishments for hanging, yet so that the general public should be unaware of the change. There was the greatest anxiety that it should not be thought that this change was out of any deference for Beccaria or his school. "In the abolition of capital punishment," said Kaunitz, "his Majesty pays no regard at all to the principles of modern philosophers, who, in affecting a horror of bloodshed, assert that primitive justice has no right to take from a man that life which Nature only can give him. Our sovereign has only consulted his own conviction, that the punishment he wishes substituted for the capital penalty is more likely to be felt by reason of its duration, and therefore better fitted to inspire malefactors with terror."

Nor was it only in Europe that Beccaria's influence thus prevailed, for as soon as the American Colonies had shaken off their English connection they began to reform their penal laws. When the Revolution began there were in Pennsylvania nearly twenty crimes punishable by death, and within eighteen years of its close the penal code was thoroughly transformed, it being ordained in 1794 that no crime should any longer be capital but murder in the first degree. It is true that this was but a return to the principles adopted by [William] Penn on the settlement of the colony, but Penn's penal code was annulled by Queen Anne, and the English Government insisted on a strict adherence to the charter from Charles II, which enjoined the retention of the Statute and the Common Law of England. When, therefore, the new Constitution was formed in 1776, the arguments of Beccaria gave fresh life to the memories of Penn.

Thus, before his death Beccaria saw torture almost entirely abolished in Europe, and a general tendency spreading to follow the spirit of the changes he advocated in other details of criminal law. Probably no other theorist ever lived to witness so complete an adoption of his principles in practice, or so thorough a transformation of the system he attacked. It is possible that he but gave body and voice to ideas of change already widely prevalent in his time; but the *Turnbull's Visit to Philadelphia Prison*, 1797.

But if the interest of Beccaria's chapter on Torture is now merely historical, an interest that is actual still attaches to his advocacy of the total abolition of capital punishment, this being the cause with which his name is most generally associated, and for which it is likely to be longest remembered. Previous writers, like Montaigne, if they deprecated the excess or severity of the death penalty, never thought of urging that it should be abolished altogether.

There is an apparent discrepancy in Beccaria's first condemning death as too severe a punishment and then recommending lifelong servitude as one of more deterrent power; but Beccaria would have said that the greater certainty of the latter more than compensated for the greater severity of the other. As regards the relative power of the two punishments, it probably varies in different individuals, some men having a greater dread of the one, and some of the other. The popular theory certainly goes too far, when it assumes that all men have a greater dread of the gallows than of anything else. When George III once granted a pardon to the female convicts in Newgate on condition of their transportation to New South Wales, though seventeen of them accepted the offer, there were yet six who preferred death to a removal from their native country. It is also stated by Howard that in Denmark the punishment in cases of infanticide, namely, imprisonment for life, with labor and an annual whipping on the place of the crime, was "dreaded more than death," which it superseded as a punishment.

It is, however, probable that the frequency of any crime bears little or no relation to the punishment affixed to it. Every criminal begins a new career, in which he thinks less of the nature of his punishment than of his chances of eluding it. Neither tradition nor example count with him for much in his balance of the chances in his own favor. The law can never be so certain in its execution as it is uncertain in its application, and it is the examples of impunity, not of punishment, to which men turn when they violate the law. So that whether the punishment for murder be an excruciating death, as in ancient Rome, or a mere fine, as in ancient England, the motives for escape are always the same, the means to effect it are always the same, and the belief in his power to effect it is correspondingly powerful in every criminal guilty of homicide.

> **Every criminal begins a new career, in which he thinks less of the nature of his punishment than of his chances of eluding it.**

Even if we assume that death is absolutely the severest penalty devisable by the law, and that as a punishment for murder it is not too severe, it remains certain, that, relatively to the circumstances of a trial for murder, to the reluctance of judges or juries to pass an irretrievable sentence, to their fear of error, to their conscientious regard for human life, it is really a much less terrible danger for a malefactor to face than a penalty which would justify fewer hopes of impunity.

Nor are such scruples to convict unreasonable, when we consider the number who on apparently conclusive evidence have been falsely and irrevocably condemned to death. Playgoers who have seen "The Lyons Mail" will remember how barely Lesurques, the Parisian gentleman, escaped punishment for the guilt of Dubosc, the robber and murderer. But the moral of the story is lost in the play, for Lesurques actually was executed for the crime of Dubosc, by reason of the strong resemblance he bore to him, the latter only receiving the due reward for his crimes after the innocent man had died as a common murderer on the scaffold. Then there are cases in which, as in the famous case of Galas, someone having committed suicide, someone else is executed as the murderer. That dead men tell no tales is as true of men hung as of men murdered, and the innocence of an executed man may be proved long afterwards or not at all.

Where there is no capital punishment, as in Michigan, a man's innocence may be discovered subsequently to conviction, and justice done to him for the error of the law. Such a case actually happened not long ago in Michigan, where a prisoner's innocence was clearly proved after ten years' imprisonment. Where capital punishment exists, there is no such hope; nor is there any remedy if, as in the case of Lewis, who was hung in 1831, another man, thirty-three years afterwards, confesses himself the murderer.

It is impossible to preclude all chances of such errors of justice. Illustrative of this is the story of the church organist near Kieff, who murdered a farmer with a pistol he stole from a priest. After his crime he placed the pistol in the sacristy, and then, when he had prevented the priest from giving evidence against him by the act of confession, went and denounced the priest as the culprit. The priest, in spite of his protestations of innocence, was sentenced to hard labor for life; and when, twenty years afterwards, the organist confessed his guilt on his deathbed, and the priest's liberation was applied for, it was found that he had died only a few months before.

That the scruple to convict diminishes the certainty of punishment, and therefore raises hopes of impunity, is illustrated by the case of two American brothers who, desirous to perpetrate a murder, waited till their victim had left their State, in which capital punishment had been abolished, and had betaken himself to a State which still retained it, before they ventured to execute their criminal intention. That such reluctance to convict is often most injurious to the public is proved by the case of a woman at Chelmsford who some years ago was acquitted, in spite of strong evidence, on a charge of poisoning, and who, before her guilt was finally proved, lived to poison several other persons

The final test of all punishment is its efficiency, not its humanity.

who would otherwise have escaped her arts. Such considerations as these will, perhaps, lead some day to the abolition of capital punishment. The final test of all punishment is its efficiency, not its humanity. There is often more inhumanity in a long sentence of penal servitude than in a capital sentence, for the majority of murderers deserve as little mercy as they get. The many offenses which have ceased to be capital in English law yielded less to a sense of the inhumanity of the punishment as related to the crime than to the experience that such a punishment led to almost total impunity. The bankers, for instance, who petitioned Parliament to abolish capital punishment for forgery, did so, as they said, because they found by experience that the infliction of death, or the possibility of its infliction, prevented the prosecution, the conviction, and the punishment of the criminal; therefore they begged for "that protection for their property which they would derive from a more lenient law."

For the same reason it is of little avail to call in question, as Beccaria does, the right of society to inflict death as a punishment. There may be a distinction between the right of society and its might, but it is one of little comfort to the man who incurs its resentment. A man in a dungeon does better to amuse himself with spiders and cobwebs than with reflections on the encroachment of the law upon his liberty, or with theories about the rights of government. Whenever society has ceased to exercise any of its powers against individuals, it has not been from the acceptance of any new doctrine as to its rights, but from more enlightened views as to its real interests, and a cultivated dislike of cruelty and oppression.

When Beccaria wrote against capital punishment, one great argument against its abolition was its practical universality. It had been abolished in ancient Egypt by King Sabaco, in the best period of the Roman Republics by the Porcian law, and in the time of the Roman Empire by Calo-Johannes. But these cases were too remote from modern times to lend much weight to the general argument. At that time Russia alone, of all the countries in the world had, from the accession of the Empress Elizabeth, afforded a practical example of the fact, that the general security of life is not diminished by the withdrawal of the protection of capital punishment. But since that time this truth has become less and less a theory or speculation, and it now rests on the positive experience of no inconsiderable portion of the world. In Tuscany, Holland, Portugal, Russia, Romania, Saxony, Prussia, Belgium, and in ten of the United States of America, the death penalty has either been abolished or discontinued; and can it be thought that the people of those countries are so indifferent to the safety of their lives as to be content with a less efficient legal protection than is vouchsafed in countries where the protection is death?

The opponents of capital punishment may fairly, therefore, draw an argument in their favor from the fact that so many parts of the world have found it not incompatible with the general security of life to erase the death penalty from their list of deterrent agencies. It is better to rely on so plain a fact than on statistics which, like two-edged weapons, often cut both ways. The frequency of executions in one country and their total absence in another may severally coexist with great numerical equality in the number of murders committed in each. It is always better, therefore, to look for some other cause for a given number of murders than the kind of punishment directed to their repression. They may depend on a thousand other things, which it is difficult to ascertain or eliminate. Thus both in Bavaria, where capital punishment has been retained, and in Switzerland, where it had been abolished in 1874, murders have increased greatly in recent years; and this fact has, with great probability, been attributed to the influence of bad habits contracted during the Franco-German War.

Capital punishment being less general in the world now than torture was when Beccaria wrote, it seems to be a fair logical inference that it is already far advanced towards its total disappearance. For the same argument which Voltaire applied in the case of torture cannot fail sooner or later to be applied to capital punishment. "If," he says, "there were but one nation in the world which had abolished the use of torture; and if in that nation crimes were no more frequent than in others, . . . its example would be surely sufficient for the rest of the world." England alone might instruct all other nations in this particular; but England is not the only nation. Torture has been abolished in other countries, and with success; the question, therefore, is decided. If in this argument we read capital punishment instead of torture, murders instead of crimes, and

Portugal instead of England, we shall best appreciate that which is after all the strongest argument against capital punishment, namely, that it has been proved unnecessary for its professed object in so many countries that it might safely be relinquished in all.

The Lessons of the Hour, Frederick Douglass (1883)

In the eyes of many white people, all Negroes look alike, and as the man arrested and who sits in the dock in irons is black, he is undoubtedly the criminal.

It is a real calamity, in this country, for any man, guilty or not guilty, to be accused of crime, but it is an incomparably greater calamity for any colored man to be so accused. Justice is often painted with bandaged eyes. She is described in forensic eloquence, as utterly blind to wealth or poverty, high or low, white or black, but a mask of iron however thick, could never blind American justice, when a black man happens to be on trial. Here, even more than elsewhere, he will find all presumptions of law and evidence against him. It is not so much the business of his enemies to prove him guilty, as it is the business of himself to prove his innocence. The reasonable doubt which is usually interposed to save the life and liberty of a white man charged with crime, seldom has any force or effect when a colored man is accused of crime. Indeed, color is a far better protection to the white criminal, than anything else. In certain parts of our country, when any white man wishes to commit a heinous offence, he wisely resorts to burnt cork and blackens his face and goes forth under the similitude of a Negro. When the deed is done, a little soap and water destroys his identity, and he goes unwhipt of justice. Some Negro is at once suspected and brought before the victim of wrong for identification, and there is never much trouble here, for as in the eyes of many white people, all Negroes look alike, and as the man arrested and who sits in the dock in irons is black, he is undoubtedly the criminal.

A still greater misfortune to the Negro is that the press, that engine of omnipotent power, usually tries him in advance of the courts, and when once his case is decided in the newspapers, it is easy for the jury to bring in its verdict of "guilty as indicted."

In many parts of our common country, the action of courts and juries is entirely too slow for the impetuosity of the people's justice. When the black man is accused, the mob takes the law into its own hands, and whips, shoots, stabs, hangs or burns the accused, simply upon the allegation or suspicion of crime. Of such proceedings Southern papers are full. A crime almost unknown to the colored man in the time of slavery seems now, from report, the most common. I do not believe these reports. There are too many reasons for trumping up such charges.

Another feature of the situation is that this mob violence is seldom rebuked by the press and the pulpit, in its immediate neighborhood. Because the public opinion which sustains and makes possible such outrages, intimidates both press and pulpit.

Besides, nobody expects that those who participate in such mob violence will ever be held answerable to the law, and punished. Of course, judges are not always unjust, nor juries always partial in cases of this class, but I affirm that I have here given you no picture of the fancy, and I have alleged no point incapable of proof, and drawn no line darker or denser than the terrible reality. The situation, my colored fellow citizens, is discouraging, but with all its hardships and horrors, I am neither desperate nor despairing as to the future.

One ground of hope is found in the fact referred to in the beginning, and that is, the discussion concerning the Negro still goes on.

The country in which we live is happily governed by ideas as well as by laws, and no black man need despair while there is an audible and earnest assertion of justice and right on his behalf. He may be riddled with bullets, or roasted over a slow fire by the mob, but his cause cannot be shot or burned or otherwise destroyed. Like the impalpable ghost of the murdered Hamlet, it is immortal. All talk of its being a dead issue is a mistake. It may for a time be buried, but it is not dead.

Keynote Address, American Social Science Annual Meeting, Francis Wayland (1883)

The Constitution of the American Social Science Association was adopted in October, 1865. In the address of the Executive Committee, issued in the following month, the nature and purposes of the Association were explained, the division into departments was announced, and several topics naturally belonging to each section were indicated. Among these a prominent place was assigned to "the vexed question of capital punishment." It is a singular circumstance that, thus far, no paper on this important subject has been presented at any of our meetings. It is not to be inferred, however, that our reticence represents the condition of the public mind. Within the last half century English and American periodicals have contained more than a hundred articles devoted to this topic. It has occupied large space in the columns of our most influential newspapers, religious and secular. It has been discussed in many sessions of many legislatures of our Union. It has again and again received the thoughtful consideration of the English Parliament.

It has been argued on Scriptural grounds, on ethical grounds, on humanitarian grounds. The old-fashioned Tory has feared that infidelity lurked behind "the attempt to set aside that great: principle which God had laid down, that 'whoso sheddeth man's blood, by man shall his blood be shed.'" The tender-hearted Quaker has pleaded for the sanctity of human life. The conservative jurist has predicted a carnival of crime if the gallows no longer bore its ghastly burden; the progressive jurist has doubted the deterrent effect of a penalty which is rarely enforced. So wise and experienced a statesman as Earl Russell thought "nothing would be lost to justice, nothing to the preservation of innocent life if the punishment of death were altogether abolished;" one of the latest public utterances of so clear-headed and humane a philosopher as John Stuart Mill was a speech in Parliament against dispensing with the hangman.

It is a very hopeful sign that while little direct effect may have been produced upon legislation by the discussion of this question, the range of profitable debate has been reduced to a comparatively narrow field. It has come to be practically conceded that society has the right to protect life, liberty and property by the adoption of any measures best fitted to secure that end. Crime is a breach of the social compact, a violation of some law enacted for the protection of the individual. The offender must pay the penalty prescribed by law for such violation.

The sanguinary instincts of the middle ages no more belong to the criminal jurisprudence of the nineteenth century than do the decrees of that merciless magistrate, Judge Lynch.

No thought of passion, or vengeance, or retribution, or expiation must dictate or shape or color this punishment. The sanguinary instincts of the middle ages no more belong to the criminal jurisprudence of the nineteenth century than do the decrees of that merciless magistrate, Judge Lynch. The sole consideration with which the legislator of today has to deal is the simple inquiry: What kind or degree of punishment will most effectually protect society from the consequences of crime?

In deciding this question, the acknowledged principles of human nature and the teachings of mature experience must alike be taken into account. It must be remembered that while undue leniency brings law into contempt, undue severity prevents the uniform enforcement of law by weakening its hold upon the moral sentiment of the community. The doctrine is at least as old as Beccaria that the certainty of punishment is of much greater value than its severity. Nothing is more conducive to the successful administration of criminal justice than the skilful adaptation of punishment to crime, because

It has been well said that the efficacy of any law in a free state depends upon its being in harmony with the spirit of the people.

nothing tends more directly to establish that intimate connection between guilt, detection and conviction which is so essential to the good order of society.

It has been well said that the efficacy of any law in a free state depends upon its being in harmony with the spirit of the people. This is only stating, in other words, the sound proposition that when a law does not reflect the popular will it cannot be enforced. When this attitude of the community toward any law is found to be inspired not by momentary excitement, but by settled conviction, the time has arrived for its repeal or its material modification. This certainly is common sense, and ought always to be the basis of legislative action.

In point of fact, however, a statute seems too often to be regarded as a sort of fetish. Even when a dead letter—possibly because it is a dead letter—it receives a certain superstitious reverence. It is worshipped, not for any power which it exerts for good or evil, but because it is what is called "an existing institution."

Many legislators appear to imagine that to repeal a statute is to manifest a culpable indifference to the offense which it was designed to punish. They even fear that they may be suspected in some way of making a compromise with crime. For these and similar reasons, "The Maine Law" was suffered to encumber the statute books of some States for years after it had been abundantly proved that convictions under its provisions could not be secured. By and by somebody proposes a practicable yet operative substitute for the unused enactment, and straightway this inheritance of less enlightened times disappears forever.

Such is conspicuously the recent history of criminal legislation in England. We find the same dreary record of stubborn conservatism ignoring the lessons of experience; of blind adherence to the fallacy that severe penalties are, *per se*, deterrent, from the beginning of the last century, when more than-a hundred and fifty offenses were punishable with death, down to our own times, when only treason and murder conduct to the gallows. In every instance, the pressure of public opinion has finally effected the reform against the fears of learned jurists and the protests of timid legislators.

When it was proposed to abolish the punishment of death for the atrocious crime of stealing to the amount of forty shillings from a dwelling house, Lord Chancellor Eldon gravely declared that such an innovation would leave his property wholly without protection. But here, and in kindred cases, when juries refused to convict, the instinct of self-preservation provided milder and more effectual remedies.

The forces of conservatism—the worshippers of the statute fetish made perhaps their most determined struggle over the proposal to abolish the punishment of death for the crime of forgery. Around this relic of a barbarous code they rallied with the courage of desperation. There is something almost pathetic in the fidelity with which they clung to their ancient and useless weapons, the gravity with which they advanced their often refuted arguments, and the earnestness with which they appealed to fears which experience had shown to be unfounded. Shall the forger go unpunished? Shall we surrender all the safeguards of property? Shall we be in league with the law-breakers?

But while the battle was being sharply fought in Parliament and in print, the stronghold of superstition and unreason was being steadily undermined. Juries continued to acquit and culprits escaped "unwhipped of justice," to renew their depredations upon the unprotected and helpless capitalist. During the ten years preceding 1831, the Bank of England alone lost by forgeries, on an average more than £40,000 per annum. Now and then, during a period of about a quarter of a century, efforts were made to pacify the public by exempting special classes of forgery from the death penalty, but juries still refused to convict.

Fauntleroy, whose confessed forgeries amounted to more than £400,000, executed in November, 1824, was the last man to die under the sentence of an English tribunal for the crime of forgery. Meanwhile, the mercantile classes were naturally alarmed at this condition of affairs. In 1830 the bankers addressed an earnest petition to Parliament, setting forth "that the infliction of capital punishment for forgery encouraged the commission of the crime, because juries refused to convict while the statute affixed this penalty to the offense." And yet it was not until 1837 that forgery of all kinds was made punishable only by imprisonment.

This measure having reconciled public opinion to the administration of justice, juries were content to give to evidence its due weight, and certainty of punishment diminished the number of offenders. Step by step, the same process of reasoning was subsequently brought to bear on other offenses, until those living in England in 1861, saw capital punishment abolished for all crimes but treason and murder.

This brief survey of English criminal jurisprudence in comparatively recent times seems to warrant us in coming to the following conclusions:

First—That with the growing intelligence of a free people there arises an increasing aversion to capital punishment.

The second conclusion we give, in the words of Sydney Smith, whose writings are not more conspicuous for their wit than for their practical wisdom: "The efficient maximum of punishment is not what the legislature chooses to enact, but what the great mass of the people think that maximum ought to be."

Third—That whenever a penalty is so far out of harmony with public sentiment that, with rare exceptions, juries refuse to enforce it, the time has arrived for its repeal.

This, it will be seen, narrows the discussion of the death penalty in case of murder to the simple question of expediency. By the very nature of the social compact, society is bound to afford the amplest possible protection to human life. Does capital punishment give such protection? It is said that one object in visiting crime with a penalty is to deter others from committing a similar offense. Does capital punishment act as such a deterrent? Does its existence on the statute book tend to strengthen or to weaken public respect for law?

It is not denied that in certain conditions of society the death penalty may be, and often is, so enforced as both to protect and deter. Murder and horse-stealing, for instance, will for a time disappear from the criminal annals of any community when it is known that the sentence of death which follows the searching investigation of a vigilance committee will be inexorably and speedily carried into execution. Here, as always, it is the certainty of punishment which deters. I was about to say that this "nearest tree justice," salutary and even necessary as it may be in the mixed and shifting population of a frontier settlement, is not desired in any State of our Union having a permanent constitution and a code of laws—but I recall the fact that in more than one of our older commonwealths this side of the Mississippi, where capital punishment has not been abolished, murders have been committed with almost absolute impunity for many years with such startling frequency that law-abiding and sober-minded citizens have cried out in the bitterness of anguish, "Oh for a single hour of Judge Lynch!"

Having in view then, in the progress of this discussion, the single consideration of expediency, let us inquire whether in our times and in this country capital punishment is so enforced as to afford adequate protection to human life; and, secondly, if not so enforced, whether the reasons for its non-enforcement are temporary and accidental, or well considered and probably permanent.

We shall be materially aided in these inquiries by reliable statistics from two States not second to any in our Union for general intelligence, respect for law and love of social order. I refer to Massachusetts and Connecticut. It will not be questioned that they are fair specimens of our best civilization, fortunate in possessing competent courts of justice, able lawyers, admirable systems of common school education and many well-endowed and well-equipped universities of learning. Whatever may be truthfully said of other communities, here the administration of justice is singularly free from political, mercenary or other corrupting influences. In these States, if anywhere in our broad land, we should expect to find laws in sympathy with the temper of the people. Certainly we should be surprised to discover an obvious reluctance to punish high crimes with suitable severity, or a manifest disposition to shield the criminal from "the due reward of his deeds." Let us see what the facts are.

Beginning with Massachusetts, we find that during the years from 1860 to 1882, both inclusive (omitting all cases which were not actually passed upon by juries), there were one hundred and seventy trials for murder in the first degree. Twenty-nine persons were convicted of the crime as charged. Twelve of the twenty-nine had their death sentences commuted to imprisonment for life. Sixteen of the seventeen whose sentences were not commuted were hung, and one committed suicide before the day fixed for execution. In twenty-six cases verdicts of murder in the second degree were rendered.

If there are any who believe that Massachusetts is controlled by a spirit of philanthropy verging somewhat too closely upon fanaticism, we call their attention to a few statistics from the neighboring Commonwealth of Connecticut, a State which no sane man has ever suspected of entertaining sentimental views of crime or its penalty. During the thirty years from January 1, 1850, to January 1, 1880, ninety-seven persons were tried for murder in the first degree. Thirteen were convicted of murder in the first degree. In six of the cases the sentence was commuted to imprisonment for life. Seven were executed. Forty-two were convicted of murder in the second degree. Seven were acquitted on the sole ground of insanity.

There are instructive statistics from New Haven County covering the same period of time. As I need not remind such an audience as this, the county seat is the City of New Haven, the home of Yale College and, until recently, one of the capitals of the State. For the thirty years preceding the year 1880, the number of trials for murder in the first degree was twenty-three. In one case the sentence was commuted to imprisonment for life. Two were hung. Three were acquitted on the sole ground of insanity. Nine were convicted of murder in the second degree.

During the same period the number of trials for the crime of burglary in the same county was three hundred. Now bear in mind that a trial for murder is not only not a hasty proceeding, commenced without much preliminary investigation and pressed forward with very little ceremony, but that it usually supposes three previous hearings—before a coroner's jury, a magistrate, and a grand jury, all for the purpose of ascertaining if there is a probability of guilt— and, farther, that in the State of Connecticut, the crime of burglary is never brought before a grand jury, but is tried on "information" of the prosecuting attorney for the County, and you will be prepared to appreciate the startling contrast presented by the fact that out of the three hundred trials for burglary to which I have alluded, two hundred and seventy- three resulted in convictions. In three cases the accused were acquitted on the ground of insanity.

In 1852, the state of Rhode Island abolished the death penalty, substituting imprisonment for life. Its most populous county is Providence, of which the county seat is the city of Providence, not exceeded in intelligence by any community in our country; possessing, like New Haven, public schools of unsurpassed excellence, to say nothing of the civilizing and enlightening influences of an ancient university. Turning to the records of this county, we find that during the thirty years next succeeding the date of the abolition of capital punishment, out of twenty-seven trials for murder in the first degree, there were seventeen convictions; considerably more than fifty per cent.

But let us take more concrete illustrations. Three trials for murder in the state of Connecticut within the last twelve years attracted extraordinary attention, not only by reason of the exceptional atrocity of the offenses as proved, but also of the astounding character of the verdicts rendered. In each case the killing was by poison administered by somebody, deliberately, systematically, persistently. There was no suggestion of insanity. It was not urged that the deed was done in self-defense, or in the heat of passion or under great provocation. There was no conceivable escape from the conclusion, either that the accused were innocent not only of any criminal intent, but of any homicidal act, or else that they were guilty of murder in the first degree. In two of these cases, the verdict was murder in the second degree, the penalty for which was, as the jury had of course been instructed, imprisonment for life. In the third case, a plea of murder in the second degree was accepted by the Court. When, a little later, one of the women—for two of the accused belonged to the gentler sex—confessed to having poisoned eight persons within twenty years, it could not have been a surprise, even to the jury who had saved her from the gallows.

About twelve years ago, in the same state, a man was tried for murder in the first degree under the following circumstances. Having a grudge against a neighbor, the accused armed himself with a shotgun, concealed himself behind a stone wall on the roadside not far from his house, and awaited his opportunity. When, presently, the unsuspecting farmer seated in his wagon was driving past the place of ambush, the assassin took careful aim and fired. As the victim fell, an arm pressed upon one of the reins and the horse obeying the impulse thus unconsciously given, bore his bleeding and dying master into the yard and before the door of his murderer. The result of the trial was a verdict of murder in the second degree. This occurred in a county in which there have been twenty-seven trials for murder within thirty years and in which the hangman's office has been a sinecure for a century.

Take another case occurring three years earlier in another county of the same state. A man after several quarrels with his wife of whom he professed to be jealous, invited her to bathe with him in a shallow stream near their home. Having in a very deliberate manner held her head under water until she was drowned, he secreted her dead body in an adjoining thicket, and subsequently transferred the remains from place to place to diminish the danger of discovery. I believe that when finally arrested, he was engaged in this somewhat unenviable if not reprehensible occupation. Tried for murder in the first degree, he was convicted of murder in the second degree. It is only fair to add that during the period to which I refer—from 1850 to 1880—Connecticut has always been represented in its criminal courts by competent prosecuting officers, abundantly able to cope with the counsel for the defense.

If it be urged that, in the cases to which I have particularly alluded and in other cases equally pertinent and significant which might be cited, courts and juries have availed themselves of a very ancient statute, peculiar, I believe to Connecticut, which provides that "no person shall be convicted of any crime punishable by death without the testimony of at least two witnesses or that which is equivalent thereto," I can only say that the very flimsiness of the pretext strengthens the argument against capital punishment.

If it be true that there are states in which statistics would show a larger proportion of cases in which the death penalty has been inflicted, it is also true that there are states in which the proportion is very much smaller. On the whole it may well be questioned whether a fairer average could be presented than in the states from which our illustrations have been drawn.

If this conclusion be correct, it seems to follow that the death penalty is not so enforced in our times and in this country as to afford adequate protection to human life. The only legitimate objects to be accomplished by any form of penalty for the crime of murder are: First—To incapacitate the convicted criminal from doing society any further injury; and, secondly, to deter others from following his example.

But, as we have seen, a trial for murder means, with infrequent exceptions, a sentence to imprisonment for life, and imprisonment for life means, according to the most reliable estimates, confinement for from twelve to fourteen years. The medical report of the state prison at Auburn, N. Y., for fifty years previous to 1868, gives instructive figures on this point. During this period, two hundred and fourteen persons were committed to that prison under life sentences. Of these, thirty-four died from natural causes, eight became insane, two committed suicide, one escaped, and ten were transferred to other prisons; leaving one hundred and fifty-nine to be accounted for. Of these, twenty-nine remained in the prison at the date of the report, and one hundred and thirty-four had been pardoned; their average period of servitude having been six years and six months. It is asserted that in Massachusetts fifty per cent, of life prisoners are pardoned. Of the fifty six committed to the Connecticut state prison during the thirty years from 1850 to 1880 on life sentences for murder or on commutation of sentence, eight died in prison, four were transferred to the State hospital for the insane; leaving forty-four to be accounted for. Of these, thirty-four were pardoned, after an average period of confinement of nine years and two months.

In view of such facts as these, the statement does not seem extravagant, "that imprisonment for life is, to all intents and purposes, an unknown punishment in this country." And it is very important that we bear in mind that verdicts of murder in the second degree as a substitute for the death penalty, are rendered with a full knowledge of the probable consequences we have described. When, therefore, juries are thus resolute in declining to send murderers to the gallows and the pardoning power is thus lavishly exercised, it is difficult to see how society is protecting human life by incapacitating the criminal from repeating his crime.

We have now to consider in the second place, the deterrent effect of the death penalty in the light of such statistics as we have been examining. It may be well to remember at the outset, that not a few thoughtful men, who have made crimes and their penalties the subject of special study, have seriously questioned whether there is any appreciable deterrent influence in punishment, or, it is said, if the offense be committed in cold blood, the offender counts upon escaping detection, and if in hot blood, he takes no thought of the future.

However this may be, it is undeniable that any power to deter which punishment may possess, depends entirely upon its being awarded certainly and enforced speedily. Doubt and delay only encourage offenders. If we repeat these axioms to weariness, it is because they are so often overlooked by the advocates of capital punishment. One of the ablest of English jurists asserts that "no other punishment deters men so effectually from committing crime as the punishment of death," and he seeks to maintain this, in part, as follows:

"This is one of those propositions which it is difficult to prove, simply because they are in themselves more obvious than any proof can make them. It is possible to display ingenuity in arguing against it, but that is all. The whole experience of mankind is in the other direction. The threat of instant death is the one to which resort has always been made when there was an absolute necessity for producing some result. Those who argue that the punishment of death does not terrify, may be challenged to answer this single question. Suppose a pistol were leveled at the head of a man proposing to commit murder, and suppose he knew that the death of his victim would immediately be followed by his own, does anyone suppose that the murder would be committed?" (Sir James Fitz James Stephens)

Probably not. Most decidedly not, we should say, if we could put ourselves in the place of the supposed assassin. Meanwhile, those who argue that the punishment of death does terrify, may be challenged to answer this single question. Suppose a man, intent on murder, were confidentially informed by a discreet friend, with due apologies for the interruption, that, if he pulled the fatal trigger, or administered the deadly poison, he might be detected; that if he did not escape he would be arrested; that after a probable delay of some months he would be brought to trial; that if he could command the means to employ the Rufus Choate of the period, or, indeed, any other able lawyer, the trial might be indefinitely prolonged; that the chances were considerably better than ten to one against his conviction; and if convicted, quite as good as ten to one against his execution, does anyone doubt that the murder would be committed, if the would-be slayer were very much in earnest?

We confess that our jurist's argumentative illustration seems to us somewhat infelicitous in view of the statement, made without contradiction on the floor of the House of Commons during; the session of 1881, that "during the twenty years between 1860 and 1881, for other crimes except murder, the number of committals in which there were convictions was seventy-six per cent; but for murder only forty-nine per cent., of which forty-six per cent, were reprieved." The analogy between this state of things and "the leveled pistol" threatening "immediate" retribution, is not, we submit, sufficiently close to be quite conclusive. That the illustration for us in our own country, in these closing years of the nineteenth century, is ludicrously inapplicable, goes without saying. And why, oh! why, does it remind us of a single sentence in a clever farce written by a fellow countryman of our gifted author? "Poppy seeds, when taken incessantly for several weeks, produce immediate dissolution."

Let us now consider the second branch of our general inquiry, viz: whether the reasons for the non-enforcement of the law providing capital punishment as the penalty for murder are temporary and accidental or well-considered and probably permanent; and therefore justifying, if not demanding its repeal.

On this point there would seem to be no room for controversy. It will, we think, be conceded by the vast majority of those who have had occasion to be familiar with proceedings in criminal courts, as well as by our most accomplished penologists, that the difficulty of securing convictions in capital cases arises almost exclusively from reluctance to take human life. In many instances, of which some examples have been given, this feeling has been so strong as to override all evidence, and set at defiance inevitable inferences from undisputed facts.

In 1864 and 1865 the general question which we are examining was considered in England by the Parliamentary Capital Punishment Commission, of which our distinguished visitor, Lord Justice Coleridge, was a leading member. In his testimony before the Commission, Lord Chancellor Cranworth stated as the result of his observation that "juries wished to rid themselves of the responsibility of finding a man guilty of a capital offense," adding by way of illustration the case of a man "who was tried for murder, attended with highway robbery, and acquitted, but was afterwards tried for robbery on precisely the same evidence and convicted." Numerous cases were cited before the Commission by eminent members of the English bar to show that capital punishment often leads to the acquittal of guilty men.

In most cases, however, refusal to convict has been caused by the belief that mistake was possible, and that the consequences of an erroneous verdict might be irreparable. Ex-Attorney General Train, of Massachusetts, whose professional prominence and extended official experience in criminal courts give great value to his opinions, says that "the danger that the innocent may be executed instead of the guilty presses upon jurymen with fearful power, so that they will return a verdict of murder in the second degree instead of in the first, where there is the slightest ground for it, and sometimes when there is not, since such a verdict does not involve the possibility of taking the life of the prisoner." And you do not need to be told that the firm attitude of a single juror will as completely foul the efforts of the prosecuting officer as a verdict of acquittal by the entire panel.

It sometimes seems as if the jury and the prisoner's counsel were joined in a conspiracy to save the accused from the gibbet. And yet, after all, the venerable anecdotes to prove that by circumstantial evidence the innocent have been condemned to die and the guilty have been screened from punishment; the well-worn stories of convictions procured by perjured testimony, and, where the edge of these familiar weapons is somewhat dulled by proof of the prisoner's confession, the easy suggestion of insanity—these and similar devices which perhaps to a spectator weighing the evidence with impartial mind because having nothing at stake, seem pitiably weak, may fill the anxious twelve with most distressing doubts. Have they not, or at all events, do they not believe that they have the life of a fellow being in their hands?

But for this predisposition to mercy among jurors founded on the fear of making a fatal mistake, murder trials would be reduced to much more moderate dimensions and the ends of justice be more speedily attained. The eclat of cheating the gallows of a victim with so many chances in his favor will usually tempt an able advocate to undertake a capital case and will stimulate him to greater zeal—not always limited to legitimate efforts—than is manifested in any other criminal proceeding where professional activity is not stimulated by a generous fee.

With what follows you are all familiar—the countless pretexts for postponing the trial; the pains taken to secure twelve men having no decided convictions on any subject; the characteristic treatment of the witnesses for the state; and last of all the fervid appeal to the weary, confused jurors to " beware how they usurp the attributes of the Almighty and allow their fallible inferences from human and therefore imperfect evidence to send a fellow creature to the scaffold;" and all the rest of it: I dare say some of you know it by heart—from the daily papers. Sometimes it has the ring of true eloquence; sometimes it is the merest rant.

But whether it be eloquence or rant, it serves to remind the jury of the sacredness of human life, the danger of being misled to the injury of the accused, and the possibility, however remote, of sacrificing an innocent man.

Over against this, as the point to be carried, the advocate masses his heaviest artillery. Hear him. "Of all penalties, capital punishment alone is irreparable. Property may be restored; reputation may be retrieved; but human life once taken, can never be recalled. Fatal mistakes have been made; will be made again," etc., etc. True, every word of it; and because true, rarely without its effect upon a jury. Moreover, we think it demonstrable that reluctance to convict on this precise ground is increasing rather than diminishing in our most enlightened communities.

Of all penalties, capital punishment alone is irreparable. Property may be restored; reputation may be retrieved; but human life once taken, can never be recalled.

But if, as will occasionally happen, the case is too clear for even a speculative doubt, and a verdict of guilty is returned, the prisoner's counsel need not despair. There remain the various expedients which we have neither space nor time to enumerate; terminating with the petition for pardon or commutation, which almost everybody seems willing to sign—all intended to set at naught the deliberate judgment of the jurors, and save the forfeited life of the convict.

Before leaving this branch of the subject, we cannot forbear to quote from remarks made by a veteran lawyer in the House of Commons, during a debate on a motion for the second reading of the bill to abolish capital punishment, in the session of 1881. "There was a great and growing distrust in the rightfulness of the punishment—at all events in its efficacy—and there was an inherent feeling in the human breast which revolted from the taking of the life even of a murderer." He ventured to say that no punishment should be inflicted which was irreversible if it were discovered that a person had been wrongfully convicted, and the consequences of which could not be removed even in a mitigated form.

The efficacy of the punishment consisted in its certainty, not in its severity; and from his own experience he knew that juries were unwilling to convict, because they felt that they were not infallible and might be dooming an innocent man to death. He had been engaged professionally in trials in which convictions for murder would have been given had it not been for the consequences which would follow. For these reasons he gave his hearty support to the bill, believing that the sentence of death did not act as a deterrent. He thought, therefore, that it would be in the interests of society if the punishment of death were removed from the statute books. They would have justice administered, sentences carried out with greater certainty and they would have convictions where they did not now obtain them. He looked to the greater certainty of convictions and of the punishment as a surer deterrent than the punishment of hanging.

Another consideration should be by no means overlooked. If capital punishment is to be retained on our statute books and is ever to be enforced, we shall still be confronted with that most embarrassing if not insoluble problem: How shall executions be conducted? Public hanging is now almost universally condemned on account of its brutalizing effect upon the spectators. Secret hanging will never be and ought never to be tolerated among a free people. If hanging is within the prison enclosure and representatives of the press are permitted to be present—and it is difficult to see how they can be excluded—then every incident, moment by moment, of the last hours of the doomed man, with all the hideous and harrowing details of the final tragedy, will soon be eagerly devoured by millions of readers from Maine to Mexico, with results hardly less demoralizing than those which accompany and follow the public enforcement of the death penalty. For it should be observed—although the gloomy picture hardly needs a more sombre tint—that one consequence of our infrequent hangings is that the clumsy because unpracticed hand and the troubled because humane heart of the executioner often turns what should be made an impressive spectacle into a scene which excites only disgust, horror and indignation among the beholders.

We are now prepared for the final inquiry: What is proposed as an effectual substitute for the death penalty?

We are well aware that by many the mere proposal will be regarded with extreme disfavor. There are some who hold, with Sir James Fitzjames Stephen, that "no other punishment gratifies and justifies in so emphatic a manner the vindictive sentiment, the existence of which is one of the safeguards against crime," and who think, we may presume, that an occasional execution, even an allowance of only one hanging in half a century, is very much better than no execution at all.

Others have a vague notion—hardly amounting to an opinion— that the taking of one life illegally can only be properly punished by taking another life judicially; that there is a law regarding that sort of thing, and, somehow taking it for granted that it is carried into effect, on the whole, rather resent any attempt to enlighten their minds on the subject.

Others, still, who, if on a jury in a capital case, would be among the very first to welcome any offered mode of escape, however illogical or even absurd, from the duty of rendering a verdict of guilty, yet cannot bring themselves to consent to the repeal of a law which has been on the statute books for so many generations; i. e., they are "in favor of the law, but opposed to its enforcement." Then, of course, there are in every community many thoughtful, intelligent, well-informed men whose deliberate opinions are entitled to great respect, and who think it wiser that the present law should be retained.

But not to prolong the classification of our opponents, all that they or any others can justly demand is that the suggested substitute shall accomplish more effectually the desirable objects sought to be obtained by the existing statute.

Let us see if imprisonment for life will not answer this reasonable requirement. As has already been remarked, the design of the death penalty is twofold. First: to incapacitate the criminal from repeating his crime: and Second: to deter others from committing a like offense. This is all. Restitution is impossible. Reformation, in the brief period between the sentence and the scaffold, is highly improbable.

But, clearly, society at large is as perfectly protected from the violence of a man who is confined in prison for life, as though he were "hung by the neck until dead." Hanging does nothing more than put him out of the way. Does imprisonment for life do less?

But observe: the convicted murderer has forfeited the right to be at large; therefore he is imprisoned for life. He has even forfeited the right to the society of those who have been guilty of crimes, but of lesser degree: therefore his only fellow prisoners should be fellow murderers. If in any given commonwealth, there should not be a sufficient number of life prisoners to warrant the erection of a separate building to confine them, it would only be necessary to add a wing to the main prison—adjoining yet distinct. A life prisoner should have regular hours of labor, nutritious food, clean and well-ventilated cells, suitable clothing; but no diversions; no relaxations; no communication with the outer world; no correspondence with relatives or friends. In a word, he must be socially dead, as much so as if his body were moldering in a felon's grave.

Solitary confinement should be reserved for additional punishment—or for violation of prison rules; perhaps permanent solitary confinement for the murder of a keeper or a fellow prisoner. In Rhode Island, where, for other murders, capital punishment is abolished, it is enacted, "that every person who shall commit murder while under sentence of imprisonment for life shall be hung." This statute was probably passed in the belief that juries would always convict under such circumstances, but within five years, in another New England state, a convict who, while endeavoring to escape, killed his keeper, was convicted of murder in the second degree. And although this was really a case of murder in the first degree, and should have received the highest punishment known to the law, yet it must always be remembered that if there are exceptionally wicked prisoners, there are also brutal keepers and a long series of exasperating indignities may transform a human being into a wild beast.

Consider now the probable deterrent effect of the suggested substitute for the death penalty. Imprisonment for life under the conditions which have been indicated, is a form of punishment which may well appall the stoutest heart. A man condemned to die and cherishing a hope, however faint, of a reprieve, may, at the lust, when all hope has fled, brace himself by a supreme effort, against the brief agony of the gallows and meet his fate with fortitude. Indeed, we know that men have done this. But how, if he look forward to the certainty of a lifelong seclusion from his fellow men? There is no room here for mock heroism or bravado. There is no spectacle: there are no spectators. Nothing which the world can give will ever minister to his enjoyment or comfort, or break the sad monotony of his weary days. There will be no tidings from home; he has no home but a cell: no horizon beyond the prison walls. He is, in sober earnest, "a man without a country."

To others, his punishment is a standing menace; a perpetual warning. The lessons taught by the gallows are short lived. The man dies and is forgotten. But the prisoner for life preaches from his lonely cell a daily sermon to deter from crime.

Again, the deterrent influence of this form of penalty will be materially enhanced by the greatly increased certainty of conviction after detection and of punishment after conviction. From the moment when it is made to appear that a possible mistake is not irreparable, trials for murder will be deprived of their anomalous and exceptional features. The gallows will no longer cast its dark shadow across the courtroom. Evidence will be weighed, and inferences drawn, and probabilities balanced, and verdicts rendered, as in other criminal cases. There will be less feverish excitement; fewer angry controversies, diminished attraction for the idle and vicious; in a word a much more wholesome atmosphere, material as well as moral, for the exercise of calm reflection and deliberate judgment. It would be strange, moreover, if much impassioned, not to say lurid, eloquence of the Old Bailey variety were not lost to the world. But our life is controlled by compensations and we should hope to be reconciled, in time, even to this result, in view of the more rapid despatch of criminal business, and, as we firmly believe, the added security to human life.

And now, if the question be asked—and certainly nothing could be more natural than such an inquiry—how can the literal execution of a life sentence be ensured? I answer: By a constitutional provision, making release from confinement impossible, until, before the court in which the prisoner was convicted, it shall be made to appear that he was innocent.

Elizabeth Fry: The Gallows And English Laws (1884)

About this period the subject of Capital Punishment largely attracted Mrs. Fry's attention. The attitude of Quakers generally towards the punishment of death, except for murder in the highest degree, was hostile ; but Mrs. Fry's constant intercourse with inmates in the condemned cell fixed her attention in a very painful manner upon the subject. For venial crimes, men and women, clinging fondly to life, were swung off into eternity; and neither the white lips of the philanthropist, nor the official ones of the appointed chaplain, could comfort the dying. Among these dying ones were many women, who were executed for simply passing forged Bank of England notes; but as the bank had plenary powers to arrange to screen certain persons who were not to die, these were allowed to get off with a lighter punishment by pleading "Guilty to the minor count." The condemned cell was never, however, without its occupant, nor the gallows destitute of its prey. So Draconian were the laws of humane and Christian England, at this date, that had they been strictly carried out, at least four executions daily, exclusive of Sundays, would have taken place in this realm.

The "Black Act," first passed in the reign of George I, and enlarged by George II, punished by hanging, the hunting, killing, stealing, or wounding any deer in any park or forest; maiming or killing any cattle, destroying any fish or fish-pond, cutting down or killing any tree planted in any garden or orchard, or cutting any hop-bands in hop plantations. Forgery, smuggling, coining, passing bad coin, or forged notes, and shop-lifting; all were punishable by death.

According to Hepworth Dixon, and contemporary authorities, the sanguinary measures of the English Government for the punishment of crimes dated from about the time of the Jacobite rebellion, in 1745. Prior to that time, adventurers of every grade, the idle, vicious, and unemployed, had found an outlet for their turbulence and their energies in warfare — engaging on behalf of the Jacobites, or the Government, according as it suited their fancy. But when the House of Hanover conquered, and the trade of war became spoiled within the limits of Great Britain, troops of these discharged soldiers took to a marauding life; the high roads became infested with robbers, and crimes of violence were frequent. Alarmed at the license displayed by these Ishmaelites, the Government of the day arrayed its might against them, enacting such sanguinary measures that at first sight it seemed as if the deliberate intent were to literally cut them off and root them out from the land. That era was indeed a bloodthirsty one in English jurisprudence.

Enactments were passed in the reign of the second George, whereby it was made a capital crime to rob the mail, or any post office; to kill, steal, or drive away any sheep or cattle, with intention to steal, or to be accessory to the crime. The "Black Act," first passed in the reign of George I, and enlarged by George II, punished by hanging, the hunting, killing, stealing, or wounding any deer in any park or forest; maiming or killing any cattle, destroying any fish or fish pond, cutting down or killing any tree planted in any garden or orchard, or cutting any hop-bands in hop plantations. Forgery, smuggling, coining, passing bad coin, or forged notes, and shoplifting; all were punishable by death. From a table published by Janssen, and quoted from Hepworth Dixon, we find that in twenty-three years, from 1749 to 1771, eleven hundred and twenty-one persons were condemned to death in London alone. The offenses for which these poor wretches received sentence included those named above, in addition to seventy-two cases of murder, two cases of riot, one of sacrilege, thirty-one of returning from transportation, and four of enlisting for foreign service. Of the total number condemned, six hundred and seventy-eight were actually hanged, while the remainder either died in prison, were transported, or pardoned. As four hundred and one persons were transported, a very small number indeed obtained deliverance either by death or pardon. In fact, scarcely any extenuating circumstances were allowed; so that in some cases cruelty seemed actually to have banished justice. It is recorded, as one of these cases, that a young woman with a babe at the breast, was hanged for stealing from a shop a piece of cloth of the value of five shillings. The poor woman was the destitute wife of a young man whom the press-gang had captured and carried off to sea, leaving her and her babe to the mercy of the world. Utterly homeless and starving, she stole to buy food; but a grateful country requited the services of the sailor-husband by hanging the wife.

The certainty of punishment became nullified by the severity of the laws. Humane individuals hesitated to prosecute, especially for forgery; while juries seized upon every pretext to return verdicts of "Not guilty." Reprieves were frequent, for the lives of many were supplicated, and successfully; so that the death penalty was commuted into transportation. Caricaturists, writers, philanthropists, divines—all united in the chorus of condemnation against the bloody enactments which secured such a crop for the gallows. Men, women, girls, lads and idiots, all served as food for it. Jack Ketch had a merry time of it, while society looked on well pleased, for the most part. Those appointed to sit in the seat of justice sometimes defended this state of things. One of the worthies of the "good old times"—Judge Heath—notorious because of his partiality for hanging, is reported to have said: "If you imprison at home, the criminal is soon thrown back upon you hardened in guilt. If you transport you corrupt infant societies, and sow the seeds of atrocious crimes over the habitable globe. There is no regenerating a felon in this life. And, for his own sake, as well as for the sake of society, I think it better to hang."

As a caricaturist George Cruikshank entered the field, and waged battle on behalf of the poor wretches who swung at the gallows for passing forged Bank of England notes. He drew a note resembling the genuine one, and entitled it "Bank note, not to be imitated." A copy of this caricature now lies before us. It bears on its face a representation of a large gallows, from which eleven criminals, three of whom are women, are dangling, dead. In the upper left hand corner, Britannia is represented as surrounded by starving, wailing creatures, and surmounted by a hideous death's head. Underneath is a rope coiled around the portraits of twelve felons who have suffered; while, running down, to form a border, are fetters arranged in zig-zag fashion. Across the note run these words, "Ad lib., ad lib., I promise to perform during the issue of Bank notes easily imitated, and until the resumption of cash payments, or the abolition of the punishment of death, for the Governors and Company of the Bank of England.—J. KETCH." The note is a unique production, and must have created an enormous sensation. Cruikshank's own story, writing in 1876, is this:

"Fifty-eight years back from this date there were one-pound Bank of England notes in circulation, and, unfortunately, many forged notes were in circulation also, or being passed, the punishment for which offense was in some cases transportation, in others DEATH. At this period, having to go early to the Royal Exchange one morning, I passed Newgate jail, and saw several persons suspended from the gibbet; two of these were women who had been executed for passing one-pound forged notes.

"I determined, if possible, to put a stop to such terrible punishments for such a crime, and made a sketch of the above note, and then an etching of it.

"Mr. Hone published it, and it created a sensation. The Directors of the Bank of England were exceedingly wroth. The crowd around Hone's shop in Ludgate Hill was so great that the Lord Mayor had to send the police to clear the street. The notes were in such demand that they could not be printed fast enough, and I had to sit up all one night to etch another plate. Mr. Hone realized above £700, and I had the satisfaction of knowing that no man or woman was ever hanged after this for passing one-pound Bank of England notes.

"The issue of my *"Bank Note: note not to be Imitated"* not only put a stop to the issue of any more Bank of England one-pound notes, but also put a stop to the punishment of death for such an offense — not only for that, but likewise for forgery — and then the late Sir Robert Peel revised the penal code; so that the final effect of my note was to stop hanging for all minor offenses, and has thus been the means of saving thousands of men and women from being hanged."

It may be that the great caricaturist claims almost too much when he says that the publication of his note eventually stopped hanging for all minor offenses; but certainly there is no denying that this publication was an important factor in the agitation.

It is said that George III kept a register of all the cases of capital punishment, that he entered in it all names of felons sentenced to death, with dates and particulars of convictions, together with remarks upon the reasons which induced him to sign the warrants. It is also said that he frequently rose from his couch at night to peruse this fatal list, and that he shut himself up closely in his private apartments during the hours appointed for the execution of criminals condemned to death.

Tyburn ceased to be the place of execution for London in 1783; from that year Newgate witnessed most of these horrors.

Philanthropists of every class were, at the period of Mrs. Fry's career now under review, considering this matter of capital punishment, and taking steps to restrain the infliction of the death penalty. The Gurney family among Quakers, William Wilberforce, Sir James Mackintosh, Sir Samuel Romilly, and others, were all working hard to this end. In 1819 William Wilberforce presented a petition from the Society of Friends to Parliament against death punishment for crimes other than murder. Writing at later dates upon this subject, Joseph John Gurney says: " I cannot say that my spirit greatly revolts against life for life, though capital punishment for anything short of this appears to me to be execrable." And, again, "I cannot in conscience take any step towards destroying the life of a fellow-creature whose crime against society affects my property only. I am in possession, like other men, of the feelings of common humanity, and to aid and abet in procuring the destruction of any man living would be to me extremely distressing and horrible."

As a banker, Mr. Gurney felt that the punishment for forgery should be heavy and sharp, but less than death. In the Houses of Parliament various efforts were made to obtain the commutation of the death penalty, and when in 1810 the Peers rejected Sir Samuel Romilly's bill to remove the penalty for shoplifting, the Dukes of Sussex and Gloucester joined some of the Peers in signing a protest against the law. The time appeared to be ripe for agitation; all classes of society reverenced human life more than of old, and desired to see it held less cheap by the ministers of justice.

According to Mrs. Fry's experience, the punishment of death tended neither to the security of the people, the reformation of any prisoner, nor the diminution of crime. Felons who suffered death for light offenses looked upon themselves as martyrs — martyrs to a cruel law — and believed that they had but to meet death with fortitude to secure a blissful hereafter. This fearful opiate carried many through the terrible ordeal outwardly calm and resigned.

Among the condemned ones was Harriet Skelton, a woman who had been detected passing forged Bank of England notes. She was described as prepossessing "open, confiding, expressing strong feelings on her countenance, but neither hardened in depravity nor capable of cunning." Her behavior in prison was exceptionally good; so good, indeed, that some of the depraved inmates of Newgate supposed her to have been condemned to death because of her fitness for death. She had evidently been more sinned against than sinning; the man whom she lived with, and who was ardently loved by her, had used her as his instrument for passing these false notes. Thus she had been lured to destruction.

After the decision had been received from the Lords of the Council, Skelton was taken into the condemned cell to await her doom. To this cell came numerous visitors, attracted by compassion for the poor unfortunate who tenanted it, and each one eager to obtain the commutation of the cruel sentence. It was one thing to read of one or another being sentenced to death, but quite another to behold a woman, strong in possession of, and desire for life, fated to be swung into eternity before many days because of circulating a false note at the behest of a paramour. Mrs. Fry needed not the many persuasions she received to induce her to put forth the most unremitting exertions on behalf of Skelton. She obtained an audience of the Duke of Gloucester, and urged every circumstance which could be urged in extenuation of the crime, entreating for the woman's life. The royal duke remembered the old days at Norwich, when Elizabeth had been know in fashionable society and had figured somewhat as a belle, and he bent a willing ear to her request. He visited Newgate, escorted by Mrs. Fry, and saw for himself the agony in that condemned cell. Then he accompanied her to the bank directors, and applied to Lord Sidmouth personally, but all in vain. It was not blood for blood, nor life for life, but blood for "filthy lucre;" so the poor woman was hung in obedience to the inexorable ferocity of the law and its administrators.

On this occasion Mrs. Fry was seriously distressed in mind. She had vehemently entreated for the poor creature's life, stating that she had had the offer of pleading guilty only to the minor count, but had foolishly rejected it in hope of obtaining a pardon. The question at issue on this occasion was the power of the bank directors to virtually decide as to the doom of the accused ones. Mrs. Fry made assertions and gave instances which Lord Sidmouth assumed to doubt. Further than this, he was seriously annoyed at the noise this question of capital punishment was making in the land, and though not necessarily a cruel or blood-thirsty man, the Home Secretary shrank from meddling too much with the criminal code of England. This misunderstanding was a source of deep pain to the philanthropist, and, accompanied by Lady Harcourt, she endeavored to remove Lord Sidmouth's false impressions, but in vain. While smarting under this wound, received in the interests of humanity, she had to go to the Mansion House by command of Her Majesty Queen Charlotte, to be presented. Thus, very strangely, and against her will, she was thrust forward into the very foremost places of public observation and repute. She recorded the matter in her journal, in her own characteristic way:

"Yesterday I had a day of ups and downs, as far as the opinions of man are concerned, in a remarkable degree. I found that there was a grievous misunderstanding between Lord Sidmouth and myself, and that some things I had done had tried him exceedingly; indeed, I see that I have mistaken my conduct in some particulars respecting the case of poor Skelton, and in the efforts made to save her life, I too incautiously spoke of some in power. When under great humiliation in consequence of this, Lady Harcourt, who most kindly interested herself in the subject, took me with her to the Mansion House, rather against my will, to meet many of the royal family at the examination of some large schools. Among the rest, the Queen was there. There was quite a buzz when I went into the Egyptian Hall, where one or two thousand people were collected; and when the Queen came to speak to me, which she did very kindly, I am told that there was a general clapp. I think I may say this hardly raised me at all; I was so very low from what had occurred before. . . . My mind has not recovered this affair of Lord Sidmouth, and finding that the bank directors are also affronted with me added to my trouble, more particularly as there was an appearance of evil in my conduct; but, I trust, no greater fault in reality than a want of prudence in that which I expressed."

The Society of Friends had always been opposed to capital punishment. Ten years previously, Sir Samuel Romilly had determined to attack these sanguinary enactments, one by one, in order to ensure success. He began, therefore, with the Act of Queen Elizabeth, "which made it a capital offense to steal privately from the person of another." William Allen records in the same year, 1808, the formation of a " Society for Diffusing Information on the Subject of Punishment by Death." This little band worked with Sir Samuel until his painful death in 1818; while Dr. Parr, Jeremy Bentham, and Dugald Stewart aided the enterprise by words of encouragement, both in public and in private. In Joseph John Gurney's Memoirs, it is stated that Dr. Lushington declared his opinion that the poor criminal was thus hurried out of life and into eternity by means of the perpetration of another crime far greater, for the most part, than any which the sufferer had committed.

The feeling grew, and in place of the indifference and scorn of human life which had formerly characterized society, there sprang up an eager desire to save life, except for the crime of murder. In May, 1821, Sir James Mackintosh introduced a bill for "Mitigating the Severity of Punishment in Certain Cases of Forgery, and Crimes connected therewith." Buxton, in advocating this measure, says truly:

The people have made enormous strides in all that tends to civilize and soften mankind, while the laws have contracted a ferocity which did not belong to them in the most savage period of our history; and, to such extremes of distress have they proceeded that I do believe there never was a law so harsh as British law, or so merciful and humane a people as the British people. And yet to this mild and merciful people is left the execution of that rigid and cruel law.

This measure was defeated, but the numbers of votes were so nearly equal, that the defeat was actually a victory.

Time went on. In 1831, Sir Robert Peel took up the gauntlet against capital punishment, and endeavored to induce Parliament to abolish the death penalty for forgery; the House of Commons voted its abolition, but the Lords restored the clauses retaining the penalty. One thousand bankers signed a petition praying that the vote of the Commons might be sustained, but in vain ; still, in deference to public opinion, after this the death penalty was not inflicted upon a forger. Nevertheless, there remained plenty of food for the gallows. An incendiary, as well as a sheep-stealer, was liable to capital punishment; and so severely was the law strained upon these points, that he who set fire to a rick in a field, as well as he who found a half-dead sheep and carried it home, was condemned without mercy. But the advocates of mercy continued their good work until, finally, the gallows became the penalty for only those offenses which concerned human life and high treason.

The World as Will and Idea, Arthur Schopenhauer (1886)

An entirely different kind of proof of the same truth is afforded by the moral fact that while the law punishes poaching just as severely as theft, and in many countries more severely, yet civil honor, which is irrevocably lost by the latter, is really not affected by the former; but the poacher, if he has been guilty of nothing else, is certainly tainted with a fault, but yet is not regarded, like the thief, as dishonorable and shunned by all. For the principles of civil honor rest upon moral and not upon mere positive law; but game is not an object upon which labor is bestowed, and thus also is not an object of a morally valid possession: the right to it is therefore entirely a positive one, and is not morally recognized.

According to my view, the principle ought to lie at the basis of criminal law that it is not really the man but only the deed which is punished, in order that it may not recur. The criminal is merely the subject in whom the deed is punished, in order that the law in consequence of which the punishment is inflicted may retain its deterrent power. This is the meaning of the expression, "He is forfeited to the law." According to Kant's explanation, which amounts to a *jus talionis*, it is not the deed but the man that is punished. The penitentiary system also seeks not so much to punish the deed as the man, in order to reform him. It thereby sets aside the real aim of punishment, determent from the deed, in order to attain the very problematic end of reformation. But it is always a doubtful thing to attempt to attain two different ends by one means: how much more so if the two are in any sense opposite ends. Education is a benefit, punishment ought to be an evil; the penitentiary prison is supposed to accomplish both at once. Moreover, however large a share untutored ignorance, combined with outward distress, may have in many crimes, yet we dare not regard these as their principal cause, for innumerable persons living in the same ignorance and under absolutely similar circumstances commit no crimes. Thus the substance of the matter falls back upon the personal, moral character; but this, as I have shown in my prize essay on the freedom of the will, is absolutely unalterable. Therefore moral reformation is really not possible, but only determent from the deed through fear. At the same time, the correction of knowledge and the awakening of the desire to work

Moral reformation is really not possible, but only determent from the deed through fear.

can certainly be attained; it will appear what effect this can produce. Besides this, it appears to me, from the aim of punishment set forth in the text, that, when possible, the apparent severity of the punishment should exceed the actual: but solitary confinement achieves the reverse. Its great severity has no witnesses, and is by no means anticipated by anyone who has not experienced it; thus it does not deter. It threatens him who is tempted to crime by want and misery with the opposite pole of human suffering, ennui: but, as Goethe rightly observes—
"When real affliction is our lot, Then do we long for ennui."

The contemplation of it will deter him just as little as the sight of the palatial prisons which are built by honest men for rogues. If, however, it is desired that these penitentiary prisons should be regarded as educational institutions, then it is to be regretted that the entrance to them is only obtained by crimes, instead of which it ought to have preceded them.

That punishment, as Beccaria has taught, ought to bear a proper proportion to the crime does not depend upon the fact that it would be an expiation of it, but rather on the fact that the pledge ought to be proportionate to the value of that for which it answers. Therefore, everyone is justified in demanding the pledge of the life of another as a guarantee for the security of his own life, but not for the security of his property, for which the freedom, and so forth, of another is sufficient pledge. For the security of the life of the citizens capital punishment is therefore absolutely necessary. Those who wish to abolish it should be answered, "First remove murder from the world, and then capital punishment ought to follow." It ought also to be inflicted for the clear attempt to murder just as for murder itself; for the law desires to punish the deed, not to revenge its consequences. In general the injury to be guarded against affords the right measure for the punishment which is to he threatened, but it does not give the moral baseness of the forbidden action. Therefore the law may rightly impose the punishment of imprisonment for allowing a flowerpot to fall from a window, or impose hard labor for smoking in the woods during the summer, and yet permit it in the winter. But to impose the punishment of death, as in Poland, for shooting an ure-ox is too much, for the maintenance of the species of ure-oxen may not be purchased with human life. In determining the measure of the punishment, along with the magnitude of the injury to be guarded against, we have to consider the strength of the motives which impel to the forbidden action. Quite a different standard of punishment would be established if expiation, retribution, *jus talionis*, were its true ground. But the criminal code ought to be nothing but a register of counter-motives for possible criminal actions: therefore each of these motives must decidedly outweigh the motives which lead to these actions, and indeed so much the more the greater the evil is which would arise from the action to be guarded against, the stronger the temptation to it, and the more difficult the conviction of the criminal—always under the correct assumption that the will is not free, but determinable by motives—apart from this it could not be got at at all. So much for the philosophy of law.

On the Genealogy of Morals, Friedrich Nietzsche (1887)

To be entitled to pledge one's word, and to do it with pride, and also to be permitted to say "Yes" to oneself—that is a ripe fruit, as I have mentioned, but it is also a late fruit:—for what a long stretch of time this fruit must have hung tart and sour on the tree! And for an even much longer time it was impossible to see any such fruit—no one could have promised it would appear, even if everything about the tree was certainly getting ready for it and growing in that very direction!—"How does one create a memory for the human animal? How does one stamp something like that into this partly dull, partly flickering, momentary understanding, this living embodiment of forgetfulness, so that it stays current?" [. . .]

This ancient problem, as you can imagine, was not resolved right away with tender answers and methods. Indeed, there is perhaps nothing more fearful and more terrible in the entire prehistory of human beings than the technique for developing his memory. "We burn something in so that it remains in the memory. Only something which never ceases to cause pain remains in the memory"—

that is a leading principle of the most ancient (unfortunately also the longest) psychology on earth. We might even say that everywhere on earth nowadays where there is still solemnity, seriousness, mystery, and gloomy colors in the lives of men and people, something of that terror continues its work, the fear with which in earlier times everywhere on earth people made promises, pledged their word, made a vow.

The past, the longest, deepest, most severe past, breathes on us and surfaces in us when we become "solemn." When the human being considered it necessary to make a memory for himself, it never happened without blood, martyrs, and sacrifices, the most terrible sacrifices and pledges (among them the sacrifice of the first born), the most repulsive self-mutilations (for example, castration), the cruelest forms of ritual in all the religious cults (and all religions are in their deepest foundations systems of cruelty)—all that originates in that instinct which discovered in pain the most powerful means of helping to develop the memory. In a certain sense all asceticism belongs here: a couple of ideas are to be made indissoluble, omnipresent, unforgettable, "fixed," in order to hypnotize the entire nervous and intellectual system through these "fixed ideas"—and the ascetic procedures and forms of life are the means whereby these ideas are freed from jostling around with all the other ideas, in order to make them "unforgettable."

The worse humanity's "memory" was, the more terrible its customs have always appeared. The harshness of the laws of punishment, in particular, provide a standard for measuring how much trouble people went to in order to triumph over forgetfulness and to maintain a present awareness of a few primitive demands of social living together for this slave of momentary feelings and desires.

We Germans certainly do not think of ourselves as an especially cruel and hard-hearted people, even less as particularly careless people who live only in the present. But just take a look at our old penal code in order to understand how much trouble it takes on this earth to breed a "People of Thinkers" (by that I mean the European people among whom today we still find a maximum of trust, seriousness, tastelessness, and practicality, and who, with these characteristics, have a right to breed all sorts of European mandarins). These Germans have used terrible means to make themselves a memory in order to attain mastery over their vulgar basic instincts and their brutal crudity: think of the old German punishments, for example, stoning (the legend even lets the millstone fall on the head of the guilty person), breaking on the wheel (the most characteristic invention and specialty of the German genius in the realm of punishment!), impaling on a stake, ripping people apart or stamping them to death with horses ("quartering"), boiling the criminal in oil or wine (still done in the fourteenth and fifteenth centuries), the well-loved practice of flaying ("cutting flesh off in strips"), carving flesh out of the chest, and probably covering the offender with honey and leaving him to the flies in the burning sun.

With the help of such images and procedures people finally retained five or six "I will not's" in the memory, and, so far as these precepts were concerned, they gave their word in order to live with the advantages of society—and it's true! With the assistance of this sort of memory people finally came to "reason!"—Ah, reason, seriousness, mastery over emotions, this whole gloomy business called reflection, all these privileges and showpieces of human beings: how expensive they were! How much blood and horror is at the bottom of all "good things"!

[. . .] In order to give at least an idea of how uncertain, how belated, how accidental "the meaning" of punishment is and how one and the same procedure can be used, interpreted, or adjusted for fundamentally different purposes, let me offer here an example which presented itself to me on the basis of relatively little random material: punishment as a way of rendering someone harmless, as a prevention from further harm; punishment as compensation for the damage to the person injured, in some form or other (also in the form of emotional compensation); punishment as isolation of some upset to an even balance in order to avert a wider outbreak of the disturbance; punishment as way of inspiring fear of those who determine and carry out punishment; punishment as a sort of compensation for the advantages which the lawbreaker has enjoyed up until that time (for example, when he is made useful as a slave working in the mines); punishment as a cutting out of a degenerate element (in some circumstances an entire branch, as in Chinese law, and thus a means to keep the race pure or to sustain a social type); punishment as festival, that is, as the violation and humiliation of some enemy one has finally thrown down; punishment as a way of making a conscience, whether for the man who suffers the punishment— so-called "reform"—or whether for those who witness the punishment being carried out; punishment as the payment of an honorarium, set as a condition by those in power, which protects the wrongdoer from the excesses of revenge; punishment as a compromise with the natural condition of revenge, insofar as the latter is still upheld and assumed as a privilege by powerful families; punishment as a declaration of war and a war measure against an enemy to peace, law, order, and authority, which people fight with the very measures war makes available, as something dangerous to the community, as a breach of contract with respect to its conditions, as a rebel, traitor, and breaker of the peace.

Human, All Too Human, Friedrich Nietzsche (1878)

Executions (70)

How is it that every execution offends us more than a murder? It is the coldness of the judges, the painful preparations, the understanding that a man is here being used as a means to deter others. For guilt is not being punished, even if there were guilt; guilt lies in the educators, the parents, the environment, in us, not in the murderer--I am talking about the motivating circumstances.

Judge not (101)

When we consider earlier periods, we must be careful not to fall into unjust abuse. The injustice of slavery, the cruelty in subjugating persons and peoples, cannot be measured by our standards. For the instinct for justice was not so widely developed then. Who has the right to reproach Calvin of Geneva for burning Dr. Servet? His was a consistent act, flowing out of his convictions, and the Inquisition likewise had its reasons; it is just that the views dominant then were wrong and resulted in a consistency that we find harsh, because we now find those views so alien. Besides, what is the burning of one man compared to the eternal pains of hell for nearly everyone! And yet this much more terrible idea used to dominate the whole world without doing any essential damage to the idea of a god. In our own time, we treat political heretics harshly and

When we consider earlier periods, we must be careful not to fall into unjust abuse. The injustice of slavery, the cruelty in subjugating persons and peoples, cannot be measured by our standards.

cruelly, but because we have learned to believe in the necessity of the state we are not as sensitive to this cruelty as we are to that cruelty whose justification wee reject. Cruelty to animals, by children and Italians, stems from ignorance; namely, in the interests of its teachings, the church has placed the animal too far beneath man.

Likewise, in history much that is frightful and inhuman, which one would almost like not to believe, is mitigated by the observation that the commander and the executor are different people: the former does not witness his cruelty and therefore has no strong impression of it in his imagination; the latter is obeying a superior and feels no responsibility. Because of a lack of imagination, most princes and military leaders can easily appear to be harsh and cruel, without being so.

Egoism is not evil, for the idea of one's "neighbor" (the word has a Christian origin and does not reflect the truth) is very weak in us; and we feel toward him almost as free and irresponsible as toward plants and stones. That the other suffers must be learned; and it can never be learned completely.

A rewarding justice (105)

The man who has fully understood the theory of complete irresponsibility can no longer include the so-called justice that punishes and rewards within the concept of justice, if that consists in giving each his due. For the man who is punished does not deserve the punishment: he is only being used as the means to frighten others away from certain future actions; likewise, the man who is rewarded does not deserve this reward; he could not act other than as he did. Thus a reward means only an encouragement, for him and others, to provide a motive for subsequent actions: praise is shouted to the runner on the track not to the one who has reached the finish line. Neither punishment nor reward are due to anyone as his; they are given to him because it is useful, without his justly having any claims on them. One must say, "The wise man rewards not because men have acted rightly," just as it was said, "The wise man punishes not because men have acted badly, but so they will not act badly." If we were to dispense with punishment and reward, we would lose the strongest motives driving men away from certain actions and toward other actions; the advantage of man requires that they continue; and in that punishment and reward, blame and praise affect vanity most acutely, the same advantage also requires that vanity continue.

The Haymarket Tragedy, Eugene V. Debs (1887)

The trial of the Chicago anarchists created throughout the country the most profound attention. Chicago, more than New York or any other great American city, had been for a number of years the converging center for a set of restless and reckless spirits, under various names—"Anarchists," "Socialists," etc.—and their immunity from arrest or interference of any kind had emboldened them in the use of language in their papers, and public harangues, which indicated a disregard for law and order, and America, with her boasted liberty, free schools, manhood suffrage, freedom of speech and freedom of press, became as odious in the eyes of anarchists as Russia, Turkey, or any other despot-cursed country under heaven. These anarchists saw nothing, or little, in American institutions worthy of favorable consideration, saturated with ideas born of European methods of government, they assumed that every wrong perpetrated by individuals or corporations against the rights and interests of workingmen was fundamental, rather than superficial; that is to say that such wrongs are inherent in the principles upon which the government was founded, rather than innovations, at war with its spirit, and hence they sought to inculcate by speech and press, opposition to institutions, which, by their liberality, permitted them to openly and defiantly antagonize them.

It is by no means surprising that men holding such views of government should attract to themselves an exceedingly dangerous element, men whose passions, the outgrowth of ignorance, make them mad and blind, and who, with or without provocation, resort to murderous methods to accomplish their own, and the ruin of their associates. It must be remembered, in this connection, that Free Speech and Free Press are the twin glories of the American government. Strike them down, throttle them, murder them in court or on the battle field, and no matter by what captivating name the government is known, it is a despotism nevertheless, as odious and as infamous as was ever known on the earth, since the devil, serpent or Satan transformed Eden into a thorn-bearing wilderness. But free speech and a free press do not mean unlicensed devilishness, and on very many occasions the courts have been required to draw the line between license and licentiousness. Such cases, however, in this country, have related to the rights of individuals, communities, states, and the federal government, have seldom been involved, and never, we think, in time of peace.

The Chicago trial of the anarchists forms an exception, though in that trial there was a blending of charges of actual felony with the menace of social safety, and the condemnation to death is the first instance in the criminal records of the country when a jury adjudged that free speech could be carried to such excess as to make the death penalty a requirement, and justifiable by the laws of the land. Judge Gary, in his sentence condemning the anarchists to be hung, said: *"It is nowhere asserted or claimed that these prisoners threw the bomb, but that their doctrines, ideas, opinions and teachings prepared the way and led to the throwing of the bomb."*

We have italicized the extraordinary words of Judge Gary, because, since the prisoners did not throw the bomb which did the killing, they are to be hung for the expression of opinions which led to the murder. These prisoners did inveigh against the government, against the laws, against the policy and practice of corporations and monopolists, and the loose and often shameful administration of the laws. They saw, or thought they saw, monstrous wrongs which enslaved some while they enriched others. They saw rich criminals go unwhipped of justice, because they could, by the use of money or social influence, transform courts into tribunals, in which technicalities had the consideration and force of letter and spirit of the law, and under cover of which they escaped the penalties due their crimes, while the poor wretch, without money or friends, was made to suffer.

The righteous denunciations of such things has not been confined to Chicago anarchists, the stump, the rostrum, the forum and the press, has ceaselessly arraigned legislatures, congresses, and political parties as being parties to such flagitious practices as being venal and corrupt to the core. The press, and men of high repute, have declared that cities, where the people's representatives meet to enact laws are little less than Sodams, and that the institutions of the country were in peril of being overthrown by corruption in high places. Anarchists, whether foreigners or native born, have had ten thousand texts, glowing with denunciations of parties and the government, of "doctrines, ideas, opinions and teachings" well calculated to breed anarchists, but whoever thought of arresting the authors of such opinions, ideas and teachings, of trying them and condemning them to be imprisoned or hung, because of their insane and incendiary utterings."

The language of Judge Gary in sentencing the Chicago anarchists, is startling. It rings like an alarm bell. He said it was "nowhere asserted or claimed" that the anarchists "threw the bombs." They were not on trial for killing. They had committed no murderous act, but had proclaimed "doctrines, ideas, opinions and teachings" which "prepared the way and led to the throwing of the bombs," and for this exercise of free speech, carried to dangerous courts, they are condemned as worthy of death. With such a decision, unrevoked, what is the situation? What is the status of free men? What are the privileges of the press? A moment's reflection leaves the mind overwhelmed in confusion. The verdict of the Chicago jury and the language of Judge Gary effectually obliterates the line separating language and overt acts; that is to say, a word is equal to a blow or a bomb, not a word in itself felonious, but a word, an opinion, an idea, a doctrine, a "teaching," which prepares the way for the overt act.

There have been strikes which were the direct outgrowth of "doctrines, ideas, opinions and teachings," and in numerous instances these strikes have resulted in various grades of felony. The Chicago verdict and the language of Judge Gary does not distinguish between the men who committed the felony and those who harangued the people against chronic and flagrant wrongs. On the contrary, for the first time in American jurisprudence the astounding declaration is made that a difference does not exist.

"It is nowhere claimed," said Judge Gary, "that these prisoners threw the bomb." It was not claimed, it was not asserted, it was not proven, that they threw the bomb, but that they had expressed doctrines, opinions and ideas which led to the throwing of the bomb.

Let this verdict stand, let it become the practice of the courts, let it have popular approval, let it go unrevoked, and free speech is as dead in America as it is in Russia, and a free press becomes a haggard aggravating misnomer, as treacherous as a mirage or an *ignia fatuas*—dead sea fruit—which tempts but to deceive, and once endorsed, the pillars of our boasted temple of liberty disappear as if by a decree of Jehovah.

In this age it will not do to hang men for their doctrines, ideas, opinions and teachings, however dangerous they may be or may appear to be, and a moment's reflection will, we think, convince rational men that the proposition is impregnable against attack, no matter from what quarter it may come. We are by no means opposed to laws which punish men for the abuse of free speech. We are not in favor of mobs, mob rule or mob law. We are unalterably opposed to the teachings of anarchists—the bomb, the torch, the using of the weapons of assassins—but we would guard with ceaseless vigilance free speech and a free press, and could we speak with the tongue of an angel, we would not condemn a man to death for inveighing the wrongs which have crept into American methods of government.

In other words, if there is no law for hanging men for holding opinions, ideas, doctrines, and for teachings, we would not hang them for such things; and if an attempt were made to enact such a law we would oppose it with all the power of mind we could command. With such a law upon the statute books, the world would begin a retrograde movement, and despotism worse than anarchy, would be reinstated. If anarchists threaten the peace of society, we would restrain them, if they commit murder we would hang them. But the bare mention that teaching certain doctrines, or holding to certain opinions of government, we care not how monstrous, are worthy of the death penalty, if it does not thrill the American mind with alarm, then it must be confessed that the American mind has reached a point on the road to despotism far more alarming than any of the insane harangues made by the Chicago cranks. Nothing was ever gained in the way of suppressing ideas and opinions by hanging or burning men for ideas and opinions. Ideas and opinions escape the death penalty, the halter, the faggot and the wheel.

WITNESS TO AN EXECUTION
Haymarket Tragedy, Mother Jones (1925)

The first of May, which was to usher in the eight-hour day uprising, came. The newspapers had done everything to alarm the people. All over the city there were strikes and walkouts. Employers quaked in their boots. They saw revolution. The workers in the McCormick Harvester Works gathered outside the factory. Those inside who did not join the strikers were called scabs. Bricks were thrown. Windows were broken. The scabs were threatened. Someone turned in a riot call.

The police without warning charged down upon the workers, shooting into their midst, clubbing right and left. Many were trampled under horses' feet. Numbers were shot dead. Skulls were broken. Young men and young girls were clubbed to death.

The Pinkerton agency formed armed bands of ex-convicts and hoodlums and hired them to capitalists at eight dollars a day, to picket the factories and incite trouble.

On the evening of May 4th, the anarchists held a meeting in the shabby, dirty district known to later history as Haymarket Square. All about were railway tracks, dingy saloons and the dirty tenements of the poor. A half a block away was the Desplaines Street Police Station presided over by John Bonfield, a man without tact or discretion or sympathy, a most brutal believer in suppression as the method to settle industrial unrest.

Carter Harrison, the mayor of Chicago, attended the meeting of the anarchists and moved in and about the crowds in the square. After leaving, he went to the Chief of Police and instructed him to send no mounted police to the meeting, as it was being peacefully conducted and the presence of mounted police would only add fuel to fires already burning red in the workers' hearts. But orders perhaps came from other quarters, for disregarding the report of the mayor, the chief of police sent mounted policemen in large numbers to the meeting.

One of the anarchist speakers was addressing the crowd. A bomb was dropped from a window overlooking the square. A number of the police were killed in the explosion that followed.

The city went insane and the newspapers did everything to keep it like a madhouse. The workers' cry for justice was drowned in the shriek for revenge. Bombs were "found" every five minutes. Men went armed and gun stores kept open nights. Hundreds were arrested. Only those who had agitated for an eight-hour day, however, were brought to trial and a few months later hanged. But the man, Schnaubelt, who actually threw the bomb was never brought into the case, nor was his part in the terrible drama ever officially made clear.

The leaders in the eight hour day movement were hanged Friday, November the 11th. That day Chicago's rich had chills and fever. Rope stretched in all directions from the jail. Police men were stationed along the ropes armed with riot rifles. Special patrols watched all approaches to the jail. The roofs about the grim stone building were black with police. The newspapers fed the public imagination with stories of uprisings and jail deliveries.

But there were no uprisings, no jail deliveries, except that of Louis Lingg, the only real preacher of violence among all the condemned men. He outwitted the gallows by biting a percussion cap and blowing off his head.

The Sunday following the executions, the funerals were held. Thousands of workers marched behind the black hearses, not because they were anarchists but they felt that these men, whatever their theories, were martyrs to the workers' struggle. The procession wound through miles and miles of streets densely packed with silent people.

In the cemetery of Waldheim, the dead were buried. But with them was not buried their cause. The struggle for the eight hour day, for more human conditions and relations between man and man lived on, and still lives on.
Seven years later, Governor Altgeld, after reading all the evidence in the case, pardoned the three anarchists who had escaped the gallows and were serving life sentences in jail. He said the verdict was unjustifiable, as had William Dean Howells and William Morris at the time of its execution. Governor Altgeld committed political suicide by his brave action but he is remembered by all those who love truth and those who have the courage to confess it.

WITNESS TO AN EXECUTION
Hanging of Albert Parsons, Lucy Parsons (1889)

There is one man whose name and life was so intimately interwoven with one of the stirring periods of this country's history that that history could not be written if his name were omitted. That man is Gen. Ulysses S. Grant. His biographers record no act of his life with more praise than the magnanimous manner in which he treated the Rebel General, Lee, when the latter surrendered his sword to him. Suppose Grant had taken the proffered sword and stabbed his antagonist with it? There would have been no word too detestable to have attached to his name. Albert R. Parsons surrendered his sword to the wild mob of millionaires when he walked into Court and asked for a fair trial by a jury of his peers. Yet the proud State of Illinois murdered him under the guise of "Law and Order;" foully murdered this innocent man. And upon the heart of her then Governor (Oglesby), who completed the atrocity by ratifying the vile conspiracy conducted by the wild howls of the millionaire rabble, by signing the death warrants of men whom he, as a lawyer, knew were innocent, there is not "one damned spot," but five, to "out."

Thus it is that history repeats itself. In this case it was the old, old cry: "Away with them; they preach a strange doctrine! Crucify them!" But the grand cause for which they perished still lives. […]

Seditious writing and inflammatory speech are not murder, but capital punishment inflicted upon men for either offense is murder.

Had the Illinois rulings been good law in Jefferson's time he might have been hanged at any period in his active political career. He was an Anarchist. Not an amateur, speculative Anarchist, but a physical-force Anarchist, and an avowed enemy of Government. His biographers have tried to explain away the "no Government" theory of Jefferson, but that he cherished and advocated the theory cannot be denied. The following quotation is not from the *Arbeiter-Zeitung* nor the Alarm; it is from Jefferson's letter excusing the Massachusetts rebellion; not the rebellion against Great Britain, but the rebellion against the United States:

God forbid we should ever be twenty years without such a rebellion. What country can preserve its liberties if its rulers are not warned from time to time that this people preserve the spirit of resistance? Let them take arms. What signify a few lives lost in a century or two? The tree of liberty must be refreshed from time to time by the blood of patriots and tyrants. It is its natural manure. Did Fielden, Parsons, or Spies utter anything more sanguinary than that, or anything more Anarchical than this: [. . .]

He referred to his wife as a "lion-hearted" woman, said his children would not feel his loss on account of their youth, and favored the turn-key with snatches from the "Marseillaise," his favorite song of liberty and death to oppressors. On being asked if he wished stimulants he answered, "No." "I wish to go off sober," said Parsons, and perhaps the temperance people will be disposed to drop a single tear of sympathy in consequence.

The moment his feet touched the scaffold, Parsons seemed to completely lose his identity and to feel that his spirit was no longer a part of his body. He stood like one transfigured. Only he—the one American—seemed to realize to the full that he must die in a manner to impress, if possible, on all future generations the thought that he was a martyr. No tragedian that has paced a stage in America ever made a more marvelous presentation of a self-chosen part, perfect in every detail. The upward turn of his eyes, his distant, far-away look and, above all the attitude of apparent complete resignation that every fold of the awkward shroud only served to make more distinct, was by far the most striking feature of the entire gallows picture.

During the reading of the death warrant his face was a study. His eyes were unnaturally brilliant, but whatever emotion he felt was firmly checked by the indomitable spirit which had hitherto sustained him. He toyed carelessly with his mustache and let his eyes rest easily upon the objects about him. As the men moved forward Parsons turned to the Jenkinses of the press, who were scrutinizing every action, and said sarcastically: "Won't you come inside?"

When the halter was placed about his neck he never faltered. He stood erect, looking earnestly yet reproachfully at the people before him. The nooses wer? quickly adjusted, the caps pulled down, and a hasty movement made for the traps. Then from beneath the hoods came these words:

Spies: "There will be a time when our silence will be more powerful than the voices you strangle today!"

Fischer: "Hurrah for anarchy!"

Engel: "Hurrah for anarchy!"

Fischer: "This is the happiest moment of my life!"

Parsons: "Will I be allowed to speak, O men of America? Let me speak, Sheriff Matson! Let the voice of the people be heard!

O! But the signal had been given, and the officers of the State performed their mission by strangling both speakers and speech.

Facts And Laws Of The Moral Life, Wilhelm Wundt (1892)

Theories of Punishment

The notion of punishment is intimately connected with that of crime. Punishment is always an act of the social will; hence, more especially, of the will of the State, since it is the State that, as a rule, expresses and fulfils the will of the legal community. The judge and the executive officer are merely the organs of this social will. In other cases also, outside of the realm of law, punishment has the same general character: the father who punishes his child embodies the social will of the family, and the teacher represents in his punishments the social will of the educational community. There is no such thing as punishment inflicted by an individual will. This is just what constitutes the complete antithesis between punishment and the action punished, which usually proceeds from the will of an individual. The moment that punishment loses this character, and, whether in public life or, as frequently enough happens, in the family or the school, assumes a form that shows it to be a mere arbitrary act of the individual will, it ceases to be punishment, and becomes revenge or ill-treatment. These facts should be kept in mind as carefully as the fundamental motive of crime, if we are to avoid wrong views of the nature of punishment.

The most frequent form of error is where the acts of the social will are regarded from the same point of view as the conflict between individual wills. Punishment then becomes retribution. This is closely akin to revenge, and hence is often wholly identified with it,—always wrongly. Revenge meets the injury received with any kind of injury whatsoever in return; retribution measures the deed and its retaliatory deed against each other, requiting good for good and evil for evil; so that in both cases the amount of good or evil returned corresponds to the merit or demerit of the act. Hence the most perfect form of retributive punishment is the *jus talionis*, to which, as a matter of fact, it was reduced by the older theories of punishment, as well as by Kant, following their example. But how can the *jus talionis* be applied to actions like fraud, perjury, or treason to one's country? And would not the penal power of the State itself become immoral, if it undertook to punish the cruelty of murder with an equal cruelty?

Retribution is the principle of private life. There it governs all our intercourse with others. Hence, so long as punishment is regarded from the point of view of individual rights, which is always the case in the older theories of law, the notion of retribution, and, so far as it is practicable, the *jus talionis* itself, are the sole ruling principles. At this stage of development punishment is still a mere reaction of one individual will against another, as is shown by the fact that it leaves the very worst forms of evil to be dealt with by the avenging will of an individual or his kinsmen. The case is different where the social will is the conscious representative of the general conception of law. It stands so high that it cannot, inflict evil on the individual merely in order to square accounts with him for the evil he has done. Such a position simply transfers the standpoint of the individual will to the social will. Since punishment is and should be an evil, it continues to involve the element of retribution which at first constituted its whole nature; but this element does not exhaust the content of the notion. Retribution and punishment are conceptual spheres that overlap partially but not completely. Punishment ceases to be identical with retribution in proportion as it ceases to be an act of private revenge, and becomes an act of public authority. Hence the barbarous conclusions, to which the retributive theory leads, especially in its older forms, are to be rejected, not for the criminal's sake, but because hatred and revenge are emotions which should have no influence on the social will. The single fact that it is, or at least ought to be, dispassionate, constitutes the immense superiority of public legislation. The postulate maintained by philosophy and religion both, that judgments about right and wrong should never be disturbed by emotion, must remain a mere ideal for the individual will. But the social will can fulfill it approximately, if not completely.

> **Punishment ceases to be identical with retribution in proportion as it ceases to be an act of private revenge, and becomes an act of public authority.**

The retributive theory makes punishment an end in itself. If the act is atoned for, the balance which it originally disturbed is restored; any further results are at least outside the sphere of punishment as such. In this respect the theory agrees perfectly with a second conception, otherwise quite dissimilar— the theory of security. This is based on the view expressed in Spinoza's phrase, "Security is the virtue of a State, but freedom is a private virtue." While the retributive theory makes individual emotion the vehicle of punishment, here, on the contrary, it is held to be essential that the State should confront wrongdoing in a wholly dispassionate spirit; hence judging it, one might say, not by its moral significance, but merely with reference to the degree in which the criminal endangers public safety. Security is to be ensured by punishments involving restraint on personal liberty; such punishments being sufficient, according to some theorists, for the majority of cases, and according to others, for all. Thus it is requisite that the punishment should last until the danger is in all probability removed. Evidently the result of this theory would be to mete out punishment, not according to the gravity of the offense, but according to the likelihood of future offenses of a similar kind.

The wife murderer, who has once for all attained his end by his action, the official who has embezzled funds and whose removal from office has destroyed his chance for further peculations, might be allowed to go at liberty; while, on the other hand, tramps and petty rascals, of whom the judge can confidently prophesy that they will steal and beg again at the next opportunity, would have to be locked up for life. It is evident that a theory so absolutely inconsistent with our moral sentiment and with the general notion of punishment must lead to error. But it seems to me that this inconsistency makes it impossible for us to predicate of the theory of security even that partial truth which belongs to the retributive theory. Punishment does not undertake to serve the end of security at all: it leaves that to the police and to the private vigilance of each individual. If it were the task of penal justice to render innocuous all those subjects who tended to become dangerous by reason of inclination to crime, habitual carelessness, propensity to drink, mental derangement and the like, then the population of a country might be divided into two classes: the one sitting under lock and key and the other keeping guard.

Conscious of this weakness in its position, the protective theory usually seeks further support by associating itself with another conception of punishment, which may also exist independently—the theory, namely, of reformation. What distinguishes this view favorably from the two preceding is the fact that it makes punishment a means to the attainment of a further end, and not an end in itself. The school of Krause, which made an especial point of the reformatory theory in its propaganda, requires that punishment be executed with direct reference to this end. It aims to bring the offender to a consciousness of the immorality of his life by teaching and moral exhortation. Of course there is nothing to be said against such efforts, so long as they are combined with punishment. But if the whole conception of punishment is exhausted in them, it ceases altogether to be punishment, that is, an evil, and thereby loses a large portion of the moral effect that it is intended to produce. When the reformatory and protective theories are combined, the next step is to make the degree of reformation attained the standard of our judgments as to whether further restraints on the criminal's freedom are necessary or superfluous. If one of the objects of punishment, reformation, is reached, the other, the security of society, follows as a matter of course. If the most dangerous of assassins has given convincing proof that he will lead a good life from now on, why should we hesitate to release him? How such proof can be obtained is another question. Requiring prison officials to take a course in criminal psychology would hardly meet the difficulty. As a matter of fact, the greatest connoisseur of human nature in the world could not predict with any degree of probability whether the promises of good behavior, made in all good faith by the culprit in prison, would really be kept under the wholly different circumstances of freedom. Moreover, since it is a well-known fact that honest repentance is oftener found among great than among petty criminals, the absurd result of this proposition, even if it were practicable, would probably be the liberation of assassins and poisoners after a brief period of custody, and the maintenance of beggars and footpads all their lives in prison at the expense of society.

Finally, the deterrent theory of punishment accords with the reformatory theory in regarding punishment as a means rather than an end, however differently it may conceive the essential nature of punishment. It agrees with the protective theory in maintaining that punishment exists not for the sake of the criminal, but for that of society. The murderer is executed, the thief imprisoned, to set an example. Aside from the fact, proved by statistics, that this result is not, as a rule, attained, since crimes tend rather to increase than to diminish in number and cruelty in proportion to the cruelty and publicity of executions, it is essentially absurd to attempt to influence by punishment a third person rather than the individual punished. The basis of this conception is apparently failure to discriminate between the existence of the legal order in general and the special cases of its application. The fact that the State has penal power is, indeed, not to be underestimated in its importance for public morality. It is the most forcible means of making the individual realize that his will is subject to a social will, and this consciousness is a prerequisite to the efficacy of all the special moral motives. But such a realization on the individual's part is quite independent of the manner in which the penal power is administered. It deters from crime, not because the latter as a particular act is met by a particular punishment, but because crime contravenes the conduct of life that is publicly sanctioned and operates in the individual conscience as the imperatives of constraint. When conscience has once been silenced, the fear of punishment is powerless. Moreover, in accordance with the universal tendency of human nature to believe what it desires, almost every criminal beguiles himself into disregard of this consideration by confidently hoping to escape discovery.

The Case Against Capital Punishment
B. Paul Neuman (1889)

1) As to the certainty of application.

"If it were possible," says Sir Samuel Romilly, "that punishment, as the consequence of guilt, could be reduced to absolute certainty, a very slight penalty would be sufficient to prevent almost every species of crime except those which arise from sudden gusts of ungovernable passion."

The converse of this proposition appears to hold good. Where the penalty is very heavy its incident is apt to become erratic and uncertain. Of all punishments used by civilized nations the punishment of death is most open to this objection. Under the old law, when death was inflicted for minor offences, this feature was even more apparent than it is at the present day. Mr. Harmer, a solicitor with a very large Old Bailey practice, said, when examined before a parliamentary committee in 1819:

"The instances, I may say, are innumerable, within my own observation, of jurymen giving verdicts in capital cases in favor of the prisoner directly contrary to the evidence. I have seen acquittals in forgery where the verdict astonished every one in court, because the guilt appeared unequivocal, and the acquittal could only be attributed to a strong feeling of sympathy and humanity in the jury to save a fellow creature from certain death. The old professed thieves are aware of this sympathy, and are desirous of being tried rather on capital indictments than otherwise."

The late Sergeant Parry on a subsequent occasion gave the following evidence:

"It is a common observation in our profession that there is nothing more difficult than to obtain a verdict of guilty from a jury where the charge is murder. It has frequently occurred that the jury have asked—Can we find a verdict of manslaughter? No, you cannot. And the prisoner is allowed to go free."

It may be objected that such evidence as this has no application at the present day, but it is easy to supplement it from more recent sources. In the course of a recent debate in the House of Commons, Sir Colman O'Loghlen said he had within the last forty-eight hours prosecuted a man in County Cork, about whose conviction, but for the penalty of death, he felt certain, but who, as it was, was acquitted. Every one of the Crown solicitors on the Munster Circuit, and, he believed, the majority of the judges, were of opinion that if capital punishment were done away with the number of convictions would be increased. The experiment of doing away with capital punishment has been tried in several of the American States, and the result throws a light upon the subject which only inveterate bigotry or stolid prejudice could venture to disregard. Take, for instance, the case of Wisconsin.

Writing to Mr. John Bright in 1864, the Governor of that State thus expresses himself:

"The evil tendency of public executions, the great aversion of many to the taking of life, rendering it almost impossible to obtain jurors from the more intelligent portion of the community, the liability of the innocent to suffer so extreme a penalty, and be placed beyond the reach of the pardoning power, and the disposition of courts and juries not to convict, fearing the innocent might suffer, convinced me that this relic of barbarism should be abolished. The death penalty was repealed in 1853. No legislation has since reestablished it, and the people find themselves equally secure."

Some years later, in 1873, we find this passage in Governor Washburne's message:

"There can be no doubt that the change in the law has made punishment more certain, and I but express the opinion of those who have most carefully considered the question, when I state that but for that change in the law, at least one half of those convicted would have escaped all punishment—so difficult is conviction when the punishment is death."

Reverting to 1864, the Governor of Michigan writes :

"Before the abolition of the death penalty murders were not unfrequent, but convictions were rarely or never obtained. It became the common belief that no jury could be found (the prisoner availing himself of the common law right of challenge) which would convict. There can be no doubt that public opinion sustains the present law, and is against the restoration of the death penalty. Conviction and punishment are now much more certain than before the change was made."

Similarly, the Chief Justice of Rhode Island, where the death penalty has also been abolished, writes :

"My observation fully justifies me in saying that conviction for murder is far more certain now in proper cases than when death was the punishment of it."

(2) As to susceptibility of graduation.

It is hardly necessary to say that scarcely any two instances of the same species of crime show precisely the same degree of turpitude; motive, provocation, surrounding circumstances, age, character, all have to be taken into consideration in estimating the amount of punishment requisite. Hence the need for graduation in the punishment. Simple imprisonment, hard labor, penal servitude, even the lash are all capable of more or less accurate graduation. Nowhere is there greater room for difference in the degree of guilt than in the case of murder, and yet the punishment inflicted is one and the same in every case. In some cases, indeed, even death may be a severer punishment to one man than to another. To a man brought up in the higher ranks of society the social infamy and the personal degradation may add a sting to the punishment which may be entirely absent in the case of one less fortunate in his birth. But this distinction which in other punishments can be taken into account and allowed for, operates, in the case of death, altogether independently of the judge. Hence it may, and no doubt often has happened, that the punishment has borne most heavily where the guilt was lightest.

(3) As to revocability.

Here again it is perfectly obvious that of all punishments, that of death is, tried by this standard, the most unsatisfactory. For although it is perfectly true that in one sense all punishment is irrevocable as soon as it has commenced to operate, yet in every other case, as long as the victim is alive, it is possible either to remit a portion of the sentence or to make substantial reparation. If, therefore, it can be shown that there is an appreciable danger of so fatal a miscarriage of justice, most people would freely admit that the case against capital punishment is a very serious one. The risk of such a miscarriage might, no doubt, be lessened by the adoption of that simple measure of reform which for so many years has clamored vainly at our gates—the creation of a Court of Criminal Appeal. Even then, however, the danger would not be removed, and the argument against capital punishment would to many minds still remain overwhelming.

Now, what are the facts of the case?

Some time ago, Sir James Mackintosh, a most cool and dispassionate observer, declared that, taking a long period of time, one innocent man was hanged in every three years. The late Chief Baron Kelly stated as the result of his experience that from 1802 to 1840 no fewer than twenty-two innocent men had been sentenced to death, of whom seven were actually executed. These terrible mistakes are not confined to England: Mittermaier refers to cases of a similar kind in Ireland, Italy, France, and Germany. In comparatively recent years there have been several striking instances of the fallibility of the most carefully constituted tribunals. In 1865, for instance, an Italian named Pelizzioni was tried before Baron Martin for the murder of a fellow-countryman in an affray at Saffron Hill. After an elaborate trial he was found guilty, and sentenced to death. In passing sentence the Judge took occasion to make the following remarks, which should always be remembered when the acumen begotten of a "sound legal training" and long experience is relied on as a safeguard against error:

"In my judgment it was utterly impossible for the jury to have come to any other conclusion. The evidence was about the clearest and the most direct that after a long course of experience in the administration of criminal justice I have ever known . . . I am as satisfied as I can be of anything that Gregorio did not inflict this wound, and that you were the person who did. "

The trial was over. The Home Secretary would most certainly, after the Judge's expression of opinion, never have interfered. The date of the execution was fixed. Yet the unhappy prisoner was guiltless of the crime, and it was only through the exertions of a private individual that an innocent man was saved from the gallows. A fellow-countryman of his, a Mr. Negretti, succeeded in persuading the real culprit (the Gregorio so expressly exculpated by the Judge) to come forward and acknowledge the crime. He was subsequently tried for manslaughter and convicted, while Pelizzioni received a free pardon.

Again in 1877 two men named Jackson and Greenwood were tried at the Liverpool Assizes for a serious offense. They were found guilty. The Judge expressed approval of the verdict and sentenced them to ten years' penal servitude. Subsequently fresh facts came to light and the men received a free pardon.

Once more, in 1879, Habron was tried for the murder of a policeman. He was found guilty and sentenced to death. An agitation for a reprieve immediately followed. The sentence was commuted to penal servitude for life. Three years after, the notorious Peace, just before his execution for the murder of Mr. Dyson, confessed that he had committed the murder for which Habron had been sentenced.

With these incidents fresh in our minds, let us turn once more to *St. Giles and St. James*, and listen to the indignant words of Douglas Jerrold:

"Oh that the ghosts of all the martyrs of the Old Bailey—and though our profession of faith may make moral antiquarians stare, it is our invincible belief that the Newgate Calendar has its black array of martyrs; victims to ignorance, perverseness, prejudice; creatures doomed by the bigotry of the council table; by the old haunting love of blood as the best of cures for the worst of ills—oh that the faces of all of these could look from Newgate walls! That but for a moment the men who stickle for the laws of death as for some sweet domestic privilege, might behold the grim mistake; the awful sacrilegious blunder of the past, and seeing, make amendment for the future."

WITNESS TO AN EXECUTION
Execution of Kemmler, Auburn State Prison (1890)

Doubtless he knew that his words will go down in history and he had his lesson well learned. He addressed his audience [in] a commonplace way and without hesitation.

"Well, gentleman, I wish everyone good luck in this world, and I think I am going to a good place, and the papers have been sa[yi]ng a lot of stuff that isn't so. That's all I have to say."

And so with a parting shot at what he was good enough to refer to not long ago as "those d—d reporters," William Kemmler took his leave of earth. The quiet demeanor of the man as he entered had made a strong impression on those in the room. His self-possession after his oratorical effort simply amazed them. He got up out of his chair as though he were anxious to try the experiment, not as though he courted death, but as though he was thoroughly prepared for it. [...]

There was no delay. Kemmler constantly encouraged the workers at the straps with "Take your time; don't be in a hurry; do it well; be sure everything is all right." He did not speak with any nervous apprehension.

Warden Durston leaned over, drawing the buckle of the straps about the arm. "It won't hurt you, Bill," he said, "I'll be with you all the time."

A minute later Kemmler said, "There's plenty of time." He said it as calmly as the conductor of a streetcar might have encouraged a passenger not to hurry.

Kemmler was pinioned so close that he could hardly have moved a muscle except those of his mouth.

The Warden took a last look at the straps. "This is all right," he said.

"All right," said Dr. Spitzka, and then bent over and said, "God bless you,

Kemmler."

"Thank you," said the little man, quietly.

"Ready?" said the Warden.

"Ready," answered the doctors.

"Goodbye," said the Warden to Kemmler. There was no response.

Gave The Signal.

The Warden stepped to the door leading into the next room. It was then forty-three and one-half minutes past six o'clock by the prison clock. "Everything is ready," said the Warden to some one hidden from view in the next room. The answer came like a flash in the sudden convulsion that went over the frame of the chair. If it seemed rigid before under the influence of the straps, it was doubly so now has it strained against them.

The seconds ticked off. Dr. McDonald, who was holding the stop-watch, said "Stop."

Two voices near him echoed, "Stop."

The Warden stepped to the door of the next room and repeated the word "Stop."

As the syllable passed his lips the forehead of the man in the chair grew dark in color, while his nose, or so much of it as was exposed, appeared a dark red.

There was very little apparent relaxation of the body, however. A fly lighted on the nose and walked about unconcernedly. The witnesses drew nearer to the chair.

"He's dead," said Spitzka, authoritatively.

"Oh, yes, he's dead," said McDonald.

"You'll notice," said Spitzka, "the post-mortem appearance of the nose immediately. There is that remarkable change that cannot be mistaken for anything else, that remarkable appearance of the nose."

The other doctors nodded assent. They looked at the body critically for a minute and then Spitzka said, "John, undo that now. The body can be taken to the hospital."

"Well, I can't let you gentlemen out of here until I have your certificates," said the Warden.

Found Signs Of Life.

It was while this businesslike conversation was going on that Dr. Balch made a discovery.

"McDonald," he cried, "McDonald, look at that rupture," he pointed at the abrasion of the skin on Kemmler's right thumb. In the contraction of the muscles the figurehead scraped against it and removed the skin, and from that little wound blood was flowing—an almost certain indication of life.

A low cry of horror went through the assemblage.

"Turn on the current," excitedly cried Dr. Spitzka. "This man is not dead."

The crowd fell back from the chair, as though they were in danger. The Warden sprang into the closed door and pounded on it with his hand.

"Start the current!" he cried. As he spoke of fluid began to drop from Kemmler's mouth and to run down his beard; a groaning sound came from his lips, repeated and growing louder each time.

It seemed an age before the card was again turned on. In fact it was just seventy-three seconds from the end of the first contact when the first sound was heard to issue from Kemmler's lips, and it was not more than a half minute] before the card was again turned on.

Recovering Consciousness.

But every second to that time the horrible sound from those groaning lips was becoming more distinct, a straining of the chest against the leather harness stronger and more evident.

The man was coming to life. The spectators grew faint and sick. Men] who had stood over dead and dying men and had cut men to pieces without an emotion grew pale and turned their heads away.
One witness was forced to lie down while one of the doctors fanned him.

But the end came at last. There was another convulsion of the body, and … it became rigid with the rigidity of iron.

"That man wasn't dead," cried Spitzka excitedly. As he spoke the body twitched again. The electrician had given the current gain new alternation and now 2,000 volts were playing in short, successive shocks down Kemmler spine. The sound ceased with the first convulsion, but the fluid continued to trip from the mouth and down the beard, making the body a sickening spectacle.

"Keep it on now until he's killed," said one of the doctors.

"Keep it on! Keep it on!" Cried Warden Durston through the door.

Silence reigned for a moment. A bell without began to toll solemnly.

Burned By The Current.

Then from the chair came a sizzling sound, as of meat cooking on hand. Following it immediately a billow of smoke came from the body and filled the air of the room with the odor of burning hair.

There was a cry from all the members of the little group, and Warden Durston cried through the door leading to the next room to turn the current off.

The Crime Of Capital Punishment,
Hugh O. Pentecost (1890)

It is a constant amazement to persons awake to the enormity of the offense, that capital punishment continues to be practised in what are called civilized countries. Every consideration of public decency, social morals, ordinary humanity, and plain common sense calls for its abrogation.

It does not prevent or tend to prevent crime. It not infrequently happens that during the week or upon the very day of an execution a murder is committed almost under the nose of the executioner.

Four men were recently hanged in New York, to the scandal of the world. Each had killed a woman—his wife or his mistress. The execution was the talk of the whole country for weeks before it occurred. Everyone knew about it. It was particularly horrible because of the large number of men who were slaughtered. If ever an execution was calculated to strike preventive terror to the heart of a prospective murderer, this one was. But there were two women murdered in New York State within two days of that execution, and the famous Luca murder occurred at about the same time.

The fear of the gallows does not tend to prevent murder committed in the heat of passion, as most murders are committed, nor to restrain the deliberate murderer, because he believes that he can conceal his deed. Both in theory and in fact it can be shown to those who are willing to see it, that capital punishment does not prevent or tend to prevent the commission of crime.

Capital punishment is an offense to enlightened thought and well-educated conscience because it is a measure of revenge, a sentiment which no person or people should harbor. It is said by apologists, that the theory of legal killing is not that of revenge, but that the killing is done merely as a warning to evil-doers and for the safety of society. But this is an afterthought, an explanation which the growing humane sentiment of the people is forcing from the barbarians who defend and practice murder by law. The real reason for capital punishment is that it is commonly supposed that one who commits murder "deserves to die." When the idea of revenge is eliminated from our habits of thought with regard to criminals, capital punishment will be esteemed an act of brutality which no community would think of permitting. When we come to clearly understand that the worse criminal a man is, the more it is our duty to deluge him with moral sympathy and help, the more clearly we shall see that the main motive for capital punishment is revenge; because, as I have already said, an execution is neither a warning to possible criminals nor a protection to society.

On the contrary, it unquestionably tends to brutalize the minds of the people and familiarize them with the thought of killing. As long as the State employs persons for the express purpose of murdering men, those who are not officially employed and paid for it will also engage in the business.

Every judge who sentences a fellow being to death, every juryman who votes for a verdict of death against a fellow being, every sheriff who carries out the sentence, every hangman who actually springs the drop, every priest or minister who assists at an execution, preparing the criminals for death by teaching them that in submitting to the crime about to be committed upon them they are conforming themselves to that which God approves, is a murderer; none the less so because they act in accordance with the statute law and social custom. Some of the most horrible crimes against humanity are committed according to statute law and common custom. And as long as some of these legal murderers are admitted to our best society, and highly honored because of the murderous offices they fill, and all of them except the wretched hangman are quite respectable, murder never will be looked upon with the abhorrence it should produce in every mind.

Wherein is the sense of legally killing a man? Does his murder restore his victim to life ? Is it right, can it be right, because one murder has been committed that another should be? A tippling Catholic priest is under sentence of death by hanging in Raleigh, N. C., charged with (although it was by no means absolutely proved) committing an outrageous assault upon a young woman. What good end will be served by hanging the man, even if he is guilty? His crime, if he committed it, was very awful, but will the maiden be any different than she is if her alleged or real assailant is hanged for the offense? There is no sense in hanging the man except for revenge, and that is a motive which cannot be defended among a civilized people. One would think that the outraged girl herself would plead for the life of the wretch who wronged her, rather than willingly go through life with the ceaseless memory that a man had been shamefully killed on her account.

I have no sympathy whatever with that sentimentality that transforms a person into a hero because he is a murderer. Carrying bouquets to criminals because they are criminals is as silly as it is unfit. A criminal should be made to feel in every possible way that, as a criminal, he has forfeited all right to the respect of his fellows. Neither have I any sympathy with the practice of carrying tracts and delivering religious homilies to criminals. There is no reason why a murderer should be rewarded for his deed by clusters of roses, or compelled to endure the dreary preaching of persons who enjoy rubbing their religion into sinners upon every possible occasion. A murderer is not worthy to be crowned with flowers, and very few of us are good enough to lecture him. We may not be murderers but we are probably not good enough to sit in judgment upon those who are. I do not believe in treating murderers to sentimental gush, or boring them with religious humbug. But neither do I think we should, from the time a man commits his crime until he expiates it on the gallows, show him nothing but the hard, vindictive side of humanity. From the moment a murder is committed, society, in the person of its policemen and prosecuting attorney, becomes a pitiless bloodhound. Clubs, handcuffs, and prison bars fill the criminal's horizon. No pity is shown him. No attempt is made to awaken the good that is in him. No effort is made to redeem him. Society becomes solely an avenger; pitiless, remorseless, thirsting for blood. The human heart turns to ice. The human hand is withheld. The human eye is averted. The human voice grows hard and dry. Society turns into an engine of death, with no more feeling than the cold blade of a guillotine.

It is no wonder that criminals become hard after the steel hand of the law once grips them. It is no wonder that so many criminals fold their arms across their stolid breasts and coolly look judge, jury, and executioner in the face, before they die, with apparent unconcern. We take all this as evidence of their bad natures, and are glad that such base beings are well hanged. We forget that no matter how brutal the murder that one man commits may be, it cannot be as cold-blooded, as base, as heartless, as the judicial murder that is conducted with all the deliberate formality of the law. The deeds of "Jack the Ripper " are fearful and cruel, but they are not so fiendish as that form of murder which conducts a human being through days, weeks, or months, of mental torture preliminary to a deliberate and heartless death at the hands of the hangman.

One of the worst phases of capital punishment, to my mind, is the invariable presence upon the scaffold, as the general assistant of the hangman, of a Christian priest or minister. At every scaffold there is a strange and significant union of Church and State. The State is there in the person of the hangman. The Church is there in the person of the priest or minister. It is the old familiar scene of the State doing deeds of violence and blood in the name of law and order, and with the sanction and concurrence of religion. It is the old combination of the secular arm doing that of which the representative of an ignoble hypothetical God approves. It is a junction of two terrible engines of unhappiness and tyranny — superstition and physical force.

It may be said that to speak of the ministers of religion in this connection and in these terms is unfair, but I think not. Most ministers of the Christian religion are upholders of capital punishment, as they are of every respectable infamy. They cooperate with the "machinery of justice " in preparing the victim of revenge for the slaughter. They are very useful coadjutors, too, because they quiet the victim's mind and, no doubt, prevent many distressing exhibitions of fear which would help to bring legal killing into disrepute. At the last execution in New York, the officiating priest actually led one of the condemned men under the noose. The poor wretch was sick with fright and likely to fall down, but the priest did part of the hangman's work for him by leading the man to the shambles to be choked to death.

It is a mystery to me how these pretended disciples of one who was himself cruelly murdered by law, and who was the very apostle of love and gentleness, can engage in this horrible business. Jesus taught that if one should smite us upon one cheek we should turn to him the other, a doctrine as wise as it is humane; that if one forcibly took our overcoat we should give him our undercoat; that we should in all ways return good for evil; that we should forgive those who injure us an indefinite number of times. The whole tenor of his teaching and practice was against everything that looked toward capital punishment. And yet his pretended disciples, the priests and ministers, take part in all the hangings, and I have yet to hear of one who ever walked out upon the scaffold and uttered his protest against the bloody performance as entirely shameful, and particularly so when practiced by a people who claim to be at least partially civilized. Instead of doing this, they do everything they can to make the prisoners feel that in quietly submitting to be murdered they are only accepting a visitation of just punishment that has come upon them by the desire of their Heavenly Judge who is also their Heavenly Father. One of the kind of fathers, it may be supposed, who takes his child into a back room and assures him that it is very painful to be obliged to flog him, and that in doing so he will hurt himself far more than he will hurt the child, and then proceeds to give the child a beating that the brute nature of the father thoroughly enjoys. No doubt these Christian priests and ministers, many of whom are estimable persons, are quite unconscious of the shameful business in which they engage, but it is none the less a fact that they are simply the hangman's assistants.

It is gratifying to know that there is slowly growing a genuine repugnance to hanging, if not to capital punishment altogether. Cases of persons having been hanged who were afterward discovered to have been innocent; cases like the man who has just been set at liberty from Auburn prison, after having been thirty-seven years serving a life sentence, commuted from hanging, it being now discovered that he is innocent; cases of bungling at the gallows, the breaking of the rope, the struggles of the strangling men, the tearing of a victim's head half off, as recently occurred, the blood ripping down on the scaffold; such specific things, added to the general horror of the performance, are gradually helping to awaken the sluggish sensibilities of the people to an appreciation of the enormity of the outrage that is being perpetrated upon the common sense and moral nature of the people in the name of law, order, and religion. It is gradually being felt that hanging is at least vulgar, if not wicked, and some other method of human slaughter is being sought for. In New York State, killing by electricity has been adopted, and one man is already condemned to die in that manner. This certainly seems to be more in keeping with the scientific spirit of the age in which we live, and it has an air of respectability about it that hanging has not, but, in my opinion, it is a more ghastly method of judicial murder than hanging. It is, in fact, a killing device that rivals in horror the worst tortures of the worst ages of the world. A chair is to be constructed, a reclining chair, in cruel imitation of those chairs that are used for restful comfort. Into this chair the person is to be strapped, to prevent his making any unseemly gestures with his legs or arms in case the treatment makes him nervous, or to prevent his leaving the chair entirely if it should occur to him that the attentions of the legal killer were distasteful. After being strapped into the chair, and tickled a little with an electric current for the highly amusing purpose of discovering, by means of the Wheatstone bridge, how much of the fatal fluid will be required to kill him, bandages are to be placed upon the victim's head, which member will have been previously shaved, and also upon other portions of the body, perhaps the feet. To these appliances are to be attached the ends of the wires that are to convey the killing fluid. When everything is ready the executioner will touch a button and the wretched mortal will be shot with a stream of electricity, a stream of fire seven times hotter than fire is wont to be. The creature may have deep holes burned into him without killing him. He may have to be finally knocked in the head with an axe. He may be slowly burned to death in the chair, his body reduced to a charred cinder — murdered and cremated at the same time. Or, if the killing machine works as it is hoped that it will, in one moment of anguish, his life will go out.

Now, supposing this wicked contrivance works to the charm of the detestable person who could be tempted by money to devise and construct it, think of the mental torture to which the condemned person is put! The victim of the common murderer is not forced to thus horribly anticipate death. He is not obliged to sit in a chair and see and hear his worse than Quilp-like slayer making, in cold blood, the preparation for his death. And then consider, too, that by the new contrivance this victim of the State is to meet his death in silence and alone. There are to be no witnesses of the grim and dastardly deed; no reporters, no crowd of special constables, no little group of spectators such as always at scenes of hanging enable the dying men to feel that they are in company in their last moments. There will be no expectation that thousands of persons will read the full account of the event the next day. There will be no sustaining sense of being the center of interest for an hour, at least. This new kind of judicial murder is to be done in secret, and anyone who is familiar with the stories of torture that come to us from the dark ages knows that there were very few of the brave victims of torture in those days who could endure the suffering in solitude.

This new system of judicial murder seems to me worse than the roastings of the savages, worse than the burnings, and pinchings, and stretchings of the Inquisition; worse than these if for no other reason than that it is to be practiced by those who claim to be enlightened, civilized beings. Nevertheless, there are some favorable points about it, one of which is that it is the result of a demand that there shall be a change in the manner of our killing; and another is that henceforth in one State judicial killing will be done in secret. This is a tacit confession that it must be done hereafter in secret or not much longer at all. When the State begins to be ashamed of what it does the practice is doomed, you may be sure.

It may now be asked what form of punishment should be substituted for the death penalty. It is not necessary to my purpose in writing this article that I should dwell upon that subject at all. This article is written mainly for the purpose of protesting against the crime of capital punishment, and not for the purpose of explaining what can or should be substituted for it. It will not, however, be out of place to say that the most natural substitute for the death penalty, under our form of government, would be imprisonment for a term sufficiently long to demonstrate that the offender might be safely allowed to go free. It is just as vicious, of course, to imprison a man for revenge, as to hang him for revenge. There is, therefore, no valid reason why a murderer should be punished at all. It is right that he should be apprehended and confined until it is determined whether he is of such a nature or disposition as to be likely to commit more murders. But if this view of the case is too nearly in accordance with humane considerations to suit this cruel and bloodthirsty age, then the obvious mode of punishment to substitute for judicial killing is imprisonment at hard labor for life. This is far too cruel a punishment to visit upon anyone for any crime done under the impulse of passion, but among a people who so frequently say: "Hanging is too good for him," and who are so given to lynching, it is as much of a modification of our present practice as we could expect to get.

It would be far better for society if instead of speculating on the forms of punishment we turned our attention to the means of preventing the crimes for which we punish the offenders. It has been observed that most of the murders occur among the poor people, and upon the top floors of tenement houses; that is to say, among the poorest of the poor. The connection between poverty and the crime of murder, like the connection between poverty and all other crime, is demonstrably close. If we could cure the social disease of poverty, the seeds of crime would be destroyed. The people rarely think of this. They think it is our business to punish crime; but it is our best business to prevent it. Our present organization of society manufactures criminals faster than we can possibly take care of them. Poverty degrades men; it robs them of leisure, which is absolutely necessary for the development of mind, and the proper control of the passions; it keeps the people hungry and fierce; it imbrutes them; it makes Ishmaels of them — their hand is against society as the hand of society is against them. Plant a generation of paupers, and you will reap a crop of criminals.

If we are wise, we will turn our attention to the most important problem of this or any age: how to so enrich the people that the temptations to crime will be minified to the last possible degree. The solution of the problem is as simple as it is important. For every millionaire we shall have a thousand tramps; for every monopolist we shall have a hundred burglars; for every woman who lives in idleness upon the fruit of others' toil, filched from them under the name of interest or rent, we shall have a score of prostitutes; for every vacant land owner and money limiter — the twin man-starvers — we shall have a murderer. One is the seed from which the other grows. Eliminate your monopolists, the king of whom is the owner of vacant land, and your problem of crime is settled. With open opportunities for men to apply their labor to natural wealth productions, tenfold more wealth would be produced and equitably distributed; and with wealth many times multiplied and equitably distributed, a criminal would be more of a curiosity than the original three-toed horse.

But we need not wait for the disappearance of criminals before we abolish the death penalty for crime.

Anarchy and its Heroes, Cesare Lombroso (1897)

In principle, I am not opposed to the death penalty when that penalty guarantees the life of many people. Nevertheless, I think it would be better not to apply it in the case of anarchists. If it is necessary to suppress born criminals or criminals like Navaho, who hide behind the anarchist mask, on the other hand we must avoid the application of the death penalty to anarchists like Vaillant, among whom the tendency to evil is cloaked in an altruistic form and who, even with their violent thirst for the new, can render service to humanity.

In any event, the suppression of anarchists would have no practical effect, for fanatics and neuropaths don't retreat before punishment. On the contrary, it is punishment that enflames their imagination and as we saw after the attacks in Barcelona and Paris, the too-severe punishment of anarchists was always followed by crimes even more violent and dangerous. An even more radical measure, especially in France, would be to cover them in ridicule. Martyrs are venerated, but madmen never. As for international agreements, of which much has been said, they are worse than useless, for the anarchists have no center that can be seized.

In order to demonstrate the uselessness of ferocious penalties it suffices to see that even the death of Ravachol, who was a true-born criminal, completely unworthy of the pity of honest men, far from being intimidating was followed by an apotheosis. After his execution certain individuals discovered a supreme anarchist-logic in his diverse crimes. It was decided that he was a symbolic assassin, tomb raider, dynamiter, guillotine. The cult of Ravachol was born. Even prior to this the anarchists had their martyrs: those hung in Chicago, those garroted in Xeres, the Germans Reinsdorf and Kuchler, executed with an axe. French revolutionaries needed, despite their internationalism, a national martyr, executed by the guillotine. And he was more than a martyr, he was Ravachol-Jesus as a party rhymer, Paul Paillette wrote. A photograph showing him standing with his crazed look, in the clogs of a prisoner between two gendarmes was reproduced in thousands of copies. Pamphlets to his glory were published: Ravachol Anarchiste, Ravachol et Carnot in Hell, etc. we even have the hymn, La Ravachole.

Just as we can't pass definitive judgment during his life on a great man, a generation can't with certainty judge the falsity of an idea, whatever it might be and, consequently, it doesn't have the right to inflict a penalty as radical as he death penalty on the partisans of that idea. It is for this reason that I proposed for all political criminals — apart born criminals — temporary punishments.

I don't care to discuss briefly the prophylaxis of anarchist crime, but I nevertheless would like to establish the following: Just as we see cholera strike the poorest and most filthy quarters, anarchy strikes in all places the least well governed. Its presence can thus serve as an indicator that all is not for the best in the countries that suffer from it, just as wherever it appears cholera indicates that there are improvements to be made in the domain of hygiene. In the presence of anarchist crimes one should not forget that painful exclamation of Vaillant's that, though coming from an hysteric, nevertheless deserves to be retained: "For too long a time," he said, "our voice is responded to with prison, the rope or the fusillade, but don't delude yourselves: the explosion of my bomb is not only the cry of Vaillant in rebellion, but is the cry of an entire class that calls for its rights and will soon join its acts to its words."

Upon The Gallows Hung A Wretch, Emily Dickinson (1896)

Upon the gallows hung a wretch,
Too sullied for the hell
To which the law entitled him.
As nature's curtain fell
The one who bore him tottered in,
For this was woman's son.
"'T'was all I had,' she stricken gasped;
Oh, what a livid boon!

Two Laws of Penal Evolution, Emile Durkheim (1893)

The variations through which punishment has passed in the course of history are of two kinds: quantitative and qualitative. The laws regarding each kind are, naturally, different.

THE LAW OF QUANTITATIVE VARIATION

It can be formulated as follows: "The intensity of punishment is greater as societies belong to a less advanced type — and as centralized power has more absolute character."

Let us first explain the meaning of these statements.

There is no great need to define the first. It is relatively easy to recognize whether a social species is more or less advanced than another: one has only to see which is more complex or, if equally complex, which is more organized. Moreover, this hierarchy of social species does not imply that the succession of societies forms a unique and linear series: on the contrary, it is certain that it is better represented as a tree with many more or less divergent branches. But on this tree societies are placed higher or lower and are found at a greater or lesser distance from the common trunk. It is only on the condition of considering them in this way that it is possible to speak of a general evolution of societies.

The second factor which we distinguished above should detain us longer. We say of governmental power that it is absolute when it encounters in the other social functions nothing which by its nature balances and efficaciously limits it. In point of fact, a complete absence of all limitation is nowhere to be found; we can even say that it is inconceivable. Tradition and religious belief serve as restraints to even the strongest governments.

This observation leads us to another which more directly concerns our subject: the fact that the more or less absolute character of the government is not an inherent characteristic of any given social type. If, in effect, it can as easily be found where collective life is extremely simple as where it is extremely complex. It does not belong more exclusively to lower societies than to others, [...j

This special form of political organization —governmental absolutism —

does not, therefore arise from the congenital constitution of the society, but from individual, transitory, and contingent conditions. This is why these two factors of penal evolution—the nature of the social type and that of the governmental organ—must he carefully distinguished. This is because, being independent, they act independently of one another, sometimes even in opposite directions. For example, it happens that in passing from a lower species to other, more advanced types, we do not see punishment decrease, as could be expected, because at the same time the governmental organization neutralizes the effects of social organization. [...]

THE LAW OF QUALITATIVE VARIATIONS

The law which we have just established relates exclusively to the magnitude or quantity of punishments. That which we are now about to consider is related to their qualitative modalities. It can be formulated as follows: Punishments consisting in privations of freedom .. and freedom alone .. for lengths of time varying according to the gravity of the crime, tend more and more to become the normal type of repression. Lower societies, are almost completely unacquainted with this kind of punishment. [...]

On first examination, it doubtless seems quite obvious that, from the day when prisons became useful to societies, men had the idea of constructing them. However, in reality, the existence of prisons assumes that certain conditions, without which they are not possible, have been realized. Prisons imply the existence of public establishments, sufficiently spacious, militarily occupied, arranged in such a way as to prevent communications with the outside, and so on. Such arrangements are not improvised on the spur of the moment: no truces of them exist in less advanced societies. [....]

But as the social horizon is extended, as collective life, instead of being dispersed into a vast number of minor foci where it cars manage only a meager existence, is concentrated about a more restricted number of points, it simultaneously becomes more intense and more continuous. Because it takes on greater importance, the dwellings of those who are in charge are transformed. They are extended and arc organized in view of the more extensive and more permanent functions which are incumbent upon them. The more the authority of those who live in them grows, the more those dwellings are singularized and distinguished from the rest. They take on a grandiose air; they are sheltered by higher walls and deeper moats in such a way as to denote visibly the line of demarcation which thenceforth separates the holders of power and the mass of their subordinates. At that point, the preconditions of the prison come into being. What leads us to suppose that prisons originated in this way is that they often first appeared in the shadow of the king's palace or among the out buildings of temples and similar institutions. [...]

Thus, at the very moment when the establishment of a place of detention became useful in consequence of the progressive disappearance of collective responsibility, edifices which could be used for this purpose were being constructed. Prisons, it is true, were as yet only preventive. But once constituted for this purpose, they quickly took on a repressive nature, at least in part.

EXPLICATION OF THE FIRST LAW

Since the penalty results from the crime and expresses the way in which it affects the public conscience, we must ask the determining cause of the evolution of penal law in the evolution of crime.

Without having to enter into the details of the proofs which justify this distinction, we think that it will be conceded without difficulty that all acts reputed to be criminal by the various known societies can be divided into two fundamental categories: some are directed against collective things (whether ideal or material), of which the principal examples are public authority and its representative mores, traditions, and religion — the others offend only individuals (murders, thefts, violence and frauds of all kinds). These two forms of criminality are sufficiently distinct to be designated as different words. The first could be called "religious criminality" because attacks against religion are its most essential element and because crimes against traditions or heads of state always have a more or less religious character. We might refer to the second category as "human" or "individual criminality." We also know that crimes of the first type comprise, almost to the exclusion of all others, the penal law of lower societies, but that on the contrary, they regress to the extent that social evolution proceeds. Meanwhile, attacks against the individual more and more occupy this entire area. For primitive peoples, crime consists almost solely in not observing the practices of the cult, in violating the ritual taboos, in deviating from the mores of ancestors, in disobeying authority where it is strongly consolidated. On the other hand, for today's European, crime consists essentially in the disruption of some human interest.

> **For primitive peoples, crime consists almost solely in not observing the practices of the cult, in violating the ritual taboos, in deviating from the mores of ancestors, in disobeying authority where it is strongly consolidated.**

Now, these two types of criminality differ profoundly because the collective sentiments which they offend are not of the same nature. As a result, repression cannot be the same for both. [...]

If we compare the present with the past, we find that we are not more tolerant of all crimes indiscriminately, but only of some of them; there are others, on the contrary, toward which we show ourselves to be more severe. However, those for which we evince an even greater indulgence happen also to be those which provoke the most violent repression. Inversely, those for which we reserve our severity evoke only moderate punishments. Consequently, to the extent that the former cease to be treated as crimes and are withdrawn from penal law to be replaced by the latter, a weakening of the average penalty must necessarily occur.

But this weakening can last only as long as does the substitution. A time must come—it has nearly arrived—when the process will have been completed, when attacks against persons will fill the whole of criminal law, when even what remains of the others will be considered to be dependent on this new form of criminality. The movement of retreat will then stop. There is not reason to believe that human criminality must, in its turn, regress in the same way as the punishments which repress it. Instead, everything leads us to predict that it will develop further, that the list of acts considered criminal will grow longer and that their criminal character will be accentuated. Frauds and injustice which yesterday left the public consciousness indifferent today arouse its revulsion. And this sensitivity will only become more lively with time. There is not a general tapering off of the entire repressive system; one particular system is giving way but is being replaced by another which, while less violent and less harsh, still has its own severities and is in no way destined to an uninterrupted decline.

The Ballad of Reading Gaol, Oscar Wilde (1898)

He did not wear his scarlet coat,
  For blood and wine are red,
And blood and wine were on his hands
  When they found him with the dead,
The poor dead woman whom he loved,
  And murdered in her bed.
He walked amongst the Trial Men
  In a suit of shabby grey;
A cricket cap was on his head,
  And his step seemed light and gay;
But I never saw a man who looked
  So wistfully at the day.

Durkheim

I never saw a man who looked
  With such a wistful eye
Upon that little tent of blue
  Which prisoners call the sky,
And at every drifting cloud that went
  With sails of silver by.

I walked, with other souls in pain,
  Within another ring,
And was wondering if the man had done
  A great or little thing,
When a voice behind me whispered low,
  "That fellows got to swing."

Dear Christ! the very prison walls
  Suddenly seemed to reel,
And the sky above my head became
  Like a casque of scorching steel;
And, though I was a soul in pain,
  My pain I could not feel.

I only knew what hunted thought
  Quickened his step, and why
He looked upon the garish day
  With such a wistful eye;
The man had killed the thing he loved
  And so he had to die.

———

Yet each man kills the thing he loves
  By each let this be heard,
Some do it with a bitter look,
  Some with a flattering word,
The coward does it with a kiss,
  The brave man with a sword!

Some kill their love when they are young,
  And some when they are old;
Some strangle with the hands of Lust,
  Some with the hands of Gold:
The kindest use a knife, because
  The dead so soon grow cold.

Some love too little, some too long,
  Some sell, and others buy;
Some do the deed with many tears,
  And some without a sigh:
For each man kills the thing he loves,
  Yet each man does not die.

———

He does not die a death of shame
  On a day of dark disgrace,
Nor have a noose about his neck,
  Nor a cloth upon his face,
Nor drop feet foremost through the floor
  Into an empty place

He does not sit with silent men
  Who watch him night and day;
Who watch him when he tries to weep,
  And when he tries to pray;
Who watch him lest himself should rob
  The prison of its prey.

He does not wake at dawn to see
  Dread figures throng his room,
The shivering Chaplain robed in white,
  The Sheriff stern with gloom,
And the Governor all in shiny black,
  With the yellow face of Doom.

He does not rise in piteous haste
  To put on convict-clothes,
While some coarse-mouthed Doctor gloats, and notes
  Each new and nerve-twitched pose,
Fingering a watch whose little ticks
  Are like horrible hammer-blows.

He does not know that sickening thirst
  That sands one's throat, before
The hangman with his gardener's gloves
  Slips through the padded door,
And binds one with three leathern thongs,
  That the throat may thirst no more.

He does not bend his head to hear
  The Burial Office read,
Nor, while the terror of his soul
  Tells him he is not dead,
Cross his own coffin, as he moves
  Into the hideous shed.

He does not stare upon the air
  Through a little roof of glass;
He does not pray with lips of clay
  For his agony to pass;
Nor feel upon his shuddering cheek
  The kiss of Caiaphas.

WITNESS TO AN EXECUTION
Execution of the Bonifacio Brothers (1898)

I received orders from General Mariano Noriel to take over Andrés Bonifacio and Procopio Bonifacio, from the place where they were detained, and to conduct them to the hill of Tala in Maragondong, Cavite. General Noriel handed to me at the same time a sealed package with orders that it be not opened until we reached the place I mentioned. I was charged to follow to the letter, the instructions contained within the package.

In compliance with these orders, I took with me the two brothers to the place mentioned, together with four soldiers under my command. On the road we conversed like friends. But I already had a presentiment of the order contained within the parcel.

On reaching Tala hill in Maragondong, I opened the order, read it, and then let the brothers read it. It was an order for the execution of the brothers. The two brothers were terror stricken; Andrés told me in Tagalog, '*Patawarin ninyo ako, kapatid.*' (Brother, forgive me.) I answered that I was very sorry, but by military discipline I had to carry out the unhappy task.

I conducted Procopio, who was stronger, to a wooded place, and on reaching the top of the hill, I ordered one of the soldiers to shoot him in the back. This done, I and the soldiers, using bayonets and bolos, dug a pit where we buried Procopio.

When I approached the place where Andrés was, he said, '*Patay na kapatid ko.*' (My brother is dead.) And he added, '*Patawarin ninyo ako, kapatid.*' I replied that I was sorry, but it was my military duty to follow the order.

Andrés Bonifacio tried to escape, but he could not go far because of the thick shrubbery around. One of the soldiers reached him, firing at him from behind and shooting him in the back. After digging one more grave with our bayonets and bolos, we buried Andrés in it.

Procopio and Andrés were not taken to Tala hill bound but free. Andrés had only one wound, in one of his arms. From the hill where Procopio was buried to the grave of Andrés, on a hill slope facing a rivulet, there were only twenty-five steps, while from Andres' grave to the brook the distance was about five brazas.

The brothers were buried in the morning. This was before the fighting with the Spaniards took place, when they captured Maragondong.

Andrés wore a white *camisa de chino* on the day of his execution. The gun used was a Remington. The four soldiers who accompanied us were natives of Kawit, and they are all dead. I am the only survivor of the occurrence.

MODERN TIMES

Heredity and Human Progress: A Remedy, William Duncan McKim (1900)

In any community, an individual's appreciation of what is really good for himself and what good for society, and of the degree to which his own interests should yield to those of his fellows, must vary with his original endowments and with the nature of his environment. Further, whatever his comprehension of these things, the strength of will wherewith to act in accordance with his sense of right must vary greatly for each individual, in accordance with conditions which he has had no part in creating. The play of motives within a man's mind may be analyzed, to a degree, by himself and even by his neighbor, but the complex influences underlying and controlling these motives are beyond human ken and measure. However it may be with the general mass of men, we all believe, when we seriously reflect upon the matter, that there are many individuals to whom, through congenital imbecility or mental disease, it is utterly unreasonable to impute any moral responsibility; and to this number we should add many individual whose conduct must be deeply influenced by mental defect or infirmity, although such condition be so subtle as to escape general recognition. Surely, this consideration must have great weight when we sit in judgment upon the moral delinquencies of our fellows. When none of us can measure our own guilt, who shall determine the moral responsibility of his neighbor? The attempt must ever be futile.

But for the practical issues of life, we have no need of such superhuman insight. In the matter of our likes and dislikes, an estimate as to moral worth may still be an important factor, for this is a question of personal taste to be decided mainly by sentiment; but in the construction of plans for the broad interests of society we must accept the degree of a man's social worth as a tangible and all-sufficient measure. From birth to death, we all exist through the toleration, and by the active support, of society. The only claim to this toleration and support which society can afford to recognize is found in our social worth. But in the conception of social worth we must have room for a broad appreciation of the possibilities of humanity: not only vigor of physique, and aptitude for the development of material resources, but aesthetic and ethical gifts, and all that tends to lift man higher above the brute, must have due recognition. We shall then have a fairly tangible criterion upon which society may base its action. By a man's deeds society must judge him. If these, when discriminately examined, appear predominantly good, in the sense of being advantageous to society, the latter must approve the man as worthy, without inquiry as to the degree of his intrinsic moral merit — a point indeterminable. If the man's actions be predominantly bad — directly or indirectly hurtful to society's deep interests — the necessary inquiry will be not as to the man's moral guilt but as to the steps requisite to prevent a recurrence of such social damage. We cannot properly say, in this case, that the man deserves punishment, for we know nothing of his true responsibility, but we may determine that the preservation of society demands that he be placed under restraint, or that he be coerced, or that his life be taken from him.

We may — and should — feel a deep pity for the man whom we thus put from us, and yet be persuaded that society cannot longer tolerate his existence. There are certain natural laws upon the observance of which the very being of society is conditional. We have not made these laws, but have been given intelligence to recognize them. Into society there are born, from time to time, individuals whose lives are so incompatible with these fundamental laws that society if it harbor them must perish. What need can we have, as practical men, to speculate here as to moral guilt? Whether such be present or absent, the essential condition is not altered: in the mere existence of these individuals lies the menace to the life-continuance of society. By the instinct of self-preservation wherewith society has been endowed, the lives of these individuals must be taken. According to the view here sketched, the idea of administering punishment as such, should be abandoned forever; but penalties must continue — if under a new name — as long perhaps as the race shall endure. With such a change in our penal philosophy, penalties should be inflicted not in wrath but in sorrow, as a kindly necessity often for the offender's own sake as well as for the preservation of society, and never as the harsh act of vengeance. Officially, then, with the moral responsibility of men, society has absolutely nothing to do ; it should concern itself with the degree of their usefulness — as understood in the broadest and most enlightened sense — and with the degree of injury which may result from their continued existence.

Now, some of my readers may agree that this disposal of the very vicious is reasonable enough and thoroughly salutary, and yet believe it unchristian and barbarous that any should be given over to death merely because of their weakness or helplessness. Let us consider this difficulty. The bond between weakness and viciousness is very close; indeed, in most cases, they are but two superficial aspects of one deep-lying constitutional degeneracy. Is it not the rule that when the child is morally very weak the man is depraved, that when the father is morally very weak the son is vicious? Shall society ignore what every man knows, and wait until useless plants have run to noxious seeds before we uproot them? To one who reflects upon the laws of growth and reproduction, such action seems madness.

The great majority of intelligent and humane people approve fully the taking of life, by judicial process, in certain cases — not only as a penalty for murder but under certain other circumstances, as, in time of war, for a soldier's desertion. Here, it must be admitted, the only authority for such action rests upon the general conviction of expediency — the consensus of opinion that the safety of society requires this extreme measure. Now, the enlightened judgment of the day is tending strongly to abandon the idea that judicial penalties are inflicted as punishment, i.e., as a kind of revenge, and to hold rather that they are used for their deterrent effect upon the tendency to crime, or for their beneficial influence upon the criminal; in other words, that penalties are applied as may seem expedient for the welfare of society. If, then, penalties are but expressions of expediency, the question of moral guilt or innocence need hardly arise in connection with their administration, and we should inflict them, within reasonable limits wherever required for social safety. The extinction of life is as justifiable, thus, in the case of those individuals who are merely weak as in the case of those who are vicious, provided that the safety of society appears to demand so stern a measure. We cannot reasonably draw the line here between the very weak and the very vicious, and if, to our great hurt, we halt in this matter, it is simply because of an unreasonable sentiment. If the safety of a nation be threatened by war, it is generally held to be right that countless lives of its best citizens should be voluntarily offered, or sacrificed under compulsion, to preserve its existence. Can it be regarded as wrong, then, to protect a nation from a far graver and more constant danger than a foreign foe — the insidious transmission of a foul and debasing heritage — by condemning certain weak, useless, contaminating lives to extinction? Our minds are

Can it be regarded as wrong, then, to protect a nation from a far graver and more constant danger than a foreign foe — the insidious transmission of a foul and debasing heritage — by condemning certain weak, useless, contaminating lives to extinction?

adjusted to the frequent execution of the vicious, but we shrink from a plan for the elimination of the very weak — the breeders of the vicious — merely because of its novelty. Were these two sad burdens similarly removed, we should soon regard the process as equally justifiable in the two cases.

But there is another aspect to the question. The weakling is usually an unhappy creature, to end whose being appears a mercy. Let us give our thought, for a moment, to the subject of happiness. That a man may be happy, his activities must be useful — whether so intended or not — to society; or, at least, they must not be hurtful. This we may state as a general rule. Happiness is the accompaniment of a free and effective play of our physical and mental powers. While engaged in such work as conduces to the general benefit, not only do we feel that our efforts are not likely to meet with great hindrance from the opposition of other men, but we have a consciousness of sympathy and approval which adds to the pleasure of mere exertion. Useful lives are thus, as a rule, the happiest. There are other lives, however, which appear to be happy, although they present, as a product, little or nothing of usefulness. Many persons seem to live enwrapt within themselves: their energies are mainly spent in abstraction from exterior things, and in study or contemplation; and, although they may produce nothing to benefit their fellows, the great happiness which they undoubtedly experience is explicable through the free play of their powers according to their bent. But in the case of those individuals whose powers are expended, not in usefulness but in injury to the race, the free play of faculty upon which happiness depends is constantly opposed by the restraints of society: these men might be happy were it not that they ever find, or fear to find, an obstacle placed by human hands in the path of their desires. It would seem that difficulties offered by infra-human nature incite in us a pleasurable desire to surmount them, whereas those put in our way by our fellow-men induce, besides an impatience to over-come them, a feeling of bitterness or rancor. The men whose energies are anti-social can but seldom find much happiness in the world, and such as they obtain cannot be of an exalted kind; and to our limited vision it appears that for them, with their meager compensation for the many grievous ills which life must bring, death can be only a relief.

If we have here portrayed in any measure the true essence of happiness, the weakling's life can have but little joy. His functions are for the most part feeble, and, with our present physiological knowledge, we cannot conceive of any but languid pleasure as the concomitants of languid powers. Through his weakness, he is more constantly a victim to disease and other adverse natural influences than the man who is fairly normal. With weakness, as we have seen, are almost always joined other manifestations of degeneracy — vicious tendencies which bring the energies of the weakling into collision with society, to the spoiling of any pleasure which might otherwise accrue to him through their activity. Finally, through his degeneracy, the weakling is at war with himself, for lacking that balance of functions which is the essential characteristic of the so-called normal man, his physical and mental powers clash together in perpetual discord, whereby there are often induced by day disquietude and pain, and by night torturing dreams, until his life is made an almost unceasing misery. We have reason to believe then, quite apart from any thought of advantage to the race, that it is well for the very weak when their abnormally burdensome life comes to an end. The test of social worth will enable us to judge fairly well as to the degree of weakness at which society should draw the line and refuse its support. It being evident to our best judgment that the child before us gives no prospect whatever of any advantage to society, and that there is an emphatic promise of misery to the poor little being itself and of injury to society, I maintain that it is our duty to the child, to ourselves, and to all posterity, that we extinguish painlessly this unfortunate life, and so fulfill the law of a far-sighted and kindly altruism.

WITNESS TO AN EXECUTION
An Australian in China, G.E. Morrison (1894)

. . . As we went out of the west gate, I was shown the spot where a few days before a young woman, taken in adultery, was done to death in a cage amid a crowd of spectators, who witnessed her agony for three days. She had to stand on tiptoe in the cage, her head projecting through a hole in the roof, and here she had to remain until death by exhaustion or strangulation ensued, or till some kind friend, seeking to accumulate merit in heaven, passed into her mouth sufficient opium to poison her, and so end her struggles.

On the gate itself a man not so long ago was nailed with red-hot nails hammered through his wrists above the hands. In this way he was exposed in turn at each of the four gates of the city, so that every man, woman, and child could see his torture. He survived four days, having unsuccessfully attempted to shorten his pain by beating his head against the woodwork, an attempt which was frustrated by padding the woodwork. This man had murdered and robbed two travelers on the high road, and, as things are in China, his punishment was not too severe.

[. . .] But the temple has not always witnessed only scenes of mercy. Two years ago, a tragedy was enacted here of strange interest. At a religious festival held here in April, 1892, and attended by all the high officials and by a crowd of sightseers, a thief, taking advantage of the crush, tried to snatch a bracelet from the wrist of a young woman, and, when she resisted, he stabbed her. He was seized red-handed, dragged before the Titai, who happened to be present, and ordered to be beheaded there and then. An executioner was selected from among the soldiers; but so clumsily did he do the work, hacking the head off by repeated blows, instead of severing it by one clean cut, that the friends of the thief were incensed and vowed vengeance. That same night they lay in wait for the executioner as he was returning to the city, and beat him to death with stones. Five men were arrested for this crime; they were compelled to confess their guilt and were sentenced to death. As they were being carried out to the execution-ground, one of the condemned pointed to two men, who were in the crowd of sightseers, and swore that they were equally concerned in the murder. So these two men were also put on their trial, with the result that one was found guilty and was equally condemned to death. As if this were not sufficient, at the execution, the mother of one of the prisoners, when she saw her son's head fall beneath the knife, gave a loud scream and fell down stone-dead. Nine lives were sacrificed in this tragedy: the woman who was stabbed recovered of her wound.

. . . On the morning of May 7th, as we were leaving the village where we had slept the night before, we were witnesses of a domestic quarrel which might well have become a tragedy. On the green outside their cabin, a husband with goitre, enraged against his goitrous wife, was kept from killing her by two elderly goitrous women. All were speaking with horrible goitrous voices as if they had cleft palates, and the husband was hoarse with fury. Jealousy could not have been the cause of the quarrel, for his wife was one of the most hideous creatures I have seen in China. Throwing aside the bamboo with which he was threatening her, the husband ran to the house, and was out again in a moment brandishing a lone native sword with which he menaced speedy death to the joy of his existence. I stood in the road and watched the disturbance, and with me the soldier-guard, who did not venture to interfere. But the two women seized the angry brute and held him till his wife toddled round the corner. Now, if this were a determined woman, she could best revenge herself for the cruelty that had been done her by going straightway and poisoning herself with opium, for then would her spirit be liberated, ever after to haunt her husband, even if he escaped punishment for being the cause of her death. If in the dispute he had killed her, he would be punished with "strangulation after the usual period," the sentence laid down by the law and often recorded in the *Peking Gazette* (e.g., May 15th, 1892), unless he could prove her guilty of infidelity, or want of filial respect for his parents, in which case his action would be praiseworthy rather than culpable. If, however, in the dispute the wife had killed her husband, or by her conduct had driven him to suicide, she would be inexorably tied to the cross and put to death by the "Ling chi," or "degrading and slow process." For a wife to kill her husband has always been regarded as a more serious crime than for a husband to kill his wife; even in our own highly favored country, till within a few years of the present century, the punishment for the man was death by hanging, but in the case of the woman death by burning alive.

Let me at this point interpolate a word or two about the method of execution known as the *Ling chi*. The words are commonly, and quite wrongly, translated as "death by slicing into 10,000 pieces"--a truly awful description of a punishment whose cruelty has been extraordinarily misrepresented. It is true that no punishment is more dreaded by the Chinese than the *Ling chi*; but it is dreaded, not because of any torture associated with its performance, but because of the dismemberment practiced upon the body which was received whole from its parents. The mutilation is ghastly and excites our horror as an example of barbarian cruelty; but it is not cruel, and need not excite our horror, since the mutilation is done, not before death, but after. The method is simply the following, which I give as I received it first-hand from an eyewitness: The prisoner is tied to a rude cross; he is invariably deeply under the influence of opium. The executioner, standing before him, with a sharp sword makes two quick incisions above the eyebrows, and draws down the portion of skin over each eye, then he makes two more quick incisions across the breast, and in the next moment he pierces the heart, and death is instantaneous. Then he cuts the body in pieces; and the degradation consists in the fragmentary shape in which

Supplice chinois.

the prisoner has to appear in heaven. As a missionary said to me: "He can't lie out that he got there properly when he carries with him such damning evidence to the contrary."

In China, immense power is given to the husband over the body of his wife, and it seems as if the tendency in England were to approximate to the Chinese custom. Is it not a fact that, if a husband in England brutally maltreats his wife, kicks her senseless, and disfigures her for life, the average English bench of unpaid magistrates will find extenuating circumstances in the fact of his being the husband, and will rarely sentence him to more than a month or two's hard labor?

WITNESS TO AN EXECUTION
The Other Side of the Lantern, Frederick Treves (1905)

A week or so before we reached Canton a man had been strangled to death on the quay by the upholders of the law for a robbery committed on a steamer. He was brought to die at the scene of his crime. Those who landed at Canton for the first time on the day of this event must be haunted by this street scene in the nightmare city. The man is suspended in a pyramidal framework of wood. On the summit of this is a horizontal board with a hole in it, just large enough to take his neck. His toes barely touch the ground, so he hangs by his head. Death comes slowly to those who find themselves in the grip of this fiendish trap. They may live a day or more, I was told.

The man who came to his end on the quay in this wise could see from the height to which his strained neck was lifted the Pearl River and the sampans skimming to and fro with light-hearted indifference. He would, no doubt, catch sight of one he knew now and then. He could see the crowd of stokers and seamen leaning over the rail of the steamer alongside, watching him die while they smoked; and the string of coolies, tramping to and fro, unloading the ship. He could see the gaping crowd about him, the man with the savage's insane glare of cruelty in his eye, the pitying woman, the half-weary friend, the curious boy, munching a handful of nuts. He would look until the blood burst into his cracking eyeballs and made all red, and in this whirling eddy of crimson, his soul would pass from out of the company of men.

The identical instrument of death can be seen outside the common gaol, and shopkeepers who sell souvenirs to tourists, sell photographs of men with black, bloated faces dying in the embrace of this machine.

There are other forms of torture sanctioned by the law, either for the purpose of extracting a confession or of inflicting punishment. They vary from mere flogging, or kneeling with bare knees on chains, to suspension by means of the thumbs or fingers, the crushing of the ankles between boards, and other less lenient processes.

Capital punishment is carried into effect by means of rapid throttling with a rope and pole, by slicing the victim to death slowly with a knife, or by the merciful process of hacking off his head with a sword. There is so little open space in Canton that the executions are performed in a potter's yard—a little muddy gap in the midst of the straightened lanes of the city. On one side is the potter's cottage; on two sides are low grey walls; while at the fourth end is an alley of shops filled with the usual pressing crowd. Men are busy in the yard moulding coarse bowls and clay stoves. They make a few less on the mornings when the upholders of the law march into the place with a criminal or two.

The victim has his hands tied behind his back. He kneels facing a blank wall, where are some rows of pots put out to dry, and his head is cut off by an expert coolie. If any blood spurts upon the potter's goods it is easily rubbed off. Children like to play in this place, because it is open, and the potters are interesting folk to watch. In a photograph of an actual execution, the faces of pigtailed children are to be seen in the gaps between the apathetic row of clay stoves. They appear to be watching the man of the sword with great admiration. The crowd, the potter's handiwork, and the children are all human enough, but there is a presentment of the terrible about that bare grey wall, grim and pitiless, upon which the eyes of so many have looked their last.

The common prison of Canton is a woeful place. There is a cavernous guardroom, dark and smoke-stained, where, amid the fumes of cooking-pots and tobacco, gaolers are squatting playing at cards. A sombre passage, jangling with keys, leads to a grating of iron which looks into a court. Here are the prisoners, huddled like beasts. The court is a mere grimy yard, a bear pit, a sty. The prisoners crowd to the grating, hold on nervously to the iron-work with filthy hands, thrust grinning yellow faces through the bars—a company of human wolves—with among them the bland, smiling countenance of the idiot, and the frowning brow of the insane. Here and there are a few pleasant-looking people, and one wonders how they have found themselves in this hellish pen.

The fate of these trapped wretches is hideous to think upon. The torture instruments are just without, while the execution yard is but a little way off. Which of these jabbering men will have his voice silenced and his neck crushed by a cord twisted with a pole? How many of these thumbs, which grip the bars, will serve to swing their owners by, and how many of these almond-shaped eyes will close upon the dreary grey wall in the potter's field ?

Lynch Law In America, Ida B. Wells-Barnett (1900)

Our country's national crime is lynching. It is not the creature of an hour, the sudden outburst of uncontrolled fury, or the unspeakable brutality of an insane mob. It represents the cool, calculating deliberation of intelligent people who openly avow that there is an "unwritten law" that justifies them in putting human beings to death without complaint under oath, without trial by jury, without opportunity to make defense, and without right of appeal. The "unwritten law" first found excuse with the rough, rugged, and determined man who left the civilized centers of eastern States to seek for quick returns in the gold-fields of the far West. Following in uncertain pursuit of continually eluding fortune, they dared the savagery of the Indians, the hardships of mountain travel, and the constant terror of border State outlaws. Naturally, they felt slight toleration for traitors in their own ranks. It was enough to fight the enemies from without; woe to the foe within! Far removed from and entirely without protection of the courts of civilized life, these fortune-seekers made laws to meet their varying emergencies. The thief who stole a horse, the bully who "jumped" a claim, was a common enemy. If caught he was promptly tried, and if found guilty was hanged to the tree under which the court convened.

Those were busy days of busy men. They had no time to give the prisoner a bill of exception or stay of execution. The only way a man had to secure a stay of execution was to behave himself. Judge Lynch was original in

This is the work of the "unwritten law" about which so much is said, and in whose behest butchery is made a pastime and national savagery condoned.

methods but exceedingly effective in procedure. He made the charge, impaneled the jurors, and directed the execution. When the court adjourned, the prisoner was dead. Thus lynch law held sway in the far West until civilization spread into the Territories and the orderly processes of law took its place. The emergency no longer existing, lynching gradually disappeared from the West.

But the spirit of mob procedure seemed to have fastened itself upon the lawless classes, and the grim process that at first was invoked to declare justice was made the excuse to wreak vengeance and cover crime. It next appeared in the South, where centuries of Anglo-Saxon civilization had made effective all the safeguards of court procedure. No emergency called for lynch law. It asserted its sway in defiance of law and in favor of anarchy. There it has flourished ever since, marking the thirty years of its existence with the inhuman butchery of more than ten thousand men, women, and children by shooting, drowning, hanging, and burning them alive. Not only this, but so potent is the force of example that the lynching mania has spread throughout the North and middle West. It is now no uncommon thing to read of lynchings north of Mason and Dixon's line, and those most responsible for this fashion gleefully point to these instances and assert that the North is no better than the South.

This is the work of the "unwritten law" about which so much is said, and in whose behest butchery is made a pastime and national savagery condoned. The first statute of this "unwritten law" was written in the blood of thousands of brave men who thought that a government that was good enough to create a citizenship was strong enough to protect it. Under the authority of a national law that gave every citizen the right to vote, the newly-made citizens chose to exercise their suffrage. But the reign of the national law was short-lived and illusionary. Hardly had the sentences dried upon the statute-books before one Southern State after another raised the cry against "Negro domination" and proclaimed there was an "unwritten law" that justified any means to resist it.

The method then inaugurated was the outrages by the "red-shirt" bands of Louisiana, South Carolina, and other Southern States, which were succeeded by the Ku-Klux Klans. These advocates of the "unwritten law" boldly avowed their purpose to intimidate, suppress, and nullify the Negro's right to vote. In support of its plans the Ku-Klux Klans, the "red-shirt" and similar organizations proceeded to beat, exile, and kill Negroes until the purpose of their organization was accomplished and the supremacy of the "unwritten law" was effected. Thus lynchings began in the South, rapidly spreading into the various States until the national law was nullified and the reign of the "unwritten law" was supreme. Men were taken from their homes by "red-shirt" bands and stripped, beaten, and exiled; others were assassinated when their political prominence made them obnoxious to their political opponents; while the Ku-Klux barbarism of election days, reveling in the butchery of thousands of colored voters, furnished records in Congressional investigations that are a disgrace to civilization.

The alleged menace of universal suffrage having been avoided by the absolute suppression of the Negro vote, the spirit of mob murder should have been satisfied and the butchery of Negroes should have ceased. But men, women, and children were the victims of murder by individuals and murder by mobs, just as they had been when killed at the demands of the "unwritten law" to prevent "Negro domination." Negroes were killed for disputing over terms of contracts with their employers. If a few barns were burned, some colored man was killed to stop it. If a colored man resented the imposition of a white man and the two came to blows, the colored man had to die, either at the hands of the white man then and there or later, at the hands of a mob that speedily gathered. If he showed a spirit of courageous manhood he was hanged for his pains, and the killing was justified by the declaration that he was a "saucy nigger." Colored women have been murdered because they refused to tell the mobs where relatives could be found for "lynching bees." Boys of fourteen years have been lynched by white representatives of American civilization. In fact, for all kinds of offenses--and, for no offenses--from murders to misdemeanors, men and women are put to death without judge or jury; so that, although the political excuse was no longer necessary, the wholesale murder of human beings went on just the same. A new name was given to the killings and a new excuse was invented for so doing.

Again the aid of the "unwritten law" is invoked, and again it comes to the rescue. During the last ten years a new statute has been added to the "unwritten law." This statute proclaims that for certain crimes or alleged crimes no Negro shall be allowed a trial; that no white woman shall be compelled to charge an assault under oath or to submit any such charge to the investigation of a court of law. The result is that many men have been put to death whose innocence was afterward established; and to-day, under this reign of the "unwritten law," no colored man, no matter what his reputation, is safe from lynching if a white woman, no matter what her standing or motive, cares to charge him with insult or assault.

It is considered a sufficient excuse and reasonable justification to put a prisoner to death under this "unwritten law" for the frequently repeated charge that these lynching horrors are necessary to prevent crimes against women. The sentiment of the country has been appealed to, in describing the isolated condition of white families in thickly-populated Negro districts; and the charge is made that these homes are in as great danger as if they were surrounded by wild beasts. And the world has accepted this theory without let or hindrance. In many cases there has been open expression that the fate meted out to the victim was only what he deserved. In many other instances, there has been a silence that says more forcibly than words can proclaim it that it is right and proper that a human being should be seized by a mob and burned to death upon the unsworn and the uncorroborated charge of his accuser. No matter that our laws presume every man innocent until he is proved guilty; no matter that it leaves a certain class of individuals completely at the mercy of another class; no matter that it encourages those criminally disposed to blacken their faces and commit any crime in the calendar so long as they can throw suspicion on some Negro as is frequently done, and then lead a mob to take his life; no matter that mobs make a farce of the law and a mockery of justice; no matter that hundreds of boys are being hardened in crime and schooled in vice by the repetition of such scenes before their eyes--if a white woman declares herself insulted or assaulted, some life must pay the penalty, with all the horrors of the Spanish Inquisition and all the barbarism of the Middle Ages. The world looks on and says it is well.

Not only are two hundred men and women put to death annually, on the average, in this country by mobs, but these lives are taken with the greatest publicity. In many instances the leading citizens aid and abet by their presence when they do not participate, and the leading journals inflame the public mind to the lynching point with scare-head articles and offers of rewards. Whenever a burning is advertised to take place, the railroads run excursions, photographs are taken, and the same jubilee is indulged in that characterized the public hangings of one hundred years ago. There is, however, this difference: in those old days the multitude that stood by was permitted only to guy or jeer. The nineteenth century lynching mob cuts off ears, toes, and fingers, strips off flesh, and distributes portions of the body as souvenirs among the crowd. If the leaders of the mob are so minded, coal-oil is poured over the body and the victim is then roasted to death. This has been done in Texarkana and Paris, Tex., in Bardswell, Ky., and in Newman, Ga. In Paris, the officers of the law delivered the prisoner to the mob. The mayor gave the school children a holiday and the railroads ran excursion trains so that the people might see a human being burned to death. In Texarkana, the year before, men and boys amused themselves by cutting off strips of flesh and thrusting knives into their helpless victim. At Newman, Ga., of the present year, the mob tried every conceivable torture to compel the victim to cry out and confess, before they set fire to the faggots that burned him. But their trouble was all in vain--he never uttered a cry and they could not make him confess.

This condition of affairs were brutal enough and horrible enough if it were true that lynchings occurred only because of the commission of crimes against women--as is constantly declared by ministers, editors, lawyers, teachers, statesmen, and even by women themselves. It has been to the interest of those who did the lynching to blacken the good name of the helpless and defenseless victims of their hate. For this reason, they publish at every possible opportunity this excuse for lynching, hoping thereby not only to palliate their own crime but at the same time to prove the Negro a moral monster and unworthy of the respect and sympathy of the civilized world. But this alleged reason adds to the deliberate injustice of the mob's work. Instead of lynchings being caused by assaults upon women, the statistics show that not one-third of the victims of lynchings are even charged with such crimes. *The Chicago Tribune*, which publishes annually lynching statistics, is authority for the following:

In 1892, when lynching reached high-water mark, there were 241 persons lynched. The entire number is divided among the following states:

Alabama	22	Montana	4
Arkansas	25	New York	1
California	3	North Carolina	5
Florida	11	North Dakota	1
Georgia	17	Ohio	3
Idaho	8	South Carolina	5
Illinois	1	Tennessee	28
Kansas	3	Texas	15
Kentucky	9	Virginia	7
Louisiana	29	West Virginia	5
Maryland	1	Wyoming	9
Mississippi	16	Arizona Ter.	3
Missouri	6	Oklahoma	2

Of this number, 160 were of Negro descent. Four of them were lynched in New York, Ohio, and Kansas; the remainder were murdered in the South. Five of this number were females. The charges for which they were lynched cover a wide range. They are as follows:

Rape.................	46	Attempted rape......	11
Murder...............	58	Suspected robbery...	4
Rioting..............	3	Larceny.............	1
Race Prejudice........	6	Self-defense........	1
No cause given........	4	Insulting women....	2
Incendiarism..........	6	Desperadoes.........	6
Robbery..............	6	Fraud................	1
Assault and battery...	1	Attempted murder....	2
No offense stated, boy and girl.............. 2			

In the case of the boy and girl above referred to, their father, named Hastings, was accused of the murder of a white man. His fourteen-year-old daughter and sixteen-year-old son were hanged and their bodies filled with bullets; then the father was also lynched. This occurred in November, 1892, at Jonesville, La.

Indeed, the record for the last twenty years shows exactly the same or a smaller proportion who have been charged with this horrible crime. Quite a number of the one-third alleged cases of assault that have been personally investigated by the writer have shown that there was no foundation in fact for the charges; yet the claim is not made that there were no real culprits among them. The Negro has been too long associated with the white man not to have copied his vices as well as his virtues. But the Negro resents and utterly repudiates the efforts to blacken his good name by asserting that assaults upon women are peculiar to his race. The Negro has suffered far more from the commission of this crime against the women of his race by white men than the white race has ever suffered through his crimes. Very scant notice is taken of the matter when this is the condition of affairs. What becomes a crime deserving capital punishment when the tables are turned is a matter of small moment when the Negro woman is the accusing party.

But since the world has accepted this false and unjust statement, and the burden of proof has been placed upon the Negro to vindicate his race, he is taking steps to do so. The Anti-Lynching Bureau of the National Afro-American Council is arranging to have every lynching investigated and publish the facts to the world, as has been done in the case of Sam Hose, who was burned alive last April at Newman, Ga. The detective's report showed that Hose killed Cranford, his employer, in self-defense, and that, while a mob was organizing to hunt Hose to punish him for killing a white man, not till twenty-four hours after the murder was the charge of rape, embellished with psychological and physical impossibilities, circulated. That gave an impetus to the hunt, and *The Atlanta Constitution*'s reward of $500 keyed the mob to the necessary burning and roasting pitch. Of five hundred newspaper clippings of that horrible affair, nine-tenths of them assumed Hose's guilt—simply because his murderers said so, and because it is the fashion to believe the Negro peculiarly addicted to this species of crime. All the Negro asks is justice—a fair and impartial trial in the courts of the country. That given, he will abide the result.

But this question affects the entire American nation, and from several points of view: First, on the ground of consistency. Our watchword has been "the land of the free and the home of the brave." Brave men do not gather by thousands to torture and murder a single individual, so gagged and bound he cannot make even feeble resistance or defense. Neither do brave men or women stand by and see such things done without compunction of conscience, nor read of them without protest. Our nation has been active and outspoken in its endeavors to right the wrongs of the Armenian Christian, the Russian Jew, the Irish Home Ruler, the native women of India, the Siberian exile, and the Cuban patriot. Surely it should be the nation's duty to correct its own evils!

Second, on the ground of economy. To those who fail to be convinced from any other point of view touching this momentous question, a consideration of the economic phase might not be amiss. It is generally known that mobs in Louisiana, Colorado, Wyoming and other states have lynched subjects of other countries. When their different governments demanded satisfaction, our country was forced to confess her inability to protect said subjects in the several States because of our State-rights doctrines, or in turn, demand punishment of the lynchers. This confession, while humiliating in the extreme, was not satisfactory; and, while the United States cannot protect, she can pay. This she has done, and it is certain will have to do again in the case of the recent lynching of Italians in Louisiana. The United States already has paid in indemnities for lynching nearly a half million dollars, as follows:

Paid China for Rock Springs (Wyo.) massacre...........	$147,748.74
Paid China for outrages on Pacific Coast...............	276,619.75
Paid Italy for massacre of Italian prisoners at New Orleans	24,330.90
Paid Italy for lynchings at Walsenburg, Col	10,000.00
Paid Great Britain, outrages on James Bain & Frederick Dawson ..	2,800.00

Third, for the honor of Anglo-Saxon civilization. No scoffer at our boasted American civilization could say anything more harsh of it than does the American white man himself who says he is unable to protect the honor of his women without resort to such brutal, inhuman, and degrading exhibitions as characterize "lynching bees." The cannibals of the South Sea Islands roast human beings alive to satisfy hunger. The red Indian of the Western plains tied his prisoner to the stake, tortured him, and danced in fiendish glee while his victim writhed in the flames. His savage, untutored mind suggested no better way than that of wreaking vengeance upon those who had wronged him. These people knew nothing about Christianity and did not profess to follow its teachings; but such primary laws as they had they lived up to. No nation, savage or civilized, save only the United States of America, has confessed its inability to protect its women save by hanging, shooting, and burning alleged offenders.

Finally, for love of country. No American travels abroad without blushing for shame for his country on this subject. And whatever the excuse that passes current in the United States, it avails nothing abroad. With all the powers of government in control; with all laws made by white men, administered by white judges, jurors, prosecuting attorneys, and sheriffs; with every office of the executive department filled by white men—no excuse can be offered for exchanging the orderly administration of justice for barbarous lynchings and "unwritten laws." Our

No American travels abroad without blushing for shame for his country on this subject.

country should be placed speedily above the plane of confessing herself a failure at self-government. This cannot be until Americans of every section, of broadest patriotism and best and wisest citizenship, not only see the defect in our country's armor but take the necessary steps to remedy it. Although lynchings have steadily increased in number and barbarity during the last twenty years, there has been no single effort put forth by the many moral and philanthropic forces of the country to put a stop to this wholesale slaughter. Indeed, the silence and seeming condonation grow more marked as the years go by.

A few months ago the conscience of this country was shocked because, after a two-weeks trial, a French judicial tribunal pronounced Captain Dreyfus guilty. And yet, in our own land and under our own flag, the writer can give day and detail of one thousand men, women, and children who during the last six years were put to death without trial before any tribunal on earth. Humiliating indeed, but altogether unanswerable, was the reply of the French press to our protest: "Stop your lynchings at home before you send your protests abroad."

WITNESS TO AN EXECUTION
A Lynching, Juliette V. Harring (1922)

As the Dyer Anti-Lynching Bill is awaiting final action by the Senate, the following account of a typical Southern lynching by an eyewitness may be of interest. I could name the State, but I will spare them that.

It was while he sat in his room by his lamp looking over his notes and jotting down some ideas which are still fresh in his mind, that he suddenly became conscious of that sense of alarm which is always aroused by the sound of hurrying footsteps in the silence of the night. He stopped writing and looked at his watch. It was after eleven. He listened, straining every nerve to hear above the tumult of his quickening pulse. He caught the murmur of voices, then the gallop of a horse, then of another and another. He was now thoroughly alarmed. After a moment he put out the light, softly opened the window-blind, and cautiously peeped out. He saw men moving in one direction, and from the mutterings, he vaguely caught a rumor that some terrible crime had been committed--murder! rape! He put on his coat and hat; it was impossible to remain in the house under such tense excitement. His nerves would not have stood it. He went out, and, following the drift, reached the railroad station.

There was gathered a crowd of men: all white; others were steadily arriving, seemingly from all the surrounding country. How did the news spread so quickly? He watched these men moving under the yellow glare of the lamps about the station, stern, comparatively silent, all of them armed, some of them in boots and spurs; fierce, determined men. He had come to know the type well--blond, tall and lean, with ragged muscles and beard, and glittering gray eyes. At the suggestion of daylight, they began to disperse in groups, going in several directions. There was no extra noise or excitement, no loud talking, only swift, sharp words of command given by those who seemed to be accepted as leaders by mutual understanding. In fact, the impression made upon this man was that everything was being done in quite an orderly manner. In spite of so many leaving, the crowd around the station continued to grow: at sunrise there were a great many women and children. By this time he also noticed some colored people; a few seemed to be going about their customary tasks; several were standing on the outskirts of the crowd, but the gathering of Negroes usually seemed in such towns was missing.

Before noon, they brought him in. Two horsemen rode abreast; between them, half dragged, the poor wretch made his way through the dust. His hands were tied behind him, and ropes around his body were fastened to the saddle horn of his double guard. The men who at midnight had been stern and silent were now yelling themselves hoarse. A space was quickly cleared in the crowd, and a rope placed about his neck, when from someone came the suggestion, "Burn him." It ran like an electric current. Have you ever witnessed the transformation of human beings into savage beasts? Nothing can be more terrible. A railroad tie was sunk into the ground, the rope was removed and a chain brought and securely coiled around the victim and the stake. There he stood, a man only in form and stature, every sign of degeneracy stamped upon his countenance. His eyes were dull and vacant, no indication of a single ray of thought in his sluggish brain. Evidently the realization of his fearful fate had robbed him of whatever reasoning power he had ever possessed. He was too stunned and stupefied even to tremble.

Fuel was brought from everywhere: oil, the torch; the flames crouched for an instant as though to gather strength then leaped up as high as their victim's head. He squirmed, he writhed, strained at his chains, then gave out cries and groans that the man who saw it says he shall always hear. The cries and groans were choked by the fire and smoke; but his eyes, bulging from their sockets, rolled from side to side, appealing in vain for help. Some of the crowd yelled and cheered and cried, "You are burning him too fast!" Others seemed appalled at what they had done, and there were a few who turned away, sickened at the sight. The horrified eyewitness was fixed to the post where he stood, powerless to turn his eyes away from what he did not want to see. Before he could make himself believe what was really happening, he was looking at a scorched post, a smoldering fire, blackened bones, charred fragments sifting down through coils of chain, and the smell of burnt flesh—human flesh—was in his nostrils.

He walked a short distance away, and sat down in order to clear his dazed mind. When he decided to get up and go back to his room, he found he could hardly stand on his feet. He was as weak as a man who had lost blood. A wave of humiliation and shame swept over him; shame for his country, that is the great example of democracy to the world, should be the only civilized, if not the only State on earth, where a human being could be burned alive and with impunity be treated worse than animals.

As a Southern woman from the State of Virginia, I am convinced that the real South, the upright, intelligent people, regret these outrages, but how long will the South remain silent? How long will the South endure the limits which are placed on free speech? How long will they cower and tremble under "Southern opinion?"

> *"They are slaves who fear to speak For the friendless and the weak;*
> *They are slaves who fear to be In the right with two or three."*

We cry out in righteous indignation when we learn of the atrocities practiced upon the Armenians by the Turks, and on the Jews by the Russians; the cry for relief from suffering beyond our shores is heard and ever responded to by generous America.

The thousands of spires on churches of every denomination, running high into the heavens, bear testimony that this is a Christian nation, or at least purports to be, and yet, actual records tell us that within the last thirty years we have lynched 3,436 human beings—3,436 blots of shame on the United States. Most of these lynchings occurred in the so-called Solid South, bringing disgrace upon the entire Southern people, and condemnation from God and man. I love the South with every fiber of my being and it is for this reason that I am appealing to her people. The Southern people are admired everywhere for their sterling qualities; and is it not possible for them to band together and eradicate this cruel custom?

I realize that the details of this ghastly horror are revolting, but I recite them that they may be brought home to you and that the people of this country may rouse themselves and demand justice. I could go on and tell you of case after case; I could tell you of a Negro being burned alive, while women with babies in their arms made themselves comfortable and looked on without shame. In another case, the victim was tortured for three and one-half hours, and the last sign of life did not disappear until a full half hour later. Red-hot pokers were used to bore out the Negro's eyes; hot irons dug gaping wounds in his back and sides, killing him inch by inch.

I realize that the details of this ghastly horror are revolting, but I recite them that they may be brought home to you and that the people of this country may rouse themselves and demand justice.

This abomination is spreading by leaps and bounds and must be stamped out. Lawlessness begets lawlessness; tolerated and unrestrained lawlessness invariably grows. The essence of lynching is not the satisfaction of the law, but revenge, and revenge is an endless chain.

The Varieties of Religious Experience
William James (1902)

Perfect conduct is a relation between three terms: the actor, the objects for which he acts, and the recipients of the action. In order that conduct should be abstractly perfect, all three terms, intention, execution, and reception, should be suited to one another. The best intention will fail if it either work by false means or address itself to the wrong recipient. Thus no critic or estimator of the value of conduct can confine himself to the actor's animus alone, apart from the other elements of the performance. As there is no worse lie than a truth misunderstood by those who hear it, so reasonable arguments, challenges to magnanimity, and appeals to sympathy or justice, are folly when we are dealing with human crocodiles and boa-constrictors. The saint may simply give the universe into the hands of the enemy by his trustfulness. He may, by non-resistance, cut off his own survival.

Herbert Spencer tells us that the perfect man's conduct will appear perfect only when the environment is perfect: to no inferior environment is it suitably adapted. We may paraphrase this by cordially admitting that saintly conduct would be the most perfect conduct conceivable in an environment where all were saints already; but by adding that in an environment where few are saints, and many the exact reverse of saints, it must be ill adapted. We must frankly confess, then, using our empirical common sense and ordinary practical prejudices, that in the world that actually is, the virtues of sympathy, charity, and non-resistance may be, and often have been, manifested in excess. The powers of darkness have systematically taken advantage of them. The whole modern scientific organization of charity is a consequence of the failure of simply giving alms. The whole history of constitutional government is a commentary on the excellence of resisting evil, and when one cheek is smitten, of smiting back and not turning the other cheek also. You will agree to this in general, for in spite of the Gospel, in spite of Quakerism, in spite of Tolstoy, you believe in fighting fire with fire, in shooting down usurpers, locking up thieves, and freezing out vagabonds and swindlers.

And yet you are sure, as I am sure, that were the world confined to these hard-headed, hard-hearted, and hard-fisted methods exclusively, were there no one prompt to help a brother first, and find out afterwards whether he were worthy; no one willing to drown his private wrongs in pity for the wronger's person; no one ready to be duped many a time rather than live always on suspicion; no one glad to treat individuals passionately and impulsively rather than by general rules of prudence; the world would be an infinitely worse place than it is now to live in. The tender grace, not of a day that is dead, but of a day yet to be born somehow, with the golden rule grown natural, would be cut out from the perspective of our imaginations. The saints, existing in this way, may, with their extravagances of human tenderness, be prophetic. Nay, innumerable times they have proved themselves prophetic. Treating those whom they met, in spite of the past, in spite of all appearances, as worthy, they have stimulated them to be worthy, miraculously transformed them by their radiant example and by the challenge of their expectation.

From this point of view we may admit the human charity which we find in all saints, and the great excess of it which we find in some saints, to be a genuinely creative social force, tending to make real a degree of virtue which it alone is ready to assume as possible. The saints are authors, *auctores*, increasers, of goodness. The potentialities of development in human souls are unfathomable. So many who seemed irretrievably hardened have in, point of fact, been softened, converted, regenerated, in ways that amazed the subjects even more than they surprised the spectators, that we never can be sure in advance of any man that his salvation by the way of love is hopeless. We have no right to speak of human crocodiles and boa-constrictors as of fixedly incurable beings. We know not the complexities of personality, the smouldering emotional fires, the other facets of the character-polyhedron, the resources of the subliminal region. St. Paul long ago, made our ancestors familiar with the idea that every soul is virtually sacred. Since Christ died for us all without exception, St. Paul said, we must despair of no one. This belief in the essential sacredness of every one expresses itself today in all sorts of humane customs and reformatory institutions, and in a growing aversion to the death penalty and to brutality in punishment. The saints, with their extravagance of human tenderness, are the great torch-bearers of this belief, the tip of the wedge, the clearers of the darkness. Like the single drops which sparkle in the sun as they are flung far ahead of the advancing edge of a wave-crest or of a flood, they show the way and are forerunners. The world is not yet with them, so they often seem in the midst of the world's affairs to be preposterous. Yet they are impregnators of the world, vivifiers and *animaters* of potentialities of goodness which, but for them, would lie forever dormant. It is not possible to be quite as mean as we naturally are, when they have passed before us. One fire kindles another; and without that over-trust in human worth which they show, the rest of us would lie in spiritual stagnancy.

Momentarily considered, then, the saint may waste his tenderness and be the dupe and victim of his charitable fever, but the general function of his charity in social evolution, is vital and essential. If things are ever to move upward, someone must be ready to take the first step, and assume the risk of it. No one who is not willing to try charity, to try non-resistance as the saint is always willing, can tell whether these methods will or will not succeed. When they do succeed, they are far more powerfully successful than force or worldly prudence. Force destroys enemies; and the best that can be said of prudence is that it keeps what we already have in safety. But non-resistance, when successful, turns enemies into friends; and charity regenerates its objects. These saintly methods are, as I said, creative energies; and genuine saints find in the elevated excitement with which their faith endows them an authority and impressiveness which makes them irresistible in situations where men of shallower nature cannot get on at all without the use of worldly prudence. This practical proof that worldly wisdom may be safely transcended is the saint's magic gift to mankind.

Not only does his vision of a better world console us for the generally prevailing prose and barrenness; but even when, on the whole, we have to confess him ill adapted, he makes some converts, and the environment gets better for his ministry. He is an effective ferment of goodness, a slow transmuter of the earthly into a more heavenly order.

In this respect, the Utopian dreams of social justice in which many contemporary socialists and anarchists indulge are, in spite of their impracticability and non-adaptation to present environmental conditions, analogous to the saint's belief in an existent kingdom of heaven. They help to break the edge of the general reign of hardness, and are slow leavens of a better order.

WITNESS TO AN EXECUTION
Witnesses Describe Czolgosz's Final Moments
Buffalo Commercial (1901)

Sheriff Caldwell and Charles R. Huntley returned from Auburn shortly after 1 o'clock this afternoon, having witnessed the execution of Leon F. Czolgosz, the slayer of President McKinley. Asked about the execution, Mr. Huntley said to a *Commercial* reporter:

There is really little to be said about it. The case has been described correctly in the newspapers. I read them on my way up from Auburn and find that they picture the proceeding accurately. Czolgosz did not show any signs of fear and he did not tremble or turn pale; he walked into the death room between two men, and walked with a firm step. He stumbled as he came into the room but did not fall, nor did his knees weaken. I was quite surprised at his demeanor, as was everyone else, I should say. He was perfectly strong and calm. He just slid himself into the chair exactly as a man might who expected to enjoy a half hour's repose. The fact that in a moment a death current was to be forced through him did not seem to perturb him in the least.

Yes, I heard him make the statements accredited to him. He spoke very plainly and in a voice which did not waver in the slightest degree. He said first that he was not sorry for having killed the President, and, as the straps which bound his jaws were put in place, he said that he was sorry he could not see his father. Everyone in the room must have heard and understood him. He had expressed a desire to speak, so it was claimed, after getting in the presence of the witnesses. He wanted everyone to hear him. It was supposed, therefore, that whatever talking he intended to do he would do before getting into the chair. It was a general surprise to hear his voice after the men had begun to affix the electrodes. The witnesses were somewhat startled and were amazed at the man's calmness. We all kept our eyes on him and listened most attentively. But the men at work beside him and in front of him, did not pause. They kept on affixing the appliances. Evidently Czolgosz had prepared something to say and what he said was part of his prepared piece. That is my thought of the matter. I wouldn't say that he tried to make a hero of himself. There was no spirit of bravado manifest at all. He said a few things just as if he felt it his duty to say them."

"Did, he tremble or grow pale as the straps were put in place?" was asked.

"No, not at all. He was collected and calm every moment, to all appearances. Sheriff Caldwell, who was with me, said he looked better and more self-possessed than he looked during the trial here in Buffalo. His face had the normal amount of color in it, and his hands didn't tremble a bit.

"The majesty of the law was perfectly sustained," continued Mr. Huntley. "There wasn't a hitch anywhere and not an incident which could merit the faintest criticism. Czolgosz was sentenced to die in the electric chair, and his death was effected quickly and certainly. It was but an incredibly short time after the murderer walked into the death chamber when the doctors in attendance pronounced him dead. There had been no scene; no one had fainted or grown excited. Everyone conducted himself with remarkable *sang-froid*. The attendants were busy right up to the moment of turning on the current, and had but stepped back when the body of the assassin was in the grasp of the powerful current. As I have said, not a thing marred the formality. Everything went off smoothly, according to a schedule carefully planned."

Sheriff Caldwell's Impression.

Sheriff Samuel Caldwell was asked by a *Commercial* reporter as to his impressions of the execution of the assassin. He replied:

"I was impressed with the idea that the assassin was a man of great nerve. Although guards had hold of his arms, the prisoner could have walked unaided to the chair. Aside from the prisoner's last words, there was not a sound in the death chamber, and the prisoner himself gave no evidence of fear.

"As soon as he had been seated in the chair and his face covered so that his nose and month were alone exposed, Warden Mead raised his hand and Electrician Davis turned on the current which snuffed out the prisoner's life as with a snap of the finger. The electrician then felt the prisoner's jugular vein. Dr. MacDonald did the same, and was followed by Prison Physician Gerin. The doctors then stepped back, and Warden Mead again raised his hand. Again the current was applied and was continued about 50 seconds.

"When the electricity was again shut off, the physicians examined the body by the usual means, and at the end pronounced that the man was dead.

The witnesses left the death chamber before the body was removed to the operating table in the autopsy room. I signed the document. swearing that I saw the electrocution of the assassin. The doctors remained for the autopsy, but I came home immediately.

"The prisoner's nerve was evidenced by his conduct from the moment he entered the death chamber. No groan escaped him, and his lips did not even move except when he was making his final statement to the effect that he did not repent his crime. When the electricity entered the assassin's body it stiffened with successive jerks, but death was so quick that he did not have time to groan."

Social Punishment Among Animals
Arthur Cleveland Hall, Ph.D. (1902)

Does crime exist among animals? If so, it must be something very different from those destructive acts by which an animal secures his food, defends himself, strengthens his own band, or weakens that of his enemies; acts which have often mistakenly been called the crimes of animals. It must be conduct distinctly harmful to his own kind, his own social group; awakening against himself general dislike and vengeance. Many facts unite to prove that such noxious individuals are occasionally found among the more intelligent animal communities, that they frequently manifest signs of degeneration, like those common among human criminals, and that severe social punishment is often inflicted upon them.

In the different groups of monkeys, writes Brehm, when the struggle for command has resulted in the dominance of some sturdy male, any monkey refusing obedience is brought to reason by force, with cuffs and bitings.

The "cinocefali" are well organized for brigandage. They post sentinels to warn the devastating horde of the approach of man, and death is the penalty inflicted if one prove faithless or negligent in the discharge of this most necessary social duty.

They post sentinels to warn the devastating horde of the approach of man, and death is the penalty inflicted if one prove faithless or negligent in the discharge of this most necessary social duty.

When the band is on the march toward the orchard destined for pillage, profound silence is compulsory. The ignorant youngster who begins to chatter is well thrashed.

From the moment he is weaned, stealing is a part of the young monkey's education. Indeed, his very life depends upon his success in theft. According to Dr. Brehm, the mother monkey robs her own child. There is no chance for him while his elders are feeding peacefully; but they are sure to wrangle over some dainty morsel and then the young monkey seizes all he can and escapes. Woe to the unskillful thief who is caught in the act. He not only loses his booty, but is severely beaten by the older monkeys. Stealing has the entire approval of the monkey race. It is not thieving, but lack of skill in thieving, which the monkeys unite to punish, — a practice said to have been customary among the Spartans also.

Here is good evidence that social punishment is inflicted by monkey bands for certain acts akin to treason, that is, active disloyalty to the community.

Here is good evidence that social punishment is inflicted by monkey bands for certain acts akin to treason, that is, active disloyalty to the community; and for lack of skill in thieving. The actions punished are thoroughly destructive of the social welfare, by preventing, or endangering, the obtaining of the food supply. They are acts in direct opposition to the strong trend of the social life, which is, education and organization of the monkey band for stealthy marauding expeditions.

Perhaps the most intelligent of the anthropoid apes is a species of chimpanzee called the Soko, discovered and most carefully described by Livingstone. "They live in communities consisting of about a dozen individuals, and are strictly monogamous in their conjugal relations. If a Soko tries to seize the female of another, he is caught on the ground and all unite in boxing and biting the offender." Here is true social punishment for adulterous, or more probably, incestuous assault.

Elephants are very sociable by nature and lovers of peace, but they occasionally expel from the herd a "rogue" elephant, always distinguished as unusually malicious. Once driven out from his own herd, the "rogue" is never admitted to another, although Saunderson found them occasionally in company with another solitary of their own species. Sir J. Tennant records, that even when driven into the keddah, a "rogue " was never allowed to enter the herd of captives with which he was enclosed. In isolation, the rogue is noted for malignant ferocity toward men as well as other elephants. His actions are often abnormal and he appears to be suffering from excitement which sometimes passes away. Good temper appears to be a fundamental condition of membership in elephant society. A malicious, unsociable fellow is punished with something like outlawry, "doubtless because of conduct obnoxious to the rest — probably aggressive."

The ferocity of the "rogue" buffalo and "rogue" hippopotamus must probably be accounted for in the same way. Intolerable to their own kind and outlawed from society, they revenge themselves by the indulgence of their malicious nature and criminal instincts. Herds of wild cattle, in northern Scotland, have been known to punish offending individuals with death. We may believe, therefore, that herds of elephants, hippopotami, buffaloes and wild cattle, punish with outlawry or death the few incurably malicious, antisocial individuals found among them.

The Changing World and Lectures to Theosophical Students, Annie Besant (1910)

I can hardly leave this subject without saying a word on Capital Punishment. That, of course, cannot find defense from anyone who realizes the principle of Brotherhood. Some of you may remember the saying of a witty Frenchman: "*Que messieurs les assassins commencent ;*" but it is not from the lower that reforms begin, but from the higher. You cannot expect your murderer to respect human life if you have taught him by your criminal legislation that the right penalty for murder is to murder again. True, one comes from passion and the other from the law; but if the law does not teach respect for human life, how should the passions of the criminal honor that sacredness? It is not only from that general principle that you make human life cheap by destroying it, but from another even more important. You cannot get rid of that murderer of yours; you can only get rid of his body, and his body is the most convenient prison in which you can keep him. You can lock up his body and prevent him from committing any further murders, but you cannot lock him up when you have driven him out of his body by the hangman's noose; you have not killed him, you cannot kill him, you have only killed his body; and you have driven him out into that next world which interpenetrates this world, and whose inhabitants are with us all the time; you have sent him out into that other world hating, cursing, full of anger and revenge against those who have cut short his life. He acts as the instigator of other murders; he stimulates other criminals into the last possibility of crime. Have you ever noticed that a brutal murder is sometimes repeated over and over again in the same community until you get a cycle of murders of one particular kind? I know, of course, that the Press, in reporting every detail of those horrors, adds the forces of imagination to the power of temptation which comes from the man you have sent to the other side. In a civilized country no such details of brutal crime should ever be given; people should understand that that stimulates the faculty of imitation, and so makes repetition of the crime more likely. Another reason why you should never send a man out like that is, that when the criminal is in your hands, remembering the lives that lie in front of him, you should try to give him something to take with him into the other world which he can turn into capacity and moral sense; you should remember he will come back again to a physical body, and it is your duty to make that next birth of his as much an improvement on the present as it is possible for human thought and human love to make it. We have a duty to these young souls around us in order that they may profit by our civilization, and not suffer from it as they too often do today.

Theodore Roosevelt: An Autobiography (1913)

The men I cared for most in the regiment were the men who did the best work; and therefore my liking for them was obliged to take the shape of exposing them to most fatigue and hardship, of demanding from them the greatest service, and of making them incur the greatest risk. Once I kept Greenway and Goodrich at work for forty-eight hours, without sleeping, and with very little food, fighting and digging trenches. I freely sent the men for whom I cared most, to where death might smite them; and death often smote them — as it did the two best officers in my regiment, Allyn Capron and Bucky O'Neil. My men would not have respected me had I acted otherwise. Their creed was my creed. The life, even of the most useful man, of the best citizen, is not to be hoarded if there be need to spend it. I felt, and feel, this about others; and of course also about myself. This is one reason why I have always felt impatient contempt for the effort to abolish the death penalty on account of sympathy with criminals. I am willing to listen to arguments in favor of abolishing the death penalty so far as they are based purely on grounds of public expediency, although these arguments have never convinced me. But inasmuch as, without hesitation, in the performance of duty, I have again and again sent good and gallant and upright men to die, it seems to me the height of a folly both mischievous and mawkish to contend that criminals who have deserved death should nevertheless be allowed to shirk it. No brave and good man can properly shirk death; and no criminal who has earned death should be allowed to shirk it.

❖❖ ❖

As regards capital cases, the trouble is that emotional men and women always see only the individual whose fate is up at the moment, and neither his victim nor the many millions of unknown individuals who would, in the long run, be harmed by what they ask. Moreover, almost any criminal, however brutal, has usually some person, often a person whom he has greatly wronged, who will plead for him. If the mother is alive she will always come, and she cannot help feeling that the case in which she is so concerned is peculiar, that in this case a pardon should be granted. It was really heartrending to have to see the kinsfolk and friends of murderers who were condemned to death, and among the very rare occasions when anything governmental or official caused me to lose sleep were the times when I had to listen to some poor mother making a plea for a criminal so wicked, so utterly brutal and depraved, that it would have been a crime on my part to remit his punishment.

On the other hand, there were certain crimes where requests for leniency merely made me angry. Such crimes were, for instance, rape, or the circulation of indecent literature, or anything connected with what would now be called the "white slave" traffic, or wife murder, or gross cruelty to women and children, or seduction and abandonment, or the action of some man in getting a girl whom he had seduced to commit abortion. I am speaking in each instance of cases that actually came before me, either while I was Governor or while I was President.

In an astonishing number of these cases, men of high standing signed petitions or wrote letters asking me to show leniency to the criminal. In two or three of the cases — one where some young roughs had committed rape on a helpless immigrant girl, and another in which a physician of wealth and high standing had seduced a girl and then induced her to commit abortion — I rather lost my temper, and wrote to the individuals who had asked for the pardon, saying that I extremely regretted that it was not in my power to increase the sentence. I then let the facts be made public, for I thought that my petitioners deserved public censure. Whether they received this public censure or not I did not know, but that my action made them very angry I do know, and their anger gave me real satisfaction. The list of these petitioners was a fairly long one, and included two United States Senators, a Governor of a State, two judges, an editor, and some eminent lawyers and business men.

In the class of cases where the offense was one involving the misuse of large sums of money, the reason for the pressure was different. Cases of this kind more frequently came before me when I was President, but they also came before me when I was Governor, chiefly in the cases of county treasurers who had embezzled funds. A big bank president, a railway magnate, an official connected with some big corporation, or a Government official in a responsible fiduciary position, necessarily belongs among the men who have succeeded in life. This means that his family are living in comfort, and perhaps luxury and refinement, and that his sons and daughters have been well educated. In such a case the misdeed of the father comes as a crushing disaster to the wife and children, and the people of the community, however bitter originally against the man, grow to feel the most intense sympathy for the bowed-down women and children who suffer for the man's fault. It is a dreadful thing in life that so much of atonement for wrong-doing is vicarious. If it were possible in such a case to think only of the banker's or county treasurer's wife and children, any man would pardon the offender at once. Unfortunately, it is not right to think only of the women and children. The very fact that in cases of this class there is certain to be pressure from high sources, pressure sometimes by men who have been beneficially, even though remotely, interested in the man's criminality, no less than pressure because of honest sympathy with the wife and children, makes it necessary that the good public servant shall, no matter how deep his sympathy and regret, steel his heart and do his duty by refusing to let the wrong-doer out. My experience of the way in which pardons are often granted is one of the reasons why I do not believe that life imprisonment for murder and rape is a proper substitute for the death penalty. The average term of so-called life imprisonment in this country is only about fourteen years.

Of course there were cases where I either commuted sentences or pardoned offenders with very real pleasure. For instance, when President, I frequently commuted sentences for horse stealing in the Indian Territory because the penalty for stealing a horse was disproportionate to the penalty for many other crimes, and the offense was usually committed by some ignorant young fellow who found a half-wild horse, and really did not commit anything like as serious an offense as the penalty indicated. The judges would be obliged to give the minimum penalty, but would forward me memoranda stating that if there had been a less penalty. I they would have inflicted it, and I would then commute the sentence to the penalty thus indicated.

In one case in New York I pardoned outright a man convicted of murder in the second degree, and I did this on the recommendation of a friend, Father Doyle of the Paulist Fathers. I had become intimate with the Paulist Fathers while I was Police Commissioner, and I had grown to feel confidence in their judgment, for I had found that they always told me exactly what the facts were about any man, whether he belonged to their church or not. In this case the convicted man was a strongly built, respectable old Irishman employed as a watchman around some big cattle-killing establishments. The young roughs of the neighborhood, which was then of a rather lawless type, used to try to destroy the property of the companies.

In a conflict with a watchman, a member of one of the gangs was slain. The watchman was acquitted, but the neighborhood was much wrought up over the acquittal. Shortly afterwards, a gang of the same toughs attacked another watchman, the old Irishman in question, and finally, to save his own life, he was obliged in self-defense to kill one of his assailants. The feeling in the community, however, was strongly against him, and some of the men high up in the corporation became frightened and thought that it would be better to throw over the watchman. He was convicted.

Father Doyle came to me, told me that he knew the man well, that he was one of the best members of his church, admirable in every way, that he had simply been forced to fight for his life while loyally doing his duty, and that the conviction represented the triumph of the tough element of the district and the abandonment of this man, by those who should have stood by him, under the influence of an unworthy fear. I looked into the case, came to the conclusion that Father Doyle was right, and gave the man a full pardon before he had served thirty days.

The Penitentiary Administration in England (1913)

The idea of using prisons for the punishment of criminals is relatively new. Before the 18th century the prisons were used for the detention of men charged with some crime and awaiting trial and for debtors. Punishment never took the form of deprivation of liberty; for the most serious crimes capital punishment was inflicted, for the less serious the whip, and brand of shame, mutilation, the pillory, the muzzle and the swing. At the same time in order to clear the country of the dangerous vagrants, they transported them to the colonies. This transportation, begun under the reign of Elizabeth (1558-1603) was continued periodically until the revolt of the American colonies. As the population and the wealth of the country increased the criminal laws became more and more severe. Capital punishment reappeared in every new law, for the legislators, suspecting with good reason that nine criminals out of ten escaped the watchfulness of the police, hoped that capital punishment inflicted publicly to the tenth would terrify the nine others to such a degree that they would lack courage to defy the law. But this severity had no preventive effect; in fact, murders and thefts had never been so frequent as at that period of English history.

At the beginning of the 19th, century great improvement is evident in the administration of justice. Capital punishment, except for the most serious crimes was abolished in 1824; in 1861 it was only inflicted in cases of murder or treason; in 1864 all executions take place within the prisons. Meanwhile the discoveries of Captain Cook suggested the idea of using these new lands for the deportation of criminals. But after forty years the increasing number of deported criminals threatening the respectable element of the colonies' Imputation, all the colonies except Western Australia forbade further deportation.

The British government had to find in England a system which would dispose of its criminals. The capacity of the old prisons was increased and for the prisoners who could not be accommodated there, they had to take recourse to the old ships out of service, anchored in the ports on the rivers. The cells were cubical compartments, made of sheet iron and juxtaposed in the center of the ship. Some of these narrow and unhealthy cells were still occupied five years ago. In spite of the endeavors of the central administration, the lodgings arranged for the prisoners remained insufficient and the government found it necessary to discharge on condition a great number of criminals chosen among the least dangerous. In 1864, a system was inaugurated which enabled a prisoner, by his good conduct to shorten his term of detention. The shortest period of detention at this time was 7 years; in 1879 it was reduced to 5 years and in 1891 to 3 years, the courts of justice at the same time being authorized to inflict two years of ordinary imprisonment for offenses which before would have been punished by a period of detention in a central prison. The result of this reform was a great diminution of the criminal population.

There is an essential difference between the ordinary prisons and the central prisons; whereas in the ordinary prisons the men are never allowed to go out, the inmates of the central prisons can be employed in outdoor work under the supervision of armed officers. They work in the quarries, on the farms, at the buildings. Moreover, the interior of their prison is a true factory where all trades are carried on. The prisoners print all the documents necessary to the administration of the prison, bind its books, etc. The reformers of the prisons of the 18th century, fearing the dangers which might arise from freedom of intercourse among the prisoners recommended cellular imprisonment and hard labor as the best means of reforming criminals. At this time two years of hard labor were considered a very serious punishment. The administration was content that the hard labor imposed should be unproductive, as for instance, the disciplinary mill or squirrel-cage and the crank. It was generally believed that the preventive effect of the hard labor was increased in proportion with its unproductiveness.

Causes And Cures Of Crime, Thomas Speed Mosby (1913)

Punishment, to serve as a deterrent by force of example, must be certain if it is to be effective. You may convince a man that he will suffer a penalty he sees inflicted upon another, provided you convince him that he will be detected. How can you convince one man that he will be caught when he sees so many others escaping? Every new crime is a proof that punishment does not deter. If conviction always followed upon the heels of crime, the situation would be vastly different. Even the certainty of detection and exposure would deter most men from crime. It would deter in all cases of deliberate crime, excepting in the case of some defectives and degenerates, and for these the only remedy is permanent isolation. The severity of punishments counts for absolutely nothing as a crime deterrent. This is amply shown in the case of capital punishment.

As practiced in the United States today capital punishment is illogical and inconsistent, both in the manner of its administration and in the reasoning by which it is ostensibly supported. These infirmities are especially apparent in the following among other important particulars: We are accustomed to justify the death penalty as a deterrent example, but we take pains to render the example as inconspicuous as possible by dispatching the victim with the utmost privacy.

Public executions are generally abolished, and are now conducted in the obscurity of a jail yard, with but a very limited number of spectators present. In our day, few indeed are the persons who are permitted to behold the gallows, even in its repose. It is safe to say that the majority of men do not know what it looks like, excepting from hearsay. Not one in ten thousand has seen one.

If the gallows is to serve as a warning against the commission of crime, it should be placed as conspicuously as possible. Men and women should be allowed to inspect it, and to point it out to their children as a thing of terror. It should be a visible manifestation of the majesty of the law, a standing monition of the wage of sin. When culprits are put to death thereon, men, women and children — especially the children — should be present, in order that they may imbibe the full measure of terror which the example should Inspire in the hearts of the people; to the end that, having witnessed the example, they may be impelled by its inspiring force to walk in the ways of righteousness and peace. Yea, more; the victim himself, after his taking off, should be made to subserve the same benign purposes, as was formerly the case, when the criminal's dissevered head was set upon the gates of the prison and his limbs distributed among the principal cities of the kingdom. In such manner was the treason of the Duke of Monmouth punished; but, unfortunately, the example, even then, was not sufficiently potent to prevent the overthrow of King James but a few years later in the Revolution of 1688. In the executions of that elder day, it was also an incident of inspiring solemnity to stick the head of the victim on the end of a pikestaff, as a gruesome reminder of the portentous truth that the way of the transgressor is hard.

By such means the example may be seen and felt, and made so plain that "he who runneth may read." If capital punishment be of any value as a public example the public should be made fully cognizant of that example. A head that is set on a pike-staff, like a city that is set on a hill, cannot be hid. It is futile to undertake to set an example that none can see. An inconspicuous warning is an ineffective warning. Why then was publicity done away with? Why does the hangman shun the light? For this reason only, and none other: Men concluded that such scenes tended to engender sentiments more barbarous than those which they were designed to suppress; i.e., that public executions were brutalizing. Private executions are said to be less brutalizing; the spiritual welfare of Jack Ketch, to be sure, being placed out of the reckoning. It is finally agreed, then, that these public killings are in themselves debasing and immoral, and instead of setting a good example, they set a bad one. And the private execution: Does it set any example at all? If so, what kind of an example? And, insofar as it affects the public mind at all, is not the effect in kind, if not in degree, precisely that which attends the public execution? It can operate as a warning only to the extent that it is known and its terrors realized. The logic that condemns public executions because of their bestializing influence cannot justify the private execution as an influence for good, because it involves a concession that in sofaras that influence extends it is harmful in character. Therefore the private execution, in so far as it exerts an influence, exerts a bad one; otherwise, by the very logic of its advocates, it should not exist.

Whenever recourse is had to do the death penalty, that penalty is applied because it is thought that life imprisonment is not sufficiently severe. Is the death penalty sufficiently severe? How are we to determine this point? If the element of severity be accounted the salient principle of criminal punishments, how can we regard any punishment as sufficiently severe which falls short of preventing crime, and why shall we not increase the penalties to the very limit of severity until crime shall cease or be reduced to its minimum? When we fail to do that, we give evidence of insincerity; we show that we do not believe that which we both preach and practice in our administration of the death penalty. Nothing is more clear than that the gallows and the electric chair do not prevent murder.

Homicidal crime appears to be increasing in the United States. If severity is to be the principal deterrent, then nothing can be plainer than that we are not sufficiently severe in our punishment of murderers. The example we make of them is not sufficiently horrible to impress upon the public mind the extremely hazardous nature of homicide as a trade or pastime. Indeed, we often hear it said of this or that criminal, that "hanging is too good for him."

If death in any manner is impressive because of the severity of the punishment, why is not torture still more impressive? In the time of Henry VIII, those who committed murder by poisoning were boiled to death, like lobsters. Now it is plain that no sane person wants to be boiled alive. Therefore, is it not reasonable to believe that men would refrain from murder if they knew that boiling would be the penalty? Or, they could be fricasseed — or sent to the packing houses, for soap grease. Ravaillac, the man who murdered Henry IV, had his flesh torn off with hot pincers. Vivisection, too, might be practiced upon them, in the interest of science. As early as the 4th century B.C., Herophilus of Alexandria dissected living criminals who were supplied by the state for that philanthropic purpose. Is it reasonable to suppose that any Southern negro would commit rape if he thought he would be turned over, alive, to the "student-doctors" and the dissecting table?

One thing is certain, and that is this: If severe punishments prevent crime, then we are woefully lacking in severity. Hanging is too mild a punishment. The advocates of the scaffold and electric chair are mere maudlin sentimentalists. If they are right in their theory of criminal punishments, they err in not going far enough; if wrong, they have erred in going too far. In either event, the argument for severity, carried to its logical conclusion, is an argument for the abolition of the death penalty as now administered.

Under its own definition of murder, society makes itself as guilty of that crime every time a legal execution occurs as is any culprit who dies upon the scaffold. After a crime has been committed, no private individual has the right, either morally or legally, to deliberately kill the criminal, it matters not how wicked or depraved that criminal may be. Any person who did so would be adjudged guilty of murder. But that which the individual would scorn to do directly, he does indirectly, and that which no private member of society is allowed to do individually is done by society in the aggregate.

The common law definition of murder, as given by Mr. Wharton, one of the greatest authorities on criminal law, is as follows: "Murder is where a person of sound memory and discretion unlawfully kills any reasonable creature in being, and in the peace of the commonwealth, with malice prepense or aforethought, either express or implied." As is well known, malice may be implied from the deliberate use of a deadly weapon, and an instrument certain to produce death is a deadly weapon; *ex. gr.*, the gallows or the electric chair. The gist of the crime in all cases is the deliberate intent to kill.

One need not spring the death trap in order to share the responsibility for a legal execution. In every case society stands by, aiding and abetting the killing.

To make one a principal in a murder it is not necessary that he should inflict the mortal wound. One need not spring the death trap in order to share the responsibility for a legal execution. In every case, society stands by, aiding and abetting the killing. Nor is it necessary, according to the accepted authorities, that the homicide, in order to constitute murder, should be the effect of the "direct" violence of the person charged with murder. If he set in motion the dangerous agency which results in the death of his victim, it may be murder. If a person intentionally do any act towards another, who is helpless, which must, necessarily, lead to the death of that other, it may be murder. It matters not how depraved the victim may be, to deliberately kill him or cause or aid another to do so, is murder. Society says so, and the law decrees it. Even to kill an alien enemy in time of war is murder, unless the killing occur in the exercise of actual warfare.

The general rule under the common law and the statutes of the majority of the American states is that justifiable or excusable homicide can exist only when the proper officer executes a criminal in strict conformity with his sentence, where an officer in the legal exercise of a particular duty kills a person who resists or prevents him from exercising it, or where the homicide is committed in preventing a forcible and atrocious crime; as, for instance, in self-defense, or where the deceased was in the act of committing robbery or murder.

The law, as will be seen, exempts the hangman; for to be a murder the killing must be done "unlawfully," and whatever else may be said of the hangman it cannot be said of him that he hangs persons in violation of the laws as they exist and are declared and construed by the courts. The hangman is merely an agent — your agent and mine. He acts deliberately and with intent to kill. He coolly plans the death of his victim and deliberately carries his plans into execution. But his act is authorized by law. For this reason, and for this reason only, it is not murder. If any other human being, not clothed with his official authority, killed the same person in the same manner, it would be murder.

Society has in the aggregate authorized a particular officer to do a particular act which any other member of society would be hanged for doing. The hangman, however, does not make the law. He can only obey, or else resign and permit its mandates to be carried out by another. But society does make the law.

To the hangman, killing is but obedience to the law. But what law does society obey when it decrees the death penalty and sets in motion the dangerous and deadly agency that destroys a human life? There is no law by which the people of any state are required to authorize capital punishment. They are not forced to do so. They do not act under duress, or any species of compulsion. It is upon their part a voluntary act, deliberately performed, decreeing death to those whom they never saw. Through the hangman, therefore, society commits a murder every time the death penalty is executed. As to society, in such cases (though not as to the hangman) every element of murder exists as defined in the indictment against the victim. Strike the word "unlawful" from the common law definition of murder, and you make the hangman as much a murderer as the man he hangs.

That word defends and acquits the hangman. But to what law society turn for its defense? Confronted with these willful and deliberate homicides done through its decree, how can it escape the charge of murder by the very definition it gives of that crime?

In vain do we search the category of justifiable and excusable homicides for a vindication of the State. You do not execute the condemned man while he is resisting an officer, or while he is attempting to commit some forcible or atrocious crime; you do not execute a criminal in a heat of passion, by accident, or in self-defense.

What, then, has society to say? Simply this: "It is necessary." The major portion of society thinks it necessary that such a one should die. Therein lies the right to kill; therein lies all the defense that can be interposed to the indictment against society for the crime of murder every time it commits a cold-blooded, intentional, deliberate homicide. The victim may think otherwise. A very considerable minority of the members of society unquestionably do think otherwise. We come, then, to this proposition: The right of any man to live depends solely upon the popular vote. Society having decreed by a majority vote that certain persons shall die, they are executed. Is that a defense to the charge of murder? It may be argued for society that the man who commits a capital crime knows in advance what the penalty will be, and that having notice of the consequences, he acts upon his own responsibility and at his own peril, when he incurs the death penalty. This suggests the story of the Texas cowboy who stole a horse. He was lynched, and the coroner's jury brought in a verdict of suicide. But the service of notice of an intention to kill cannot mitigate the crime; it simply emphasizes the murderous intent, and aggravates the element of premeditation, which is the chief constitutive element of the crime of murder.

Having by popular vote determined that in certain cases human beings should be put to death, society has taken unto itself to say when a man shall live and when he shall die; it is the sole judge of the expediency and of the necessity. If it have this right, human existence, then, must depend upon the will of society. If it have the right to say whether or not a man shall die it has, by the same process of reasoning, the same right to say whether he shall be born, and the right which builds the gallows implies the right to commit abortion— or infanticide, as did the Ephora under the constitution of Lycurgas.

It is a distortion of terms and a trifling with words to call this power a right. It is neither more nor less than the exercise of inborn and inherent power, regardless of abstract considerations of right or wrong; and it is the same power which the individual murderer exerts when he slays his victim.

However benevolent the general purpose of legal executions, as to the helpless victim himself their purpose is annihilation, predetermined and premeditated, and the motive is one of murderous malignity. Whether society should continue to commit these deliberate murders may be an open question; but that society does commit murder in the instances mentioned does not admit of doubt.

From the foregoing considerations it appears that our death penalty is an

We do privately that which we would not do openly, we do in part that which we would not do entirely, we do collectively that which we would not do individually and we convict ourselves of the very crime we condemn in others.

anomaly in logic and in law; that it is conceived in ignorance, maintained by falsehood and consummated in murder; that it is inconsistent with itself, with right reason and sound morality, and repudiated by the very logic that seeks to sustain it; that in its administration we do privately that which we would not do openly, we do in part that which we would not do entirely, we do collectively that which we would not do individually and we convict ourselves of the very crime we condemn in others. [. . .]

Singularly enough, so accurate a thinker as Gabriel Tarde, who otherwise writes with great intelligence, appears to attempt a justification of the death penalty, as well as of war, upon the basis of the theory of Malthus and that of Darwin. Neither, however, can be said to offer convincing support to capital punishment. This is easily apparent. In his "Essay on Population," Dr. Malthus attempts to show that population increases more rapidly than the means of subsistence — a proposition by no means demonstrable, because although we may, from our knowledge of the nature of man, be able to forecast to some extent the growth of population, we can by no means and by no manner of possibility estimate the future productivity of the world. New means and methods of production are being discovered every day, so that in some instances an acre of ground is made to yield a hundred times more in food values than it would have yielded at the time when Malthus wrote his essay. The trouble with the Malthusian school of materialists is that they totally ignore the factor of intelligence and the inventive powers of man. But, even if Malthus were correct, that would not cause his doctrine to lend support to capital punishment. On the contrary, it would lend much greater support to murder. Once we reach the conclusion that the human race is multiplying too rapidly and that society is benefited by those things which tend to limit population, we are forced to admit that the professional murderer is to some extent a public benefactor. The death penalty, in that event, would be a very bad thing because it would discourage murder — if it does discourage murder (and M. Tarde thinks that it does).

As to the Darwinian theory of natural selection and the survival of the fittest, that is always a better doctrine for plants and lower animals than it is for men. Besides, homicide committed by the State in administration of the death penalty is not natural selection; it is artificial selection. The law of natural selection would permit the strong to devour or destroy the weak. But, when one attempts that, you hang him for it, and we have "resolution thus fobbed as it is with the rusty curb of old father antic, the law." Fie upon such natural selection. Is that Darwin's theory? By no means. And as to the survival of the fittest — who are they? The eugenists are opposing war because the fittest are usually slain. In Mexico, where assassinations and executions, both legal and illegal, wars and murders, are playing a retaliatory game, we should like to know if the fittest will survive. They will break a Mexican precedent if they do.

All history seems to bear out Beccaria's principle that, in the matter of crime prevention, the certainty of punishment is of far more avail than its severity. If mere severity could avail anything, England would be more lawless today than she was three hundred years ago. But it is known that at no time was thieving so general, and at no time were the rights of property less secure, than during the time when every petit larceny was punishable by death, and thieves were hanged twenty at a time. During the reign of Henry VIII, 70,000 thieves were hanged in England. Commercial paper is more secure in England today than it was when every petty forgery was punishable by death, notwithstanding the fact that when Parliament was considering the bill for the abolition of the death penalty for forgery, the bankers of London protested against the bill upon the ground that its enactment would destroy the value of commercial paper in Great Britain.

Konrad Celtes wrote: "Women who have been brought into disrepute because of witchcraft or superstitious practices, or have been guilty of infanticide or abortion, have various punishments inflicted upon them; being either sewed up in sacks and drowned, or even burned to death, or buried alive. Yet these cruel punishments are not sufficient to prevent their continually adding crime to crime." Historians are advised that there was not as much crime in Rome under the Valerian and Porcian laws, when capital punishment was abolished, as there was in later times, when every tyrant's frown meant a subject's death.

Prof. Ferri says that in the statistics of capital punishment at Ferrara, during nine centuries, he discovered the significant fact that there was a succession of notaries executed for forgery, frequently at very short intervals, in the same town. "This," says he, "attests the truth of the observation made by Montesquieu and Beccaria, as against the deterrent power of the death penalty, for men grow accustomed to the sight; and this again is confirmed by the fact mentioned by M. Roberts, a jail chaplain, and M. Birenger, a magistrate, that several condemned men had previously been present at executions, and by another act mentioned by Despine and Angelucci, that in the same town, and often in the same place, in which executions had been carried out, murders are often committed on the same day."

A similar occurrence was detailed by the late Justice Fox of the Supreme Court of Missouri. While he was "on circuit" a large concourse assembled to witness an execution, in one of the counties of his circuit, in the days of the public hangings. Various affrays occurred in the crowd, and two men were stabbed, one of them fatally. Indeed, one of the reasons for making all executions private in the United States, was the fact that the public execution was usually the occasion for the assembling of a disorderly crowd, in which bloodshed was by no means a rare occurrence.

WITNESS TO AN EXECUTION
An Alienist: Personal And Professional
Allan Mclane Hamilton (1916)

Several years ago I was called to testify in behalf of a street railway company in Brooklyn, engaged in defending a suit brought by the widow of a passenger who had been killed by the passage of an electric current through his body as the result of some alleged defect in insulation of the trolley connection. I had given much expert testimony, theoretical and otherwise, in my direct examination, for I had had much experience in the effect of dangerous currents of electricity upon the human body, and had written a book over thirty years before which was then an authority. Whatever good effect my testimony produced upon the jury was evidently minimized by the first question put to me by my friend Herbert Smyth, a clever and quick-witted lawyer who appeared for the other side. It was this: "Doctor, have you ever seen a man killed by a strong electric current?" To which I was forced to reply in the negative.

As the result of this experience I determined at the first opportunity to qualify myself for any subsequent appearance upon the witness stand in any other possible case of this kind, and within a few months I was invited to attend an electrocution at the State's Prison at Ossining, the hour being fixed at six o'clock in the morning. After a rather sleepless night at a small local hotel, I went at the break of dawn to the low-lying grey prison, a mile away. The winter morning was cold and still, but the sharp snap of the exhaust from the engine ahead, preparing to supply the terrible force which was to crush out the life of the wretched murderer, reached my ears as I walked along the snow-crusted road. In the prison office I found several silent and decidedly nervous men who, like myself, were to be present as the guests of the tall, cadaverous warden; who, after the last late-comer arrived, beckoned us to follow him out and around the corner to an insignificant brick building.

As we entered, most of the small room was in darkness, but in the center was an ugly, cumbersome wooden chair upon which was placed a number of glowing electric bulbs, all harmless enough in themselves, but horrible in their suggestion that their resistance was typical of what was in store for the unfortunate who was later to take their place. The ugliness of the chair and its business-like character were striking, for no such piece of furniture could be used for anything but torture, and it forcibly called up the old wood cuts of the Inquisition that I collect. As I entered the door there was a semi-circle of absorbed, silent men seated behind a rope stretched across the end of the room — with a grim suggestion of a dead minstrel troupe without an "interlocutor" or the end men. In the center of the room were business-like doctors and the warden, who tried the straps and patted the chair as if it were a living thing, while dodging behind a switch-board was an insignificant-looking little man who tried his apparatus with seeming enjoyment, peering at the chair and lamps

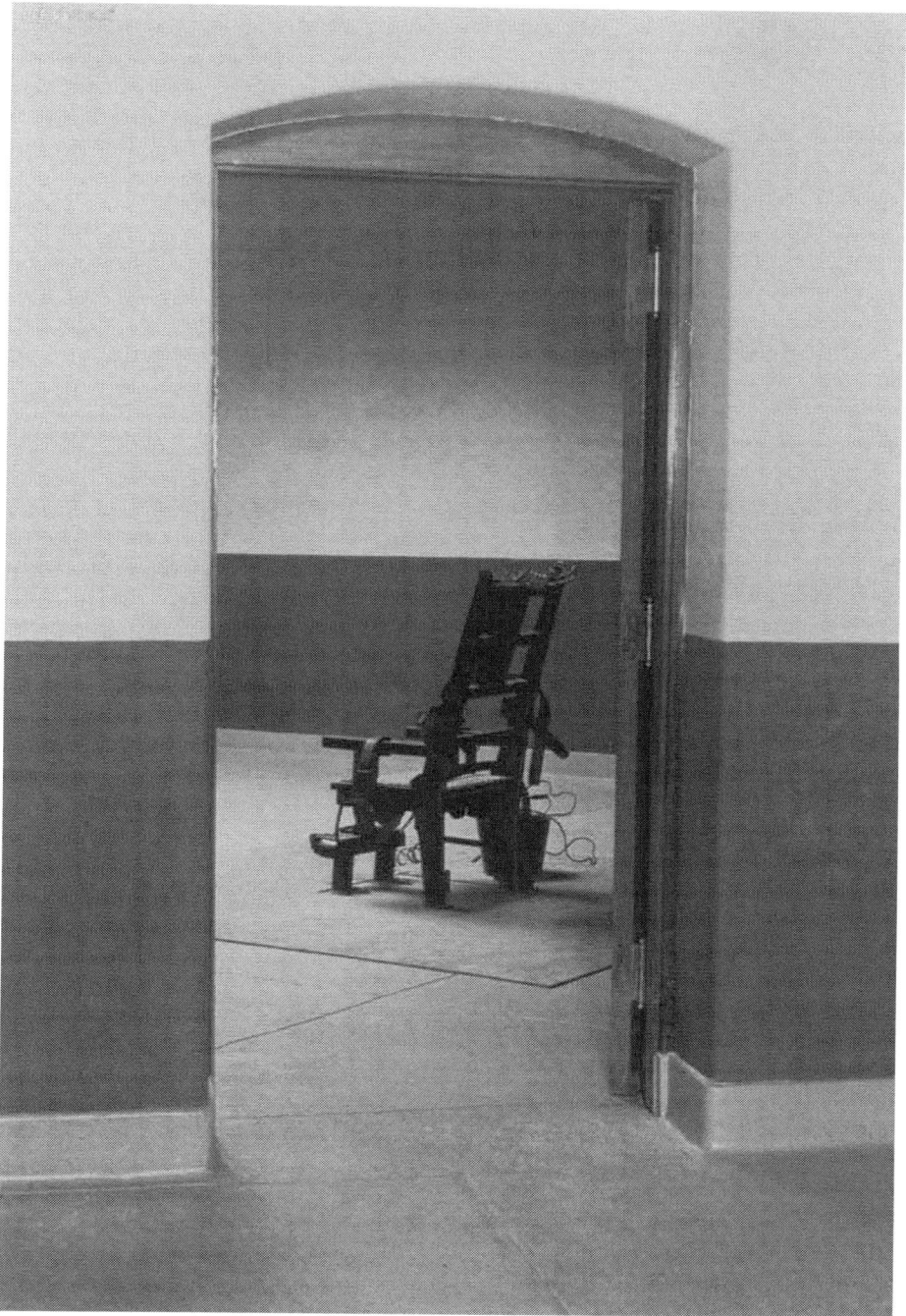

occasionally, until finally everything was in order.

Presently a slight noise was heard at the north end of the room, and through a small door came a wretched, bareheaded man in a shirt and trousers only, supported on either side by two priests who mumbled prayers with him and placed in his hands a crucifix. After being rapidly strapped in the chair, one electrode was fastened upon his shaven head and the other was affixed to the calves of his legs. The tall warden then gave what was to us an imperceptible signal; the executioner pulled his knife-switch open, and the condemned sank, and, after a general convulsion, became a limp thing and had apparently lost in stature. Coincidentally he raised his crucifix, which was held in his right hand, to his lips. The doctors examined his pupils, and after some discussion it was decided to apply the current a second time, which was evidently sufficient, for the pupillary reflexes were lost, and the man pronounced dead. It was but a matter of moments for the attendants to unlimber and take him to an adjoining room, where he was stripped and left for the autopsy which was to follow in a short time.

All this had scarcely happened before another slight disturbance attended the entry of a fresh victim—this time it was a burly German who had strangled his wife in a fit of jealous rage a year previously, in the city of New York. His excursion from "the little door" to the chair was quite as striking an evidence of torpor and indifference as that of the degenerate Italian whose still warm body at that moment was awaiting the knives of the pathologists. This time the killing was more difficult, and when the warden said to the electrician, "You had better give him another," the increased current was sufficient to form a tiny arc beneath the rim of the head electrode, so that the smell of burned flesh and hair was distressingly perceptible and horrid. It was not long before my nervous system and stomach rebelled and I hurried to the cool outer air and left Sing Sing as soon as I could.

Although I have seen many dreadful things during the past forty years, I don't think any other has ever raised my gorge as this had done, and for weeks my dreams were filled with the details of that half hour. I had seen men hung years before in the yard of the Tombs—and for the most part these executions were solemn affairs. Even the ward politician and political heeler who had "got a ticket" were awed, and reverently followed the prayer of the black-robed priests, and everything seemed to be decent and in order; meanwhile scores of white pigeons fluttered on the heads of the condemned men or even alighted on the top of the scaffold.

I am sorry to say that the method of electrical execution did not give this impression, and there was a more or less decided feeling that everyone thought more of the success of the procedure than that a human being, no matter how wicked, was being sent out of the world with so short a shrift. I was impressed on this occasion, as I have been on others, with the fact that the condemned criminal—at least so far as his actions are concerned—does not suffer as might be supposed, and by a wise provision of nature, becomes at the last so indifferent to his fate that he rather welcomes the noose or the current. I can recall only a few exceptions— chiefly among young people. When three brothers who had committed a murder at Hudson were electrocuted a few years ago, their terror was pitiable, and they resisted till the last moment. Others have gone to their death protesting their innocence, like Carlyle Harris, the wife poisoner, or exhibited actual insanity as did Czolgosz.

The long months in the death house, after the Court of Appeals refuses to interfere, does the work, and the gruesome camaraderie of the many others likewise awaiting their fate minimizes the awful terrors of the last scenes. The man without hope often grows actually fat, gaining from ten to thirty pounds in weight.

Roland B. Molineux, who was twice tried for criminal poisoning and finally acquitted, spent many months in the death chamber, and graphically describes the dreadful anticipation of the occupants of its ten cells which are always brilliantly lighted in the daytime by glass skylights and at night by gas and electric light. "It is," he said, "like living, eating, sleeping, and bathing in a searchlight. It is like being alive, yet buried in a glass coffin."

The pursuits of the doomed men are varied. They play checkers upon home-made boards, calling the moves to each other; sing, learn new languages, and read. One even raised onions, using discarded tobacco as soil, in which they flourished. One German trained the mice he lured to his cell with bread crumbs and made pets of them as Silvio Pellico did with his bird.

Everyone knew when the number was reduced by the passage of a victim through the little door beyond, and one man became violently insane as the result of the suspense and horror. I remember once a terrible scene at the City Prison when three Negroes, who had murdered a peddler at New Rochelle, were executed together, which is an exception to what I have said. Neither of them exhibited any cowardice when led into the square, but after the rope that held the sand bag counterweight was cut, and their bodies shot up, the younger prisoner, who was in the middle, contrived to raise his legs and entwine them about the neck of the man next to him; so that the knot was shifted and for a time he was conscious. It was not long, however, before he changed his position and submitted to the inevitable. In one way, it was a suicide.

When Mr. Elbridge Gerry and other philanthropists some years ago objected to hanging, and wrote to some of us for suggestions that we should name a better substitute, I advocated the lethal chamber, which is a humane and inexpensive method of execution without the attendant publicity. My idea was to sentence the prisoner, as is now the case, to be put to death in a certain week. The death chamber might be very readily fitted with pipes through which carbon dioxide or monoxide should be introduced at night to the unsuspecting condemned man, who would never awaken from his last sleep, and have none of the horrid fear of the actual execution. The absolute painlessness of this death and its freedom from preliminary horror recommends it strongly.

Charcoal gas poisoning, which is so popular in France, and so generally used there, is the same thing. It is inexpensive, absolutely certain, and no complicated apparatus is required. All that is needed is a furnace, or receptacle for liquefied carbonic oxide, which is connected with a hidden aperture in the cell of the condemned. When the prisoner is asleep this cell can be hermetically sealed at the appointed time in a noiseless way, and the gas valve turned on. As carbonic acid gas is heavier than air, it of course falls to the lower part of the room and engulfs the sleeping prisoner.

The more dramatic and complicated method was, however, adopted, and in inexperienced hands is capable of great misapplication and harm. In the early days of electrocution in this state, at least one man was half killed, subsequently restored, and taken back to the chair "to get a heavier dose," which was sufficient to comply with the law.

A current of 1,260 volts was turned on at a given signal, and with a crash the legs shot forward and upward, tearing the standard and entire front from the chair. For 52 seconds this condition was sustained and the current was shut off. For twenty seconds the condemned man appeared to be dead, but then he gasped.

On July 27th, 1893, a murderer named William G. Taylor was electrocuted at the Auburn prison. A current of 1,260 volts was turned on at a given signal, and with a crash the legs shot forward and upward, tearing the standard and entire front from the chair. For 52 seconds this condition was sustained and the current was shut off. For twenty seconds the condemned man appeared to be dead, but then he gasped. The executioner tried again to turn on the current, but there was some hitch. Within half a minute the pulse beats reappeared, faintly at first but distinctly later, and respiration became evident. The breathing was stertorous and the subject resembled a patient in an apoplectic state. He next moved both hands, arms and legs and rolled from side to side. Morphine in large doses was given hypodermically and, this failing, the man was chloroformed. He objected at first, but was carried to the electric chair and received a current with a voltage of 1,260, which finally killed him.

This was one of the earlier cases and the query immediately arises whether today, in places where electrocution is adopted, there is not sometimes bungling of which nothing is said. It does not appear that at Sing Sing any such sickening accidents have happened.

While I do not wish to make an unprovable and perhaps unjust charge, I do believe it possible that there have been occasions where the causation of actual death is a matter of doubt. Of course the autopsy made within two hours will settle this question, but if the electrical current is to be used, the public officials should avail themselves of the teachings of modern physiologists who have shown that the passage of a sufficient current directly through the heart is certain to kill, and this they have not yet done. A perusal of the many reports of people who have lived even after the receipt of currents of enormous voltage and amperage suggests the important idea that the present method of application of the electrodes is defective. Arsonoval has reported cases where currents of 5,000 voltage have by some system of surface connection passed out of the body without doing any great harm. The immediate effect is in such cases, the production of burns and unconsciousness, and in a few a trance-like condition has remained in a way resembling "hysterical catalepsy," which is often mistaken for actual death.

The late Dr. Francis Harris of Boston, who was for many years the local

Medical Examiner, and whose duty compelled him to be present at electrical executions, wrote me before he died about his strong abhorrence of this form of punishment; he believed it brutal and unscientific, and that it should be abolished, and said that in every case in which he officially appeared he feared some dreadful miscarriage would occur.

The inventive genius of New England has been exercised to make more merciful and successful the use of hanging, which in many ways is better than electrocution. My attention was directed in 1894 to an "automatic gallows" devised by the Superintendent of the Connecticut State Prison at Weathersfield. This consisted of a platform upon which the condemned man stood, connected with a hidden system of complicated levers and heavy weights. The ingenious part of the apparatus was a small receptacle filled with gunshot which were gradually released, allowing a superimposed light iron weight to release the levers which actuated a greater one of three hundred and fifty pounds—quite enough to do what was required. The shot-receptacle emptied itself in forty seconds, a period of time which was recorded by a grim-looking dial and hand, or the contents could be released en masse, producing an immediate effect. It was copied after an "automatic water gallows" in Colorado; but as the life of the condemned man in one instance I heard of had been snuffed out despite the efforts to stop another machine when a reprieve was on its way, this gruesome possibility was avoided by the use of a foot lever which enabled the warden to check the operation of the shot box at any time, avoiding such a deplorable eventuality.

It would seem as if the element of theatrical display were indispensable to public execution in this country alone, for abroad nowadays the taking off of the condemned is conducted with secrecy and decency, especially in Germany and England. It is only a year or two ago that the newspapers were filled with accounts of special trains being run to an execution in the southwestern part of the United States, and just such hysterical scenes were enacted as might have occurred in the Place de la Roquette in the flourishing days of the guillotine—yet I doubt if there was then the same vulgarity and heartlessness that now exist among our own countrymen at such a hanging, or the occasional burnings which too often occur.

Except upon extraordinary occasions, I believe capital punishment can do no good, for most murder is committed by individuals who are degenerates or insane criminals, and isolation with sterilization and hard work would serve the same purpose. In Italy, the plan of utilizing small islands, like Ponza, off the coast, where condemned murderers support themselves and are of use to the State, works very well. There is a species of savagery in the cruel and vengeful life-imprisonment in a dungeon in political cases which is a virtual immuration, the result being a quickly induced insanity and speedy death. To those advanced criminologists who are interested in eugenics, the idea of capital punishment, which, after all, is but a part of the vengeful Mosaic Law, is today in disfavor, as it deserves to be.

WITNESS TO AN EXECUTION
Memoirs Of Sarah Bernhardt (1907)

Well, everything was now explained to us. The goods train which had started before us ran off the line, but no great damage was done, and no one was killed. The St. Louis band of robbers had arranged everything, and had prepared to have this little accident two miles from the Little Incline, in case their comrade crouching under my car had not been able to unhook it. The train had left the rails, but when the wretches rushed forward, believing that it was mine, they found themselves surrounded by the band of detectives. It seems that they fought like demons. One of them was killed on the spot, two more wounded, and the remainder taken prisoners. A few days later, the chief of this little band was hanged. He was a Belgian, named Albert Wirbyn, twenty-five years of age. I did all in my power to save him, for it seemed to me that unintentionally I had been the instigator of his evil plan.

If Abbey and Jarrett had not been so rabid for advertisement, if they had not added more than six hundred thousand francs worth of jewelry to mine, this man, this wretched youth, would not perhaps have had the stupid idea of robbing me. Who can say what schemes had floated through the mind of the poor fellow, who was perhaps half-starved, or perhaps excited by a clever, inventive brain? Perhaps when he stopped and looked at the jeweler's window he said to himself: "There is jewelry there worth a million francs. If it were all mine I would sell it and go back to Belgium. What joy I could give to my poor mother, who is blinding herself with work by gaslight, and I could help my sister to get married." Or perhaps he was an inventor, and he thought to himself: "Ah, if only I had the money which that jewelry represents I could bring out my invention myself, instead of selling my patent to some highly esteemed rascal, who will buy it from me for a crust of bread. What would it matter to the *artiste*?

"Ah, if only I had the money! Ah, if I had the money!" — perhaps the poor fellow cried with rage to think of all this wealth belonging to one person. Perhaps the idea of crime germinated in this way in a mind which had hitherto been pure. Ah, who can tell to what hope may give birth in a young mind? At first it may be only a beautiful dream, but this may end in a mad desire to realize the dream. To steal the goods of another person is certainly not right, but this should not be punished by death—it certainly should not. To kill a man of twenty-five years of age is a much greater crime than to steal jewelry even by force, and a society which bands together in order to wield the sword of Justice is much more cowardly when it kills than the man who robs and kills quite alone, at his own risk and peril. Oh, what tears I wept for that man, whom I did not know at all— who was a rascal or perhaps a hero! He was perhaps a man of weak intellect, who had turned thief, but he was only twenty-five years of age, and he had a right to live.

How I hate capital punishment! It is a relic of cowardly barbarism, and it is a disgrace for civilized countries still to have their guillotines and scaffolds. Every human being has a moment when his heart is easily touched, when the tears of grief will flow; and those tears may fecundate a generous thought which might lead to repentance.

I would not for the whole world be one of those who condemn a man to death. And yet many of them are good, upright men, who when they return to their families, are affectionate to their wives, and reprove their children for breaking a doll's head.

I have seen four executions, one in London, one in Spain, and two in Paris.

In London the method is hanging, and this seems to me more hideous, more repugnant, more weird than any other death. The victim was a young man of about thirty, with a strong, self-willed looking face. I only saw him a second, and he shrugged his shoulders as he glanced at me, his eyes expressing his contempt for my curiosity. At that moment I felt that individual's ideas were very much superior to mine, and the condemned man seemed to me greater than all who were there. It was, perhaps, because he was nearer than we all were to the great mystery. I can see him now smile as they covered his face with the hood, while, as for me, I rushed away completely upset.

In Madrid I saw a man garroted, and the barbarity of this torture terrified me for weeks after. He was accused of having killed his mother, but no real proof seemed to have been brought forward against the wretched man. And he cried out, when they were holding him down on his seat before putting the garrote on him, "Mother, I shall soon be with you, and you will tell them all, in my presence, that they have lied."

These words were uttered in Spanish, in a voice that vibrated with earnestness. They were translated for me by an attaché to the British Embassy, with whom I had gone to see the hideous sight. The wretched man cried out in such a sincere, heartrending tone of voice that it was impossible for him not to have been innocent, and this was the opinion of all those who were with me.

The two other executions which I witnessed were at the *Place de la Roquette*, Paris. The first was that of a young medical student, who with the help of one of his friends, had killed an old woman who sold newspapers. It was a stupid, odious crime, but the man was more mad than criminal. He was more than ordinarily intelligent, and had passed his examinations at an earlier age than is usual. He had worked too hard, and it had affected his brain. He ought to have been allowed to rest, to have been treated as an invalid, cured in mind and body, and then returned to his scientific pursuits. He was a young man quite above the average as regards intellect. I can see him now, pale and haggard, with a dreamy, far-away look in his eyes, an expression of infinite sadness. I know, of course, that he had killed a poor, defenseless old woman. That was certainly odious, but he was only twenty-three years old, and his mind was disordered through study and overwork, too much ambition, and the habit of cutting off arms and legs and dissecting the dead bodies of women and children. All this does not excuse the man's abominable deed, but it had all contributed to unhinge his moral sense, which was perhaps already in a wavering state, thanks to study, poverty, or atavism. I consider that a crime of high treason against humanity was committed in taking the life of a man of intellect, who, when once he had recovered his reason, might have rendered great service to science and to humanity.

The last execution at which I was present was that of Vaillant, the anarchist. He was an energetic man, and at the same time mild and gentle, with very advanced ideas, but not much more advanced than those of men who have since risen to power.

My theatre at that time was the Renaissance, and he often applied to me for free seats, as he was too poor to pay for the luxuries of art. Ah, poverty, what a sorry counselor art thou, and how tolerant we ought to be to those who have to endure misery!

One day Vaillant came to see me in my dressingroom at the theatre. I was playing Lorenzaccio, and he said to me: "Ah, that Florentine was an anarchist just as I am, but he killed the tyrant and not tyranny. That is not the way I shall go to work."

A few days later he threw a bomb in a public building, the Chamber of Deputies. The poor fellow was not as successful as the Florentine, whom he seemed to despise, for he did not kill any one, and did no real harm except to his own cause.

I said I should like to know when he was to be executed, and the night before, a friend of mine came to the theatre and told me that the execution was to take place the following day, Monday, at seven in the morning.

I started after the performance, and went to the *Rue Merlin*, at the corner of the *Rue de la Roquette*. The streets were still very animated, as that Sunday was *Dimanche Gras* [*Shrove Sunday*]. People were singing, laughing, and dancing everywhere. I waited all night, and as I was not allowed to enter the prison, I sat on the balcony of a first floor flat, which I had engaged. The cold darkness of the night in its immensity seemed to enwrap me in sadness. I did not feel the cold, for my blood was flowing rapidly through my veins. The hours passed slowly, the hours which rang out in the distance, *L'hettre ext morte. Vive Theure!* I heard a vague, muffled sound of footsteps, whispering, and of wood which creaked heavily, but I did not know what these strange, mysterious sounds were until day began to break. I saw that the scaffold was there. A man came to extinguish the lamps on the *Place de la Roquette*, and an anæmic-looking sky spread its pale light over us. The crowd began to collect gradually, but remained in compact groups, and circulation in the streets was interrupted. Every now and then a man, looking quite indifferent, but evidently in a hurry, pushed aside the crowd, presented a card to a policeman, and then disappeared under the porch of the prison. I counted more than ten of these men: they were journalists. Presently the military guard appeared suddenly on the spot, and took up its position around the melancholy-looking pedestal. The usual number of the guard had been doubled for this occasion, as some anarchist plot was feared. On a given signal swords were drawn and the prison door opened.

Vaillant appeared, looking very pale, but energetic and brave. He cried out in a manly voice, with perfect assurance, "*Vive l'anarchie!*" There was not a single cry in response to his. He was seized and thrown back over the slab. The knife fell with a muffled sound. The body tottered, and in a second the scaffold was taken away, the place swept; the crowds were allowed to move. They rushed forward to the place of execution, gazing down on the ground for a spot of blood which was not to be seen, sniffing in the air for any odor of the drama which had just been enacted.

There were women, children, old men, all joking there on the very spot where a man had just expired in the most supreme agony. And that man had made himself the apostle of this populace; that man had claimed for this teeming crowd, all kinds of liberties, all kinds of privileges and rights.

I was thickly veiled so that I could not be recognized, and accompanied by a friend as escort.

I mingled with the crowd, and it made me sick at heart and desperate. There was not a word of gratitude to this man, not a murmur of vengeance nor of revolt.

I felt inclined to cry out: "Brutes that you are! Kneel down and kiss the stones that the blood of this poor madman has stained for your sakes, for you, because he believed in you."

But before I had time for this a street urchin was calling out, "Buy the last moments of Vaillant! Buy, buy!"

Oh, poor Vaillant! His headless body was then being taken to Clamart, and the crowds for whom he had wept, worked, and died were now going quietly away, indifferent and bored. Poor Vaillant! His ideas were exaggerated ones, but they were generous.

I Cannot Be Silent, Leo Tolstoy (1908)

I take up today's paper. Today, the 9th of May, it is something awful. The paper contains these few words: Today in Kherson on the Strelbitsky Field, twenty peasants were hung for an attack made with intent to rob, on a landed proprietor's estate in the Elizabetgrad district.

Twelve of those by whose labor we live, the very men whom we have depraved and are still depraving by every means in our power—from the poison of vodka to the terrible falsehood of a creed we do not ourselves believe in, but impose on them with all our might — twelve of these men, strangled with cords by those whom they feed and clothe and house, and who have depraved and still continue to deprave them. Twelve husbands, fathers, sons, from among those on whose kindness, industry and simplicity alone rests the whole of Russian life, were seized, imprisoned and shackled. Then their hands are tied behind their backs lest they should seize the ropes by which they would be hung, and they are led to the gallows. Several peasants similar to those who are about to be hung, but armed, dressed in clean soldiers' uniforms, with good boots on their feet and with guns in their hands, accompany the condemned men. Beside them walks a long-haired man, wearing a stole and vestments of gold or silver cloth, and bearing a cross. The procession stops. The manager of the whole business says something: the secretary reads a paper; and when the paper has been read, the long-haired man, addressing those whom other people are about to strangle with cords, says something about God and Christ. Immediately after these words, the hangmen (there are several, for one man could not manage so complicated a business) dissolves some soap, and having soaped the loops in the cords that they may tighten better, seize the shackled men, put shrouds on them, lead them to a scaffold and place the well-soaped nooses around their necks.

And then, one after another, living men are pushed off the benches which are drawn from under their feet, and by their own weight suddenly tighten the nooses round their necks, and are painfully strangled. Men, alive a minute before, become corpses dangling from a rope; at first slowly swinging, and them resting motionless.

All this is carefully arranged and planned by learned and enlightened people of the upper class. They arrange to do these things secretly at daybreak so that no one shall see them done, and they arrange that the responsibility for these iniquities shall be so subdivided among those who commit them that each may think and say that it is not he who is responsible for them. They arrange to seek out the most depraved and unfortunate of men and, while obliging them to do this business planned and approved by themselves, still keep up an appearance of abhorring those who do it. Even such a subtle device is planned as this; sentences are pronounced by a military tribunal, yet it is not the military but civilians who have to be present at the execution. And the business is performed by unhappy, deluded, perverted and despised men, who have nothing left them but to soap the cords well, that they may grip the necks without fail, then to get well drunk on poison sold them by these same enlightened upper-class people, in order more quickly and fully to forget their souls and their quality as men. A doctor makes his round of the bodies, feels them, and reports to those in authority that the business has been done properly; all twelve are certainly dead. And those in authority depart to their ordinary occupations, with the consciousness of a necessary though painful task performed. The bodies, now grown cold, are taken down and buried.

The thing is awful!

And this is not done once, and not to these twelve unhappy, misguided men from among the best class of the Russian people only, but is done unceasingly for years, to hundreds and thousands of similar misguided men, misguided by the very people who do these awful things to them.

And not this kind of dreadful thing alone is being done, but on the same plea and with the same cold-blooded cruelty, all sorts of other tortures and violence are being perpetrated in prisons, fortresses and convict settlements.

And while this goes on for years all over Russia, the chief culprits of these acts — those by whose order these things are done, those who could put a stop to them — fully convinced that such deeds are useful and even absolutely necessary, either devise methods and make up speeches how to prevent the Finns from living as they want to live, and how to compel them to live as certain Russian personages wish them to live; or else publish orders to the effect that "In Hussar regiments, the cuffs are collars of the men's jackets are to be of the color of the latter, while the pelisses of those entitled to wear them are not have braid round the cuffs over the fur."

This is awful!

Capital Punishment of Mentally Defective Murderers
The Calcutta Journal of Medicine (1908)

Our attention is almost daily called to the problem of disposition of murderers, who show more or less plainly mental defects. In practically every case of homicide in which self-defense, absolute lack of intent to kill or other obvious excuse or justification is not manifest, the plea of insanity is either made or seriously contemplated by the defense. Neurology has also, within the last few years, recognized many phases of mental perturbation and deficiency, not generally recognized as constituting insanity. Thus, self-interest, on the part of the slayer and his family, abstruse scientific conclusions and humanity have united to emphasize the importance of mental aberration in regard to the subsequent dealings of the State with the slayer.

Our caption is faulty in two respects; first, we believe that the legal killing of those who have killed their fellows should not primarily be regarded as punishment; secondly, the term murderer is not technically applicable to one who kills without intention, or full realization of the nature of the act.

Why do we put to death or sentence to life imprisonment those who have killed other men? Unquestionably, up to less than a century ago, the proper answer would have been to avenge a wrong. Indeed, even the word revenge might have been applicable. Unquestionably, too, there is a survival of this attitude in a large part of the community. According to this sentiment, the death penalty or that of life imprisonment may rightly be considered a punishment. A broader spirited view of legal punishment of crime brings into prominence two other factors—reformation of the criminal and determent of potential criminals through fear of consequences.

These two factors are, however, less conspicuous in regard to manslaughter than in regard to any other crime. In the first place, popular sentiment always has and probably always will demand either actual death or the living death of permanent imprisonment for murderers as the term is commonly and not very accurately employed. Such punishment obviously renders reformation, except in the moral and religious sense as applied to one permanently removed from human society, out of the question. Again, in a large proportion of homicides, especially those to which the term murder is strictly applicable, the ultimate reason leading to the killing is so personal and so obsessive, that no penalty will deter anyone contemplating murder nor, on the other hand, will the lack of penalty predispose to crime.

Criminal acts in general may be classified as impersonal and personal. Those against property are, as a rule impersonal, at least when perpetrated for the immediate interests of the criminal. Very occasionally theft, burglary, etc., are committed as acts of revenge, but damage to property from personal motives usually takes the form of arson or other wanton destruction. So too, perjury is usually committed in the immediate interest of the criminal and only rarely with the object of getting a particular individual into trouble. On the other hand, killing, assault, etc., is peculiarly frequent as an expression, of personal hatred although we must also recognize such acts as dependent upon mental perversion — when they are rather apt to be associated with sexual perversion — in which an inexplicable pleasure is had in injury and death without regard to individuality of the victim; and as dependent upon other forms of criminality, usually dishonest acquisition of property. In the last group of cases, we must further distinguish the burglar, highwayman, etc., who kills merely incidentally, perhaps very reluctantly or even unintentionally, the one who combines dishonesty with cruelty and the one who happens to be actuated by personal malice.

Now, viewing the matter impartially, without either bitterness or sympathetic weakness, it seems to us that the sole excuse and justification of the death penalty is to remove permanently from human society an excessively dangerous member. Life imprisonment meets the same end but less certainly and less economically. On the other hand, the abolition of capital punishment marks a general elevation of the moral and religious tone of the community though we would not go so far as to advocate it. To avoid confusion, let us eliminate all cases of manslaughter which are commonly recognized as justifiable—for instance self-defense either against actual assault or in dealing with burglars, etc.—or entirely unintentional and not due to criminal carelessness, or committed by persons at the time recognized as insane, *non compos mentis*—as in the case of young children who kill their companions in sport and without any realization of the nature of what they are doing, etc.

The remaining cases include a large group in which there is no reasonable danger of the repetition of the act further than that, having once usurped the functions of the judiciary, the perpetrator of the crime may rightly be considered liable to repeat the offense in the future. In many such instances, aside from the unwisdom of allowing any individual to usurp the prerogative of the whole people, public sentiment upholds him and regards his act as definitely useful. In many other instances, embarrassment is avoided by the immediate suicide of the slayer. In a second large group, the slayer is a professional criminal, a menace and expense to the community even if he kills no one and there is no question that he should be put out of the way. In a third group, to which we allude particularly, careful review of the case in retrospect, shows more or less mental warping of the slayer.

For instance, Dr. S. Grover Burnet in the Medical Fortnightly of December 25, 1907, studies the histories of three criminal epileptics who have taken eleven lives. There has also recently occurred the second trial of Thaw, the defense concentrating their efforts on the plea of insanity, although apparently, no one had ever thought of him as insane prior to his killing of White. At the risk of seeming brutal, we would advocate that, for this entire group of cases, the only safe rule is to regard capital punishment or its substitute, life imprisonment, not as punishment in any true sense of the word, but as a means of ridding society of dangerous members.

From this standpoint, it makes little difference whether we can make out a distinct mental warping or not. From the practical standpoint such cases are of greater danger to society than the unquestionably sane murderer who, without previous criminality and with deliberate purpose takes the law into his own hands and kills some individual against whom lie has a bitter grudge. They are of even greater potential danger than the criminal who kills in the pursuit of burglary or highway robbery. The latter may be rendered honest by reformatory methods or the natural process of maturity, and if reformed so far as honesty is concerned he is not likely to commit murder again. The great danger in the insanity plea with regard to murderers is that they will be discharged from custody as insane, while retaining the characteristics which have led them to commit the first murder. Even in custody in proper asylums, they remain a source of danger to companions and custodians.

Moreover, to take a particular instance, there is no reasonable question but that the acquittal of Thaw was on account of his financial resources, whereas, exactly the same circumstances repeated in low life would already have led to a conviction. Generally speaking it is exceedingly difficult, even impossible, to distinguish sharply between mere folly and lunacy, between a bad temper and a moral idiocy, between the immediate effects of alcohol and its permanent effect on the brain. Strictly speaking, it is illogical and unethical to hold a man accountable for criminal acts perpetrated while he is drunk. Men have been hauled for murders committed under the influence of alcohol, although they couldn't even remember the deed. Yet, as a matter of practical utility it seems impossible to consider drunkenness as an excuse for crime.

As an academic proposition, it is fairly questionable whether a person who is mentally normal will never kill either himself or others, yet, in the crude practical sense, we must recognize sane suicides and murderers. In many instances the question of insanity is not raised by the defense simply because the murderer does not wish to save his life or because there is no one to take sufficient interest in his defense. There are obvious ethical difficulties in the way of allowing a state of affairs which will necessarily let wealth or influence play an important part on the disposition of criminals. It is equally unethical to allow the choice between capital punishment and imprisonment to rest in any sense with the murderer. If, on the other hand, capital punishment is abandoned, it is only a matter of a comparatively short time when we shall have undergoing life imprisonment hundreds of persons, perfectly sane, perfectly well disposed, virtually different in every way from the men condemned for murder—just as different, for example, as you and we are at our maturity or in our senility from the immature cubs we once were.

What shall be done with these persons? It will be unjust to keep them in captivity. It will be sociologically uneconomic, for many murderers are men of ability and excellent qualities. If the pardoning power is exercised, we shall have the same play of financial and personal influence as in the original trial; we shall have under the present rule of gubernatorial discretion, displays of individual temperament varying from cold-bloodedness to maudlin sympathy. Mistakes will be made which will turn loose on the community crafty criminals who have nursed their vengeance for years and have covered it with a cloak of hypocrisy, or mental defectives who have shown apparent recovery under the routine of confinement. We can see no simple and satisfactory way out of the dilemma but strongly incline to the idea that, in the absence of ample justification, capital punishment, not as a matter of vengeance, but as a safeguard to society, is the best method of dealing with the slayer of man, without regard to impracticable refinements of neurology.

Against Capital Punishment (*Eine Ehrenpflicht*)
Rosa Luxemburg (1918)

We did not wish for amnesty, nor for pardon, in the case of the political prisoners, who had been the prey of the old order. We demanded the right to liberty, to agitation, to revolution for the hundreds of brave and loyal men who groaned in the jails and in the fortresses because, under the former dictatorship of Imperialist criminals, they had fought for the people, for peace, and for socialism.

They are all free now.

We find ourselves again in the ranks, ready for the battle.

It was not the clique of Scheidemann and his bourgeois allies, with Prince Max of Baden at their head, that liberated us. It was the Proletarian Revolution that made the doors of our cells spring open.

But another class of unfortunate dwellers in those gloomy mansions has been completely forgotten. No one, at present, thinks of the pale and morbid figures which sigh behind prison walls because of offenses against ordinary law. Nevertheless these are also the unfortunate victims of the infamous social order against which the Revolution is directed – victims of the Imperialistic war which pushed distress and misery to the very limit of intolerable torture, victims of that frightful butchery of men which let loose all the vilest instincts.

The justice of the bourgeois classes had again been like a net, which allowed the voracious sharks to escape, while the little sardines were caught. The profiteers who have realized millions during the war have been acquitted or let off with ridiculous penalties. The little thieves, men and women, have been punished with sentences of Draconian severity.

Worn out by hunger and cold, in cells which are hardly heated, these derelicts of society await mercy and pity.

They have waited in vain, for in his preoccupation with making the nations cut one another's throats and of distributing crowns, the last of the Hohenzollerns forgot these miserable people, and since the Conquest of Liege there has been no amnesty, not even on the official holiday of German slaves, the Kaiser's birthday.

The Proletarian Revolution ought now, by a little ray of kindness, to illuminate the gloomy life of the prisons, shorten Draconian sentences, abolish barbarous punishments – the use of manacles and whippings – improve, as far as possible, the medical attention, the food allowance, and the conditions of labor. That is a duty of honor!

The existing disciplinary system, which is impregnated with brutal class spirit and with capitalist barbarism, should be radically altered.

But a complete reform, in harmony with the spirit of socialism, can be based only on a new economic and social order; for both crime and punishment have, in the last analysis, their roots deep in the organization of society. One radical measure, however, can be taken without any elaborate legal process. Capital punishment, the greatest shame of the ultra-reactionary German code, ought to be done away with at once. Why are there any hesitations on the part of this Government of workers and soldiers? The noble Beccaria, two hundred years ago, denounced the ignominy of the death penalty. Doesn't its ignominy exist for you, Ledebour, Barth, Daeumig?

You have no time, you have a thousand cares, a thousand difficulties, a thousand tasks before you? That is true. But mark, watch in hand, how much time would be needed to say: "Capital punishment is abolished!" Would you argue that, on this question also, long discussions followed by votes are necessary? Would you thus lose yourselves in the complications of formalism, in considerations of jurisdiction, in questions of departmental red tape?

Ah! HOW German this German Revolution is! How argumentative and pedantic it is! How rigid, inflexible, lacking in grandeur!

The forgotten death penalty is only one little isolated detail. But how precisely the inner spirit, which governs the Revolution, betrays itself in these little details!

Let one take up any ordinary history of the great French Revolution. Let one take up the dry Mignet, for instance.

Can one read this book except with a beating heart and a burning brow? Can one, after having opened it, at no matter what page, put it aside before one has heard, with bated breath, the last chord of that formidable tragedy? It is like a symphony of Beethoven carried to the gigantic and the grotesque, a tempest thundering on the organ of time, great and superb in its errors as well as in its achievement, in victory as well as in defeat, in the first cry of naive joyfulness as well as in the final breath.

And now how is it with us in Germany?

Everywhere, in the small as in the great, one feels that these are still and always the old and sober citizens of the defunct Social-Democracy, those for whom the badge of membership is everything and the man and the spirit are nothing.

Let us not forget this, however. The history of the world is not made without grandeur of spirit, without lofty morale, without noble gestures.

Liebknecht and I, on leaving the hospitable halls which we recently inhabited – he, among his pale companions in the penitentiary, I with my dear, poor thieves and women of the streets, with whom I have passed, under the same roof, three years and a half of my life – we took this oath as they followed us with their sad eyes: "We shall not forget you!"

We demand of the executive committee of the Council of Workers and Soldiers an immediate amelioration of the lot of all the prisoners in the German jails!

We demand the excision of capital punishment from the German penal code!

During the four years of this slaughter of the peoples, blood has flowed in torrents. Today, each drop of that precious fluid ought to be preserved devotedly in crystal urns.

Revolutionary activity and profound humanitarianism – they alone are the true breath of socialism.

A world must be turned upside down. But each tear that flows, when it could have been spared, is an accusation, and he commits a crime who with brutal inadvertency crushes a poor earthworm.

WITNESS TO AN EXECUTION
The Execution of Mata Hari (1917)

The first intimation she received that her plea had been denied was when she was led at daybreak from her cell in the *Saint-Lazare* prison to a waiting automobile and then rushed to the barracks where the firing squad awaited her.

Never once had the iron will of the beautiful woman failed her. Father Arbaux, accompanied by two sisters of charity, Captain Bouchardon, and Maitre Clunet, her lawyer, entered her cell, where she was still sleeping — a calm, untroubled sleep, it was remarked by the turnkeys and trusties.

The sisters gently shook her. She arose and was told that her hour had come.

"May I write two letters?" was all she asked.

Consent was given immediately by Captain Bouchardon, and pen, ink, paper, and envelopes were given to her.

She seated herself at the edge of the bed and wrote the letters with feverish haste. She handed them over to the custody of her lawyer.

Then she drew on her stockings, black, silken, filmy things, grotesque in the circumstances. She placed her high-heeled slippers on her feet and tied the silken ribbons over her insteps.

She arose and took the long black velvet cloak, edged around the bottom with fur and with a huge square fur collar hanging down the back, from a hook over the head of her bed. She placed this cloak over the heavy silk kimono which she had been wearing over her nightdress.

Her wealth of black hair was still coiled about her head in braids. She put on a large, flapping black felt hat with a black silk ribbon and bow. Slowly and indifferently, it seemed, she pulled on a pair of black kid gloves. Then she said calmly:

"I am ready."

The party slowly filed out of her cell to the waiting automobile.

The car sped through the heart of the sleeping city. It was scarcely half-past five in the morning and the sun was not yet fully up.

Clear across Paris, the car whirled to the *Caserne de Vincennes*, the barracks

of the old fort which the Germans stormed in 1870.

The troops were already drawn up for the execution. The twelve Zouaves, forming the firing squad, stood in line, their rifles at ease. A subofficer stood behind them, sword drawn.

The automobile stopped, and the party descended, Mata Hari last. The party walked straight to the spot, where a little hummock of earth reared itself seven or eight feet high and afforded a background for such bullets as might miss the human target.

As Father Arbaux spoke with the condemned woman, a French officer approached, carrying a white cloth.

"The blindfold," he whispered to the nuns who stood there and handed it to them.

"Must I wear that?" asked Mata Hari, turning to her lawyer, as her eyes glimpsed the blindfold.

Maitre Clunet turned interrogatively to the French officer.

"If Madame prefers not, it makes no difference," replied the officer, hurriedly turning away.

Mata Hari was not bound and she was not blindfolded. She stood gazing steadfastly at her executioners, when the priest, the nuns, and her lawyer stepped away from her.

The officer in command of the firing squad, who had been watching his men like a hawk that none might examine his rifle and try to find out whether he was destined to fire the blank cartridge which was in the breech of one rifle, seemed relieved that the business would soon be over.

A sharp, crackling command and the file of twelve men assumed rigid positions at attention. Another command, and their rifles were at their shoulders; each man gazed down his barrel at the breast of the women which was the target.

She did not move a muscle.

The under-officer in charge had moved to a position where from the corners of their eyes they could see him. His sword was extended in the air. It dropped. The sun — by this time up — flashed on the burnished blade as it described an arc in falling. Simultaneously the sound of the volley rang out. Flame and a tiny puff of greyish smoke issued from the muzzle of each rifle.

Automatically the men dropped their arms.

At the report, Mata Hari fell. She did not die as actors and moving picture stars would have us believe that people die when they are shot. She did not throw up her hands nor did she plunge straight forward or straight back.

Instead she seemed to collapse. Slowly, inertly, she settled to her knees, her head up always, and without the slightest change of expression on her face. For the fraction of a second it seemed she tottered there, on her knees, gazing directly at those who had taken her life. Then she fell backward, bending at the waist, with her legs doubled up beneath her. She lay prone, motionless, with her face turned towards the sky.

A non-commissioned officer, who accompanied a lieutenant, drew his revolver from the big, black holster strapped about his waist. Bending over, he placed the muzzle of the revolver almost — but not quite — against the left temple of the spy. He pulled the trigger, and the bullet tore into the brain of the woman. Mata Hari was surely dead.

Politics as a Vocation, Max Weber (1919)

What do we understand by politics? The concept is extremely broad and comprises any kind of independent leadership in action. One speaks of the currency policy of the banks, of the discounting policy of the *Reichsbank*, of the strike policy of a trade union; one may speak of the educational policy of a municipality or a township, of the policy of the president of a voluntary association, and, finally, even of the policy of a prudent wife who seeks to guide her husband. Tonight, our reflections are, of course, not based upon such a broad concept. We wish to understand by politics only the leadership, or the influencing of the leadership, of a political association, hence today, of a state.

But what is a 'political' association from the sociological point of view? What is a 'state?' Sociologically, the state cannot be defined in terms of its ends. There is scarcely any task that some political association has not taken in hand, and there is no task that one could say has always been exclusive and peculiar to those associations which are designated as political ones: today the state, or historically, those associations which have been the predecessors of the modern state. Ultimately, one can define the modern state sociologically only in terms of the specific means peculiar to it, as to every political association, namely, the use of physical force.

"Every state is founded on force," said Trotsky at Brest-Litovsk. That is indeed right. If no social institutions existed which knew the use of violence, then the concept of 'state' would be eliminated, and a condition would emerge that could be designated as 'anarchy,' in the specific sense of this word. Of course, force is certainly not the normal or the only means of the state—nobody says that—but force is a means specific to the state. Today the relation between the state and violence is an especially intimate one. In the past, the most varied institutions—beginning with the sib—have known the use of physical force as quite normal. Today, however, we have to say that a state is a human community that (successfully) claims the monopoly of the legitimate use of physical force within a given territory. Note that 'territory' is one of the characteristics of the state. Specifically, at the present time, the right to use physical force is ascribed to other institutions or to individuals only to the extent to which the state permits it. The state is considered the sole source of the 'right' to use violence. Hence, 'politics' for us means striving to share power or striving to influence the distribution of power, either among states or among groups within a state.

> **A state is a human community that claims the monopoly of the legitimate use of physical force within a given territory.**

Punishment and Reformation
Frederick Howard Wines (1919)

Death is the most ancient of all penalties, and the most common in antiquity, as it still is among savages. It is the most effectual mode of getting rid of troublesome or offensive characters; and the feeling of revenge, when in active operation and unrestrained by the considerations which appeal to the intellect and conscience of civilized men, is an impulse which grows by what it feeds upon, and very easily runs to excess, nor stops short until the extreme limit of possible agony has been inflicted upon the sufferer.

Among the modes of taking human life which are or have been practiced by conquerors and rulers, may be mentioned: burning, beheading, hanging, drawing and quartering, breaking on the wheel, crucifixion, strangulation, suffocation, drowning, precipitation from a height, stoning, sawing asunder, flaying alive, crushing beneath wheels or the feet of animals, throwing to the wild beasts, compulsory combat in the arena, burying alive, boiling, impaling, pressing, piercing with javelins, shooting, starving, poison, the troughs, melted lead, serpents, blowing from the mouth of a cannon, and electrocution. I have named about thirty different ways of taking life, under some of which a number of sub-varieties may be specified.

Burning, for instance, is a very ancient method. It is mentioned in the book of Genesis; Judah proposed to burn Tamar, his daughter-in-law, when she was found to have lapsed from virtue. Moses ordained burning as the penalty of incest. Achan was burned. The three Hebrew children, captives in Babylon, were cast alive into a furnace of fire. In the worship of Moloch, a hollow image of the god, of brass, with folded arms, was erected; babes were laid, as living sacrifices, in the idol's arms, and killed by the heat of the flames from a fire kindled within.

Caesar tells us that the Gauls and Britons of his day thrust captives in mass into a wicker image of gigantic stature, then piled wood around, lighted it, and, in the midst of the smoke which concealed the god and his victims from sight, the image and its living contents tumbled together into the fire, where they were consumed. In the early history of England, slaves were burned for theft; female slaves were burned by women—eighty other female slaves were compelled to assist at the ceremony. Burning was the mode of execution of slaves also in Rome. The Theodosian code prescribed this punishment for witchcraft.

In the Middle Ages, burning was the usual punishment for sacrilege, parricide, poisoning, arson, and the crime against nature. Under the term *sacrilege* were included heresy, witchcraft, atheism, blasphemy, and the like. It was customary to drive a stake in the ground, build a platform around it, set straw and fagots in order under or upon this platform, leaving an opening for the introduction of the condemned, then bind him to the stake by iron bands about the neck and waist, and light the bonfire. If it was desired to abbreviate the agony of the victim, a cord passed around his neck was secretly tightened

from behind, before setting fire to the pile; or his heart was pierced, through the flames, by an iron dart at the end of a long hooked pole used to stir the fire. A handful of ashes was thrown in the air at the conclusion of the ceremony. In the *auto-da-fe*, or act of faith, the accused was given an opportunity to recant, upon the platform, in the hearing of the spectators; and, if he failed to avail himself of the opportunity mercifully given him to save his life, the ceremony proceeded. In London the ordinary place for kindling the sacred flame was at Smithfield; and the frequency of this punishment under one of the English queens has fastened upon her the title of Bloody Mary.

England, to her everlasting shame be it spoken, demanded the death of Joan of Arc, who was burned at the stake as a heretic. Under Henry IV, of England, a law was enacted which authorized sheriffs to burn heretics without a writ; for this reason, no estimate can be formed of the number burned in that country. Burning was also the penalty of treason. Even women were thus punished, under English law; and it is only about a hundred years ago that burning for treason was abolished. Other modes of burning have been in vogue in other parts of the world. Nero smeared the bodies of the early Christians with pitch, and, it is said, used them to light the streets of Rome. In Persia, the punishment invented by Sefi II, known as the illuminated body, consisted in piercing the body with numberless holes, in which burning wicks were inserted. In China a woman is credited with the invention of *pao-lo*, which was a tall metal tube, to the top of which the victim was bound, with arms and legs encircling the tube, and a fire kindled at the bottom was kept up until his remains were reduced to ashes.

The Beheading of the Rebel Lords on Great Tower Hill.

So, too, there have been many ways of beheading men sentenced to die. The Romans used a short sword called the *glaive*, with which, no doubt, John the Baptist was beheaded in prison. The method followed in China and Japan is described as follows:

"The criminal is carried to the place of execution in a bamboo cage, and by his side is a basket in which his head will drop when removed. He is pinioned in a very effective manner. The middle of a long thin rope is passed across the back of his neck, and the ends crossed on his chest and brought under the arms; they are then twisted around the arms, the wrists are tied together behind the back, and the ends are fastened to the portion of the rope on his back. A slip of paper containing his name, crime, and sentence is fixed to a reed and fastened at the back of his head. On arriving at the place of execution, the officials remove the paper and take it to the presiding mandarin, who writes on it in red ink the warrant for execution. The paper is then replaced, a rope loop is passed over the head of the culprit, and the end given to an assistant, who draws the head forward, so as to stretch the neck, while a second assistant holds the body from behind, and in a moment the head is severed from the body. The instrument is a sword made expressly for that purpose. It is a two-handed weapon, very heavy, and has a very broad blade. The executioners pride themselves on their dexterity in its management. After the execution, the culprit's head is taken away, and generally hung up in a bamboo cage near the scene of the crime, with a label bearing the name and the offense of the criminal."

Beheading was not practiced in England before the year 1035. Prisoners sentenced to lose their heads had them taken off, in the Tower, upon a block, with an axe. Macaulay, in commenting upon the blundering and tragic execution of the Duke of Monmouth, says:

"Within four years the pavement of the chancel was again disturbed, and hard by the remains of Monmouth were laid the remains of Jeffreys. In truth, there is no sadder spot on the earth than that little cemetery. Death is there associated, not, as in Westminster Abbey and St. Paul's, with genius and virtue, with public veneration and imperishable renown; not, as in our humblest churches and churchyards, with everything that is most endearing in social and domestic charities; but with whatever is darkest in human nature and in human destiny, with the savage triumph of implacable enemies, with the inconstancy, the ingratitude, the cowardice of friends, with all the miseries of fallen greatness and of blighted fame. Thither have been carried, through successive ages, by the rude hands of jailers, without one mourner following, the bleeding relics of men who had been the captains of armies, the leaders of parties, the oracles of senates, and the ornaments of courts. Thither was borne, before the window where Jane Grey was praying, the mangled corpse of Guilford Dudley. Edward Seymour, Duke of Somerset and Protector of the Realm, reposes there by the brother whom he murdered. There has mouldered the headless trunk of John Fisher, Cardinal of Saint Vitalis, a man worthy to have lived in a better age, and to have died in a better cause. There are laid John Dudley, Duke of Northumberland, Lord High Admiral, and Thomas Cromwell, Earl of Essex, Lord High Treasurer. There, too, is another Essex, on whom nature and fortune had lavished all their bounties in vain, and whom valor, grace, genius, royal favor, popular applause, conducted to an early and ignominious doom. Not far off sleep two chiefs of the great house of Howard—Thomas, fourth Duke of Norfolk, and Philip, eleventh Earl of Arundel. Here and there, among the thick graves of unquiet and aspiring statesmen, lie more delicate sufferers : Margaret of Salisbury, the last of the proud name of Plantagenet, and those two fair queens who perished by the jealous rage of Henry. Such was the dust with which the dust of Monmouth mingled."

Sonorous and pathetic as is this passage, it makes no mention of Sir Thomas More, Sir Walter Raleigh, Algernon Sidney, Archbishop Laud, and the unfortunate Charles I; names which, for one reason or another, interest us more than some of those with ponderous titles, which the brilliant historian has selected to adorn his pages.

Beheading in France has been reduced to high art, by the adoption and use of the guillotine. In its primitive form, this is a very ancient instrument of decapitation, by which Manlius, the Roman, is said to have lost his life. There are numerous mediaeval engravings representing the execution of Manlius, one of which is by Albert Dürer. It was called, in the criminal statutes of the Netherlands, in 1233, the *Panke* or *Diele*; in France, in the fifteenth century, *la*

The Halifax Gibbet.

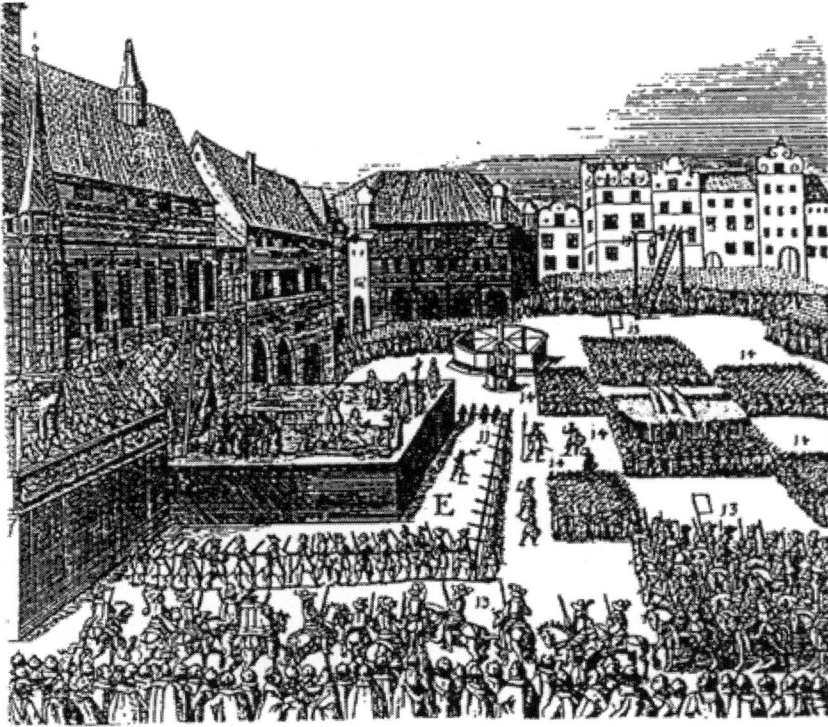

doloirc; in Italy, in the sixteenth, the *mannaia*. Beatrice Cenci was beheaded after this fashion. Jean d'Autun, the contemporary and biographer of Louis XII, relates that in 1507, Demetrius Giustiniani, of Genoa, for sedition, was condemned to kneel upon the scaffold and lay his neck upon a block, when it was cut in two by a falling *bascule*, operated by a cord in the hand of the executioner. At Florence, Sept. 7, 1629, by a similar device, Lorenzo Zei had his head severed from his body. The nature of the instrument is well indicated by the old German name for it, the *fall-beil*, or falling axe. Marshal Montmorency of France was guillotined at Toulouse, in 1652. The "gibbet of Halifax," in use before and during the Commonwealth, and last used in 1650, consisted of two parallel upright beams, and a transverse beam, the latter heavily weighted with lead, and having a sharp, cutting edge in the form of a chopping-knife about a foot square, attached to the lower side; this cross-beam was upheld at a height of about ten feet, by a pulley; when the rope was cut by the stroke of a sword, it fell upon the victim's neck, which was securely held in place between them. Lord Morton, Regent of Scotland, having seen it, was so taken with it, that he introduced it at home, where, on the third of June, 1587, he was the first to test its efficacy in practice. For this reason, the Scotch gave it the name of the "Maiden." It is preserved in the Antiquarian Museum of Edinburgh.

The guillotine is so called after its reputed inventor, Dr. Guillotin, who was, during the French Revolution, a member of the Assembly. A motion offered by him to abolish the immemorial distinction in penalties for the same offenses committed by the aristocracy and the common people was agreed to, Dec. 1, 1789, four months and a half after the overthrow of the Bastille. On the 25th of September, 1791, in the penal code that day adopted, it was further provided that the only mode of execution should thenceforth be by beheading, a privilege which formerly pertained to the nobles, vulgar criminals having to put up with hanging. The motive of both these innovations was humane. Louis XVI had already abolished preliminary torture. The assembly put an end to all torture, and to the confiscation of estates, as well as to the practice of declaring the posterity of offenders infamous.

Equally humane was the intention of Dr. Guillotin in the invention of a machine, still in use in France, by which he designed to reduce the pain of death "to a shiver," as, in his enthusiasm, he explained to his colleagues. It is an instrument substantially like a pile-driver, with grooved posts, between which a heavy axe falls with sufficient force to cut off a human head. The criminal, tightly bound, is laid with his face downward and his neck resting in a curved depression in the block which receives the knife; the blade strikes him from behind, and his head falls into a basket. It was first tried upon three cadavers conveyed from the hospital to the prison at Bicetre, in Paris, for that purpose. The son of Samson, the notorious executioner, said to his father, at this preliminary trial, that it would interfere with their business; to which the old man responded (with prophetic vision, alas!) that it would make cutting heads off so easy, that the trade would be brisker than ever. This was on the 17th of April, 1792; a week later, it was set up on the Place de Greve. Originally the blade was at right angles with the upright standards between which it moved, but the king suggested that it would work better, if set diagonally; and, nine months afterward, he benefited by his own suggestion.

The reception of the new invention by the mercurial people of France was shocking in its levity. It was the theme of numberless songs and jests. Models of it were made in wood, in ivory, in silver, and in gold, and sold as parlor ornaments and toys for children. A somewhat fashionable closing ceremony, with which to wind up a dinner in an aristocratic house, was for the noble hostess to produce a *figurante* supposed to represent Danton, Robespierre, or Marat, and with a toy guillotine cut off his head, when, instead of blood, a tiny stream of crimson perfume flowed from the neck, in which the ladies at the table hastened to dip

their dainty lace handkerchiefs. The revolutionists, on the other hand, adopted it as a seal.

Hanging is another very ancient method of execution. Haman, you remember, was hanged on the gallows which he erected for Mordecai. Constantine the Great practiced it. In France, the criminal was conveyed to the gibbet seated in a cart, with his back to the horse, his confessor at his side, and his executioner before or behind him. In this order he was taken through the crowded streets. On arrival at the place of execution, he was made to ascend a ladder leading up to the gallows; the executioner preceded him, mounting backwards, so as to assist the prisoner. The confessor followed. After he had confessed him upon the scaffold, three ropes were attached to the prisoner's neck, two of them knotted, and the third intended to swing him off the ladder. The confessor then descended to the ground, leaving the culprit standing on the ladder, and the executioner upon the platform above him. The latter pushed away the ladder with his foot, swung the prisoner off, and then, horrible to relate, taking hold of the rope in order to steady himself, he jumped upon the prisoner and kicked him to death. In England, however, the cart was driven out from under, and the man's neck was broken by the fall. Executions in France are public. In England, the law now requires them to be private; and in Newgate prison not even the official witnesses required to certify the death see the contortions of the expiring convict, whose body falls into a sort of well, out of sight of all but the executioner and the attending physician. When the physician announces that death has taken place, the witnesses come forward, identify the corpse, and sign the necessary attestation.

Drawing was a mediaeval punishment by which a man was dragged to death by horses. Brunehilda is said to have been executed in this manner.

When a prisoner was drawn and quartered, he was attached to a platform facing the sky, by two iron bands, one around his chest and arms, the other around his thighs. The weapon with which he had killed his murdered victim was placed in his hand, which was filled with sulphur, tied, and the sulphur fired, so that his hand was burned off him. Next, he was torn with hooks upon the breast and legs, and a composition of melted lead, rosin, wax, and sulphur poured into the wounds. After that, ropes fastened to whippletrees were attached to his arms and legs, each rope secured by two sailor-knots, and the horses attached to the whippletrees pulled him to pieces.

Haman, you remember, was hanged on the gallows which he erected for Mordecai.

A paling was erected around the spot to keep off the eager, curious crowd. The mangled remains were burned in a fire.

This mode of execution was reserved for offenders guilty of *lese-majesty*. One of the most terrible executions upon record was that of Damiens, a poor fool who attempted, it was said, to assassinate Louis XV. He pierced his side slightly with a knife. The king received the attack with courage. Damiens, when questioned as to his motive, said that he did not want to kill Louis, but to give him a warning—to prick him a little, because he was a great tyrant, in order to show him what might happen. All of the parliaments of France were invited to make suggestions as to the manner in which the assassin should be tortured. It would torture the reader to quote the many recommendations gravely submitted in response to this royal request. Pending a decision, in order to prevent his escape, he was tied to an iron bed. The boot was finally agreed to be the most terrible form of suffering, and he was subjected to it for an hour and a half, then taken away to be drawn and quartered, but his sinews were so tough, that he was drawn for an hour, without avail, and a knife had to be used with which to quarter him, while still alive. A woman who was looking on, seeing, from the balcony where she stood, the frantic efforts of the horses to pull harder, exclaimed, "Oh, the poor horses!"

Breaking on the wheel, authorized by Francis the First in 1534, was really a way of pounding a man to death. The wheel was in the form of a cross of Saint Andrew, with four arms of equal length sloping slightly toward the point of intersection, upon which the prisoner was laid, with his face upward. Supports were nailed to the arms of the cross, so as to come half way between the shoulder and the elbow, the elbow and the wrist, the hips and the knees, and the knees and the ankles. With a heavy iron bar the upper and forearms, the thighs and shinbones, could each be broken into three pieces. After being thus rudely disjointed, the body was bent backward, until the head and heels met, when it was attached to a wheel, with the hubs sawed off, which was rapidly revolved on a pivot, until the sufferer was relieved by death. John Calvin is sometimes reproached with theological asperity for having burned Servetus at the stake, as if his religious opinions had prompted that inexcusable cruelty, instead of its being a custom of the age in which Calvin lived. But, as an offset, it may be mentioned that, less than a century and a half ago, Voltaire, who represents the opposite pole of religious thought, in one of his private letters, expresses his gratitude to God for the breaking of the priest Malacreda upon the wheel, and in another the comfort which it was to him to hear that three Jesuits had been burned alive at Lisbon. This form of punishment was known in Greece, where it was applied to slaves. In Athens it was proposed to break Phocion. This was really a form of beating to death, accomplished by the natives of South Africa in a more primitive way, with clubs. By the law of the Twelve Tables, *læsa majestas [public enemies]* were punished by flogging to death.

As to crucifixion, Darius is said to have crucified, on one occasion, two thousand Assyrians, and, upon another, three thousand Babylonians at once. Regulus was crucified, but not until he had been rolled down hill in a barrel driven through from the outside with iron spikes. On the cross his eyelids were removed, that his eyes might be exposed continuously to the sun.

There are two modes of empaling, one by forcing a stake or spear through the prisoner's body and pinning him to the ground, the other by forcing his body upon a sharpened point. The latter is closely allied to crucifixion. In Siam a stake is driven longitudinally through the criminal's body, and the body is then elevated upon this stake, which is firmly driven into the ground. Suspension on hooks has been practiced in the West Indies; also, for abjuring the Mohammedan religion, in Algeria and in India.

Strangulation, as described in Homer's "Odyssey," appears to have been by hanging. In Sparta, it was effected by two executioners, who pulled at the opposite ends of a rope which encircled the victim's neck. Different modes of execution are looked upon as more or less infamous in different countries; in Turkey, the bow-string is reserved for the nobility. In China, too, strangulation is regarded as more honorable than decapitation. The Spanish garrote is a mode of strangulation, no longer accomplished, as formerly, by ropes and cords, but by enclosing the neck in an iron ring, which can be tightened from behind by a screw, which is turned until the point of it pierces the spinal column. Strangulation before burning was an act of mercy.

Death by suffocation is mentioned in the Old Testament; Hazael the Syrian murdered Benhadad by dipping a thick cloth in water and spreading it over the king's face. Also in the Apocrypha, where it is said that Antiochus Eupator put Menelaus to death, at Berea, "as the manner is in that place." The Bereans had built a tower fifty cubits high, full of ashes, which could be stirred by some round instrument, possibly a wheel, "hanging down on every side into the ashes." Into this ash-heap Menelaus was thrown, as a punishment for sacrilege. Prisoners have also been suffocated by smoke, especially that given off by burning sulphur. Marshal Pelissier destroyed a force of Algerians who had taken refuge in a cave by smoking them to death.

Drowning is, of course, a mode of suffocation. Jesus Christ possibly alludes to the legal punishment of drowning in Matthew 18:6. The story of the drowning of the Duke of Clarence is thus quaintly told by Sir Thomas More in "The Pitiful Life of King Edward the Fifth."

"George, Duke of Clarence, was a goodly and well-featured prince, in all things fortunate, if either his own ambition had not set him against his brother, or the envy of his enemies had not set his brother against him; for

440

were it by the Queen or the nobles of her blood, which highly maligned the King's kindred (as women commonly, not of malice, but of nature, hate such as their husbands love), or were it a proud appetite of the Duke himself intending to be King, at the leastwise, heinous treason was laid to his charge, and finally, were he in fault, or were he faultless, attainted was he by Parliament, and judged to death; and thereupon hastily drowned in a butt of Malmsey within the Tower of London. Whose death King Edward (although he commanded it), when he wist it was done, piteously he bewailed and sorrowfully repented it"

The manorial pits for drowning or half drowning women, like the manorial gibbets for hanging men, were highly prized prerogatives of the early English nobility.

Burying is the terrene equivalent of drowning. When the Third Crusade started from Europe for the Holy Land, certain rules for the government of its members were adopted, and it was announced that their violation would be punished, if at sea, by throwing the offender into the water, but if on land, by interring him alive. In Rome, vestal virgins guilty of a breach of the vow of chastity were thus buried.

Sefi, the eighth Shah of Persia, whose name is a synonym for cruelty, believing that an unsuccessful attempt had been made to poison him, buried forty of the women of his seraglio, including his mother. Tacitus records the fact that lewd women were buried alive, by the Gauls, in swamps. Jews were buried

by Pepin of France. In some parts of Germany, even since the beginning of the last century, this was the penalty for infanticide.

In 1347, two counterfeiters were boiled alive at Paris. This penalty for counterfeiting was in force in the sixteenth century. The boiling was sometimes done in oil. French law tolerated it until 1791, though it had long fallen into practical disuse. Under Henry VIII of England, poisoning was for ten years regarded by law as treason, and it was punishable in this manner. The Bishop of Rochester's cook, a man named Rose, was publicly boiled at Smithfield, in 1630, for throwing poison into the yeast-tub in the kitchen of the episcopal palace. His occupation may have suggested the mode of his death.

Stoning, common among the ancient Hebrews, was regarded by them as the most infamous of punishments. The execution took place outside of the camp or city, and the witnesses were required to throw the first stone, but all the people took part in the ceremony. Æschylus was condemned to suffer death by stoning for having written a tragedy which was thought to be irreverent, but the sentence was not executed. Among the Romans this was a military punishment. Stoning was forbidden by Constantine. A law of Æthelstan, in the tenth century, prescribed it as the punishment of male slaves for theft; the thief was stoned by eighty fellow-slaves, and if any of them missed the mark three times he was thrice whipped.

Pressing to death was a mode of execution known to the Carthaginians. The instrument of torture known as the scavenger's daughter, in use in the Tower of London, will be described below, under "Torture." The judgment of penance,

referred to at the close of the last chapter, was in these words: "That you be taken back to the prison whence you came, to a low dungeon into which no light can enter; that you be laid on your back on the bare floor, with a cloth around your loins, but elsewhere naked; that there be set upon your body a weight of iron as great as you can bear—and greater; that you have no sustenance, save, on the first day, three morsels of the coarsest bread, on the second day three draughts of stagnant water from the pool nearest to the prison door, on the third day again three morsels of bread as before, and such bread and such water alternately from day to day until you die."

Among the punishments mentioned in the Epistle to the Hebrews is sawing asunder, or "dichotomy," which is the penalty for horse-stealing in Tartary, for poisoning in Persia, and was formerly, with obvious fitness, inflicted for bigamy in Switzerland. The Bodoveresta, prescribed by Zoroaster, the Persian lawgiver, against incompetent physicians and mothers who killed their offspring, was very similar to the Chinese penalty entitled *ling-chee* or "cutting into a thousand pieces," while still alive.

Compare with the horrible torture just mentioned the sentence pronounced, in the reign of Edward the Second, against the Earl of Carlisle, for high treason: "The award of the court is that you be drawn, and hanged, and beheaded; that your heart, and bowels, and entrails, whence came your traitorous thoughts, be torn out, and burnt to ashes, and that the ashes be scattered to the winds; that your body be cut into four quarters, and that one of them be hanged

upon the Tower of Carlisle, another upon the Tower of Newcastle, a third upon the Bridge of York, and the fourth at Shrewsbury; and that your head be set upon London Bridge, for an example to others that they may never presume to be guilty of such treason as yours against their liege lord."

Precipitation from a height, another of the punishments forbidden by Constantine, was the form of death inflicted upon Æsop, the writer of fables. Pygmalion, King of Tyre, visited it upon two priests guilty of having eaten the flesh of human sacrifices. In the history of the Maccabees it is written that Jewish mothers, with their infants in their arms, were thrown from the walls of Jerusalem. The Tarpeian rock at Rome was a place set apart for this mode of execution, chiefly practiced upon slaves guilty of theft.

The Carthaginian general, Hasdrubal, before throwing his Roman prisoners from a rock, flayed them alive. Excoriation is named as a penalty in the laws of Henry the First of England. The general reader will observe occasional references in historical and other works to the ancient practice of nailing up human skins where they could be seen by the public, and the minds of those predisposed to crime be stricken with terror at the hideous spectacle.

Deserters from the army are, since the invention of firearms, usually shot to death. The fact is perhaps not generally known that, in some at least of the Western territories, convicts sentenced to endure capital punishment are given their choice whether they will be hung or shot. The author was shown, in a territorial prison, the location of the convict against the wall, and the spot where the tent is pitched in which the armed guards are concealed; to one or more of them are given guns loaded with blank cartridges. The spot where the Paris communists shot Archbishop Darboy, within prison walls, is shown to visitors, and excites much interest; the marks made by the bullets are still visible. The ancient equivalent form of death was by piercing the victims with javelins, which was also a military punishment.

Prisoners have sometimes been starved to death, either by withholding from them all food, or by feeding them on bread and water, or other provisions known to be inadequate to sustain life.

The Athenians forced Socrates, Phocion, and many others, to drink a poisonous decoction, and so to end their own lives. Years afterward, statues were erected to both these heroes; and the remains of Phocion were brought back from Megara and interred in Athens, at the expense of the public treasury. Somewhat similar was the ancient Moslem punishment for wine-drinking, namely, pouring melted lead down the offender's throat.

Daniel was thrown, by Darius the Mede, into a den of lions. In Siam prisoners are sometimes thrown to crocodiles. The Roman arena was the place of martyrdom of thousands of the early Christians; the remains of Roman amphitheatres may still be traced in Great Britain. In China faithless wives are given to elephants to be by them trampled underfoot. This was the mode of punishment of deserters adopted by Hamilcar, the Carthaginian general.

Criminals have also been thrown into dens of serpents, or tied down in forests where it was certain that they would be bitten by serpents. The Roman penalty for parricide at one time consisted in sewing up the rebellious child in a leather sack, together with a live serpent, a cock, and a goat, and throwing the sack and its contents into the sea.

Plutarch, in his memoir of Artaxerxes, describes one of the most terrible of all recorded punishments, which was inflicted upon Mithridates, by order of the Persian monarch, for boasting, when overcome with wine, that he, and not Artaxerxes, had in truth slain the mighty Cyrus. He was encased in a coffin-like box, from which his head, hands, and feet protruded, through holes made for that purpose; he was fed with milk and honey, which he was forced to take, and his face was smeared with the same mixture; he was exposed to the sun, and in this state he remained for seventeen days, until he had been devoured alive by insects and vermin, which swarmed about him and bred within him.

Barbarous as are these tales of cruelty and hatred, was the blowing of the sepoys from the mouths of British cannon in India any less shocking?

Many travelers have seen, in the torture chamber at Nuremberg, the figure of a woman constructed in such a manner as to embrace a victim thrust into her arms, and pierce him to death with knives. A similar instrument was invented by Nabis, a Spartan tyrant, who named it the Apega, after his wife.

The Hangman at Home, Carl Sandburg (1920)

WHAT does the hangman think about
When he goes home at night from work?
When he sits down with his wife and
Children for a cup of coffee and a
Plate of ham and eggs, do they ask
Him if it was a good day's work
And everything went well or do they
Stay off some topics and talk about
The weather, baseball, politics
And the comic strips in the papers
And the movies? Do they look at his
Hands when he reaches for the coffee
Or the ham and eggs? If the little
Ones say, Daddy, play horse, here's
A rope—does he answer like a joke:
I seen enough rope for today?
Or does his face light up like a
Bonfire of joy and does he say:
It's a good and dandy world we live
In. And if a white face moon looks
In through a window where a baby girl
Sleeps and the moon gleams mix with
Baby ears and baby hair—the hangman—
How does he act then? It must be easy
For him. Anything is easy for a hangman,
I guess.

Capital Punishment, George Bernard Shaw (1922)

The Obstacle Of Stupidity.

Another difficulty is the sort of stupidity that comes from lack of imagination. When I tell people that I have seen with these eyes a man (no less a man than Richard Wagner, by the way) who once met a crowd going to see a soldier broken on the wheel by the crueier of the two legalized methods of carrying out that hideous sentence, they shudder, and are amazed to hear that what they call medieval torture was used in civilized Europe so recently. They forget that the punishment of half-hanging, unmentionably mutilating, drawing and quartering, was

on the British statute book within my own memory. The same people will read of a burglar being sentenced to ten years' penal servitude without turning a hair. They are like Ibsen's *Peer Gynt*, who was greatly reassured when he was told that the pains of hell are mental: he thought they could not be so very bad if there was no actual burning brimstone. When such people are terrified by an outburst of robbery with violence, or sadistically excited by reports of the White Slave traffic, they clamor to have sentences of two years' hard labor supplemented by a flogging, which is a joke by comparison. They will try to lynch a criminal who ill treats a child in some sensationally cruel manner; but on the most trifling provocation they will inflict on the child the prison demoralization and the prison stigma which condemn it to crime for the rest of its life as the only employment open to a prison child. The public conscience would be far more active if the punishment of imprisonment were abolished, and we went back to the rack, the stake, the pillory, and the lash at the cart's tail.

Blood Sports Disguised As Punishment Are Less Cruel Than Imprisonment But More Demoralizing To The Public.

The objection to retrogression is not that such punishments are more cruel than imprisonment. They are less cruel, and far less permanently injurious. The decisive objection to them is that they are sports in disguise. The pleasure to the spectators, and not the pain to the criminal, condemns them. People will go to see Titus Gates flogged or Joan of Arc burnt with equal zest as an entertainment. They will pay high prices for a good view. They will reluctantly admit that they must not torture one another as long as certain rules are observed; but they will hail a breach of the rules with delight as an excuse for a bout of cruelty. Yet they can be shamed at last into recognizing that such exhibitions are degrading and demoralizing; that the executioner is a wretch whose hand no decent person cares to take; and that the enjoyment of the spectators is fiendish. We have then to find some form of torment which can give no sensual satisfaction to the tormentor, and which is hidden from public view. That is how imprisonment, being just such a torment, became the normal penalty. The fact that it may be worse for the criminal is not taken into account. The public is seeking its own salvation, not that of the lawbreaker. It would be far better for him to suffer in the public eye; for among the crowd of sightseers there might be a Victor Hugo or a Dickens, able and willing to make the sightseers think of what they are doing and ashamed of it. The prisoner has no such chance. He envies the unfortunate animals in the zoo, watched daily by thousands of disinterested observers who never try to convert a tiger into a Quaker by solitary confinement, and would set up a resounding agitation in the papers if even the most ferocious man-eater were made to suffer what the most docile convict suffers. Not only has the convict no such protection: the secrecy of his prison makes it hard to convince the public that he is suffering at all.

Judicial Vengeance As An Alternative To Lynch Law.

Thus we see that of the three official objects of our prison system: vengeance, deterrence, and reformation of the criminal, only one is achieved; and that is the one which is nakedly abominable. But there is a plea for it which must be taken into account, and which brings us to the root of the matter in our own characters. It is said, and it is in a certain degree true, that if the Government does not lawfully organize and regulate popular vengeance, the populace will rise up and execute this vengeance lawlessly for itself. The standard defense of the Inquisition is that without it no heretic's life would have been safe. In Texas today the people are not satisfied with the prospect of knowing that a murderer and ravisher will be electrocuted inside a jail if a jury can resist the defense put up by his lawyer. They tear him from the hands of the sheriff; pour lamp oil over him; and burn him alive. Now the burning of human beings is not only an expression of outraged public morality: it is also a sport for which a taste can be acquired much more easily and rapidly than a taste for coursing hares, just as a taste for drink can be acquired from brandy and cocktails more easily and rapidly than from beer or sauterne. Lynching mobs begin with Negro ravishers and murderers; but they presently go on to any sort of delinquent, provided he is black. Later on, as a white man will burn as amusingly as a black one, and a white woman react to tarring and feathering as thrillingly as a Negress, the color line is effaced by what professes to be a rising wave of virtuous indignation, but is in fact an epidemic of Sadism. The defenders of our penal system take advantage of it to assure us that if they did not torment and ruin a boy guilty of sleeping in the open air, the British public would rise and tear that boy limb from limb.

Now the reply to such a plea, from the point of view of civilized law, cannot be too sweeping. The government which cannot restrain a mob from taking the law into its own hands is no government at all. If Landru can go to the guillotine unmolested in France, and his British prototype who drowned all his wives in their baths can be peaceably hanged in England, Texas can protect its criminals by simply bringing its civilization up to the French and British level. But indeed the besetting sin of the mob is a morbid hero worship of great criminals rather than a ferocious abhorrence of them. In any case nobody will have the effrontery to pretend that the number of criminals who excite popular feeling enough to risk lynching is more than a negligible percentage of the whole. The theory that the problem of crime is only one of organizing, regulating, and executing the vengeance of the mob will not bear plain statement, much less discussion. It is only the retributive theory over again in its weakest form.

Crime: Its Cause and Treatment, Clarence Darrow (1922)

The question of capital punishment has been the subject of endless discussion and will probably never be settled so long as men believe in punishment. Some states have abolished and then reinstated it; some have enjoyed capital punishment for long periods of time and finally prohibited the use of it. The reasons why it cannot be settled are plain. There is first of all no agreement as to the objects of punishment. Next, there is no way to determine the results of punishment. If the object is assumed, it is a matter of conjecture as to what will be most likely to bring the result. If it could be shown that any form of punishment would bring the immediate result, it would be impossible to show its indirect result although indirect results are as certain as direct ones. Even if all of this could be clearly proven, the world would be no nearer the solution. Questions of this sort, or perhaps of any sort, are not settled by reason; they are settled by prejudices and sentiments or by emotion. When they are settled they do not stay settled, for the emotions change as new stimuli are applied to the machine.

A state may provide for life imprisonment in place of death. Some especially atrocious murder may occur and be fully exploited in the press. Public feeling will be fanned to a flame. Bitter hatred will be aroused against the murderer. It is perfectly obvious to the multitude that if other men had been hanged for murder, this victim would not have been killed. A legislature meets before the hatred has had time to cool and the law is changed. Again, a community may have capital punishment and nothing notable happens. Now and then hangings occur. Juries acquit because of the severity of the penalty. A feeling of shame or some bungling execution may arouse a community against it. A deep-seated doubt may arise as to the guilt of a man who has been put to death. The sentimental people triumph. The law is changed. Nothing has been found out; no question has been settled; science has made no contribution; the public has changed its mind, or, speaking more correctly, has had another emotion and passed another law.

In the main, the controversy over capital punishment has been one between emotional and unemotional people. Now and then the emotionalist is reinforced by some who have a religious conviction against capital punishment, based perhaps on the rather trite expression that "God gave life and only God should take it away." Such a statement is plausible but not capable of proof. In the main, religious people believe in capital punishment. The advocates of capital punishment dispose of the question by saying that it is the "sentimentalist" or, rather, the "maudlin sentimentalist" who is against it. Sentimentalist really implies "maudlin."

But emotion, too, has its biological origin and is a subject of scientific definition. A really "sentimental" person, in the sense used, is one who has sympathy. This, in turn, comes from imagination which is probably the result of a sensitive nervous system, one that quickly and easily responds to stimuli. Those who have weak emotions do not respond so readily to impressions. Their assumption of superior wisdom has its basis only in a nervous system which is sluggish and phlegmatic to stimuli. Such impressions as each system makes are registered on the brain and become the material for recollection and comparison, which go to form opinion. The correctness of the mental processes depends upon the correctness of the senses that receive the impression, the nerves that transmit the correctness of the registration, and the character of the brain. It does not follow that the stoic has a better brain than the despised "sentimentalist." Either one of them may have a good one, and either one of them a poor one. Still, charity and kindliness probably come from the sensitive system which imagines itself in the place of the object that it pities. All pity is really pain engendered by the feelings that translate one into the place of another. Both hate and love are biologically necessary to life and its processes.

Many people urge that the penalty of imprisonment for life would be all right if the culprit could be kept in prison during life, but in the course of time he is pardoned. This to me is an excellent reason why his life should be saved. It is proof that the feeling of hatred that inspired judge and jury has spent itself and that they can look at the murderer as a man. Which decision is the more righteous, the one where hatred and fear affect the judgment and sentence, or the one where these emotions have spent their force?

Everyone who advocates capital punishment is really ashamed of the practice for which he is responsible. Instead of urging public executions, the most advanced and sensitive who believe in killing by the state are now advocating that even the newspapers should not publish the details and that the killing should be done in darkness and silence. In that event, no one would be deterred by the cruelty of the state. That capital punishment is horrible and cruel is the reason for its existence. That men should be taught not to take life is the purpose of judicial killings. But the spectacle of the state taking life must tend to cheapen it. This must be evident to all who believe in suggestion. Constant association and familiarity tend to lessen the shock of any act however revolting. If men regarded the murderer as one who acted from some all-sufficient cause and who was simply an instrument in an endless sequence of cause and effect, would anyone say he should be put to death?

It is not easy to estimate values correctly. It may be that life is not important. Nature seems extravagantly profligate in her giving and pitiless in

That capital punishment is horrible and cruel is the reason for its existence.

her taking away. Yet death has something of the same shock today that was felt when men first gazed upon the dead with awe and wonder and terror. Constantly meeting it and seeing it and procuring it will doubtless make it more commonplace. To the seasoned soldier in the army, it means less than it did before he became a soldier. Probably the undertaker thinks less of death than almost any other man. He is so accustomed to it that his mind must involuntarily turn from its horror to a contemplation of how much he makes out of the burial. If the civilized savages have their way and make hangings common, we shall probably recover from some of our instinctive fear of death and the extravagant value that we place on life. The social organism is like the individual organism: it can be so often shocked that it grows accustomed and weary and no longer manifests resistance or surprise.

So far as we can reason on questions of life and death and the effect of stimuli upon human organisms, the circle is like this: Frequent executions dull the sensibilities toward the taking of life. This makes it easier for men to kill and increases murders, which in turn increase hangings, which in turn increase murders, and so on, around the vicious circle.

In the absence of any solid starting point on which an argument can be based; in the absence of any reliable figures; in the absence of any way to interpret the figures; in the absence of any way to ascertain the indirect results of judicial killings, even if the direct ones could be shown; in the impossibility through life, experience or philosophy of fixing relative values, the question must remain where it has always been, a conflict between the emotional and unemotional; the "sentimental" and the stolid; the imaginative and the unimaginative; the sympathetic and the unsympathetic. Personally, being inclined to a purely mechanistic view of life and to the belief that all conduct is the result of certain stimuli upon a human machine, I can only say that the stimuli of seeing and reading of capital punishment, applied to my machine, is revolting and horrible. Perhaps as the world improves, the sympathetic and imaginative nature will survive the stolid and selfish. At least one can well believe that this is the line of progress if there shall be progress, a matter still open to question and doubt.

Real Crimes and Imaginary Mysteries
G. K. Chesterton (1923)

When these lines are written, the Press and public are still under the shadow of a tragedy which ended on the scaffold. The shadow comes to most of us through a transparency of newspapers, which makes the tragedy much too like a shadow pantomime. It is now ended, but the same newspapers are already filled with the same sort of stories that may probably have the same sort of end. It is not without any particular criminal problem that I am concerned here but with the general moral problem of the journalistic treatment of it. I am never comfortable about capital punishment; but in any case I think it should be the punishment of certain kinds of treason and tyranny, rather than of all kinds of killing. But while I do not think homicide necessarily the worst of our crimes, neither do I think capital punishment the worst of our abuses. And I wish to inform the newspapers that I, for one, am not so much troubled about whether a murderer ate a hearty breakfast, as I am about some thousands of other people who have had no breakfast, and yet have committed no murders.

So long as a murder story really is a mystery story, I think curiosity about it is very natural and pardonable. Personally, I prefer imaginary mysteries about imaginary murders, where a more perfect policeman runs after a more ideal crook [. .] I like them so much that, when I cannot get any to read, I am driven to the dreadful course of thinking of some to write. [. . .] Where I think the sensational Press is altogether indefensible is not so much as being sensational about the crime as sensational about the punishment. It is even more horrible when it is not only sensational but also sentimental. Sentiment is for comedy; it is only tolerable as a fanciful and fragile thing. Real tragedy ought really to purify the emotions with pity and terror. But a study of the Sunday Press leaves me doubtful about whether all my fellow journalists have had their emotions purified.

But there is also a moral point of mortal or immortal moment. Everybody seems to have forgotten that punishment is supposed to be expiation. The only excuse for it is that it is supposed to clear all scores. If we have really come to the dreadful decision that a man must die, he has at least already achieved the independence of death. He has already passed beyond us, and certainly beyond all our loud gossip and scandal-mongering sensationalism; with human death he regains human dignity. He is no longer a mystery; he is a man. He has a right to the last of his private life, like one who is making some private atonement. We have no business whatever to be told about his breakfast, to spy upon his private movements or eavesdrop on his private words. If we had public executions we should at least have the advantage of publicity, and he would know he had to die like a public man. But it is the very vilest spirit to shout reports about him, like secrets stolen from a private man. He is no longer news; he is no longer a subject for copy, and hardly for conversation. We have no real right to talk about him at all, unless our philosophy permits us to pray for his soul. While we are about it we it would perhaps be even better if we were to pray for our own; for there is one sense in which he is probably better than all of us, and stands above and alone. He is doing what none of the rest of us have ever done yet. He is paying his debts.

The truth is there are two views of crime and punishment; many would call them opposite extremes, and I should say that the extremes meet and are really the same evil. Anyhow, there are two ways of talking about these things which I personally detest beyond expression. The first is the sort police routine and legal cant that cuts people up like a sausage-machine; which sees a series of poor, shabby criminals merely like a procession of pigs into the pork factories of Chicago. The appalling dullness and staleness of this state of mind is such that it really seems to regard it as an ordinary thing that a man should be hunted and killed by men. It is only a question of how, when and where this easy, everyday habit should be indulged, and of whether we have kept certain complicated rules of law, which are about as ethical and eternal as the rules of lawn tennis.

But if the one evil spirit is that which would have men butchered like swine, the other evil spirit is that which holds them blameless like swine. The other view, which repels me not quite so much but in exactly the same way, is that which suggests that criminals cannot help being criminal, just as swine cannot help being swine. It is the attitude of the humanitarian, who declared that the criminal has a criminal skull or a criminal nose, as the rhinoceros has a horn or the elephant a trunk. In other words, he also regards the criminal class as a separate species or tribe of animals; only, instead of killing the animals in a sort of forensic Coliseum, he would keep them in cages in a sort of psychological "zoo."

To my mind, the humanitarian is more inhuman even than the inhuman legalist. But there is one notion that never comes into the head of either of them; and that is the simple reminder that he himself is a man, that he is also an animal, that he also might be thrown into that arena or shut up in that cage. And the two types are obviously alike in everything else. For these two things are really the same thing; these two opposite extremes are really the same evil.

The evil is materialism, in the moral sense even when not in the philosophical sense. It is the general idea that men are like monkeys, that some men are very like monkeys, and that the only difference between the case for shooting the monkey in the jungle and staring at a monkey in the monkey-house. It is a part of this philosophy, of course, that the more simian sort of man is always the more impecunious sort, and to the eye of some of the philosophers the difference between a monkey and the Italian organ-grinder is quite indistinguishable.

The criminal lawyers have no opportunity of considering whether the hanging of a millionaire was or was not sound law; and it is comparatively seldom that the skull of a duke appears as a diagram in the books of the more benevolent criminologists. Among many other matters of agreement, the two share the conviction that the criminal class is not likely to contain anything classy. But their serious point of agreement is on the fatal necessity of crime for the criminal. The criminal lawyer is convinced that the prisoner has committed the murder. The more humane psychologist is only convinced that he will commit it.

The fundamental difference, therefore, is not, to my mind, merely between a particular punishment and a particular pardon. Of two men, one may be for punishment and another for pardon, but both for the same reason, and that the wrong reason. Of another two, one may be for pardon and the other for punishment, yet they may both be in agreement and both be right. A man may be pardoned in the hope of reform or punished on the ground of responsibility; but both views are founded on the idea that his responsibility is the only basis of his reform. An offense may be punished because it is an act of free will, or a pardon may be valued because it is a free pardon, but both are rooted in the idea of freedom. On the other side there is even less difference between the superior person who would pardon his crime because it is inevitable, and the other superior person who would kill the criminal because he is incurable. Neither would think of appealing to the criminal to decide for himself whether he would be a criminal or no.

The abyss is between those who respect a man enough to punish him and those who despise him enough to forgive him. The man who respects may also forgive, and the man who despises may also punish; but the difference is none the less the same. And one practical form of it is that he who respects a man enough to make him the victim of such a vindication will not make him the victim of vulgar advertisement, or a cock-shy for the comic papers.

My Friend Julia Lathrop, Jane Addams (1931)

The last months of her life were filled with concern over the impending execution of a young criminal from Rockford who was still a minor in years and certainly in development. She possessed that horror over the deliberate taking of life on the part of the state which has overshadowed some of the greatest minds in each generation during the last two centuries. For Julia Lathrop, so long identified with governmental service to the country, the state and the nation, official violence such as an execution held almost an element of complicity on her part which may have been well nigh unendurable.

In August 1931, Russell McWilliams, a seventeen-year-old Rockford boy, held up the passengers on a streetcar, shooting and killing the motorman. He was arrested the next day and charged with murder. At the first trial in the circuit court, Russell pleaded guilty and was sentenced to be electrocuted in December 1931. A few days after the sentence Julia Lathrop wrote a public letter which contains the following: "Such a death sentence pronounced against a boy of that age is against public policy. Condemning to death so young and undeveloped a person is a profound miscarriage of justice."

She immediately organized an appeal against the execution of minors which became nation wide. Many letters and petitions were sent to the Governor of Illinois and publicity was obtained through several powerful newspapers whose policy was against capital punishment. Miss Lathrop, with an attorney from Rockford, two distinguished attorneys from Chicago, and Jessie F. Binford, the Superintendent of the Juvenile Protective Association, undertook the responsibility for the boy's legal defense and also for financing the case. This was the beginning of one of the most widely publicized trials of a juvenile in the United States, lasting from October 1931 to April 1933, with three trials in the Rockford Circuit Court, each of which resulted in a death sentence, two appeals in the Illinois Supreme Court, each of which resulted in remanding the case for retrial. The Illinois Supreme Court remanded the case to the Rockford Court on the ground that "further testimony should be heard in mitigation as well as aggravation," and reminded the lower court that the youth of the defendant entitled him to special consideration in fixing the penalty. Appeals to two Illinois governors – as an election had taken place during the year and a half – followed two hearings before the State Board of Pardons where the case was ably presented. [. . .]

On May 23rd when the date set for the execution was drawing near the boy wrote: "God will take care of me. The old devil Satan cannot take me unless God says it is O.K." Then he wrote Dr. Van Waters again: "The truth is that I don't expect any 30-day stay. Mother and I were arranging things for my funeral. It was a terrible thing to talk about, but just in case I did die, I wanted to know."

On April 13 1933, the newly-elected governor of Illinois, acting on the recommendation of the new Pardon Board, commuted the sentence of Russell McWilliams from death to imprisonment for 99 years. This commutation was issued a year after Julia Lathrop's death in the Rockford hospital on April 15, 1932.

WITNESS TO AN EXECUTION
The Case of Sacco and Vanzetti in Cartoons from *The Daily Worker* (1927)

Hastily, as these cartoons go to press, the roasted bodies of Sacco and Vanzetti, still unburied, are placed in state in the "cultured" city of Boston. The world is still ringing with the protests of workers and liberals against one of the foulest of the innumerable foul crimes of the capitalist class. Demonstrations continue to storm the doors of the American embassies and consulates in two hemispheres; and the American workers are preparing to perpetuate the memory of the two working class heroes who, innocent of any crime except the "crime" of fighting for the emancipation of humanity from capitalist oppression, were tortured for seven long years and finally murdered as a challenge to the revolutionary movement.

These cartoons were drawn from day to day during the tense period immediately preceding the murder of Sacco and Vanzetti. They appeared in *The Daily Worker*. Many elements and many publications tried to save the two men from the vengeance of the ruling class. None was as clear and persistent in pointing out the CLASS nature of the judicial murder as *The Daily Worker*; in clarifying the case as a symbol of the titanic struggle between capital and labor.

This policy explains in part the power of these cartoons. The most vigorous cartoons in this country appear in the revolutionary press. At its best the cartoon has always been a political weapon in the hands of a revolutionary class. Hogarth and Daumier drew their spiritual sustenance from the young and progressive bourgeoisie; their work, satirizing the powers that were, radiated with technical strength and conceptual greatness. The very word "cartoon" (the encyclopaedia tells us) was first applied to political caricature in the case of a "Punch" drawing attacking class injustice. It was called, significantly enough, "Substance and Shadow: The Poor Ask for Bread and the Philanthropic State Accords—an Exhibition."

[. . .] The drawings in this book are aflame with the idea of class struggle, from the one where the two martyr's sit on the trap of the working class enemy to the one where their murdered bodies dangle over the slogan: CARRY ON!

The last words were Sacco and Vanzetti's message to their fellow workers. These drawings —like their conduct —call not for mourning but for struggle.

WITNESS TO AN EXECUTION
An Execution In Paris, Frank Harris (1930)

Ihad heard about Henry, the anarchist, from one of his friends, had
been told of his wild idealism and quaint beliefs, of his kindness,
too, and amiability, and suddenly a journalist acquaintance, H.B.,
asked me to go with him to witness the execution. I had never seen one: reason
or curiosity suggested that it was an experience which perhaps I ought to go
through: it might teach me something: in an evil hour I made up my mind to go.

I got the journalist's special permission without any difficulty, besides
my *coupe-file*; I was to go with two or three Parisian writers; one of them, the
gigantic H.B., declared that it was usual to make a night of it; he proposed we
should sup first on the spot, and then go down to the show. I allowed myself to
be persuaded; we supped in a room looking on the fatal square; my friends told
stories, talked about other executions, did everything to pass the time, but time
crawled on leaden feet. When I first looked at my watch (my heart was in my
mouth) I thought it must be four o'clock; it was barely two.

The window was thrown open, the night was clear and starlit, a faint
breeze sighed across the void square. There was a certain animation in the Place:
the windows were lighted, the cafes all doing brisk business. As I looked towards
the dark prison, my whole inside seemed to shrink: almost I made up my mind
to say that I would not stay; but a sort of false shame was upon me, and the old
foolish arguments came back — experiences enrich life and so forth — I turned
again to the room.

The talk began again, and the meaningless stories, chiefly now mere
egoistic braggings. I sat and watched my friends; they seemed to me my real,
grotesque masks; I wondered whether Henry was sleeping or waking; what his
thoughts were. My heart was wrung with pity.

It was H.B. who turned my thought and distracted my attention by telling
of a new play he had written for some little theater on an outside boulevard.
It was a gruesome story, but splendidly mimed, and the telling of it and the
discussion it led to relieved me of the obsession of the one thought. Interested in
my turn, I forgot.

All of a sudden we heard the tramp of men: again the windows were
thrown open, and we looked out. It was near dawn; the stars were paling. A
crowd now fringed the Place, and in the center the Republican Guard had made
a cordon, a great square, which was kept free, save for perhaps a dozen or twenty
people, who, I was told, were journalists like ourselves. All the preparations
oppressed me: I could scarcely draw my breath; the waiting was terrible. I felt it,
weak with apprehension. I was afraid to think of the condemned man; I hoped
he was sleeping—unconscious. But I could not help seeing, feeling, thinking. . . .

In the square the crowd talked, laughed; snatches of song broke out from
windows near, or wild whoopings, "*A bas l'assassin!*" The beat was taken up—
"*l'assassin, l'assassin, l'assassin,*" the first two syllables pronounced quickly, the

third dwelt upon—a ghastly imitation of the three knocks at the theater to show that the audience was becoming impatient—*"l'assassin, l'as-sassin."* The brutes! I thought, the brutes! It suddenly struck me that this ribaldry was perhaps a pretense in order to remove the dreadful apprehension that was weighing me down, that must be weighing everyone down. But I was mistaken: the exclamations grew more frequent, the witticisms riper, and behind all the vile refrain rose more imperious —*"l'assassin, l'assassin!"* More people tried to sing; shrieks of laughter pealed out here and there; squeals as of women tickled, and all the while--*"l'assassin, l'assassin, l'assassin!"*

The incongruity between what went on around us and the menacing silent square and the gloomy prison front was too horrible. I said weakly:

"I've had enough of this: I'll go home to bed."

"Nonsense, nonsense!" my friends cried. "The fun's going to begin." Fun! "M. de Paris will arrive soon. Here he is! On time always!"

A burst of cheering rose from the square and the open windows, and, fascinated, I watched the great *fourgons* drive up and enter the guarded enclosure.

"Let's go down, or we'll be too late," proposed H.B.

The bill was called for and paid; and we trooped down the stairs and made our way as quietly as possible through the crowd into the central guarded square: *"Pardon, monsieur; pardon, madame."* The people made way....

The executioner and his assistants had begun to set up the guillotine. We walked inside the file of soldiery, inside the picket of mounted men, and stood looking on. The men worked very quickly. While the assistants were putting up the guillotine I noticed that time, which had been so laggard, was now racing; everything was done swiftly, silently; not a pause, not a check anywhere; the men seemed to be racing; piece moved to piece, the thing went together of itself, and soon the hideous bare outline was there against the pale sky and the dying stars. I could hear my heart thump — that wicked triangle — the long, slanting edge against the pale turquoise sky. . . .

The executioner went over and pressed a button, and the knife fell with a swish. I almost choked. Another touch, and the knife slid up into its place again. The deadly blade was eager to be at work: it was all ready, waiting—my mouth was dry with fever.

Scarcely had the guillotine been erected and tried when a sharp order was given, and the soldiers began to move the crowd back. One saw faces everywhere: eager, curious faces, framing us in; terrible faces, pallid, gray, menacing! And still time hurried and the sky got lighter and lighter, and suddenly there was a loud word of command, and at once the square of soldiers opened out, and we saw straight to the prison. A moment's pause, and there came a clang, and the prison doors flew open, and in the black hollow a little group of men appeared, hurrying towards us. I could have shrieked. Insensibly, we were drawn towards them. I could scarcely keep up with the rest; but I was in a trance: life had stopped still with me. . . . Suddenly the knot of men was quite close to me, the priest in front of Henry, who kept waving him away; the priest moved backward, repeating phrases — prayers, in a distressed, quick monotone.

I could see the sweat of the man's forehead — ghastly! Again Henry waved him aside, and as he moved I saw him. His face was not white, but green, a sort of greenish yellow, the eyes set! The shirt had been cut away from round the neck in jagged cuts; his mouth was pressed together, his eyes fixed — staring. Suddenly I felt that he was staring at the guillotine, and the solid ground waved under my feet. There might have been resolution in his face: there was resolution in it — a man's resolution; but his feet had been tied together so tightly that he could scarcely hobble. Every time he attempted to step like a man he stumbled, and had to be held up by the men walking on either side of him who hurried him along. ... It was all degrading, dreadful!

Suddenly shouts broke forth, wild shriekings. "*A bas l'assassin! L'assassin a la veuve! A la veuve!*" Shrieks of inhuman triumph, of gloating expectation. Were these human beings?

Henry stopped, and his eyes fell on them; the next moment he was pushed forward almost on his face, then held up from falling, and hurried on, dragged and pushed forward. The needless appalling indignity of it!

I followed unconscious; I was standing by the guillotine. The two assistants caught hold of Henry, and pulled him roughly to the *bascule*. One stooped, tying his legs to it; the other slid the strap round his chest and buckled it. Haste, breathless haste! Suddenly the *bascule* operated, and instead of standing, he was slung forward on his face: his head was in the *lunette*, but not through; an assistant on the other side got hold of his ears in both hands and dragged his head through — tore it through into position. The next second he moved back, withdrawing his hands quickly; the executioner stepped forward, one glance to see that all was in order, then he touched the button. Again, the swish as of tearing silk and the head jumped forward from the body into the basket like a carrot chopped off with a knife, while the trunk spouted streams of blood. The next moment the body was cast off and flung into the basket, too, and while we stood appalled at the ghastly speed of it all, unable to think as quickly as the event, the assistants had begun to take the whole thing to pieces, and H.B. caught me by the arm: "Quick work, eh?"

I could not speak: my tongue stuck to my dry mouth. I gasped for breath; the others were talking around me, the crowds outside singing and laughing as they dispersed.

"The savages!" I said to myself. "The brute beasts! Oh, the brutes! They can shout and laugh;" and again I saw the man trying to be brave and dragged forward, stumbling. . . . . Oh, what brutes men are!

END NOTES

Without the magic of the Internet this book would have taken a lifetime to research and compile. All Web addresses were checked on July 29, 2009.

Part I: In the Beginning

p. 3 - Code of Hammurabi (1790 BCE) The Code of Ur-Nammu is the oldest known tablet containing a law code surviving today. It predates the Code of Hammurabi by some 300 years. Its first law is "If a man commits a murder, that man must be killed."

p. 7 — **The Ancient Hebrew Law of Homicide**, Mayer Sulzburger (1915) <books.google.com/books?id=bxd3CVb6sfEC&dq> (Chapter 1.) Sulzburger was a prominent Philadelphia judge and Jewish community leader.

p. 10 — **A History of Greece from the Earliest Times to the Present**, Telemachus Thomas Timayenis (1883) <books.google.com/books?id=73qzI5CkAlAC> Timayenis (1853-1918) was a Greek immigrant who was a champion of oppressed Greek peddlers in Boston.

p. 12 – **The History Of The Peloponnesian War**, Thucydides (431 BCE) <www.greektexts.com/library/Thucydides/History_of_The_Peloponnesian_War_-_Book_III/eng/48.html>

p. 14 — **The Laws**, Plato (360 BCE) <classics.mit.edu/Plato/laws.html> (From book V)

p. 16 — **Crito**, by Plato (360 BCE) <classics.mit.edu/Plato/crito.html>

p. 17 — **The Death of Socrates**, Plato (360 BCE) This is from **Phædo**. <www.wsu.edu:8080/~wldciv/world_civ_reader/world_civ_reader_1/phaedo.html>

p. 18 — **Nicomachean Ethics**, Aristotle (350 BCE) <www.constitution.org/ari/ethic_00.htm> (From Book V, sec. 1)

p. 20 — **A History of Continental Criminal Law: Aristotle**, Carl Ludwig von Bar (1916) <books.google.com/books?id=WlcpAAAAYAAJ> (From part II, chap 1, section 76, p. 386)

p. 21 — **Conspiracy of Catiline**, Gaius Sallustius Crispus (63)<forumromanum.org/literature/sallust/catilinae.html> (from chapters 50, 51 & 55)

p. 27 — **The Execution of Mithridates**, Plutarch (75) This is from *Artaxerxes*, translated by John Dryden. <classics.mit.edu/Plutarch/artaxerx.html>

p. 28 — **On Mercy (***De Clementia***)**, Seneca (1st Century) <www.stoics.com/seneca_essays_book_1.html> These were a series of letters written to the Emperor Nero.

p. 29 — **Execution of Aper** (284) is from Edward Gibbons **Decline and Fall of the Roman Empire** (1901), Vol. 1, ch. 12 <ancienthistory.about.com/library/bl/bl_text_gibbon_1_12_3.htm>

p. 29 — **The Tenth Persecution under Diocletian** (303) <www.gutenberg.org/files/22400/22400.txt> (from **Foxe's Book Of Martyrs**, Or *A History Of The Lives, Sufferings, And Triumphant Deaths Of The Primitive Protestant Martyrs From The Introduction Of Christianity To The Latest Periods Of Pagan, Popish, And Infidel Persecutions Embracing, Together With The Usual Subjects Contained In Similar Works*. It was first published in 1563.

p. 32 — **City of God (***De Civitate Dei***)**, Augustine of Hippo (5th Century) <www.ccel.org/ccel/schaff/npnf102.iv.ii.xxii.html>

p. 32 — **Summa Theologica**, Thomas Aquinas (1264-1275) This is from The Second Part of the Second Part (*Secunda Secundæ Partis*) <www.newadvent.org/summa/3064.htm>

p. 34 — *Utopia*, Sir Thomas More (1516) <www.online-literature.com/more/utopia/> (From the first chapter, *Discourses of Raphael Hythloday*)

p. 39 — **The Prince**, Niccolò Machiavelli. (1532) (From Chapter XVII: *Concerning Cruelty And Clemency, And Whether It Is Better To Be Loved Than Feared*.) <www.constitution.org/mac/prince00.htm>

p. 41 — **The Execution of Archbishop Cranmer** <englishhistory.net/tudor/pcranmer.html> This is attributed to an anonymous bystander. Cranmer, a leader in the Protestant Reformation, was executed for heresy and treason when the Catholic Mary I ascended the English throne.

p. 43 — **Martyr's Mirror** (1569) <www.homecomers.org/mirror/dirk-willems.htm> First published in 1660, **The Bloody Theater** or *Martyrs Mirror of the Defenseless Christians who baptized only upon confession of faith, and who suffered and died for the testimony of Jesus, their Saviour, from the time of Christ to the year A.D. 1660,* describes the persecution and execution of thousands of Anabaptists in the Low Countries between 1524 and 1660.

p. 44 — **Execution of Mary Queen of Scots** (1587) This is an anonymous eyewitness account. <home.earthlink.net/~zzz12/eyewitness2.htm>

p. 46 — **Of Experience**, Michel de Montaigne (1588) <essays.quotidiana.org/montaigne/experience/> In Florio's translation of Montaigne's *Essays* (1603) you will find it in Book III, Chap. XIII. This was Montaigne's last essay.

p. 48 — **Disputations on Controversial Matters:** *De Laicis* — Saint Robert Bellarmine's Treatise on Civil Government, Chapter 21 (1596) <catholicism.org/de-laicis.html/21>

p. 54 — **Auto Da Fe**, Madrid (1682) <www.gutenberg.org/files/22400/22400.txt> This excerpt is also from **Foxe's Book of Martyrs**. *Auto da Fe* , literally "act of faith," was the ritual of public penance of condemned heretics and apostates between the trial and punishment phases during the Spanish and Portuguese Inquisitions.

p. 55 — **The Spanish Inquisition**, Count Joseph de Maitsre (1822) <www.archive.org/details/lettersonspanis00maisuoft>

p. 63 — **On Revenge**, Sir Francis Bacon (1597) <www.bartleby.com/3/1/4.html>

p. 64 — **The Rights of War and Peace**, Grothius (Hugo deGroot) (1625) The extracts are all from Book 1, Chapter XX, "*On Punishments*." <oll.libertyfund.org/?option=com_staticxt&staticfile=show.php%3Ftitle=553> Grotius laid the foundations for international law.

Part II: The Best of Times, The Worst of Times

p. 81 — **Leviathan**: *Of Punishments and Rewards*, Thomas Hobbes (1660) From Chap. 28 <publicliterature.org/books/leviathan/xaa.php> Hobbes most famous saying occurs in chap. 13, where he characterizes the life of man as "solitary, poor, nasty, brutish, and short."

p. 73 — **Blaise Pascal, Letter XIV** (1656) This is one of the *Provincial Letters*, written anonymously (they were considered heretical), attacking the Jesuits for "casuistry," or case-based reasoning as opposed to rule-based reasoning. <oregonstate.edu/instruct/phl302/texts/pascal/letters-contents.html>

p. 87 — **Hanging of General Harrison**, Samuel Pepys (1660) This is from the Pepys *Diary*, Saturday 13 October. <www.pepysdiary.com/archive/1660/10/13/>

p. 87 — **Hanging Not Punishment Enough**, Basil Montagu, Esq. (1701) <books.google.com/books?id=ks0DAAAAQAAJ> This pamphlet was originally published anonymously, but achieved its widest circulation in this 1812 edition, which bears Montagu's name on the cover and includes an introduction by him.

p. 92 — **Theodicy**: *Essays on the Goodness of God, the Freedom of Man and the Origin of Evil*, Gottfried W. Liebniz (1710) <www.gutenberg.org/files/17147/17147-h/17147-h.htm>

p. 96 — **A London Hanging** (1726) <www.eyewitnesstohistory.com/londonhanging.htm>

p. 98 — **Going To Be Hanged**, Jonathan Swift (1727) <books.google.com/books?id=dC4JAAAAQAAJ&pg=PA437>. You'll find this on page 437.

p. 99 — **An Enquiry Concerning Human Understanding**, David Hume (1748) The extracts here are from Sect. VIII: *Of Liberty and Necessity*, part 1. <www.infidels.org/library/historical/david_hume/human_understanding.html>

p. 100 — **Spirit of Laws**, Charles de Secondat, Baron de Montesquieu (1748) <www.constitution.org/cm/sol-02.htm> These selections are from Book VI, *Consequences of the Principles of Different Governments with Respect to the Simplicity of Civil and Criminal Laws, the Form of Judgments, and the Inflicting of Punishments.*

p. 103 — **Essays on the Mind**, Claude Adrien Helvétius (1758) <books.google.com/books?id=IijEooaXqCYC> This extract begins on page 189.

p. 104 — **The Rambler 114**, Samuel Johnson (1750) </books.google.com/books?id=YyEVAAAAQAAJ> *The Rambler* was a magazine published by Dr. Johnson on Tuesdays and Saturdays from 1750 to 1752.

p. 107 — **An Account Of Corsica**, *The Journal of a Tour to That Island*, James Boswell (1765) <books.google.com/books?id=_jQVAAAAQAAJ>

p. 109 — **The Theory of the Moral Sentiments,** Adam Smith (1759) This extract is from Part II: *Of Merit and Demerit; or, of the Objects of Reward and Punishment Consisting of Three Parts* ; Section II: *Of Justice and Beneficence; Chap. III: Of the Utility of this Constitution of Nature* <books.google.com/books?id=xVkOAAAAQAAJ>

p. 115 — **The Social Contract**, Jean-Jacques Rousseau, (1762) <www.constitution.org/jjr/socon.htm> Book II, Chap. 5. *The Right of Life And Death.*

p. 116 — **Second Treatise of Government**, John Locke (1764) <www.gutenberg.org/dirs/etext05/trgov10.txt>

p. 120 — **Of Crimes and Punishments**, Cesare Beccaria From Chap. 28, *Of the Punishment of Death.* (1764) <books.google.com/books?id=G0kGAAAAQAAJ> Thomas Jefferson had a heavily marked-up copy of Beccaria's book in his library.

p. 125 — **A Commentary on the Book, Of Crimes And Punishments**, Voltaire (1764) <books.google.com/books?id=G0kGAAAAQAAJ> This is from a 1788 English edition.

p. 126 — **Principles of Penal Law**, William Eden, Lord Auckland (1771) This is Chapter III: *Of the Infliction of Death.* <books.google.com/books?printsec=titlepage&id=PswiAAAAMAAJ>

p. 129 — **Memoirs of the Year Two Thousand Five Hundred**, Louis-Sébastien Mercier (1772) This is from the chapter *"Execution of a Criminal."* The French title of this Utopian novel is *L'An 2440, rêve s'il en fut jamais* ("The Year 2440: A Dream If Ever There Was One.") <books.google.com/books?id=VI0TAAAAQAAJ>

p. 130 — **A Hanging at Tyburn** (1777). This is from **Hand-book of London,** Peter Cunningham (1850). <books.google.com/books?id=0BQNAAAAYAAJ> It describes the execution of a Dr. Dodd for the forging of bonds in the name of Lord Chesterfield. From pages 514-517 is a history of executions on the Tyburn gallows in London.

p. 130 — **Execution of Tupac Amaru II**, José Antonio de Areche (1781). This extract is reprinted in **The Peru Reader** By Orin Starn, Carlos Iván Degregori, Robin Kirk (Duke University Press, 1995)

p. 133 - **Thoughts on Executive Justice: with Respect to our criminal laws, by** A sincere well-wisher to the public (1785) <books.google.com/books?id=ZK0DAAAAQAAJ>. Published anonymously, the author was a lawyer turned Methodist minister, Martin Mandan.

p. 136 — **The Right of Punishing,** Immanuel Kant (1790) This is from **The Science of Right** <philosophy.eserver.org/kant/science-of-right.txt> From the chapter *Acquisition Conditioned by the Sentence of a Public Judiciary.*

p. 141 — **Against Granting the King a Trial**, Robespierre, (1792) <books.google.com/books?id=HrDgrnNmJJ4C> This extract is taken from a 1900 anthology, **The World's Greatest Orators**, by Guy Carleton Lee.

p. 142 — **The Execution of Louis XVI**, Henry Essex Edgeworth (1792.) This is from **The Historical Cabinet;** *containing authentic accounts of many remarkable and interesting events, which have taken place in modern times* (1838) <www.archive.org/stream/historicalcabine00phil> Edgeworth was an Irish priest and the confessor of Louis XVI. His memoir was published in 1815.

p. 144 — **The Life of Thomas Paine**, Moncure Daniel Conway (1793) <books.google.com/books?id=az9twvi_RyIC>

p. 146 — **On Punishing Murder by Death**, Benjamin Rush (1792) <press-pubs.uchicago.edu/founders/documents/amendVIIIs16.html> Rush was a signatory of the Declaration of Independence and attended the Continental Congress. Later in life, he became a professor of medical theory and clinical practice at the University of Pennsylvania and is considered the father of American psychiatry.

p. 148 — **Philosophy in the Bedroom**, Marquis de Sade, (1795) <www.sin.org/tales/Marquis_de_Sade--Philosophy_in_the_Bedroom.pdf> This is from *"Yet Another Effort, Frenchmen, If You Would Become Republicans,"* an interlude between Dialogues V and VI.

p. 149— **Execution of Governor Wall**, Don Manual Alvarez Espriella (1809.) <www.archive.org/stream/lettersfromengla01soutuoft#page/x/mode/2up> This is from Volume I of **Letters from England:** by Don Manuel Alvarez Espriella. Translated from the Spanish by Robert Southey (1809) Don Manuel is a fictional creation of Southey.

p. 152 — **The Execution of Governor Wall**, John Thomas Smith. This is from *"A Book for a Rainy Day"* (1861). <books.google.com/books?id=a0EBAAAAQAAJ> The account starts on page 165.

p. 153 — **The Nottingham Frame-Breaking Bill**, House of Lords Speech, Lord Byron. (1808) <everything2.com/title/Lord%2520Byron%2520Speaks%2520to%2520Parliament> This was Lord Byron's maiden speech in the house of Lords; "frame-breaking" was the destruction of new technology by Luddites.

p. 155 — **An Execution in Rome**, Lord Byron (1817) This is from a letter to his publisher, John Murray, May 30. <engphil.astate.edu/gallery/byron7.html>

p. 156 — **Capital Punishment And The Ordeal**, Frederick von Schlegel.(1810) This essay is taken from **A Course of Lectures on Modern History**, published in 1849. The extract was taken from lecture II, *The Germans*. <books.google.com/books?id=II14Yr_E5NwC>

p. 157 — **The Philosophy of Right**, Georg Wilhelm Friedrich Hegel (1820) <www.marxists.org/reference/archive/hegel/prindex.htm> These extracts are from Part I (*Abstract Right*) Sect. iii (*Wrong*)

p. 158 — **The Saint Petersburg Dialogues**, Joseph de Maistre (1821) <maistre.ath.cx:8000/st_petersburg> de Maistre, an opponent of the rationalism of the Enlightenment, was one of the fathers of European conservatism.

p. 160 — **The Rationale of Punishment**, Jeremy Bentham (1830) <www.archive.org/details/rationalepunish00bentgoog>

p. 179 — **Lectures on Witchcraft**, *Comprising A History: The Delusion In Salem, in 1692.* Charles W. Upham (1831) <books.google.com/books?id=A2CXUuHlG9UC> Upham was a member of the Massachusetts House of Representatives and a Unitarian minister in Salem.

p. 181 — **On Witchcraft**, Harriet Martineau (1836) From: **Miscellanies**, Vol. II, p. 387ff <www.archive.org/details/miscellanies05martgoog> Martineau was an English writer and philosopher, controversial journalist, political economist, abolitionist and life-long feminist. She been called the first female sociologist and the first female journalist in England.

p. 182 — **The Execution of Davy Crockett**, Lt. Col. José Enrique de la Peña (1836) <www.cah.utexas.edu/exhibits/Pena/translation.html>

p. 183 — **On The Punishment Of Death: A Fragment**, Percy Bysshe Shelley (1815) <books.google.com/books?id=IvoFAAAAQAAJ>

p. 187 — **Sonnets Upon The Punishment Of Death**, William Wordsworth (1839) <www.bartelby.org/145/ww923.html>

p. 192 — **William Wordsworth, his life, works, and influence**, George McLean Harper (1916) <books.google.com/books?id=DEEzAAAAMAAJ>. This extract starts on page 423.

p. 193 — **Going To See A Man Hanged**, William Makepeace Thackeray (1840) <www.exclassics.com/newgate/courv.htm> Another interesting piece by Thackeray is "The Case of Peytel," included in **The Paris Sketchbook** <www.online-literature.com/view.php/paris-sketch-book/16?term=peytel>

p. 203 — **Concerning Political Justice And Its Influence On Morals And Happiness**, William Godwin.(1842) <www.archive.org/details/enquiryconcernin02godwuoft> This is from Vol. II; all of Book VII concerns crime and punishment. Godwin is now mostly remembered as the husband of the pioneering feminist, Mary Wollstonecraft and father of Mary Shelly, author of "Frankenstein," but he was extremely influential in his own time.

p. 208 — **A Hanging in Wisconsin** (1842) <boards.ancestry.myfamily.com/surnames.caffee/57/mb.ashx>

p. 210 — **The Execution of the Mexican Assassins**, Lewis H. Garrard (1847) This extract is taken from the book **Eyewitness to the Old West** by Richard Scott (Roberts Rhinehart, 2002), pp 85-87. The account originally appeared in the book **Wah-To-Yah and the Taos Trail** (Cincinnati, OH: A. S. Barnes and Company. Publishers, 1850.) These hanging took place during what is called in New Mexico "The Revolt of 1847." An account of the events leading up to these hangings was written by Robert J. Torrez, the NM State Historian, available online at <www.newmexicohistory.org/filedetails.php?fileID=21394>

p. 212 — **Speech to the Legislative Assembly**, Victor Hugo (1848.) This speech is included in *"The Speaker's Garland and Literary Bouquet"* (1876.) <books.google.com/books?id=zRlKAAAAIAAJ>

p. 213 — **The Execution of Tapner**, Victor Hugo (1856.) <www.archive.org/details/victorhugolifere00hugouoft> Hugo was living in exile on the British island of Guernsey; this letter was addressed to Lord Palmerston, the Home Secretary. Also included in this biography, written by his adoring wife, is a letter written prior to Tapner's execution, addressed to the people of Guernsey.

III: After the Enlightenment

p. 219 — **Essays on The Punishment Of Death**, Charles Spear (1844.) <www.archive.org/details/essaysonpunishm05speagoog>This is from Essay II, *"Revengeful."* Spear was a Universalist preacher and editor of a national newspaper, *"The Prisoner's Friend."*

p. 222 — **Capital Punishment**, based on Professor Karl Josef Anton Mittermaier's "Todstraffe" (1846.) <books.google.com/books?id=hqgMAAAAYAAJ&dq> This is from chap. II: *Humanitarian Doctrines: Their Bearing on the Theory of Capital Punishment.* Mittermaier was a jurist, journalist and politician; a central figure in German liberalism.

p. 238 — **Capital Punishment**, Margaret Fuller (1846) This book review is taken from a collection of her essays, **"Life Without and Life Within."** <books.google.com/books?id=ZEkLAAAAIAAJ&pg=PA199>. The particular book by John Barrell Cheever that Fuller so venomously reviewed does not appear to be online but a similar volume can be read at <www.archive.org/stream/capitalpunishme00sulgoog#page/n15/mode/1up>

p. 239 — **Horray for Hanging!**, Walt Whitman (1846) This is the first series of columns about the death penalty that Whitman wrote for the *Brooklyn Eagle* in 1846, collected in *"The Gathering of the Forces"* (1920), edited by Cleveland Rodgers and John Black. The letters start on page 97. <books.google.com/books?id=YtjQAAAAMAAJ>

p. 241 — **Letters to the Daily News**, Charles Dickens (1846) <home.earthlink.net/~bsabatini/Inimitable-Boz/etexts/dickens_on_capital_punishment.html> In later years, Dickens became more conservative and moderated his position. In an 1863 letter to a friend he wrote: *"I am sorry to confess that I do now believe Capital Punishment to be necessary in extreme cases; simply because it appears impossible otherwise to rid Society of certain members of whom it must be rid, or there is no living on this earth. But I believe a public execution to be a savage horror far behind the time, affording an indecent and fearful gratification to the worst of people."*

p. 248 — **Horsemonger Lane Execution**, Charles Dickens (1849) <http://books.google.com/books?id=wS8NAAAAYAAJ> This is on page 120 of **The Men Of The Time In 1852, Or, Sketches Of Living Notables**, by David Bogue (1852)

p. 250 — **The Philosophy of Poverty**, Pierre-Joseph Proudhon (1847) <trotsky.org/reference/subject/economics/proudhon/philosophy/index.htm> This is in Chapter 7: *Police or Taxation.*

p. 253 — **The Death Penalty Is Atheistical In Doctrine**, W.Y Emmet (1849) <http://books.google.com/books?id=-QXP1PDIbq0C>

p. 255 — **Model Prisons**, Thomas Carlyle (1850) <books.google.com/books?id=qlImAAAAMAAJ> This is from Chap. 2 of **Latter Day Pamphlets**.

p. 260 — **Neapolitan Trials for Political Offences**, W. E. Gladstone. (1851) <faculty.ed.umuc.edu/~jmatthew/naples/gladstone.html> Gladstone was four times Liberal Party Prime Minister of the United Kingdom.

p. 263 — **Defence of Slavery!** A Series of Letters to Harriet Beecher Stowe. Nicholas Brimblecomb, Esq. (1853) <books.google.com/books?id=NFCh3E11SuwC&dq> Brimblecomb is a pseudonym; the author is unknown. Although most sources treat his letters seriously, there is speculation that they are perhaps satire, along the lines of Jonathan Swifts "A Modest Proposal."

p. 266 — **Karl Marx** in *The New-York Tribune* (1853.) <www.marxists.org/archive/marx/works/1853/02/18.htm> In the early 1850s, Karl Marx wrote news summaries about events in Europe for the *New York Daily Tribune*.

p. 269 — **A London Fête**, Coventry Patmore (1854.) <oldpoetry.com/opoem/101691-Coventry-Patmore-A-London-F-te>

p. 270 — **Capital Punishment Speech**, Wendell Phillips (1859.) This is from **The Free Speaker** by William Bentley Fowle (1859), which is a collection of "speeches for declamation." <books.google.com/

books?id=NpoXpk2aZEsC&pg=PA82>
Phillips, a Boston lawyer, was an American anti-slavery activist, advocate for Native Americans, and orator.

p. 272 — **The Execution of John Brown**, John T. L. Preston (1859.) This letter is cited in **The Military History of the Virginia Military Institute from 1839 to 1865** by Jennings Cropper Wise (1915) p. 108. <books.google.com/books?id=INmKsEB4LWAC>

p. 276 — **The Execution of John Brown**, Thomas J. "Stonewall" Jackson (1859.) <www.vmi.edu/archives.aspx?id=4919> This letter is from the Virginia Military Institute online research center.

p. 277 — **Burning Human Beings Alive at the Stake**, William Henry Fey (1860) This is from the *Republican Campaign Handbook*. <www.archive.org/details/bookcampaignrep00repurich>

p. 283 — **Execution of 38 Sioux**, Isaac Heard (1863.) <books.google.com/books?id=HlMgJlHtdukC> This extract is from the book **History of the Sioux War and Massacres of 1862 and 1863**. Lincoln refused to pay the Santee Sioux $1.5 million owed them by terms of two 1851 treaties (Traverse des Sioux and Mendota) and three 1858 treaties for the sale of 24 million acres, including most of Minnesota. In 1862, after a crop failure, famine broke out among the Indians. Local authorities refused to supply the starving Indians with the food stockpiled for them in accordance with the terms of the treaties. The Sioux, Cheyenne, and Chippewa responded with the Great Sioux Uprising of 1862, in which over 800 white men, women, and children were massacred. The war ended with this execution.

p. 287 — **Guillotining in Paris**, George Alfred Townsend (1864.) </books.google.com/books?id=BZTTdvoYgrQC> This is from the book *Campaigns of a Non-Combatant*, p. 321. Couty de la Pommerais was a homeopathic doctor convicted of killing his lover. Townsend was a noted war correspondent during the American Civil War, and a later novelist.

p. 291 — **The Execution of The Lincoln Conspirators**, Clara E. Laughlin (1865/1909.) <www.archive.org/details/deathlincolnsto00lauggoog> Laughlin was an author; travel specialist; journalist; editor and radio broadcaster.

p. 293 — **Horace Greeley** (1867.) This letter to Marvin Bovee was reprinted in **Reasons**

for Abolishing Capital Punishment <books.google.com/books?id=vZ4XAAAAYAAJ> p. 100. Greeley was editor of the *New York Tribune*, a reformer and politician.

p. 294 — **Use of the Death Penalty**, John Stuart Mill (1868.) <www.mnstate.edu/gracyk/courses/web%20publishing/Mill_supports_death_penalty.htm> Mill delivered this speech before the British Parliament on April 21, 1868 in opposition to a bill banning capital punishment.

p. 300 — **Mark Twain Witnesses a Hanging** (1868.) From the Nevada State archives <nevadaculture.org/nsla/index.php?option=com_content&task=view&id=1574&Itemid=95>

p. 302 — **Letter to Marvin H. Bovee**, Elizabeth Cady Stanton (1868.) <books.google.com/books?id=vZ4XAAAAYAAJ> This letter is included in the book **Reasons for Abolishing Capital Punishment**, by Marvin Henry Bovee (1878), pp. 173-175. Bovee was a Wisconsin legislator, Quaker and social activist who dedicated his life to the abolishment of capital punishment.

p. 303 — **The Program of the International Brotherhood**, Mikhail Bakunin (1869.) <www.marxists.org/reference/archive/bakunin/works/1869/program.htm> Bakunin was a well-known Russian revolutionary and theorist of collectivist anarchism.

p. 305 — **The Algerian Executioner (1873.)** From an unsigned article, *"The Roumi In Kabylia,"* from **Lippincott's Magazine Of Popular Literature And Science**, April, 1873. <www.gutenberg.org/files/13145/13145-h/13145-h.htm>

p. 306 — **The Principles of Sociology**, Herbert Spencer, (1873-74.) <www.archive.org/details/principlesofsoci02spen> This extract is from Vol. 2, Part V (*Political Institutions*) Chap XIII, (*Judicial and Executive Systems*.) The following chapter, "Laws," is also interesting.

p. 310 — **The General Influence Of Beccaria On Legislation**, James Anson Farrer (1880.) <www.archive.org/details/crimesandpunish00farrgoog> This is from Chap. II of a lengthy introduction to a translation of Beccaria.

p. 316 — **The Lessons of the Hour**, Frederick Douglass (1883.) <antislavery.eserver.org/legacies/the-lessons-of-the-hour/the-lessons-of-the-hour.pdf> This is from an address delivered in the Metropolitan AME Church in Washington, D.C. on April 16, on the 21st anniversary of emancipation in Wash. D.C..

p. 317 — **Keynote Address, American Social Science Annual Meeting**, Prof. Francis Wayland (1883) <books.google.com/books?id=vDIJAAAAIAAJ> This is Francis III, a Lt. Gov. of Connecticut and Dean of Yale Law School.

p. 330 — **Elizabeth Fry: The Gallows and English Laws** (1884) <books.google.com/books?id=2xwIAAAAQAAJ> This is from Chap. VIII of Emma Raymond Pitman's biography of Elizabeth Fry (1884); Fry died in 1845. Fry was a prominent Quaker abolitionist and prison reformer.

p. 336 — **The World as Will and Idea**, Arthur Schopenhauer (1886) <books.google.com/books?id=92sOAAAAIAAJ> This is from the Fourth Book, Chap. XLVII, starting on p. 412.

p. 338 — **On the Genealogy of Morals**: A Polemical Tract. Friedrich Nietzsche (1887) <records.viu.ca/~johnstoi/Nietzsche/genealogytofc.htm> These extracts are from the Second Essay, "*Guilt, Bad Conscience, and Related Matters.*"

p. 340 — **Human, All Too Human**, Friedrich Nietzsche (1878) <nietzsche.holtof.com/Nietzsche_human_all_too_human/index.htm>

p. 342 — **Haymarket Tragedy**, Eugene V. Debs (1887) — <books.google.com/books?id=2DooAAAAYAAJ&pg=PA12&lpg=PA12> Although this editorial from the Locomotive Fireman's Magazine, Brotherhood of Locomotive Firemen, is unsigned, the editor of the magazine was Eugene V. Debs, candidate for President of the United States as a member of the Social Democratic Party in 1900, and later as a member of the Socialist Party of America in 1904, 1908, 1912, and 1920.

p. 345 — **Haymarket Tragedy**, Mother Jones (1925) <www.angelfire.com/nj3/RonMBaseman/mojones1.htm> This extract is from **The Autobiography of Mother Jones**, Chap. II, *Haymarket Tragedy*. Mary Harris Jones was an American labor and community organizer.

p. 346 — **Hanging of Albert Parson**s, Lucy Parsons (1889) <www.archive.org/details/lifeofalbertrpar00pars> These extracts are from **The Life of Albert Parsons**, written by his wife, an anarchist leader and writer in her own right.

p. 348 — **Facts and Laws Of The Moral Life**: Theories of Punishment, Wilhelm Wundt (1892) <books.google.com/books?id=j2sAAAAAMAAJ> Wilhelm Maximilian Wundt (1832 - 1920) was a German medical doctor, psychologist, physiologist, and professor, known today as one of the founding figures of modern psychology.

p. 351 — **The Case Against Capital Punishment**, B. Paul Neuman (1889) <www.archive.org/stream/capitalpunishartic00fannrich/capitalpunishartic00fannrich_djvu.txt> This article was reprinted in **Full text of 'Selected articles on capital punishment,'** a debate handbook published in 1909. It contains 33 articles both for and against capital punishment.

p. 355 — **Execution of Kemmler**, Auburn State Prison (1890) <www.mindfully.org/Reform/Kemmler-Torture-Death7aug1890.htm>

p. 357 — **The Crime Of Capital Punishment**, Hugh O. Pentecost (1890) From *The Arena*, January 1890, Vol. 1, no. 2, pp. 175-83.

p. 363 — **Anarchy and its Heroes** , Cesare Lombroso (1897) <ww.marxists.org/subject/anarchism/lombroso.htm> Lombroso was an Italian criminologist: using concepts drawn from physiognomy, early eugenics, psychiatry and Social Darwinism, Lombroso's theorized that criminality was inherited, and that someone "born criminal"' could be identified by physical defects.

p. 365 — **Upon The Gallows Hung A Wretch**, Emily Dickinson (1896) This is poem XXII from **Poems by Emily Dickinson, Three Series, Complete**, edited by Charles Dudley Warner. <infomotions.com/etexts/gutenberg/dirs/1/2/2/4/12242/12242.htm>

p. 365 — **Two Laws of Penal Evolution**, Emile Durkheim (1900) This extract is available from several sources, including **Readings from Emile Durkheim** By Émile Durkheim, (Kenneth Thompson, Margaret A. Thompson Routledge, 1985) Durkheim addresses similar issues in **The Division of Labor in Society** (1893)

p. 368 — **The Ballad of Reading Gaol**, Oscar Wilde (1898) <books.google.com/books?id=MzIWAAAAYAAJ> This is the first of six parts of the poem. Wilde was sentenced to two years of hard labor in prison after being convicted of homosexual offences in 1895. During his imprisonment, Charles Thomas Wooldridge, found guilty of slitting his wife's throat with a razor, was hanged, profoundly effecting Wilde.

p. 371 — **Execution of the Bonifacio Brothers** (1898.) <opinion.inquirer.net/inquireropinion/columns/view/20090515-205102/The-execution-of-Bonifacio> Andrés Bonifacio y de Castro (November 30, 1863 – May 10, 1897) was a Filipino nationalist and revolutionary, a founder and leader of the Katipunan movement which sought independence from Spain and started the Philippine Revolution. He is celebrated as a national hero of the Philippines.

IV: Modern Times

p. 375 — **Heredity and Human Progress**, William Duncan McKim (1900.) <www.archive.org/details/heredityandhuma00mckigoog> This extract is from chapter V: "*A Remedy.*" McKim, a physician, advocated mercy killing for alcoholics, criminals and people with disabilities, noting that all that stood in his way was "the unreasonable dogma that *all* human life is intrinsically sacred."

p. 378 — **An Australian in China,** George Ernest Morrison (1894.) <gutenberg.net.au/ebooks05/0500681h.html> Morrison was an Australian adventurer and *The Times* Peking correspondent.

p. 381 — **The Other Side of the Lantern**, Frederick Treves (1905.) <www.archive.org/details/othersideoflante00trevuoft>. Treves was a prominent British surgeon, now most famous for his friendship with Joseph Merrick, the Elephant Man.

p. 382 — **Lynch Law In America**, Ida B. Wells-Barnett (1900.) <courses.washington.edu/spcmu/speeches/idabwells.htm> Wells-Barnett was an African American journalist and newspaper editor and owner. An early leader in the civil rights movement, she documented the extent of lynching in the United States. She was also active in the women's rights and suffrage movements.

p. 389 — **A Lynching,** Juliette V. Harring (1922.) <womhist.alexanderstreet.com/lynch/doc16.htm> First published in the Macon, Georgia *Daily Telegraph*. Harring was from Virginia.

p. 392 — **The Varieties of Religious Experience**, William James (1902) <www.archive.org/details/varietiesreligi02jamegoog> This excerpt is from Lectures XIV and XV, grouped together under the heading "*The Value of Saintliness.*"

p. 394 — **Witnesses Describe Czolgosz's Final Moments,** *Buffalo Commercial* (1901.) <ublib.buffalo.edu/libraries/exhibits/panam/law/execution.html> One of seven children of Polish immigrants, Leon Frank Czolgosz was the assassin of President William McKinley.

p. 396 — **Social Punishment Among Animals**, Arthur Cleveland Hall, Ph.D. (1902.) From **Crime in Its Relations to Social Progress**, <www.archive.org/details/crimeinitsrelati00hallrich> Hall was a Fellow in Sociology at Columbia University.

p. 398—**The Changing World and Lectures to Theosophical Students,** Annie Besant (1910.) <www.archive.org/details/changingworldlec00besauoft> From Chapter 4: *Brotherhood Applied To Social Conditions*, p. 95. Besant was a prominent Theosophist, women's rights activist, writer and orator and supporter of Irish and Indian self rule.

p. 399—**Theodore Roosevelt: An Autobiography** (1913.) <www.archive.org/details/theodorerooseve11roosgoog>

p. 401—**The Penitentiary Administration in England.** (1913.) <books.google.com/books?id=uOEtAAAAIAAJ> This an unsigned article from the *Journal of the American Institute of Criminal Law and Criminology*.

p. 403—**Causes and Cures Of Crime**, Thomas Speed Mosby (1913.) <www.archive.org/details/causesandcuresc00mosbgoog> This extract is from Part III (*Therapeutics*), Chapter VII (*The Theory of Punishment*) starting on page 225. Mosby was an attorney in Missouri who often wrote about criminal matters, including the intriguingly titled "Mothers of Bad Boys."

p. 410—**An Alienist: Personal And Professional** , Allan Mclane Hamilton (1916.) <books.google.com/books?id=vxB1MkycaiAC> This extract is from Chap. XXIII, "*Capital Punishment.*" Alienist is an archaic word for psychiatrist. Hamilton testified as a prosecution witness at murder trials of Guiteau (President Garfield's assassin) and Harry Thaw (murderer of architect Stanford White.) He was professor of mental diseases at Cornell University Medical College.

p. 416 — **Memoirs Of Sarah Bernhardt** (1907.) <books.google.com/books?id=oJq0zkaJqwoC> This extract is from **My Double Life**, Ch. XXVII. The legendary French actress was described by Alexandre Dumas, *fils*, as "a legendary liar."

p. 420 — **I Cannot Be Silent**, Leo Tolstoy (1908.) <en.wikisource.org/wiki/I_Cannot_Be_Silent>

p. 421 — **Capital Punishment Of Mentally Defective Murderers** (1908) <books.google.com/books?id=wPdXAAAAMAAJ> This unsigned article is from the *Calcutta Journal of Medicine*, April, 1908, attributed to *The Medical Times*, March 1908.

p. 424 — **Against Capital Punishment** (*Eine Ehrenpflicht*), Rosa Luxemburg (1918.) <www.marxists.org/archive/luxemburg/1918/11/18c-alt.htm> Luxemburg was a Polish-Jewish-German Marxist theorist, socialist philosopher, and revolutionary.

p. 427 — **The Execution of Mata Hari** (1917.) <www.eyewitnesstohistory.com/matahari.htm> Mata Hari (Margaretha Geertruida "Grietje" Zelle)was a Dutch-Frisian exotic dancer and courtesan who was executed by firing squad for espionage during World War I

p. 429 — **Politics as a Vocation**, Max Weber (1919) <en.wikisource.org/wiki/Politics_as_a_Vocation>

p. 430 — **Punishment and Reformation**, Frederick Howard Wines (1919.) <books.google.com/books?id=s8dMAAAAIAAJ> This extract is from Chapter 5, "*Intimidation and Torture*." Wines, a lawyer, was Secretary of the State Charities Aid Association and a prison visitor.

p. 446 — **The Hangman at Home**, Carl Sandburg (1920) This is from **Smoke and Steel** (1922), ch. II: *People Who Must*. <bartleby.com/231/0226.html>

p. 446 — **English Prisons Under Local Government**, George Bernard Shaw (1922.) <books.google.com/books?id=y8kMAAAAYAAJ> This is extracted from a lengthy introduction to a book by Beatrice and Sidney Webb, well worth reading in its entirety. In balance, Shaw comes down in favor of the death penalty, judging it less cruel than lengthy imprisonment for "incorrigible" criminals.

p. 449 — **Crime: Its Cause and Treatment**, Clarence Darrow (1922.) <www.archive.org/stream/crimeitscauseand12027gut/12027-8.txt>

p. 451 — **Real Crimes and Imaginary Mysteries**, G. K. Chesterton (1923) This essay is from **The Collected Works of G.K. Chesterton**: *The Illustrated London News*, 1923-1925, Vol 33, edited by Lawrence J. Clipper and George J. Marlin (Ignatius Press 1990) Chesterton's prolific output included journalism, philosophy, poetry, biography, Christian apologetics, fantasy and detective fiction.

p. 454 — **My Friend, Julia Lathrop**, Jane Addams. Addams book was published in 2004 by the University of Illinois Press, edited and with an introduction by Anne Firor Scott.

p. 455 — **The Case of Sacco and Vanzetti in Cartoons** from the Daily Worker (1927) <archive.lib.msu.edu/DMC/AmRad/sacoovanzetticartoons.pdf>

p. 457 — **An Execution In Paris**, Frank Harris (1930) <www.archive.org/stream/confessional014664mbp/confessional014664mbp_djvu.txt> This is from his book **Confessional: A Volume of Intimate Portraits, Sketches and Studies** (New York: Panurge Press, 1930.) He died in 1931.

The etymologies in the introduction are from the Online Etymology Dictionary, copyright 2008, Doug Harper <www.etymologyonline.com>.

Index of Proper Names

Alphabetical Index of Titles

Acknowledgements

My heartfelt thanks to every author included in this anthology – even the ones I heartily disagree with – for taking the time to record their thoughts on this most important topic.

Joan Cheever, in addition to graciously agreeing to write the foreword, helped immensely with proofreading. We have agreed to disagree about commas and, of course, any reaming mistakes are totally mine.

As always, thanks to my friends and colleagues at the peaceCENTER for their love and support, even when I am obsessed.

YOU MIGHT ALSO ENJOY

DEATH SENTENCES

34 CLASSIC SHORT STORIES ABOUT THE DEATH PENALTY BY CHEKHOV, TOLSTOY, POE, DUNBAR, BALZAC, TWAIN, KAFKA, DICKENS & MORE GREAT WRITERS

Susan Ives, editor

with a foreword by
Jay Brandon

& an afterword by
Roger C. Barnes, Ph.D.

AVAILABLE SUMMER 2009
peaceCENTER Books
www.salsa.net/peace/ebooks & on Amazon.com

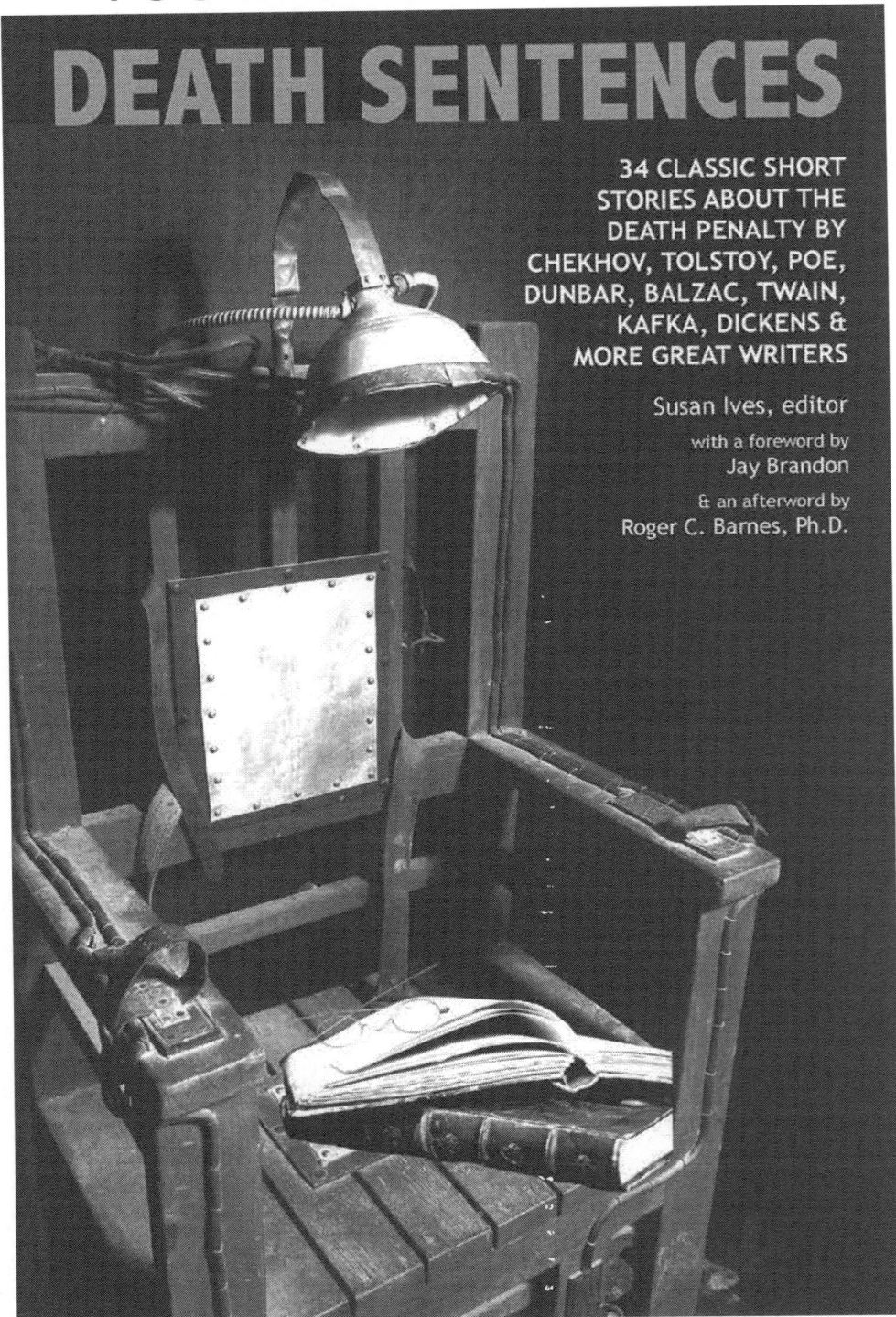

AVAILABLE SUMMER 2009
peaceCENTER Books
www.salsa.net/peace/ebooks & on Amazon.com

END OF THE LINE
five short novels about the death penalty

Last Days of a
Condemned Man
by Victor Hugo

The Seven Who
Were Hanged
by Leonid Andreyev

Lois The Witch
by Elizabeth Gaskell

Billy Budd
by Herman Melville

The Dead Alive
by Wilkie Collins

Susan Ives, editor

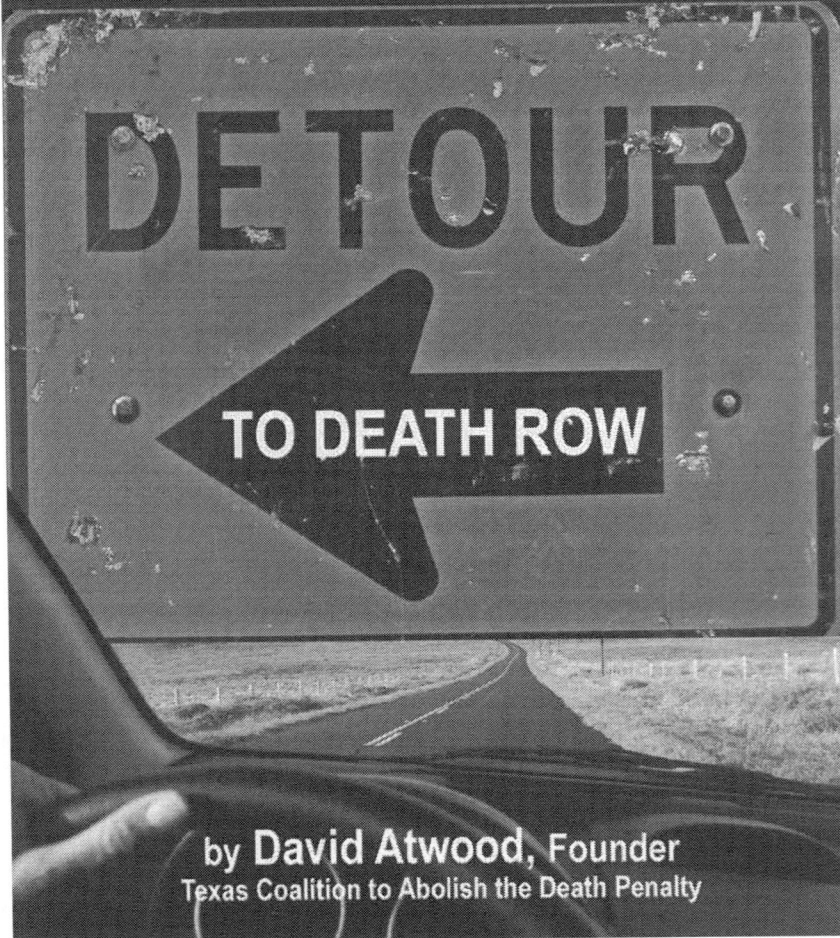

"Who would have thought that an engineer working for an oil company would one day be leading the fight to abolish the death penalty in the state which leads the nation in executions?"
Sister Helen Prejean, CSJ, author of *Dead Man Walking*

DETOUR
TO DEATH ROW

by **David Atwood**, Founder
Texas Coalition to Abolish the Death Penalty

AUGUST 2008   peaceCENTER Books
www.salsa.net/peace/ebooks & on Amazon.com

"David takes us on a pilgrimage from Hell to Paradise in a small Dante's Comedy, a journey to death row where we hear astonishing stories and meet incredible human beings."
Mario Marazziti, spokesperson for the Community of Sant'Egidio & co-founder of the World Coalition Against the Death Penalty

About peaceCENTER Books

Since 2007, the San Antonio peaceCENTER has been conducting an experiment in community-based publishing, distributing time-tested information written from decades of collective grassroots experience, designed for all who seek peace, teach peace, demonstrate peace and celebrate peace.

Books are available for purchase from Amazon.com and from the peaceCENTER Web site, www.salsa.net/peace/ebooks. Please contact the peaceCENTER for information about bulk discounts for activists, classes, community organizations and book stores. Profits generated by peaceCENTER books support the work of the peaceCENTER.

Capital Ideas: 150 Classic Writers on the Death Penalty, from the Code of Hammurabi to Clarence Darrow, Susan Ives (editor)

Cerca de la Cerca: Near the Border Fence photographs and commentary by María Teresa Fernández

Death Sentences: 34 Classic Short Stories about the Death Penalty Susan Ives (editor) with a foreword by Jay Brandon

Detour to Death Row by David Atwood, founder, Texas Coalition to Abolish the Death Penalty

End of the Line: Five Short Novels about the Death Penalty, Susan Ives (editor)

Facilitator's Manual for the Class of Nonviolence by Susan Ives; foreword by Colman McCarthy

Hajj Journal by Narjis Pierre, with an introduction & photographs by Ali Moshirsadri

Insights on the Journey: *Trauma, Healing and Wholeness.* An Anthology of Women's writing compiled by Maureen Leach, OSF

Peace is Our Birthright: *the p.e.a.c.e. process and interfaith community development* by Ann E. Helmke and Rosalyn Falcón Collier, with a foreword by Arun Gandhi

Shall We Ever Rise? A Holy Walk Lenten collages by Rosalyn Falcón Collier and Ann E. Helmke

Visualize Whirled Peas: Vegan Cooking From the San Antonio peaceCENTER by Susan Ives

Working It Out! *Managing and Mediating Everyday Conflicts* by Rosalyn Falcón Collier

"Wherever they burn books they will also, in the end, burn human beings."
Heinrich Heine

Focused on the vision of Peace in our lives, the interfaith peaceCENTER supports the learning of peace through prayer and education; and supports the demonstration of peace through nonviolent actions and community.
The peaceCENTER is a 501(c)(3) nonprofit organization
1443 S. St. Mary's, San Antonio, TX 78210
210.224.HOPE   pcebooks@yahoo.com

5589416R0

Made in the USA
Lexington, KY
26 May 2010